AN APPRENTICESHIP IN ARMS

An Apprenticeship in Arms

The Origins of the British Army
1585–1702

ROGER B. MANNING

OXFORD
UNIVERSITY PRESS

OXFORD
UNIVERSITY PRESS

Great Clarendon Street, Oxford OX2 6DP

Oxford University Press is a department of the University of Oxford.
It furthers the University's objective of excellence in research, scholarship,
and education by publishing worldwide in

Oxford New York

Auckland Cape Town Dar es Salaam Hong Kong Karachi
Kuala Lumpur Madrid Melbourne Mexico City Nairobi
New Delhi Shanghai Taipei Toronto

With offices in

Argentina Austria Brazil Chile Czech Republic France Greece
Guatemala Hungary Italy Japan Poland Portugal Singapore
South Korea Switzerland Thailand Turkey Ukraine Vietnam

Oxford is a registered trade mark of Oxford University Press
in the UK and in certain other countries

Published in the United States
by Oxford University Press Inc., New York

British Library Cataloguing in Publication Data

Data available

Library of Congress Cataloging in Publication Data

Data available

Typeset by Newgen Imaging Systems (P) Ltd., Chennai, India
Printed in Great Britain
on acid-free paper by
Biddles Ltd., King's Lynn, Norfolk

ISBN 0–19–926149–0   978–0–19–926149–9

1 3 5 7 9 10 8 6 4 2

For Clayton Roberts

Preface

The seventeenth-century origins of the British army as a standing military force are complex and varied, and draw upon the military experiences of numerous officers and enlisted men from the British Isles who served in the armies of the Three Kingdoms as well as in the armies of mainland Europe. The officers usually began their careers in the French, Dutch or various Scandinavian armies as gentlemen volunteers, while those who served in the ranks were frequently impressed and sent into exile by their governments and military enterprisers who filled the manpower needs of continental armies. English and Scots soldiers comprised nearly half of the field armies of the Dutch Republic in the age of Maurice of Nassau, contributed significantly to the successful Dutch struggle for independence from Spain and continued to serve in the Dutch army until the beginning of the Age of Revolution. Scots soldiers, who were seemingly ubiquitous, made their way into the armies of the Scandinavian kingdoms, Russia, Poland and France, constituted one-sixth of the fighting forces of Gustavus Adolphus of Sweden and campaigned extensively in Germany during the Thirty Years War. The Irish were particularly drawn to the Spanish Army of Flanders following the end of the Irish wars of the late sixteenth century when the earls of Tyrone and Tyrconnell fled with many of their followers. By the middle of the seventeenth century these 'wild geese' were also to be found in the French army; following the Williamite conquest of Ireland, when almost the entire Irish army of James II passed into the service of Louis XIV, Irish soldiers were becoming as numerous in the French royal army as the Swiss.

The inability or unwillingness of the early Stuart monarchs to maintain permanent military forces in the Three Kingdoms drove swordsmen to seek employment abroad in the European religious and dynastic wars. Clearly, religious fervour explains the motivation for many of these men seeking military service abroad, but others sought economic opportunity, adventure or the chance to validate their honour on the field of battle. Others—especially in Ireland and Scotland—followed leaders to whom they owed fealty or loyalty. The aristocratic society and culture of England had been remilitarized to a significant degree by 1640, while those of Scotland and Ireland had never been demilitarized in the first place. The continuing vitality of a martial culture and contact with the European military world introduced the cult of duelling into England and the Lowlands of Scotland, while cattle-raiding, poaching forays and other forms of feuding and symbolic warfare continued in the borderlands and Celtic areas of the British Isles. As government attempts to curb such violence intensified, those who had committed notorious acts of revenge and violence often found it convenient to flee justice or prosecution by 'fire and sword'.[1] This apprenticeship in arms exposed these officers and men to the technological innovations of the military revolution and contributed to a fund of professional expertise which the leaders of the various armies that fought in the British and Irish civil wars drew upon when the veterans of the Thirty Years and Eighty Years Wars returned to seek employment in their native lands after 1638.

The experiences of the English, Irish, Scots and Welsh veterans of the mainland European wars were varied and in their years of exile they had formed allegiances which contributed to religious, political, military and social conflict at home. The Wars of the Three Kingdoms led to the extensive mobilization of the manpower resources of the British Isles; after more than a decade of conflict many soldiers found it difficult to return to civilian life. During the Commonwealth and Protectorate, the New Model Army continued to be needed to garrison the recently conquered Celtic kingdoms, and found employment in military adventures on the continent and in Jamaica. The existence of a large standing army, together with the reception of Tacitean and Machiavellian modes of thought, helped to revive the old debate about whether a select militia led by members of the best county families would not be preferable to a standing army consisting of professional officers or mercenaries who were devoted to keeping wars going and themselves in employment. With the Restoration of the monarchy, the political and military settlement provided only for a small standing army consisting of 'guards and garrisons' supplemented by a select militia, but no provision for raising and training field armies. This, along with similar small-scale military establishments in Scotland and Ireland, was barely equal to discharging constabulary duties. Since these minimal standing military forces could provide employment for only a few of the demobilized officers and soldiers of the Cromwellian and Royalist armies, an exodus of soldiers of fortune resumed. They made their way into the armies of the Dutch Republic, France, Spain, Venice, Portugal, and Imperial Austria. The Scandinavian kingdoms provided fewer opportunities in the latter part of the seventeenth century, but Muscovite Russia had need of experienced officers—especially Scots.

The officer corps of mainland European armies in the seventeenth century remained aristocratic, but service in the Dutch and Swedish armies exposed volunteers from the British Isles to military systems in which merit and seniority weighed as much as social status in awarding commissions and promotions. As military theory and practice became more technical and military organization grew more complex, the conflict between social and military hierarchies intensified. Amateur gallants frequently sought military action for a few campaigning seasons in order to validate their honour and to seek personal glory. Such motives could not always be reconciled with the more rational political and military objectives of

---

[1] Many of these themes are discussed in the companion volume to this present book, R. B. Manning, *Swordsmen: The Martial Ethos in the Three Kingdoms* (2003).

the state, and, moreover, these aristocratic amateurs were often not amenable to military discipline and accepting orders from persons of a lesser social rank. In the wars of the earlier seventeenth century, military commanders were sometimes oblivious to the need to conserve resources of military manpower and to avoid secondary conflicts with civilian populations resulting from plunder or unrestrained foraging. Later in the century, styles of command evolved in which the ability to motivate men in battle and to direct and manage violence in a focused and rational manner and to limit the destructiveness of war came to be valued in military commanders. All of these needs promoted professionalization among the officers who served in the Wars of the Three Kingdoms. However, the restored Charles II recognized that his most loyal supporters during the civil wars had been found among the peers and gentry, and when he conferred commissions in the armies of the Restoration period, political necessity frequently obliged him to prefer loyal aristocrats who were military amateurs over more experienced and competent officers of lesser social stature. Thus the Restoration political and military settlement caused the decay of a military tradition that had been built up over the previous eighty-five years since the official English intervention in the Dutch war of independence, as professional soldiers were obliged to seek their fortunes in foreign armies.

Some of these officers and men spent their formative years in the British Brigades in France and Portugal or fighting Moors in Charles II's new colony of Tangier. Perhaps the most talented group of expatriate officers—mostly English and Scots, but including some Irish—was to be found in the Anglo-Dutch and Scots Brigades of the Dutch army after William III became stadholder of the United Provinces and captain-general of the States' Army in 1672. Once again the Orange court and officer corps of the States' Army became a 'nursery of soldiers' as it had been in the time of Maurice of Nassau. Many of these same English and Scots officers and soldiers constituted the core of William III's invasion force of 1688 when he landed at Torbay, after mounting one of the largest and most successful amphibious operations ever assembled before the twentieth century. Augmented with regiments of James VII and II's army, which because of a dispirited and divided officer corps had failed to oppose William's 'descent on England', William's force of English, Scots, Irish Protestants, French Huguenots and German and Danish mercenaries then subdued Scotland and conquered Ireland during the Williamite wars. When that task was completed, William II and III could devote his energies and British resources of men and treasure to halting Louis XIV's advance upon the Low Countries during King William's War or the Nine Years War. Although the British army was not formally created until after the Act of Union of 1707, the military successes in the Nine Years War and the War of Spanish Succession of the English army, augmented by Irish, Scots and Huguenot regiments, in halting Louis XIV's advance, gave birth to the modern British army and restored a military tradition which had been in abeyance for a generation.

Acknowledgements

In a commonwealth of knowledge one incurs many debts of gratitude in undertaking a research project and preparing a manuscript for publication. This present volume began as part of my previous book *Swordsmen* (2003), but was detached upon the good advice of the anonymous readers of the Oxford University Press. Financial assistance for research and travel came from a senior fellowship awarded by the National Endowment for the Humanities and Fletcher Jones and Mellon fellowships at the Huntington Library as well as a sabbatical leave and grants from the College of Graduate Studies of Cleveland State University. Research was carried out in the British Library, the Public Record Office (now the National Archives), the Institute of Historical Research, University of London, the Cleveland Public Library, the Huntington Library, and the College of Law and the University Libraries of Cleveland State University. The librarians and staff of the latter institution never blink an eye when I submit mountains of requests for new books, inter-library loans and microfilm. The online English Short Title Catalogue greatly facilitates the task of locating rare books or microfilm copies. To all the archivists and librarians of these esteemed institutions I give my thanks for numerous acts of kindness.

Colleagues and friends have been most helpful and encouraging. Jane Ohlmeyer read Chapters 1–6 and offered an abundance of useful advice and bibliographical assistance in the fields of Irish and Scottish history. The anonymous readers of the Oxford University Press have always been very generous in supplying constructive evaluations of the manuscript. Others have also been helpful and encouraging, and I wish particularly to mention Barbara Donagan, Robert Ritchie, Mary Robertson, Joyce Mastboom, Donald Ramos and Scott Hendrix.

The editorial staff of the Oxford University Press have, as always, been encouraging, helpful and patient, and I wish particularly to acknowledge the kind assistance of Anne Gelling, the history editor, Kay Rogers, the production editor and Jeff New, the copy-editor.

As always my greatest debt of gratitude is to my wife, Anne Brown Manning, who has encouraged me to engage in scholarship and provided me with the leisure to do so for the past forty-five years.

R.B.M.

Cleveland, Ohio
2005

Contents

List of Tables

List of Maps

Note on the Text

The spelling, punctuation and capitalization of all quotations taken from contemporaneous manuscripts and printed books have been modernized. However, the actual spelling of titles of books printed before 1800 has been retained in footnote citations and in the Select Bibliography, although punctuation and capitalization have been modernized. Wordy titles have been shortened with the omissions indicated by ellipses. Where the author has used different editions of the same work, the actual edition consulted is cited in the footnote, but only the earliest edition or the most accessible modern edition is listed in the Bibliography.

The year is assumed to begin on 1 January rather than 25 March. The day and the month are given according to old style or new style and so indicated where such precision is possible.

Abbreviations

AHR	*American Historical Review*
APSM	*American Philosophical Society Memoirs*
AQ	*Army Quarterly*
APC	*Acts of the Privy Council of England*, ed. J. R. Dasent, 46 vols. (London, 1890–1964)
BARSEH	British Academy, Records of Social and Economic History
BC	Bannatyne Club
BHS	Bedfordshire Historical Society
BIHR	*Bulletin of the Institute of Historical Research*
BL	British Library, London
Carlton, *GW*	C. Carlton, *Going to the Wars: The Experience of the British Civil Wars, 1638–1651* (1992)
Childs, *AC*	J. Childs, *The Army of Charles II* (1976)
Childs, *AJGR*	—— *The Army, James II and the Glorious Revolution* (1980)
Childs, *BAW*	—— *The British Army of William III, 1689–1702* (1987)
Childs, *NYW*	—— *The Nine Year' War and the British Army, 1688–1697: The Operations in the Low Countries* (1991)
CHJ	*Cambridge Historical Journal*
CJH	*Canadian Journal of History*
Clarendon, *RCW*	Edward Hyde, earl of Clarendon, *The History of the Rebellion and Civil Wars in England*, ed. W. D. Macray, 6 vols. (1888)
CM	*Camden Miscellany*
CS	Camden Society
CSP	*Calendar of State Papers* (different editors and series)
DNB	*Dictionary of National Biography*, 22 vols. (Oxford, 1990 edn.)
DRS	Dorset Record Society
EHR	*English Historical Review*
EHQ	*European Historical Quarterly*
ERO	Essex Record Office, Chelmsford
ES	*English Studies*
ESR	*European Studies Review*

Firth, *CA*	C. H. Firth, *Cromwell's Army: A History of the English Soldier During the Civil Wars and the Protectorate* (repr. 1962)
Firth, *Ludlow*	—— *The Memoirs of Edmund Ludlow . . . 1625–1672*, 2 vols. (1894)
Fissel, *EW*	M. C. Fissel, *English Warfare, 1511–1642* (2001)
Fissel, *W&G*	—— *War and Government in Britain, 1598–1650* (1991)
Gentles, *NMA*	I. Gentles, *The New Model Army in England, Ireland and Scotland, 1645–1653* (1992)
HEH	Henry E. Huntington Library, San Marino, Calif.
HJ	*Historical Journal*
HLQ	*Huntington Library Quarterly*
HM	*Harleian Miscellany* (various editions and editors)
HMC	*Historical Manuscripts Commission*
HR	*Historical Research*
HRS	Hertfordshire Record Society
HS	Hakluyt Society
HSP	*Huguenot Society Proceedings*
HT	*History Today*
IHS	*Irish Historical Studies*
IS	*Irish Sword*
JHI	*Journal of the History of Ideas*
JMH	*Journal of Military History*
JSAHR	*Journal of the Society for Army Historical Research*
Luttrell, *RSA*	Narcissus Luttrell, *A Brief Historical Relation of State Affairs from September 1678 to April 1714*, 6 vols. (1857; repr. 1974)
McClure, *LJC*	N. E. McClure (ed.), *The Letters of John Chamberlain*, 2 vols. (1939)
Macdougall, *S&W*	N. Macdougall (ed.), *Scotland and War, AD 79–1918* (1991)
Macinnes, *CC*	A. I. Macinnes, *Clanship, Commerce and the House of Stuart, 1603–1788* (1996)
Manning, *H&P*	R. B. Manning, *Hunters and Poachers: A Cultural and Social History of Unlawful Hunting in England, 1485–1640* (1993)
Manning, *R&S*	—— *Religion and Society in Elizabethan England* (1969)
Manning, *Swordsmen*	—— *Swordsmen: The Martial Ethos in the Three Kingdoms* (2003)
Manning, *VR*	—— *Village Revolts: Social Protest and Popular Disturbances in England, 1509–1640* (1988)

MC	Maitland Club
MHI	T. Bartlett and K. Jeffery (eds.), *A Military History of Ireland* (1996)
Monro, *Expedition*	Robert Monro, *Monro his Expedition with the Worthy Scots Regiment (called Mac-Keyes Regiment)* (1637)
NH	*Northern History*
NLWJ	*National Library of Wales Journal*
NNAS	Norfolk and Norwich Archaeological Society
Northants RS	Northamptonshire Record Society
NRS	Navy Record Society
NH	*Northern History*
NS	*Northern Scotland*
ODNB	*Oxford Dictionary of National Biography*, ed. H. C. G. Matthew and B. Harrison, 60 vols. (Oxford, 2004)
OED	*Oxford English Dictionary*
ORS	Oxford Record Society
Parker, *MR*	G. Parker, *The Military Revolution: Military Innovation and the Rise of the West, 1500–1800*, 2nd edn. (1996)
PHSL	*Proceedings of the Huguenot Society of London*
P&P	*Past and Present*
PRO	Public Record Office, London (now The National Archive)
PS	Percy Society
RC	Roxburghe Club
Redlich, *GME*	F. Redlich, *The German Military Enterpriser and his Work Force*, 2 vols., *Vierteljahrschrift für Sozial- und Wirtschaftsgeschichte*, 47–8 (1964–5)
Redlich, *DPM*	—— *De Praeda Militari: Looting and Booty, 1500–1800*, *Vierteljahrschrift für Sozial- und Wirtschaftsgeschichte*, 39 (1956)
RHS	Royal Historical Society
RPCS	*Register of the Privy Council of Scotland* (various editors)
RQ	*Renaissance Quarterly*
RSLC	Record Society of Lancashire and Cheshire
Rushworth, *HC*	John Rushworth, *Historical Collections*, 8 vols. (1688–1701)
SAHR	Society for Army Historical Research
SC	*Seventeenth Century*
SC	Spalding Club

SCJ	*Sixteenth Century Journal*
Schwoerer, *NSA*	L. G. Schwoerer, *No Standing Armies! The Antiarmy Ideology in Seventeenth-Century England* (1974)
SHR	*Scottish Historical Review*
SJH	*Scandinavian Journal of History*
SRS	Somerset Record Society
SS	Surtees Society
SSNE	S. Murdoch and A. Grosjean, 'Scotland, Scandinavia & Northern Europe, 1580–1707' <database@univ.abdn.ac.uk/history/datasets/ssne>
ST	*Scottish Tradition*
T&C	*Technology and Culture*
THSLC	*Transactions of the Historic Society for Lancashire and Cheshire*
TRHS	*Transactions of the Royal Historical Society*
TT	Thomason Tracts (British Library)
Walker, *HAC*	G. G. Walker, *The Honourable Artillery Company, 1537–1937* (1954)
WHR	*Welsh Historical Review*
WMQ	*William and Mary Quarterly*
YAJ	*Yorkshire Archaeological Journal*

PART I

A MILITARY APPRENTICESHIP
1585–1640

1

The Irish wars

For empire and greatness, it importeth most that a nation do profess arms as their principal honour, study and occupation.

Sir Francis Bacon, *The Essayes and Counsells, Civill and Morall*, ed. M. Kieran (1985), 95.

He that would England win,
Must with Ireland first begin.

George Story, *A Continuation of the Impartial History of Ireland* (1693), 319.

Better be hanged at home than die like dogs in Ireland.

Old Cheshire proverb, quoted in R. Bagwell, *Ireland under the Tudors*, 3 vols. (1885–90; repr. 1963), iii. 249.

Prior to the beginning of the Anglo-Spanish War in 1585, Elizabethan Englishmen had enjoyed many years of domestic peace. But some of the queen's subjects did not regard this as a blessing. For swordsmen, the years of peace during the queen's reign gave rise to a false sense of security which had bred contempt for the exercise of arms and the study of war, and had also elicited a 'despising of soldiers and martial discipline'.[1] Although the king of Spain had amply demonstrated his hostility to English interests throughout the British Isles and northern Europe by this date, William Cecil, Lord Burghley, the lord treasurer of England and leader of the peace party, had argued that England could not afford a war with Spain and dared not count upon the loyalty of the commonalty.[2] By 1584, following the assassination of William the Silent and the collapse of the Protestant Union of Utrecht backed by Holland and Zeeland, it became apparent that if the Dutch Revolt failed, and the Spanish reconquered all the Netherlands, they would next turn their eyes across the Narrow Seas to England. Although a Spanish invasion of England may not have been inevitable, Robert Dudley, earl of Leicester,

---

[1] Robert Barret, *The Theorick and Practicke of Moderne Warres* (1598), 2.
[2] William Camden, *Annales: or the History of the Renowned and Victorious Princesse Elizabeth*, 3rd edn. (1635), 493.

and Sir Francis Walsingham, the leaders of the war party in England, argued that it was. By the Treaty of Nonsuch of 10 August 1585, Elizabeth agreed to take the United Provinces under her protection and assist the Dutch struggle for independence with a limited military force of 5,000 foot and 1,000 horse to be commanded by an Englishman of noble rank.[3]

The decision that the English forces in the Netherlands should be commanded by an Englishman of 'quality' rather than an experienced professional soldier set the tone for the late Elizabethan wars, whether in the Netherlands, Ireland or elsewhere; the Elizabethan government usually got what it bargained for and no more. Although the English, with their Dutch and Huguenot allies, succeeded in keeping the Spaniards out of England (but not Ireland), and kept the Dutch resistance going, it became painfully obvious that warfare had changed since English armies last campaigned on the continent of Europe, and English military leaders had much to learn about conducting armies under the new conditions. Whether driven by a desire for martial glory, religious zeal, exile, impressment or simple poverty, swordsmen and soldiers from the Three Kingdoms of England, Ireland and Scotland would serve in the armies of continental Europe in considerable numbers during the religious and dynastic conflicts of the late sixteenth and seventeenth centuries. Although the Three Kingdoms may have been minor powers during this period, the continental powers regarded the peoples of the British Isles as an important source of military manpower and competed with one-another to secure their services. Often holding the very highest ranks in the armies of the Dutch Republic, Spanish Flanders, Denmark, Sweden, France and Imperial Austria, many of these soldiers returned home to participate in the British and Irish wars of 1638–51 after having served an apprenticeship in arms under commanders such as Maurice of Nassau, prince of Orange, and Gustavus Adolphus, king of Sweden. This apprenticeship in arms was the foundation upon which the subsequent feats of arms of the British army rested after 1689.

As an island kingdom, Tudor England had been little bothered by or involved in continental European affairs, and, unlike Spain and France, was less exposed to invasion. The two latter states had been compelled to develop standing armies composed of mercenary soldiers, but, before 1585, England had not. Elizabeth's government maintained small garrisons at the Tower of London, Berwick-upon-Tweed and elsewhere, but these forces were static in nature and could not be deployed as field armies. The perpetual warfare of Ireland necessitated a military organization of somewhat larger proportions, but it retained the characteristics of garrison forces which sometimes ventured out against the Irish rebels. The origins of an English standing army in the reign of Elizabeth are to be traced primarily to the English military establishment in Ireland and the forces sent to assist the Dutch in 1585. The English and Scottish soldiers in the army of the States

---

[3] R. B. Wernham, *Before the Armada: The Emergence of the English Nation, 1485–1588* (repr. 1972), 367–71.

General would be particularly significant in the British military experience because, exposed to combat with the formidable *tercios* of the Spanish Army of Flanders—at that time the best in the world—and initiated into the methods of the new siege warfare, service in the Dutch army provided 'a nursery of soldiers'. From this cadre of professional English soldiers in Ireland and the Netherlands, Elizabeth's government was able to assemble in 1588 at Tilbury Camp and at Plymouth considerable forces to repel a Spanish invasion which, besides the county trained bands, included 'soldiers disciplined and trained in the wars in Ireland and the Netherlands'.[4]

It could be argued that the balance of power had shifted to England's disadvantage since the late medieval Angevin and Lancastrian interventions in France, and both Spain and France possessed greater demographic and economic resources at the end of the sixteenth century. In fact, the military exertions of the great powers exceeded their demographic resources and financial means, and this had a levelling effect in warfare which operated to the advantage of the lesser powers such as England. Every army experienced serious problems supplying, victualling and paying their soldiers in a timely fashion, but the careful oversight of military expenditures by Lord Burghley and other members of the Privy Council may have given the English forces a slight advantage in their confrontations with Spanish military and naval forces.[5]

Elizabethan armies and naval expeditions were always constrained by limited fiscal resources and underdeveloped logistical support systems, and the martialists such as Sir Philip Sidney and, later, Robert, second earl of Essex, were always disappointed that Elizabeth did not allow her military and naval commanders to campaign more aggressively against the Spanish in the Low Countries and elsewhere. Elizabeth and Burghley were always sceptical about what could be accomplished by military force, and it is debatable how much the queen understood about military strategy. One might fairly ask the same question about some of Elizabeth's military commanders. Leicester analysed battles in terms of martial honour gained rather than military objectives achieved, and the second earl of Essex regarded any opposition to the war with Spain as 'dishonourable and treacherous' whether that war was achieving strategic goals or not, and Essex had a large following of swordsmen.[6] Elizabeth always distrusted the ambition of martialists, and did not wish to have to contend with military commanders puffed up with pride and honour gained from recent victories.

Even experienced soldiers, such as Sir John Smythe, found the late sixteenth-century wars in France and the Netherlands chaotic and bewildering.[7]

[4] S. Adams, 'Tactics or Politics? "The Military Revolution" and the Hapsburg Hegemony, 1525–1648', in J. A. Lynn (ed.), *Tools of War: Instruments, Ideas and Institutions of Warfare, 1445–1871* (1990), 38; [Daniel Defoe?], *A Brief Reply to the History of Standing Armies in England* (1698), 3; J. S. Nolan, 'The Militarization of the Elizabethan State', *JMH* 58 (1994), 392–3.

[5] P. Anderson, *Lineages of the Absolutist State* (repr. 1979), 122–3; Adams, 'Tactics or Politics?', 45–6.   [6] Camden, *Annales* (1635 edn.), 493–4.

[7] Sir John Smythe, *Certain Discourses Military*, ed. J. R. Hale (1964), 6.

The 'chivalric revival' instilled a value system which ill equipped swordsmen for the new style of warfare. 'Battles do not now decide national quarrels and expose countries to the pillage of conquerors as formerly. For we make war more like foxes than lions, and you will have twenty sieges for one battle; in which sieges the scarcity of victuals, the certainty of blows and the uncertainty of plunder ... renders the usual parts of war full of sufferings and dangers and of little profit to the soldiers.'[8] Most swordsmen recognized that they had a lot to learn if they were to become proficient soldiers, and insisted upon the need for an apprenticeship in arms emphasizing experience and discipline before accepting commissions as officers. Since swordsmen of the Three Kingdoms served as officers and volunteers in all of the armies of Europe, this constituted an initiation into a European martial culture as well as an exposure to the principles and practices of the so-called 'military revolution'. Experienced soldiers as well as interested scholars at home began to compile, translate and write military treatises and training manuals for English-speaking readers. The more intellectual swordsmen hired scholars, such as Gabriel Harvey, the poet and student of Livy, and John Sadler, the translator of Vegetius, to research Roman military practice and to meet with groups of martialists to discuss appropriate military policies, tactics and soldierly behaviour.[9]

Matthew Sutcliffe, who served as judge-advocate-general of the English forces in the Netherlands, was sensitive about the sometimes undisciplined performance of English soldiers in the Low Countries and France at the end of the sixteenth century. The English had been renowned for their military prowess in the past, but were slow in adopting modern military practice at the end of the Elizabethan period, which Sutcliffe thought was a reflection of how much the rules and methods of warfare had changed. The military performance of English soldiers in France and in the Netherlands needs to be put into perspective by remembering that, in both cases, they were fighting on the weaker side and lacked sufficient money, victuals and equipment.[10] The more experienced continental European commanders who preferred sieges to more risky pitched battles were following the sound example not only of medieval precedent, but of Roman military writers such as Vegetius. The outcome of sieges was usually more predictable than pitched battles, because the strongest of fortresses could always be starved into submission if the besieging army had the patience and staying power. In actuality, far too

---

[8] Roger Boyle, 1st earl of Orrery, *A Treatise of the Art of War* (1677), 15.

[9] Parker, *MR*, esp. ch. 1. For estimates on the number of men from the Three Kingdoms who served in the Thirty Years War, cf. Carlton, *GW* 19–21. On the dialogue between swordsmen and scholars concerning Roman military practice, cf. L. Jardine and A. Grafton, 'Studied for Action: How Gabriel Harvey Read his Livy', *P&P* 129 (Nov. 1990), 35–40, and *The Foure Bookes of Flavius Vegetius Renatus*, trans. John Sadler (1572; repr. 1968), dedication; Manning, *Swordsmen*, ch. 4. For a discussion of military treatises, cf. H. J. Webb, *Elizabethan Military Science: The Books and the Practice* (1965), and for a full bibliography of the military books of the period, see M. J. C. Cockle, *A Bibliography of English Military Books up to 1642 and Contemporary Foreign Books* (1900).

[10] Matthew Sutcliffe, *The Practice, Proceedings and Lawes of Armes* (1593), 70.

many English commanders preferred frontal assaults to methodical sieges; they were thirsty for instant honour and glory, but they were also amateurs. The preference for frontal assaults and pitched battles on the part of English commanders was evident in the late Elizabethan wars, and this remained true through the Wars of the Three Kingdoms.[11]

Most English commanders and officers had yet to learn the principles of good military leadership. The social gulf between aristocratic officers and private soldiers, who were conscripted by sweeps of vagrants and petty criminals for service in Elizabethan overseas military expeditions, was wide and communications across that gulf must have been difficult. Sir Walter Raleigh's experience with common soldiers was that they were unmoved by motives of patriotism and religious zeal; only the prospect of plunder would motivate them to attack the enemy. Otherwise, thought Raleigh, they were quick to mutiny.[12] English officers were indifferent about the welfare of the men who served under them. Following a battle in which his servant was seriously wounded, Sir Roger Williams said of him: 'if he dies, it makes no great matter. He was a lackey of mine, which carried my headpiece.'[13] Most officers assumed that their main function in battle was limited to providing an example of courage to their men. They could have learned from Vegetius that since few men are born with courage, it could be acquired only by training and discipline, which would have required a lot of hard work for both commissioned and non-commissioned officers.[14] This emphasis upon training would begin during the period when English and Scottish soldiers served under the leadership of Maurice of Nassau, prince of Orange, as captain-general of the Dutch army.

The demeaning attitude of English officers towards their soldiers derived from a continuing debate concerning who made the best foot soldiers. Sir Francis Bacon asserted the widely repeated maxim that the principal strength of an army was its infantry, and yeomen made the best foot soldiers. Smallhold tenants, cottagers and labourers were too servile to make resolute soldiers, and vagrants and vagabonds were unstable and lacked suitable physiques.[15] In Tudor and Stuart England, the government and its gentry and merchant supporters were prejudiced in favour of a military system based upon a select militia which drew heavily upon yeomen and householders. Consequently, overseas military expeditions were recruited from amongst the vagrants and masterless men swept up by county and municipal authorities in their hundreds.[16]

---

[11] F. Tallett, *War and Society in Early Modern Europe, 1495–1715* (1992), 52–3.

[12] Sir Walter Raleigh, *The History of the World* (1617), iv. 2. 4 (p. 178). See also *A Breefe Declaration of that which happened . . . without Ostend sithence the vii. of Januarie 1602* (1602), 3.

[13] R. B. Wernham, *After the Armada: Elizabethan England and the Struggle for Western Europe, 1588–1595* (1984), 437.   [14] *Foure Bookes of . . . Vegetius*, sigs. Aiir, Gir, and fo. 49v.

[15] Sir Francis Bacon, *History of King Henry VII*, in *The Works of Francis Bacon*, ed. J. Spedding, 14 vols. (1857–74; repr. 1963), vi. 93–5; J. McGurk, *The Elizabethan Conquest of Ireland: The 1590s Crisis* (1997), 32.

[16] John Stow, *The Annales or Generall Chronicle of England . . . continued by Edmund Howes* (1615), 791; HEH, Hastings MSS. 1(8).

The argument concerning whether foreign mercenaries or subjects made the best soldiers, and whether the English military forces should recruit yeomen or lesser breeds of men, was also related to the question of what was the preferred weapon for equipping the English foot. The archers of Lancastrian armies possessed considerable firepower combined with accuracy and rapidity of fire, and Sir John Smythe was able to argue plausibly that the English longbow was, in the late sixteenth century, superior to the heavy and awkward prototypes of the musket. But, the drafts of impressed men arriving in the Netherlands or Ireland contained not yeomen archers bred in that skill since childhood, but lesser men. Experienced officers knew that it was easier to train such people in the use of firearms than longbows. Besides, archers were never meant to act as shock troops, and, in the line of battle or assaults upon fortifications, that function was now discharged by pikemen, who were more usually drawn from gentlemen volunteers, and were interwoven into the line of battle with musketeers.[17]

In late medieval warfare, the role of shock troops was usually performed by mounted cavalry, but the needs of siege warfare and the restricted topography of the Dutch and Irish landscapes left little room for cavalry to manoeuvre. The high cost of transporting horses to the Netherlands and feeding them necessarily limited their numbers. In any case, Henry VIII's wasteful and extravagant use of equine resources had caused a shortage of warhorses in Elizabethan England. Cavalrymen in England were usually drawn from aristocratic and gentry households, and these persons, serving as gentlemen volunteers, more usually functioned as pikemen in the Dutch wars. The Thirty Years War and the British civil wars would see a revival of the employment of cavalry.[18]

Service in the Low Countries or northern France brought English military men into contact with a European martial culture which included certain rules of engagement as well as the belief that prisoners of war should be treated as men who had been worthy enemies at the moment of surrender. Although there were certainly instances when discipline broke down and atrocities occurred, generally speaking, a shared martial culture among the polyglot armies of continental Europe contributed to the movement to limit the destructiveness and cruelty of war which began to emerge during the seventeenth century.[19] English soldiers who went to Ireland, on the other hand, encountered an entirely different situation, because the English government regarded the Irish as rebels to whom the rules of war did not apply and as barbarians who were so savage as to be beyond the bounds of Christian civilization. Although the Anglo-Norman conquerors and colonizers had recognized the inhabitants as Christian, the Elizabethan adventurers found Irish religious life so alien to their Protestant culture that they

---

[17] Smythe, *Certain Discouses Military*, ed. Hale, p. lxii; H. H. Turney-High, *Primitive War: Its Practice and Concepts* (1971), 11; T. Esper, 'The Replacement of the Longbow by Firearms in the English Army', *T&C* 17 (1965), 382–93.

[18] Webb, *Elizabethan Military Science*, 108–23; J. Thirsk, *Horses in Early Modern England: For Service, for Pleasure, for Power* (1978), 7–8; Adams, 'Tactics or Politics?', 36–8.

[19] On the limitation of war, cf. J. T. Johnson, *Just War Tradition and the Restraint of War: A Moral and Historical Inquiry* (1981), 187–91.

supposed the Irish to be pagan. The English military adventurers, some of whom had fought against the Turks or had knowledge of or contact with the Indian peoples of the New World, placed the Irish in the same category of barbaric peoples. This judgement partly rested upon the observation that the Irish followed pastoral ways based upon transhumance rather than arable agriculture, and thus could not be regarded as civilized until they acquired more settled ways, accepted English law and yielded up their weapons.[20]

Ireland had never been entirely conquered in medieval times because the English monarchs of that period were preoccupied by their continental possessions or the need to suppress rebellions and fight civil wars at home. Sir John Davies, the Jacobean attorney-general for Ireland, assumed that the Irish were a warlike people and could not be subdued except by a war fiercely waged; at the same time, he understood that the English monarchs had failed to recognize the Irish as subjects and provide them with justice and protection, which might have attached them by loyalty to English rule. Rather, they were regarded as rebels and enemies of the crown. English law was at first extended only to the Old English settlers in the twelve counties of the provinces of Leinster and Munster. In the wild, boggy and wooded parts of Ireland, which the English usually avoided, it was not a crime in English law to kill an Irishman.[21] The English, like the Romans, never felt comfortable fighting in bogs, woods and mountains, where the distinctively Celtic methods of fighting put them at a disadvantage.[22] Because the methods of warfare of the English and Irish differed so much, the rules of war prevalent in Europe never found acceptance in Ireland where warfare had taken a particularly brutal form since medieval times and before. It was the practice of the medieval English rulers of Ireland to license local magnates to make war on rebels, and mercy was not encouraged by the practice of putting a price on the heads of their leaders. The custom of bringing in the heads of rebels was of long standing in medieval Ireland and continued through the seventeenth century, when it was sanctioned by proclamation. When Richard II went to Ireland in 1394, he took with him the largest military expedition ever sent to Ireland before the Tudor period, and his methods of warfare included destroying villages and their inhabitants and driving away their cattle so as to deny any survivors the means of sustenance.[23]

[20] N. Canny, 'The Ideology of English Colonization: From Ireland to America', *WMQ* ser. 3, vol. 30 (1973), 584–6; Barnabe Rich, *Alarme to England foreshewing What Perilles are Procured where the People live without regarde of Martiall Lawe* (1578), sigs. Ej r–v. Cf. also A. Lawrence, 'The Cradle to the Grave: English Observation of Irish Social Customs in the Seventeenth Century', *SC* 3 (1988), 63–84.

[21] Sir John Davies, *A Discovery of the True Causes Why Ireland Was never Entirely Subdued*, ed. J. P. Meyers (1612; repr. 1988), 70–1, 107–9, 116–17, 126, 130; S. O'Domhnaill, 'Warfare in Sixteenth-Century Ireland', *IHS* 5 (1946–7), 39–41.

[22] Davies, *True Causes*, 162–3.

[23] J. F. Lydon, *The Lordship of Ireland in the Middle Ages* (1972), 195, 234; George Story, *A Continuation of the Impartial History of the Wars of Ireland* (1693), 58–9; K. Simms, 'Warfare in the Medieval Gaelic Lordships', *IS* 12 (1975–6), 98–104.

Map 1.1. The late Elizabethan wars in Ireland

The invasion of Ireland by Edward Bruce in 1315 led to the importation of Scots mercenary soldiers known as gallowglasses who came to be associated with an especially brutal kind of warfare. While armies recruited from among the native Irish were certainly destructive of property, it did not make sense to kill civilians in a land that was underpopulated. The gallowglasses, however, resorted to the wanton killing of noncombatants. Thereafter, the use of gallowglasses by Irish chieftains spread throughout the four provinces and is indicative of the militarization of late medieval Irish society. The use of gallowglasses by both Irish lords and chieftains and English viceroys persisted into the sixteenth century, when they became assimilated into Irish society. By the end of the sixteenth century they were replaced by the recruiting of the so-called 'redshanks', who came into Antrim from the Western Isles and West Highlands of Scotland to provide soldiers for the rebellious lords of Ulster.[24]

The harshness of war intensified in sixteenth-century Ireland. The enforcement of the Reformation in Ireland presented greater problems than was the case in England, and a predominantly Catholic Ireland invited the intervention of continental Catholic powers, such as Spain. The resources which would have been needed for preaching the reformed religion were daunting, and the English government responded by the free use of the sword but very few sermons.[25] English commanders in Ireland of the Elizabethan period practiced a particularly brutal kind of warfare which did not distinguish between combatants and non-combatants. Sir James Croft, who had served as lord deputy under Edward VI, protested such actions by his successors as being unnecessary and without justification, and he thought that officers who perpetrated such acts were unchristian and lacking in military expertise.[26]

Anglican divines such as Thomas Becon insisted that the act of rebellion itself was unchristian. Indeed, Becon compared the sin of rebellion to witchcraft in its heinousness. The example of the Irish rebellion was often cited to show that the rules of war did not apply to the suppression of rebellion, and there was no requirement to distinguish non-combatants from combatants since it could be presumed that the families of Irish warriors who followed the warrior bands were aiding the rebels. This belief in the need to punish Irish camp-followers and dependants received the approbation of writers such as Thomas Churchyard and Edmund Spenser. Spenser asserted that Irish military traditions were confined to internecine tribal warfare. He thought the Irish were so primitive and barbaric in their methods of warfare that they must have been descended from the Scythians.

[24] J. F. Lydon, 'The Scottish Soldier in Medieval Ireland: The Bruce Invasion and the Gallowglass', G. G. Simpson (ed.), *The Scottish Soldier Abroad, 1247–1967* (1992), 1–8, 12; O'Domhnaill, 'Warfare in Sixteenth-Century Ireland', 37; C. Falls, *Elizabeth's Irish Wars* (1970), 76–9; A. McKerral, 'West Highland Mercenaries in Ireland', *SHR* 30 (1951), 1–13.

[25] B. Bradshaw, 'Sword, Word and Strategy in Reformation Ireland', *HJ* 21 (1978), 496–7, 501.

[26] D. B. Quinn, *The Elizabethans and the Irish* (1966), 133; V. Carey, 'The Irish Face of Machiavelli: Richard Beacon's *Solon his Follie* (1594) and Republican Ideology in the Conquest of Ireland', in H. Morgan (ed.), *Political Ideology in Ireland, 1541–1641* (1999), 86–9.

Spenser also believed that it was a mercy to execute Irish rebels by martial law, because if they were tried under English law by a court of record, their lands would be forfeited to the crown and their heirs beggared.[27]

The English government asserted that the English crown held title to Ireland by right of conquest dating to the Norman invasion of Ireland. Queen Elizabeth assumed that once the rebellious Irish chieftains were defeated, her Irish subjects would be entitled to the same rights and protection as her English subjects, whereas the Scots were trespassers and could be ejected. The breakdown of this policy of treating the Irish as subjects entitled to protection dates from two separate events—the Rathlin Island massacre of July 1575, and the appointment of Sir Humphrey Gilbert as military governor of Munster to suppress the rebellion led by Gerald Fitzgerald, fifteenth earl of Desmond. In the former instance, Walter Devereux, first earl of Essex, was campaigning against the O'Neills of Ulster and sought to lure the leader of the redshank mercenaries, Sorley Boy MacDonnell, out of the Glynns, or Antrim Highlands, to do battle. The MacDonnells had left their families on Rathlin Island off the north coast of Antrim, where some of the redshanks had settled. Essex ordered Sir John Norris, with a naval flotilla, to menace the MacDonnell families. Sorley Boy refused to come out and fight and had to watch as Norris and his men slaughtered 600 women and children on Rathlin Island.[28]

After Sir Henry Sidney was appointed lord deputy in 1565, he made a tour of Munster and observed that the misrule of the Irish earls, Desmond, Thomond and Clanricarde, was a source of oppression and disorder. He determined to end their feudal jurisdictions and ability to raise private armies. This he proposed to do by establishing a permanent military presence outside the Pale by erecting presidencies or military governorships in each of the three provinces of Connaught, Munster and Ulster, beginning with Connaught in 1569 and Munster the following year. This was to be accomplished by the erection of fortresses defended by permanent garrisons. Only military men were appointed to the presidencies, and their task was to suppress the private armies of the earls and chieftains and to dispense martial law until a system of English common law could be established.[29] Sidney had already sent Sir Humphrey Gilbert into Munster in 1569 to crush the Desmond resistance, with the rank of colonel and the powers of a military governor. From the start, Gilbert employed the ruthless methods of fire and sword. Castles in the hands of Irish lords were given only one opportunity to surrender. If that offer was rejected, all inhabitants were put to the sword when the castle was

[27] Thomas Becon, *The Governance of Vertue* (1566), fos. 96v–98v; Johnson, *Just War Tradition*, 55, 57–9; Thomas Churchyard, *A Generall Rehearsall of Warres, called Churchyardes Choice* (1579), sig. Qij; Edmund Spenser, *A View of the State of Ireland* (1763), 6, 143, 163–4, 169, 182.

[28] Canny, 'Ideology of English Colonization', 579–80; J. M. Hill, *Fire and Sword: Sorley Boy MacDonnell and the Rise of Clan Ian Mor, 1538–1590* (1993), 1; J. Bardon, *A History of Ulster* (1992), 83–5.

[29] N. P. Canny, *The Elizabethan Conquest of Ireland: A Pattern Established, 1565–76* (1976), 47–8, 50, 54–5; J. B. Black, *The Reign of Elizabeth, 1558–1603* (1936), 391–2.

taken. Those Irish lords and chieftains who did make submission were compelled to approach Gilbert's tent by walking between two rows of severed heads. When the accusation was made that his tactics were cruel, Gilbert replied that he only used the methods of warfare which the Irish had long employed against the English.[30] In fact, the use of such extreme methods appears to have originated with Gilbert, and Elizabeth and her Privy Council accepted the argument that they were justified. The policy of making war 'by fire and sword' (the phrase derives from the commission to execute martial law given to Gilbert) was continued by subsequent lord deputies and presidents of provinces. Sir Humphrey Gilbert's half-brother, Sir Walter Raleigh, while serving as a captain in Ireland, learned to make use of the guerilla tactics of the Irish kernes, or foot soldiers, and, on one occasion, ambushed and captured a band of them and then hanged every last man summarily.[31] The Desmond Rebellion was not easily crushed, and, indeed, was prolonged by the strategy of the West Country adventurers, such as Sir Warham St Leger and Sir Richard Grenville, of provoking the Gaelic lords to rebel so that they could obtain the rebels' forfeited lands. Thus, the suppression of the Desmond Rebellion and the plantation of Munster became inextricably linked.[32]

Sir John Perrott, who had been one of the queen's champions at her accession, was the first president of Munster to be so styled. He took up his duties in 1572 and immediately began to mop up in the aftermath of Desmond's Rebellion. Desmond's seneschal, James Fitzmaurice, defied the new president by hanging the mayor of Kilmallock from the market cross and plundering the town. Perrott went to the town and took up residence in a half-burnt house, where he summoned the burgesses to begin rebuilding. Perrott then raised a punitive expedition consisting of English troops plus hired gallowglasses and kernes and pursued the rebels into a bog where the rebels thought the president would not follow them. His troops killed fifty of the 200 rebels and brought their heads back to Kilmallock, where they were displayed in the market-place. In order to please Lord Burghley and save money, which was always in short supply for the English forces in Ireland, Perrott made it a practice to hire gallowglasses and kernes to supplement his meager English troops, and he trained and equipped them in the methods of modern warfare. He was subsequently accused of treason, called home and much blamed for arming the Irish. The Irish, having been trained in the methods of modern warfare by Perrott, now became more difficult to subdue and required the expenditure of more money and larger armies to conquer, according to his critics.[33]

[30] *The Voyages and Colonizing Enterprises of Sir Humphrey Gilbert*, ed. D. B. Quinn, 2 vols., HS, 2nd ser. 83–4 (1940), i. 16–17; Churchyard, *Generall Rehearsall*, sigs. Q1–R1; Canny, 'Ideology of English Colonization', 581–3.

[31] Canny, *Elizabethan Conquest*, 81–2.

[32] Raphael Holinshed, *Chronicle of England, Scotland and Ireland*, 6 vols. (1807–8), vi. 437; M. MacCarthy-Morrough, *The Munster Plantation: English Migration to Southern Ireland, 1583–1641* (1986), 28–30.

[33] [Richard Rawlinson], *The History of... Sir John Perrott* (1728), 47–8, 73, 79–83, 106–12; Camden, *Annales* (1630 edn.), bk. iii, p. 127; Sir Robert Naunton, *Fragmenta Regalia, or Observations*

When Sir George Carew became president of Munster in 1600, he would accept the surrender of Irish rebels only if they could persuade large numbers of followers to do the same. At the ceremony where they surrendered, the rebels were made to grovel and crawl on their knees to him. Lesser rebels were simply dealt with by fire and sword. Nor was it particularly beneficial to enjoy Carew's protection, as Edmund Fitzgibbon, the so-called 'White Knight' and sheriff of co. Clare discovered. One of Carew's captains burned a house in one of the White Knight's towns, before an old soldier told him that he had made a mistake. The White Knight's son, John Fitzgibbon, sought revenge against Carew's captain and sixty people died in the ensuing clash. Ireland was a nervous and volatile place.[34]

Sir Richard Bingham, who began his military career as a gentleman volunteer in an English troop of horse in the French Wars of Religion, was sent as governor of Connaught in the 1580s to suppress the rebellion of the Bourkes in co. Mayo with inadequate forces. These were further depleted by drafts sent to reinforce garrisons in the Netherlands, so Bingham was forced to hire kernes while the Bourkes brought in gallowglasses from Antrim and redshanks from Scotland. Bingham demanded eldest sons from the Bourkes as pledges, but that did not prevent them from rebelling a second time. Bingham reduced the seat of the Bourkes, Castle Barry, without artillery, which could not be hauled around in the trackless wilderness of the west of Ireland, and all of the Bourkes who garrisoned the castle died in its defence. The kernes, who fought on both sides of the Bourke Rebellion, were armed mostly with bows and arrows.[35] While the remaining ships of the Spanish Armada were making their way home off the west coast of Ireland in 1588, a party of 200 Spaniards surrendered to Bingham upon 'mercy'. When Bingham heard a rumour that another much larger party of armed Spaniards had also landed, he slaughtered the 200 prisoners. Fearing to surrender to Bingham, some 800 Spaniards put to sea in a decayed Irish vessel and all perished. By contrast, Elizabeth ransomed the 1,200 Spanish soldiers and mariners who cast up on the shores of England and were taken prisoner. Bingham lost his nerve once again during yet another rebellion of the Bourkes, and massacred a batch of prisoners awaiting trial upon hearing that the rebellion was more widespread than he had previously supposed. Bingham was briefly imprisoned in the Fleet Prison in London in 1596 for his excesses, but he was soon released and returned to Ireland in 1598, where he continued to function as a provost marshal.[36]

---

upon Queen Elizabeth, Her Times and Favorites, ed. J. S. Cervoski (1641; repr. 1985), 65–6. For a detailed discussion of Sir John Perrott's career as lord deputy between 1584 and 1588, cf. H. Morgan, *Tyrone's Rebellion: The Outbreak of the Nine Years War in Tudor Ireland* (1993), ch. 3.

[34] Thomas Stafford, *Pacata Hibernia: Ireland Appeased and Reduced* (1633), 47, 63–4, 73–4; *DNB, sub* Edward Fitzgibbon (1552?–1608).

[35] BL, Harley MS. 35 ('Richard Bingham's Relation of the Suppression of the Bourkes in co. Mayo, Province of Connaught, 1586'), fos. 222v–35r.

[36] Churchyard, *Generall Rehearsall*, sig. A1v; *Triumphs of Nassau*, trans. W. Shute (1613), 79; Richard Beacon, *Solon His Follie* (1594), 16, 19; *DNB, sub* Richard Bingham (1528–99).

The English government could not ignore Ireland, because if foreign powers intervened in or invaded Ireland, England would be strategically vulnerable. Both Elizabeth of England and Philip of Spain were aware of the inconsistency of her intervention in the Netherlands to support a revolt against another Christian prince and her attempt to suppress a rebellion in Ireland, and the awkwardness of this situation was certainly a consideration when Elizabeth refused the offer of the Dutch States General to assume sovereignty over the United Provinces. Although one can argue that the English viceroys and adventurers might have been less truc-ulent in their dealings with the Irish lords and chieftains—not to mention the peasants—one must not forget that the leaders on both sides were martialists and not diplomats. It would be difficult to imagine the Irish accepting a peaceful solu-tion since Irish society was, by nature, bellicose and highly militarized, and both sides assumed that the normal way of settling disputes was by war. The prospect of establishing a stable government in the Netherlands, with its thriving commerce and middle-class culture, could, perhaps, be posited, but Ireland presented an entirely different set of circumstances.

Old Irish society regarded war as a sport. Aristocratic households in Ireland still swarmed with large numbers of idle swordsmen, who, since childhood, had never known any other way of life than that of the warrior and scorned any other occupation. Among the Old English inhabitants, feudal lords professed loyalty to the crown at the beginning of Elizabeth's reign, but they kept private armies of retainers, including gallowglasses, on the pretext that they would provide a buffer against the Gaelic Irish. However, by the sixteenth century such bands of retainers were kept for display, pursuing feuds and cattle-raiding. Whether undertaken by bandits, unemployed kernes or magnates, cattle-raiding was a widespread pastime in Ireland. It was also a simulation of war which, perhaps, substituted for more bloody depredations, but the threat to political stability was clear enough.[37]

Until the mid-Elizabethan period, the costs of the Irish wars and the maintenance of royal troops in Ireland were largely borne by the English government. Thereafter, the costs were increasingly shifted onto Irish society, whether the sol-diery fought for the rebels or the English government. Under such circumstances, any possibility of agricultural prosperity eluded the Irish farmer and all prospect of the emergence of a civil society faded. In the more anglicized areas of south-eastern Ireland, the custom of coigne and livery obliged the husbandman to pay the soldier 'mansmeat, horsemeat and money', when so demanded. This was an adaptation among the Old English of the Irish *bonaght*, a similar form of extortion where gallowglasses and kernes were billeted and fed at the expense of the peasantry. Since Ireland was on a warlike footing throughout the sixteenth century, the various forms of war taxation encouraged idleness among the Irish peasantry because it was too risky to accumulate wealth. This situation was

---

[37] Quinn, *Elizabethans and the Irish*, 15–16, 39; Canny, *Elizabethan Conquest*, 21–2; Spenser, *State of Ireland*, 6; Manning, *Swordsmen*, 167, 171–2.

unlikely to change until a strong central authority could restrain the lords and chieftains and pacify the land.[38]

The Old English of the Pale[39] and other Anglo-Norman settlements along the coast of Munster should have been natural political supporters of the Elizabethan Irish government, since they regarded themselves as being English in culture. Although they had at first supported Sir Robert Sidney as lord deputy, the Old English turned against Sidney because he wished to establish a permanent standing army in Ireland to take the place of the 'hosting' or muster of their own retainers. Sidney's standing army was to be supported by a tax on all householders instead of the more traditional system of purveyance which fell upon peasant households only. Sidney had also bypassed the Irish Parliament in introducing new policies, and the Old English perceived an alarming transfer of military and political power from them to the officials at Dublin Castle and the New English settlers. There was also a religious cleavage between the two groups, since most of the Old English remained Catholics and felt an affinity for the new, more militant Tridentine Catholicism.[40]

The New English plantation of Ireland began in earnest after the appointment of Sir Henry Sidney as lord deputy in 1565. Sidney's colonizing efforts were motivated by his recognition that the O'Neills of Ulster could never be reconciled to English rule nor could the Scots mercenaries be ejected without establishing a military presence by colonization. Sidney had learned much about the Spanish colonial experience during the three years he spent in Spain as a diplomat in the 1550s. He also discovered that there was extensive trade between Spain and Munster and that this was the source of many Irish weapons. Those who answered Sidney's summons to make their fortunes in Ireland were usually landless younger sons, many from the West of England, who were veterans of the Wars of Religion in France and privateering voyages against Spain. Some of them were Dudley adherents, such as the Carews and the Champernouns who had earlier been involved in Wyatt's Rebellion of 1554. Like the Spanish *conquistadores*, these gentlemen went to Ireland as officers and volunteers hoping to carve out estates or at least garner booty. John Clapham believed that the English captains who coveted Irish estates 'devised means to nourish and prolong [the] wars for private advantage'. Although English swordsmen always played an important role in colonization, Sidney did not favour purely military colonies, because the martialists had little in the way of capital, and he had learned not to expect financial assistance from Elizabeth. Therefore, Sidney sought to involve merchants in colonization schemes to help provide the necessary capital investment.[41]

[38] Davies, *True Causes*, 173–5; Quinn, *Elizabethans and the Irish*, 4–5; Canny, *Elizabethan Conquest*, 211–12.

[39] The English Pale included the counties of Dublin, Meath, Louth, Kildare and Westmeath.

[40] N. P. Canny, *The Formation of the Old English Elite* (1975), 2, 4–7, 22–4, 28–9.

[41] Id., *Elizabethan Conquest*, 66–8, 71–3, 75–7; Quinn, *Elizabethans and the Irish*, 106–7; id., *Raleigh and the British Empire* (1949), 24–7; Churchyard, *Generall Rehearsall*, sigs. D2r & v; R. Bagwell, *Ireland under the Tudors*, 3 vols. (1885–90; repr. 1963), iii. 250–1; *Elizabeth of England:*

The plantation of Munster in the early 1570s did not get off to an auspicious start, because the first grants of land which dispossessed Irish tenants (who were usually kernes) made violent conflict inevitable. The New English settlers soon learned that their position was very vulnerable unless they extirpated the Irish or drove them westward. In order to secure English settlements in Munster, the western part of Leinster and in Ulster, it became necessary to establish new towns (a novelty to the Irish) which extended beyond the original Anglo-Norman coastal and riverine settlements. These towns needed to be walled about and the streets laid out in a regular grid pattern in order to make control easier. They usually contained a small garrison—a practice which tied English forces down and made them less mobile. Altogether, some fifty-six towns in Ireland were walled. Although the British civil wars made urban fortifications redundant on the main island, they continued to be quite necessary in Ireland until the Williamite conquest was completed in 1692. These towns were intended to be outposts of civility, symbolized by English speech, dress and law, as well as military strongholds set down in the Irish wilderness. English law did not extend beyond these garrison towns, and outside the walls the Irish remained subject to martial law in the absence of English law and judges. The larger towns such as Dublin had some sort of militia guild or company to which only those 'of English name and blood' might belong. The first earl of Essex had begun a town at Belfast in 1573, and other towns were begun in eastern Ulster at a day's march from Belfast, which proved to be of great military significance during the suppression of Tyrone's Rebellion in the 1590s. Carrickfergus was added on the Antrim coast of Belfast Lough to provision the English forces in Ulster from Chester.[42]

The native Irish were ill equipped both tactically and psychologically to besiege fortresses or to fight battles in the European manner. Traditional Irish warfare was based upon guerilla tactics on ground of their own choosing—river fords, mountain passes or in the vicinity of bogs and forests. Moreover, until the Tyrone Rebellion of 1593–1601, Irish kernes and gallowglasses relied heavily upon long battle-axes, bows and arrows, hand-thrown darts and broadswords and targes, and made little

---

Certain Observations concerning the Life and Reign of Queen Elizabeth by John Clapham, ed. E. P. and C. Read (1951), 58–9.

[42] E. M. Hinton, *Ireland through Tudor Eyes* (1935; repr. 1978), 650; R. Gillespie, *Colonial Ulster: The Settlement of East Ulster, 1600–1641* (1985), 168; S. M. Jack, *Towns in Tudor and Stuart Britain* (1996), 5–8, 14; P. Somerville-Large, *Dublin* (1979), 85, 87; Davies, *True Causes*, 166, 252. Professor Canny points out that the plantation of Ireland provided a model for planting colonies across the Atlantic, and thus a garrison mentality was carried into the New World. In the North American colonies, as in Ireland, authority was vested in the hands of colonial officials with few limits placed upon the exercise of that authority. Because they were usually soldiers, seventeenth-century colonial governors were disposed to use military action against the native inhabitants and to dispossess them (*Kingdom and Colony: Ireland in the Atlantic World, 1560–1800* (1988), 29). Especially noticeable was the predilection of the British and the colonists to build fortresses in the wilderness to overawe and pacify the 'savages'. John Keegan notes that by the end of the French and Indian (Seven Years) War in 1763, 'North America was one of the most fortified regions in the world', and many more forts would continue to be constructed between the eighteenth and the early twentieth centuries (*Fields of Battle: The Wars for North America* (1995), 62–3).

use of cavalry or artillery. Although the Irish lived in close proximity to the technologically and militarily developed parts of Western Europe, they resisted the reception of modern military theory and practice. The Gaelic Irish, like the Highland Scots, relied upon variations of the Celtic or Highland charge to gain a psychological advantage over military forces of more technologically advanced cultures, making maximum use of the elements of surprise, unrestrained fury and familiar terrain. Their style of fighting depended upon individual prowess and personal honour, and their chiefs led by example from the front. Such warfare was most effective when carried out by small, highly mobile warrior bands which could take cover in bogs, mountains or forests.[43]

The English encroachment on Ulster had precipitated a crisis by the 1590s. The English policy of compelling the Irish lords and chieftains to surrender their feudal powers in exchange for the regrant of their lands with English-style titles stripped of military power together with expanding English settlements posed a fundamental challenge to the hegemony of the Irish leaders. The resulting clash, which gradually became more overt and violent, posed the greatest challenge to English rule in Ireland of the Elizabethan period.

The Tyrone Rebellion was based in Ulster, the most Gaelic and inaccessible part of Ireland, and was led by Hugh O'Neill, the most powerful of all Irish lords, known to the Irish as 'The O'Neill', and to the English as the third baron of Dunganon and second earl of Tyrone. O'Neill was at first Machiavellian enough to hope that he could obtain what he wanted by diplomacy and deceit rather than by war. He probably would have been content with some sort of permanent delegation of authority from Elizabeth, but that was incompatible with her concept of sovereignty and policy of centralization. O'Neill had no hope of expelling the English from Ireland, but he did hope to drive them back into the Pale. He and his fellow lords of Ulster could see that the conquest of Munster, Connaught and eastern Ulster by fortress-building and maintaining permanent garrisons was bearing fruit, and that it was but a matter of time before their lordships were broken up, divided into shires and subjected to English law. O'Neill's strategy was to delay the process of anglicization by defensive war, to make political concessions, to negotiate truces and to buy time until the English were exhausted by their various wars or the queen was dead, giving him a chance to obtain a better settlement from James VI of Scotland.[44]

O'Neill had persuaded the Irish to abandon their medieval edged weapons and accept firearms. The kernes were trained in the use of calivers and muskets, and the gallowglasses and redshanks, who regarded themselves as gentlemen, were taught to wield pikes. Some of O'Neill's *bonaghts* or mercenaries had seen service under the Spanish, and he could put 2,000 of them into the field at any one time. Although this force represented the beginnings of a modern, permanent Irish army, they

[43] J. M. Hill, *Celtic Warfare, 1595–1763* (1986), 1–4.

[44] G. A. Hayes-McCoy, 'Strategy and Tactics in Irish Warfare, 1593–1601', *IHS* 2 (1940–1), 256–7; Morgan, *Tyrone's Rebellion*, ch. 8.

continued to prefer guerilla tactics within a defensive strategy. O'Neill's men were best at skirmishes and large-scale ambushes, but usually avoided sieges and pitched battles because they were vulnerable to even the lightest field artillery, and because under the stress of battle the Irish soldiers would sometimes revert to the traditional methods of Irish warfare. In order to avoid sieges, Tyrone abandoned his own castles, but he made one exception to this rule when, in 1594, he ordered his lieutenants to attack Enniskillen Castle, which controlled communications between Ulster and Connaught. Although he still remained in the background at this date, O'Neill wished to coordinate the resistance in Ulster with that in other parts of Ireland. O'Neill was able to unite the Irish of Ulster (no small achievement in itself), and to win battles such as that at the Yellow Ford in 1598, but ultimately he failed to unite the Irish into a nation, nor could he overcome the localism or displace the archaic martial cultures of the chieftains.[45] Moreover, like all of the so-called English conquests of Ireland in the sixteenth and seventeenth centuries, Tyrone's Rebellion was also a civil war between different factions of Irish lords, some of whom, like the *bonaghts*, allied themselves with the New English officials and adventurers.

Irish resistance was not easily or quickly crushed. In dealing with the earl of Tyrone, the English commanders in Ireland, although certainly aware of changes in warfare on the European mainland, were less willing to recognize that Tyrone was modernizing his army and that the lessons learned in the wars of the Low Countries were applicable to Ireland. When the English government sent Sir John Norris to Ireland in 1594 with a regiment of experienced veterans of the Brittany campaign, the lord deputy, Sir William Russell, insulted Norris by saying that his soldiers were ragged and looked like they had been culled from prisons. Russell and Norris, who became the military commander in Ireland, were thereafter at odds with one another. Again, when the second earl of Essex came to Ireland as lord deputy in 1599, he offended veterans of the Irish wars by publically and pointedly expressing a preference for veterans of the Dutch wars and, by inference, disparaging the capabilities of those officers whom he held responsible for the defeat at the Battle of Blackwater or the Yellow Ford. These veterans were subsequently denied positions of command by Essex. The English forces in Ireland were riven by factionalism, as when a quarrel broke out between Henry Wriothesley, third earl of Southampton, the lieutenant-general of the horse, and Thomas, fifteenth Lord Grey of Wilton, over the latter's failure to obey orders during a recent skirmish. Grey also came into conflict with Essex over his attempt to become lieutenant-general of the infantry in succession to Roger Manners, fifth earl of Rutland. When rebuffed by Essex, Grey declared that he was shifting his allegiance to Sir Robert Cecil, 'and shortly, the Lord Grey went to England where he did the lord lieutenant no good offices'.[46]

[45] Hayes-McCoy, 'Strategy and Tactics', 261–3, 265; Falls, *Elizabeth's Irish Wars*, 38; Hill, *Celtic Warfare*, 4–5, 22–5, 29–30.

[46] Sir James Perrott, *The Chronicles of Ireland, 1584–1608*, ed. H. Wood, IMC (1933), 89–90, 93–7, 161–2, 164. Perrott was the bastard son of the late lord deputy, Sir John Parrott, and governor

Because so many of the English forces in Ireland were scattered among garrisons in the numerous small forts, it was impossible to gather together a field army of significant size. Sir James Perrott described the English forces as 'disheartened' and subject to the depredations of corrupt captains, who cheated and abused their men and returned false musters. Many captains were frequently absent from their posts and left their duties to subordinates, and it was found necessary to cashier a number of them. New drafts of recruits from England melted away before they reached their remote garrisons, and it became necessary to replace them with Irish *bonaghts*. Although the regulations stated that captains were to employ no more than three native Irish per company of 100 men, Barnabe Rich insisted that in the 1590s it was not unusual for more than half of the men in English companies to be Irish. Irish chieftains took advantage of this opportunity to send their retainers to join such companies, and, after having availed themselves of training in the use of modern weapons, these *bonaghts* would then desert, often taking their weapons with them, and return to their chieftains to serve under O'Neill. Some of the English captains, such as Thomas Lee, were actually accused of direct dealings with O'Neill.[47]

The appointment of Charles Blount, eighth Lord Mountjoy, as lord deputy in 1600, inaugurated the decisive and final phase of the Tyrone Rebellion. Lord Mountjoy was the most competent and determined of all of the Elizabethan military commanders in Ireland. Mountjoy abandoned the strategy of holding a large number of small forts, whose garrisons sapped manpower, and retained only those necessary to supply his troops in the field. He taught his men how to overcome the difficulties of the Irish terrain and how to campaign in the winter to the enemy's disadvantage. He ferreted out the Irish rebels when the trees were bare of foliage, when their provisions were low, and thus forced them to abandon guerilla tactics and meet him in more open engagements. Mountjoy also struck ruthlessly at the civilian population with fire-and-sword tactics, so that they could not supply the Irish warriors. Mountjoy and his subordinates, such as Sir George Carew, also employed diplomacy and sought to detach and win over O'Neill's confederates such as Florence MacCarthy, the MacCarthy More, an important leader in Munster. Mountjoy also made effective use of sea power and, in May 1600, Sir Henry Docwra led a force of 4,000 men into the heart of Ulster and landed them near Derry at the head of Lough Foyle.[48]

of Newry. He presented a martialist view of Irish history that was hostile to courtier influence (ibid., p. vi).

[47] Ibid. 8, 98, 159; Barnabe Rich, *The New Description of Ireland* (1610), 109–10; H. H. Davis, 'The Military Career of Thomas North', *HLQ* 12 (1948–9), 320; J. P. Meyers, ' "Murdering Heart . . . Murdering Hand": Captain Thomas Lee of Ireland, Elizabethan Assassin', *SCJ* 22 (1991), 47–60.

[48] C. Lennon, *Sixteenth-Century Ireland: The Incomplete Conquest* (1995), 299; Bardon, *History of Ulster*, 103–4; [Thomas Gainsford], *The . . . History of the Earl Tirone* (1619), 32; Hill, *Celtic Warfare*, 30; Hayes-McCoy, 'Strategy and Tactics', 269; McGurk, *Elizabethan Conquest*, 224–5.

Until this time, O'Neill had fought a largely defensive war, maintaining his position in the rugged fastness of Ulster. The possibility that the Spanish might send assistance to him in the south meant that he had to keep his lines of communication with Connaught and Munster open. When a Spanish force under Don Juan Áquila landed at Kinsale with additional outposts at Castlehaven, Berehaven and Baltimore in September 1601, O'Neill was forced to come out into the open and march south to assist the Spanish, which meant employing offensive tactics. O'Neill set up his camp surrounding the English besiegers at Kinsale. In order to break through to the Spanish lines O'Neill planned a pitched battle, hoping to take the English by surprise in the early dawn hours of Christmas Eve 1601, but Mountjoy, with a force half the size of the combined Spanish and Irish armies, prevailed. In the articles of surrender, the Spanish army, which never engaged the English, was allowed to depart with all their arms, ordnance, munitions and ensigns. O'Neill fled northward into the forests. Mountjoy offered O'Neill a pardon in early 1603, and he surrendered on 30 March—unaware that Queen Elizabeth had died six days earlier.[49]

Under the generous terms offered by James VI and I, O'Neill could have lived out his remaining years in peace with his estates largely intact but for an English military presence in Ulster. However, his pride was such that he could not accept a superior authority in his lordships of Clandeboye and Tyrone. So, in 1607, O'Neill and Roderick or Rory O'Donnell (the brother of O'Neill's late co-conspirator Hugh Roe O'Donnell, lord of Tyrconnell), who had been created earl of Tyrconnell by James I, took ship in Lough Swilly and fled to Spanish Flanders with a number of their kinsmen and supporters. This 'flight of the earls' represents the beginning of the dispersal of the 'wild geese' who, like O'Neill's son Henry, served in the Spanish Army of Flanders and other European armies until the end of the eighteenth century. The flight also opened the way for the English settlement of Ulster.[50]

Both English and Irish veterans of the English forces were encouraged to settle in Ulster and were frequently taken on as tenants by their former officers. Loyalty was regarded as more desirable than knowledge of agricultural techniques. Their sense of camaraderie marked them as a distinctive community and made them vulnerable to attack during the rebellion of 1641.[51] Sir John Harington, himself a veteran of the Irish wars and one of Essex's knights, told Sir Robert Cecil that the government of Ireland had been entrusted too much to military men, who relied on the use of martial law where they ought to have attempted to resolve disputes by legal means. He also thought that military men had no interest in peace because they feared that they would not find employment, and he cited

---

[49] J. J. Silk, *Kinsale: The Spanish Intervention in Ireland at the End of the Elizabethan Wars* (1970), 1–7, 53–5; Hayes-McCoy, 'Strategy and Tactics', 270; E.J., *A Letter from a Souldier of Good Place in Ireland* (1602), 3, 11–12, 19–23; Lennon, *Sixteenth-Century Ireland*, 300–1.

[50] Bardon, *History of Ulster*, 115–18; N. Canny, 'The Flight of the Earls, 1607', *IHS* 17 (1971), 380, 390–1. [51] Canny, *Kingdom and Colony*, 95–6.

Machiavelli's *Art of War* to show that mercenary soldiers can never make virtuous citizens.[52] Because the laws of England had not been extended to much of Ireland before the final suppression of the Tyrone Rebellion, there had been no other way to enforce English policy except by military force. Although Sir John Davies thought that Ireland was much better governed under James VI and I, he did admit that it was still necessary to continue a standing army in Ireland to serve as a 'seminary of martial men' and to be available for use by the lord deputy to enforce English law and policy.[53]

The Irish wars provided an important training ground for late Elizabethan soldiers to undergo an apprenticeship in arms, but the lessons learned while conducting war against a foe who employed guerilla tactics and refused to be drawn out into pitched battles were more applicable to fighting Indians in North America. Although Ireland was a useful place to garrison permanent military forces which could not well be kept in England because of objections to standing armies and mercenary soldiers, Ireland was also a land that had the reputation of being a graveyard for military reputations. Swordsmen were drawn there more by the hope of plunder and lands for colonization than the expectation of military honour and glory. Elizabeth never provided enough money and men to complete the conquest of Ireland until the final phase of Tyrone's Rebellion under Lord Deputy Mountjoy. Earlier lords deputy were often too arrogant or unimaginative to adapt to the conditions of warfare in Ireland, and wasted their meagre resources building and garrisoning many small forts, and consequently could not gather together enough men to constitute a field army of sufficient size to subdue the Irish. Moreover, few of them possessed the diplomatic skills to reconcile the Old English to more direct English rule, nor did they possess the authority to offer the protection of English common law and courts to the native Irish whom, in any case, they regarded as being beyond the pale of civilization. The lords deputy and the governors of Munster, Connaught and Ulster were almost invariably military men by inclination, experience and profession and were used to dispensing martial law when not actually deploying military force. Their background and garrison mentality furnished a prototype for many of the men who were later to govern English and British colonies overseas, and anticipated the attitudes and patterns of behaviour which were to characterize the relationship between governors, colonists and native peoples—especially in the New World.[54]

[52] Sir John Harington, *A Short View of the State of Ireland, Written in 1605* (1879), 5–6, 9.

[53] Davies, *True Causes*, 5–7, 261–2; Morgan, *Tyrone's Rebellion*, 3. The judges in the common-law courts of Ireland held that the Irish were not reputed to be subjects of the king nor subject to English law because they were aliens, and consequently they did not enjoy the protection of common law unless they purchased charters of denization, which were often not available when a native Irish person applied for them (ibid. 107–10).

[54] S. S. Webb, *The Governors-General: The English Army and the Definition of Empire, 1569–1681* (1979), 110–11, 179, 440–1; L. Boynton, 'The Tudor Provost-Marshal', *EHR* 77 (1962), 440–2; R. A. J. Tyler, *Bloody Provost* (1980), 52–7.

The captains of the English companies in Ireland, like their counterparts in the States' Army in the Netherlands, tended to be corrupt entrepreneurs, who cheated their men out of pay, provisions and clothing and returned false musters or hired Irish mercenaries in defiance of military regulations. Lacking discipline and obedience to orders themselves, they set a poor example for their soldiers and lacked the professionalism so necessary for training a modern army. They resembled nothing so much as the Elizabethan sea dogs who were more interested in plunder than military objectives. The apprenticeship in arms of the English in both Ireland and the Netherlands must have been a dispiriting experience for those more high-minded soldiers whose attention was focused on containing Spanish power.

2

The Low-Countries wars

War is the remedy for a state surfeited with peace: it is a medicine for commonwealths sick of too much ease and tranquility...it carrieth a reforming nature, and it is part of justice.

Sir William Cornwallis, *Discourses upon Seneca the Tragedian*
(1601; repr. 1952), sig. H1*r*.

The Netherlands wars were the queen's seminaries and nurseries of many brave soldiers, and so likewise were the civil wars of France, whither she sent five several armies, the fence schools that inured the youth and gallantry of the kingdom, and it was a militia wherein they were daily acquainted with the discipline of the Spaniards.

Sir Robert Naunton, *Fragmenta Regalia, or Observations on Queen Elizabeth, Her Times, and Favorites*, ed. J. S. Cervoski
(1641; repr. 1985), 57.

There were fundamental differences between the Elizabethan conquest of Ireland and the English intervention in the Dutch war of independence. The former was a brutal and ruthless war waged to extirpate Catholicism, Gaelic culture and law and to replace the native Irish with English settlers. As rebels the enemy were denied the status of combatants. The strategic objective was to end Spanish and Scottish influence in Ireland. This enterprise offered the prospect of acquiring wealth and estates, but because the war in Ireland was fought against what the English military adventurers regarded as an unworthy and uncivilized enemy, it afforded small opportunity to display virtue and win honour.[1] By contrast, the swordsmen who went as volunteers to the Netherlands were conscious of participating in a

---

[1] Although Edmund Spenser tried to invest the military conquest and colonization of Ireland with an aura of chivalry, his literary efforts were far removed from reality (cf. A. B. Ferguson, *The Chivalric Tradition in Renaissance England* (1986), 71). Spenser's ignorance of the rules of engagement and of how wars were fought needs to be emphasized. Arthur, 14ᵗʰ Lord Grey of Wilton, whom Spenser served as secretary, was recalled from his post as lord deputy of Ireland by Elizabeth's government to face charges for the brutal excesses with which he waged war against the Irish rebels (M. West, 'Spenser's Art of War: Chivalric Allegory, Military Technology and the Elizabethan Mock-Heroic Sensibility', *RQ* 41 (1988), 667, 684–5).

Protestant crusade in which they felt a strong bond of fellowship with Dutch Calvinists and French Huguenots whom they encountered in the Netherlands and on the various military expeditions to northern France to assist Henry IV.[2] Through contact with neo-Stoic thinkers and classical scholars, these volunteers assimilated an ideology of constancy, duty and service to a cause which ennobled their efforts and helped to provide a code of behaviour which facilitated the process of military professionalization.[3] Although the commanders, officers and volunteers adjusted haltingly to the new conditions of static siege warfare in the Netherlands, they were forced to admit that the Spanish Army of Flanders was a formidable and worthy opponent and that there was much to be learned by serving in the Dutch army, which was organized specifically to confront the veteran professionals of this Spanish force.

When Elizabeth finally consented to send a military expedition to the aid of the Dutch, it was too late to prevent the break-up of the seventeen provinces of the Low Countries. The Dutch were leaderless, William of Orange having been assassinated in June 1584, and Antwerp, the chief city of the southern Low Countries, which had been besieged for many months by Alexander Farnese, prince of Parma, commander of the Spanish Army of Flanders, was finally starved out and capitulated in April 1585. England thus became exposed to invasion from Spanish Flanders. Leicester did not arrive in the Netherlands until December 1585, and the troops which he brought with him, having been inadequately trained and equipped, were far from ready to go into action. There were already in the Netherlands some 7,000 English troops under the command of Sir John Norris, an experienced professional soldier, who were trained and ready to fight. Norris had been forced into a subordinate position by the arrival of Leicester, who proceeded to establish a rival chain of command staffed with his own followers. Although Norris had already secured and garrisoned the cautionary towns and was ready for an offensive, the queen obliged him and his troops to assume a defensive posture.[4]

Elizabeth never was comfortable with the Dutch alliance and the prospect of a strong military effort in the Low Countries aimed at Spain. This policy had been

[2] Paul Hammer stresses the differences not only between strategies, but also between values of the Essexians, who favoured confronting Spanish power directly whether in the Low Countries, France, or on the high seas, versus the Cecilians, who wished to avoid continental involvement and regarded Ireland as the place to check foreign influences. Virtue was best displayed in a continental or naval war, whereas victory in Ireland tended to reward the followers of Lord Burghley and Sir Robert Cecil, who controlled the patronage networks of the Irish government (*The Polarisation of Elizabethan Politics: The Political Career of Robert Devereux, 2nd Earl of Essex, 1585–1597* (1999), 393–4).

[3] D. J. B. Trim emphasizes that a chivalric ethos, which was apparently widespread among the Dutch nobility, was in no way incompatible with the comparatively high degree of military professionalization to be found in the States' Army in the time of Maurice of Nassau ('Army, Society and Military Professionalism in the Netherlands during the Eighty Years' War', in Trim (ed.), *The Chivalric Ethos and the Development of Military Professionalism* (2003), 269, 278–87).

[4] Sir C. Wilson, *Queen Elizabeth and the Revolt of the Netherlands* (1970), 61, 63, 84; J. Israel, *The Dutch Republic: Its Rise, Greatness, and Fall, 1477–1806* (1995), 219–20; J. S. Nolan, *Sir John Norreys and the Elizabethan Military World* (1997), 84–92.

advocated by Leicester and the war party, and the Essexians would continue to urge it in the 1590s. Although Elizabeth had been offered the sovereignty of Holland and Zeeland and, later, the title of protector, she refused both and took no interest in the Netherlands until English interests were challenged more directly. She sent money and men to the Netherlands grudgingly and only upon the security of retaining possession of the so-called cautionary towns of Brill, Bergen-op-Zoom, Flushing and the adjacent coastal fortress of Rammekens. After the troops which had been under Leicester's command were absorbed into the States' Army, Elizabeth considered those who held Dutch military commissions, such as Sir Francis Vere, to be men of divided allegiance. When Vere sought the position of governor of Brill in 1597, Elizabeth rejected him because of this conflict of allegiance and also because he was not of noble rank.[5]

Not only Elizabeth, but many swordsmen who volunteered for service in the States' Army, felt uncomfortable about the location of sovereignty in the emerging Dutch state. Many of the Dutch leaders recognized their anomalous position, and that was why the sovereignty had been offered to the duke of Anjou and then to Queen Elizabeth. This was always a contentious issue in Dutch politics, and this is why the position of stadholder (or provincial governor) and captain-general of most of the Dutch provinces remained in the possession of the House of Orange-Nassau. Among those who sought an aristocratic or princely leader of the Dutch revolt, it was assumed that the bourgeois Dutch, unlike the ancient Romans or Swiss, lacked the virtues of Spartan living and discipline which could sustain the martial culture necessary to defend republican liberty. When Sir Philip Sidney resolved to fight under the leadership of the House of Orange, he assumed that an independent Netherlands would be governed by a prince; he did not realize, apparently, that many of the Dutch leaders were thinking of a republic. Sidney probably agreed with those who thought a republic was out of the question because the Dutch nobility and commonalty were thought to be effeminate and lacking that special military quality of virtue which could grow only from a Roman-like emphasis upon the continual exercise of arms. Justus Lipsius, who had much influence on Sidney and his fellow volunteers, thought that princely rule was the best way to promote virtue in a commonwealth, and he insisted on the need for a standing army as the practical means to foster that virtue. Lipsius had rejected the Machiavellian idea of a civic militia. This had the effect of marginalizing the role of the Dutch militia guilds which best embodied the martial tradition in Holland and Zeeland.[6]

    [5] R. M. Smuts, *Court Culture and the Origins of a Royalist Tradition in Early Stuart England* (1987), 19–20; *Sir Thomas Overbury's Observations in his Travels upon the State of the Seventeen Provinces* (1626) in C. H. Firth (ed.), *Stuart Tracts, 1603–1693* (1903; repr. 1973), 214; *The Commentaries of Sir Francis Vere* (1657), in *Stuart Tracts*, 135–7.
    [6] M. van Gelderen, *The Political Thought of the Dutch Revolt, 1555–1590* (1992), 171–2, 180; id., 'The Machiavellian Moment and the Dutch Revolt: The Rise of Neostoicism and Dutch Republicanism', in G. Bock, Q. Skinner and M. Viroli (eds.), *Machiavelli and Republicanism* (1990), 208; B. Worden, *The Sound of Virtue: Philip Sidney's* Arcadia *and Elizabethan Politics* (1996), 234–5.
    In all fairness, it must be said that the Dutch nobility were much reduced in numbers by the end of the sixteenth century; only in Friesland did nobility remain numerous. They retained a tradition of

Map 2.1. The English intervention in the Low-Countries wars

The Elizabethan chivalric revival as a literary movement closely coincides with the declaration of war against Spain in 1585 and Leicester's expedition to the Netherlands. The proponents of this militant Protestant activism were led by Sir Philip Sidney and Edmund Spenser, who sanctioned raids on Spanish treasure fleets, military conquests and plantations in Ireland and the New World, and service

serving in both military and civil offices (J. de Vries, *The Dutch Rural Economy in the Golden Age, 1500–1800* (1974), 35–41).

in the Huguenot and Dutch armies as volunteers. Although he had not been in battle for thirty years, none was more caught up in this quest for chivalric honour than Leicester himself, but Elizabeth repeatedly thwarted his military ambitions by denying him adequate financial means to keep his army effective and by reprimanding him for seeking political and military honours above his social rank.[7]

The literary revival of chivalry publicized the endeavours of court gallants like Leicester and Sidney, but, in fact, English and Scottish volunteers and professional soldiers had been fighting for the Dutch for many years. The first English company to go to the Netherlands was raised by Sir Thomas Morgan of Pencarn in 1572. It contained 300 volunteers, of whom 100 were gentlemen—among them his kinsman Sir Roger Williams. Williams came of a poor but old gentry family seated in Penrhos, Monmouthshire, and he readily admitted that he went to war primarily for money. However, the Dutch army was not as regularly paid under William of Orange as it was in the seventeenth century, and after almost two years service with the Dutch, Williams entered the Spanish Army of Flanders, where he spent the next four years. He returned to the States' Army between 1578 and 1587. Williams's courage and skill as a soldier were respected by allies and foes alike, but he often found the Dutch to be jealous and ungrateful employers who regularly discharged their soldiers when the campaigning season concluded. At the end of an unsuccessful campaign to relieve Louis of Nassau at Mons in Hainault, the English soldiers when returning north were refused entry into Flushing by their supposed Dutch allies. They were very discouraged, and despite William of Orange's attempt to retain them under his command, most of the English soldiers went home.[8] Morgan's original band of volunteers eventually grew into an English regiment, successively commanded by Sir Humphrey Gilbert and Roger Williams. Although given to plunder, they were more regularly paid, better disciplined and more effective soldiers than the badly led impressed men who constituted most of Leicester's expedition.[9]

---

[7] Ferguson, *Chivalric Tradition*, 66, 70–2; R. C. McCoy, *The Rites of Knighthood: The Literature and Politics of Elizabethan Chivalry* (1989), 46–7.

The Dutch historian Pieter Geyl cannot bring himself to speak of Leicester and the English efforts to assist the Dutch in their struggle for independence except with the greatest distaste (*The Revolt of the Netherlands, 1555–1609* (1932), 196, 201, 203, 209–17).

[8] Sir Roger Williams, *The Actions of the Low Countries*, ed. D. W. Evans (1618; repr. 1964), pp. i–xiii, 49–53, 57; William Camden, *The History of the Most Renowned and Victorious Princess Elizabeth*, 4th edn. (1688; repr. 1970), 507; L. V. D. Owen, 'Sir Roger Williams and the Spanish Power in the Netherlands', *AQ* 34 (1937), 53, 58–9.

Another well-known literary figure who volunteered to fight in the Dutch army in 1572 was the poet George Gascoigne. He also came home with a poor opinion of the Dutch as allies and wrote a number of poems expressing his disillusionment with war (R. C. Johnson, *George Gascoigne* (1972), 86–95, esp. 93).

[9] Williams, *Actions of the Low Countries*, 57; Sir C. Oman, *The Art of War in the Sixteenth Century* (1937; repr. 1991), 548–50.

Another regiment of English mercenaries commanded by Sir Edward Chester served in the States' Army for several months in 1574. One company was retained by the Dutch after the remainder of the regiment was dismissed. Chester held the rank of colonel of the States' Army when he died in

The literary revival of chivalry was preceded by a more prosaic effort to elicit patriotic sentiments and anti-Catholic feeling in prospective gentlemen volunteers. Some thirty-one military newsbooks were published between 1578 and the end of Elizabeth's reign, to provide more accurate information about the Low-Countries wars than could be gathered from discharged soldiers, merchants and Dutch refugees. The quality of the newsbooks varied, but among the best were George Gascoigne's *The Spoyle of Antwerp*[10] and a couple of works put out by Leicester's muster-master-general, Thomas Digges.[11]

At a higher level, contact with European neo-Stoicism began with Sir Philip Sidney and his circle, and provided an intellectual foundation for a Protestant martial culture which was passed on to the followers of the second earl of Essex in the 1590s and, in the next reign, to the court of Henry, prince of Wales, and, of course, to the third earl of Essex and his circle. Among the more important links were Samson Lennard, Sidney's companion-in-arms at Zutphen, who later translated *The Mystery of Iniquity* (1611), an anti-papal propaganda piece by Sidney's close friend, the Huguenot and politique counsellor to Henry IV of France, Philippe Duplessis-Mornay. In the Netherlands, contact with the Flemish humanist scholar Justus Lipsius provided a more religiously neutral version of neo-Stoicism which inculcated an engagement with political issues and a dedication to discharging one's duty to the state. On a more practical level, contact with humanist scholars of the classics brought to the attention of those undergoing an apprenticeship in arms detailed advice on how the Romans trained and disciplined their armies.[12]

Sidney had been banished from court after criticizing the proposed marital alliance between Elizabeth and the duke of Alençon, and the queen never entirely trusted him again. His writings made oblique and veiled references to Elizabeth's refusal to champion the Protestant cause in Europe and to the employment of her knights in the tiltyard rather than on the battlefield. In his correspondence with the Huguenot scholar Hubert Languet, Sidney was more open about his intention to seek honour and glory with his uncle Leicester's expedition. He was already acquainted with François de la Noue, the 'Huguenot Paladin', who held command in the States' Army and was a 'pillar' of the Orangist camp in the Netherlands.[13]

1577 (Williams, *Actions of the Low Countries*, 135–6). Sir John Norris was also the colonel-proprietor of a large regiment in Dutch service in the 1580s (Nolan, *Sir John Norreys*, 33, 41–3).

[10] (1579).

[11] [Thomas Digges], *The Militarie Services done in the Low Countries by the Erle of Leicester* (1587); id., *Proceedings of the Earle of Leycester for the Reliefe of the Town of Sluce, 1587* (1590). These newsbooks had little impact upon the recruiting of ordinary soldiers (H. G. Webb, 'Military Newsbooks During the Age of Elizabeth', *ES* 33 (1952), 241–51.

[12] A. McCrea, *Constant Minds: Political Virtue and the Lipsian Paradigm in England, 1584–1650* (1997), pp. xx, xxiii; J. H. M. Salmon, 'Stoicism and the Roman Example: Seneca and Tacitus in Jacobean England', *Journal of the History of Ideas*, 50 (1989), 206–8; *Foure Bookes of... Vegetius*, dedication; H. G. Webb, *Elizabethan Military Science: The Books and the Practice* (1965), 11–12.

[13] McCrea, *Constant Minds*, 32–3; *The Correspondence of Sir Philip Sidney and Hubert Languet*, trans. and ed. S. A. Pears (1845), 137–8, 159 n.; J. H. M. Salmon, *The French Religious Wars in English Political Thought* (1959), 26, 184.

Other gallants displayed similar motivation. Peregrine Bertie, thirteenth Lord Willoughby de Eresby, began his career as Elizabeth's ambassador to Denmark, but discovered that he had a greater aptitude for military matters than diplomacy. He went to the Netherlands as Leicester's lieutenant-general, and later succeeded Leicester. At the Battle of Zutphen, Willoughby threw himself into the thick of the fight and was utterly heedless of his own safety.[14] Robert Cary, later first earl of Monmouth, fell in with some swordsmen who were seeking military action and glory. He went to the Netherlands with George Clifford, third earl of Cumberland, aboard the latter's bark and joined his brother Edmund's company at Ostend, where he appears to have stayed for only one season of campaigning. He decided that little action and less glory were to be found there under the earl of Leicester, for whom he had the greatest of contempt: 'Many things in that time were attempted; nothing of worth performed, I, finding no hope of any good action to be performed ... returned to England and found by that little experience that a brave war and a poor spirit in a commander never agree well together.'[15] Yet, English gallants continued to volunteer their services in the States' Army. When Maurice of Nassau invaded Flanders in 1600 with a force of 1,600 foot, he was accompanied by Sir Francis Vere, Sir Robert Sidney, Lord Grey of Wilton and twenty-four English companies. Among those peers who announced their intention of joining Maurice were Henry Percy, thirteenth earl of Northumberland; Roger Manners, fifth earl of Rutland; William, Lord Herbert, heir of Henry Herbert, second earl of Pembroke; Henry, fifth Lord Windsor; and William Parker, fourth Lord Monteagle and eleventh Lord Morley.[16] When Elizabeth ordered the second earl of Essex to remove his friend Henry Wriothesley, third earl of Southampton, from the command of the cavalry in Ireland, and then denied Southampton the governorship of Connaught after Lord Mountjoy had commended him for bravery, Southampton left Ireland for the Low Countries, where he joined the States' Army.[17]

When the first English soldiers went to the Netherlands, they did not appreciate how much warfare had changed, and how long it took to learn the technical aspects of modern warfare. Sir Roger Williams candidly provides many examples of this lack of experience and expertise. After Sir Humphrey Gilbert arrived at Flushing in 1572 with ten English companies of foot (subsequently turned into a regiment), most were sent to relieve Louis of Nassau at Mons. The commander of the Army of Flanders, Fernando Alvarez de Toledo, duke of Alva, played for time by engaging Gilbert and the Dutch commander, Jerome Tseraerts, in a parley, and then, leading them to believe that he meant to lift the siege, drew them into a trap where he bombarded them with artillery. When the English forces withdrew, they left themselves open to attack because of the disorderly way in which they

---

[14] Emmanuel van Meteren, *A...Discourse Historicall of the Succeeding Governors in the Netherlands and the Civill Warres*, trans. Thomas Churchyard (1602), 103–4.
[15] Robert Cary, earl of Monmouth, *Memoirs* (1759), 13.   [16] McClure, *LJC* i. 100–1.
[17] A. L. Rowse, *Shakespeare's Southampton: Patron of Virginia* (1965), 150–1.

marched. Another example which Williams provides was the defence of Haarlem in 1573 against a besieging force of '26,000 good soldiers' of the Spanish army. The defence of that town was undertaken by William of Orange—more out of a sense of honour than any rational military calculation; Gilbert's forces numbered only 6,500 infantry, half of whom were 'poor-spirited burgesses' of the civic militia. The town capitulated and most of the defenders were executed by Alva. 'Thus were we overthrown with ill directions and ignorant government.'[18]

The Dutch war of independence saw few pitched battles or general actions. The military leaders of the Dutch, William of Orange and Maurice of Nassau, were very cautious and fought an essentially defensive war. Leicester found it difficult to adapt to what he called 'these defensive garrison wars', and he was hard-pressed to raise the money and manpower to carry on this kind of warfare. Thomas Digges, the mathematician whom Leicester selected to serve as his muster-master-general, had published in 1579 an important treatise on modern military science dedicated to Leicester, in which he argued that it was necessary for gentlemen to study mathematics if they intended to pursue military careers. This would provide them with the necessary skills to construct fortifications, organize and march large bodies of men through confined spaces in an orderly manner and undertake the planning of encampments. After 1585 Digges, in his official capacity as muster-master-general, made recommendations about how to repair the fortifications of the English cautionary towns and how to improve discipline among the English forces. However, the elaborate fortress system of the United Provinces swallowed up large numbers of troops to serve in garrisons and left few men for field armies. Indeed, very few towns in the northern Netherlands were without such fortifications.[19]

Leicester was thus forced to face the Spanish with an inadequate field army. In July 1586 he told Sir Francis Walsingham that although he had been reinforced with between 11,000 and 12,000 foot, as many as 2,000 had deserted. Half of the remainder were scattered among small garrisons and he could not put together a field army of more than 5,000. In September of that year the same field army, which had stripped bare the Dutch and English garrisons of the northern and eastern Netherlands, consisted of 4,500 English foot, 1,300 English and Dutch horse and 1,100 mixed Dutch and Scottish foot. With this force, Leicester was obliged to resist a Spanish field army of 3,000 horse and 8,000 to 10,000 foot.[20] Many of the fortified English garrisons such as Sluis and Bergen-op-Zoom lay south of the Rhine

---

[18] Williams, *Actions of the Low Countries*, 66–70, 90; T. Digges, *Arithmeticall Militarie Treatise*, sig. A4v. Professor Israel (*Dutch Republic*, 178–81) argues that since Haarlem had just been officially Protestantized, it made sense to stand up to Avila, who elsewhere displayed extreme cruelty and massacred whole town populations.

[19] Digges, *Arithmetical Militarie Treatise*, sig. A4v; Webb, *Elizabethan Military Science*, 17–25; S. Adams, 'Tactics or Politics? The Military Revolution and the Hapsburg Hegemony, 1525–1648', in J. A. Lynn (ed.), *Tools of War: Instruments, Ideas, and Institutions of Warfare, 1485–1871* (1990), 41; D. Parrott, *Richelieu's Army: War, Government and Society in France, 1624–1642* (2001), 56–9.

[20] J. Bruce (ed.), *Correspondence of Robert Dudley, earl of Leycester during his Government of the Low Countries*, CS os 27 (1844), 374, 408.

estuaries in States Flanders or Brabant, and were therefore highly exposed to Spanish sieges. It probably would have made sense to sit out these sieges in the manner of William of Orange and Maurice of Nassau, if the Dutch naval forces could have supplied and supported the English garrisons. But Leicester engaged in political activities hostile to the States General, which made that body less willing to provide naval and logistical support for the relief of Sluis when it was besieged by the prince of Parma in 1587. Leicester failed to relieve Sluis, which was commanded by Sir Roger Williams, and his meddling in Dutch politics (with Elizabeth's connivance) ended his usefulness in the Netherlands. The dissension which Leicester allowed to develop among his officers provided another reason for his recall in 1587.[21]

English officers proved to be too impatient to sit out sieges; they preferred frontal assaults and hand-to-hand combat. This led, for example, to factionalism in the garrison of the cautionary town of Bergen-op-Zoom, where the captains of the horse told the governor, Sir William Drury, that their honour required that they sally forth and attack the Spanish camp, but other officers supported Drury. The factionalism was intensified when Queen Elizabeth replaced Drury with Sir Thomas Morgan. The garrison was now divided between the Scots and the Dutch who favoured Morgan, who was Welsh, while the English contingent continued to support Drury. Lord Willoughby, Leicester's successor, sought to appease the factions by giving the government of the town to Morgan and control of the forts to Drury. The strife between the two rivals and their factions continued through the Siege of Bergen in 1588 and 1589—even after Willoughby threatened to imprison Morgan.[22]

When the Spanish Siege of Sluis began, Sir Roger Williams had only 1,600 men, including pioneers, to defend fortifications with a perimeter of two-and-a-half miles. He held out for sixty days, and when he surrendered only 700 of his soldiers remained. Williams's men had been subjected to heavy bombardment, had repelled five assaults through breaches in the walls, and had engaged in hand-to-hand combat for nine straight days. Yet, the States General cashiered Williams and his English troops without payment because they thought Williams should have held out longer—reminding him that Haarlem had withstood a siege of ten months. Williams thought that the States General wasted men's lives and expected the impossible in defending a garrison of limited military usefulness—especially since the main target of the Spanish Army of Flanders was Ostend.[23]

The Spanish Army might have followed up such victories with devastating effect had not their own ranks been plagued with frequent mutinies provoked by uncertain and irregular payment of their soldiers. Leicester's army was also prevented from mounting counter-offensives because the English subsidies arrived late, and the Dutch never paid the amount of money agreed upon for the support

[21] Digges, *Proceedings of the Earle of Leycester for the Reliefe of . . . Sluce*, sig. A2r, pp. 7–9; R. B. Wernham, *Before the Armada: The Emergence of the English Nation, 1485–1588* (repr. 1972), 378–9, 388–9; G. Bertie, *Five Generations of a Noble House* (1845), 137, 141.
[22] *The Triumphs of Nassau*, trans. W. Shute (1613), 89–90.
[23] Sir Roger Williams, *A Briefe Discourse of Warre* (1590), 49–53.

of the English forces. Both Dutch and English troops suffered privations as a result, and both were frequently on the verge of mutiny.[24]

The States' Army went on the offensive in the 1590s and regained many of the earlier losses in the south. During Maurice's invasion of Flanders in 1600, his troops suffered heavy losses, and the English and Scots contingents suffered particularly. Twenty-two Scots companies were cut to pieces on 30 June 1600 at the Battle of Nieuwpoort, which was part of the larger campaign to retain Ostend for the States General. Sir Francis Vere, who commanded the infantry and cavalry forces of the States' Army, suffered three separate wounds and had his horse shot out from under him. He climbed back up behind Sir Robert Drury and led his men in a running battle in which they chased the Spanish for four miles. Five hundred English soldiers died on the sand-dunes of Ostend, along with five of their captains. Vere claimed all of the honour for himself and then for his English regiments, ignoring the Dutch. Vere and the other English officers probably understood by then that they could expect no gratitude and little payment from the States General. A committee of the States General, like modern military commissars, had accompanied Maurice's field army in order to participate in military decisions, and much carping ensued. Although Johan van Oldenbarnevelt, the advocate of Holland, praised Vere's bravery, Vere was later criticized for giving up the attempt to relieve the Siege of Ostend. Vere's supporters, in a pamphlet war, replied that the English troops bore the brunt of the fighting and that the States General failed to furnish enough troops to enable Vere to break through the Spanish lines. As it was, Vere had great difficulty in maintaining discipline in a polyglot army consisting of French, Walloons and German besides the English, Scots and Dutch. The Spanish also conducted an effective campaign of psychological warfare against the troops of Vere's army by firing arrows into their midst bearing written messages stirring up factionalism and offering the States' troops better wages if they would join the Spanish army. Nonetheless, the defenders of Ostend endured the siege for more than three years.[25]

Because serving in the Dutch army was regarded as a kind of Protestant crusade, such gentlemen volunteers and officers who did so were never regarded as mercenaries—despite notable exceptions such as Sir Roger Williams. They had maintained a considerable presence in the States' Army ever since the first English company went to the Low Countries in 1572. The high social status of the volunteers who accompanied Leicester in 1585 undoubtedly ensured that they

---

[24] F. G. Oosterhoff, *Leicester and the Netherlands, 1586–1587* (1988), 37, 86; G. Parker, *The Army of Flanders and the Spanish Road, 1567–1695: The Logistics of Spanish Victory and Defeat in the Low Countries War* (1972), 185–206; Oman, *Art of War*, 546–7; Bertie, *Five Generations*, 172–3; *Discourse . . . of the Lord Willoughby, Gouvernour of hir Majestie's Succours in the United Provinces of the Low Countries* (1589), 1–19.

[25] McClure, *LJC* i. 102–4; C. Dalton, *Life and Times of General Sir Edward Cecil, Viscount Wimbledon*, 2 vols. (1885), i. 51–2; Anon., *Extremities pressing the lord General Sir Francis Veare to offer the late anti-parle with the Arch-duke Albertus* (1602), 3, 5–6, 8–9; Israel, *Dutch Republic*, 258–60; A.U., *The Memorable Siege of Ostend* (1604), 223.

would be esteemed in England, if not in the Netherlands. Leicester's following included Edward Vere, seventeenth earl of Oxford; Lord Willoughby; George Touchet, eleventh Lord Audley; Roger, second Lord North; and 600 or 700 knights, esquires and gentlemen volunteers.[26] Although most sought honour and glory, they did hope to recoup at least some of their expenses from the legitimate spoils of war, since they could expect little from Queen Elizabeth or the States General. Edward, earl of Oxford, had not only accompanied Leicester in 1585, but had also hired ships at his own expense to sail against the Armada in 1588. In this way, he spent much of his fortune. Lord Willoughby was compelled to mortgage his lands to pay the cost of his military office, and looked to the ransoming of noble prisoners as a way of discharging his debts. A quarrel over the ransom of a cavalry commander captured from the Spanish Army of Flanders caused a falling out between Leicester and Willoughby.[27] Ralph Bostock's career as a gentleman volunteer and officer had brought him few tangible rewards in eighteen years of military service. He wrote to Sir Robert Cecil in 1600 complaining that, after serving many years in the Netherlands, with Essex in France, in Ireland and on the Portugal expedition, he had spent £1,000 of his patrimony and had been reduced to being an ex-captain without employment.[28]

The Dutch desperately needed English and Scots manpower, but they found that English standards of military command and administration were deplorable. When Dutch troops, who had been used to the command of the late prince of Orange, came under English commanders, friction developed. For example, when a Dutch regiment was placed under the command of Sir Philip Sidney, Sidney ignored the practice in that regiment and other regiments in the States' Army of promoting officers from within the ranks of the regiment and began commissioning 'strangers'. The Dutch soldiers complained and presented a petition through Counts Hohenlohe, Solms and Overstein, asking that the former practice of commissioning subalterns from the ranks be restored and that their English officers pay them on time. Leicester and the other English officers were highly offended upon receiving the petition, and showed themselves quite unable to accept criticism from more experienced officers. Sir Edward Norris challenged Count Hohenlohe to a duel—although this was forbidden by Dutch military law under pain of death. The matter was resolved by a printed apology from Hohenlohe. Despite his prickly behaviour, the States General trusted Norris more

---

[26] William Blandy, *The Castle, or Picture of Pollicy* (1581), fo. 19; [T. Digges], *Reporte of the Militarie Service done in the Low countries by the Erle of Leicester*, unpaginated. E. M. Tenison (*Elizabethan England*, 12 vols. (1932), vi. 45–7) lists the names of 239 peers, knights, esquires and gentlemen volunteers who served in the cavalry and were mustered and paid at The Hague. However, the names are not always correctly listed.

[27] Arthur Collins, *Historical Collections of the Noble Families of Cavendish, Holles, Vere, Harley* (1752), 264–6; Bertie, *Five Generations*, 110–13, 137, 248–9.

[28] R. Bagwell, *Ireland under the Tudors*, 3 vols. (1885–90; repr. 1963), iii. 250–1. Sir Edward Cecil had to raise £500 to purchase command of a cavalry troop when it was offered to him by Sir Francis Vere in 1599. The previous captain, Sir Nicholas Parker, used the money to retire to England (Dalton, *Sir Edward Cecil*, i. 13–14, 29–30, 36, 41).

than any other English officer. But the Dutch officers perceived that Leicester held them in low esteem—especially after he executed several Dutch officers of good reputation for surrendering the town of Grave, which was no longer defensible.[29]

Of all the contemporaneous writers who observed the late Elizabethan wars in the Netherlands, only Leicester's client, Thomas Digges, ever described him as anything but incompetent. The officers who served under Leicester were an extension of his patronage network rather than members of a disciplined and orderly military hierarchy, and their military functions remained largely underdeveloped. Although two-thirds of Leicester's captains had prior military experience, in most cases that experience dated back to the military expeditions of the 1560s. Lacking professional military expertise himself, Leicester neglected to ensure that his subordinates discharged their military duties without factionalism among themselves and friction with their Dutch allies. He failed to observe the Treaty of Nonsuch with regard to maintaining the troop strength of the English regiments and garrisons, despite repeated Dutch insistence on holding regular musters. Consequently, Leicester never really knew how many troops he had at his disposal at any particular moment for putting together a field army.[30]

The States General also became exasperated with Leicester's inability to maintain discipline among the English troops. Besides Leicester's own personal responsibility for this situation, matters were made worse by the widespread dishonesty of English captains, who cheated their men of pay and victuals and failed to follow accounting procedures prescribed by both Dutch and English fiscal officials. A muster of the English garrison at Bergen-op-Zoom in 1589, although after Leicester's time, illustrates this seemingly intractable problem. Of the nominal strength of 1,970 men for whom the English government provided pay, 247 were listed as absent in England and elsewhere, 217 were Dutch or a nationality other than English (in other words, they were impostors temporarily recruited to stand in for absent English soldiers) and eighty-five were sick. Thus, only 1,421 men could be accounted for. Since the captains and the commander were legally allowed 10 per cent dead-pays,[31] this reduced the number by something like another 211, yielding 1,210 effectives. The strength of the five English troops of cavalry, made up largely of gentlemen malingerers, was even more depleted: Sir Robert Sidney's troop was 35 per cent under strength, and, at the other extreme, Sir John Burgh's was 61 per cent under its official complement of

---

[29] Edward Grimestone, *A Generall Historie of the Netherlands* (1627), 817–18, 820, 824; *DNB*, *sub* Sir Edward Norris (d. 1603).

[30] Grimeston, *Historie of the Netherlands*, 806–7, 811–12, 955; S. Adams, 'A Puritan Military Crusade? The Composition of the Earl of Leicester's Expedition to the Netherlands, 1585–6', in Adams, *Leicester and the Court: Essays on Elizabethan Politics* (2002), 178; Webb, *Elizabethan Military Science*, 64–5; Monmouth, *Memoirs*, 2–13.

[31] In this sense, pay was allowed to the captain for men who did not actually serve in his company or troop and were not listed on the muster roll. This had the effect of increasing the captain's remuneration, but unscrupulous officers manipulated the system by falsifying muster rolls and illegally collecting more than the specified number of dead-pays.

100 troopers.[32] In August 1588 most of the eight English garrisons in the Netherlands were approximately one-third under strength.[33]

The consequence of the failure to pay the soldiers of the English regiments in a full and timely fashion was widespread desertion and mutiny. In July 1586 Leicester confessed to Walsingham that 500 men had deserted in the space of two days, including 'a great many to the enemy'. Of the 500, 200 were recaptured on the coast and returned, and 'divers' were hanged as an example.[34] The soldiers of the English garrison at Ostend were in a state of mutiny over their arrears of pay in 1590 and actually placed their officers under arrest. They sent a petition to the queen complaining that they had not received a month's pay in two-and-a-half years. Also, because the garrison was depleted as a result of their captains keeping their companies at half strength in order to collect extra dead-pays, the soldiers were much fatigued from standing watch at night more frequently than was customary. When Sir Edward Norris arrived to become the new governor of Ostend, he told the troops of the garrison that the queen 'does not regard them as subjects', and, if he had been on the spot when the mutiny occurred, it would have 'been a bloody day'. The English troops defending Geertruidenberg, lacking food and pay, mutinied during the months of February and March 1588 while the town was under siege by the Spanish. The mutiny was ended by the personal intervention of Lord Willoughby; Maurice and the States General refused to accept Willoughby's negotiated agreement for a pay-settlement promising the soldiers twenty-four months pay for thirty-one months in arrears until late July 1588, when there could be no doubt that the Spanish Armada would soon be bearing down upon the Flemish coast and the Dutch leaders were fearful that the English mutineers would hand their towns over to the Spanish.[35] The mutinies of this period were not limited to the English contingents of the States' Army. Several Dutch garrisons in the Province of Utrecht mutinied in 1587 over lack of pay, and members of the civic militia and even villagers had to be empowered to deal with the mutineers where they had gathered at Gooiland near the city of Utrecht. It was reported in the States of Holland that 1,500 soldiers had died of hunger for want of pay.[36]

Leicester's politicizing of the English contingent of the States' Army and his interference in Dutch politics left a most unfortunate legacy. His successor, Lord Willoughby, found that Leicester's court captains had entrenched themselves in their positions, and because of the queen's interference, he could not discipline or reward officers serving under his command; in 1588, during the Armada threat, he asked to be relieved of his command and expressed preference for serving in the

---

[32]. Grimeston, *Historie of the Netherlands*, 806–7; *CSP Foreign, Jan.–July, 1589*, pp. xxxviii–xxxix, 142–3.   [33] Israel, *Dutch Republic*, 238, table 6.

[34] Bruce (ed.), *Correspondence of Robert Dudley*, 338.

[35] *Discourse . . . of the Lord Willoughby*, 1–19; *CSP July–Dec., 1588*, 188–9. This document is misdated 'before September 1588'. Norris did not become governor of Ostend until 1590.

[36] *Discourse . . . of the Lord Willoughby*, 1–19; F. J. S. ten Raa and F. de Bas, *Het Staatsche Leger*, 8 vols. (Breda, 1911–80), i. 74; J. S. Fishman, *Boerenverdriet: Violence between Peasants and Soldiers in Early Netherlands Art* (1979), 5.

ranks.[37] The treason of Sir William Stanley, who gave Deventer to the Spanish in 1587, and Rowland Yorke, who delivered up Zutphen Sconce, was also blamed on Leicester and led to an anti-English reaction among the supporters of Oldenbarnevelt, the States General and those who wished to concentrate more power in the States of Holland. These defections occurred at roughly the same time as the military mutinies in both the English and Dutch garrisons, and led to legislation by the States General enhancing the military authority of Maurice of Nassau.[38]

Matthew Sutcliffe blamed the indiscipline and mutinies on the corruption of the captains of companies, who withheld pay, provisions, clothing and equipment from their soldiers and returned false musters. Sutcliffe insisted on the need to give rewards and accord honour—even to those in the ranks—and he also advocated commissioning officers from the ranks.[39] These 'Low-Country captains'[40] were held in great contempt, not only because they cheated their men, but because they disdained to lead them into battle. Sir John Smythe wrote that such infantry officers, 'mounted upon horses of swift careers ... either have accompanied their footmen upon flanks or rearward, or else have put themselves into some bands of horsemen as though it were against their reputation to serve on foot, amongst their soldiers, or rather, as it may be thought, that upon any hard accident they may be ready, leaving their soldiers to slaughter, to save themselves rather with the force of their heels and spurs than any dint of sword'.[41]

Sir Thomas Sherley and his sons, Thomas the younger and Anthony, were all captains of companies under Leicester's command in the Netherlands. Although Anthony did lead his men into battle, Sir Thomas and the younger Thomas were 'court captains' who spent more time away from their companies than with them.

[37] Bertie, *Five Generations*, 197–9.

[38] Oosterhoff, *Leicester and the Netherlands*, 145–6; Israel, *Dutch Republic*, 229–30. A Scottish officer, Col. Patton, who was governor of Guelders and commanded a Scots regiment, also betrayed his town to the Spaniards. Apparently, Patton was driven to this treachery by Leicester's threat to cashier him (Grimeston, *Historie of the Netherlands*, 835).

[39] Matthew Sutcliffe, *The Practice, Proceedings and Lawes of Armes* (1593), 298–9; *APC 1586–1587*, 374.

[40] The term 'Low-Country captains' refers to company commanders, especially of the foot, who had a proprietary interest in their companies and into whose hands was delivered their soldiers' pay. They regarded their offices as a business enterprise from which a profit was to be made and a species of property which ultimately could be sold to recover the purchase price plus profit. Military regulations did allow them a certain number of dead-pays—usually 10%—as their margin of profit, but false musters could increase the profits, and it was common practice to delay or even withhold what remained of the soldiers' wages. Moreover, every regiment contained a colonel's company and a lieutenant-colonel's company with larger complements than ordinary companies, which made field-grade officers, as company commanders themselves, complicit in these dishonest practices (C. G. Cruickshank, 'Dead-Pays in the Elizabethan Army', *EHR* 53 (1938), 93–5.

[41] Sir John Smythe, *Certain Discourses Military*, ed. J. R. Hale (1964), 20. For other literary references to 'Low-Country captains', cf. F. Cunningham (ed.), *The Works of Ben Jonson*, 3 vols. (1910–12), vol. i, pp. x–xi, and epigram CVII (iii. 249–50); also *The ... Epigrams of Sir John Harington* (1618; repr. 1970), epigram no. 28 (p. 30). Jonson was a volunteer in the Netherlands, and Harington accompanied Essex to Ireland in 1599.

Sir Thomas was a confidant of Leicester, and, while retaining his company, he also became treasurer of war in Leicester's expedition, an office which he used for large-scale embezzlement and fraud. Lord Willoughby thought Sir Thomas Sherley had embezzled one-fifth of the £100,000 paid out annually to maintain the English forces in the Netherlands.[42]

Sir John Smythe claimed that some of the Low-Country captains went so far as to farm their companies out to their lieutenants for a 'yearly rate'. It was a common practice for such corrupt officers in the Netherlands to encourage their men to plunder the local peasants and to run up large debts with their landlords which they had no intention of ever paying in the towns where they were garrisoned. Consequently, secondary warfare sometimes broke out between peasants and plundering soldiers, and fatalities were not unusual.[43] Some English troops and companies acquired such an evil reputation that Dutch towns, which were usually walled, sometimes refused to accept them into their garrisons. One such troop was commanded by Sir Thomas Sherley the younger, which he left in the care of his lieutenant. When Sherley's troop was posted to Zwolle in Overijssel, the townsmen refused to admit them. The lieutenant left the young cornet in command of the troopers, who camped outside the walls of Zwolle, while he went to secure authority from Lord Willoughby to gain admittance to the town. During the lieutenant's absence, the troopers drank and slept despite intelligence that a Spanish company of infantry was only a mile away. The Spanish fell upon them and killed the cornet and thirty men together with sixty-three horses, who had been betrayed by the townsmen of Zwolle, according to the Spanish captain. Another twenty men were missing, and only a third of the troop, together with a few horses, survived. Willoughby sought to relieve Thomas Sherley the younger of his command, but his orders were countermanded, and it took Willoughby a year-and-a-half to get the younger Sherley transferred to Ireland, where he was promptly knighted by Sir William Fitzwilliam, the lord deputy, upon his arrival.[44]

Sir John Smythe also claimed that Low-Country captains, having cheated men out of their pay, allowed them 'to go *à la picorée*', that is, 'to rob and spoil the boors [peasants]'.[45] Anthony Sherley's cavalry troop, while stationed at Gorcum in Holland, counterfeited coins. Members of the garrison of Bergen-op-Zoom under the governorship of Sir Thomas Morgan became highwaymen and pirates and preyed upon those travelling the roads and waterways of Brabant. While the Spanish Armada was passing through the Narrow Seas, Sir John Conway, governor of Ostend, sent men and ships he could hardly spare to capture and plunder a

---

[42] D. W. Davies, *Elizabethans Errant: The Strange Fortunes of Sir Thomas Sherley and his Three Sons* (1967), 10–13, 18–20.

[43] Smythe, *Certain Discourses Military*, 15. Smythe's *Discourses* were suppressed by the Privy Council because of Smythe's criticism of Leicester and Elizabeth's government.

[44] Davies, *Elizabethans Errant*, 24–8.

[45] Smythe, *Certain Discourses Military*, 21–2. For a succinct discussion of picaresque culture in Spain and the Spanish Netherlands, cf. Parker, *Army of Flanders*, 179–80.

Spanish vessel which had become separated from the Spanish fleet.[46] The States General, dominated as it was by regents drawn from a middle-class culture and society, were sensitive to concepts and rights of private property; not only soldiers, but officers and volunteers as well, needed to be taught the difference between the legitimate booty of war and plundering the subjects of allies, which was robbery.[47]

Elizabethan swordsmen had much to learn about military discipline, chains of command and the conduct of war. Gentlemen volunteers, in particular, tended to be undisciplined, and generals found it necessary to insert in their articles of war a prohibition against gentlemen volunteers enrolling in their armies except under the authority and command of captains of companies.[48] The second earl of Essex remained convinced that he was entitled to command the expedition of 1589 to Spain and Portugal by his social rank, even though he lacked the queen's commission. Although he accompanied that expedition as a mere volunteer, he arranged to have all of the key subordinate commands given to his kinsmen, friends and followers so that he might retain a commanding influence although he did not command in name. On the Cadiz expedition of 1596, a whole regiment of gentlemen volunteers was raised, and when Essex captured the city of Cadiz, 1,000 troops accompanied him, of whom at least one-quarter were gentlemen volunteers and personal followers.[49] Such aristocratic patronage networks did not mesh well with military hierarchies, which were cobbled together for each expedition and thus lacked continuity and the force of tradition. As long as considerations of honour remained uppermost in martial culture, even experienced commanders such as Sir John Norris felt compelled to make decisions which more prudent military commanders might have avoided. When French Royalist officers proposed an assault through a breached wall of the Spanish-held town of Guingamp in Brittany, Norris felt obliged to comply in order to preserve his honour despite the fact that he thought the town would be difficult to take by assault, and the French Royalist foot had refused to charge. Patiently laying siege to the town was not an option that Norris considered, and he did not regard loss of life among his own soldiers as important.[50]

---

[46] Davies, *Elizabethans Errant*, 28–30; van Meteren, *True Discourse Historicall*, 106–9; *Triumphs of Nassau*, trans. Shute, 76.

[47] Late Elizabethan Articles of War, in HMC, *Salisbury MSS.*, xiv. 299; Redlich, *DPM* 14–15. An unqualified concept of private property did not emerge in England until later in the seventeenth century (Manning, *VR* 4–6).

[48] Francis Markham, *Five Decades of Epistles of Warre* (1622), 27–8.

[49] R. B. Wernham (ed.), *The Expeditions of Sir John Norris and Sir Francis Drake to Spain and Portugal, 1589*, NRS 127 (1988), pp. xxxv–xxxvi; H. A. Lloyd, *The Rouen Campaign, 1590–92: Politics, Warfare and the Early Modern State* (1973), 87–9; Sir Francis Vere, 'The Journey of Cadiz', BL, Harleian MSS. 3638, fos. 160–8; Markham, *Epistles of Warre*, 27–8.

[50] *The... Service in Britanie Performed lately by... Sir John Norreys* (1591), sigs. A2r, A3v–A4v, B1r; van Meteren, *Discourse Historicall*, 134–42. Nolan (*Sir John Norreys*, 184) passes quickly over this incident and insists that the assault on Guingamp was not a difficult operation since the town was surrounded by high medieval walls rather than low, thick ramparts.

While military adventurers might look to Ireland as a place where one could acquire experience and perhaps land, the Netherlands was the chief theatre for demonstrating virtue and honour, and the swordsmen who followed Leicester, Sidney and the third earl of Essex looked to the Low-Countries wars to pursue a Protestant crusade and to learn modern military theory and practice. Essex and his followers turned to Ireland only out of desperation, knowing that the distribution of military and civil offices remained largely within the orbit of Cecilian patronage. The 'chivalric revival' in England blossomed at the same time as the English intervention in the Netherlands, and the philosophical inspiration for this movement owed much to contact with neo-Stoic philosophers, classical scholars and Huguenot political theorists and swordsmen; it owed little to the English court, and many English swordsmen began turning their backs on courtly culture in the late Elizabethan and Jacobean periods.

Those who looked to the Low-Countries wars to establish their fortunes or to gather booty found that in the latter part of the sixteenth century the States General were grudging and unreliable paymasters and discouraged the plundering of burghers and boors. Moreover, the corrupt practices of the Low-Countries captains—many of them followers of Leicester—skimmed off the profits and drove their soldiers to desperation. Such impecunious volunteers might turn instead to service in the Spanish Army of Flanders or to opportunities for privateering.

Whatever their choice of theatres of action, swordsmen of the British Isles found plenty of opportunities for serving an apprenticeship in arms, and this, in turn, contributed to the remilitarization of the aristocracies of the Three Kingdoms and their gentlemen followers. Swordsmen and gallants of this period were often undisciplined and tended to focus upon individual exploits and feats of valour rather than upon military objectives. Consequently, under the leadership of Leicester and his clients, this was not a glorious period for English arms—at least in land battles. But those who remained in the Netherlands and persisted in learning the new methods of warfare in the reorganized States' Army under the great commander Maurice of Nassau found that their efforts were rewarded. Their military experiences would later contribute much to the exploits of English and British arms.

3

British manpower and the States' Army

At Holland's Leaguer[1] there I fought,
But there the service prov'd too hot,
Then from the League[r] returned I,
Naked, hungry, cold and dry.[2]

'The Joviall Broome Man' (broadside ballad, c.1640), *The Roxburghe
Ballads*, ed. W. Chapell, 9 vols. in 8 (1869; repr. 1966), i. 503.

In the nature and discipline of a private soldier, there are three parts generally
required: courage, strength and obedience. Courage is the foundation of war,
is the soul of strength and by obedience [he] becomes a reasonable soul.

Sir Edward Cecil, Lord Wimbledon, 'The duty of a Private Soldier',
BL, Harley MS. 3638, fo. 159.

Pay well and hang well, makes a good soldier.

Anon., *Advice to a Soldier* (1680), in *HM*, ed. T. Park,
10 vols. (1808–13), i. 480.

Although allowed by the Union of Utrecht, citizens of the Republic were rarely
conscripted into the Dutch army. Limited conscription was permitted in Holland
in 1629 under threat of Spanish invasion, but burghers could hire substitutes to
take their places. Service in the army was not only divorced from patriotism and
religious sentiment, it was incompatible with Dutch political culture. Service in
the Dutch navy was more acceptable to the peoples of maritime Holland and
Zeeland, but even the navy was dependent upon mariners from Scandinavia and
England.[3] Because of reasonably regular pay and strong discipline, mutinies
became rare, although not unheard of, in the States' Army. There had been a
mutiny over lack of pay among the English troops defending Ostend as late as

---

[1] Military camp, from the Dutch word *leger*.
[2] Devoid of payment or satisfaction.
[3] Although soldiers in the States' Army were better paid than in other armies (when they were
paid in full), sailors in the Dutch navy were paid even more, and mariners in the merchant fleet could
earn considerably more than naval personnel. Wages in the Netherlands—especially in Holland and
Zeeland—were the highest in Europe (J. Israel, *The Dutch Republic: Its Rise, Greatness and Fall,
1477–1806* (1995), 352).

1602, but thereafter Maurice of Nassau's military reforms made pay more regular except for a brief period in the 1620s. The Dutch had little liking or respect for the army, although better-disciplined garrisons improved relations between citizens and soldiers, and the inhabitants of garrison towns in States Brabant and Flanders and along the more rural eastern frontier became economically dependent upon the army.[4]

The Dutch army was a mercenary force consisting mostly of foreigners. The popular perception of the States' Army as an alien institution was not helped by the fact that it contained many Catholics. Official surveys taken in 1622 and 1637 estimated that the army contained between 58 and 68 per cent foreigners, but these estimates are surely low. Moreover, most of the native Dutch soldiers came from Friesland and the eastern provinces, and were probably more numerous in the cavalry than in the infantry. The foreign mercenaries included French, Walloon, German, Swiss, Danish, Irish, English and Scottish soldiers as well as a few Italians. In 1609 Sir Thomas Overbury estimated that English troops made up one-third of the States' Army, but at times the proportion of English and Scots rose to as much as one-half of the Dutch foot. Certainly, Maurice relied heavily upon the English and Scots when he constituted field armies. Of the 146 companies present with Maurice at the Siege of Juliers (Gulick) in the summer of 1614, fifty-two were English and twenty were Scots. Thus, on that occasion, the English and Scots, under the command of Sir Horace Vere, comprised 49 per cent of the Dutch infantry.[5] Maurice preferred English soldiers in his army because he admired their courage, and they were often used to spearhead assaults in battle and sieges. Sir William Temple's explanation was that the English soldiers were not usually from the peasantry and were better fed than other foreign auxiliaries, and, presumably, possessed better physiques.[6]

Discipline was strict in the States' Army, but one should not conclude that it was easy to maintain order. The foreign troops were more likely to be sent into the field, while the native Dutch troops remained in garrison. At the Siege of Ostend in 1601, Sir Francis Vere had complained of the difficulty in preserving unity and maintaining order among the 'hotch-pot' of nations in the Dutch army. The Spanish practiced a kind of psychological warfare by disseminating propaganda

[4] *A Dialogue... upon the Siedge of Oostend* (1602), sig. B2r; M. 't Hart, *The Making of a Bourgeois State: War, Politics and Finance during the Dutch Revolt* (1993), 35–6; J. H. Huizinga, *Dutch Civilization in the Seventeenth Century* (1968), 34–5; A. T. van Deursen, 'Holland's Experience of War during the Revolt of the Netherlands', in A. C. Duke and C. A. Tamse (eds.), *Britain and the Netherlands*, vol. 6: *War and Society* (1977), 31–5; S. Schama, *The Embarrassment of Riches: An Interpretation of Dutch Culture in the Golden Age* (1987), 246–7.

[5] Table 4.2; 't Hart, *Bourgeois State*, 35, 64 n.; Sir Thomas Overbury, *Observations... upon the State of the Seventeen Provinces, 1609*, in C. H. Firth (ed.), *Stuart Tracts, 1603–1693* (1903; repr. 1973), 214; Henry Peacham, *A Most True Relation of the Affairs of Cleve and Gulick* (1615; repr. 1973), sigs. B2v–B3r, B4r & v. Cf. also H. L. Zwitzer, *De Militie van den Staat: Het Leger van de Republiek der Verenigde Nederlanden* (1991), 44, 61, 240.

[6] Sir William Temple, *Observations... upon the United Provinces of the Netherlands* (1673; repr. 1932), 109, 111–12.

aimed at stirring up factionalism or encouraging desertion among the foreign troops of the States' Army. Remembering the defection of Stanley at Deventer and Yorke at Zutphen Sconce, the Dutch military authorities followed the policy of never trusting the soldiers of one nation only to stand watch. Consequently, one encounters frequent complaints of soldiers fatigued by what was regarded as excessive guard duty. At the Siege of Ostend, Vere said that not only did the English soldiers carry the brunt of the assault, but they were also obliged to stand guard every other night for six months and many of them became ill. It is not surprising that the English often were contemptuous of the Dutch because they neglected the martial arts and engaged in commercial pursuits in the midst of perpetual war.[7]

English and Scottish aristocrats and gentlemen enthusiastically sought service as officers and volunteers in the States' Army, but few of the private soldiers of the English regiments shared that enthusiasm, because they were usually recruited by press gangs. According to international law, the widespread practice of one country lending part of its military or naval forces to a foreign country or recruiting soldiers for a belligerent power did not necessarily involve the government of that country in a state of war with the opposing belligerent power.[8] However, in England, the practice of impressing soldiers for service in foreign wars was definitely regarded by most common lawyers as illegal. Sir Edward Coke states that the king cannot compel a soldier of any social rank to serve in a military capacity in Ireland or any foreign land, nor can he compel anyone, even with the consent of Parliament, to contribute to the cost of a foreign war. Coke allowed that the king could recruit volunteers, provided they were paid out of his own resources and not from taxes raised from his subjects. There was a universal obligation for all male subjects between 16 and 60 years of age to serve in the militia if called upon to do so, and tenants-in-chief of the crown had a particular obligation to help the king by military service or financial assistance, but such obligations did not extend beyond a defensive war fought within the realm. Although the legality of impressing soldiers for foreign service was dubious, no one ever questioned the legality of impressing mariners for naval service. Moreover, there was no clear distinction between serving aboard ships as sailors or as soldiers (or marines as we should call them).[9]

Commissions of array were a familiar legal instrument for recruiting men into the king's service in Tudor England. Earlier in the sixteenth century, the constitutional limitations on employing commissions of array for more than forty days of military service or foreign wars was conveniently forgotten. Edwardian and Marian Acts of

---

[7] Anon., *Extremities pressing… Sir Francis Vere, to offer the Late Anti-Parle with the Arch-duke Albertus* (1602), 3, 5–6; Overbury, *Observations*, 216–17; Barnabe Rich, *Alarme to England fore-shewing What Perilles are procured where the People live without regarde of Martiall Lawe* (1578), sig. Fiiijr & v; Temple, *Observations*, 152.

[8] Sir G. Clark, *War and Society in the Seventeenth Century* (1958), 59–60.

[9] Sir Edward Coke, *The Second Part of the Institutes of the Laws of England*, 4th edn. (1671), 48, 528; C. Clode, *The Military Forces of the Crown: Their Administration and Government*, 2 vols. (1869), i. 16–17; F. W. Maitland, *The Constitutional History of England* (1909), 280.

Parliament accepted the fact of overseas service or explicitly sanctioned the practice of recruiting for foreign military service. In 1596 the English Privy Council imprisoned Sir John Smythe for making a speech at a militia muster in Colchester to the effect that soldiers could not be recruited for service abroad without parliamentary approval. By the time of James I and Charles I, there was confusion and sharp debate about the constitutionality of the impressment of soldiers.[10]

Despite the questionable legality of impressing the king's subjects for foreign wars, Protestant divines could be found to justify compulsory service in the armies of Protestant powers as a crusade. It was an honourable calling for gentlemen to take up the sword 'against Moab',[11] said Thomas Barnes, and the 'meaner and vulgar sort' should not begrudge going forth with them as pressed men. Richard Bernard also thought that it was lawful to impress men for a just war.[12] Barnes provided another widely accepted justification for impressment: it was an instrument for social control and the means 'to cleanse the city and rid the country of such as may be straggling vagrants and lewd livers . . . which do swarm amongst us'. God sometimes used wicked men to punish other wicked men. Moreover, being in the presence of death might help lewd men become better men by making them think about their souls.[13] Like many military commanders who had to discipline such persons and lead them into battle, Thomas Palmer, in a sermon preached to the Artillery Company of Bristol in 1635, strongly disagreed with the practice of enlisting criminals, vagrants and masterless men to defend the Protestant cause:

The body of an army should not (like Hannibal's) consist of the scum of the seas, of the excrement of the land. A commander should have more than a common care in the choice of the common soldier. . . . War is now counted but the spleen of a body politique, to drain out the ill humours. When occasion of service is offered, tattered gaol-birds and masterless vagrants are the greatest part of master constable's choice. . . . It is no Christian policy to choose such sinful instruments for such a serious action. God will not be the leader of that army when [he] reigns in the main battle.[14]

When raising an army in late Elizabethan or Stuart England, it was not difficult to find experienced officers who had previously served in Ireland, the Netherlands or in one of the expeditions to France, Spain, Portugal or the Islands. The main problem was always enlisting suitable recruits for the ranks. In the States' Army under Maurice of Nassau, experienced old soldiers were much sought after, were better paid and were granted privileges such as exemption from standing guard at night. Foreign governments desiring to recruit soldiers in England or Scotland first needed to secure licences from the English or Scottish Privy Councils. They

---

[10] Maitland, *Constitutional History*, 275–6, 278; C. G. Cruickshank, *Elizabeth's Army*, 2nd edn. (1968), 5–14.

[11] The 'people of Moab' was a pejorative term for Catholics in the 17th century (*OED*).

[12] Thomas Barnes, *Vox Belli: or, an Alarum to Warre* (1626), 40; Richard Bernard, *The Bible Battells, or Sacred Art Military* (1629), 63–5.   [13] Barnes, *Vox Belli*, 9, 14–15.

[14] Thomas Palmer, *Bristoll's Military Garden* (1635), 220–1.

would then send recruiting parties headed by English or Scots or English-speaking officers 'to beat the drum'.[15] No compulsion was employed in recruiting volunteers by beat of the drum, but recruiting officers were not above using a few tricks. James Batson recalled, in his autobiographical memoir, that he was persuaded to enlist by 'two of those sorts of soldiers called decoy-ducks who serve to draw in others when there are levies'. Batson notes that there were also plenty of confidence-tricksters who took advantage of inexperienced recruiting officers:

After some discourse, they [the decoys] told me that they were going my way, being informed that at Colchester there was a captain raising men, and that none who 'listed under him would ever want....' The next day we got to that town, and being kindly received by the captain, and, listed, we lived in clover for a fortnight, making our landlords furnish us with dainties, and demanding impossibilities. At last we received orders to march, and having left the town, our captain moved like a snail ... because the towns paid him to be exempted. He continued this cheat three days; but on the fourth, as we were passing by a wood, all his men, about thirty in number, left him with only the colours, drum and ensign, and five wenches who went with the baggage; for he is not likely to keep up a company who contrives only how to make his own advantage of them, without considering that it is easy to find a captain, and no less difficult to get thirty soldiers.[16]

When the earl of Leicester and the second earl of Essex were selected by Elizabeth to lead military expeditions, they began their recruiting efforts in the medieval fashion by calling upon their tenants and raising men by feudal levy. In 1585 Leicester raised two companies of 200 men each from among his tenants in North Wales. These were joined by another company of men raised in South Wales by impressment. All three companies accompanied Leicester to the Netherlands. Grants of land carrying an obligation of military service were still being made to gentlemen, freeholders and smallhold tenants in the Marches of Wales as late as the 1570s. A distinction should be made between the infantry soldiers who were raised from among Leicester's tenants and those recruited from among his servants, who were of higher social status and served in troops of horse. Robert, second earl of Essex, never had much trouble raising volunteers from among his followers and tenants in Staffordshire and elsewhere, and many of them were experienced veterans. When Essex put together his Normandy expedition of 1590–2, no troops were impressed from Staffordshire and the Welsh Marches for fear that the resulting force would resemble nothing so much as Essex's private army. Instead, the impressed men came from Gloucestershire and elsewhere. They totalled 4,000 men.[17]

[15] H. A. Lloyd, *The Rouen Campaign, 1590–1592: Politics, Warfare and the Early Modern State* (1973), 87–9; 't Hart, *Bourgeois State*, 36.

[16] Autobiographical memoir by James Batson (b. *c.*1603; executed for murder, 1666), in J. L. Rayner and G. T. Crook (eds.), *The Complete Newgate Calendar*, 5 vols. (1926), i. 189. The captain was apparently recruiting for the Dutch army, but being laughed at when he arrived in London, he decided to go Barcelona as a volunteer in the Spanish army, where he was given command of a company (ibid. i. 190).

[17] S. L. Adams, 'The Gentry of North Wales and the Earl of Leicester's Expedition to the Netherlands, 1585–1586', *WHR* 7 (1974), 133–4; id., 'A Puritan Crusade? The Composition of the

The Tudor and Stuart governing classes agreed that yeomen and husbandmen made the best foot soldiers—a prejudice which was reinforced by reading Roman military writers and historians. A corollary of that proposition was that rogues, vagrants and other masterless men—especially those from the cities—made the worst recruits. However, agrarian developments in early modern England and Wales conspired to reduce the number of smallhold tenants and increase the number of agricultural labourers, cottagers and masterless men. Landlords who were more oriented towards making profits than making war were not disposed to give up good tenants, and in any case the trained bands had first call upon copyholders and freeholders, so tenants were less likely to be conscripted for overseas service unless the authorities were desperate to fill impressment quotas or a landlord wanted to get rid of a troublesome tenant. Consequently, magistrates and constables increasingly turned to vagrants and masterless men to press for soldiers, and military commanders complained about the intractable rogues who arrived with each draft. Sir Francis Vere himself came to England in April 1602 to beat the drum for volunteers for the States' Army, but he was so unsuccessful in this endeavour that he was compelled to ask the authorities for a press of 3,000 men.[18]

When the English Privy Council imposed quotas upon the localities, other considerations besides military needs motivated magistrates and constables. As in other countries of Europe, local officials seized the opportunity to cleanse their communities of undesirables and to send rogues and gaol-birds into foreign parts. Masterless men were seldom accorded legal rights in early modern England, and the use of impressment for social cleansing undoubtedly justified the dubious legality of conscription in the minds of the propertied classes and ratepayers. In 1697 John Locke submitted a poor-relief scheme to the Board of Trade which included a proposal for conscripting vagrants and masterless men who were physically fit for service in the army overseas.[19]

Between 1585 and 1602 nearly 106,000 soldiers were raised in the towns and countryside of England and Wales for service in the Netherlands, Ireland, France and the expeditions to Spain, Portugal and the Azores. Although spread out over sixteen years, this approached two-fifths of the men eligible for military service and constituted more than 2 per cent of the total population. In northeast Hertfordshire, the total number of men impressed for overseas service between 1587 and 1602 was 12 per cent of those named as eligible for military service in 1583, but the more footloose members of the population probably escaped being enrolled in militia lists. Also, contemporary observers generally

Earl of Leicester's Expedition to the Netherlands, 1585–6', in Adams (ed.), *Leicester and the Court: Essays on Elizabethan Politics* (2002), 176–7; Lloyd, *Rouen Campaign*, 87–9.

[18] *Foure Bookes of... Vegetius*, sig. Aiir; Manning, *VR* 5, 78; William Harrison, *The Description of England*, ed. G. Edelen (1968), 258–9, 327–9; F. J. Fisher (ed.), 'The State of England Anno Dom. 1600, by Thomas Wilson', *CM XVI*, CS 3rd ser. 52 (1936), 34; Matthew Sutcliffe, *The Practice, Proceedings and Lawes of Armes* (London, 1593), 62–3; Barnabe Rich, *A Path-Way to Military Practice* (1587; repr. 1969), sig. G3; McClure, *LJC* i. 139, 143, 146.

[19] G. Henry, *The Irish Military Community in Flanders, 1586–1621* (1992), 25; Barnabe Rich, *The Fruits of Long Experience* (1604), 62; M. Cranston, *John Locke: A Biography* (1957), 424–5.

agreed that higher proportions of the population of military age were impressed from London and other urban areas. Given the wastage rates in English military units sent overseas during this period, few of these soldiers were likely ever to return home. Of the total number of men raised from England and Wales between 1585 and 1602, probably about 32,000 or 30 per cent were sent to the Netherlands.[20]

Although the population of England and Wales had doubled in the sixteenth century, late Elizabethan England did not have abundant reserves of manpower for war. When Sir Francis Drake and Sir John Norris were putting together the force for their expedition to Spain and Portugal in 1589, they planned on raising 12,000 men. Lord Burghley told them to ask the Dutch if they could borrow 4,000 experienced English infantry out of the Netherlands to be matched by 8,000 men, including pioneers, to be raised in England. The Dutch insisted that the 4,000 infantry be replaced by fresh recruits from England. An unspecified number of masterless men were swept up in the streets of London and impressed. They were supplemented by 500 volunteers from the Protestant refugee churches of London and 1,500 English volunteers. The 1,500 volunteers were dispatched to help relieve the siege of Bergen-op-Zoom. The total number of troops actually raised in England is unknown, but it fell short of the 8,000 authorized, and consequently, the Dutch contribution was less than expected and the departure of the fleet was delayed.[21]

The various military and naval expeditions of the 1620s necessitated recruiting on a scale comparable to the Elizabethan war years. However, particular years, such as 1624, when 12,000 men were raised for the Mansfeld expedition to the Palatinate, and 1625, when 10,000 men were levied for the Cadiz expedition, exceeded the annual averages of 5,000–6,000 of the Elizabethan war years. The recruiting was especially heavy in London, where one-third of the 10,000 men authorized for the Cadiz expedition were pressed. From the mid-1590s a significant number of discharged soldiers and sailors had gathered in the city and suburbs and were ripe for plucking by constables and provost-marshals. Again, social cleansing took precedence over military needs.[22]

The authorities of London and Middlesex and the provost-marshals who were employed in the metropolis in the 1590s were certainly more cooperative about sweeping up masterless men for impressment than were the magistrates in rural

[20] Cruickshank, *Elizabeth's Army*, 25–7, 290–1; J. McGurk, *The Elizabethan Conquest of Ireland: The 1590s Crisis* (1997), 55; A. J. King (ed.), *Muster Books for North and East Hertfordshire, 1580–1605*, HRS 12 (1996), 8–27, 50–82, 88–107, 114–29, 152–64. I am assuming that the population of England in 1601 was 4.1 million (D. M. Palliser, *The Age of Elizabeth: England under the Later Tudors, 1547–1603*, 2nd edn. (1992), 40). See also I. A. A. Thompson, 'The Impact of War', in P. Clark (ed.), *The European Crisis of the 1590s* (1985), 265–6, for a more conservative estimate of the demographic impact of military recruiting.

[21] R. B. Wernham (ed.), *The Expeditions of Sir John Norris and Sir Francis Drake to Spain and Portugal, 1589*, NRS 127 (1988), pp. xxv–xxvi, 11, 35–6, 69.

[22] S. J. Stearns, 'Conscription and English Society in the 1620s', *JBS* 11: 2 (1972), 4–8; Manning, *VR* 193–4.

districts in meeting their quotas. Local officials in farming communities often conspired to prevent the impressment of substantial tenants and married men, because their families might become dependent upon parish poor relief, and so they preferred to conscript bachelors and strangers. After the mid-1590s it would not have made sense, as Sir John Smythe had earlier asserted, for landlords to connive at the impressment of their own tenants so that they could profit from a turnover of tenants and collect extra entry fines. In Norfolk in the late 1620s, Sir John Hobart was reprimanded for saying that his fellow deputy-lieutenants had accepted money for discharging impressed men. The sums had been large enough, Hobart complained, to drive those persons offering bribes to try to recoup their expenditure by theft or other unlawful means. Because of such problems and the likelihood that the pressed men would try to desert, impressed men were immediately given the king's shilling, the acceptance of which constituted a binding contract and made the new recruit subject to military law and its penalties. It then required considerable effort and vigilance to maintain discipline and conduct the pressed men to the ports of embarkation.[23] An English officer, writing from Flushing in 1605, complained that the latest draft of troops from the North of England were ill-disciplined, feigned sickness and were generally regarded by their officers as utterly useless.[24]

Having concluded peace and initiated a pro-Spanish foreign policy, James VI and I was never happy about allowing the Dutch States General to recruit soldiers in England, but nonetheless he did allow the Privy Council to issue licences to do so. After the beginning of the Twelve Years Truce (1609–21) between Spain and the Dutch Republic, when the States' Army began to reduce its forces, James committed himself to sending 4,000 English and Scots soldiers, who had been detached from the States' Army, to protect the Duchy of Cleve in the Lower Rhineland from Imperial aggression.[25] Public opinion forced James to back off from his pro-Spanish policy in the 1620s, and James gave his permission to the States General in 1624 to raise 5,000 volunteers by beat of the drum for four new English regiments. The four new English regiments were viewed as a first line of defence for England and a means to protect the interests of his daughter Elizabeth, lately queen of Bohemia, and his grandchildren in the Rhenish Palatinate.[26]

In the reign of Charles I, the Protestant princes, now heavily engaged against the Spanish and Imperialist forces, stepped up their recruiting of British manpower. The English Privy Council justified raising troops in England while England was at peace by arguing that it was merely a continuation of the policy followed by James I, and by pretending that the men levied were all volunteers.

[23] Manning, *VR* 178–85 (for commissions of martial law and provost-marshals); K. Sharpe, *The Personal Rule of Charles I* (1992), 24–5; Sir John Smythe, *Certain Discourses Military*, ed. J. H. Hale (1964), pp. xxxiv–xxxv; W. Rye (ed.), *State Papers Relating to Musters, Beacons, Shipmoney in Norfolk*, NNAS (1907), 65–91, 102–3.   [24] HMC, *De L'Isle and Dudley* (1925), iii. 205.
[25] A. J. Loomie, 'Gondomar's Selection of English Officers in 1622', *EHR* 88 (1973), 575; Sir Ralph Winwood, *Memorials of Affairs of State in the Reigns of Queen Elizabeth and King James*, comp. Edmund Sawyer, 3 vols. (1725), iii. 112–15.   [26] PRO, SP 84/118, fo. 98.

Responding to an attempt by Ambrose Spinola, the able commander of the Spanish Army of Flanders, to link up with an Imperialist army in the Rhineland and strike at the heart of the Dutch interior across the River IJssel in 1626, Frederick Henry, the new stadholder, had increased the strength of the States' Army to 77,000 men. In the spring of 1629 he prepared to launch an offensive against the Spanish, and put together an exceptionally large field army of 28,000 men to besiege the key border fortress of 's-Hertogenbosch. The States of Holland raised 5,000 civic militia men to replace troops stripped from nearby Dutch garrison towns. Throughout the summer, recruiting parties were beating the drum in England to reinforce the Dutch army at 's-Hertogenbosch, which surrendered in September. Because of an inability to persuade the States General to appropriate the money for another offensive, the Dutch army was reduced in size by 15,000 men at the end of 1629, and a considerable number of English officers in the States' Army found themselves unemployed.[27]

The Protestant powers were on the offensive again in the early 1630s. The king of Sweden had conquered Pomerania and Frankfurt-an-der-Oder and was advancing into Silesia. Gustavus Adolphus raised 3,000 Scots and 3,000 Englishmen in 1631 to be commanded by the marquis of Hamilton, and, in 1634, 12,000 men were levied for Swedish military service—mostly in Scotland. Earlier, in 1627 and thereafter, press gangs had been busy in East Anglia rounding up 'volunteers' for service in the king of Denmark's army. After 1632, when the Dutch army resumed the offensive, recruiting agents were in England each year to bring the English regiments of the States' Army up to strength.[28]

What distinguished the recruiting efforts of the English local authorities in the 1620s and 1630s was that, as the requests for military manpower from foreign governments increased, the constables and magistrates became more desperate and indiscriminate in selecting those to be impressed, and even householders, subsidy men and members of the trained bands found themselves swept up and sent overseas. Those with money could buy their way out. Many of those impressed in East Anglia for Danish service mutinied and tried to desert. They were threatened with hanging, and the Privy Council ordered that 'exemplary justice should be done upon the mutineers'. Usually, the pressed men of the Caroline period ended up in the Danish, Swedish or Dutch armies, but one English captain who was conducting a company through the Netherlands for service under the elector palatine had some of his men forcibly seized for service in the army of the Dutch West India Company.[29]

[27] BL, Stowe MS. 133, fo. 268; Israel, *Dutch Republic*, 507; William Whiteway of Dorchester, *His Diary, 1618 to 1635*, DRS 12 (1991), 106; A. Searle (ed.), *Barrington Family Letters, 1628–1632*, CS 4th ser. 28 (1983), 113–14, 256.

[28] Whiteway, *Diary*, 117, 141; *CSP Dom., 1627–1628*, 146; PRO, SP 84/148, fos. 53, 56, 59, 61, 63, 66–7.

[29] Stearns, 'Conscription and English Society', 5–6; *CSP Dom., 1627–1628*, 146; PRO, SP 84/155, fo. 5.

The Privy Council of Scotland also pursued a policy of encouraging or compelling unemployed soldiers and vagrants to serve in the armies of the northern
Protestant powers. Among the first Scottish soldiers to serve in the Dutch army were
those who were swept up in Edinburgh in 1572 during a period of dearth and
famine. After the capture of Edinburgh Castle from the supporters of Mary, queen
of Scots, in 1573, the Peace of Perth ended the Scottish Civil War and left many
Scots soldiers without employment. The Scottish Privy Council continued to
license the levying of troops and to profess that they were fighting for the Protestant
cause, although many ended up fighting for the Catholic powers. The presbytery
courts of the Kirk of Scotland also aided recruiting efforts by hounding young men
of notorious behaviour out of their parishes. A much higher proportion of the
Scottish population had experience of the trade of Mars during the Thirty Years War
than was the case with the English; something like 25,000 Scots, or 10 per cent of
the male population, served with foreign armies during that conflict. Although the
Scots soldiers were led by officers of noble status, one Scot complained of the tendency of the Dutch and English to regard the English who served in foreign armies—
especially the States' Army—as volunteers and to put the Scots down as mercenaries
since they were thought to be as ubiquitous on the battlefields of Europe as lice and
rats. The Scottish regiments serving in the States' Army came to be organized into
the Scots Brigade, which remained in the service of the States General until the eve
of the French Revolution. The officers of the Scots Brigade were drawn from the
same Lowland families generation after generation. Their surnames included
Stewart, Balfour, Murray, Hamilton, Seton, Patton and Nisbet.[30]

Overseas military expeditions were a constant drain upon manpower of the
British Isles in the late sixteenth and seventeenth centuries. Because of wastage, a
military term covering death in battle, mortality resulting from disease, malnutrition and exposure as well as desertion, there was a continuing resort to impressment to fill up the various expeditions and the British and Irish garrisons and units
in foreign armies. The wastage rates varied, and most losses are accounted for by
death from disease or desertion rather than from battlefield casualties. Perhaps as
many as one out of every two private soldiers recruited for service abroad never
returned home.[31] Of the 11,000 soldiers and 2,500 mariners who went on the
expedition to Spain and Portugal of 1589, only 6,000 (or 44 per cent) returned.
The high death rate was attributed to insufficient provisions, indiscipline, drunkenness and the failure to provide sufficient surgeons. Good military surgeons were
hard to come by at that date because few had any experience on how to treat gun
wounds.[32] Of the 11,000 or 12,000 men sent to the Netherlands in the autumn of

---

[30] J. Ferguson (ed.), *Papers Illustrating the History of the Scots Brigade in the Service of the United Netherlands, 1572–1782*, 2 vols. (1899), i. 3–7; J. H. Burton (ed.), *RPS 1569–1578* (1878), ii. 148; W. MacRay (ed.), *Records of the Presbyteries of Inverness and Dingwall, 1643–1688*, SHS 24 (1896), 59–60; Carlton, *GW* 19.   [31] Parker, *MR* 53–5.

[32] *A . . . Discourse written by a Gentleman employed in the late Voyage of Spaine and Portingale* (1589; repr. 1972), 9–12.

1586 to serve under Leicester, 2,000 deserted upon landing. There is no indication of how many deserted in England between the time of impressment and embarkation. Sir Roger Williams's loss of nearly half of his 1,600-man force in the defence of Sluis illustrates the cost in human terms of a besieged garrison. Of the 11,000 English soldiers who perished in Normandy between 1589 and 1592, fewer than 1,100 died as a result of battle wounds. At any given time, a muster would have barely yielded 1,100 to 1,200 effectives.[33] The Spanish siege of the Dutch garrison of Ostend which lasted three years and three months, ended in 1603 with a loss of nearly 77,000 Spanish troops and 50,000 men of the States' Army. Probably, 45 per cent of the men of the Dutch army who died in the ultimately futile defence of Ostend were English and Scots.[34]

Rough calculations of the wastage through illness have been worked out by David Stewart. When an expeditionary force was sent to Lough Foyle in Ulster in 1601, the percentage of those who were sick at any given moment during the campaigning season varied between 14 per cent (in July) and 52 per cent (in September). However, non-effective rates at Lough Foyle could range as high 61 per cent in the middle of the winter. The differences between the sick rates and the non-effective rates are explained by mortality from sickness and battle, dead-pays, and those discharged as invalids. This represents a sampling of troops in the field. Sickness rates of troops in garrison (taken from musters at Havre in 1563, Berwick-upon-Tweed in 1563–4 and Zutphen in 1568) reveal sick rates varying between 1½ per cent and 10 per cent (when the plague broke out at Havre while the garrison was under siege). In the same garrisons, non-effective rates could vary between 5 per cent and 32 per cent. Sick rates of about 8 per cent were usual in garrison.[35]

A number of variables stand out in calculating sickness and non-effective rates. Sickness rates were higher in newly formed units than in more 'seasoned' units. Sick rates were usually higher in Ireland because of the damp climate, and the autumn season in the Low Countries was also thought to be conducive to illness. Observers noted that Scots soldiers appeared to be hardier and more resistant to disease than English troops. Finally, desertion contributed as much to wastage as illness, and an army in the field could lose half its strength in six months.[36]

For those soldiers who remained with the colours until the battle was over, no pensions were provided for the maimed and disabled. This was justified by the argument that they were recruited from among the lawless in the first place.

---

[33] J. Bruce (ed.), *Correspondence of Robert Dudley, Earl of Leicester during his Government of the Low Countries*, CS 27 (1844), 374; Sir Roger Williams, *A Briefe Discourse of Warre* (1590), 49–53; R. B. Wernham, *After the Armada: Elizabethan England and the Struggle for Western Europe, 1588–1595* (1984), 407, 417–18.

[34] *An Historical Account of the British Regiments Employed since the Reign of Queen Elizabeth and James I in the Formation and Defence of the Dutch Republic* (1794), 12–14; A.U., *Historie of the... Siege of Ostend... translated out of French by Edward Grimeston* (1604), 223.

[35] D. Stewart, 'Sickness and Mortality Rates of the English Army in the Sixteenth Century', *Journal of the Royal Army Medical Corps*, 91 (1948), 24, 29.   [36] Ibid. 32, 34.

Officers left the States' Army with the selling price of their commissions and
perhaps a bit of profit garnered from booty and ransoms. However, Sir Edward
Cecil complained in 1625 that he had lost £900 a year ever since he entered the
Dutch army. He told Sir Edward Conway that he wished to retire and enter the
service of the duke of Buckingham, but it was difficult for officers and soldiers of
the English regiments of the Dutch army to obtain discharges because of high
attrition rates and the difficulty which the States General faced in replacing them.
It was considered a particular mark of favour that when Horace, Lord Vere, retired
from the Dutch army in 1634 he was granted a pension of £30 per month by the
States General.[37]

As the 'cockpit of Europe' during the Eighty Years War, the Low Countries saw
the intervention of most of the powers of central and western Europe. Its cost in
both human and economic terms was staggering. Francisco Gómez de Quevedo y
Villegas, writing in the 1630s, claimed that more than 2 million people had died
in that struggle to date. This was the cost of freeing a population which never
exceeded 1,950,000 at its highest level (1672) during the seventeenth century.
The southern Low Countries suffered more than the Dutch Republic, and many
towns and villages lost one-half to two-thirds of their population—mostly in the
last thirty years of the sixteenth century. The economic costs certainly contributed
to the collapse of Spain as a great power.[38]

While it is difficult to extract reliable statistics concerning troop strengths of
early modern armies from official records and literary evidence,[39] it is still possible
to make some very rough estimates of the manpower drawn from the peoples of
the British Isles and serving in the States' Army during the Eighty Years War and
how that manpower was employed. The contribution of England and Scotland to
the Dutch army was very large in the late sixteenth century, and at all times constituted a larger proportion of that army than any other single nation. In 1586
Leicester's reinforced expedition probably made up 57 per cent of the entire
Dutch army. In 1595, the 4,150 English and 1,100 Scottish foot together constituted 18 per cent of the 30,000 men of the States' Army. The year 1609 saw the

---

[37] J. R. Hale (ed.), *On a Tudor Parade Ground: The Captain's Handbook of Henry Barrett, 1562* (1978),
54 n.; *Cabal Sive Scrinia Sacra: Mysteries of State*, 3rd edn. (1691), i. 167–8; Whiteway, *Diary*, 143.
Cecil probably spent much of that money maintaining a mess for his officers. Professional soldiers
believed in living well, not saving. Gervase Holles summed up the net worth of his kinsman, Sir
George Holles, the younger son of a sword family, in these words: 'This is the sum of his last will. . . . It
was not much that he left behind him saving a good wardrobe, and some plate and jewels. He
continued all his life unmarried (binding up his posterity in his own stock of honour), and so cared
for no more than whilst he lived to live nobly. He lies buried in the chapel of St John the Evangelist in
Westminster Abbey next to his kinsman and first commander, Sir Francis Vere' (*Memorials of the
Holles Family, 1493–1656*, ed. A. C. Wood, CS 3rd ser. 60 (1937), 77).

[38] G. Parker, 'War and Economic Change: The Economic Costs of the Dutch Revolt', in J. M.
Winter (ed.), *War and Economic Development* (1975), 49–51, 54–5; Israel, *Dutch Republic*, 620.

[39] S. Adams, 'Tactics or Politics? "The Military Revolution" and Hapsburg Hegemony,
1525–1648', in J. A. Lynn (ed.), *Tools of War: Instruments, Ideas and Institutions of Warfare,
1445–1871* (1990), 301.

Table 3.1. English and Scottish soldiers in the States' Army, 1586–1650

Date	English foot	Scots foot	Total English and Scots	Total States' Army[a]
1586	2,000+	—	[57% of total][d]	—
1588	—	—	—	21,000
1594	3,767	—	—	—
1595	4,150	1,100	5,250 (18% of total)	30,000
1598	—	—	—	32,000
1605	8,900	—	—	—
1607	—	—	—	50,000+
1608	—	—	—	47,000
1609[b]	6,000	4,100	10,100 (39% of foot)	(26,000 foot) 29,000
1610	—	2,060	—	—
1617	—	2,300	—	—
1618	—	1,490	—	—
1621[c]	—	2,320	—	48,000
1623	9,550	3,870	13,420 (22% of total)	60,250
1624–5	[19,100][d]	[3,870]	[22,970 (28% of total)]	80,725
1626	—	—	—	55,000
1627	—	—	—	65,000
1629	—	—	—	77,000
1635	—	—	—	79,135
1642	—	—	—	60,430
1650	—	—	—	30,000

Notes:

 [a] This total includes infantry, cavalry and troops in the garrisons of fortresses.
 [b] After the beginning of the Twelve Years Truce.
 [c] Following the resumption of the Eighty Years War.
 [d] Numbers in brackets are my estimates based upon incomplete official statistics.

Sources: ten Raa and de Bas, *Staatsche Leger*, ii. 35, 49–63; iii. 173–8, 182–91; iv. 218–58; Israel, *Dutch Republic*, 263–4, 479, 498–9, 507; Winwood, *Memorials of Affairs of State*, iii. 41–2; 't Hart, *Making of a Bourgeois State*, 43–4; H. L. Zwitzer, 'The Eighty Years War', in M. van der Hoeven (ed.), *The Exercise of Arms: Warfare in the Netherlands, 1568–1648* (1997), 47; H. L. Zwitzer, 'De Militie van den Staat': Het Leger van der Republiek der Verenigde Nederlanden (1991), 45, 175.

beginning of the Twelve Years Truce and a reduction of forces, but the English and Scots foot still made up 35 per cent of the total Dutch military establishment and 39 per cent of the infantry forces. The Eighty Years War resumed in 1621, and by 1623 the four old English regiments with 9,550 men and the three Scots regiments with 3,870 men made up 22 per cent of the States' Army. Four new English regiments were raised by the 'military earls'[40] and sent to help reconquer the Rhenish Palatinate which had been overrun by the Imperialist forces. This

---

 [40] Henry Wriothesley, 3rd earl of Southampton; Robert Devereux, 3rd earl of Essex; Henry de Vere, 18th earl of Oxford; and Robert Bertie, 14th Lord Willoughby de Eresby and later 1st earl of Lindsey (ten Raa and de Bas, *Staatsche Leger*, iii. 169–91).

Table 3.2. Composition of Dutch field armies, 1586–1637

Date	English foot	Scots foot	Total English and Scots	Total field army
1586	4,500	[1,100 mixed Dutch and Scots foot][a]	68%+	6,600
1595	1,600	1,100	2,700 (35%)	7,800
Early 17th century	45 companies	19 companies	64 companies (59%)	109 companies of foot
1610	10 companies	6 companies	16 companies (33%)	48 companies of foot
1614	28 companies	8 companies	36 companies (43%)	84 companies of foot
1614	52 companies	20 companies	72 companies (49%)	146 companies of foot
1632	4 regiments	3 regiments	7 regiments (47%)	15 regiments of foot
1637	55 companies	[25 companies][a]	[80 companies (33%)][a]	246 companies of foot

Note:

[a] Numbers in brackets are my estimates.

Sources: ten Raa and de Bas, *Staatsche Leger*, ii. 35; Bruce (ed.), *Correspondence of Robert Dudley*, 374, 408; Cruso, *Militarie Instructions for the Cavallrie*, 60–7, 104–5; Peacham, *True Relation of the Affaires of Cleve and Gulick*, sig. B4r & v; Henry Hexham, *A Journall of the Taking in of Venlo, Roermont, Strale, the Memorable Siege of Mastricht, the Towne and Castle of Limburch* (1633), preface, 2, 35–40; id., *Siege of Breda*, 1–2.

brought the English foot to approximately 19,100 and the Scots to about 3,870, which constituted at least 28 per cent of the total Dutch military establishment.[41]

If one examines the composition of field armies, most of them personally commanded by Maurice of Nassau, the contribution of the English and Scots foot is even more preponderant. Usually, one-half of the infantry of such field forces was British. The proportion could rise as high as 68 per cent, as in 1586, but did not fall below one-third of the total.[42] When the Dutch army was increased to 77,000 in 1629 during the threatened Spanish invasion, foreign troops were transferred from garrisons to field forces and replaced by Dutch militia.

Following the Maurician reforms, field armies were usually divided into three brigades on the march. When they went into battle, the medieval practice of calling the three brigades the vanguard or van, the battle or main battle and the rearguard was retained. In European martial cultures where soldiers clung to the ancient preference for face-to-face combat, it was considered a great honour to be part of the

[41] Cf. Table 3.1. It cannot be assumed that the English and Scottish regiments consisted solely of members of those nations. At the same time we know that the regiments raised by the Dutch provinces or Dutch noblemen contained many who were not Dutch and they certainly included English and Scots.   [42] Table 3.2.

vanguard, and commanders, eager for honour and glory, vied for the forward position. Of course, marching in the rearguard also required reliable soldiers who could be depended upon not to turn and run. The less seasoned troops could be placed in the middle of the main battle. Leonard and Thomas Digges, writing in the 1570s, thought that it was a bad practice to always give one nation the honour of marching into battle in the vanguard, and tended to promote jealousy in a polyglot army. Yet in Dutch field armies of the Maurician period it appears that the English foot always marched in the vanguard, and often bore the brunt of the losses, as Sir Francis Vere had complained in 1600 during the Battle of Ostend. In 1610 the vanguard consisted entirely of English and Scots, with the Dutch, Frisians, Germans and Walloons, in the main battle. In 1622 it was reported that the English, along with some Dutch battalions, were in the vanguard, and the Scots were mingled among the Dutch in the rearward 'like beans and peas among the chaff'. 'These [Scots] are sure men, hardy and resolute, and their example holds up the Dutch.'[43]

In contrast to the preponderance of British infantry in the States' Army, England and Scotland supplied insignificant numbers of cavalrymen. Although heavy cavalry had formed the core of medieval European armies, English armies made but little use of horse troops during the sixteenth century. One of the explanations for this decline of cavalry, besides the obvious trouble and expense of carrying horses in overseas expeditions, was the increasing reliance on infantry, but it also needs to be emphasized that the English had not kept up with other European armies in their adaptation of cavalry tactics to modern warfare. Henry VIII's wasteful employment of horses in his wars caused a shortage of good warhorses which persisted into the reign of Elizabeth. Horses were expensive to maintain and cost more to feed than their grooms. Official efforts to encourage the breeding of cavalry mounts were not very successful. Cavalry troops formed no part of the trained bands, and cavalry, when required for suppressing domestic rebellions or supplying the few troopers carried in overseas expeditions, could be recruited only from among the households of peers and the greater gentry.[44]

The 1,300 cavalry which Leicester carried with him to the Netherlands in 1585–6 were to a large degree raised by summons from among his own clients,

---

[43] Sir C. Oman, *The Art of War in the Sixteenth Century* (1937; repr. 1991), 34; *A Military Dictionary... by an Officer* (1702), sub 'Van or Vanguard'; Leonard and Thomas Digges, *An Arithmeticall Militaire Treatise named Stratioticos* (1579; repr. 1968), 149; Henry Hexham, *The Second Part of the Principles of the Art Militaire Practized in the Warres of the United Provinces* (1638), 8; Arthur Collins, *Historical Collections of the Noble Families of Cavendish, Holles, Vere, Harley* (1752), 308–9, 316–18; [John Cruso], *Militarie Instructions for the Cavallrie* (1632), 10–15; C. Dalton, *Life and Times of General Sir Edward Cecil, Viscount Wimbledon*, 2 vols. (1885), ii. 17.

It was also a practice of English armies to send forward a detachment of 300 or so musketeers in advance of the front line of the infantry to break the force of the first line of enemy and throw them into confusion (C. H. Firth, *Cromwell's Army* (repr. 1962), 102). This detachment was called *les infants perdus* or 'the forlorn hope'.

[44] H. J. Webb, *Elizabethan Military Science: The Books and the Practice* (1965), 108–23; J. Thirsk, *Horses in Early Modern England: For Service, for Pleasure, for Power* (1978), 7–8, 15, 21; Cruickshank, *Elizabeth's Army*, 33–4. Also, *infra* Ch. 8.

servants and friends among the gentry of North Wales. The essentially feudal nature of these horsemen is demonstrated by the fact that although they were nominally organized into fifteen troops, when they finally mustered at The Hague in 1586, they were identified as belonging to the retinues of particular lords and gentlemen. Moreover, each of the 1,300 lances required several grooms and servants to function. They were not ready for modern warfare, and it is little wonder that the States General took only 300 of them into their pay and service. Of the forty-six troops of cavalry carried on the Dutch military establishment between *c.*1585 and 1609, only four were English and three were Scottish. Sir Edward Cecil, who began his military career in Sir Nicholas Parker's troop, said that many of the English horse were killed at the Battle of Nieuwpoort in 1600, and the English troops of horse were never again recruited up to strength with Englishmen. Cecil had to fill his own troop with Dutch troopers because skilled horsemen were no longer easy to recruit in England. When the Dutch cavalry establishment was increased to sixty-six troops between 1609 and 1625, the number of troops commanded by English and Scots officers remained at seven. Even when the number of Dutch cavalry troops rose to eighty between 1625 and 1648, the English and Scottish contingent continued at seven troops. The cheapest and most convenient place to recruit cavalrymen was Germany, and most of the Dutch cavalry troops were manned by German reiters.[45]

Leicester's lances, besides being untrained and expensive to maintain, were singularly ill-equipped to operate within the confines of the Dutch landscape and had no place in siege warfare. Dutch cavalry troops were divided into cuirassiers and harquebusiers. All operated as pistoleers, while the latter, in addition, carried carbines which were shorter and lighter versions of muskets. Harquebusiers wore only a light headpiece for armour and anticipated the functions of the mounted infantry who were later called dragoons. The Dutch cavalry performed much better after being subjected to the Maurician tactical reforms and contributed to the notable victory at the Battle of Turnhout in 1597. Under the leadership of able cavalry commanders such as Louis, count of Nassau, and the Scotsman John Hamilton, the Dutch horse conducted cavalry raids called *cavalcados* or cavalcades into enemy territory to plunder and pillage. This was a useful tactic for armies which were short of money, provisions and fodder as the Dutch were in the early days of the Eighty Years War. Such cavalcades benefited from the element of surprise, but the retreats had to be conducted with great skill and required good discipline. Since cavalry troopers were regarded as gentlemen, punishments could not be as severe as they were in the infantry. Cavalry regiments, unlike battalions of foot, did not have provost-marshals and disciplinary infractions were dealt with by councils of war.[46]

---

[45] Adams, 'Gentry of North Wales and the Earl of Leicester's Expedition', 137–8, 145–6; ten Raa and de Bas, *Staatsche Leger*, ii. 109–33; iii. 150–63, iv. 186–212; BL, Royal MS. 18. C. xxiii ['Of Divers Parts of War, Especially the Discipline of the Cavalry', by Sir Edward Cecil, Lord Wimbledon], pp. 77–8; Oman, *Art of War*, 547–8.

[46] BL, Royal MS. 18. C. xxiii, pp. 48–9, 77–81; [John Bingham], *Tactics of Aelian* (1616; repr. 1968), 157–8; J. W. Wijn, *Het Krijgswezen in den Tijd van Prins Maurits* (1934), 441–2.

It is difficult to make an accurate assessment of the state of morale among the Scottish and English troops of the States' Army. However, a few fragments of evidence suggest that problems of morale continued even after the days of Leicester when pay was uncertain and desertions were massive. Officers were not permitted to abuse soldiers in the Dutch army and private soldiers were aware that they had certain rights. A decree issued by the States General in the early 1620s encouraged soldiers to denounce their officers for false musters and collecting unauthorized dead-pays, and English officers complained that this bred rebelliousness in the ranks. James Howell remarked that it was only the regularity of pay that prevented large-scale desertion: otherwise 'I believe they would be insolent enough...and...few or none would serve them'.[47]

In fact, the pay of the English regiments in Dutch service became notably irregular in the 1620s, and desertion rates soared. As semi-private entrepreneurs, captains in the Dutch army had to borrow money in order to meet payrolls because the States General and the individual provinces were slow to pay the captains. In November 1623 the colonels of the four old English regiments complained that the States General failed to pay them in a timely fashion and their men were no longer able to subsist. They asked the English ambassador to The Hague, Sir Dudley Carleton, to support their plea to the prince of Orange on their behalf. English and Scottish regiments on detached service, such as those sent to the Palatinate or Denmark, were in even worse straits. In 1625 the English government held up reinforcement and payment of the four new English regiments in the Palatinate and insisted that the Dutch first make satisfaction for the execution of English merchants by Dutch East India Company officials at Amboina in the Moluccas in 1623. The English Council of War had delayed issuing warrants to pay the English government's share of the upkeep of troops in 1626, while the Dutch paymaster Callandrini had stopped payment of the Dutch share of the remuneration for the four new English regiments upon pretence of defective musters. The prince of Orange lent the colonels money for two weeks' pay out of his private funds, but asked that the officers assume responsibility for one-third of the pay of their soldiers. The officers were obliged to go into debt to pay their men, but in July of 1626 the English and Scottish colonels told the English Privy Council that their resources were exhausted and their regiments were at the point of dissolving for lack of pay. This, they said, was bound to reflect upon the king's honour.[48]

In November 1626 the colonels of three of the new English regiments, the third earl of Essex, Sir Charles Morgan and Sir John Borlase (who had assumed command upon the death of the earl of Southampton in 1624), together with Sir James Livingstone who commanded a Scots regiment, stated that their regiments were assigned the most dangerous of tasks, were kept constantly in the field

---

[47] HMC, *Thirteenth Report*, Appendix II (Portland MSS.) (1891), 112; James Howell, *Epistolae Ho-Elianae, or the Familiar Letters of James Howell*, 2 vols. (1907), i. 159.

[48] 't Hart, *Bourgeois State*, 38; PRO, SP 84/112, fos. 217r & v, 35r; 126, fo. 216r; 127, fo. 186r; 130, fo. 81r; 131, fo. 117r & v; 132, fos. 1r, 29r and v.

on the most distant frontiers rather than in garrisons like the Dutch troops and yet were not paid by the States General nor provided with shelter. More recently, they had been withdrawn from the frontiers but not given time to refresh themselves before being immediately seconded to Danish service and told to make ready to embark. Sir Charles Morgan was appointed colonel-general of the four regiments and ordered to clothe and equip them for cold weather. New recruits were sent out from England and the captains were instructed not to enlist any but Englishmen. The English and Scottish colonels again complained that they lacked sufficient money to clothe and equip their men, but the States General refused to make up back pay. The colonels also stated that their monarch should have been consulted about their posting to Denmark, and took the position that since the States General refused to pay them their oath of allegiance was nullified when they were ordered to Denmark. Frederick Henry, prince of Orange and stadholder, grew angry when this argument was presented, and told the four colonels that they remained in Dutch service and were bound by their oath of allegiance.[49]

Morale must have sunk very low in the four regiments under Sir Charles Morgan's command. The winter of 1626–7 was exceptionally cold and the ships which the English and Scots soldiers were to embark upon at Amsterdam were frozen at anchor. The soldiers were not properly clothed for cold weather and the new recruits were not sufficiently hardened. Many of the officers were absent from their duties and some appear to have resigned. Numerous soldiers died from exposure or lost fingers and toes to frostbite. The States General refused to take responsibility for the pay or care of sick and disabled soldiers and warned that they would not care for any soldiers left behind when the four regiments sailed for Denmark. They also refused to pay for the four chaplains who had been appointed to accompany the regiments. It is unclear when the expedition sailed for Denmark, but a muster taken on 3 April 1627 revealed, predictably, that nearly half of the strength of each of the four regiments (or 2,236 out of 4,708 men) had deserted.[50] In early November 1638 the English colonels in Dutch service jointly complained that they had been paid by the English government for only two out of the previous eighteen months. The English Privy Council's reply was that those who had been seconded to Danish service had no reason to complain since they were paid at double the rate of pay that they would have received in Charles I's service.[51]

How much comfort the English soldiers in the States' Army derived from their chaplains is questionable. Samuel Bachiler, a chaplain in the English camp, reproved soldiers 'who are ready for any employment in wars, whether against friend or foe they care not so they may find pay, booty and prey, regarding only their private ends and particular gains'. Having said that, Bachiler tried to convert English participation in the war against the Spanish into a holy war.[52] It is not clear

[49] PRO, SP 84/132, fos. 147–8; 133, fos. 15*r* & *v*, 98–9.   [50] Ibid.
[51] PRO, SP 84/138, fos. 132*r* & *v*, 233*r*, 235*r*.
[52] Samuel Bachiler, *Miles Christianus, or The Campe Royal* (1628), 712–13.

that a chaplain was assigned to every English and Scottish regiment. In 1597 one of the chaplains to a Scots regiment in Dutch service was Andrew Hunter, who had been forced into exile from Scotland for serving as a chaplain to the forces of Francis Steuart Hepburn, fifth earl of Bothwell, during the rebellion of the Catholic lords against James VI. He continued as a chaplain until *c.*1630, when his widow was awarded a pension by the States General. In 1586 the States General appropriated 4,000 guilders to build a chapel for the English garrison at Flushing. Another chaplain to the English forces between 1610 and 1616 was Thomas Potts, a Presbyterian who remained behind as a *predikant* when the English garrison moved elsewhere. The chaplains to the Scots and Anglo-Dutch Brigades in the Netherlands were expected to minister to English and Scots civilian residents as well as the soldiers in the local garrisons. They might serve more than one regiment and, like the officers and soldiers, their pay was often in arrears.[53]

In the early days of the Dutch revolt, the irregular naval forces known as Sea Beggars, with their ferocious behaviour and plundering habits, were barely distinguishable from the duke of Alva's troops, but from the 1580s military authorities promulgated codes of justice which were intended not only to impose strict discipline, but also to prevent the plundering and destructiveness associated with war. Both garrison towns and camps in the field were walled and fenced about, and soldiers who left such enclosures without leave were subject to the death penalty, as were those men who attacked, molested, abused and robbed persons in the households where they were billeted.[54] Dutch military law, as codified in the *Krijgsrecht* of 1590, was also very strict and precise about matters such as dead-pays, the ransom of prisoners and what constituted lawful booty and how it was to be distributed between soldiers and officers. To muster under a false name, or in more than one company or with a horse other than one's own, was punishable by death. All prisoners taken were to be reported to one's commander before the end of each day. High-ranking prisoners of war were to be taken to the commanding officer immediately, but the soldier doing so received a reward of up to 5,000 guilders. Severe penalties were specified for those who allowed a prisoner to escape after being bribed. Since medieval times, the Church had encouraged the practice of ransoming and exchanging prisoners of war rather than killing them. In 1602 the States General and the Spanish viceroy in the Low Countries concluded a protocol which established a schedule of ransoms for officers and soldiers differentiated by rank and branch of service.[55]

Officers of noble status who believed in living well in the field found a more spartan life forced upon them by the *Krijgsrecht*, which imposed limits on the number of wagons in the baggage train and prohibited carrying women in them.

[53] A. C. Dow, *Ministers to the Soldiers of Scotland* (1962), 62–3.

[54] HMC, *Salisbury MSS*, 21 vols. (1883–1970), xiv. 299.

[55] Henry Hexham, *The Principles of the Art Militarie Practiced in the Warres of the United Provinces* (1637), app., 3–8, 9–15; [Cruso], *Militarie Instructions for the Cavallrie*, 20–2; Redlich, *DPM* 39 (1956), 30–1.

Officers also were not to absent themselves from their companies without the permission of their superiors.[56]

Most military commanders believed that it was a salutary practice to hang a soldier every now and then for the sake of example and the preservation of discipline. But it is very doubtful if the death penalty was exacted for every capital offence specified in the Dutch Articles of War. Provident commanders came to realize in the seventeenth century that military manpower was a valuable resource which could not be wasted. Mutiny and desertion in the face of the enemy were the worst crimes imaginable to a military man, but the Roman practice of decimation, which the earl of Essex revived while he was in Ireland, came to be widely adopted—at least in the English forces. Decimation was the practice of having condemned mutineers and deserters draw lots in order to determine who would live or die, and then executing only every tenth man. The condemned men would discover who was actually to die only at the very last moment, and officers were satisfied that a little bit of terror went a long way.[57]

The re-chivalrization of English aristocratic society resulted from a change of values which occurred among the peerage and gentry—partly in response to contact with foreign noblemen, and especially those of France in the age of the Religious Wars. The remilitarization of the lower social orders in England, on the other hand, came about by compulsion, and most soldiers were recruited for overseas service by impressment. Their reluctance to accept this calling is demonstrated by their desertion in large numbers whenever pay and provisions dried up and morale sank. Mercenary soldiers from Ireland or Scotland were recruited, as we shall see in the next chapter, by poverty, forced exile and the endeavours of military entrepreneurs. Although Scots and Irish military officers may have entered foreign service for different motives than their English counterparts, they all came to participate in the same pan-European martial culture. That the impressment of subjects in England was illegal and unconstitutional was forgotten as aristocratic volunteers and divines attempted to justify participation in foreign wars as a holy crusade and a manifestation of virtue and honour. Magistrates and constables were glad to sweep up vagrants and masterless men in the cities, but landlords were usually reluctant to allow good tenants to be impressed and their families beggared and forced upon parish poor relief. The men of the British Isles who were impressed, exiled or otherwise recruited were legally invisible in their own countries; they went to the Netherlands to fight in the place of Dutchmen who did not perceive any connection between patriotism and military service—a concept which was not inaugurated until the French revolutionary government proclaimed the *levée-en-masse* and the concept of the nation-in-arms in August 1793.

Through the heavy contribution of men and resources, the early Stuart monarchs were drawn into the Eighty Years War and the Thirty Years War despite

---

[56] [Cruso], *Militarie Insructions for the Cavallrie*, 20–2.

[57] M. Smuts, 'Court-Centred Politics and the Use of Roman Historians, *c.*1590–1630', in K. Sharpe and P. Lake (eds.), *Culture and Politics in Early Stuart England* (1993), 27; Edward Davies, *The Art of War and England's Traynings* (1619; repr. 1968), 67.

James VI and I's avowed policy of peace with Spain. Public opinion persuaded him to allow troops to be raised to intervene in Bohemia and the Palatinate, and close ties with the ruling dynasty of Denmark made it difficult to refuse requests for troops to be employed by the Danish monarchs in pursuit of their ambitions in Germany. The pro-war party at home could argue that the fortresses of the Dutch Republic were England's first line of defence against Hapsburg aggression, but Thomas Mun noticed that the English contributions in manpower and treasure was disproportionately heavy and freed the Dutch to conquer and plunder the East Indies.[58] While the presses of men for the States' Army and the overseas military and naval expeditions of the Elizabethan period took mostly vagrants and masterless men, the recruiting efforts for the various expeditions of the 1620s together with the drafts for foreign armies grew so indiscriminate that they conscripted householders and subsidy men. The illegality of the Elizabethan impressments were easier to overlook than those of the 1620s, and, together with the issues of martial law and extra-parliamentary taxation occasioned by the military and naval expeditions of the 1620s, the practice of impressment indirectly contributed to the Petition of Right of 1628.[59]

Although numerous historians and political scientists have asserted that soldiers of the Dutch army were the best and most regularly paid in Europe, there were times—especially in the 1580s and the 1620s—when lack of pay, provisions and clothing caused such appalling conditions among the English and Scottish regiments of the States' Army that morale plummeted to the point where these corps were on the verge of dissolution as a result of massive desertions. This was because there was a faction in the States General and individual provincial States which was willing to cripple the war effort against Spain by delaying appropriations in order to restrict the military and political power of the princes of Orange and the Orangist party. English contributions to the pay of these regiments was delayed by the bad feeling which followed upon the Amboina 'Massacre' of 1623. The memory of this incident was not forgotten, and can be cited as a minor cause of the Anglo-Dutch wars later in the century.[60]

[58] Thomas Mun, *England's Treasure by Forraign Trade* (1664; repr. 1965), 78–9. Actually, the army of the Dutch East India Co. was largely made up of Germans.

[59] Although many of the disorders complained of in the Petition of Right were occasioned by or associated with the impressment of unwilling recruits, it is interesting that the Petition of Right focuses largely upon the unlawfulness of the use of martial law within England and extra-parliamentary taxation rather than the violation of the civil rights of English subjects by illegal impressment. Thus, the men impressed into the army remained legally invisible.

[60] An English gentleman named Fairfax, writing in 1631 to a kinsman in Yorkshire, reported that three Dutch merchants at a tavern near Strasbourg had boasted to a group of countrymen how they had with their own hands participated in torturing and executing the English merchants at Amboina. When word of this was carried to two English captains of horse in Imperial service, the English officers, accompanied by a troop of cavalry, ambushed the Dutch merchants in a wood and summarily hanged fifteen of them, sparing the sixteenth to carry news of their revenge to the States General in The Hague (Thomas Birch, *The Court and Times of Charles I*, ed. R. F. Williams, 2 vols. (1848), ii. 109–10).

4

Recruiting in the British Isles for mainland European armies

A young cavalier, desirous of honour and greedy of good instruction, could have learned from this king [Gustavus Adolphus]. . . . Such a general would I gladly serve, but such a general I shall hardly see, whose custom was to be first and last in danger himself. . . .

Monro, *Expedition*, ii. 16.

Oh, woe unto these cruel wars / That ever they began!
For they have reft[1] my native isle / Of many a pretty[2] man.
First they took my brethren twain[3] / Then they wiled[4] my love frae me,
Oh, woe unto the cruel wars / In Low Germany.[5]

Fragment of an old Scots ballad printed in B. Hoenig, 'Memoiren englischer Officere im Heere Gustav Adolf's und ihr Fortleben in der Literatur', *Beitrage zur neuerer Philologie Jakob Schipper dargebracht* (1902), 326.[6]

The peoples of the British Isles served in most of the armies of continental Europe besides that of the Dutch Republic during the seventeenth century. The need for military manpower increased when the Thirty Years War began in 1618 and the Eighty Years War resumed in 1621. Gentlemen volunteered for reasons of religious fervour, honour, glory, military adventure and experience, while humble folk were more often recruited under compulsion. Young men of military age from Scotland and Ireland were also susceptible to the inducements of lairds and clan chieftains, and some Irish and Scottish regiments contained sizeable kinship and clan groups. The governments of the Three Kingdoms assisted this compulsory recruitment because they wished to rid their realms of idle swordsmen and vagrants and send them into what often amounted to perpetual exile. However,

---

[1] Robbed.   [2] Brave.   [3] Took my brothers away.   [4] Lured.
[5] Another version reads 'High Germany'.
[6] This fragment appears to have been worked into an early 19th-century ballad by the Scottish poet Allan Cunningham in *The Songs of Scotland, Ancient and Modern*, 4 vols. (1825; repr. 1975), iv. 213–15. It was a common practice for Romantic lyric poets such as Cunningham and Robert Burns, to rework old ballads.

the efforts of military enterprisers, who recruited whole companies and regiments for profit, were successful beyond the sporadic efforts of officials of the Three Kingdoms. While most Englishmen preferred to serve in the States' Army, the Scots were to be found everywhere, but especially in the Swedish army in the time of Gustavus Adolphus and in the army of Denmark-Norway under Christian IV. The Catholic Irish, urged on by their priests, preferred Spanish service—especially in the Army of Flanders—but also maintained a significant presence in the French army after that country entered the Thirty Years War in 1635.

Following the regal union of England and Scotland in 1603, the possibility of war between those two kingdoms diminished, and Scottish soldiers were no longer needed at home. Likewise in Ireland, the end of the Tyrone Rebellion or Irish Nine Years War and the Anglo-Spanish War made soldiers—whether English or Irish—redundant in that kingdom. The governments of both Scotland and Ireland embarked upon a policy of supplying the needs of military enterprisers recruiting for mainland European armies and making life difficult for swordsmen who tarried too long before accepting enlistment and exile.[7] That discharged soldiers and idle swordsmen were a threat to domestic stability had long been recognized. Sir William Stanley's Regiment, which defected from the States' Army to the Spanish Army of Flanders, had been recruited from among English and Irish soldiers discharged from the English army in Ireland. Although Stanley's desertion with his whole regiment gave Irish soldiers a bad reputation among Protestant princes and military commanders, one Captain Dawtrey asked Sir Robert Cecil in July 1594 to be allowed to raise a regiment of 1,500 to 2,000 native Irish for service in Brittany. Dawtrey insisted that the native Irish made very good soldiers when sent overseas, and that Cecil should not be influenced by Stanley's bad example.[8]

All governments regarded discharged soldiers as a threat to stability. In England, after 1588 government policy and legislation also attempted to discourage discharged soldiers and sailors from returning from overseas expeditions by treating them as vagrants and masterless men. Discharged soldiers and sailors were especially troublesome when demobilized without full pay—as often happened—and despite official discouragement, congregated in London and its suburbs where they participated in riots during the war years of the 1590s and 1620s.[9]

Following the end of the Tyrone Rebellion and the Anglo-Spanish War, the English government of Ireland decided that Irish swordsmen must be removed because, being regarded as uncivilized, adverse to labour, unregenerate and stubbornly Catholic, they could not be incorporated into planter society. Under the terms of the Anglo-Spanish Peace Treaty of 1604, the British Isles became neutral

---

[7] Macdougall, *S&W*, p. xii; G. Henry, *The Irish Military Community in Flanders, 1586–1621* (1992), 42–3.

[8] Henry, *Irish Military Community*, 24–5; HMC, *Salisbury MSS.*, iv. 566–7.

[9] Henry, *Irish Military Community*, 24–5; Manning, *VR* 187, 193–4, 203, 210, 214–17.

territory for recruitment by foreign armies. In 1609 the Irish government estimated that there were some 12,000 idle swordsmen who continued to be followers of the Irish lords and chieftains, and, from the time of Lord Mountjoy, the lords deputy had encouraged them to follow their martial inclinations elsewhere. With the inauguration of this policy down until the Irish Rebellion of 1641, the Irish and English governments did not much care where Irish swordsmen went as long as they were gone. They actively cooperated with military contractors and recruiting officers to pack them off to the Protestant powers of the Netherlands, Denmark and Sweden, but also allowed Irish recruiting officers from Poland, Spain and Imperial Austria to come to Ireland and enlist volunteers.[10]

The earlier drafts of Irish soldiers for the Spanish Army of Flanders—especially those of 1586, 1605 and 1621—appear to have been made up mostly of volunteers, but many of those who went elsewhere were impressed. Sir Arthur Chichester, lord deputy from 1604 to 1614, claimed to have sent 6,000 men to Sweden. Following the flight of the Irish earls in 1607, 1,200 of Tyrone's own vassals and retainers were forced to enter the service of Sweden and Muscovy in one year alone. In a battle between the Russians and the Poles, seven companies of Irish deserted the Muscovite army, and the Russians killed the remaining two companies of Irish in retaliation. Those Irish sent to serve the kings of Denmark and Sweden were also disgruntled, and their priests, who accompanied them disguised as common soldiers, incited mutinies. After 1631 Gustavus Adolphus refused to accept any more Irish troops.[11]

Military enterprisers and contractors in Ireland found it easy to practise their trade because the English lords deputy and provincial governors made life difficult for idled soldiers. The death of Lord Mountjoy in 1606 deprived Tyrone and the other Irish earls and chieftains of a sympathetic ear in the Irish government. The enfranchisement of the inhabitants of Ulster as English subjects in 1605 effectively deprived the Irish lords and chieftains in that province of their authority and contributed to the flight of the earls in 1606. The president of the province of Munster, Sir George Carew, declared his intention 'to hunt' the idled soldiers, and he proposed employing Catholic prisoners of war to fight the remaining rebels so that they might consume one another. Any who remained after this sweep through the woods and bogs could be dispatched to the Indies, Virginia or the Low Countries, where 'three parts of four were likely never to return'. The English Privy Council discouraged sending them to the States' Army, but did not care if they went to the Spanish Army of Flanders. The further away the better was the

---

[10] N. Canny, *Kingdom and Colony: Ireland in the Atlantic World, 1560–1800* (1988), 103–4; R. D. Fitzsimon, 'Irish Swordsmen in the Imperial Service in the 30 Years War', *IS* 9 (1969–70), 22–4; Henry, *Irish Military Community*, 26, 29–30.

[11] Henry, *Irish Military Community*, 71–2; Fitzsimon, 'Irish Swordsmen', 22–3; G. Parker, *The Army of Flanders and the Spanish Road, 1567–1659: The Logistics of Spanish Victory and Defeat in the Low Countries' Wars* (1972), 28–9, 52–3; M. K. Walsh, 'The Wild Goose Tradition', *IS* 17 (1987–90), 6; A. Åberg, 'Scottish Soldiers in the Swedish Armies in the Sixteenth and Seventeenth Centuries', in G. G. Simpson (ed.), *Scotland and Scandinavia* (1990), 91.

rule that English officials followed, and voyages to the Indies were ideal since tropical conditions exacted such a high toll.[12]

Recruiting policies throughout the Three Kingdoms appear to have been driven by official concerns for domestic stability regardless of the impact on foreign relations. Thus, contractors for the Spanish Army of Flanders were allowed to recruit in Ireland even though this was prejudicial to Dutch interests. Recruiting for the Spanish army was briefly prohibited following the discovery of the Gunpowder Plot of 1605, but by 1606 at least four Spanish recruiting parties were busy in Ireland because Dublin Castle assigned a higher priority to cleansing Ireland of swordsmen. James I also encouraged English Catholics to serve in the Spanish army, despite the fact that this facilitated communications of Catholic recusants in England with their friends and kinsmen in Flanders, permitted young men from English Catholic families to be educated overseas and made it easier for priests, disguised as soldiers, to return home. While it was lawful for subjects of the king of England to serve in foreign armies, it was made a felony to leave the country for that purpose without first having sworn an oath not to be reconciled to the pope and not to be a party to any conspiracy or plot against the king. For their part the Spaniards never missed an opportunity to subvert the king's subjects. Thus, William Trumbull wrote to Sir Dudley Carleton from Brussels in 1619 that Archibald Campbell, seventh earl of Argyll, who was scorned at home, was 'caressed' by the Spaniards and given an annual pension of £1,500. The Irish earls and their gentlemen retainers who went to Flanders found a welcome from kinsmen who had already settled there and a government which was happy to educate—and indoctrinate—their sons.[13]

The number of men from the British Isles who volunteered, were recruited by military enterprisers and contractors or were impressed for service in the various armies of mainland Europe during the Thirty Years War was at least 55,000 and may have totalled as many as 80,000. The number of Englishmen was between 10,000 and 15,000; the total of the Irish probably exceeded 15,000; and the Scots, who appear to have been everywhere, certainly numbered at least 25,000, but could have been as numerous as 50,000.[14] The dates of the Thirty Years War

---

[12] Henry, *Irish Military Community*, 42–3; Fynes Moryson, *Itinerary*, 4 vols. (1907–8), ii. 279; *Cal. S.P., Ireland, 1600*, 401; D. B. Quinn, *The Elizabethans and the Irish* (1966), 119–20; Sir John Davies, *A Discovery of the True Causes Why Ireland was Never Entirely Subdued*, ed. J. P. Meyers (1612; repr. 1988), 22–3.

[13] Henry, *Irish Military Community*, 27–9, 48–9; G. Anstruther, *Vaux of Harrowden: A Recusant House* (1953), 440; I. R. Bartlett, 'Scottish Mercenaries in Europe, 1570–1640: A Study in Attitudes and Policies', *ST* 13 (1984–5), 16; Statute of 3 & 4 Jac. I, c. 4 [1605–6], printed in G. W. Prothero (ed.), *Select Statutes and Other Constitutional Documents Illustrative of the Reigns of Elizabeth and James I*, 4th edn. (1913; repr. 1963), 259–60; S. R. Gardiner (ed.), *Letters and Documents Illustrating the Relations between England and Germany at the Commencement of the Thirty Years War*, 2 vols., CS 90, 98 (1865, 1868), ii. 68; J. Casway, 'Henry O'Neill and the Formation of the Irish Regiment in the Netherlands', *IHS* 18 (1972), 481–8.

[14] Carlton, *GW* (1992), 19; A. I. Macinnes, *Charles I and the Making of the Covenanting Movement, 1625–1641* (1991), 311.

as usually given are, of course, arbitrary and merely represent the widening of a number of conflicts; nor did the Peace of Westphalia (1648) end the conflict between France and Spain, in whose armies substantial numbers of soldiers from Scotland and Ireland served. Perhaps as many as 20,000 Irish soldiers had already fought in the Spanish Army of Flanders between 1586 and 1611.[15] Although only 4,000 Irish were serving in that army in 1623, one must remember that wastage rates of 50 per cent a year when armies were in the field were not unusual. As many as 25,000 Irishmen, assigned to seven regiments, probably served in the French army between 1635 and 1664.[16]

Twenty-five thousand soldiers from Scotland seems like a great many, since this would represent one-tenth of the adult male population of Scotland, yet there is good reason for thinking that such a figure is a low estimate. Twenty-five thousand soldiers from the British Isles served with the Swedish army during a three-year period between 1629 and 1631. The Swedish army at one time had thirteen Scottish regiments, each with an authorized strength of 1,008 men. Donald Mackay, first Lord Reay, the busiest of all Scottish military enterprisers, alone recruited 10,000 Scots for the Swedish army between 1629 and the mid-1630s. The Danish army employed 10,000 to 12,000 Scots and English soldiers before its participation in the Thirty Years War collapsed. Because of poverty, as many as 100,000 Scots (10 per cent of the total population) emigrated from Scotland in the early seventeenth century, and Allan Macinnes estimates that half of them were soldiers.[17]

We know more about the motivation of officers and gentlemen volunteers who fought in foreign armies than we do about that of the men in the ranks. Despite the demilitarization of aristocratic values in the early Elizabethan period, it remained possible for gentlemen to find military adventure and honour by travelling overseas. Sir John Smythe had helped to suppress the rebellions of 1549 in both Norfolk and in the West, and he subsequently fought in France. Later, he obtained permission to go abroad to fight the Turks in the service of Maximilian II. He stated that he always fought 'as an adventurer [i.e., volunteer] at mine own charges' in all the armies he served with because he wanted to be 'free and at liberty in all actions to accompany the lieutenant general . . . and other principal officers'.

---

[15] G. Henry, ' "Wild Geese" in Spanish Flanders: The First Generation, 1586–1610', *IS* 17 (1989), 192; J. M. McGurk, 'Wild Geese: The Irish in European Armies (sixteenth to eighteenth centuries)', in P. O'Sullivan (ed.), *The Irish World Wide: History, Heritage, Identity*, vol. 1: *Patterns of Migration* (1992), 40.   [16] Parker, *MR* 49; id., *Army of Flanders*, 52.

[17] M. E. Ailes, 'From British Mercenaries to Swedish Nobles: The Immigration of British Soldiers to Sweden during the Seventeenth Century', Univ. of Minnesota Ph.D diss. (1997), 37–8, 41–2; S. Murdoch, *Britain, Denmark-Norway and the House of Stuart, 1603–1660* (2000), 202–8, 225; J. Grant, *Memoirs and Adventures of Sir John Hepburn* (1851), p. viii; Macinnes, *Covenanting Movement*, 31; E. M. Furgol, 'Scotland Turned Sweden: The Scottish Covenanters and the Military Revolution', in J. Morrill (ed.), *The Scottish National Covenant and its British Context* (1990), 136. Cf. Also I. Roy, 'England Turned Germany? The Aftermath of the Civil War in its European Context', *TRHS* 5th ser. 28 (1978), 130.

As a Catholic recusant and a cousin of the queen through the Seymour connection, Smythe was highly visible, and she called him home in 1569 and kept him hanging about the court. Consequently his military career was frustrated, although he was given a few diplomatic assignments and made a colonel of the Essex trained bands in 1585.[18]

Even when professional soldiers were more fastidious about their allegiance, their career choices might be restricted. After William the Silent discharged the English Regiment in January 1574, Sir Roger Williams found himself unemployed. The English government had intended to send the members of the regiment to Ireland, but being short of money, Williams tried to join the prince of Condé's army in Germany, which Williams knew would be marching back into France to help the Huguenot cause in the French Religious Wars, but Condé was not ready to proceed and could not offer employment immediately. On his way back to England through Brabant, Julian Romero offered Williams a commission in the Spanish Army of Flanders, and he decided to accept because he was in desperate financial circumstances, but also out of a desire for travel and adventure. He made the most of his experiences to learn from his Spanish masters about the new methods of warfare, and he closely observed Spanish military organization and tactics. After serving the Spanish for four years, Williams eventually returned to the Netherlands with a commission in Sir John Norris's Regiment after overcoming the prince of Orange's distrust of him for serving the Spanish. He drew upon his experiences in the Low Countries to write the *Brief Discourse of War* (1590), in which he advocated the new military practices which he had learned while serving in the two opposing armies involved in the Eighty Years War.[19]

William, Lord Craven, was more constant in his loyalties. The son of a wealthy London merchant and lord mayor from Yorkshire, he began his military career in the States' Army under Maurice of Nassau. He helped Frederick, king of Bohemia, in his attempt to recover the Palatinate and commanded the English troops under Gustavus Adolphus. He became a lifelong admirer of Frederick's queen, Elizabeth, and the companion of Prince Rupert of the Rhine, and shared Rupert's imprisonment at the hands of the Imperialists in 1638. He lived into his nineties, held the rank of lieutenant-general under James II and was ordered by that monarch to hand over the duty of guarding Whitehall Palace to William III's Dutch Blue Guards in 1688.[20]

Many swordsmen, attracted by the martial culture of France and reputation of the French military nobility, preferred to begin their careers in the French Royal or Huguenot armies. Sir Nicholas Malby saw his first action during the Siege of St Quentin. At the conclusion of the French Religious Wars, Malby served as a

---

[18] Sir John Smythe, *Certain Discourses Military*, ed. J. R. Hale (1964), pp. xiii–xxv.

[19] Sir Roger Williams, *The Actions of the Low Countries*, ed. D. W. Davies (1618; repr. 1964), pp. xiii–xvii, 27, 112–13.

[20] P. Morrah, *Prince Rupert of the Rhine* (1976), 38–9; *DNB*, *sub* William Craven, earl of Craven (1606–1697).

gentleman volunteer in Ireland. As was generally the custom, he always paid his own expenses, but, at the same time, he displayed an inordinate concern with garnering booty. Sir Edward Cecil, later Viscount Wimbledon, was also drawn to serve his military apprenticeship in the French Royal army, whose military culture, he thought, provided the best opportunity for demonstrating feats of valour and establishing a reputation. Like many old-fashioned swordsmen, Wimbledon thought that serving in the cavalry made a man more daring and resolute than fighting on foot.[21]

George Gordon, second marquis of Huntly, was a military peer who, when he rebelled against the Covenanters in 1639, knew the geography of France better than his native Scotland. The family's Catholic connections would have made service in the French Royal army more congenial than fighting under Gustavus Adolphus. Like his two sons, George, Lord Gordon, and James, Viscount Aboyne, Huntly had served his 'apprenticeship in the school of Mars' in a company of Scottish *gens d'armes*, which he commanded.[22] Robert Monro had also served his apprenticeship in arms in the French Royal army, which presumably reflected his personal preference. When Donald Mackay, first Lord Reay, began raising his famous regiment in 1626, Monro felt obliged to join because his cousin, Robert Monro, baron of Foulis, the chief of his clan, had asked him to do so. When Monro sat down to write his military memoirs, he dedicated the book to Frederick, king of Bohemia and elector palatine; the audience to which he addressed his book included 'all worthy cavaliers favouring the laudable profession of arms'.[23]

Sir James Turner was not quite 17 when he graduated from Glasgow University. His father and grandfather wished him to continue his studies, but Turner rebelled. It was not that he did not have a scholarly bent of mind, for he was very interested in history and literature and well versed in religious controversy. He lived for a year with his father at Dalkeith until he decided that he wanted to be a soldier.

Before I attained to the eighteenth year of my age, a restless desire entered my mind to be, if not an actor, at least a spectator of these wars which at that time made so much noise over all the world, and were managed against the [Holy] Roman emperor and the Catholic League in Germany under the auspicious conduct of the thrice famous Gustavus Adolphus, king of Sweden. Sir James Lumsden was then levying a regiment for that service, and with him... I engaged to go over [as] ensign to his brother, Robert Lumsden, eldest captain.[24]

---

[21] Thomas Churchyard, *A Generall Rehearsall of Warres* (1579), sigs. D2r & *v*; Sir Edward Cecil, Lord Wimbledon, 'Of Divers Parts of War, Especially the Cavalry', BL, Royal MS. 18. C. xxiii, pp. 4–5, 16.
[22] James Gordon, parson of Rothiemay, *History of Scots Affairs*, 3 vols., SC 1, 2, 4 (1841), ii. 215–16.   [23] Monro, *Expedition*, preface, i. 3, 18, 45, 88.
[24] Sir James Turner, *Memoirs of his own Life and Times, 1632–1670*, BC 31 (1829), 3–4.

Scottish peers and gentlemen played a prominent role in the officer corps of the Swedish army in the time of Gustavus Adolphus. Sir Alexander Leslie was a field marshal and later commanded the Scots Covenanting Army during the British civil wars. Another Scot, Robert Douglas of Whittington, later rose to that same rank and was created baron of Skälby and count of Skeminge in the Swedish nobility. General Sir James Spens of Wormiston, who commanded all the Scots and foreign troops in the Swedish army, was also granted a patent of Swedish nobility as baron of Orreholmen in Västergötland and was employed as an ambassador to the court of James VI and I and other European courts. Sir James King, who came from the Orkney Islands, was lieutenant-general to Sir Alexander Leslie in both the Swedish and Scots Covenanting armies. He was later raised to the Scottish peerage as Baron Eythin. Sir Patrick Ruthven of Bandean, who served as lieutenant-general to the Swedish Field Marshal Johan Banier or Banèr, was later general-in-chief of Charles I's Royalist army, and was created earl of Brentford and Forth in the English and Scottish peerages in addition to his Swedish title of count. Twelve Scottish officers achieved the rank of major-general under Gustavus Adolphus, and as many as 121 Scots were colonels of regiments or lieutenant-colonels. There were twenty-seven field officers and eleven captains who bore the surname of Monro, and many of them were kinsmen of Robert Monro. Other Scottish surnames occurring among the officers of Gustavus Adolphus's army included Forbes (seven), Hamilton and Leslie (five), Lumsden and Lindsay (four), as well as three Ruthvens, three Douglases, two Sinclairs and two Ramsays. Scottish officers in Swedish service included five peers or heirs of peerages (among them Lord Reay; Alexander Lindsay, fourteenth earl of Crawford; George Lindsay, third Baron Spynie; and Alexander, master of Forbes, who became the eleventh Lord Forbes and clan chieftain), besides those Scots who were subsequently ennobled in the peerages of England and Scotland on their return home to participate in the Wars of the Three Kingdoms. Not all Scottish colonels in the Swedish army led regiments composed of soldiers of their own nation; many commanded Dutch, Finnish and Swedish regiments.[25] In addition, four Englishmen, colonels Austin, Cassels, Thomas Conway and George Fleetwood, also commanded regiments in the Swedish army in the time of Gustavus Adolphus.[26] It was more difficult for foreigners to enter the nobility of Denmark-Norway through meritorious military service than was the case in Sweden, but nonetheless eight Scots were ennobled in the late sixteenth and early seventeenth centuries.[27]

---

[25] Monro, *Expedition*, ed. W. S. Brockington (1999 repr. edn.), 113–16; Grant, *Memoirs...of Sir John Hepburn*, 252–8; [Daniel Defoe], *The Scots Nation and Union Vindicated* (1714), 25–8; A. Grosjean, *An Unofficial Alliance: Scotland and Sweden, 1569–1654* (2003), 22–38.

[26] Fleetwood, whose brother was the regicide, parliamentary commander and son-in-law of Cromwell, served his whole career in the Swedish military and diplomatic services. He was promoted lieutenant-general and created a Swedish baron by Queen Christina (*DNB*, *sub* George Fleetwood (1605–1667)).   [27] Murdoch, *Britain, Denmark-Norway and the House of Stuart*, 189.

Scottish officers serving in foreign armies were regarded by members of the English nobility as being 'mere soldiers of fortune, men low-born and illiterate'. Scottish writers were at pains to point out that such persons were rarely 'low-born', but were bred as gentlemen. Moreover, many were well educated, and Scots in the seventeenth century had better access to a university education than did Englishmen. A number of Scots officers with extensive professional experience came to serve in both the English Royalist and Parliamentarian armies, and English peers and magnates resented the fact that Scots officers had attained high rank through merit and experience rather than noble status. This was certainly very galling to many aristocrats—both English and Scottish—and English aristocrats had trouble relating to the social status of untitled barons, lairds and considerable freeholders who came to be called gentry only from the time of Charles I.[28] However, it certainly is true that a lack of opportunities at home caused Scots to look overseas for honourable employment and military careers, and they must have been aware that military service in time of war provided the fastest entrée into the nobility.[29]

Sir Thomas Urquhart was at pains to defend the honour of Scots soldiers against the 'infamy' incurred by Presbyterian Covenanters and by 'money-grubbing' Scottish merchants and bankers—especially those living in London. Urquhart could count the names of seventy-one Scots who served as Swedish general officers and colonels who were subsequently created Swedish barons, as well as those who were Scottish peers or were subsequently created peers.[30] A more recent study of this problem of social status reveals that of the generation of Scots officers who served under Gustavus Adolphus, thirty-five persons representing twenty-seven Scottish families and one English family were ennobled by the Swedish crown; in the next generation, forty-five officers from twenty-seven Scottish military families were granted patents of nobility in Sweden. Those Scots who were ennobled in Sweden and remained in Sweden or Finland usually married women descended from Scots families. Thus, the Scottish military families in Sweden remained a tightly knit community.[31]

The famous Mackay's Regiment, mostly recruited from among Highlanders, furnishes a case study of the backgrounds of 105 gentlemen volunteers and how they subsequently fared in their careers. Their proprietary colonel, Lord Reay, was of course a peer, but between 1626 and 1634 six sons or brothers of peers served in the regiment, together with two knights and two who were subsequently knighted. They might have done better had not fifty-two of the 105 been killed,

[28] [Sir David Dalrymple, Lord Hailes], *The Life of Sir James Ramsay, a general officer in the armies of Gustavus Adolphus of Sweden* (1787?), 1; Macinnes, *Covenanting Movement*, 2–3, 7–8.

[29] K. M. Brown, *Kingdom or Province? Scotland and the Regal Union, 1603–1715* (1992), 43–4.

[30] Sir Thomas Urquhart of Cromarty, *ΕΚΣΚΥΒΑΛΑΥΡΟΝ [EKSKIBALAVON]: or, The Discovery of a Most Exquisite Jewel* (1652), in *Works*, MC 30 (1834), 212–20.

[31] Ailes, 'From British Mercenaries to Swedish Nobles', 73–4, 81–2; T. A. Fischer (*The Scots in Sweden* (1907), 120, 259–64) says that a total of 80 Scots in the Swedish army were ennobled in the 17th century.

wounded or died on active service with the regiment during that eight-year period. As it was, their ranks would come to include five lieutenant-colonels, eight majors, forty-one captains, fifteen lieutenants and ten ensigns. One subsequently became a general in Swedish service, thirteen became field-grade officers in the Swedish army, four in the Dutch army, three in the English Royalist or Parliamentary armies, and one in the army of a German prince. At least six of the junior officers subsequently became captains in Swedish service.[32]

The Swedish army in the seventeenth century was an organization where promotion was based upon merit, and one can find in it examples of Scots soldiers who rose through the ranks. Jacob MacDougall, known in Swedish as Duwall, was born in Makerstone, Scotland, in 1589, and emigrated to Mecklenburg and later to Sweden. He enlisted in the Swedish army as a musketeer in 1607. He was subsequently promoted captain and became lieutenant-colonel in 1621. By 1625 he was colonel of a Swedish regiment from Norland, and later raised two German regiments. He was commandant of the Swedish garrison at Frankfurt-an-der-Oder in 1631, and commanded an army in Silesia before his death in 1634. He is regarded as the founder of a Swedish military dynasty, and eight of his brothers also were officers in the Swedish army.[33]

From the perspective of English aristocrats, mercenaries were soldiers who fought for profit and plunder regardless of religious allegiance. Sir James Turner admitted that many professional soldiers were not careful about bestowing their allegiances in the continental religious wars: 'I had swallowed, without chewing, in Germany a very dangerous maxim which military men there too much follow, which was that so we serve our master honestly, it is no matter what master we serve.'[34] Sir Thomas Urquhart held a similar opinion that Scottish soldiers who served in mainland European armies paid little heed to religious allegiances when entering upon military service.[35] Fritz Redlich argues that there were many Protestant soldiers who fought on the Imperial or Catholic side in the Thirty Years War, but only a few Catholics, such as Ernst, count von Mansfeld, and Sir John Hepburn, who fought on the Protestant side. Redlich insisted that religious divisions were not as clearly drawn as they seem to us with the advantage of hindsight, and that personal allegiances, based upon feudal fealty or other considerations, often prevailed over religious allegiances.[36] Sir James Hepburn, a Scots Catholic, had originally entered the service of Elizabeth, queen of Bohemia, out of personal devotion to a lady who possessed the ability to charm many gallants. However, Hepburn

---

[32] J. Mackay, *An Old Scots Brigade, Being the History of Mackay's Regiment* (1885), 204–8. Cf. Also [Defoe], *Scots Nation and Union Vindicated*, 23–4.

[33] J. Berg and B. Lagercrantz, *Scots in Sweden* (1962), 32.   [34] Turner, *Memoirs*, 14.

[35] Urquhart, *ΕΚΣΚΥΒΑΛΑΥΡΟΝ*, 218.

[36] Redlich, *GME* i. 188. Steve Murdoch observes that a number of Catholic officers also fought in the army of Denmark-Norway. One needs to remember that the dynastic aspect of the Thirty Years War was as important as the conflict between religious ideologies (*Britain, Denmark-Norway and the House of Stuart*, 209–11).

served in a regiment commanded by a Catholic colonel, Sir Andrew Gray. Hepburn later served with great distinction in the Swedish army. His regiment was a large unit numbering more than 8,000 men divided into forty-eight companies, and probably a large number of these men were Catholics. At least one of the two regimental chaplains, Joseph de Tremblay, was a priest and a Capuchin friar.[37]

Although Hepburn and his regiment served Gustavus Adolphus faithfully, it was not without friction. The king of Sweden had entrusted Hepburn with the command of the Scots Brigade of the Swedish army, but he also exerted pressure on him to become a Protestant. Probably because of his religion, Hepburn never achieved a rank higher than colonel in the Swedish army. There were other points of contention between the king and Hepburn before the latter exploded and declared to Gustavus that he would never again draw his sword in the king's service, and, as colonel-proprietor, took his regiment into French service. Gustavus had upbraided Hepburn for the extravagance of his armour and apparel, and Hepburn and a number of other Scottish officers resented the fact that the king had allowed Swedish soldiers to make the final assault on the castle keep of Marienberg after the Scots had, at great cost, fought their way through the outer defences of the fortress. There was also the belief that Gustavus had treated the marquis of Hamilton and other Scottish officers less than generously on a number of occasions. Hepburn's Regiment was accepted into the French army in 1633 and became known as the Regiment d'Hebron. Hepburn was killed in a siege in French service three years later.[38]

These events undoubtedly soured relations between the governments of Sweden and Scotland. For their part, the General Assembly of the Church of Scotland attempted to furnish adequate chaplains for every regiment in foreign service. Two chaplains were provided for the earl of Irvine's Regiment, raised for French service in 1643, at a cost of Scots £1,000 or 1,000 marks.[39] Three chaplains accompanied another Scots regiment levied for the service of the duke of Guelder in 1647. However, distrust of Scots Catholics in the Swedish army endured, and when it was reduced in size in the 1650s, a Scots-Swedish major-general named Arfvid Forbes recommended cashiering the Catholics and married men among the Scots first.[40]

According to Robert Monro, the presbyterian chaplains furnished by the General Assembly earned their pay. When Mackay's Regiment entered Swedish service, Gustavus Adolphus continued the practice of paying for two regimental chaplains. They not only preached to the soldiers, but helped to maintain discipline and were prepared to lead the men into battle. During the Bishops' Wars, it

---

[37] Mackay, *Old Scots Brigade*, 178; A. C. Dow, *Ministers to the Soldiers of Scotland* (1962), 52–3; Murdoch, *Britain, Denmark-Norway and the House of Stuart*, 209–11.

[38] Grant, *Memoirs . . . of Sir John Hepburn*, 190–2; Mackay, *Old Scots Brigade*, 178, 189–90, 193–4.

[39] When James VI became king of England in 1603 the exchange rate was set at Scots £12 = £1 Sterling.   [40] Dow, *Ministers*, 53–6; Fischer, *Scots in Sweden*, 125.

Map 4.1. Military activities of the Scots in the Swedish army

was a common practice, according to an English observer, for Scots chaplains in the Covenanting Army to carry swords, pistols and carbines, although Robert Baillie, who had himself served as a chaplain, insisted that he did so only to protect himself against bandits. An English observer, who had visited the camp of Sir Alexander Leslie, earl of Leven, noted that the Scots chaplains were learned and godly men who preached appropriate sermons, in contrast to the Anglican chaplains in Charles I's army.[41]

The Irish and the English serving in foreign armies probably demonstrated more commitment to religious allegiances than the Scots. Thomas Raymond observed that when English soldiers of the States' Army were campaigning in Catholic areas of the southern Low Countries, they were not content to 'steal and plunder', but also made a point of desecrating and destroying sacred pictures and images.[42] For their part, English and Irish Catholics showed a strong preference for employment by Catholic princes, and Catholic priests were very active in recruiting for the Spanish Army of Flanders and the Imperialist forces.[43] English and Irish Catholic troops who were forced to serve in the armies of Protestant princes were likely to mutiny or desert. The Spanish Army of Flanders had obtained their first English and Irish units by desertion from the States' Army, and thereafter they began to recruit directly from the British Isles; after 1605 this was done by licence from the English and Irish governments. In the 1620s and 1630s as many as 4,000 soldiers from the British Isles served in the Spanish Army of Flanders at any given time, except between 1625 and 1630, when England and Spain were at war.[44]

The practice of allowing English recusants to serve in the Spanish Army of Flanders perpetuated the tradition of military service among Catholic swordsmen. In 1622 Edward, fourth Lord Vaux, was licensed to raise a regiment of mostly English Catholics for Spanish service which joined the Scots regiment raised by Archibald, seventh earl of Argyll. Vaux's Regiment usually maintained a strength of 1,500–1,800 men, but Argyll's appears to have been considerably smaller.[45] James VI and I had allowed the levying of these regiments despite abundant proof that Guy Fawkes and his fellow conspirators were veterans of the Spanish Army of Flanders and had acquired their knowledge of sapping and mining while in Spanish service.[46] Veterans of Lord Vaux's Regiment who returned to England formed a secret society which was said to number more than 160 men, who met openly in taverns and flaunted distinctive symbols and mocked those Protestant gallants who had taken part in the disastrous voyage to Cadiz in 1625. The boldness of these Catholic

---

[41] Monro, *Expedition*, i. 52; Fischer, *Scots in Sweden*, app., 280–1; Robert Baillie, *The Letters and Journals of Robert Baillie*, ed. D. Laing, 3 vols., BC 73 (1841–2), i. 211; C. S. Terry, *The Life and Campaigns of Alexander Leslie, First Earl of Leven* (1899), 73.

[42] G. Davies (ed.), *Autobiography of Thomas Raymond*, CS 3rd ser. 28 (1917), 42.

[43] McGurk, 'Wild Geese', 41; Fitzsimon, 'Irish Swordsmen', 25.

[44] Parker, *Army of Flanders*, 52–3, 241.   [45] Anstruther, *Vaux of Harrowden*, 431–6.

[46] Parker, *Army of Flanders*, 41 and n.; A. J. Loomie, *Guy Fawkes in Spain: The 'Spanish Treason' in Spanish Documents*, BIHR, Spec. Supplement, 9 (1971), 10–11.

veterans led to fears of a Catholic conspiracy, and the gentlemen pensioners, who rode with the king, were remounted and each armed with a brace of pistols.[47]

Few were so fickle in their allegiance as Sydenham Poyntz. After having been a Turkish prisoner and galley slave, Poyntz was converted to Catholicism by Austrian Franciscan friars. He later entered the employ of a Protestant prince, the duke of Saxony, and commanded a troop of his Life Guards. When he was captured by an Irish soldier in the Imperial Austrian army, Walter, Count Butler, who had been ennobled for his part in the assassination of the Imperialist general, Wallenstein, Poyntz was offered his choice of imprisonment or service in the Imperialist army. When the duke of Saxony failed to ransom him, Poyntz chose to serve under Butler, who, as his patron, gave him command of a troop of horse and found him not one, but two wives in succession. After both wives had died and his property had been destroyed, Poyntz returned to England. Later, when he was the Parliamentary commander of the Army of the Northern Association, Poyntz was highly offended when he was accused of being a papist and summoned before the House of Commons to answer the accusation. He denied it.[48]

When the fortunes of war resulted in soldiers of the same nation but different allegiances confronting one another on the field of battle, many found the experience profoundly disturbing. At the Siege of Bergen-op-Zoom in 1622, Sir Edward Cecil said 'it grieved me to see English colours against English colours and that his Majesty should lose his subjects' blood both ways'. This refers to the encounter with Lord Vaux's Regiment. Both Lord Vaux and his men felt that they had been deceived by the Spanish, who apparently had told them that they would be fighting Hollanders who, instead, turned out to be English soldiers. Vaux was very reluctant to fight against Sir Horace Vere, and some of the soldiers of Vaux's Regiment actually deserted rather than fight their countrymen. At the Battle of Altenberg, the Scots Brigade of the Swedish army encountered two regiments of Scots and Irish in the Imperial army commanded by Colonel John Gordon and Major Walter Leslie. They and their regiments were captured and subsequently released by Gustavus Adolphus as a tribute to their valour.[49]

In most European armies of the early seventeenth century, military administration was not sufficiently developed to undertake the task of recruiting. Instead, an entrepreneurial system prevailed in which military enterprisers or proprietary colonels undertook to raise regiments and pay the expenses of transporting them to the prince or government which contracted for them.[50] In England during the late

---

[47] McClure, *LJC* ii. 530; J. S. A. Adamson, 'Chivalry and Political Culture in Caroline England', in K. Sharpe and P. Lake (eds.), *Culture and Politics in Early Stuart England* (1993), 166.

[48] *Relation of Sydenham Poyntz*, ed. Goodrick, 55, 60, 75, 125–30, 145; Fitzsimon, 'Irish Swordsmen', 30.

[49] C. Dalton, *The Life and Times of General Sir Edward Cecil, Viscount Wimbledon*, 2 vols. (1885), ii. 7 and n.; G. Roberts (ed.), *Diary of Walter Yonge, Esquire*, CS OS 41 (1847), 51; Grant, *Memoirs ... of Sir John Hepburn*, 189. Cf. also Monro, *Expedition*, i. 11; ii. 18–19.

[50] The classic study of this system is Redlich, *GME*, cited above. For the French army, this can be supplemented by J. A. Lynn, *Giant of the Grand Siècle: The French Army, 1610–1715* (1997), chs. 7 and 11.

Elizabethan wars, commissions of array, which gave authority to the holder to recruit soldiers between the ages of 16 and 60, had been used to raise troops for the Irish and Dutch wars. This method of removing swordsmen was not used in Ireland because the expense of transporting, feeding and clothing the recruits fell upon the government. Private contractors or military enterprisers were preferred, since that method was cheaper. However, it was illegal to raise soldiers without a commission of array, and the fiction had to be preserved that the Irish swordsmen sent to Sweden and Flanders in the early seventeenth century were all volunteers.[51]

The Scottish Privy Council actively assisted military recruiters and issued licences to facilitate the process, but military enterprisers raised many more soldiers for foreign armies than can be accounted for by licences recorded in the Privy Council Registers. Although the Scottish Privy Council attempted to prevent Scottish soldiers being raised for the armies of Catholic princes, and James VI and I sought to forbid his subjects serving any prince at war with his brother-in-law, King Christian IV of Denmark, the government of Scotland lost control of the recruiting process to military enterprisers early on.[52] The second marquis of Huntly, who was a Catholic, had no trouble raising soldiers from among his Lowland and Highland tenants, who owed him feudal loyalty. He was later able to raise a force of 3,000 men to oppose the Covenanters.[53]

When Gustavus Adolphus succeeded to the Swedish throne in 1611, only a few Scots soldiers were to be found in the Swedish army. Since the young king was not inclined to peaceful solutions to disputes with his neighbours, the army needed to be expanded. Sir James Spens became one of the earliest Scots military enterprisers through personal contacts in Sweden and Scotland. Spens apparently had already left Scotland under a cloud for illegally attempting to colonize the Isle of Lewis in the Hebrides. His brother David was at that time serving in the Swedish army, and suggested that James would be willing to recruit Scots soldiers for Swedish service. The first of these troops were recruited by Spens, but commanded by Andrew Ramsay, a personal favourite of James VI and I, whose brother John had helped to save James's life during the Gowrie conspiracy. Spens had already accepted a Swedish military commission from Gustavus Adolphus's predecessor Charles IX, which gave him diplomatic powers to travel to England to negotiate with James to raise mercenaries, and Gustavus renewed those powers. Spens continued in Swedish military and diplomatic service for thirty years, and his son James also acted as a miliary enterpriser. King James took little interest in these matters until his brother-in-law, the Danish king, lodged a complaint that the Scottish soldiers in Swedish service, recruited mostly from among vagrants and criminals, were being used in Sweden's war with Denmark. James attempted to put a stop to this by specifying that, thereafter, Scots soldiers in Swedish service were to be employed only against the Muscovites.[54]

[51] Henry, *Irish Military Community*, 40–1.
[52] Bartlett, 'Scottish Mercenaries in Europe', 16–18.
[53] Gordon, *History of Scots Affairs*, ii. 215–17.
[54] Fischer, *Scots in Sweden*, 74–7, 87; Ailes, 'From British Mercenaries to Swedish Nobles', 135.

Before James's order was implemented, George Sinclair of Caithness had raised a regiment of 900 Sinclairs. They were recruited specifically to fight the Danes, who were unpopular in Scotland because of their privateering. During the Kalmar War between Denmark and Sweden, they could not be sent to Sweden through the Danish Straits, so Robert Stewart, the pirate earl of Orkney, was employed to transport them from Caithness to the Norwegian coast, where they disembarked in the Romsdalfjorden to proceed overland to Sweden. On 19 August 1612 the Sinclairs, as yet unarmed, were marching through a valley known as the Gudbrandsdalen in Oppland when they were ambushed at the Kringelen Pass by Norwegian peasants. All but eighteen were massacred, and of these fifteen were impressed into the Danish army. Some of the officers were spared because they could be ransomed. A Danish court-martial found that, although it was usually the practice for drafts of recruits for the Swedish army marching across Norway to take hostages to guarantee their security, the Sinclairs had not done so on this occasion nor had they molested the peasants. The massacre of the Sinclairs has long been celebrated in Norwegian history, literature and song as a great and heroic act.[55]

The contracts under which military enterprisers levied regiments for Swedish service specified that the colonel was responsible for raising, equipping and commanding the regiment (although command in the field was usually delegated to the lieutenant-colonel). The soldiers recruited undertook to obey their officers, to build fortifications and dig trenches and to observe the Swedish Articles of War. Discipline was strict in the Swedish army, and the commission issued to Lord Reay also specified that he was to appoint four provosts, an executioner, a court-martial clerk, a court-martial beadle and two orderlies for his regiment to carry out punishments. Although the Swedish crown promised to pay the soldiers once a month and to ransom both officers and soldiers when they became prisoners of war, these undertakings were honoured more in the breach than in the observance by the chronically insolvent Swedish government.[56]

Mackay's Regiment was apparently the first regiment raised by Lord Reay, and was originally intended for Count Mansfeld's army in the service of the elector palatine. It actually entered service under the Danish flag before transferring under the field command of Robert Monro to the army of Gustavus Adolphus. Reay had licence to raise 5,000 men between 1626 and 1628, and half of those men would have gone into Mackay's Regiment, which had between 2,400 and 3,000 foot divided into twelve companies. Two more regiments, probably both of Highlanders, raised by Reay were bestowed on Robert Lumsden of Invergellie and John Monro of Obisdale, a major from Mackay's Regiment. In 1629 Reay also

[55] Grant, *Memoirs... of Sir John Hepburn*, 31, 34–8; Fischer, *Scots in Sweden*, 75–83; Berg and Lagercrantz, *Scots in Sweden*, 27–8. Col. George Sinclair, the commander of this regiment, is not to be confused with Sir James Sinclair of Murkle, who raised another regiment for Gustavus Adolphus.

[56] Ailes, 'From British Mercenaries to Swedish Nobles', 136; T. A. Fischer, *The Scots in Germany* (1902), app., 280–1.

subcontracted with Sir Thomas Conway to raise a regiment in England for Gustavus Adolphus. Three companies of Lumsden's Regiment drowned in a shipwreck on their way to Germany. Reay's recruiting activities extended throughout the British Isles—even to Ireland, where he subcontracted with Sir George Crosby, an Irish knight, who was to levy three regiments of foot for the Swedish army as well as a dragoon regiment which later served as a guard to Gustavus Adolphus.[57] Gustavus must have been desperate for manpower at this point, since he usually did not trust Irish troops.

Sir Donald Mackay of Farr, created Lord Reay by Charles I, was chief of the Clan Mackay. His territories were located on the Strathnaver peninsula, a Gaelic outpost in the extreme north-west of the Scottish mainland. In its original incarnation, Mackay's Regiment was unique because it was composed entirely of Highlanders dressed in plaids and armed with bows and arrows and muskets. The Scots Brigade of the Swedish army, commanded by Sir John Hepburn, was called the 'Green Brigade' after the hue of the Mackay Highlanders' tartans. They were called 'Irish' by contemporary observers, including Scots Lowlanders, because being Gaelic in speech, they were more comparable to the Irish than to English-speaking Lowlanders. Within a year of sailing from Cromarty to Holstein only 900 of them remained. Six weeks later, after the defence of Stralsund, all but 400 were dead. Of these, 300 had sustained wounds.[58]

After regiments from the British Isles joined the Swedish army in Germany or the Baltic, they seldom remained distinctively Highland or Lowland or English, because of high mortality and wastage rates. Consequently, Scottish and English officers came to command Swedish, Finnish, German or Dutch regiments of Gustavus's army, and regiments such as Mackay's Highlanders lost their distinctive character. As he continued to raise new drafts, Lord Reay also accepted men swept up from amongst vagrants and freed from prisons such as the Tolbooth in Edinburgh. Although the Scottish Privy Council believed that military discipline might reform such persons, their belief in the redemptive qualities of military life did not extend so far as to welcome home those who survived the rigours of foreign campaigning; those vagrants and prisoners who were pressed for mainland European armies were admonished not to return to Scotland upon pain of death.[59]

Lord Reay was supposed to be paid Scots £1 per head for every soldier he enlisted and embarked for Sweden, plus a salary of Scots £150 per month for service as a Swedish colonel, but because the money he was promised did not always materialize, he found it necessary to discharge some of the 3,600 Highlanders he had originally enlisted in 1626. This so alarmed the Scottish Privy Council that

[57] Mackay, *Old Scots Brigade*, 2–7, 108–13, 125, 232, 235–6; Grant, *Memoirs . . . of Sir John Hepburn*, 30–2.

[58] I. Grimble, *Chief of Mackay* (1965), 11, 79–83, 89, 93–4; Åberg, 'Scottish Soldiers in the Swedish Armies', 90–9.

[59] Ailes, 'From British Mercenaries to Swedish Nobles', 138; D. Masson (ed.), *RPCS, 1625–1627*, 2nd ser. (1899), i. 385.

they advanced him Scots £500 on the promise that he would not discharge any more. Charles I also gave him another £2,000, but it was not enough to help him avoid mortgaging his lands. It is possible that Lord Reay's elevation to the Scots peerage was partial payment from Charles I for some of the money owing to him.[60]

Sweden's expansive foreign and military policies in the seventeenth century generated manpower needs which peaked in the late 1620s and 1630s. When Lord Reay returned to the north of Scotland in 1628 to recruit more troops, he discovered that other military enterprisers were competing with him. Alexander Forbes, a colonel who commanded a Scots regiment in the Swedish army, entered into an agreement with a cousin of the same name to recruit 500 men in good health and of a certain minimum height to bring his regiment up to strength. The sum agreed upon was 1,500 Swedish 'Rixdalers'. The troops were to be embarked at Glasgow for a German port. Alexander Lindsay, second Lord Spynie, also had a licence from the Scottish Privy Council to raise a regiment from among vagrants and imprisoned felons, while Sir James Sinclair of Murkle was authorized to levy 3,000 men for the king of Denmark.[61] In 1631 Lord Reay and the other Scottish military enterprisers found themselves in competition with James, third marquis of Hamilton (and later first duke of Hamilton), a favourite of Charles I who had undertaken to raise 6,000 men in Scotland to serve in the Swedish army to help recover the elector palatine's lands in Germany. Hamilton was unsuccessful in his recruiting efforts in Scotland and could find only 400 men. His efforts were hampered partly by the depletion of Scottish manpower, but also by the hostility of old soldiers in Scotland and Germany who resented the harsh treatment of James Stewart, Lord Ochiltree, who had been punished for slander at Hamilton's insistence. Ochiltree and Reay had been behind a plot to discredit Hamilton by accusing him of seeking the throne of Scotland, and Reay seems to have been able to obstruct the recruiting efforts of Hamilton's agents by spreading these rumours against him. Reay apparently resented the fact that Hamilton was to command a force of six regiments to be sent to Germany.[62] Because of Lord Reay's successful obstruction of Hamilton's recruiting efforts in Scotland, Hamilton was compelled to look to England and Ireland. Some of Hamilton's men were levied in East Anglia, but many were vagrants, masterless men and underemployed watermen from London and its suburbs. Hamilton also contracted with Sir Piers Crosby, an Irish Catholic military enterpriser, to supply an Irish regiment—perhaps what was left of the one which had accompanied the duke of Buckingham on the Isle of Rhè

---

[60] Grimble, *Chief of Mackay*, 107–8.

[61] Ibid. 110; Åberg, 'Scottish Soldiers in the Swedish Armies', 97; G. Parker, 'The Soldiers of the Thirty Years War', in *Krieg und Politik: Europäische Probleme und Perspektiven* (1988), 305.

[62] Thomas Birch, *The Court and Times of Charles I*, ed. R. F. Williams, 2 vols. (1848), ii. 125–6; H. L. Rubinstein, *Captain Luckless: James Hamilton, First Duke of Hamilton, 1606–1649* (1975), 27, 29, 30–1; Gilbert Burnet, *The Memorials of . . . James and William, Dukes of Hamilton and Castle-Herald* (1852), 15–19. For a discussion of a public duel between Reay and one of Hamilton's followers, which Charles I at first sanctioned and then cancelled at the last minute, see Manning, *Swordsmen*, 224.

expedition. Hamilton's drafts sailed from Yarmouth in a convoy of thirty-eight ships commanded by Admiral Penington, and disembarked two weeks later on the Island of Usedom at the mouth of the River Oder. Although adequately provisioned, the cramped conditions aboard ship bred disease, and Hamilton's men were decimated upon landing. Gustavus Adolphus immediately rejected Crosby's Regiment, because he thought it was full of Catholics. The Swedish army gave Hamilton's force provisions adequate for four months to sustain them on their march to the Rhenish Palatinate; beyond that Swedish field armies in Germany were supposed to live off of the land. Hamilton's men engaged in a couple of minor skirmishes en route, but one-third of his army were dead before they ever entered battle. Only 100 of the original 6,000 men survived the campaign. The Swedish chancellor Oxenstierna blamed Hamilton for not taking better care of his men, and Hamilton, for his part, was offended because, instead of an independent command, Gustavus had made him subordinate to Sir Alexander Leslie, a commoner and a bastard to boot. Having lost his army, Gustavus refused to give him another command, or even a commission. Instead, Hamilton served as a volunteer, and returned to England in the summer of 1632 on the pretext of raising another army, but never returned to Germany.[63]

From the mid-sixteenth century until the early eighteenth century, the Swedish state was almost completely organized for war, and indeed was at war for some 150 years. This took a terrible toll, not only upon the population of Sweden, but also upon the populations of those countries which supplied much of the Swedish manpower. At the beginning of the seventeenth century Sweden had a population base of 1 million with another 200,000 living in the Duchy of Finland. Sweden in the age of Gustavus Adolphus possessed a well-developed system of national conscription, but its population was never adequate to furnish the military manpower needed to sustain the ambitions of its rulers. Although Swedish soldiers were, for the most part, assigned to garrison duties, deaths on active service—mostly the result of illness—could push up the mortality rates of individual villages such as Brygdeå, which lost 46 per cent of its adult male population as military casualties between 1621 and 1639. In the latter days of the Thirty Years War, foreign mercenaries—mostly from Germany and Scotland—made up more than half of the Swedish army. Moreover, they were the ones who bore the brunt of the fighting.[64]

[63] Rubinstein, *Captain Luckless*, 31–2, 34–6, 38; W. Rye (ed.), *State Papers Relating to Musters, Beacons, Shipmoney, &c. in Norfolk*, NNAS (1907), 168; Macinnes, *Covenanting Movement*, 209 n.; P. Dukes, 'The Leslie Family in the Swedish Period (1630–5) of the Thirty Years War', *ESR* 12 (1982), 412–13, 415; James Howell, *Epistolae Ho-Elianae, or the Familiar Letters of James Howell*, 2 vols. (1907), ii. 21; Birch, *Court and Times of Charles I*, ii. 14–17, 162–3; A. Clarke, 'Sir Piers Crosby, 1590–1646: Wentworth's "tawney ribbon" ', *IHS* 26 (1988), 14–60.

[64] M. Roberts, *Gustavus Adolphus: A History of Sweden, 1611–1632*, 2 vols. (1953, 1958), ii. 201–2; A. Åberg, 'The Swedish Army, from Lützen to Narva', in M. Roberts (ed.), *Sweden's Age of Greatness* (1973), 266–7; Ailes, 'From British Mercenaries to Swedish Nobles', 10; J. Lindegren, 'The Swedish "Military State", 1560–1720', *SJH* 10 (1985), 317.

The manpower needs of the Swedish and Danish armies drove military enterprisers and their agents in Scotland not only to sweep up vagrants, beggars and even felons, but also to kidnap householders. One Scotswoman claimed that a recruiting agent had kidnapped her husband, her son and their servant and sold them to Captain George Ogilvie for the sum of Scots £40. Scottish landlords, in an essentially feudal system, could still compel their tenants to volunteer, and those who were also clan chieftains were particularly adept at levying men. There is good reason to think that Lord Reay resorted to impressment to recruit Highlanders for his various regiments. Recently discovered evidence from Swedish archives suggests that a much larger proportion of Scots soldiers in Swedish service were Highlanders than was previously supposed. Most of them came from the eastern rather than the western Highlands.[65]

James VI had pursued a policy of clearing the Highlands of some of the more troublesome clans by issuing to certain magnates commissions of 'fire and sword' in order to suppress endemic clan warfare. Archibald Campbell, seventh earl of Argyll, had been licensed in 1607 to drive out the Macdonalds and Macleans from the Kintyre Peninsula and the Southern Isles and to extirpate the notorious Macgregors in Glenmorchy, and the commission of fire and sword was renewed in favour of his heir Lord Lorne. Similarly, Kenneth Mackenzie, created Lord Kintail in 1609, was employed in the north-western Highlands to suppress the Macleods of Lewis. The consequence of these wholesale evictions was to create a pool of idle swordsmen and vagrants which military enterprisers such as Lord Reay could exploit.[66]

Denmark also drew heavily on the military manpower of the British Isles. Scots had served in Danish armies for at least a century before the outbreak of the Thirty Years War in 1618. They had fought in both the Danish and the Swedish armies during the Northern Seven Years War (1563–70). It remained a policy of the Danish kings to prefer foreign mercenaries because they did not trust their own subjects—something that the Danish nobility had complained of as early as the reign of Christian II (1513–23) when they had rebelled against him.[67] The king of Denmark's army recruited from all over the British Isles. In 1611–12 Robert Bertie, twelfth Lord Willoughby de Eresby, attempted to raise an expedition of 4,000 men consisting of four regiments. Willoughby and Sir Edward Cecil were

[65] T. C. Smout, N.C. Landsman and T. M. Devine, 'Scottish Emigration in the Seventeenth and Eighteenth Centuries', in N. Canny (ed.), *Europeans on the Move: Studies in European Migration, 1500–1800* (1994), 83–4; Åberg, 'Scottish Soldiers in the Swedish Armies', 95–6; K. M. Brown, *Noble Society in Scotland: Wealth, Family and Culture, from the Reformation to the Revolution* (2000), 2; James Fraser, *Chronicles of the Frasers*, ed. W. Mackay, SHS 1st ser. 47 (1905), 155–6; A. and H. Tayler, *The House of Forbes* SC 3rd ser. 8 (1937), 177; Masson (ed.), *RPCS, 1625–1627*, 2nd ser., i. 247.

[66] R. A. Dodgshon, ' "Pretense of Blude" and "Place of their Duelling": The Nature of the Scottish Clans, 1500–1745', in R. A. Houston and I. D. Whyte (eds.), *Scottish Society, 1500–1800* (1989), 182–3; G. Donaldson, *Scotland, James V to James VII* (1965), 229–30; B. Lenman, *England's Colonial Wars, 1550–1688: Conflicts, Empire and National Identity* (2001), 153.

[67] T. L. Christensen, 'Scots in Denmark in the Sixteenth Century', *SHR* 49 (1970), 125–6; Turner, *Memoirs*, 126–30.

to command two English regiments together with a Scottish regiment to be commanded by Richard Preston, second Lord Dingwall (created earl of Desmond in the Irish peerage in 1619), and an Irish regiment under the command of Richard Bourke, fourth earl of Clanricarde.[68] Christian IV had the reputation of inadequately provisioning his armies, failing to pay his troops and deserting his army after his defeat by Tilly in 1627. The four English and Scots regiments which were transferred from Dutch to Danish service in 1626 experienced massive desertions before they ever sailed for Denmark; experience of Christian IV's leadership brought them to the verge of mutiny in 1627. Those few who survived mostly re-entered Dutch service.[69] When Mackay's Regiment entered Danish service, a number of the Scots officers had at first refused to accept Danish colours, and only a purge of the mutinous officers brought the remainder to heel.[70] After Mackay's Regiment was discharged from Danish service, Robert Monro, the lieutenant-colonel of the regiment, took advantage of his connections within the extensive network of Scots in the Swedish army to arrange for the transfer of the regiment to Swedish service.[71]

That there was an inherent distrust of mercenaries in general and Scots in particular felt by the Swedish government at the beginning of the seventeenth century is, perhaps, understandable. The first Scots were employed by the Swedish crown under less than auspicious circumstances. King Eric XIV had employed three troops of Scottish horse and one of English horse during the Northern Seven Years War. Eric was overthrown by his brother John III, who wished to expand his territory at the expense of Muscovy, but dared not enlist native Swedish soldiers because of the insecurity of his position. King John employed Archibald Ruthven, younger brother of Patrick, third Lord Ruthven (the chief assassin of David Rizzio, Mary, queen of Scots' private secretary), to recruit 3,000 Scottish foot for a war against the Muscovites. However, not trusting foreign soldiers led by a man from such a violent family, King John gave orders that the Scots were not to be admitted to any of his fortresses, nor did he intend to pay them until they engaged the Russians in battle in Estonia. Ruthven's Scots landed near modern-day Gothenburg and marched across southern Sweden to the Baltic Sea ports of Norköpping and Södderköpping to be transported across the Baltic to Estonia. This was a formula for disaster. Ruthven's Scots, who had recently been employed in the successful siege of Edinburgh Castle at the end of the Scottish Civil War and then forcibly embarked for Sweden, were compelled to make their own way across southern Sweden without pay or provisions. Consequently, they spent the summer of 1572 plundering King John's peasants. They resisted being sent to Estonia until they were paid, which was the middle of October of that year. In order to pay the Scots, King John stopped the pay of his German mercenaries in Estonia, who

    [68] McClure, *LJC* i. 314.
    [69] BL, Add. MS. 46,188, fos. 105–6; E. A. Beller, 'The Military Expedition of Sir Charles Morgan to Germany, 1627–9', *EHR* 43 (1928), 528–39.   [70] Monro, *Expedition*, i. 2–3.
    [71] Ibid. i. 85.

resented this. After landing at Reval, John, in his wisdom, then placed the Scots alongside the Germans in preparation for attacking the Russians at Narva. A tavern brawl between the Scots and the Germans, both in a state of mutiny, led to a pitched battle in which the German cavalry rode down the Scots infantry and killed more than 1,400 men.[72]

The indiscipline of the Scots foot was matched by the conspiracies of the Scottish officers against their Swedish employers—although their discontent was certainly understandable. King John had failed to pay them, or provide equipment and mounts, and some of the Scots officers had plotted to assassinate the Swedish king under cover of performing a sword dance at the court. The conspiracy was discovered before the assassination could be carried out, and the Scots officers were required to execute the chief culprit, William Cahen, themselves before leaving for Estonia. The battle between the Scots and the Germans in the Swedish army in Estonia led to another Scots officer, Gilbert Balfour,[73] being executed for treason; their colonel, Archibald Ruthven, died in prison awaiting his fate. The remaining Scots were dismissed from the Swedish army. Only 500 of the original 3,000 men in Ruthven's army survived, and the Scottish Privy Council was so disturbed by reports of Swedish abuse of Scottish soldiers that they ceased issuing licences to recruiting contractors of the Swedish army until after 1591.[74]

Although the discipline of the Scots officers and soldiers in Swedish service improved in the early seventeenth century, and they gave their loyalty to Gustavus Adolphus more readily than to John III, gentlemen officers and volunteers still found it difficult to accept strict Swedish discipline. In 1631 the Swedish governor of Stettin hanged Andrew Monro, gentleman volunteer of Mackay's Regiment, for having, in a fit of anger, beaten a citizen of Stettin to death in the home where he had been billeted. Monro had served with distinction at the Siege of Stralsund, where he was badly wounded, but pleas of mercy from various noble ladies did not avail.[75]

The sixty-year-long War of Succession between Sweden and Poland, which began when the Catholic Sigismund Vasa was deprived of his throne and driven from Sweden in 1598, necessitated more recruiting of foreign mercenaries by Sigismund's usurping uncle, Charles IX. When Gustavus Adolphus succeeded to the throne in 1611, he found himself also involved in the Kalmar War between Denmark and Sweden. Because of past mutinies by Scottish soldiers, the Swedish crown was reluctant to recruit soldiers directly from Scotland, but instead preferred to seek out Scottish veterans of the States' Army, who were more used to discipline. The marquis of Huntly was one of the military enterprisers plying this

[72] Berg and Lagercrantz, *Scots in Sweden*, 12–17; S. P. Oakley, *War and Peace in the Baltic, 1560–1790* (1992), 29–31, 33, 37; J. Dow, *Ruthven's Army in Sweden and Esthonia* (1965), 3–9, 30–1, 37.

[73] Gilbert Balfour was the brother of Sir James Balfour, who had been involved in the murder of Cardinal Beaton.

[74] Dow, *Ruthven's Army*, 25–7, 32–5, 40; Fischer, *Scots in Sweden*, 52–64; Ailes, 'From British Mercenaries to Swedish Nobles', 27–8.

[75] Mackay, *Old Scots Brigade*, 152–3; *Grant, Memoirs . . . of Sir John Hepburn*, 86.

trade, and he furnished troops to Sir James Spens. Because Charles IX lacked the funds to pay these mercenaries in advance, it was difficult to meet recruiting quotas, and loans had to be arranged on the security of Swedish copper and iron mines. The continuing inability of the Swedish crown to pay their mercenaries caused many troops to desert to the Polish army, and there probably were Scots among them.[76]

Mutinies among Scottish troops continued after Gustavus Adolphus succeeded to the throne of Sweden. The soldiers of Samuel Catron's Regiment at Narva in 1615 dragged the head of the Swedish army commissariat into a field to interrogate him concerning whether their officers had been issued the funds to pay them. Gustavus Adolphus pardoned the mutineers after reprimanding them, but he did not pay them. Another mutiny among Scottish soldiers broke out in Livonia at the same time for the same reason. A provost-marshal hanged one of the soldiers as an example, but the soldier's commanding officer had the provost-marshal shot. When General Sir Patrick Ruthven was governor of Memel under Gustavus Adolphus during the Thirty Years War, he frequently complained of the lack of pay and provisions. The Swedish army in Germany was expected to live off of the land, which frequently involved them in secondary conflicts with peasants who laid ambushes for their foraging parties.[77]

This random plunder of Germany was replaced during the Thirty Years War by a system of *Kontributionen*, which was, in effect, organized and controlled plunder. The Swedish crown issued ordinances specifying how much bread, meat and beer a private, a non-commissioned officer or an officer was entitled to daily, and the local officials, preferring this to unrestrained plunder, collected the required provisions and fodder for distribution to the troops. Those soldiers billeted in households were provided with their rations by their hosts. At the end of the Thirty Years War 915 Swedish companies were scattered among 127 garrisons across Germany. Including the French and Imperialist armies, 250,000 men were under arms, and between 150,000 and 175,000 of these were Swedish. The size of the Swedish armies in Germany was the consequence of assigning a large part of those garrison and field forces to the task of collecting the *Kontributionen*.[78]

Because the necessity of feeding an army was always the highest priority, logistical concerns were always more important than strategy in the Thirty Years War, and warfare tended to become divorced from political objectives. As the *Kontributionssystem* spread from enemy territory to that of allies and subjects, warfare became perpetual and irrational. Some of the Scots officers in the early part of the Thirty Years War, such as General Sir Patrick Ruthven (known to his soldiers as *Rotwein*) while Swedish governor of Ulm, prospered from their

[76] Oakley, *War and Peace*, 40–2; Fischer, *Scots in Sweden*, 65–6.

[77] Fischer, *Scots in Sweden*, 84–6; Brockington (ed.), Monro, *Expedition*, 252–3.

[78] Redlich, *GME* i. 502; Parker, 'Soldiers of the Thirty Years War', 303; D. A. Parrott, 'Strategy and Tactics in the Thirty Years War: The Military Revolution', *Militärgeschichtliche Mitteilungen*, 18:2 (1985), 18.

plunder, but Sir James Turner, who was a young ensign in Lumsden's Regiment towards the end of the war, recalled that during his service in the Swedish army in Germany he often was reduced to a diet of bread and water and not infrequently went without eating at all. Tired of being cheated of his pay by his Swedish employers and his senior officers, Turner left the Swedish army in 1639.[79] Robert Monro noted that there was a constant turnover of company-grade officers in Mackay's Regiment; after they had gained experience in the Swedish army, they sought better employment elsewhere.[80]

Since Swedish troops were used mostly for garrison duties at home, Gustavus Adolphus's mercenaries bore the brunt of the fighting in Germany. Although junior officers and private soldiers might grumble about the lack of pay and provisions, their colonels were eager for personal honour and glory, and the Scots were usually in the vanguard of assaults on fortresses. The regiments of Sir John Hepburn and Sir John Lumsden led the assault at the Siege of Frankfurt-an-der-Oder; the regiments of Sir John Hamilton of Priestfield and Sir James Ramsay were employed to storm the outer-works and castle of Würzburg. However, in the latter instance Gustavus used a Swedish regiment for the final assault, because he said he wanted to preserve what was left of Hamilton's Regiment after very heavy losses. However, 'the valiant colonel [Sir John Hamilton] made another interpretation of the king's meaning'—that he wanted the glory to be had by Swedish soldiers. Again, the vanguard of the assault on Oppenheim was led by Mackay's, Ramsay's and Hepburn's Regiments, while the vanguard at the Siege of Kreuznach in the Nahe Valley was led by William, Lord Craven, who commanded an English regiment in the service of the elector palatine, and Lieutenant-Colonel George Douglas, who led a contingent of Scots in Swedish service. It was a slighting of the honour of his regiment (which was, of course, bound up with his personal honour) after the Siege of Marienberg, where his regiment was in the vanguard, that contributed to the quarrel between Gustavus and Hepburn and which caused Hepburn to withdraw himself and his regiment from Swedish service.[81]

Like the Scots in the Swedish army, the Irish soldiers in the Spanish Army of Flanders were noted for their preference for frontal assaults on fortifications and their fierceness of attack. The Spanish took note of this élan and made good use of it, believing that a large enough concentration of Irish in an assault could bring victory, and consequently Irish *tercios* in Flanders suffered heavy losses.[82]

The practice of recruiting Irish soldiers for the Spanish Army of Flanders began in 1587 with the defection of Sir William Stanley's Regiment from the Dutch

[79] Parrott, 'Strategy', 19–20; Turner, *Memoirs*, 4–12.   [80] Monro, *Expedition*, i. 85.

[81] *The Swedish Intelligencer* (1632), i. 90; ii. 13–14, 76–82; Roberts, *Gustavus Adolphus*, ii. 206; [Dalrymple], *Life of Sir John Ramsay*, 2, 5; Monro, *Expedition*, ii. 101; Grant, *Memoirs . . . of Sir John Hepburn*, 190–2. James Grant (ibid. 126) says that it was after the Siege of Marienberg in Franconia that Hepburn, the marquis of Hamilton, Sir John Hamilton of Priestfield and Sir James Ramsay all resigned from the Swedish army because of various slights received from Gustavus Adolphus.

[82] R. A. Stradling, *The Spanish Monarchy and Irish Mercenaries: The Wild Geese in Spain, 1618–68* (1994), 25; Parker, *Army of Flanders*, 29.

army. Spain no longer possessed sufficient manpower to field armies without extensive use of foreign mercenaries. Stanley's Regiment, as originally recruited for the States' Army, had a strength of 1,100 men. Most of the ninety officers were English, and the enlisted men were evenly divided between Old English veterans of the Elizabethan army from Munster and Irish kernes.[83] Leicester and others had singled out the bravery of Sir William Stanley's lieutenant-colonel, Edward Stanley, in the assault on Zutphen Sconce, which was later delivered up to the Spanish by Stanley's co-conspirator Rowland Yorke. Edward Stanley was knighted, Sir William Stanley made governor of Deventer and Rowland Yorke appointed governor of Zutphen for their courage—although the States General did not approve because Yorke and Sir William Stanley had both previously served in the Army of Flanders. Although Stanley and Yorke were assailed as traitors, it was understood that their religious allegiances had prevailed over their political loyalties. Moreover, their regiments had not been paid by the States General, and the wavering of allegiance in Stanley's Regiment was probably influenced by the presence of some 200 English Catholic gentlemen volunteers.[84]

The religious allegiances of the exiled Irish swordsmen, urged on by their chaplains, led the majority of them to continue to serve in the Spanish Army of Flanders during the seventeenth century. By 1635, when the entry of France into the Thirty Years War meant that the Army of Flanders faced a war on two fronts, there may have been as many as 7,000 Irishmen serving in that army at any one time, which was about 10 per cent of that establishment. Stanley continued to command a regiment until at least 1595, and it was brought up to strength by fleshing it out with English and Scots as well as Irish troops. Thereafter, the Spanish appear to have segregated the three nations and the Irish served in independent companies until 1605, when they were regimented under the command of Henry O'Neill, son of the earl of Tyrone, and reinforced with fresh levies from Ireland, yielding a strength of 1,700 men. Most of the officers were Old English from Munster with a sprinkling of Old Irish.[85] O'Neill's Regiment was disbanded in 1606, and the Irish presence in Flanders declined during the Twelve Years Truce. At the end of that truce, a group of English Catholic volunteers from Lord Vaux's circle informed the Spanish ambassador of their desire to revive the English Regiment, and James I gave his support by suspending the Statute of 3 Jac. I, c. 4, which required volunteers in foreign service to take an oath of

[83] Parker, *Army of Flanders*, 17; G. Henry, 'The Emerging Identity of an Irish Group in the Spanish Netherlands, 1586–1640', in R. V. Comerford *et al.* (eds.), *Religion, Conflict and Coexistence in Ireland* (1990), 53–4; ead., *Irish Military Community*, 53; E.C.S. *The Government of Ireland under . . . Sir John Perrot* (1626), 112.

[84] J. Bruce (ed.), *Correspondence of Robert Dudley, Earl of Leycester during his Government of the Low Countries*, CS OS 27 (1844), 427–30; Edward Grimeston, *A Generall Historie of the Netherlands* (1627), 805; Anon., *The Rebels' Doom* (1684), 75; Sir Roger Williams, *The Actions of the Low Countries*, ed. D. W. Davies (1618; repr. 1964), 109–10; Henry, *Irish Military Community*, 55; S. Adams, 'Stanley, York and Elizabeth's Catholics', *HT* 37 (1987), 46.

[85] Walsh, 'Wild Goose Tradition', 5; Stradling, *Irish Mercenaries*, 17; Henry, *Irish Military Community*, 57, 62–3, 68–70.

allegiance to the crown before leaving the realm. At this time the two regiments commanded by Lord Vaux and the seventh earl of Argyll were raised. The names of twenty-six individuals were nominated by the English court for the two regiments, and the Spanish ambassador accepted twenty-one and rejected five who were non-Catholics. Thirteen of the volunteers were commissioned as officers in Vaux's Regiment, and three were assigned to Argyll's.[86]

By the mid-1630s the Irish soldiers of the Army of Flanders were organized into four *tercios* or regiments; they were commanded by Owen Roe O'Neill (this regiment was known as *el Tercio Viejo Irlandes*, or the Old Irish Regiment), Thomas Preston, son of the fourth Viscount Gormanston (and himself later Viscount Tara), Hugh O'Neill, titular earl of Tyrconnel, and Patrick Fitzgerald. These colonels had recruited men in Ireland with the permission of both the English and Irish Privy Councils. Although it was easier and cheaper, when the weather was favourable, to ship the new recruits directly from Ireland to Flanders, the officers of Preston's Regiment—some sixty-three in number—made their way to Flanders across southern England with much swaggering and commotion. This alarmed the populace in the countryside, and the Dutch and French ambassadors complained to the secretary of state. Consequently, Charles I was obliged to suspend recruiting in Ireland for the next couple of years.[87]

One of the young officers who joined the earl of Argyll's Regiment some time after it was raised in 1606 was Henry Gage, who came of the Gages of Firle, Sussex. He had been educated in Flanders since the age of 10, travelled in Germany and the Netherlands and had 'trailed a pike' in the garrison of Antwerp Castle before accepting a commission under Argyll as captain of a company. He served at the sieges of Bergen-op-Zoom, Breda and Maastricht. He later joined Sir Edward Parham's Regiment and was the sergeant-major of Sir William Tresham's Regiment before acquiring command of his own regiment, which helped to defend St Omer against a French siege. When the English Civil War broke out, Gage was able to divert a shipment of arms from the Parliamentarians to the Royalists, and later brought several hundred soldiers with him to England to fight for Charles I. After helping to defend Banbury and Basing House, he was knighted by the king and made governor of Oxford. He served in that capacity for only three weeks before being killed in battle at Abingdon.[88]

Gerrat or Gerald Barry spent thirty-three years in the Spanish army—the first four as a marine. By 1625 he was a captain in the regiment of Shane or John O'Neill, titular fifth earl of Tyrone, in the Spanish Army of Flanders. He was

[86] A. J. Loomie, 'Gondomar's Selection of English Officers in 1622', *EHR* 88 (1973), 574–81.

[87] Stradling, *Irish Mercenaries*, 25; B. Jennings (ed.), *Wild Geese in Spanish Flanders, 1587–1700: Documents Relating Chiefly to Irish Regiments, from the Archives Générales, Brussels*, IMC (1964), 10, 28, 30–1.

[88] Edward Walsingham, *Alter Britannia Heros: Or the Life of … Sir Henry Gage* (1645), 2–9, 19, 21; *DNB*, *sub* Sir Henry Gage (1597–1645). For a discussion of the Gages of Firle, one of the chief recusant families of Sussex, cf. Manning, *R&S* 40, 138–40, 143, 152–6, 164, 250, 269.

probably a kinsman of David Barry, first earl of Barrymore, to whom he dedicated a drill manual which he wrote and published for the use of the English-speaking infantry of the Spanish forces. He was one of the defenders of Breda in 1625 during the Dutch siege, and he praised the way his commander, Ambrose Spinola, sustained the morale and discipline of the garrison by keeping them busy constructing fortifications during the siege. Although the Spanish defenders were well provisioned at the beginning, they were eventually starved into submission rather than being taken by assault. Barry later held the rank of colonel in the rebel forces during the Irish Rebellion of 1641 and was outlawed by the Irish government.[89]

Wastage rates among the Irish soldiers of the Army of Flanders resulting from disease and desertion were always very high. Although conditions varied from one commander to another, the Irish troops were not well provisioned, their pay was comparatively low and always in arrears. Since there was no provision for leave or discharge except for officers, the desertion rate was high. In 1601 Lord Mountjoy had estimated that only one-quarter of the Irish swordsmen sent abroad would ever return. The Old Irish Regiment (O'Neill's) lost two-thirds of its complement during 1607 because of illness; mortality rates while the Irish were in the field ran between 2 and 7 per cent per month. In 1726 a Spanish observer estimated that since it had first been raised, the Old Irish Regiment had lost 12,000 men—most of them in battle.[90]

After the beginning of the war between Spain and France in 1635, the two countries began to compete for manpower from the British Isles. Besides sending letters to Queen Henrietta Maria to win official support from Charles I, the French also suborned Irish officers from the Army of Flanders to help recruit men, and the French were willing to pay more and provide inducements such as beer and wine to compete with Spanish recruiting efforts. Philip IV ordered that the Irish colonels in Flanders be treated with all respect and esteem so that they might exert their influence to prevent defections from the Army of Flanders.[91]

Even before the Dutch army in the time of Maurice of Nassau and Frederick Henry had become a 'school of war', English and Scots swordsmen had been drawn to the French *compagnies d'ordonnance* as places where volunteers of aristocratic status could gain experience on the battlefield as heavy cavalrymen. Sir Nicholas Malby, later president of Connaught, together with his younger brother John, began their military careers in this fashion. Sir Robert Dallington observed that Henry IV had a royal guard called *les cent gentilhommes de la garde*, which consisted of 200 Scots and Swiss. The reason for their presence in this elite guard

---

[89] Gerrat Barry, *A Discourse of Military Discipline* (1634), sig. A2; id., *The Siege of Breda* (1627) 39–43.
[90] Henry, ' "Wild Geese" in Spanish Flanders', 201; ead., *Irish Military Community*, 39; Parker, *Army of Flanders*, 207–18; Walsh, 'Wild Goose Tradition', 5.
[91] Jennings (ed.), *Wild Geese*, 29–30. Cf. also C. H. Firth (ed.), *The Clarke Papers*, 4 vols., CS NS 49, 54, 61, 62 (1891–1901), iii. 110–11.

corps was that the Swiss were the hereditary enemies of the Hapsburgs and the Scots were the ancient enemies of the English.[92]

In the reign of Louis XIII, some eighteen Scottish regiments served in the French army—most of them raised after France's entry into the Thirty Years War in 1635. They appear to have been quite large regiments: James Campbell, Lord Kintyre (and later earl of Irvine), was licensed by the Scottish Privy Council to levy 4,500 men for his regiment; and Sir John Hepburn's Regiment, after he transferred from the Swedish to the French army, consisted of 8,316 men divided into forty-eight companies.[93]

Between 1635 and 1640 seven, or possibly eight, regiments were raised in Ireland for the French army. Cardinal Richelieu had requested this levy with the full approval of Charles I and the qualified support of Thomas Wentworth, earl of Strafford, the lord deputy. Two Irish Franciscans were employed to try and bring over John O'Neill, commander of the Old Irish Regiment, and Hugh O'Donnell, son of the earl of Tyrconnell, and his regiment from the Spanish Army of Flanders. Of the new Irish colonels in the French army one of the most well known was Sir Piers Crosby, a Catholic military enterpriser, who wished to raise a number of regiments but was limited by Strafford to two. Strafford had other plans for this manpower by 1640 or 1641.[94]

The Irish and the Scots also made their way into the Imperial Austrian and Polish armies. There were at least six members of the Butler family, Catholic kinsmen of the earls of Ormond, who served in various mainland European armies. James Butler was an officer in the Polish army who recruited soldiers in Ireland and raised a regiment with Irish officers for Polish service. He had a son or a nephew who also commanded a regiment in the Imperial army. The most well known of the Butlers was Colonel Walter Butler. His family's estates in Roscrea, co. Tipperary, had been confiscated in 1616, at which time he appears to have sought service with the Hapsburgs. He and his Irish officers fought against Mackay's Regiment at Frankfurt-an-der-Oder, and Robert Monro regarded Butler as an honourable and worthy opponent. Walter Butler, although a very able soldier, is best remembered as the leader of a band of Irish and Scots officers who, at the behest of the emperor, assassinated Albert von Wallenstein, the ambitious

[92] D. Bitton, *The French Nobility in Crisis, 1560–1640* (1969), 154; Churchyard, *Generall Rehearsall of Warres*, sig. A3v; Sir Robert Dallington, *The Viewe of France, 1604* (repr. 1936), sigs. I4v–K1r.

[93] Donaldson, *Scotland, James V to James VII*, 253–4; Grant, *Memoirs...of Sir John Hepburn*, 211–13, 231, 247–9. Hepburn's Regiment was reorganized when it entered French service and was combined with several other corps, including Sir Andrew Gray's Regiment, first levied for the Bohemian and Palatinate expeditions, and the Scottish Archers. Hepburn became a marshal of France, but died in battle before that commission could reach him. He was no more than 38 years old at the time of his death. In the reign of Charles II, Hepburn's Regiment was commanded by George Douglas, earl of Dumbarton, and subsequently became the Royal Scots, the first of the line in the British army.

[94] Walsh, 'Wild Goose Tradition', 7; P. Gouhier, 'Mercenaires irlandais au service de la France (1635–1664)', *IS* 7 (1955–6), 58–62.

Imperial commander, at Eger in 1634. The murder was actually carried out by Captain Walter Devereux and a company of Butler's Irish dragoons. As a reward, Butler was made a count of the Holy Roman Empire, and John Gordon and Walter Leslie, Butler's fellow conspirators, who were Protestant Scots, also received estates confiscated from the possessions of Wallenstein in Bohemia and Moravia. Gordon converted to Catholicism in order to receive his properties.[95]

Scots and English had also fought for the rulers of Muscovy since at least the time of Ivan the Terrible (1533–84), if not earlier. A cavalry force consisting of three squadrons of Scots, English and French had also served Boris Godunov before defecting to his rival, the first 'False Dimitri', during the Time of Troubles (1598–1613). Two cavalry regiments, one each of Scots and Irish, remained in the service of Czar Michael Romanov after the Time of Troubles. Most Scots and English entered Russian service by way of the Danish or, especially, the Swedish armies. This was occasioned by the conflict between Sigismund (Vasa) III and his uncle, Charles IX, who had driven him out of Sweden in 1598. Sigismund never gave up his claim to the Swedish throne, and sought to make trouble for Charles by invading Muscovy during the Time of Troubles and appropriating Russian resources for use against him. Czar Basil (Shuiski) IV, a boyar upstart, accepted military help from Charles IX to counteract Polish influence in Russia. This pitted Scots in the Swedish-Muscovite armies, led by the Franco-Swedish commander, Pontus de la Gardie, against English and Scots in the Polish army. In response, the Muscovites increased their efforts to recruit more Scottish mercenaries, who were raised and commanded by one Colonel Calvin, a Scot; they made their way to Russia through Sweden and Finland and then marched across the ice to Muscovy.[96]

Although Russia and Sweden were to become rivals in the later seventeenth century, during the reigns of Charles IX and Gustavus Adolphus the Swedes were anxious to build up the Muscovite army to counter the powerful Polish army. In 1629–30 Gustavus sent a military mission to Moscow to advise Czar Michael on modernizing his army on the Swedish model. The mission was headed by General Alexander Leslie, a kinsman of Field Marshal Alexander Leslie, who later became earl of Leven. General Leslie, who had been released from the Swedish army, was sent by the czar to Sweden and then England and Scotland to buy muskets and to recruit soldiers. With Charles I's licence and the help of an English officer, Thomas Sanderson, General Leslie returned to Moscow with 2,000 English and Scottish soldiers, including a number of felons liberated from the Fleet Prison in

---

[95] Fitzsimon, 'Irish Swordsmen in the Imperial Service in the Thirty Years War', 26–30; *DNB, sub* James Butler (*fl.* 1631–1634) *et* Walter, Count Butler (d. 1634); Redlich, *GME* i. 348; Grant, *Memoirs . . . of Sir John Hepburn*, 73; T. M. Barker, *Army, Aristocracy and Monarchy: Essays on War, Society and Government in Austria, 1618–1780* (1982), 14–15, 17–18, 19; D. Worthington, *Scots in Habsburg Service, 1618–1648* (2004), 142–76.

[96] P. Dukes, 'The First Scottish Soldiers in Russia', in G. G. Simpson (ed.), *The Scottish Soldier Abroad, 1247–1967* (1992), 47–50; J. W. Barnhill and P. Dukes, 'North-east Scots in Muscovy in the Sixteenth Century', *NS* 1 (1972), 50–3; Henry Brereton, *Newes of the Present Miseries of Russia* (1614), 32–3, 42–4; Oakley, *War and Peace*, 44–5.

London. They arrived in Archangel in 1634. Unfortunately the English and Scots officers did not get along well, and during the Smolensk War, Leslie quarrelled with Sanderson and shot him dead. Although exonerated by a court martial, the divisiveness in the Muscovite ranks obliged the Russians to negotiate peace with the Polish invaders.[97]

When one compares the recruiting methods of the States' Army in England with the recruiting efforts of other continental powers in the British Isles, a number of striking conclusions emerge. First of all, it was more difficult to find military manpower in England than in Ireland or Scotland, despite the fact that the latter two kingdoms had smaller populations. Although the English Privy Council and local magistrates scoured urban streets and rural byways for vagrants and masterless men, and resorted to the illegal practice of impressment during the late Elizabethan wars and in the 1620s, this level of recruiting could not be sustained throughout the early Stuart period as it was in the other two kingdoms because there was not as much surplus manpower to be swept up. England's population growth was beginning to slow down in the early seventeenth century, and Englishmen could find employment, or at least the means of subsistence, more readily in a developing economy. Hunger did not assist recruiting efforts to the degree that it did in Scotland and Ireland or continental countries. Although magnates such as the first earl of Leicester and the second earl of Essex could recruit tenants for cavalry troops, they had to turn to the Privy Council and local authorities to impress men to fill up their infantry companies. Without resorting to the more draconian and disruptive recruiting methods which came with the English civil wars, there were limits on the extent to which tenant loyalty, obligations or the reputation of a nobleman could influence recruiting efforts in England, and that is why resort was had to the impressment of vagrants and criminals. The Dutch army preferred to train its own recruits and was distrustful of undisciplined armies raised by military enterprisers such as Ernest von Mansfeld.[98] Military enterprisers like those who operated in Ireland and Scotland did not suit the needs of the Dutch army and did not flourish in the English situation.

By contrast military enterprisers drawn from the aristocracies of Ireland and Scotland, although exploiting smaller populations, could make use of clan loyalties and feudal obligations in very effective ways to tap military manpower for continental armies in the early seventeenth century. Later, during the Wars of the Three Kingdoms, the ability of Irish and Scottish lords, lairds and clan chieftains to recruit from among their tenants and followers continued to amaze English observers. The successful suppression of rebellions in both countries at the end of the sixteenth century had, of course, made swordsmen redundant, and both the

---

[97] P. Dukes, 'The Leslie Family', 402–11, 419–21; id., 'Scottish Soldiers in Muscovy', in *The Caledonian Phalanx: Scots in Russia* (1987), 12–14; S. Murdoch, 'The House of Stuart and the Scottish Professional Soldier', in B. Taithe and T. Thornton (eds.), *War: Identities in Conflict, 1300–2000* (1998), 48.   [98] *Infra* Ch. 5.

Irish and Scottish governments were anxious to send idle soldiers into permanent exile. At the same time, mainland European governments—especially those of Spanish Flanders, the Dutch Republic, Denmark-Norway, Poland, Sweden and France, were eager to draw upon the resources of military manpower in the British Isles. Moreover, the English, Scots and Irish enjoyed the reputation of being aggressive and courageous soldiers, and were employed in the field armies of the Netherlands and Sweden out of all proportion to their numbers and often predominated in the vanguards of those armies going into battle. Whatever their faults in accepting discipline, the Swedish chancellor Axel Oxenstierna found the Scots to be more tractable and apt for learning new methods of fighting than the German mercenaries who provided the greatest pool of military manpower.[99] Mainland European governments were undoubtedly guided by national stereotypes in their recruiting strategies.

Maurice of Nassau appears to have been one of the few military commanders of this period who husbanded military manpower—preferring sieges to pitched battles. This was because sieges, properly conducted, were more sparing of the lives of soldiers, who, Maurice understood, represented a substantial investment of time and money in training and maintenance. In his early novel, *Memoirs of a Cavalier*, Daniel Defoe depicts his cavaliers as preferring the tactics of Gustavus Adolphus, who, although profligate with the lives of his soldiers, was thought to be more 'gallant' because he aggressively sought battle with his enemies.[100] But the governments of the Three Kingdoms in the early seventeenth century had regarded idle soldiers and vagrants as a social liability and were glad to see the last of them—understanding that few were likely ever to return. As the English government became more militarily minded in the latter part of the seventeenth century, England's rulers—especially James VII and II and William II and III— realized that the manpower of the British Isles offered the prospect of great military might.

The experience of the many Scots officers and soldiers who served in the Swedish army under the command of the widely admired Gustavus Adolphus, whose ideals and leadership were greater than his kingdom's resources, provided an example of a soldier-king trying to shape a godly army to fight for the cause of Protestant liberties in Germany. That he died leading his soldiers into battle from the front only enhanced his image as a Protestant exemplar. Moreover, as Robert

---

[99] Roberts, *Gustavus Adolphus*, ii. 205 n.

[100] Daniel Defoe, *Memoirs of a Cavalier: or a Military Journal of the Wars in Germany and the Wars in England: From the Year 1632 to the Year 1648* (1720 edn.; repr. 1972), 139.

Defoe failed to sort out the chronology of the careers of Maurice of Nassau and Gustavus Adolphus. Defoe's anonymous cavalier began his military career in 1632 as an English volunteer with Gustavus Adolphus in Germany. He could not have known Maurice except by reputation since Maurice died in 1625. Defoe's cavalier spent most of his time in the campaigns of Gustavus serving under Scottish commanders such as Sir John Hepburn, and his view of Maurice's style of fighting may well represent the prejudices of Scottish soldiers in the Swedish army. Defoe's early novel has the ring of authenticity because he had the opportunity to talk to veterans of those wars.

Monro had insisted, officers and volunteers could learn much from him as an innovator in battlefield tactics comparable to Maurice of Nassau—even if the logistics of his army exposed his own soldiers and the people of Germany and Bohemia to severe privations. Thus, when the Scottish Covenanters raised an army to make war on their own king, who notably lacked the martial image and godly zeal of Gustavus Adolphus, it was only natural that they would turn to the Swedish army as a godly, disciplined force to serve as a model.[101]

One cannot help but notice that there was always a certain degree of friction between the different nations of the British Isles when they served together in foreign armies. But the English, Welsh, Scots and Irish—especially the officers and volunteers, when they shared the same religious and personal allegiances—gradually got used to one another's proximity, and could work and fight together for the same goals. Although a certain amount of mistrust would always remain, this mingling of men from the Three Kingdoms and the four nations in foreign armies as well as in the armies of the British and Irish civil wars, together with the recognition—at least among the officers and gentlemen—that they increasingly shared a common European martial culture, must have helped to smooth the path towards the integration of these elements in the English and British armies of the late seventeenth and early eighteenth centuries.

[101] Roberts, *Gustavus Adolphus*, ii. 245–68.

5

Military and naval expeditions
of the 1620s

King Charles, in the entrance to his reign, proceeds with preparations for a war begun in his father's time; the militia[1] of the kingdom, through long continued peace, were much decayed, and the musters of the trained bands were slight, seldom taken, and few of the commons were expert in the use of arms.

John Rushworth, *Historical Collections*, 8 vols. (1682–1701), i. 168.

Our Army's lingering so long at the Isle of Rhé . . . hath been the occasion of the greatest and shamefulest overthrow the English have suffered since we lost Normandy. . . .

[Mr Beaulieu] to the Revd. Joseph Mead, 16 Nov. 1627, printed in Thomas Birch, *The Court and Times of Charles I*, ed. R. F. Williams, 2 vols. (1848), i. 285.

They rank the duke[2] with Bevis,[3]
This skirmish[4] they do place
Before the cow of Dunmowe Heath[5]
And next to Chevy Chase;[6]
And swear that through our chronicles
We far and near do wander,
Before that such an one we find
Employed as a commander.

Anonymous song about Buckingham written sometime after the Isle of Rhé expedition of 1627, in *Poems and Songs relating to George Villiers, duke of Buckingham, and his Assassination by John Felton, August 23, 1628*, ed. F. W. Fairholt, PS 29 (1850), 16–17.

[1] In this sense, the armed forces of the crown, including the trained bands.

[2] Charles Villiers, 1st duke of Buckingham.

[3] The tale of *Bevis of Hampton* (c.1324) is a chivalric romance which exists in a number of versions in Norman French and Middle English and concerns a knight of obscure birth who battles dragons and giants and has many other improbable adventures. One version of the tale was written by Geoffrey Chaucer.

[4] Buckingham's capture of the town of St Martin on the Isle of Rhé, which was empty of soldiers and contained only their wives and children whom he drove into the citadel of St Martin by shooting at them so that the soldiers and their dependants would consume the provisions of the fortress and force the garrison to surrender sooner. This was Buckingham's first and only 'battle'.

[5] This is possibly a reference to one of the well-governed husbands of the Wife of Bath in Chaucer's *Canterbury Tales*, 'Wife of Bath's Prologue', ll. 218–19.

[6] A late medieval popular ballad depicting a fictional bloody encounter between Earl Percy and Earl Douglas in which several thousand die in a poaching foray across the River Tweed. It reflected the

When John Rushworth, successively secretary to the council of war of the New Model Army, Lord General Fairfax and Lord Protector Cromwell, began to compile his famous *Historical Collections*, he originally intended to begin this monumental work with the opening of the Long Parliament in November 1640; but as he delved deeper into the sources, he became convinced that the Rebellion and Civil Wars had their origins in the failed attempt to restore the Rhenish Palatinate to Frederick V, the elector palatine, who had been driven out of Bohemia and the Palatinate by Imperial and Spanish forces beginning in 1618. This had the effect of linking the English civil wars, and indeed all of the Wars of the Three Kingdoms, to the continental wars of religion. The mismanagement of the English military and naval expeditions of the 1620s—particularly the count of Mansfeld's 1624–5 expedition to the Palatinate, the 1625 expedition to Cadiz and the 1627 expedition to the Isle of Rhé—led not only to the attempted impeachment and, later, the assassination of the court favourite, the duke of Buckingham, but also to a crisis of confidence in the trustworthiness and competence of Charles I to lead and command the military forces of the crown.[7]

At the same time that James I's failure to send military forces to assist his daughter Elizabeth and his son-in-law Frederick in a timely manner exposed the military weakness of the crown, the outbreak of the Bohemian revolt and its suppression also stimulated an assertiveness, a bellicosity and a determination to go to the aid of the Palatines among the English and Scottish aristocracies and helped to define the military nobility. It also happened that some of the so-called 'military earls', such as Robert Devereux, third earl of Essex, Henry Wriothesley, third earl of Southampton, and Henry de Vere, eighteenth earl of Oxford, were by descent connected with earlier chivalric heroes such as Sir Philip Sidney and Robert, second earl of Essex, who were remembered by James I and his courtiers as being associated with resistance to the crown.[8] Both James I and Charles I failed to see that popular loyalty was directed towards the image of a militantly Protestant and martial monarchy; the court of the first two Stuart monarchs did not fit that image because court favourites, such as Buckingham, and his military followers, such as Sir Edward Cecil, were regarded as being militarily ineffective.[9] The traditional dislike of the professional soldier was also intensified by the mismanagement by Buckingham and Cecil of the military and naval expeditions of the 1620s, while the expedients for raising, paying, housing and disciplining those military and naval forces by means of impressment, forced loans, billeting of troops upon civilian households and the issuing of commissions of martial law were politically

nature of Anglo-Scottish border warfare in late medieval times (*The... History of the Memorable but Unhappy Hunting on Chevy Chase* (1710), unpaginated).

[7] Rushworth, *HC*, vol. i, sig. B2*r* & *v*; J. Scott, 'England's Troubles, 1602–1702', in R. M. Smuts (ed.), *The Stuart Court and Europe: Essays in Politics and Political Culture* (1996), 28–9.

[8] R. C. McCoy, 'Old English Honour in an Evil Time: Aristocratic Principle in the 1620s', in Smuts (ed.), *Stuart Court and Europe*, 133–5.

[9] I. Archer, 'Popular Politics in Sixteenth- and Seventeenth-Century London', paper presented at the Midwest Conference on British Studies, University of Chicago (23 Oct. 1999).

unpopular or of dubious legality or both, and provoked protests by Parliament in the Petition of Right of 1628. The mobilization of military manpower for these expeditions was the largest since the 1590s, and because James I had allowed the institutions of military administration to wither, the English government lacked the ability to provide logistical support for such large military and naval forces.[10]

James I feared being drawn into the religious wars of mainland Europe, and he genuinely hoped to arrange a peace between the Catholic and Protestant powers. This he proposed to do by negotiating a treaty of marriage and alliance which would match Prince Charles with the Spanish Infanta. This was an unpopular policy from the beginning, and rumours circulated about the contents of the proposed treaty. One rumour had it that a condition of the marriage treaty would have been the recall of English and Scottish soldiers serving in the States' Army under the command of Prince Maurice. According to Sir Simonds D'Ewes, these amounted to 11,000 men and were 'the [chief] strength' of the Dutch army.[11] Following the breakdown of the negotiations for the marriage alliance with Spain in 1623 and growing evidence of Spanish hegemony in Europe, James was drawn into close alliance with his relations among the Protestant princes. In 1613 James had married his daughter Elizabeth to Frederick V, the elector palatine, after a number of other prospects had failed. Frederick turned out to be a bellicose prince with poor judgement, and the match had effectively made James, for a time, the leading Protestant prince in Europe. Frederick's acceptance of the Bohemian crown, an appanage of the Holy Roman Empire, contrary to James's advice, invited the wrath of the emperor against Frederick and his rebellious Bohemian subjects, and destroyed the Jacobean peace. Consequently, not just England, but the governments of Scotland and Ireland alike were obliged to engage in large-scale military spending for the construction and repair of coastal fortifications, the manning and equipping of the English and Scots navies and, of course, the costly but ineffectual naval and military expeditions under discussion. Moreover, James was also pressured into sending troops to assist his brother-in-law, Christian IV of Denmark, who was campaigning in northern Germany. James also renegotiated an alliance with the Dutch Republic, which was not formalized until after his death in 1625, and his successor, Charles I, concluded a militarily worthless but costly marital alliance with France.[12]

Prince Charles and the duke of Buckingham had gone to Spain in 1623 in order to persuade King Philip IV and the count-duke of Olivares to agree to an

---

[10] Schwoerer, *NSA* 19–20; K. Sharpe, *The Personal Rule of Charles I* (1992), 23; M. Bennett, 'The Officer Corps and Army Command in the British Isles, 1620–1660', in Trim (ed.), *Chivalric Ethos*, 294.
[11] E. Bourcier (ed.), *The Diary of Sir Simonds D'Ewes, 1622–1624* (1974), 70.
[12] A. I. MacInnes, *Charles I and the Making of the Covenanting Movement, 1625–1641* (1991), 42–3; S. J. Stearns, 'The Caroline Military System, 1625–1627: The Expeditions to Cadiz and Rhé', Ph.D diss., Univ. of California, Berkeley (1967), 9–10, 19; S. Adams, 'Spain or the Netherlands? The Dilemmas of Early Stuart Foreign Policy', in H. Tomlinson (ed.), *Before the English Civil War: Essays on Early Stuart Politics and Government* (1983), 79–80.

honourable resolution of Frederick's claim to Bohemia and the Palatinate, and the proposal to marry Charles to the Infanta was only part of the diplomatic mission. In Madrid, Charles and Buckingham found abundant evidence that the marriage negotiations were being conducted in a deceitful manner and that the Spaniards had no intention of lending their assistance to the return of Bohemia or the Palatinate. Charles returned from Spain in a very belligerent mood, and felt that honour compelled England to intervene in the war in Germany. Before Charles's distaste for parliaments forced a policy of peace upon him, his inclination was to project the martial image of a warrior-king clad in armour and mounted upon a warhorse. Many of Charles's subjects also desired to see him play the soldier and intervene in the Thirty Years War.[13]

Earlier, the expulsion of the Palatines had obliged King James to reconsider his policy of peace, and he summoned Parliament in 1621 to discuss the financing of a military campaign in Germany. The unpopularity of the Jacobean peace reached a peak during the meeting of Parliament. James, however, was reluctant to abandon hope of a negotiated settlement, and the wily Spanish ambassador, Diego Sarmiento de Acuña, count of Gondomar, skilfully played upon his hopes for avoiding war. Because negotiations for a royal marriage were regarded as part of the royal prerogative, parliamentary leaders dared not question the matter, so instead they focused their criticism on the king's unwillingness to go to the aid of the Palatines. At the same time, however, the opposition leaders in the House of Commons had no inclination towards an expensive intervention in the Palatinate and, instead, preferred a more profitable war of diversion against the Hapsburgs at sea, which would provide opportunities to plunder Spanish merchantmen and to intercept the annual treasure fleet. Like Prince Charles, the king had also concluded that his honour required direct intervention in Germany, and this permitted no discussion of an alternative strategy. Parliament would not agree to finance this plan, and this gave James the excuse to abandon intervention in the Palatinate except for soliciting voluntary contributions and raising several regiments of volunteers who went there under the command of Sir Horace Vere.[14]

There was considerable sympathy among both swordsmen and English Puritans who favoured intervention in aid of fellow Protestants on the European mainland for a Palatine expedition, but by its very nature such a campaign posed logistical nightmares. After James I had committed himself to the defence or recovery of the Palatinate, he appointed a Council of War composed of experienced military and naval commanders, and charged them to determine the size and cost of raising an expedition to accomplish that purpose. Their estimates of

[13] T. Cogswell, *The Blessed Revolution: English Politics and the Coming of War, 1621–1624* (1989), 60–4; R. Lockyer, *Buckingham: The Life and Political Career of George Villiers, First Duke of Buckingham* (1981), 168–71.

[14] W. S. Maltby, *The Black Legend in England: The Development of Anti-Spanish Sentiment, 1558–1660* (1971), 101–2; Stearns, 'Caroline Military System', 11–15; Lockyer, *Buckingham*, 82–5.

the cost of levying and maintaining a force of 5,000 horse and 25,000 foot were absurdly low. Moreover, because James did not at that time wish to cooperate with the Dutch Republic, it would be very difficult to send the troops by water up the Rhine to the Palatinate because the estuaries were all controlled by the Dutch. It seems that James could see no connection between the Eighty Years War and the Thirty Years War.[15]

Meanwhile, while James was dithering about foreign and military policy, the drum was beaten in London beginning in March 1620 to enlist volunteers for the regiment which Sir Horace Vere was raising to go to the aid of the Elector Frederick in the Palatinate. The force of 2,250 men got under way in June and arrived at Dordrecht in July. Although James wished to have nothing to do with the Dutch rebels (as he regarded them), it happened that Vere was a serving officer in the Dutch army, and the Republic, knowing that the Twelve Years Truce would soon expire, had an interest in distracting Spinola's Spanish Army of Flanders which was fighting the Palatine forces along the upper reaches of the Rhine.[16] Another regiment was recruited by Sir Andrew Gray, a Scottish Catholic officer in the Elector Frederick's service, from amongst volunteers in England and Scotland and also impressed men from the latter kingdom. Gray had requested permission from King James to borrow money from English bankers, after James had refused to help with the costs. Instead, the cost of transporting Gray's Regiment to Bohemia was guaranteed by a consortium made up of James Hay, Viscount Doncaster (and later earl of Carlisle), James's ambassador to the Palatinate and the earl of Essex's cousin, along with Ludovic Stuart, duke of Lennox, James, second marquis of Hamilton, and Philip Herbert, fourth earl of Pembroke. Another Scot in Bohemian service, Colonel John Seton, also commanded a regiment, but nothing is known of how, when or where it was recruited.[17]

Recruiting for Sir Horace Vere's Regiment allowed many gallants to display their martial spirit, and the regiment seems to have contained an unusually large proportion of peers and gentlemen. The earls of Oxford and Essex, Thomas, fourth Lord Cromwell, Robert Sidney, Viscount Lisle (and later second earl of Leicester), Gilbert, second Lord Gerard, Sir Edward Sackville, Sir John Burgh, Sir John Borlase, Sir Charles Rich, Sir John Wentworth and Sir William Fairfax all commanded companies or served as officers or volunteers. Robert Rich, second earl of Warwick, and Grey Brydges, fifth Lord Chandos, indicated that they intended to join after the regiment arrived in the Netherlands. The earl of Essex on his initial campaign with Vere's expedition brought with him a draft of 300

---

[15] William Whiteway of Dorchester, *His Diary, 1618–1635*, DRS 12 (1991), 23–6; *The Interpreter* (1622), quoted in C. Hill, *Society and Puritanism in Pre-Revolutionary England* (1966 edn.), 21; S. L. Adams, 'Foreign Policy and the Parliaments of 1621 and 1624', in K. Sharpe (ed.), *Faction and Parliament: Essays on Early Stuart History* (1978), 150–1.

[16] Whiteway, *Diary*, 26, 28, 35.

[17] V. F. Snow, *Essex the Rebel: The Life of Robert Devereux, the Third Earl of Essex, 1591–1646* (1970), 93; J. V. Polišensky, 'Gallants to Bohemia', *Slavonic and East European Review*, 25 (1947), 391–3, 398.

men, of whom 100 were gentlemen. Essex himself served first as a volunteer pikeman, before being commissioned captain. The Fairfaxes were kinsmen of the Veres, and Sir William and his brother John had served their military apprentice-ships under Sir Francis Vere. Now professional officers in the Dutch army, they were subsequently joined by their 'white-haired father', Sir Thomas Fairfax (later first Lord Fairfax) in the Palatinate. Like Sir Thomas, knights such as Sir George Smith were content to trail pikes as volunteers.[18]

Among the volunteers serving in Sir Andrew Gray's Regiment was Sir John Hepburn, who later commanded a regiment together with the Scots, or Green, Brigade in the Swedish army under Gustavus Adolphus.[19] Hepburn was also a Catholic, and was a kinsman of the late James Hepburn, fourth earl of Bothwell. He came from a tumultuous Border family seated in East Lothian; he and Robert Munro had been schoolfellows and toured France together. Hepburn and Gray and other Scots soldiers were very attached to Elizabeth of Bohemia, who had been born in Falkland Palace and who always stayed in touch with her fellow Scots. Among the 1,500 or so men raised in Scotland for Sir Andrew Gray's Regiment were 120 'mosstroopers', who had been arrested by the warden of the Middle March for their habitual lawlessness and assigned to Gray. The regiment sailed from Leith and marched to Bohemia by way of the Netherlands and other friendly states. After the Imperialist victory at the Battle of White Mountain in November 1620 drove Frederick and Elizabeth out of Bohemia, Gray's Regiment served in the Palatinate under the command of Ernst, count of Mansfeld, marshal of the Bohemian and Palatine armies. Later, Gray's Scots helped the Dutch defend Bergen-op-Zoom and were part of Mansfeld's fatal 1625 Palatinate expedition.[20]

John Taylor, the 'water poet', accompanied Sir Andrew Gray's Regiment as far as Rotterdam, and then, taking a different route, he rejoined them in Prague where they served as the royal guard of Frederick and Elizabeth. Taylor was entertained by the officers and soldiers of the regiment—both Scottish and English—and remarked upon the widespread illness among the soldiers. An important eyewitness and volunteer who accompanied Sir Horace Vere's Regiment to the Palatinate was Arthur Wilson, the earl of Essex's secretary and companion. After a number of false starts as an apprentice merchant, a clerk in the Exchequer and a would-be poet, Wilson obtained a position in Essex's household. One day he rescued a drowning maid from the moat at Chartley, the earl's seat in Staffordshire. Essex took a liking to Wilson, and gave him the post of secretary.

[18] C. Dalton, *The Life and Times of General Sir Edward Cecil, Viscount Wimbledon*, 2 vols. (1885), i. 332–3; G. W. Johnson (ed.), *The Fairfax Correspondence*, 2 vols. (1848), vol. i, pp. xxx–xxxi, xli; BL, Add. MS. 30, 305, fo. 29*r* & *v*; 'The Life of Mr Arthur Wilson the Historian . . . Written by Himself', in Francis Peck, *Desiderata Curiosa*, 2 vols. (1732–5), II. xii. 11.   [19] *Supra* Ch. 4.
[20] J. Grant, *Memoirs . . . of Sir John Hepburn* (1851), 2–8, 12–14, 18; *Munro His Expedition with the Worthy Scots Regiment called Mac-Keys*, ed. W. S. Brockington (repr. 1999), p. xvi; *DNB, sub* Sir John Hepburn (1598?–1636).

Being now immersed in the aristocratic culture of honour, Wilson fought many duels and never ignored a slight. But he also took the time to leave an account of the Palatinate expedition of 1620.[21] William Fairfax carried with him on his campaign in the Palatinate antique manuscripts and Roman coins which he was collecting for John Selden, the antiquarian and legal scholar. Some of these were lost on the journey from Gravesend to Amsterdam. He left instructions for his brother to forward them to Selden if they were recovered.[22]

Unable to persuade Parliament to finance a sizeable military force to send to the Palatinate, James permitted the Dutch Republic and the king of Denmark to raise troops in England and Scotland. He had, of course, already allowed members of the aristocracies of the Three Kingdoms to volunteer for military service after 1620. The earl of Essex returned to England after the campaigning season of 1620 was over so as not to miss the hunting season, but also to raise troops for Prince Maurice of Orange, who was preparing for the end of the Twelve Years Truce in April 1621. In return for their assistance in recruiting soldiers in England and Scotland, Maurice committed himself to helping James recover the Palatinate for Frederick. Maurice's agents were authorized to raise and arm 8,000 troops in England. After the campaigning season of 1620, Essex, usually with his friend, Lord Cromwell, spent the next three campaigning seasons in Dutch garrisons rather than returning to the Palatinate, until in 1624 he was given command of one of the four new English regiments which were to be raised for the States' Army.[23]

James had earlier discouraged British and Irish peers from joining foreign armies except for those whom he wished to clear out of Ireland, or those, in his Hispanophile phase, whom he allowed to join the Spanish Army of Flanders.[24] In about 1617–18 the earl of Oxford and Edward, first Lord Herbert of Cherbury, had each resolved to raise regiments for the Venetian Republic, but Herbert was headed off by his appointment as ambassador to the king of France. Oxford took volunteers with him to Venice and was present at the siege of Grandisca. In 1620 Oxford brought a regiment of 2,200 men (probably raised on the continent) to join Sir Horace Vere's campaign in the Palatinate, but when he returned home in 1621 he was briefly imprisoned by James for indiscreet words. Buckingham later secured his release in order to serve under him as vice-admiral. When the earl of Essex came home during the winter of 1620–1, he conspicuously avoided all court festivities and only showed up to accept his appointment to the newly formed Council of War. The earl of Southampton had also wished to go as a volunteer with Vere's Palatinate expedition of 1620, but James had refused him permission to do so.[25]

    [21] John Taylor, *Taylor his Travels* (1620), sigs. B2*v*, D1*v*; 'Life of Mr Arthur Wilson the Historian', 8–9; Arthur Wilson, *The Life and Reign of James I, The First King of Great Britain* (1653), repr. in [White Kennett], *Complete History of England*, 3 vols. (1706), ii. 721b–725b.
    [22] BL, Add. MS. 30,305, fo. 29*r* & *v*.
    [23] Snow, *Essex*, 99–100, 111–14; 'Life of Mr Arthur Wilson the Historian', II. xii. 13–15; *supra* Ch. 4.   [24] *Supra* Ch. 4.
    [25] J. M. Shuttleworth (ed.), *The Life of Edward, First Lord Herbert of Cherbury, Written by Himself* (1976), 88–9; Arthur Collins, *Historical Collections of the Noble Families of Cavendish, Holles, Vere,*

Sir Horace Vere's Regiment had no cavalry, which made it vulnerable, so Prince Maurice detached 2,000 horse and 400 musketeers from the Dutch garrison of Juliers (or Gulik) to escort the English troops up the Rhine. They arrived close upon the heels of Spinola's Spanish Army of Flanders with 4,000 horse and 26,000 foot.[26] The Dutch troops did not remain long with the English, and the decision was made to garrison three of the principal towns of the Palatinate. Sir Horace Vere occupied Mannheim and appointed Sir Gerrard Herbert as military governor of Heidelberg, while Frankenthal was secured by Sir John Burgh.[27] Thus, Spinola was left free to roam the countryside.

Vere's expedition carried little or no provisions and his men were seldom paid, because James I had provided no funds and the elector palatine had little treasure remaining. Arthur Wilson says that the earl of Essex paid many in his company out of his own pocket. Captains had to borrow money to pay their men without knowing how they could repay such loans. William Fairfax was entirely dependent on an annuity he received from Lady Shrewsbury. Moreover, English soldiers and officers found that the exchange rate for their English money was one-tenth of what they would have received in the Netherlands. Lacking regular pay and food, many of Vere's soldiers deserted. To make matters worse, Count Mansfeld, after having surrendered his army in Bohemia, broke his parole not to fight the Imperialist forces again, returned to the Palatinate and began to impress the local peasants to replace his own soldiers, who often deserted when he did not pay them—which he never did. Both Mansfeld's troops and the English foraged mercilessly and consequently became distracted by secondary wars with the peasants. Thus, Frederick's Palatine subjects had no reason to favour his cause, and many preferred the better disciplined and better paid Spanish troops under Spinola.[28]

After fleeing Bohemia in disguise, the Elector Frederick, whom Arthur Wilson thought was better suited to a counting house than any 'vigourous or masculine heat', returned to the Palatinate to take command. In all fairness, no commander could have held out much longer under the circumstances. In September 1622 the Catholic League forces under Johan, count of Tilly, assaulted Heidelberg and the remnant of the English garrison surrendered and were allowed to march out under honourable terms with their colours and arms. At Mannheim, Sir Horace Vere not only withstood a siege of seven weeks, but also launched several furious

---

Harley (1752), 266–8; Snow, *Essex*, 99–100; *Acts PC, 1619–1621*, 333; M. Heinemann, 'Rebel Lords, Popular Playwrights and Political Culture: Notes on the Jacobean Patronage of the Earl of Southampton', *The Yearbook of English Studies*, 21 (1991), 66.

[26] Wilson, *Life and Reign of James I*, ii. 723a & b. John Fairfax said that Spinola had 9,000 horse and 52,000 foot who were reinforced with 3,000–4,000 Italians after arriving in the Palatinate. These numbers are probably inflated, but they may also include the armies of German princes assigned to assist Spinola by Imperial authority (Johnson (ed.), *Fairfax Correspondence*, vol. i, pp. xlii–xliii).

[27] N. Tucker, 'Volunteers in the Thirty Years War', *NLWJ* 16 (1969–70), 63–4.

[28] Ibid.; BL, Add. MS. 30,305, fos. 301, 33; Johnson (ed.), *Fairfax Correspondence*, vol. i, p. xl; Dalton, *Life and Times of . . . Sir Edward Cecil*, ii. 8; Wilson, *Life and Reign of James I*, ii. 723b–724a.

sallies against Tilly's forces. On the verge of starvation, he and his garrison also yielded upon honourable terms in November. Sir John Burgh fought on at Frankenthal until the next spring, when he surrendered in response to a direct order from King James.[29]

For others, the cost was heavier. Sir Thomas Fairfax's sons, John and William, died defending Frankenthal. Sir Thomas had also lost two other of his six sons in 1621: Thomas had been killed fighting the Turks, and Peregrine died as a volunteer in the French Royal army during the assault on the Huguenot stronghold of Montauban. Five of the Fairfax sons had been swordsmen, including the eldest, Fernando, later second Lord Fairfax. Only one, Charles, stayed at home; he became a barrister of Lincoln's Inn.[30] The earl of Essex and Arthur Wilson, preferring to return to England by way of France, encountered a hostile and menacing crowd of 500 persons, including stone-throwing friars, while passing through a French town, and were only saved from an unpleasant fate by the timely arrival of a French cavalry officer.[31]

James I remained determined to recover the Palatinate for Frederick despite the structural and logistical problems which Sir Horace Vere's expedition of 1620–3 had revealed. It was after the failure of the Spanish marriage negotiations that Buckingham's role at court evolved from royal favourite to paramount minister of the crown, and he began pushing the idea of another military expedition to the Palatinate. Buckingham also came up with the idea of employing the mercenary commander, Ernest, count of Mansfeld, as its leader. Mansfeld had been in the service of the Elector Frederick in Bohemia and the Palatinate during 1620–2, but he had acquired a questionable reputation. He had been briefly in French employ, before turning up in England in April 1624 with a scheme for leading a joint Anglo-French expedition to recover the Palatinate. James liked the Mansfeld proposal because he was told that it would cost him only £40,000, and might advance the plan for a French marriage alliance. Parliament refused to grant subsidies for a Palatinate expedition without a declaration of war on Spain, and that was something that James still hoped to avoid.[32]

Mansfeld was the illegitimate son of Peter Ernest von Mansfeld, prince of the Holy Roman Empire, who had been a military enterpriser for the Spanish crown and governor of Luxembourg. Although Mansfeld had distinguished himself as a young officer, he had suffered humiliations as a bastard relation in the service of his stepbrother Karl. In the War of Juliers Succession, Mansfeld was taken prisoner, and his lord, the Archduke Leopold, had failed to ransom him. Although

[29] Wilson, *Life and Reign of James I*, ii. 724b–725a; Tucker, 'Volunteers in the Thirty Years War', 65; Edward Grimeston, *A Generall Historie of the Netherlands* (1627), 1467; Whiteway, *Diary*, 4; Robert Markham, *Memoirs of the Military Transactions of Sir John Burroughs, Knt* (1758), 8.

[30] Johnson (ed.), *Fairfax Correspondence*, vol. i, pp. xlv, li, lviii.

[31] 'Life of Mr Arthur Wilson the Historian', II. xii. 12.

[32] Lockyer, *Buckingham*, 168–223; Adams, 'Foreign Policy and the Parliaments of 1621 and 1624', 158.

he was subsequently set free he did not forget the slight, and he led many of the archduke's troops into the camp of the Protestant Union. The duke of Savoy ennobled him in 1618, and he entered the service of the Elector Frederick V. Mansfeld developed a reputation as a resourceful commander who could keep an army in the field, although he rarely paid them because his employers seldom paid him. Of course, the consequence was that his army laid waste any area which it occupied or marched through. When Mansfeld arrived in Bohemia to take up his duties as great marshal of Frederick's army, he found a mutiny in progress among Frederick's forces, and the mutineers immediately proceeded to attack his house. His officers and household servants successfully beat off the mutineers.[33]

Following the collapse of the negotiations for a Spanish marriage, Prince Charles's and Buckingham's advocacy of war against Spain caused a realignment of court factions. Peers, such as the third earl of Southampton and the eighteenth earl of Oxford, who had been sent to the Tower of London for their criticism of the royal favourite, were now drawn to support the new anti-Spanish policy by their ambition for military command and martial fame. They, along with the third earl of Essex, had all served in English regiments in the Dutch army. Their hatred of the Spanish temporarily overcame their dislike of Buckingham. Robert Rich, second earl of Warwick, who had ambitions for a naval command, also joined the aristocratic recruits to Charles's and Buckingham's anti-Spanish coalition. Warwick was a cousin of the third earl of Essex, and his rapprochement with Buckingham had been arranged by his younger brother, Henry Rich, Lord Kensington (and later first earl of Holland). A cloud had hung over the third earl of Essex because of his father's execution as a traitor. He had avoided the court by service in the Dutch army and espousing the cause of the Palatines.[34]

This group of military peers had their own agenda. They initiated a propaganda campaign to support the plan to send a military expedition to the Palatinate, to coordinate the military efforts of England with the Dutch Republic and to promote their own undertaking to raise regiments for the Dutch army which would accompany any military expedition to the Palatinate.[35] Henry, third earl of Southampton, appears to have had a particularly ambitious agenda. His association with militant Protestantism and even republicanism derived from his earlier acquaintance with Henry Cuffe, a Puritan and a translator of Tacitus as well as secretary to the second earl of Essex. Cuffe had been executed for his part in the Essex conspiracy. Southampton was also associated with the anti-Spanish militancy of Sir Edwin Sandys both in Parliament and in the Virginia Company. Sandys was an advocate of an alliance with the Venetian Republic in order to counter papal influence. When the Imperialist forces invaded the Palatinate in 1618,

---

[33] Redlich, *GME* i. 211–15; S.W., *The Apollogie of... Prince Ernestus, Earle of Mansfield* (1622), 3, 5, 33–5, 40. [34] Cogswell, *The Blessed Revolution*, 102–3.
[35] Gervase Markham, *Honour in his Perfection* (London, 1624), unpaginated; [William Crosse], *The Dutch Survay* (1625), sig. A2, p. 29.

Southampton had sought to raise a force of volunteers and lead them there, but he was prevented from doing so because his anti-Spanish tendencies endangered James's pro-Spanish policy. In 1623 Southampton had been imprisoned and inter-rogated, but was released when James's foreign policy shifted to an interventionist stance. Southampton was then allowed to command one of the four new English regiments to be raised for the Dutch army. Southampton subsequently appointed as chaplain of his new regiment John Knight, a Puritan cleric whom he had met during his imprisonment. Knight had been committed to the Tower for saying that subjects had the right to take up arms against their sovereign when opposing the Spanish marriage negotiations. However, Southampton and his son and heir, James, Lord Wriothesley, died of the plague in a Dutch military camp in 1624, before they ever saw action.[36]

King James and the duke of Buckingham made the decision to raise an army to send to the Palatinate in the face of contrary advice from both the Council of War and the Privy Council. The Privy Council had wished to wait until they were assured by Louis XIII and Cardinal Richelieu that France would participate. Once the decision to go forward was taken, the military peers and their followers began to press James for commissions as colonels and captains in the four new English regiments to be raised for the States' Army. John Chamberlain told Sir Dudley Carleton that they had flocked to James's hunting lodge at Theobalds in early June 1625, but the king had refused to meet with them. It seems to have been a fore-gone conclusion that three of the regiments would go to Essex, Southampton and Oxford. Among those considered for the fourth regiment were William Douglas, earl of Morton, Sir John Borlase and Robert Bertie, fourteenth Lord Willoughby de Eresby (created first earl of Lindsey in 1626). In the event, Willoughby won out and the four became known as the 'military earls'. Chamberlain wondered that they were content to serve as colonels rather than generals: 'It hath seldom been seen that men of their rank . . . should hunt after so mean places in respect of the countenance our ancient nobility was wont to carry, but it is answered [that] they do it to raise the companies of voluntaries by their credit, which I doubt will hardly stretch to furnish 6,000 men without pressing, for our own people do apprehend too much the misery and hard usage of soldiers in these times. And now in the very nick comes news how barbarously the Hollanders have dealt with our men in the East Indies.'[37]

'The drums began to beat to raise men for the new colonels' on 1 July 1624, wrote Chamberlain. At first the recruiting officers proclaimed that those who volunteered would serve in the States' Army and fight the king of Spain and the regent of the Spanish Netherlands, but King James must have objected, and the next day all reference to the Spanish as enemies was dropped. Instead of

[36] *DNB*, *sub* Henry Cuff *or* Cuffe (1563–1601); Heineman, 'Rebel Lords, Popular Playwrights and Political Culture', 66–8, 84–5; *supra* Ch. 3.

[37] Dalton, *Sir Edward* Cecil, ii. 75–8; McClure, *LJC* ii. 562. The last reference is to the massacre of the English merchants at Amboina in the Moluccas by officials of the Dutch East India Company.

concerning themselves with military strategy and the logistical problem of how to transport their regiments to the Palatinate, the four colonels fell out with one another over the question of precedence—'the earl of Southampton pretends precedence as having been a general of horse'. Although Parliament had finally voted a subsidy for an expedition to the Palatinate sufficient to raise 25,000 men, James chose to send only the 6,000 recruits raised for the four new English regiments. His immediate strategic objective was to get the four military peers out of the country. The earl of Essex's name and reputation were sufficient to fill his regiment, but most of the other recruits were impressed men. During the summer of 1624 the four new English regiments joined a Dutch field army of 4,000 men at the siege of Breda, which Prince Maurice wished to retain as an ancestral possession, although strategically vulnerable. In the autumn of 1624 the plague swept over the Dutch camp and killed Southampton and Wriothesley and many of their men, who were already weakened by malnutrition, and rendered Prince Maurice too ill to command. Maurice would not survive the winter, and the earl of Oxford died of wounds received in a skirmish. Bogged down as they were at Breda, the four new English regiments were of little use for a Palatinate expedition. Essex and his men, under the command of the new stadholder and captain-general, Prince Frederick Henry, attempted to defend Breda when the Spanish siege resumed in May 1625, but the Dutch governor of Breda decided that the garrison could not hold out any longer and surrendered to Spinola.[38]

Count Mansfeld came into England in early November 1624 to begin raising troops for the joint Anglo-French intervention in the Palatinate. Twelve thousand men were to be raised in England and another 10,000 in Scotland, plus an unspecified number of cavalry to be commanded by Theophilus Clinton-Fiennes, fourth earl of Lincoln. The 12,000, raised largely by impressment, were to be organized into six regiments, to be commanded by the earl of Lincoln, Viscount Doncaster, Lord Cromwell, Sir Charles Rich, Sir John Burgh and Sir Andrew Gray. The captains in the English contingent included Sir Edward Fleetwood, Sir Ralph Hopton, Sir Nathaniel Rich and Sir James Ramsay. The English troops appear to have been impressed from London and southern England, and on the way to the port of embarkation at Dover the untrained and undisciplined recruits 'committed great spoils and rapines', which included 'pulling down houses and taking away cattle'. Local magistrates requested commissions to execute martial law until the pressed men could be put aboard the Danish and Hamburg ships which were to carry them to Calais. When Mansfeld came to England, he brought with him 6,000 experienced German mercenaries and 1,000 reiters. He asked the king if he could land his mercenaries ashore while they awaited the arrival of the English recruits, but the Privy Council feared that Mansfeld's men, who

---

[38] McClure, *LJC* ii. 567; Dalton, *Sir Edward Cecil*, ii. 62–3, 75–8; Francis Grose, *Military Antiquities Respecting a History of the British Army*, 2 vols. (1786–7), i. 350–5 (misdated 18 June 1620); Snow, *Essex*, 118–24.

were rarely paid, might fall into their wonted habits of pillage and spoil. They were finally allowed ashore without their weapons, and behaved themselves. When the English pressed men arrived they were immediately put aboard ships at Dover and along the Kentish coast.[39]

As part of the negotiations for the marriage treaty with France, Buckingham had secured some vague understandings from Richelieu about an alliance against the Hapsburgs, but the cardinal could not be pinned down. Buckingham's plans for the Palatinate expedition were predicated on the assumption that Mansfeld's army would land at Calais and march overland through eastern France to the Palatinate. At the last minute, Richelieu refused permission for the English and Scottish troops to land at Calais. This seems to have been part of a stratagem devised by Richelieu to get the English embroiled with the Spanish and to divert Mansfeld's men to assist at the defence of Breda. The transport ships were therefore compelled to seek another route to the Palatinate and proceeded towards the Dutch coast with only five days' provisions. Buckingham neglected to inform the Dutch that Mansfeld's 25,000 men were about to descend upon them until they appeared off Flushing and the Zeeland coast. The Dutch were utterly unprepared to feed so many men. As it was, they had trouble maintaining and provisioning much smaller armies in the field, and it was not the custom of Dutch communities along the River Maas to maintain large stocks of grain since they could usually depend upon river navigation remaining open to replenish their granaries. At first the Dutch were reluctant to allow so many unpaid, unprovisioned and undisciplined soldiers to disembark, and Mansfeld himself wished to keep his men aboard the ships for fear that they would desert. The transport ships were dispersed in the river estuaries. Some anchored along the marshy shores of the Walcheren Islands in Zeeland; others were strung along the south bank of the Maas in the Langstraat region near Geertruidenberg and across the river from Dordrecht.[40]

Some of Mansfeld's troops remained aboard their transports well into February. They were without provisions, and the few who had money to buy food found the food prices very high, and the Dutch officials refused to waive the usual excise taxes on their purchases. The winter of 1624–5 was unusually cold, and the estuaries began to freeze. Malnutrition, exposure and disease caused a fearful mortality. Lacking fresh water, the soldiers began drinking salt water. The dead went unburied, their bodies thrown overboard along with the comatose. The corpses remained strewn along the beaches until spring. Edward Grimeston tells us that 'this was a dismal sight for the surviving English . . . that they should be so inhospitably dealt with by those for whose succour they came to adventure their

[39] Rushworth, *HC* i. 153–4; Whiteway, *Diary*, 64–8; Dalton, *Sir Edward Cecil*, ii. 74–8; Tucker, 'Volunteers in the Thirty Years War', 68.

[40] Rushworth, *HC* i. 153–4; Stearns, 'Caroline Military System', 26–8; Dalton, *Sir Edward Cecil*, ii. 78–80; Tucker, 'Volunteers in the Thirty Years War', 69; [Garrat Barry], *The Siege of Breda* (1627), 98–9; HMC, *Thirteenth Report*, Appendix II (Portland MSS.), 116.

lives'. Many soldiers deserted. Some settled in the Netherlands; others sought refuge with the Spanish.[41]

When Mansfeld's expedition sailed from Dover, he was expressly forbidden by King James to become embroiled in the war between the Dutch and the Spanish. However, Mansfeld knew that his impressed English soldiers were in no condition to confront Tilly's veterans in the Palatinate. Indeed, some of his men were so poorly trained that they thought that the proper way to load a musket was to fill the barrel with powder 'from the breech to the muzzle'. Mansfeld decided that he would do better to lead his men to the relief of Breda, although his English colonels refused to disobey their sovereign's orders. When James died in March 1625, Charles I reversed his father's prohibition about allowing Mansfeld's army to assist at the relief of Breda. When the remnant of the 12,000 English soldiers who had sailed from Dover in November 1624 marched from Geertruidenberg to Breda in the spring of 1625, possibly only 7,000 remained, and that number was reduced by a half within two months. Very few lived long enough to die in battle. When Breda surrendered, perhaps 500 or 600 survived. Lord Cromwell's regiment probably fared better than most, with 220 surviving. Mansfeld retreated into the duchy of Cleve with the remainder, while Buckingham contemplated yet another military expedition.[42]

After the destruction of Mansfeld's expedition of 1624–5, Charles and Buckingham abandoned the Palatinate and the Palatine family, knowing that they could not expect further funding from Parliament for a land war. Despite official efforts to suppress popular discussion of Bohemia and the Palatinate, individual agents of the Palatines continued to raise money through collections in parish churches, and a number of English gallants remained devoted to the cause of Elizabeth of Bohemia, their 'queen of hearts'. Following the successful Dutch recovery of Breda in 1637, the new elector palatine, Charles Louis, successor to Frederick V, gathered together a small army consisting of about 4,000 cavalry, a single regiment of foot-guards recruited from among the veterans of the siege of Breda, and, together with some Swedish foot, attempted to regain the Palatinate. This expedition was notable because the future commander of the Royalist armies, Prince Rupert of the Rhine, accompanied his elder brother, the elector, and carried with him a number of English gallants who remained devoted to Rupert's mother, Elizabeth of Bohemia, such as Spencer Compton, second earl of Northampton, William, Lord Craven and Sir Richard Crane. In a battle with Imperialist forces at Lemgo, on the edge of the Teutoburg Forest, Rupert, Craven and Crane were taken prisoner by Colonel Walter Devereux, one of the assassins

---

[41] HMC, *Thirteenth Report*, 116; Grimeston, *Generall Historie of the Netherlands*, 1502–3; [Barry], *Siege of Breda*, 98–9; BL, Add. MS. 46,188, fo. 110.

[42] Grimeston, *Generall Historie of the Netherlands*, 1526; Dalton, *Life and Times of ... Sir Edward Cecil*, ii. 78–80, 110–11; G. Roberts (ed.), *Diary of Walter Yonge, Esquire*, CS OS 41 (1847), 81. Buckingham was apparently still trying to recruit another 1,000 men to send to Mansfeld as late as March 1625 (BL, Harley MS. 3638, fos. 98*v*–99*v*).

of Wallenstein, and his Irish Dragoons, and carried to the fortress of Linz on the Danube in Austria. During the three years which Rupert spent as a prisoner of war, he perfected his drawing skills and acquired his famous dog 'Boye'. Upon his release in 1641 he went to England and offered his services to his uncle, King Charles. Lord Craven had to pay £20,000 for his release.[43]

While the last tattered remnants of Mansfeld's force, which had been intended for the Palatinate, were perishing in the defence of Breda, Buckingham and Charles were contemplating a naval assault on Spain. No other option remained, because the opposition in Parliament would not vote the subsidies for another land campaign. Indeed, the sentiment was growing that Buckingham should not remain in control of military matters. In a speech to the House of Commons on 30 June 1625, Sir Robert Phelips reminded the House that there was no declaration of war against Spain, and no accounting had been made to Parliament of what happened to the men recruited for Mansfeld's expedition to the Palatinate or of how the subsidies appropriated had been spent. 'It was not wont to be so when God and we held together, witness that glorious queen [Elizabeth I], who with less supplies, defended herself, consumed Spain, assisted the Low Countries, relieved France, [and] defended Ireland.'[44]

The failure of the military and naval expeditions of the 1620s resulted not just from logistical deficiencies; they were also failures of command. The military and naval commanders who sailed to the coast of Spain in 1625 and the Isle of Rhé in 1627 lacked precise orders in both instances because Charles and Buckingham had not bothered to work out clear strategies in advance or to share their plans with immediate subordinates.[45] The command and logistical failures were a consequence of the Jacobean policy of peace; during James's reign military institutions were allowed to wither and martial values were disdained. Court favourites such as Buckingham had catered to the king's vices, and so dominated patronage that no room remained for counsellors of a martial disposition.[46] Advice was available from English, Irish and Scots veterans of the continental European wars, but although councils of war were constituted, their advice was ignored.

The practice of military commanders consulting councils of war was a well established part of the European military tradition in the sixteenth and seventeenth centuries, and wise generals valued the advice of such councils, which were usually composed of immediate subordinates and experienced colonels.[47] James I had established the Council of War in January 1621 to advise him on the technical aspects of raising and paying for a military expedition to the Palatinate. It was not

[43] Whiteway, *Diary*, 33, 158; E. Warburton, *Memorials of Prince Rupert and the Cavaliers*, 3 vols. (1849), i. 82–92; Fissel, *EW* 272–3; *DNB, sub* William Craven, earl of Craven (1606–1697); *supra* Ch. 4.

[44] Stearns, 'Caroline Military System', 33–5; S. R. Gardiner (ed.), *Debates in the House of Commons in 1625*, CS NS 6 (1873; repr. 1965), 31.

[45] Cf. R. W. Stewart, 'Arms and Expeditions: The Ordnance Office and the Assaults on Cadiz (1625) and the Isle of Rhé (1627)', Fissel, *W&G*, 112–32.

[46] M. Smuts, *Culture and Power in England, 1585–1685* (1999), 70.

[47] Robert Ward, *Animadversions of Warre* (1639), 209–10.

conceived of as a permanent organ of government, and its role was purely advisory. After the Council of War had met together for a month in 1621 and told James that an expedition to the Palatinate would require 25,000 men and cost in excess of £1 million for the first year—an estimated cost which was twice the royal income for one year—the king lost interest and the Council did not meet again.[48] The Council of War of 1624 was intended to be a more permanent body and was meant to appease the complaints from Parliament about control of expenditure. The new Council of War had an expanded membership, which included members of the Privy Council, and was also expected to advise on naval matters, which, of course, offended officials of the Admiralty Office. The desire of Parliament to gain some control over expenditure was, however, frustrated by the fact that the expertise of the members of the Council of War was military and not fiscal, although Fulke Greville, first Lord Brooke, had served as treasurer of the wars and chancellor of the Exchequer under Elizabeth.[49]

Buckingham liked to gather experienced soldiers around him during this period of war—especially if they were old Elizabethan veterans—but he did not allow them much latitude. Any orders which they wished to issue required validation by the Privy Council. The members of the Council of War were mostly kept busy doing small things, such as recommending unemployed officers who had been in Dutch service for commissions, negotiating rates of pay, coordinating the supplies and provisions for the naval and military expeditions and planning for home defence. They tried to speed up disbursements for soldiers and mariners whose pay was in arrears. They also took on the function of a superior court-martial, and they were allowed access to what foreign intelligence the government had gathered. But they were never allowed to determine strategy, which always remained in the hands of Buckingham, who had no military experience prior to the Isle of Rhé expedition. The Council of War was called upon, instead, to adjudicate questions of precedence among colonels. They cannot have been happy about this, but when the House of Commons called upon members of the Council of War to testify about the conduct of military affairs, they were all reluctant to do so, except for Sir Robert Mansell, who was ambitious for naval command.[50]

Patronage and symbolic gestures were probably more important to Buckingham than careful planning and strategy. When he was selecting officers for the projected naval expedition to the Iberian Peninsula, he gave command of a regiment to Sir Ralph Hopton, who was known for his personal devotion to Elizabeth of Bohemia. Hopton had escorted Elizabeth out of Prague following the Battle of White

[48] Stearns, 'Caroline Military System', 129–30. The Council of War of 1621 included military men such as Robert Sidney, 2nd earl of Leicester, Robert, 3rd earl of Essex, Henry, 18th earl of Oxford, Sir Charles Wilmot, 1st Viscount Wilmot of Athlone, Henry, Lord Danvers (later 1st earl of Danby), Toby, 1st Lord Caulfield of Charlemont, Sir Edward Cecil and John Bingham. All were veterans of the Irish and Dutch wars or had served under Sir Horace Vere on the first expedition to the Palatinate.

[49] Ibid. 134–5.

[50] Ibid. 134–5, 144–52; PRO, SP 84/118, fos. 200, 233; Rushworth, *HC* i. 213.

Mountain, and when the roads became too rough to continue by coach, the queen of Bohemia rode behind him on his horse; Hopton boasted about this singular service which he had rendered Elizabeth throughout his career as a soldier. By making use of Hopton, who was by this time an experienced soldier, Buckingham made the point that a descent on the Iberian coast 'was meant to avenge the wrongs done to the king and queen of Bohemia'.[51] Buckingham was motivated by Charles's resolve to make war on the Hapsburgs, whether in the Palatinate or Spain, because if he could earn a reputation for military honour and valour, it could bring him popularity and make his position as the king's favourite more secure. Moreover, as lord admiral, Buckingham would profit from any successful naval action because his office entitled him to 10 per cent of all prize money.[52]

Buckingham consulted the Council of War only in the broadest of terms, and came up with a strategy which was never refined. An Anglo-Dutch fleet of nearly 100 ships was to be assembled to carry an amphibious force of 10,000 soldiers in a raid on Iberian ports. This armada was to destroy naval and merchant ships, at anchor if possible, spoil provisions in magazines and secure possession of a naval base which the English navy could occupy in order to blockade the Iberian coast and possibly intercept the annual Spanish treasure fleet. The Spanish coast was thought to be especially vulnerable at this time, because a sizeable part of the Spanish and Portugese naval forces had been sent to Brazil in 1624 in order to put an end to the Dutch occupation of the north-eastern coast of Brazil. The instructions given to the commander of the expedition would be loose enough to permit part of the fleet, after achieving its objective of capturing a naval base on the Iberian coast, to sail to the West Indies to pillage port towns in order to recover the expenses incurred in outfitting the expedition, since Parliament was unwilling to pay the full costs.[53]

As had been the case when the first earl of Leicester commanded the English expedition to the Netherlands in 1585, it was believed that the honour of the English monarch required that the projected expedition be commanded by a nobleman of high rank. This was to have been the duke of Buckingham, but since Buckingham was recovering from an illness and apparently felt that he could not be spared from the diplomatic negotiations with friendly powers for the purpose of forging an anti-Hapsburg coalition, he appointed as his second-in-command Sir Edward Cecil. Cecil was an experienced soldier who had served in the Dutch army, but who was not a peer at the time of his appointment.[54] Thus, Cecil did not possess sufficient social stature to preside over the disputes about precedence which inevitably arose in any military operation of that time. His authority was also limited by the terms of his commission and military custom which dictated that he not undertake any action which was not supported by a majority of his council of war.[55]

[51] Lockyer, *Buckingham*, 275–6; Dalton, *Sir Edward Cecil*, ii. 98–9 and n.

[52] Cogswell, *Blessed Revolution*, 65–6.   [53] Stearns, 'Caroline Military System', 33–5.

[54] Cecil was promised a peerage, but was not actually created Viscount Wimbledon until his return from Cadiz.   [55] Stearns, 'Caroline Military System', 37–8.

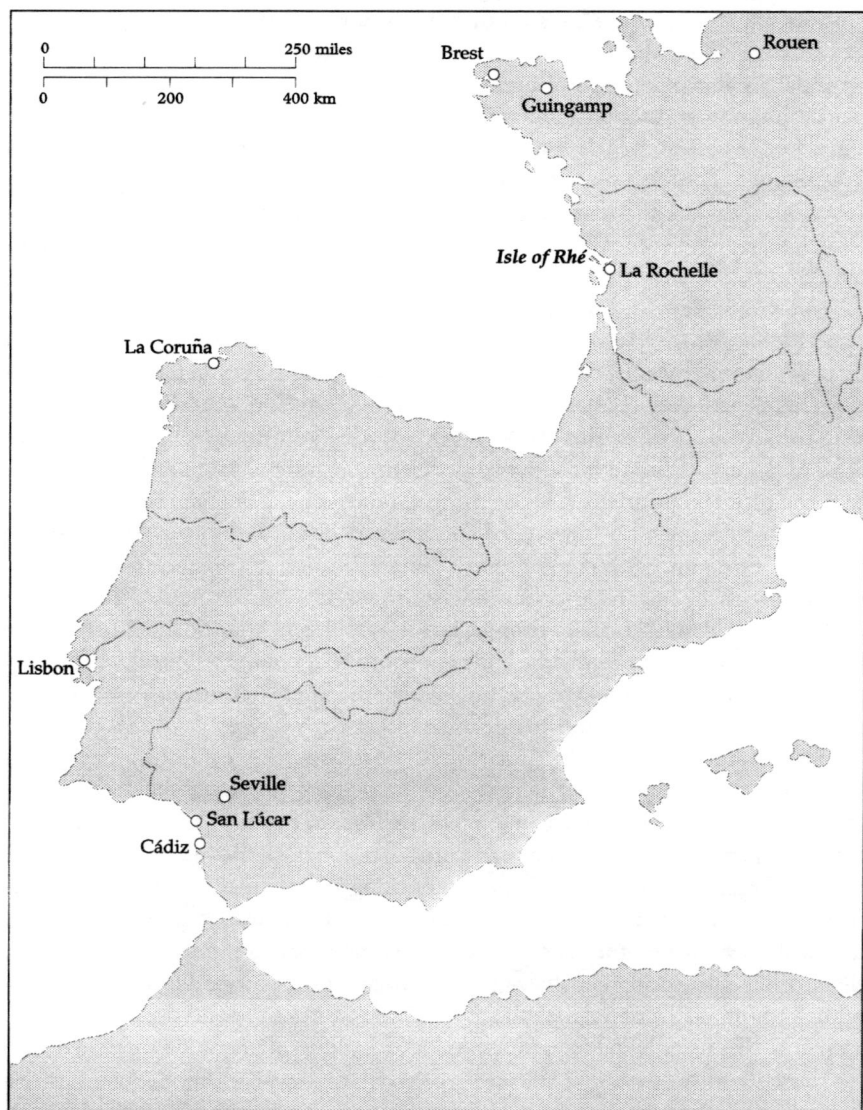

Map 5.1. English joint military and naval operations in the 1620s

There was bound to be bickering among Cecil's subordinates. King Charles had wished to see the earl of Essex assume a leading role in the naval expedition because of the prestige which attached to his name, and wished to appoint him a vice-admiral. But Buckingham had no wish to share glory with Essex, and the latter was instead offered the colonelcy of a regiment. Essex at first refused to accept the commission, which would have meant serving under Cecil, whom he regarded as a social inferior. A number of Charles's advisers were determined to have Essex accompany the expedition, so Buckingham was forced to offer him the position of second-in-command under Cecil with the rank of colonel-general in place of Sir John Ogle, a veteran of the Dutch wars with more experience than Essex. Essex again refused. The king himself intervened and persuaded him to accept the position of vice-admiral and commander of one of the three naval squadrons as well as colonel of a regiment of foot. Essex could not very well refuse his sovereign's command.[56]

There was widespread disapproval of placing Cecil in charge of the expedition to the Iberian Peninsula—both among his subordinate officers and the public at large. William Whiteway thought that Essex and others among Cecil's subordinate officers 'were very ready and forward to any service'. It would also have made sense to have placed Sir Robert Mansell, the vice-admiral of England, in command of the expedition if his superior the lord admiral could not lead, and indeed, the naval officers complained when this did not happen, but Mansell did not get along with Buckingham. Joint naval and military or amphibious operations have always been fraught with danger in any century, especially when sea officers and generals-at-sea are not in the habit of consulting one with another.[57]

That the fleet sailed from Plymouth late in the North Atlantic hurricane season (8 October) was undoubtedly the fault of subordinates in the Admiralty office and sea officers. Even when they sailed out of Plymouth Haven many ships were not adequately provisioned and some proved unseaworthy. Most ships had to reduce rations a few days after getting under way. The flagship *Anne Royal* was beset with loose masts and 5,000-pound pieces of ordnance careering across the decks, which Cecil blamed on the negligence of officers. Because of the lax discipline among the ships' masters, the fleet, which was composed of both Royal Navy ships and impressed merchantmen, had difficulty holding together; this may explain why Cecil, whom his naval subordinates called 'Sitstill', delayed calling a council of war until they reached the Iberian coast, when he revealed the secret orders to his fellow officers. Buckingham had given Cecil a choice of four Iberian ports, San Lucar, Lisbon, Cadiz or Seville, one of which he was to seize and use as an English naval base. But, with inadequate charts and little in the way of intelligence, it was difficult to determine which port offered the best conditions and the best prospect of a successful assault. Cecil and members of his council of war had also neglected to question the masters of merchantmen which they had encountered concerning conditions in the Iberian ports. Cecil scrupulously followed the advice of his council of war, but they often gave him bad advice. The evidence upon which they usually offered advice was hearsay in nature and was gathered in a

[56] Snow, *Essex*, 125–9.

[57] Whiteway, *Diary*, 77; *Epistolae Ho-Elianae, or the Familiar Letters of James Howell*, 2 vols. (1907), i. 316–19; Dalton, *Sir Edward Cecil*, ii. 191.

haphazard manner. Even as they arrived off the coast of Spain such basic strategic questions as whether to go after the plate fleet (the annual treasure fleet) first or secure a naval base were as yet unresolved.[58]

Cecil's fleet was scattered and failed to maintain secrecy, as beacons along the Portuguese coast revealed. Cecil and his council of war considered raiding San Lucar, but rejected that idea when they learned that there were sandbars at the mouth of the harbour. The decision was then taken to descend upon Cadiz, but then they learned that the city of Cadiz was strongly fortified and defended by heavy guns. Cecil might have benefited from a surprise attack on the ships anchored in the Bay of Cadiz, but the English captains and masters failed to obey his orders to put on full sail, maintain a tight formation and be cleared for action as they sailed into the Bay of Cadiz. This gave the Spanish naval fleet and merchantmen time to cut their cables and shelter under the guns of Fort Puntal at the narrowest part of the bay. Only Essex's squadron had obeyed orders. The fire from the eight large guns of Fort Puntal was deadly and accurate, and the Anglo-Dutch fleet had difficulty drawing close enough to bombard the fortress. Their naval guns had no effect, so Cecil ordered that soldiers be landed close to Puntal to take it by assault or threat of assault. The amphibious operation was hampered by bickering concerning precedence among the colonels and their regiments, but eventually Sir John Burgh and his men secured the surrender of Fort Puntal and its garrison of 119 men.[59]

At the same time that he ordered Sir John Burgh to assault Fort Puntal, Cecil also issued the command to his sea officers to attack the Spanish merchantmen of the West Indies fleet, which were preparing to sail and were still at anchor in the Bay of Cadiz. It was expected that as more troops and provisions were unloaded in order to lessen the draft of the ships they would be able to move closer to shore and be within range to begin the bombardment. However, the supplies and provisions were stored in such a way that they could not be unloaded regiment by regiment, and Sir John Burgh's Regiment and some other contingents went ashore without biscuit and water in their knapsacks. Some of the soldiers had also been assigned the task of filling the ships' casks with fresh water, which was running very low. The ships' captains refused to carry out the orders to bombard the Spanish merchantmen, and the soldiers complained that they could not march without refreshment. Cecil then gave the order to raid nearby wine-cellars and give out measured amounts of wine, but it turned out that huge amounts of wine had been stored for the West Indies fleet, and discipline broke down as the soldiers became

---

[58] Sir Edward Cecil, Viscount Wimbledon, *A Journal and Relation of the Action... upon the Coast of Spaine, 1625* (1626), 3–4, 6–8; BL, Harley MS. 3638 [Edward Cecil, Viscount Wimbledon's 'Journal of the Spanish Expedition'], fos. 109–13; Dalton, *Sir Edward Cecil*, ii. 191; Stearns, 'Caroline Military System', 38–41; N. A. M. Rodger, *The Safeguard of the Sea: A Naval History of Britain, 660–1649* (1997), 358; PRO, SP 16/10/67. Dalton thought the author of this last item, a manuscript journal of the Cadiz expedition, was Sir William St Leger.

[59] Cecil, *Journal, 1625*, 9–16; PRO, SP 16/10/67; BL, Harley MS. 3638, fos. 109–13.

drunk by whole regiments consuming a beverage to which they were not accustomed. Much of the expedition's beer had been stored aboard the *Dreadnought*, and when Cecil asked that beer be delivered ashore, the crew mutinied and refused to do so. The captain of the *Dreadnought* then compounded the offence by attempting to conceal the mutiny. With the Spanish army marching towards them, there was nothing to do but retreat towards Fort Puntal, but not before 2,000 English soldiers, in a drunken stupor, were cut down by the enemy. There was not even a skirmish.[60]

Back aboard his flagship, Cecil called another council of war. The city of Cadiz was much more strongly fortified than it had been in 1596 when the second earl of Essex had stormed it, and it had been recently reinforced. The English had landed no siege guns, so an assault was ruled out. Sir Samuel Bagnall and the other ships' captains had failed to attack the West Indies fleet, pleading low tides and contrary winds. The council of war recommended instead that they pursue the annual Spanish treasure fleet, but before they got very far it became apparent that they lacked sufficient provisions and water to continue the pursuit and make it home. Moreover, sickness and death had so depleted the number of seamen that there were not enough remaining to man the sails and stand watch. Of the 150-man crew of the *Anne Royal*, by the time it reached Kinsale, Ireland, on 11 December 1625, 130 sailors had been cast overboard after dying, and the water in the hold was growing dangerously deep. Cecil and the *Anne Royal*, after completing repairs, did not get under way until 28 January 1626, and did not reach the Downs until 28 February.[61]

Sir Edward Cecil was widely blamed for the disasters which befell the Cadiz expedition of 1625 and for the failure to intercept the Spanish treasure fleet. Given the vagueness of his orders and the lack of intelligence, he could hardly have anticipated that the treasure fleet had sailed along the North African Atlantic coast—further south than it had done for the previous forty years. Although Cecil was a professional soldier, his experience was mostly confined to the regimental level of command. Moreover, he was only the deputy of Buckingham, and his orders from Buckingham, who had no military experience of any kind, were both vague and restrictive, and allowed Cecil little freedom without providing any specificity of strategy. Cecil was furnished with old, leaky vessels, such as his flagship the *Anne Royal*, which had been partially rebuilt from the *Ark Royal*, launched in 1587. The naval ships totalled only thirteen of the nearly 100 vessels in the Cadiz fleet, which consisted mostly of merchantmen and Newcastle colliers plus twenty Dutch vessels, and were rigged with rotten canvas and cordage. Competent vice-admirals, such Sir John Penington and Sir Henry Palmer, were employed elsewhere, and the captains and masters who accompanied Cecil were ill-disciplined and insubordinate. One captain, Sir Michael Geere, had actually

---

[60] PRO, SP 16/10/67; BL, Harley MS. 3638, fos. 109–13; Cecil, *Journal*, 13–17, 25; Stearns, 'Caroline Military System', 48–53.

[61] BL, Harley MS. 3638, fos. 109–13; Cecil, *Journal, 1625*, 20–3.

gone missing for five days 'wilfully' and 'without leave', and beat the master of his ship with a cudgel when the latter remonstrated with him about the need to follow Cecil's orders. Geere had earlier refused to obey orders when sent to reconnoitre the anchorage of the Spanish ships at Fort Puntal. The spoilage by dampness of food and gunpowder and the inaccessibility of the arms and provisions when landing the troops at Puntal was the fault of Henry Power, Lord Valentia, the expedition's master of the ordnance. Although siege guns had been carried with the fleet, they could not be located and unloaded prior to the attack on Fort Puntal. Cecil became the scapegoat for the disasters of the expedition, and was blamed for incompetence and irresponsibility which were pervasive.[62]

Charges of mismanagement were brought against Cecil before the Privy Council of England on 6 March 1626 by the earl of Essex and nine other naval and military officers who had been Cecil's subordinates, together with Sir Edward Conway, the secretary of state. Notable among Cecil's accusers were Lord Valentia and Sir Michael Geere. Of the ten subordinates of Cecil who complained to the Council, only Sir John Burgh and Sir Edward Harwood could be considered professional officers with battlefield experience. The others were either amateur gallants or creatures of Buckingham. Although Essex had accompanied Sir Horace Vere to the Palatinate in 1620, he did not stay long enough to experience battle, and spent most of his time recruiting or hunting at Chartley. Only a few professional officers, such as Sir William St Leger and Sir Richard Grenville, remained loyal and refused to be drawn into the conspiracy to make Cecil the scapegoat. This conspiracy represents a split between the experienced professional soldiers, who were mostly loyal to Cecil, and the inexperienced amateurs, such as Essex, who lacked a concept of military hierarchy, discipline or loyalty, and who pursued honour and reputation rather than military objectives. Buckingham's creatures dared not blame him for the Cadiz fiasco, but the members of the Parliament of 1626, called by Charles to vote more subsidies, did not hesitate to do so; they began impeachment proceedings against Buckingham instead of voting the taxes requested by the king.[63]

One would think that after two disastrous military and naval expeditions Charles and Buckingham would have paused to consider the wisdom of sending out a third. However, the decision to attack the Isle of Rhé was not as irrational as it might appear, although it cannot be said that Charles and Buckingham had learned anything from their previous mistakes. The decision was made in response to Cardinal Richelieu's failure to keep the pledge which he had made in the so-called 'French League'. This consisted of an agreement by Charles not to enforce the Recusancy Statutes against Catholics and to loan seven naval ships to

[62] Dalton, *Sir Edward Cecil*, ii. 191; BL, Harley MS., fos. 109–13; Cecil, *Journal*, 25; Stearns, 'Caroline Military System', 41–2, 66–7; Rodger, *Safeguard of the Sea*, 357–8; Stewart, 'Arms and Expeditions', 284.

[63] Dalton, *Sir Edward Cecil*, ii. 248–52; Lockyer, *Buckingham*, 313–15. Among the leaders associated with John Pym and Sir John Eliot in the impeachment proceedings against Buckingham was John Holles, 1st earl of Clare (Gervase Holles, *Memorials of the Holles Family, 1493–1656*, ed. A. C. Wood, CS 3rd ser. 60 (1937), 102).

the French in exchange for their support for the Mansfeld expedition of 1624–5. The French, of course, did not provide that assistance, even though Charles had agreed to toleration for Catholics. The French had also used the seven English naval vessels to blockade La Rochelle, the last remaining fortified stronghold of the French Huguenots, whom Charles had promised to help. This had proved to be very embarrassing for Charles and caused problems with Parliament. So the Isle of Rhé expedition was, once again, intended to vindicate Charles's frequently wounded honour as well as to carry out his pledge to assist the Huguenots.[64]

King Charles gave Buckingham complete authority over the expedition to assist the Huguenots in retaining La Rochelle. Although everyone anticipated war between the French crown and the Huguenots, hostilities had not actually begun. Considering the difficulties, the maintenance of secrecy would probably have given the English an advantage, but Buckingham bragged about his coming exploits before the expedition sailed, so the French were forewarned and had time to strengthen their defences on the Isle of Rhé which guarded the entrance to the harbour of La Rochelle. Indeed, Buckingham wasted valuable time enjoying masques and farewell feasts while his soldiers, pent up in transport ships anchored in the Thames, were dying at the rate of fifty per day. The main part of the fleet finally sailed from Portsmouth on 27 June 1627. In all, there were 100 ships carrying not quite 6,000 foot, organized into seven regiments, and 1,000 horse, the latter of which were mostly drawn from the household servants and followers of Buckingham. Many of the foot were recently pressed, but some of the troops were veterans of Cadiz who had been kept standing and billeted along the southern coast from Kent to Devon, where they had spent their time quarrelling with their landlords instead of training.[65]

Buckingham held one council of war on the voyage to La Rochelle. Unlike the terms specified in Sir Edward Cecil's commission for the Cadiz expedition, Buckingham was not obliged to accept the advice of his council, and he frequently rejected it. William Fleetwood, whose views accurately represented those of professional soldiers, complained that Buckingham would not accept any recommendations which 'circumspect commanders under him propounded as behoveful', and was determined not to do anything 'but what proceeded from his study and approbation'. Even Lord Herbert of Cherbury, an amateur gallant whom Buckingham had appointed ambassador to the king of France, thought that the time was inopportune and that the expedition lacked clear objectives. Since many of

[64] S. L. Adams, 'The Road to La Rochelle: English Foreign Policy and the Huguenots, 1610–1629', *HSP* 22 (1975), 425–8; T. Cogswell, 'Prelude to Ré: The Anglo-French Struggle over La Rochelle, 1624–7', *History*, 71 (1986), 1–21; id., 'Foreign Policy and Parliament: The Case of La Rochelle, 1625–1626', *EHR* 99 (1984), 244; BL, Add. MS. 18,979 (Fairfax Correspondence), fo. 11; William Fleetwood, *An Unhappy View of the Whole Behaviour of my Lord Duke of Buckingham at . . . the Isle of Rhee* (1648), in Sir W. Scott (ed.), *Somers Tracts*, 13 vols. (1809–15), v. 399.

[65] Stearns, 'Caroline Military System', 83–8; Thomas Birch, *The Court and Times of Charles I*, ed. R. F. Williams, 2 vols. (1848), i. 225; Fleetwood, *Unhappy View*, v. 399; Fissel, *EW* 263; Whiteway, *Diary*, 89

the regimental commanders who sat on the council of war were relatives and followers of Buckingham, they seldom questioned his decisions. Because the Huguenot leaders of La Rochelle still hoped to negotiate with Richelieu when Buckingham's expedition arrived, they were not yet ready to accept English help, so Buckingham landed instead on the Isle of Rhé. Because of continuing financial problems, the fleet was not adequately provisioned, and the Isle of Rhé offered poorer prospects for victualling than the mainland. Nor could Buckingham be sure that reinforcements and more provisions would follow.[66]

The Isle of Rhé had not been the primary objective of Buckingham's expedition, but the governor of the island's garrison was in a position to obstruct an English descent on La Rochelle, so the island had to be secured. Under cover of a bombardment by the English fleet, a landing was effected within the space of three hours, which was more orderly than the landing at Puntal on the Cadiz expedition. However, the amphibious forces failed to reconnoitre and secure the sand-dunes behind the beaches, and French foot and horse were able to exact a terrible toll as some of the soldiers broke ranks and drowned in the surf. Buckingham's council of war advised him to capture Fort de la Prée, the lesser of two fortifications on the island, in order to protect a retreat if necessary. Buckingham, thirsting for a taste of military glory, ignored this advice, and instead chose to lay siege to the citadel of St Martin, which the professional soldiers on his council of war regarded as nearly impregnable. In the only battle in which he ever participated—more of a mock battle than a real engagement— he led his army in the capture of the town of St Martin, which was inhabited largely by the wives and children of the French garrison. Buckingham drove them into the citadel with gunfire so as to consume the garrisons' provisions the sooner. After calling upon the governor of the garrison to surrender and receiving a negative answer, Buckingham ordered siege trenches to be dug and began a two-month siege. He came close to compelling the French to surrender, but a French naval squadron was able to break the English blockade of Rhé and reprovision the fortress, while Buckingham's forces were almost at the end of their victuals. There was no hope of lifting the French royalist siege of La Rochelle after Richelieu, who had personally assumed command, began to build a mole across the harbour. Buckingham had no choice remaining but to withdraw from Rhé. But this was not before he attempted, against the advice of his council of war, a frontal assault on the citadel of St Martin in order to vindicate his honour. Many were killed, wounded or captured, whom he abandoned upon his withdrawal.[67]

[66] Stearns, 'Caroline Military System', 95–113; Fleetwood, *Unhappy View*, v. 399; Lockyer, *Buckingham*, 375; Edward, Lord Herbert of Cherbury, *Expedition to the Isle of Rhé* (1860), 42–5, 50.

[67] Stearns, 'Caroline Military System', 92–103; Herbert, *Expedition to the Isle of Rhé*, 84; Sir Philip Warwick, *Memoirs of the Reign of King Charles I* (1813), 21–8; Sir Richard Grenville, *Two Original Journals of Sir Richard Granville... II. Of the Expedition to the Isle of Rhee in France, Anno 1627* (1724), 263–5.

The assault on the citadel of St Martin had not only been made against the recommendations of the members of his council of war, who went to the length of putting their advice in writing, but it was also poorly executed. A delay in beginning the assault gave the French royalists time to land an additional 4,000 men on Rhé, which left Buckingham's forces outnumbered. The assault was begun in a heavy rain, with scaling ladders which were far too short to reach the parapets. The earl of Holland had failed to arrive from England with promised reinforcements and provisions after he had 'trifled away the time' in Plymouth. A convoy of thirty Scottish ships carrying 5,000 soldiers was on its way to reinforce Buckingham in October 1627 when it was broken up by a storm off the Norfolk coast and some of the ships driven aground. Buckingham's mismanagement at Rhé and the loss of forty-two officers (not to mention thousands of ordinary soldiers) caused 'much muttering', but the death of Sir John Burgh, Buckingham's second-in-command, was especially regretted. The professional officers and soldiers on the expedition would have preferred to have been commanded by Burgh, and their open discontent had led to factional disputes which Burgh had tried to compose. Burgh died in the trenches, according to Fleetwood, 'being clear out of all danger of the fort ... with a musket shot by an unknown hand. . . . The news and manner of this bred a new hurly-burly in camp, and ready we were to die upon each other's swords.' Sir Richard Grenville thought that the last hope of success on the Isle of Rhé perished with the mysterious death of Burgh. Burgh was given an elaborate funeral at the king's expense, accompanied by 1,200 soldiers of the London trained bands with their colours, pikes and muskets trailed. 'His body was interred near the tomb of Sir Francis Vere [in Westminster Abbey], whose pupil he had been in the art of war. . . .'[68]

If Sir John Burgh was made the heroic martyr of the Rhé expedition, Buckingham was despised and his name vilified. William Fleetwood's hostile account claimed that on the day that the French launched a major sally from the citadel, Buckingham was afraid to appear, and sent a subordinate dressed in his clothes. Buckingham also counterfeited wounds in order to affect valour, before his deceit was discovered a couple of days later. Fleetwood also reported that a French prisoner had asserted that the garrison of the citadel was near collapse, and that had Burgh lived they could not have held out much longer. The truth is that Buckingham behaved with more courage than Fleetwood would credit him with, but many of the officers and volunteers who followed Buckingham to Rhé found his courage, competence and leadership to be deficient. After the evacuation of

[68] Stearns, 'Caroline Military System', 95–103; Warwick, *Memoirs of the Reign of King Charles I*, 21–8; M. A. E. Green (ed.), *Diary of John Rous, Incumbent of Santon Downham, Suffolk, from 1625 to 1642*, CS OS 66 (1861; repr. 1968), 12–13; Granville, *Two Original Journals*, 14–17; Fleetwood, *Unhappy View*, v. 400; Birch, *Court and Times of Charles I*, ed. Williams, i. 281; Robert Markham, *The Description of that ever to be famed Knight, Sir John Burgh, Colonel-General of his Majesties Armie* (1628), unpaginated preface and 6–7; id., *Memoirs ... of Sir John Burroughs*, 12–14 . Cf. also Francis Rogers, *A Sermon preached ... at the Funerall of William Proud* (1633), sig. C3.

Rhé, two more fleets were prepared to relieve the defenders of La Rochelle: the first was led by William Feilding, earl of Denbigh, in April 1628, and the second by Admiral of the Fleet the earl of Lindsey in August. Denbigh 'said that he had no commission to hazard the king's ships in a fight and returned shamefully to Portsmouth'. In any case, they would have encountered difficulty breaching the mole and palisades which Richelieu was building across the narrow entrance to the harbour of La Rochelle.[69]

The perception by professional soldiers that the duke of Buckingham's mismanagement of the Isle of Rhé expedition had brought shame and dishonour upon their king and country provoked much scurrilous verse. The following excerpt from a widely circulated eclogue emphasizes the contempt of hard-core swordsmen for courtiers such as Buckingham, who was addressed as 'Thou great commander of the all go naughts [i.e., argonauts]':

> Stay, stay at court, and now at tennis play,
> Measure French galliards, or go kill a grey,[70]
> Venus's pavilions become thee best,
> Periwigs with helmets used not to be prest,
> To overcome Spain, win Cales and conquer France,
> Requires a soldier's march, no courtier's dance.[71]

Failing to secure, if not a victory, at the least an honourable display of martial prowess, individuals were driven to solitary acts of bravado: a gentleman volunteer rode his horse close to walls of the citadel and fired his pistols in defiance. For his pains he was killed by a musket shot, but the governor of the citadel ordered his horse to be returned to the English lines. An English captain of horse, encountering a French royalist squadron of 120 horse while on patrol, challenged a French cavalier to a single combat. George Monck began his military career inadvertently when his father, wishing to wait on the king when he came to inspect the forces at Plymouth, had his person attached for debt by the undersheriff of Devon (contrary to the latter's promise not to do so); Monck left the undersheriff close to death, and quickly volunteered to go to the Isle of Rhé. Monck went under the tutelage of his kinsman, Sir Richard Grenville, and later became an ensign in Sir John Burgh's Regiment.[72]

Many of the soldiers and mariners who returned from the Isle of Rhé were kept on active service for another year, but their pay fell in arrears, which caused outbreaks of mutiny among both officers and men in London, Westminster and Portsmouth. A mutiny began in Portsmouth on 22 August 1628 when a sailor who had insulted the duke of Buckingham a week earlier was condemned to die

---

[69] Fleetwood, *Unhappy View*, v. 401–2; Lockyer, *Buckingham*, 399–400; Rodger, *Safeguard of the Sea*, 360; Whiteway, *Diary*, 96–8.   [70] A badger.

[71] Green (ed.) *Diary of John Rous*, 22.

[72] Granville, *Two Original Journals*, 7; Herbert, *Expedition to the Isle of Rhé*, 51–2; Thomas Gumble, *The Life of General Monck, Duke of Albemarle* (1671), 1–4. Monck subsequently served in the Earl of Oxford's Regiment in the Dutch army.

by a court-martial presided over by Buckingham himself. News of this brought out a crowd of 300 sailors armed with cudgels and stones who attempted to rescue the condemned man as he was being escorted by a guard to prison. The mutiny was put down by soldiers, whose officers ordered them to fire over the heads of the mutineers, but several sailors were nonetheless killed. Officers of the fleet then arrived on the scene, followed by Buckingham at the head of 200 horsemen, who drove the sailors, at swordpoint, back aboard their ships. Two more sailors were killed and many cut down. When they were aboard, the duke accompanied the condemned sailor to the place of execution, where he was hanged by another mutinous sailor in exchange for his life. The following day Buckingham was assassinated by John Felton, a lieutenant in the army, who had served in both the Cadiz and Rhé expeditions. At the duke's funeral, companies of the London trained bands, having been ordered to trail their pikes, muskets and colours and to beat a slow march when marching in the funeral cortège, refused orders and, instead, shouldered their pikes and pieces and beat a more spirited tempo.[73]

Following the assassination of the duke of Buckingham, there was a resurgence of factional politics as various groups vied for Charles I's attention. The king grew more rigid in his views and more concerned with domestic than foreign affairs. The faction led by the earl of Holland and the duke of Hamilton attached themselves to the court of Henrietta Maria and favoured closer ties with France in order to cooperate with that government and the Dutch Republic in a military alliance to restore the Palatinate to Charles Louis. The birth of Prince Charles in 1630 weakened the Palatine claim to the English throne. Charles I revived interest in a marriage alliance with Spain; he disliked France and distrusted the Dutch because of their republican and Calvinist tendencies. He also regarded them as naval and commercial rivals. Effectively, Charles had abandoned the Palatines.[74]

For more than two years, from the winter of 1625–6 to the autumn of 1628, Charles I kept a standing army. That it was ill-disciplined and unpaid heightened the impact of war upon southern England where it was billeted, and led to the issuance of commissions of martial law and the use of the London trained bands to control mutinies and riots committed by soldiers, sailors and pressed men on the way to ports to be put aboard ships for the various expeditions of the 1620s or for service in sundry foreign armies. In late 1626, 300 unpaid sailors rioted outside the house of Sir William Russell, the treasurer of the navy, in Clerkenwell, and his house thereafter had to be guarded by militiamen from the London trained bands. Close to the same time, six captains who had served in Ireland without being paid burst into Buckingham's chamber in Whitehall Palace to

---

[73] W. H. Long (ed.), *The Oglander Memoirs: Extracts from the MSS. Of Sir John Oglander, Kt., of Nunwell, Isle of Wight* (1888), 45–6 n.; Green (ed.), *Diary of John Rous*, 27, 31; Lockyer, *Buckingham*, 453.

[74] L. J. Reeve, *Charles I and the Road to Personal Rule* (1989), 180–1; Sharpe, *The Personal Rule of Charles I*, 174.

demand their pay. The duke's threat to try them by martial law and hang them did not deter the officers in the least, so Buckingham became more conciliatory and promised to obtain their pay. Thereafter, Buckingham dared not appear in public without a guard. Demonstrations continued through the winter of 1626–7, and again, the London trained bands had to be called upon to keep order and to guard Whitehall Palace and York House, where the duke lived. Unpaid officers continued to petition for their pay, frequently demonstrating, and refusing to accept a partial payment. In February 1627 the Privy Council accused some of these officers of imputing tyrannical behaviour to the king. Unpaid and unemployed officers were involved in riots at the Inns of Court, and in July 1629 two captains were hanged for murders committed during riots at the Temple in which six citizens of London were slain and eighty wounded.[75]

Charles I's brief attempt to keep a royal army standing created a number of problems, and none were adequately addressed. Charles had raised an army which conscripted 1 per cent of the population. Although Elizabeth's government had impressed double that proportion of the total population, that levy had been spread over more than fifteen years, whereas the Caroline mobilization was concentrated into a period of about four years. The late Elizabethan wars had generally enjoyed the support of Parliament and the political nation; the Caroline war aims did not. This concentrated recruiting effort precipitated disorder and placed a severe strain upon the lords-lieutenant, the deputy lieutenants and the local magistrates and constables who had to carry out these tasks. The use of commissions of martial law, issued to urban magistrates and deputy lieutenants in the shires, raised serious legal problems. No one doubted the legality of martial law when used to maintain discipline in camps and on expeditions outside the realm, but most judges and lawyers believed that martial law was illegal at home as long as the common-law courts were still functioning. Yet, plainly, a military force at home awaiting embarkation for foreign parts could not well be held together without the use of martial law. These commissions were first issued in December 1624 to the mayor and other magistrates of Dover to execute martial law upon the many soldiers and mariners passing through that town. Parliament was especially anxious to avoid having the deputy lieutenants of counties employ commissions of martial law against impressed men passing through or billeted upon their counties, because it was conceivable that those officers might extend the use of martial law to the trained bands. It was widely believed that the deputy lieutenants had committed many abuses in the exercise of their offices by illegally impressing men, taking bribes to pass others over, by billeting soldiers and mariners upon civilians as well as by their abuses of martial law. Sir John Eliot recounted to Parliament the story of a Devon gentleman whose house was broken into by soldiers quartered in

[75] Birch, *Court and Times of Charles I*, ed. Williams, i. 175–6, 189, 191, 193; Whiteway, *Diary*, 94–6, 105; Manning, *VR* 214–17; K. Lindley, 'Riot Prevention and Control in Early Stuart London', *TRHS* 5th ser. 33 (1983), 109–26.

the neighborhood. When he complained to the commissioners of martial law, he was placed under arrest. Eliot saw similarities between the behaviour of the impressed men and the Roman standing army—an observation which was sure to strike a raw nerve in men who knew their Tacitus.[76]

Parliament was not prepared to pay the full costs of these expeditions without major political concessions, which Charles was unwilling to make—and probably not even then. Thus Charles resorted to raising money by means of the so-called Forced Loan. The members of the political community had been willing to accept the impressment of vagrants and masterless men as a means of social cleansing, but Charles was also determined to impress subsidy men who refused to contribute to the Forced Loan. Members of the Privy Council, including martial men, tried to tell the king that this was illegal, and in a couple of instances his orders were countermanded. However, there can be no doubt that taxpayers were impressed for service in the English regiments of the Dutch army seconded to the king of Denmark's army under the command of Sir Thomas Morgan. Some of them refused to be impressed, and the question was raised whether they could be punished by martial law. Lord Keeper Coventry was at first reluctant to question the king's actions and kept silent, but when urged by his colleagues to render an opinion, he said that the subsidy men who had resisted being impressed could not be punished by martial law unless they had actually accepted press money and subsequently deserted their colours.[77]

The provinces of England felt the impact of war in other ways as well. Many port towns experienced an economic slump because of the wars of the 1620s. Exeter was hit especially hard because most of its trade originated in France and Spain. Also, large numbers of mariners and other artificers were impressed into naval and military service. Because the armadas sent to Cadiz and the Isle of Rhè required many of the ships of the Royal Navy, large parts of the British Isles were left unprotected and exposed to the depredations of pirates from Dunkirk, the Barbary Coast and elsewhere. When ships carrying provisions for the English forces on the Isle of Rhè were damaged by a storm off the coast of Ireland, they were plundered by Irish wreckers and pirates at Youghal. The lord deputy, Henry Carey, first Viscount Falkland, blamed the incident on the lack of naval ships to patrol the Irish coast.[78]

[76] F. W. Maitland, *The Constitutional History of England* (1909), 279–80; Schwoerer, *NSA* 19–20, 29–31; T. G. Barnes, 'Deputies not Principals, Lieutenants not Captains: The Institutional Failure of Lieutenancy in the 1620s', in Fissel, *W&G*, 61–8, 70, 77; B. W. Quintrell (ed.), *The Maynard Lieutenancy Book, 1608–1639*, ERO, Essex Hist. Documents, 3 (1993), pp. lxxiv–lxxv; V. L. Stater, *Noble Government: The Stuart Lord Lieutenancy and the Transformation of English Politics* (1994), 40–4; id., 'War and the Structure of Politics: Lieutenancy and the Campaign of 1628', in Fissel, *W&G*, 86–109; C. Russell, *Parliaments and English Politics, 1621–1629* (1979), 358–9, 380.

[77] R. Cust, *The Forced Loan and English Politics, 1626–1628* (1987), 56–7, 322–3; Birch, *Court and Times of Charles I*, ed. Williams, i. 208; Rushworth, *HC* i. 419–20, 422; *supra* Ch. 3.

[78] W. B. Stephens, *Seventeenth-Century Exeter: A Study of Industrial and Commercial Development, 1625–1688* (1958), 14–15; Rodger, *Safeguard of the Sea*, 361–2; BL, Add. MS. 11,033 (Correspondence of Henry Carey, 1st Viscount Falkland), fo. 103.

When soldiers for overseas military expeditions were recruited and sent to ports to await embarkation, a substantial part of the cost was paid out of local rates, which did not require the approval of Parliament. Ratepayers in the counties underwrote the cost of 'coat and conduct money' as well as the expenses of feeding and billeting the newly impressed soldiers. They also bore the cost of maintaining Charles's short-lived standing army during most of 1626–7 and 1627–8. The cost of billeting Sir Piers Crosby's Irish Regiment during the winter and spring of 1627–8 was assessed upon the county of Essex, and produced much resentment which contributed to the St Patrick's Day Riots of 1628 in Witham. The soldiers had not been paid in many months, and so could not pay the bills presented to them by their landlords. The expense of billeting the soldiers appears to have been a greater grievance than their Irishness.[79] William Douglas, seventh earl of Morton's Scottish Regiment, originally intended for the Isle of Rhé, was billeted on the Isle of Wight awaiting further orders after Buckingham's return from Rhé. Sir John Oglander wrote that they were 'a proud beggarly nation . . . especially the redshanks or the Highlanders, being as barbarous in nature as their clothes'. Oglander claimed that they committed numerous felonies and left behind seventy bastards that he personally knew of. Just how dangerous and undisciplined soldiers billeted in southern England during the winter of 1627–8 could be is indicated by the disorders caused by a challenge to a duel between two officers of a company billeted in Woodbridge and a captain of the Suffolk trained bands. The captain of the trained bands, Sir William Withepole, and his second were both Catholics. The two army officers were Protestants. After an initial conflict left Withepole's second seriously wounded, the two army officers marched their company from Woodbridge while Withepole mustered his company of trained bands. They met and exchanged musket fire on Martlesham Heath. One soldier had his brains blown out by another soldier standing in the rank behind him. Withepole was made the scapegoat and committed to prison for trial by the Court of King's Bench.[80]

The military and naval expeditions of the 1620s, from Sir Horace Vere's inadequately supported campaign in the Palatinate in 1620 to the duke of Buckingham's botched expedition to the Isle of Rhé in 1627, demonstrated that Charles I lacked the political will, the necessary institutions, the competence of leadership and the financial resources to intervene in the continental religious wars on the Protestant side—a cause supported by many of the political nation of

---

[79] M. Braddick, *The Nerves of State: Taxation and the Financing of the English State, 1558–1714* (1996), 22–3; G. E. Aylmer, 'St Patrick's Day 1628 in Witham, Essex', *P&P* 61 (1973), 139–48. Crosby's Regiment defended the rearguard in the evacuation of Rhé, and Crosby was one of the few commanders who gained credit from that expedition. Despite the fact that Crosby was a Catholic, his regiment was briefly carried on the Irish establishment (A. Clarke, 'Sir Piers Crosby, 1590–1646: Wentworth's "Tawny Ribbon" ', *IHS* 26 (1988), 14–60; K. Ferguson, 'The Expedition to Rhé, 1627', *IS* 13 (1979), 369–72; BL, Add. MS. 11,033, fo. 92).

[80] Long (ed.), *Oglander Memoirs*, 36–42; Green (ed.), *Diary of John Rous*, 22–3.

England. This militant pan-Protestantism had been advocated by swordsmen and Puritans since before the official English intervention in the Dutch war for independence from Spanish rule in 1585. However, the apprenticeship of the English and Scottish officers and volunteers in the Dutch army had exposed those persons to modern military theory and practice, had gotten them used to the tedious routine of siege warfare and garrison life and had inculcated an increasingly professional and disciplined attitude towards their duties and an acceptance of the expectation which pervaded European martial culture that promotion and command, whatever one's social rank, were the rewards of long experience, beginning in the ranks, together with a measure of competence. James VI and I's policy of peace and his fear of the ambition of military men had discouraged peers from volunteering for service in foreign armies, and thus had diminished the available pool of military experience among the current generation of English nobility. Charles's sense of honour demanded revenge for the humiliations which he had suffered negotiating marital alliances with first Spain and then France, and he was briefly inclined to play the warrior-king without having the slightest idea of what this required under seventeenth-century conditions. His sense of honour also required that his armies be commanded by a nobleman of high rank—an idea which had caused failures of leadership even in the late Elizabethan wars. The duke of Buckingham had gathered around him old Elizabethan warhorses such as Sir Edward Conway, amateur gallants such as the earl of Holland, and a few competent professionals such as Sir John Burgh, but he was unwilling to listen to the advice of those who were experienced. Buckingham's management of these military campaigns emphasized the quest for military honour and glory, but his style of command did not lead to clear military objectives or coherent strategy. His failures brought shame and dishonour upon England in the eyes of swordsmen and the political nation, and ultimately precipitated a crisis of confidence in the ability and trustworthiness of the king to raise, manage and command the military forces of the crown. There were also symptoms of an increasing alienation between courtiers and swordsmen and, within the ranks of the latter, between amateur gallants and professional soldiers—although these fissures would not become fully evident until the end of the first English Civil War. Amateur gallants, such as the earls of Southampton and Essex, had continued to be more concerned with maintaining the social hierarchy within military forces and cultivating the chivalric virtues of valour and honour than in adapting their exertions to the changes in warfare brought about by the so-called military revolution.[81]

The experience of Caroline England with a standing army before the outbreak of the Wars of the Three Kingdoms was a brief one, but the disorders and depredations of untrained and undisciplined troops awaiting transport for overseas military expeditions—unredeemed by any military victories—was more than enough to awaken Tacitean prejudices against a Roman-like standing army. After 1628

---

[81] Fissel, *EW* 286.

Charles I preferred to invest his limited financial resources in the navy to insulate and protect England's shores, and to train a 'perfect militia' to mobilize yeomen and smallholder militiamen as England's ultimate line of defence. Without the partnership of Parliament and adequate funding no other course of action was possible, but these strategies did not take into consideration the possibility of invasion by Charles's own Scottish subjects, led by competent officers with experience in mainland European armies, across an undefended northern frontier.

6

The *campus martius*: the domestic school of war

Walled towns, stored arsenals and armouries, chariots of war...ordnance,
artillery and the like: all this is but a sheep in lion's skin except the breed and
disposition of the people be stout and warlike.... Neither is money the sinews
of war (as is trivially said) where the sinews of men's arms, in base and effeminate people, are failing.... Therefore let any prince or state think soberly of his
forces, except his *militia* of natives be good and valiant soldiers.

> Sir Francis Bacon, *Essayes or Counsels, Civill and Morall,*
> ed. M. Kiernan (1985), 91–2.

The Romans appointed a long and spacious field which they called *campus
martius*, wherein they exercised their youth in the knowledge of martial feats;
they likewise invented glorious triumphs which was to no other end but to
stir up the minds of the people to magnanimity and martial exercises.

> Barnabe Rich, *A Path-Way to Military Practices*
> (1587; repr. 1969), sig. A2*v*.

These are strange spectacles to this nation in this age that we have lived thus
long peaceably without noise of drum or shot, and we have stood neuters and
in peace when all the world besides hath been in arms.[1]

> *Original Memoirs Written during the Great Civil War, Being the Life of
> Sir Henry Slingsby* (1806), 22–3.

Lacking a standing army for home defence, England depended upon a select militia system which kept the more substantial householders at home and sent abroad
those socially less desirable persons whom the deputy lieutenants and constables
wished to be rid of. The training and modernization of the militia, begun in the
mid-Elizabethan period, was neglected during the Jacobean peace, but the outbreak of the Thirty Years War in Germany reminded Englishmen that the realm

---

[1] A meditation of Sir Henry Slingsby as a deputy lieutenant for the West Riding of Yorkshire upon
viewing the training of the light horse in 1639 in preparation for participation in the Bishops' Wars
against the invading Scots.

was exposed to invasion. This revived the old debates about the wisdom of arming the populace as well as the question of what was the best model for reforming the trained bands. Rejecting the concept of a standing army, many looked for guidance to the Roman *campus martius*—not only because the reception of Machiavellian thought in England favoured citizen soldiers over mercenaries, but also because of the belief that the exercise of arms fostered moral virtue. The command of the county trained bands would remain in the hands of lords-lieutenant chosen from among noblemen and courtiers, who were, for the most part, amateurs rather than professional and experienced soldiers. This would help to perpetuate, during the Wars of the Three Kingdoms and beyond, the growing tension between professional soldiers and amateur gallants which so troubled the military endeavours of the Three Kingdoms.

Training in modern tactics, close-order drill and weaponry was accomplished by sending to each county muster-masters who were professional soldiers and experienced veterans of the Dutch army. The cost of paying the muster-masters and providing for the training of the trained bands had been shifted from the crown to the county communities, and the militia rates for the upkeep of the trained bands nearly equalled the amounts of money raised by parliamentary subsidies and extra-parliamentary assessments, and angered ratepayers. It also made the members of local communities distrustful of the powers of the lieutenancy, which they perceived as no longer representing and guarding their particular interests. At the same time, the increasing burdens of administering the trained bands, impressing and billeting soldiers and collecting the militia rates, together with an unrealistic pace of officially warranted militia reform, weighed heavily upon the lords-lieutenant and the deputy lieutenants and accomplished little in the way of improving military preparedness, as was demonstrated by the poor performance of the trained bands during the Bishops' Wars. The best efforts at raising the level of military proficiency were demonstrated by municipal military societies such as the artillery companies of London and provincial cities, which, however, were often infiltrated by Puritans and manipulated for ideological purposes. The Honourable Artillery Company of London trained a cadre of officers for the City of London trained bands, many of whom gave their allegiance to Parliament during the English civil wars. Under their leadership and equipped with this training, the London trained-band regiments furnished the best infantry in the early days of the First Civil War, but, again, this mostly benefitted the parliamentary forces. Otherwise, the most competent officers and soldiers of the various English, Scottish and Irish armies of the Wars of the Three Kingdoms were drawn from among the veterans of the mainland European armies discussed in earlier chapters.

There were many reasons why England needed a trained militia in the late sixteenth and early seventeenth centuries. Before the middle of the seventeenth century England could not afford to keep an army standing for any length of time. Henry VIII had dissipated much of his monastic spoils on his numerous military adventures in Scotland and France. Charles I was unwilling to make the necessary compromises with Parliament which would have disposed that body to be more generous with parliamentary subsidies, and in any case, there is no reason to suppose that the taxpayers would have paid higher taxes unless subjected to the draconian measures for raising revenue to support permanent military forces which were employed in the 1640s.[2] Thus, a trained militia remained the only line of defence. England had a long tradition of an armed citizenry, dating back to at least the Statute of Westminster of 1285, and this principle of a universal military obligation for all males between the ages of 16 and 60 had been reaffirmed by Tudor legislation and practice. Although the county trained bands never developed into an effective military force before 1642, it helps to put the problem into perspective if one remembers that the English militia was the most highly developed system of obligatory military service in Europe, and with proper leadership, more frequent drill and adequate financial support something could have been made of it. In the days when archery skills were more widespread in the male population and a knowledge of the use of arms was not dependent on militia drill, an armed citizenry had served Henry VIII and his predecessors well, and if some of Henry's campaigns failed, it was because of the failure to give adequate consideration to strategy.[3]

The militia was not the best system of defence for England, but it was the only one which was compatible with English political culture before the Wars of the Three Kingdoms. The reception of Machiavellian and Tacitean thought was extensive and had reinforced an ungovernable prejudice in the political nation against standing armies and mercenary soldiers. It was a fundamental precept of Machiavellian thought that 'good laws and good arms' were the principal foundations of all viable political societies, and that citizens must bear arms and be prepared to go to war. A monarch who projected the image of being a successful warrior-king might have furnished a better focal point for the allegiance of his subjects than Charles I. Lacking such a leader, members of the trained bands and the artillery companies were apt to think of themselves as the defenders of the commonwealth, which is why foreign observers such as Montesquieu viewed England as a republic disguised as a monarchy.[4] A greater emphasis upon the duties of subjects to undergo military training and to be prepared to defend their country against foreign invaders was bound to promote political awareness and an interest in and a disposition to be critical of Charles I's foreign and military policy.

This did not lead to unanimity of opinion about the need to reform the militia. Returned soldiers such as Sir Edward Cecil, Lord Wimbledon, thought that one of the consequences of the long Jacobean peace and the neglect of the exercise of

---

[2] Fissel, *EW* 14, 19; J. S. Wheeler, *The Making of a World Power: War and the Military Revolution in Seventeenth-Century England* (1999), 14–15.

[3] A. Corvisier, *Armies and Societies in Europe, 1494–1789* (1979), 33–5; Fissel, *EW* 7–8; J. L. Malcolm, *Guns and Violence: The English Experience* (2002), 27–8.

[4] Niccolò Machiavelli, *The Prince*, trans. T. Bergin (1947), 34; Manning, *Swordsmen*, 21–2; M. Peltonen, *Classical Humanism and Republicanism in English Political Thought, 1570–1640* (1995), 209–13.

arms was the urgent need to convince many that England needed a well trained militia—especially after the revival of the mainland European wars. There had existed, he said, the assumption that being an island fortress, England did not need to be defended, but Wimbledon reminded his audience that England had been invaded before and could be invaded again, and modern methods of warfare made this an even greater danger. Writers and poets in the 1630s, such as Sir Richard Fanshawe, were certainly aware of this possibility. Fanshawe had written an ode in 1630 on the occasion of the king issuing a proclamation ordering the gentry to depart London and return to their country seats. Fanshawe assumed, in traditional Roman fashion, that the city was a place of temptation and corruption and that a return to the countryside would breed virtue. In the countryside, the gentry could better attend to their duties as deputy lieutenants and officers in Charles I's 'perfect militia'. At the same time, the muster-masters were keenly resented, not only for the increased expenditure on military equipment and training, but also for being instruments of innovation and outsiders in the county communities.[5]

For English military writers of the Elizabethan and early Stuart periods who wished to promote reform of the militia, the ideal model was invariably the Roman *campus martius*. Thomas Procter's *Of the Knowledge and Conducte of Warres* (1578) recommended reading the classical Roman historians to supplement the regular exercise of arms, and in particular, he urged the writings of Vegetius upon his audience.[6] Barnabe Rich insisted that the Romans exceeded all others in 'nobleness of courage and desire of martial glory', and held up the *campus martius* as a model for the early Stuart artillery garden. Like most military writers, Rich maintained that the exercise of arms in the *campus martius* instilled virtue and promoted good laws and the prosperity of the commonwealth. Neglect of the same brought the downfall of kingdoms.[7] George Wyatt says that his father, Sir Thomas Wyatt the younger, and his friends, including Sir William Pickering, Sir James Wilford, Sir James Crofts, Leonard Digges, the mathematician and military writer, and others, some of them professional soldiers, would meet periodically at 'martial banquets', where they would share their experiences and observations on military matters gathered from abroad so that they might be

[5] BL, Royal MS. 18. C. xxiii, p. 69; B. Donagan, 'Halcyon Days and the Literature of War: England's Military Education Before 1642', *P&P* 147 (May 1995), 65–7; G. Parry, 'A Troubled Arcadia', in T. Healy and J. Sawday (eds.), *Literature and the Civil War* (1990), 38–40; M. C. Fissel, 'Tradition and Invention in the Early Stuart Art of War', *JSAHR* 65 (1987), 133–47.

[6] [Thomas Procter], *Of the Knowledge and Conducte of Warres* (1578), preface. Subsequent editions of Procter's book were bound together with the English translation of *The Foure Bookes of Flavius Vegetius* by John Sadler (1572).

[7] Barnabe Rich, *Alarme to England foreshewing What Perilles are Procured where the People live without regarde of Martiall Lawe* (1578), sigs. Bijr & v; id., *A Path-way to Military Practice* (1587), sigs. A2v–A5r. The belief that the exercise of arms in the *campus martius* promoted virtue and countered effeminacy, sloth, lust and drunkenness is also expressed by Thomas Dekker, *The Artillery Garden: A Poem dedicated to all those Gentlemen, who practize Military Discipline* (1616; repr. 1952), sigs. C3–C4; Thomas and Dudley Digges, *Foure Paradoxes, or Politique Discourses* (1604), 40, 100; and Jean Bodin, *The Six Bookes of a Commonweale*, ed. K. D. MacRae (1606; repr. 1962), 603.

ready to serve their country in time of need. They wrote down such experiences and observations to compile a volume of military exercises which they 'did distribute among themselves', and which they had hoped to make available for use by Lord Protector Northumberland's government. Although the volume was lost, George Wyatt remembered enough of it, along with his extensive reading of Greek and Roman historians, to compose a 'Treatise of the Militia', *c*.1590.[8] Giles Clayton, who was a soldier for sixteen years in the Low Countries and Ireland, wrote in another military treatise intended for use by militia officers, that all great military commanders of antiquity had devised warlike games, such as the Greek Olympic games, for fostering martial skills and had provided public places such as the *campus martius* for the public exercise of arms.[9] Gervase Markham, who wrote a training manual for muster-masters, said that the original *campus martius* in Rome was situated next to the River Tiber so that Rome's citizen-soldiers could learn to swim as part of the exercise of arms.[10]

Inspired by the example of the Roman *campus martius*, proponents of the artillery garden movement in early Stuart England were also aware of the propaganda possibilities of theatrical displays. In 1638 William Bariffe, who later was to serve during the civil wars as a major in John Hampden's Regiment, together with fellow officers of the London Artillery Garden, staged a kind of military masque in the Merchant Taylors Hall in which 'Saracens' and 'Christians' engaged in a mock battle followed by displays of martial music with horns, pipes and 'Turkey-drums',[11] and the marching and counter-marching of trained-band militiamen to the accompaniment of fifes and drums. The theme of holy war and martial music offered a stark contrast to court masques of that period which celebrated the supposed halcyon days of the 1630s.[12] The poet Richard Niccolls, who as a boy had accompanied Charles Howard, earl of Nottingham, on the Cadiz expedition of 1596, reminded his readers of the ancient martial tradition of the citizens of London, which dated as far back as the time of Sir John Walworth, who slew Wat Tyler at Mile End in 1381, and according to the received version of those events, thereby preserved London and the kingdom from destruction at the hands of the rebels. Niccolls also quoted Tacitus on the usefulness of public funerals for military heroes for instructing young men about 'the soldiers' bloody game'. Niccolls derived part of his income from writing funeral orations.[13]

---

[8] George Wyatt, 'Treatise of the Militia (*c*.1590)', in D. M. Loades (ed.), *The Papers of George Wyatt, Esquire*, CS 4th ser. 5 (1968), 53–5, 57–61, 102; Digges and Digges, *Foure Paradoxes*, 40.

[9] Giles Clayton, *The Approved Order of Martiall Discipline* (1591; repr. 1973), sigs. A3*v*, A4*r*.

[10] Gervase Markham, 'The Muster-master', ed. C. L. Hamilton, *CM XXVI*, CS 4th ser. 14 (1975), 71.

[11] i.e., timpani or kettle-drums.

[12] William Bariffe, *Mars His Triumph* (1639), 1–7, 36; W. Hunt, 'Civic Chivalry and the English Civil War', in A. Grafton and A. Blair (eds.), *The Transmission of Culture in Early Modern Europe* (1990), 231.

[13] Richard Niccolls, *London's Artillery* (1616), 15, 39; *DNB*, *sub* Richard Niccols (1584–1616).

By 1626 the example of the citizens of London exercising arms in the Artillery Yard in Finsbury Fields led to the erection of military gardens in Westminster, Southwark and the liberties of the Duchy of Lancaster. Thomas Trussel openly stated what other military writers only dared hint at—that the monarch and his royal court should not only encourage the exercise of arms, but should also 'love arms', and by their own public example encourage their subjects to do the same. Before his death in 1612 Henry, prince of Wales, had done just that by exercising with a pike in the Westminster Artillery Garden.[14]

The imitation of traditions associated with the *campus martius* could be slavish and absurd. Since Roman soldiers did not possess stirrups among their equestrian accoutrements and customarily mounted their horses by vaulting, Gervase Markham insisted that modern cavalry officers and troopers should emulate the Romans by practising vaulting onto wooden horses! John Bingham, captain-commandant of the Honourable Artillery Company of London, was of the opinion that the greatest battles ever fought were those of antiquity, although he was willing to concede that some of those fought in the Low Countries, such as the Battle of Nieuwpoort, might rival these. Writing in the Restoration period, Sir James Turner had no use for 'speculative soldiers' or armchair theorists who had never been on a battlefield, who found foreign armies better than their own or who thought only the Romans had got it right. Among the 'speculative soldiers' whom Turner mentions with evident distaste were Machiavelli and Justus Lipsius.[15]

The English tradition of a universal military obligation of all adult males reached back to medieval times, but the emergence of the modern trained militia was shaped by attitudes assimilated from classical historians—especially Roman. The first characteristic of the select militia system which began to emerge during the reign of Elizabeth was that it was to be composed of the king's subjects rather than foreign mercenaries, and commanded by peers and gentlemen who were also magistrates, drawn, like the rank and file of the trained bands, from the same locality. By definition, the system was composed of part-time amateurs rather than full-time professionals. The social hierarchies of the county and municipal communities were to be preserved, which is one of the reasons why the urban trained bands preferred to muster separately—and protected from the corrosive effects of military hierarchies, which inevitably crept into martial culture as a result of prolonged warfare under modern conditions.[16]

A basic corollary of a militia which was to undergo training in the use of firearms was that a well governed state should never arm the poor. They were still subject to the universal military obligation, and were useful as pioneers and labourers for

---

[14] Thomas Trussel, *The Souldier Pleading his owne Cause*, 3rd imp. (1626), sigs. C5r, D2r.

[15] Markham, 'Muster-master', 701; John Bingham, *The Art of Embattailing an Army, or The Second Part of Aelian's Tacticks* (1629; repr. 1968), sig. A3r; Sir James Turner, *Pallas Armata: Military Essayes of the Ancient Grecian, Roman and Modern Art of War* (1683; repr. 1968), 353.

[16] Wyatt, 'Treatise of the Militia', 53–103; Sir Henry Knyvett, *The Defence of the Realme* (1906), 11; Matthew Sutcliffe, *The Practice, Proceedings and Lawes of Armes* (1593), 70; Schwoerer, *NSA* 13.

digging trenches and constructing fortifications and the like, but only property-owners should possess arms, armour and warhorses and undergo training in arms. The category of property-owners who were thought suitable to serve as trained-band soldiers included freeholders, farmers, copyholders of inheritance and other substantial householders. The weapons and armour of the trained-band soldiers as well as the mounts of the horse-bands were to be provided by clergy and laity with an income of at least £5 p.a. If their income was less, they were to band together with other individuals to furnish and maintain a weapon or a piece of armour, which was kept in a small armoury—perhaps located in the parish church.[17]

In a military treatise apparently written for King Charles I, Sir Edward Cecil said that a cavalry arm of the county militia was very useful for repressing civil rebellion and military mutinies, and bands of the gentry and their servants had played an important role in suppressing the Tudor rebellions and the Midland Revolt of 1607. These household servants of the gentry and aristocracy—most of whom were lesser gentry and yeomen—were never fully integrated into the county trained bands and did not appear at the common musters. Sir Henry Knyvett thought that these mounted bands of household servants should be merged with the horse-bands of the county militia. However, he wanted the horse-bands to be strictly limited to peers and gentry and their servants, and always to appear at the common musters. One suspects that he felt that this was necessary to preserve order among the foot-band soldiers.[18]

By general agreement, there were two constitutionally sanctioned methods of raising military forces for the defence of the realm. One was, of course, the levying of the trained bands; the other was the feudal array, whereby lords of manors called up tenants whose tenures specified an obligation to render military service. Such military tenures were still common in the north and along the Welsh border in the late sixteenth century. When invasion by the Spanish Armada threatened England in 1588, the nobility were still expected to levy private military forces from among their household servants, who were exempt from militia obligations, and from among their retainers and tenants, who were not. The array of the nobility's tenants and retainers on this occasion had the disastrous effect of depleting the trained bands. Again, this favoured the preservation of the social hierarchies of local communities over the military needs of the state, and illustrates the persistence of the conflict between the feudal idea of service to one's lord and the modern concept of service to the state.[19]

[17] Sir Walter Ralegh, 'Maxims of State', in *The Works*, ed. Thomas Birch, 8 vols. (1751; repr. 1829), viii. 27–8; C. Hill, *The World Turned Upside Down: Radical Ideas During the English Revolution* (repr. 1991), 19–20; C. Russell, *The Crisis of Parliaments: English History, 1509–1660* (1971), 244; L. Boynton, *The Elizabethan Militia, 1558–1638* (1967), 57; J. Wake (ed.), *The Montagu Musters Book, AD 1602–1623*, Northants. RS 7 (1935), pp. xxvi–xxviii, 55.

[18] BL, Royal MS. 18. C. xxiii, pp. 52–3; Boynton, *Elizabethan Militia*, 30–1; Knyvett, *Defence of the Realme*, 27.

[19] Schwoerer, *NSA* 13; Boynton, *Elizabethan Militia*, 301, 161–2; A. L. Rowse, *The Expansion of Elizabethan England* (1955), 362.

The early stages of the civil wars would demonstrate that both the feudal array and the trained bands were of limited effectiveness in raising troops for a prolonged war. Their survival into the 1640s was based upon the assumption of an inherent aristocratic superiority in military matters, and they were seen as the best means of preserving aristocratic power in the military affairs of the kingdom. Any effort to improve the standards of militia training and to increase royal control over the trained bands was perceived as evidence of royal tyranny. Although Lawrence Stone argued that the development of the Elizabethan trained bands 'destroyed the concept of a military elite', the holding of command in the militia reinforced the status of the peerage and gentry and also helped to revivify the martial elements in aristocratic and gentry culture.[20] The first qualification for the office of lord-lieutenant was always high rank within the peerage, and military writers always insisted that the company-grade officers of the trained bands should only be chosen from among peers, knights and gentlemen inhabiting the shires where the trained bands were levied. However, Charles I disrupted this militia system by purging those peers who opposed the Forced Loan, were suspected of being Catholic sympathizers or had to give way for favourites of Charles and Buckingham. These purges upset local patronage networks and were harmful to the effectiveness of the local trained bands.[21] Very few officers of the militia had actual experience, but that does not mean that they were indolent and ignorant. William Whiteway obtained his commission in 1622 as a subaltern in the Dorset militia because of his interest in and concern for the Protestant cause at the beginning of the Thirty Years War. He already knew enough French to read historians in that language, and his realization of the importance of the Netherlands in military affairs motivated Whiteway to begin learning Dutch. Bernard Mandeville thought that although the martial pose of militia officers was often affected, it served a useful purpose by elevating their character and providing a focus for their civic spirit or patriotism.[22]

At the beginning of the reign of Queen Elizabeth, activities at militia musters, which in times of peace occurred every three years or so, consisted of counting the number of men attending and viewing weapons and armour. No attempt was made to train the men, because the officers lacked the knowledge and experience to do so, and practical drill manuals and handbooks remained scarce until after 1585. Faced with the threat of invasion as well as the possibility of domestic rebellion, the crown began requiring that selected persons from the county militia should undergo training in the use of more modern weapons on a regular basis, which was specified as ten days in every year. The transition to the use of firearms in the hands of a selected group was very difficult, because detailed lists of trustworthy

---

[20] Schwoerer, *NSA* 15; L. Stone, *The Crisis of the Aristocracy, 1558–1641* (1965), 255–6; F. Heal and C. Holmes, *The Gentry of England and Wales, 1500–1700* (1994), 172.

[21] Knyvett, *Defence of the the Realme*, 30–2; V. L. Stater, *Noble Government: The Stuart Lord Lieutenancy and the Transformation of English Politics* (1994), 16.

[22] William Whiteway of Dorchester, *His Diary, 1618 to 1635*, DRS 12 (1991), 46, 49, 119; [Bernard Mandeville], *The Fable of the Bees: or, Private Vices Publick Benefits* (1714), 107–8.

men had to be drawn up, weapons were in short supply and there was at first a lack of officers sufficiently familiar with the new firearms to instruct the men in their use. In Lancashire, the deputy lieutenants undertook this task, but were unwilling to spend the amount of time needed for thorough instruction and drill. It was not until 1585 that the practice of employing professional soldiers as muster-masters to train the militia began. They were usually drawn from the queen's Yeomen of the Guard or veterans of the Low-Countries wars. The cost of maintaining these 'trained bands' was burdensome and eventually fell entirely on the county rate-payers. By the late 1580s the government was insisting that 40 per cent of the foot-bands be trained in the use of calivers and muskets. This imposed a financial hardship on counties such as Northamptonshire, where there was a shortage of firearms. At first the requirement of regular training was enforced only in the maritime counties, but with the threat of invasion from Spain the inland counties also had to conform to the more stringent training requirements. Northamptonshire's quota of foot-bands was set at 1,200 in 1587, but this was subsequently reduced to 600 because of the shortage of weapons and armour and the fact that 200 men were taken from the county for service in the Netherlands.[23]

In modern warfare, the effective use of infantry small-arms fire on the battle-field requires frequent and intensive training—especially for men who have never handled firearms. This was especially true in our period, since the type of firearms used by the trained bands changed from the mid-Elizabethan through the end of the Jacobean periods from arquebuses to calivers to muskets. Even with annual musters of ten days a year (which occurred only when foreign invasion threatened), this amount of training would have been inadequate for the 'trained-bands shot', those of the foot who were armed with firearms. Actually, the training at musters appears to have been supplemented by musketry training by corporals who were in charge of sections of twenty to twenty-four men, and was provided close to their homes on a more frequent basis, which, in Hertfordshire, worked out to two days each summer. Here they drilled in the French manner in files, and learned the intricate exercises for loading and firing their pieces in volleys without injuring the ranks in front of them. How much firing they actually did is another question, since the government was very parsimonious and allowed an expenditure for the purchase of gunpowder and shot of only £3 per company. It is also unlikely that they learned much about tactics.[24]

---

[23] J. R. Hale, *On a Tudor Parade-Ground: The Captain's Handbook of Henry Barret, 1562* (1978), 2–3; B. Coward, 'The Lieutenancy of Lancashire and Cheshire in the Sixteenth and Early Seventeenth Centuries', *THSLC* 119 (1967), 50; J. Goring and J. Wake (eds.), *Northhamptonshire Lieutenancy Papers . . . 1580–1614*, Northants. RS 27 (1975), pp. xx–xxiii, 13–14.

[24] J. Wake (ed.), *A Copy of Papers Relating to Musters, Beacons, Subsidies, Etc. in the County of Northampton, A.D. 1586–1623*, Northants. RS 3 (1925), pp. lxxxi–lxxxiv; Gervase Markham, *The Souldiers Exercise* (1639; repr. 1974) [also published under the title *The Souldiers Accidence* (1635)], 8; A. J. King (ed.), *Muster Books for North and East Hertfordshire, 1580–1605*, HRS 12 (1996), 44. The corporals of the shot in the trained bands, when presiding over these special training sessions for the musketeers, were under the supervision of the muster-master rather than the captain of the company.

It was the clear intention of the Privy Council to convert the armaments of the trained bands from 'bills and bows' to 'muskets and pikes' as quickly as possible. The transition took much longer than was anticipated because of financial problems, the scarcity of firearms in the counties and the dead weight of conservatism. The transition was not assisted by the sentimental attachment of late Elizabethan authors of military treatises, such as Sir Henry Knyvett and Sir John Smythe, to the English longbow-man. Knyvett's military experience reached back to the Siege of Leith in 1560 and he never commanded more than a company, so his knowledge of the art of war was somewhat limited. In 1588 he was the muster-master of the Wiltshire trained bands, and the fact that three of his daughters married military earls gave him more influence than he merited. Sir John Smythe had extensive experience as a soldier of fortune in the European wars before he was dismissed from the colonelcy of an Essex trained-band regiment at the instigation of the earl of Leicester for questioning the legality of impressment and other intemperate remarks. Smythe also incurred the wrath of the government for saying that the official policy of denying arms and military training to the propertyless was pursued by tyrants who had good reason to fear popular revolts.[25] Robert Barret's *The Theoricke and Practicke of Modern Warres* (1598) was better suited to the needs of a militia making the transition to firearms, but Barret was unrealistic in thinking that the ideal captain of a trained-band company would be an experienced professional soldier who had risen through the ranks. Professional soldiers who had spent their careers overseas were out of touch with the realities of landed society at home, where aristocratic amateurs expected to be given militia commissions based on their social rank and were not tolerant of professional soldiers.[26]

In the summer of 1588, when it became clear that a Spanish invasion was preparing, the Privy Council began establishing quotas of train-soldiers which each county was to send to London to defend the queen and court. Northamptonshire was at first assessed 400 of the 600 men enrolled in the foot-bands to join an army of 4,000, but later the Council ordered the deputy lieutenants to send all 600 footmen plus 100 horsemen and 200 archers if they could be found. The gentry of the county complained that they could not furnish the 100 horsemen. The county trained bands were summoned to London in late July and early August and lodged in the suburbs, towns and villages environing the metropolis; 4,000–5,000 men assembled at Tilbury, where they were reviewed by the queen accoutred in her silver cuirass. A larger number of troops gathered under Leicester in Kent. In London, one of the four trained-band regiments mustered every twenty days and trained for a full day under the command of a sergeant-major.[27] In many counties

[25] Knyvett, *Defence of the Realme*, pp. vii, x, xvi, xxiii, xxxi, 1–4; Fissel, *EW* 93; Peltonen, *Classical Humanism and Republicanism*, 112–13; Sir John Smith, *Instructions, Observations and Orders Mylitarie* (1595), sigs. ¶3v–4r.

[26] Robert Barret, *The Theoricke and Practicke of Modern Warres* (1598), 24–6.

[27] Goring and Wake (eds.), *Northampton Lieutenancy Papers*, pp. xxii–xxv; John Stow, *A Survey of the Cities of London and Westminster*, rev. John Strype, 2 vols. (1720), ii. 455b; Boynton, *Elizabethan Militia*, 161–3.

the trained bands ceased to train regularly until the threat of another Spanish invasion in 1595. As many as one-third of the trained bands in many counties still continued to be armed with bills and bows rather than muskets and pikes. Whether the trained bands exercised or not seems to have depended upon the individual lord-lieutenant. Left to themselves the deputy lieutenants were unenthusiastic about their military duties and found it difficult to persuade the ratepayers to pay the costs of impressing and conveying soldiers overseas and mobilizing and training the militia. In August 1599 the trained bands from many southern counties again mustered and assembled in London, where they trained at Mile End for the better part of a month in expectation of another Spanish invasion.[28]

Fortunately, there was no major Spanish landing in England and Wales, and the trained bands were never put to the test. The reign of King James I brought a period of peace between England and Spain and neglect of military preparedness. In 1604 the government moved Parliament to repeal the Marian Statutes of 1558 for holding musters and compelling landowners to breed warhorses and be ready to furnish light horsemen with arms and armour. The government seems to have regarded this legislation as defective and probably meant to enact new laws. The Militia Statutes of 1558 had been difficult to enforce and involved justices of the peace in militia administration—especially the collection of militia rates. The JPs had not been supportive of the Marian Horse and Armour Act of 1558, because the methods for making assessments for horses, armour and weapons were perceived to be inequitable. The deputy lieutenants were less interested in an equitable system because they felt pressure to get the job done. They had found the JPs to be obstructive and wanted them excluded completely from the militia administration. The repeal of the Militia Acts of 1558 caused confusion and mistrust among subjects, but the government assumed that it could rely upon the royal prerogative to muster the militia or to make assessments for militia rates. The issue of the legality of doing so was put aside because the government ceased to hold militia musters and training for several years. But when the government of James I found it necessary to resume mustering the trained bands following the Gunpowder Plot of 1605 and, later, the resumption of the European wars, the repeal of the Marian Militia Statutes provided critics with a pretext for linking resistance to the centralizing tendencies of the government and the lieutenancy to larger issues of constitutional principle.[29]

[28] Goring and Wake (eds.), *Northamptonshire Lieutenancy Papers*, pp. xxii–xxv; John Stow, *The Annales or Generall Chronicle of England . . . Continued by Edmund Howes* (1615), 788; B.W. Quintrell (ed.), *Maynard Lieutenancy Book, 1608–1639*, ERO, Essex Hist. Documents, 3 (1993), p. lxii.

[29] Boynton, *Elizabethan Militia*, 209–10; A. Hassell Smith, 'Militia Rates and Militia Statutes, 1558–1663', in P. Clark, A. G. R. Smith and N. Tyacke (eds.), *The English Commonwealth, 1547–1663* (1979), 100–1; J. Malcolm, *To Keep and Bear Arms: Origins of an Anglo-American Right* (1994), 7–8; R. Ashton, *The English Civil War: Conservatism and Revolution, 1603–1649* (1978), 56–7.

Despite his pacifism, James I was capable of energizing the militia if he felt personally threatened, as he did after the discovery of the Gunpowder Treason Plot in 1605. The militia officers also could respond to a sense of emergency, but with few exceptions, the Jacobean Privy Council, the lieutenants and deputy lieutenants failed to focus upon the lack of preparedness of the trained bands and to hold regular musters. The disinclination of the country gentry to breed warhorses and to practise equestrian skills made it increasingly difficult to keep up the horse-bands. The modernization of the foot-bands lagged behind, and bills and bows were not totally banished in favour of pikes and calivers until early in the Jacobean period, by which time the shot should have completed the change to muskets with their heavier firepower. The trained bands of the maritime counties were slightly better trained than those of the inland counties, but much depended upon the energy of individual lieutenants such as Thomas Cecil, first earl of Exeter, in Northamptonshire and Henry Hastings, fifth earl of Huntingdon, in Leicestershire, whose conscientiousness incurred the wrath of their county communities.[30]

The musters of the trained bands resumed in 1613 after a lapse of five years because of the fear of invasion by Ambrose Spinola's Army of Flanders. From this date, more attention was paid to training and modernizing the trained bands. The fear of an internal uprising, generated by the Gunpowder Plot, had not subsided, and the deputy lieutenants' orders in Northamptonshire cited 'the boldness and assurance which the recusants had taken of late' as another reason for reviving the musters of the trained bands. The increased need for weapons and armour, which continued to be in short supply, also provided another excuse for confiscating those of the recusant gentry. The earl of Exeter's enthusiasm for mustering and training tended to run ahead of that of his deputy lieutenants in Northamptonshire, who engaged in considerable foot-dragging. The latter better understood the popular resentment of the expense of Exeter's frequent musters of the trained bands, which they knew had not been authorized by the Privy Council, and so they obliquely questioned his authority to do so.[31]

Beginning in 1616, the Privy Council began ordering annual musters of the trained bands. In a further effort to modernize the trained bands, the Council specified that all calivers were to be replaced by muskets, each of which cost 26*s*. Their immediate replacement would have entailed considerable expense for the ratepayers. Contrary to the Council's orders, the deputy lieutenants of Northamptonshire took it upon themselves to replace the calivers gradually.

---

[30] C. H. Firth, *Cromwell's Army: A History of the English Soldier during the Civil Wars, Commonwealth and Protectorate* (repr. 1962), 6; Quintrell (ed.), *Maynard Lieutenancy Book*, pp. lxii, lxvi–lxvii, 135; Edward Davies, *The Art of War and England's Traynings* (1619; repr. 1968), preface; T. Cogswell, *Home Divisions: Aristocracy, the State and Provincial Conflict* (1998), 21–2; A. Fletcher, *A County Community in Peace and War: Sussex, 1600–1660* (1975), 182–3.

[31] Boynton, *Elizabethan Militia*, 212–14; Wake (ed.), *Montagu Musters Book*, pp. xliii, xlv, liv, lv; K. Sharpe, *The Personal Rule of Charles I* (1992), 26–7.

Although most of them had been replaced by 1617, the process of rearming was still incomplete. The lord-lieutenant, the earl of Exeter, was also unhappy with the failure of the deputy lieutenants to muster more horse. He wanted 100 horse mustered in the same place and at the same time (to prevent the same person and the same horse appearing more than once). This would have been in conformity with Elizabethan standards for the horse-bands, and Exeter could not understand why the deputy lieutenants failed to muster that number, since 'so many gentlemen do inhabit' Northamptonshire.[32] Victor Slater has observed that before the mainland European wars resumed after 1618, the function of militia musters was 'more social and political than military', and helped to promote a sense of community which, to some extent, worked against the ever-present tendency towards factionalism in the county community. Little was accomplished in the way of reforming the trained bands during the reign of James I. Indeed, the efforts of the more conscientious and active lieutenants to create a more efficient militia system severely strained the relationship between the crown and the local communities.[33]

Perhaps nothing poisoned these relations as much as the intrusion of professional soldiers and outsiders into the training of the county trained bands. Before the mobilization of the trained bands at the time of the Armada of 1588, muster-masters were often local men appointed by the Privy Council and their salaries were paid by the Exchequer. Thereafter, the Council urged the employment of professional soldiers, made the county ratepayers responsible for their salaries and gave the patronage of the office to the lords-lieutenant. It was a recipe for disaster. The muster-masters were paid between £20 and £40 p.a. at first and later as much as £80 p.a. for a few days of work each year. The cost was resented and the muster-masters perceived as mercenaries and intruders. Although they were supposed to train the captains, lieutenants and ensigns as well as the non-commissioned officers, some of the muster-masters, who acted on the parade ground as sergeant-majors, apparently regarded the trained-band officers as an irrelevance and gave their orders directly to the corporals of the files, who were the ones who actually trained the men. The professional muster-masters also spent more time and money on training and expended more gunpowder than did the militia officers, who, being drawn from the local communities, worried more about the cost; they also expected the train-soldiers to demonstrate competence rather than merely putting on a brave show. When the subsidymen refused to pay the muster-master's stipend, he refused to work.[34]

There was no going back to using local gentry unless they happened to be experienced professionals. So great was the reputation of Maurice of Nassau and his training practices that the use of English veterans of the Dutch army became all but obligatory, and was strongly supported by writers of military manuals such

---

[32] Wake (ed.), *Montagu Musters Book*, pp. lvii–lviii, 135.

[33] Stater, *Noble Government*, 24–5.

[34] Boynton, *Elizabethan Militia*, 178–81, 287–91; Cogswell, *Home Divisions*, 112, 196; Barret, *Moderne Warres*, 24.

as Henry Hexham.[35] At first muster-masters with experience in the Dutch army were scarce, but during the Eleven Years Truce they became more readily available. In 1617 James I began borrowing officers from the States' Army for periods of three months to instruct the trained bands, and he also had drill manuals printed for distribution. James told the Privy Council that he wanted the militia officers instructed on a daily basis by the Anglo-Dutch muster-masters and some of the train-soldiers mustered twice a week while the Anglo-Dutch officers were available.[36] However, James's efforts to improve the trained bands were too sporadic to bear any fruit.

The project to employ serving officers of the States' Army to improve the proficiency of the trained bands was revived by the duke of Buckingham in January 1626, and 100 'old soldiers' were to be seconded to the service of Charles I to serve as muster-masters, with two assigned to each of the counties of England and Wales. At first, the agreement was that the muster-masters were to be on leave from the Dutch army for only three months, but some of the officers of the English regiments indicated that they were willing to serve on a more permanent basis at home as muster-masters.[37] Gervase Markham, who had been a soldier in the Netherlands and Ireland in his youth, wrote a manual for use by the Caroline trained bands in about 1630. It was never printed until 1975—probably because of the offence Markham gave by accusing some of the lords-lieutenant of returning false musters. Markham also claimed that although Charles I had made an effort to improve the performance of the trained bands, they were not exercised as frequently as they had been during the late Elizabethan wars. In some counties the militia mustered only once every two or three years.[38]

The military duties of the lieutenants of the counties in the late Elizabethan and early Jacobean periods had included ordering musters, exercising the trained bands and pioneers and oversight of the maintenance and repair of coastal forts, magazines and warning beacons. With the coming of war between 1624 and 1628, the lieutenants and their deputies were also charged with many unpopular tasks such as pressing soldiers for overseas service, and clothing, equipping and billeting them when they were not actually overseas. The indiscipline of impressed soldiers gave the English a taste of the miseries of war, and the lieutenants also oversaw the work of the provost-marshals and collected Charles I's forced loans. Even before England became involved in European wars, militia rates nearly equalled parliamentary subsidies. Whereas the soldiers for the Elizabethan wars

---

[35] K. Roberts, 'Citizen Soldiers: The Military Power of the City of London', in S. Porter (ed.), *London and the Civil War* (1996), 92–3; Henry Hexham, *The Second Parte of the Principles of the Art Militarie: Practized in the Warres of the United Netherlands* (1637), dedication.

[36] BL, Add. MS. 46,188, fo. 81*r* & *v*.

[37] Whiteway, *Diary*, 79; BL, Add. MS. 46,188, fo. 93; Gervase Holles, *Memorials of the Holles Family, 1493–1656*, ed. A. C. Wood, CS 3ʳᵈ ser. 60 (1937), 75–6.

[38] Markham, 'Muster-master', 52, 60; E. Cope, 'Politics Without Parliament: The Dispute about Muster Masters' Fees in Shropshire in the 1630s', *HLQ* 45 (1982), 271–84; *Sir John Corbett* vs. *the earl of Bridgewater*, HEH, Ellesmere MSS. 7693, 7697.

had been drawn from among vagrants and cottagers, during the Caroline wars the authorities resorted to impressing householders and sometimes whole companies of the trained bands (who were supposed to be exempt from impressment). Local communities had not minded contributing money and men for their own defence during the invasion scares, but impressment required levying men—often neighbours who were unlikely ever to return home again. As the duties of the lieutenancy increased in the 1620s and 1630s, more officials were needed and this increased the scope of the lord-lieutenant's patronage and power, which was already resented. The assessments for militia rates, billeting and coat-and-conduct money had always been resented and ratepayers complained about the extortionate behaviour of deputy lieutenants, the taking of bribes to avoid impressment or the vindictiveness of impressing neighbours to settle old scores. Thus, the lieutenants of the counties had been placed in the increasingly difficult position of trying to act both as agents of the crown and the patrons of local communities.[39]

For these reasons, the lieutenants were not in a strong position to carry out reforms of the militia which Charles I called the 'exact' or 'perfect' militia. The term 'exact militia' derives from a set of instructions sent out by James I in 1623 to the lieutenants of the counties complaining that the training of the militia needed to be made more 'exact', as it was in the best model armies of mainland Europe such as the Netherlands. The idea for this order probably derived from the example of William, second Lord Compton (later first earl of Northampton), who, as president of the Council of Wales, had trained the militia in his jurisdiction to more exacting standards. It is likely that Sir Edward Cecil and Sir Edward Conway, both professional soldiers and members of the Council of War, also urged upon the king the necessity of raising the standard of training in the militia and imposing stricter discipline. This was probably done with the support of Buckingham, who feared a foreign invasion. Thus, in the reign of Charles I the term 'exact militia' became shorthand for carrying out a remodelling of the militia.[40]

The trained bands remained incapable of dealing even with minor disorders. In the spring of 1636 Sir Hugh Cholmley, a deputy lieutenant and colonel of a regiment of trained bands in the North Riding of Yorkshire, had occasion to muster 200 train-soldiers to deal with some Dutch ships which had seized a Spanish ship in Scarborough Haven; he found them so untrained that none knew how to handle their firearms except for a few former mariners. The trained bands were rarely used for suppressing popular disorders, because their reliability could not be taken for granted. On one occasion where a trained-band company was called out for use against rioters in Selwood Forest in 1631, they arrived on the

[39] Quintrell (ed.), *Maynard Lieutenancy Book*, pp. xlix–l; Cogswell, *Home Divisions*, 117–18; Wake (ed.), *Papers Relating to Musters, Beacons and Subsidies*, p. lxxxiii; T. G. Barnes, 'Deputies not Principals, Lieutenants not Captains: The Institutional Failure of Lieutenancy in the 1620s', Fissel, *W&G* 601; Stater, *Noble Government*, 22, 32–3, 38–9; Boynton, *Elizabethan Militia*, 287–91; Fletcher, *County Community*, 193–200.

[40] Fletcher, *County Community*, 240–1; T. G. Barnes, *Somerset, 1625–1640: A County's Government during the 'Personal Rule'* (1961), 244–5.

scene with insufficient powder and shot, and the musketeers refused to light their match when ordered to do so.[41]

At the general musters, the unpreparedness of the militia was evident. Robert Ward complained of the air of frivolity which characterized muster-days, and said that they were occasions for heavy drinking and feasting and that the officers set a bad example in this regard and in the neglect of their duties. Ward added that drinking was a great fault of the English nation and was particularly characteristic of English martial culture, and got in the way of performing duties even in the thick of battle in the Low Countries.[42] In trying to persuade the trained-band officers to take their duties more seriously, Thomas Palmer drew a disheartening picture of Caroline trained-band musters: 'We ... have a customary annual training of our counties. But sometimes so trivial, so superficial, that it improves rather our sport than our skill. The ignorant rustics wink when they give fire. The captain winks at it, and the spectators laugh at it. Such a military discipline is fitter for a May-game than a field. It may be heartily wished that their martial instructors were more industrious, their training more frequent and serious.'[43] The foot-bands of the Lancashire Militia appear to have been reasonably well trained during the Caroline period, but the horse-bands were not. The latter met for only one day at a time, whereas the foot-bands underwent training for several days when they mustered. The horse were poorly equipped and armed, and when they mustered in 1625, twenty-eight of the 149 horsemen did not show up. Absenteeism remained a problem throughout the Caroline period. Although the soldiers of the foot-bands were supposed to be freeholders and farmers, in fact only a small number actually met that qualification—six out of 100 in Amounderness Hundred and approximately the same number in Salford Hundred. The substantial freeholders were more frequently found among the untrained members of the militia.[44]

The difficulty in securing attendance of the horse-bands at county musters was part of the larger problem of recruiting cavalry units in England for overseas service. Besides the shortage of warhorses, which dated back to the end of Henry VIII's reign, a decline of equestrian skills and martial prowess had occurred among those peers and gentry who had stayed at home and did not volunteer for overseas expeditions. Formerly, the households of the peers and gentry had furnished horses and men for bands of cavalry, and still performed that service as late as the Midland Revolt of 1607, but that tradition was vanishing in the early part of the seventeenth century. In any case, riding down a couple of hundred peasants was hardly the same as facing the cavalry of the Spanish Army of Flanders. The heavy expense of finding

[41] Sir Hugh Cholmley, *Memoirs* (1787), 55–8; B. Sharp, *In Contempt of all Authority: Rural Artisans and Riot in the West of England, 1586–1660* (1980), 120–1.

[42] Robert Ward, *Animadversions of Warre* (1639), 30–1.

[43] Thomas Palmer, *Bristoll's Military Garden* (1635), 25, 27–9.

[44] D. P. Carter, 'The "Exact Militia" in Lancashire, 1625–1640', *NH* 11 (1975), 89–91, 97–9.

mounts and furnishing the horse-bands of the county militias increasingly fell upon less wealthy individuals who banded together to find and equip horsemen.[45]

There had existed a traditional obligation for gentlemen to serve in the militia mounted on their own horses, and age was not an excuse for failing to attend; if very old, a gentleman might send his son in his place, but not a servant. Yet Sir Edward Cecil remembered that when he was a deputy lieutenant in Surrey, many gentlemen refused to serve as horsemen in the trained bands and sent their serving-men instead. Moreover, the horse-bands of the militia were supposed to be commanded only 'by the nobility and prime gentry'. In Essex, captaincies of the horse-bands changed hands with great frequency in the 1590s—a sure sign that all was not well. The disdain of the Essex horse-bands continued through the 1620s. Instead, the officers were relatives and hangers-on of Robert Radcliffe, fifth earl of Sussex, the lord-lieutenant. The horsemen of the bands were no longer yeomen, because of the decay of that social group.[46]

Sir Edward Cecil blamed the English gentry's lack of interest in and aptitude for the horse-bands upon the fact that there were no equestrian academies to train cavalry officers in England such as existed in France, where gentlemen excelled in horsemanship. Cecil proposed that the king establish a body of royal horse guards which could serve as a school of horsemanship. Cecil had begun his own military career in the French army, and he was probably thinking of something like the *gens d'armes*, or heavy cavalry, which might serve as an equestrian equivalent of the artillery companies which were spreading from London into provincial towns in early Stuart England.[47] As it was, those gentlemen who did attend the musters of the horse-bands were notoriously less amenable to discipline than men of more humble social rank—a trait which carried over to the royalist cavalry during the English civil wars. Cavalry ranks in the Caroline militia appeared to be filling up with men who had no claim to gentility, and the 'ancient distinction and difference between cavalry and infantry as to their birth and breeding' was 'wholly taken away' and 'not regarded or inquired after'.[48]

From the beginning of the first attempts to form a select militia in Elizabethan times until the early Stuart efforts to remodel the trained bands, numerous difficulties were encountered in administering the county militia system. There were very few paid full-time clerks, and military affairs came to take up more and more time of the office-holding gentry as commissioners of musters, militia officers and deputy lieutenants. At the end of the 1620s, following the unsettling years of war,

---

[45] Boynton, *Elizabethan Militia*, 181–3; Manning, *VR* 232; Wake (ed.), *Papers Relating to Musters, Beacons and Subsidies*, 16–18; Fletcher, *County Community*, 185–6.

[46] Sir Edward Cecil, Lord Wimbledon, 'Of Divers Parts of War, Especially the Discipline of the Cavalry', BL, Royal MS. 18.C.xxiii, pp. 16, 19–24; Quintrell (ed.), *Maynard Lieutenancy Book*, pp. lxiii–lxiv, lxx. For similar developments in Somerset and Northamptonshire, cf. Barnes, *Somerset*, 251, and Goring and Wake (eds.), *Northamptonshire Lieutenancy Papers*, pp. xviii–xiv, 7–10.

[47] BL, Royal MS. 18.C.xxiii, pp. 16, 19–24. See also *The Advice of that Worthy Commander, Sir Edward Harwood, Colonel* (1642), in T. Park (ed.), *HM* iv. 273, for similar views.

[48] Carlton, *GW* 22; Turner, *Pallas Armata*, 166.

the lords-lieutenant and their deputies grew more lax, and were anxious not to offend their county communities by more onerous demands, and were careful to look after their reputations in those communities. This meant that they served the local community first and were less than enthusiastic about providing King Charles with his 'perfect militia'. Hence, the growing infrequency of annual musters. The lieutenants and their deputies resisted being turned into agents of the crown, spending all of their time carrying out the Privy Council's orders.[49]

In 1635 the Council specifically ordered a general muster and made sure that their orders were carried out. Professor Barnes suggests that this was done not only to improve the standards of training for the defence of the realm, but also to help justify the issuance of writs of ship money. The fact that the militia leadership and administration was closely interwoven with the duties of assessing and collecting militia rates and extra-parliamentary exactions such as ship money harmed the prestige of the leaders of the county militias, because the problem of inequitable assessments was never addressed. A. Hassell Smith thinks that this was one of the reasons for the collapse of Charles I's 'exact militia' system. Also, beginning in 1635, the Council decided that untrained members of the militia should also be organized into foot-bands and provided with training in the use of firearms. Thus, the distinction between the trained bands and the untrained members of the militia began to disappear—a trend observable in some counties which dated back to the 1620s. Although the rank and file of the trained bands of foot were supposed to be filled by substantial householders, it was becoming increasingly difficult to secure their cooperation, and the trained bands filled up with their servants instead. The officers of the militia companies came to be drawn from the middling rather than the office-holding gentry, and they lacked the prestige to fill up the ranks of their companies.[50]

Incorporated towns had stubbornly refused to obey orders to join the musters of the county trained bands. It was cheaper to hold their own musters locally than to send their citizens and burgesses to a distant place. London claimed to be a county unto itself, and the Cinque Ports refused to obey any orders which did not come from the lord warden of the Cinque Ports. Towns with artillery companies, such as Bristol, preferred to have one of their own captains drill their militias rather than accepting the bothersome oversight of lieutenants of counties and the expense of paying for county muster-masters. By default, the corporate towns which had their own artillery societies came to be answerable only to the crown.[51] The war years in late Elizabethan London saw popular tumults associated with the impressment of soldiers and the steady concourse of ill disciplined troops passing through the metropolis. This, together with the fear of foreign invasion, led to a revival of the Honourable Artillery Company of London, the premier military

[49] Boynton, *Elizabethan Militia*, 7; Stater, *Noble Government*, 45–7.

[50] Barnes, *Somerset*, 267; Carter, 'Exact Militia in Lancashire', 97–8; Hassell Smith, 'Militia Rates and Militia Statutes', 94; Quintrell (ed.), *Maynard Lieutenancy Book*, pp. lxxi–lxxii.

[51] Boynton, *Elizabethan Militia*, 37–8; Fissel, 'Tradition and Invention', 143.

guild of the realm, originally founded in 1537. Members of the HAC exercised arms every Thursday throughout the year, and, rotating in their turn through all ranks from corporal to captain, learned the duties of each office. During the early years of the Jacobean peace the HAC appears to have become defunct, until revived again in 1610, when the company was refounded by royal warrant.[52]

The HAC showed more activity over the next few years, and the fear of war produced an outpouring of martial enthusiasm in provincial cities which led to the founding of new artillery companies or societies patterned after the HAC and which practised in artillery 'gardens' or grounds.[53] By the time of the Great Muster of 1614, the HAC had become a kind of academy for training militia officers for the London trained bands, which had come to be organized into four regiments of foot, each containing five companies composed of 300 pikes and shot totalling 6,000 train-soldiers. Because they were used to keeping order during the frequent demonstrations of London apprentices, the London trained bands drilled more frequently than the county trained bands. In 1616 Henry, prince of Wales, became the patron of the Westminster Artillery Company, which drilled in Tothill Fields, and upon his death Prince Charles took his place. The HAC had successfully petitioned the king to increase their membership from 250 to 500, and the Westminster Artillery Company had a long waiting-list for membership. However, this initial enthusiasm for founding artillery societies persisted only a few years, and by 1621 the membership of the HAC had declined to 200.[54]

The HAC was the only institution in pre-civil war England which provided something approaching adequate training for officers of the militia. There were several locations where this took place. The first was the King's or Old Artillery Ground in Finsbury Fields, adjoining Moorfields and Bunhill. As membership expanded, the HAC also began exercising in two new locations. The New Artillery Yard was located in Bishopgate, where a new armoury, which took the place of Armourers' Hall, was built in about 1641. Another artillery garden was located in St Martin's Fields. The Military Company of Westminster dated from 1611, and there was another artillery garden at Horsleydown in Southwark.[55] Members of the HAC were keenly aware that their artillery garden was their

[52] Stow, *Survey*, rev. Strype, ii. 45a & b.

[53] The term 'artillery' originally meant archery, and the HAC had begun as a company of archers; by the beginning of the 17th century the term was used to denote all missile weapons, including firearms, which were carried by foot soldiers. *Infanterie* remained a French word known only to military professionals and did not enter common discourse until later in that century. Ordnance or 'great ordnance' was the term reserved for what would today be called artillery. The HAC did not actually contain gunners until 1781 (William Gouge, *The Dignitie of Chivalrie . . . a Sermon Preached before the Artillery Company of London* (1626), 43; *OED*; R[ichard] N[iccolls], *London's Artillery* [1616], sig. B1r; Walker, *HAC* 25).

[54] Stow, *Survey*, rev. Strype, ii. 456a & b, 457a & b; Boynton, *Elizabethan Militia*, 212–16; Walker, *HAC* 25–6; Manning, *VR* 213–14; K. Lindley, 'Riot Prevention and Control in Early Stuart London', *TRHS* 5th ser. 33 (1983), 109–26.

[55] Firth, *Cromwell's Army*, 10–11; Stow, *Survey*, rev. Strype, ii. 456a & b; W. Emberton, *Skippon's Brave Boys: The Origins, Development and Civil War Service of London's Trained Bands* (1984), 31; Walker, *HAC* 32, 41.

campus martius, and, like their Roman exemplars, they took pride in being citizen-soldiers (most of the members of the London trained bands were substantial householders). Their senior officers and chaplains force-fed them on Roman history—not to mention Machiavellian readings of Tacitus—and they had no use for mercenary soldiers or standing armies. Country gentlemen came to watch their exercises, so that they could go home and improve the drill of the county trained bands. The HAC could pride themselves on being the best-drilled military body in the kingdom. The captain-commandant in the early 1620s was John Bingham, a veteran of the Low-Countries wars, a member of the Council of War and the author of *Aelian's Tacticks*. In the 1640s, and probably earlier, Colonel William Bariffe was a senior member of the HAC. He was the author of a widely used military manual originally written for the HAC, which went through six editions in twenty-six years. Many military manuals, intended for the county trained bands, provided drills and exercises only for foot companies. Bariffe added instructions for drilling whole brigades on the Swedish model. Lieutenant-Colonel Richard Elton, also an author of a military manual widely used by officers of the Parliamentary army, belonged to the military garden in Westminster in the 1650s; he thought that the two artillery companies of London and Westminster were the 'great nurseries or academies of military discipline' in England.[56]

Many of the country gentry who led the county trained bands were slow to appreciate how rapidly the international situation was deteriorating. But London merchants and citizens, who maintained close relations with Antwerp and the mercantile centres of Flanders, were shocked to observe how the duke of Parma's successful siege of Antwerp had led to popular disorder and economic collapse because of the 'neglect of that most notable exercise of arms and martial discipline in times of wealth and peace' by the burghers of Antwerp.[57] Many of the Dutch patriots were refugees from the Flemish cities, and the Dutch learned the necessity of protecting their cities against both external enemies and violent popular tumults from within. When the HAC was refounded in 1613, the London artillerymen consciously used the Dutch *schuttersgilden* or militia guilds as a model. These Dutch militia guilds were medieval in origin, but had been reorganized in the 1570s and 1580s for defensive purposes, and membership was regarded as a civic duty. Although fellowship and commensality remained important aspects of membership, the imposition of military hierarchies upon the militia guilds was a step towards improved discipline and military proficiency. The influence of the Dutch model continued as such esteemed veterans of the Dutch army as Sir Horace Vere and Sir Edward Conway were retained by the HAC to assess the training of its members. While it must be acknowledged that the

[56] Walker, *HAC* 25–6, 29, 31, 36–7; Stow, *Survey*, rev. Strype, ii. 456a & b; Niccolls, *London's Artillery*, sig. B1r & v; Bingham, *Art of Embattailing an Army*; William Bariffe, *Military Discipline, or the Young Artilleryman*, 2nd edn. (1639), preface, 313; B. Donagan, 'Halcyon Days and the Literature of War: England's Military Education before 1642', *P&P* 147 (1995), 79–81.

[57] Stow, *Survey*, rev. Strype, ii. 457a & b; Ralph Norris, *A Warning to London by the Fall of Antwerp* (1585), 1; P. Geyl, *The Revolt of the Netherlands, 1555–1609*, 2nd edn. (1958; repr. 1962), 197–201.

colonels of the London trained-band regiments were appointed to their posts because they were prominent members of the aldermanic class rather than because of military skill, it remains true that the company- and field-grade officers of the London trained bands received excellent instruction in the military gardens of the metropolis.[58]

The founding and refounding of military societies in London and provincial towns in the early seventeenth century is evidence of the spread of martial culture to the upper levels of urban society. This phenomenon parallels the rechivalriza-tion of aristocratic society and culture which is associated with the literary efforts of authors such as Edmund Spenser, Philip Sidney, Fulke Greville and Ben Jonson and others who volunteered for or sanctioned military service against the Catholic forces. The chaplains and preachers in the artillery societies of London and the provincial towns persuaded the citizen-soldiers that they could participate in the martial culture of aristocratic chivalry. Such preachers frequently referred to the membership of the military gardens as consisting of 'gentlemen' and 'citizens' who shared the aristocratic qualities of honour and generosity. Their martial exercises were blessed by God because they were called to fight in the eternal war between the forces of Christ and Antichrist. Unless they combined courage and martial skills with Christian faith and righteousness, they could expect to be punished in the same way that the burgers of Antwerp, Magdeburg and other continental European cities had been smitten. This concept of civic chivalry and a calling to be members of a military elite based upon participation in the artillery societies manifested a tendency to undermine the privileged status of aristocrats who did not heed the call to arms to defend international Protestantism. Such a message was also a thinly veiled condemnation of James I's foreign and military policies of peace with the Hapsburgs. One preacher, addressing the artillery garden at St Martins-in-the-Fields in 1618, went so far as to speak of courtiers who supported the Jacobean policy of peace as 'wanton, base, drunken, coward-like carpet-knights'. Little wonder that James I viewed this movement of civic bellicism with great suspicion.[59]

Civic chivalry appealed to a wider audience than the apprentices who came from a gentry background. Although chivalric values and behaviour were usually associa-ted with high-born status, the popular literature of chivalry maintained that true

---

[58] Roberts, 'Citizen Soldiers', 92–7, 112; P. Knevel, *Burgers in het geweer: De Schutterijnen in Holland, 1550–1700* (1994), 411–13.

[59] W. Hunt, 'Civic Chivalry and the English Civil War', in A. Grafton and A. Blair (eds.), *The Transmission of Culture and the English Civil War* (1990), 206, 220–7; Roberts, 'Citizen Soldiers', 92–7; Geoffrey Gates, *The Defence of Military Profession* (1579), 52–4; Richard Johnson, *The Nine Worthies of London* (1592), in W. Oldys and T. Park (eds.), *HM* 10 vols. (1808–12), viii. 437.

Professor Schwoerer (*NSA* 8–11, 14–15) argues that the development of a militia based upon trained bands 'predisposed men to an antimilitary attitude', because the trained bands were com-manded and officered by peers and gentry who disliked professional soldiers and 'who resented any effort to centralize control'. The artillery societies were more free to develop without such constraints and were subjected to Puritan influences. Puritanism and 'militarism' were more compatible in early Stuart England than bellicism and monarchy (as James I well understood).

honour derived from 'virtuous deeds' rather than ancestry alone. Thus, men of humble birth could achieve honour through noble deeds.[60] Military writers, poets and preachers recommended the exercise of arms in military gardens not only because of the need to provide up-to-date military training for militia officers but also because they believed that military drill as a form of recreation fostered moral virtue, and they called for the establishment of artillery societies in provincial cities. The successful example of the London artillery gardens led to provincial and colonial towns inaugurating artillery companies in Bury St Edmunds, Yarmouth, Ipswich, Coventry, Nottingham, Bristol, Chester and Boston, Massachusetts, besides Westminster and Southwark. This process often involved the approbation of noble patrons. Thomas Palmer's *Bristoll's Military Garden* (1635) was dedicated to Philip Herbert, earl of Pembroke and Montgomery, who had presented the petition to establish an artillery society in Bristol to the king. Pembroke had himself exercised arms in the Artillery Yard at Westminster in the time of Henry, prince of Wales, who had awarded a prize to him for dexterity in exercises.[61]

At the same time that provincial merchants and gentry, influenced by the revival of the HAC, began to spread the new military practices and discipline learned in the London artillery gardens back to their own counties and towns, grammar schools began hiring veterans of the Low-Countries wars to provide military training to schoolboys. Lucy Hutchinson's memoir of her husband, Colonel John Hutchinson, states that he received his first military training at Lincoln Grammar School. The boys were eager to emulate their elders, and in some instances initiated the military exercises themselves. Noblemen and gentlemen sometimes hired private tutors for instruction in military drill as well as fencing and swordsmanship. In 1642, after he had committed himself to the parliamentary cause, Edmund Ludlow says that he and some friends from the Inns of Court retained an experienced soldier to teach them to exercise arms at the London Artillery Garden. After hostilities began, Ludlow and his friends joined the earl of Essex's Life Guard as gentlemen volunteers. Essex's Life Guard was essentially a training corps for prospective officers, consisting of 100 troopers. Ludlow served for eight months in this elite corps before being commissioned. A number of his fellow gentlementroopers later became distinguished parliamentary commanders.[62]

---

[60] John Bunyan, born the son of a cottager, confessed in later life that as a child one of his sinful indulgences was reading chivalric romances such as *Bevis of Southampton* (M. Spufford, *Small Books and Pleasant Histories: Popular Fiction and its Readership in Seventeenth-Century England* (1981), 6–7).

[61] Hunt, 'Civic Chivalry', 208; Trussell, *The Souldier Pleading his owne Cause*, sigs. C5r, D2r; William Gouge, *Dignitie of Chivalry . . . A Sermon Preached before the Artillery Company of London*, 2nd edn. (1631), repr. in *God's Three Arrowes*, 430, 432; Walker, *HAC* 30–1, 41; Palmer, *Bristoll's Military Garden*, sigs. A2r, A3r & v; P. McGrath, *Bristol and the Civil War* (1981), 7; L. G. Wickham Legg (ed.), *A Relation of a Short Survey of 26 Counties* (1904), 91–2; Samuel Kem, *The New Fort of True Honour Made Impregnable* (1640), sig. A2, pp. 24–5.

[62] Stow, *Survey*, rev. Strype, ii. 457b; Sir G. Clark, *War and Society in the Seventeenth Century* (1958), 21–2; Hunt, 'Civic Chivalry', 220; Lucy Hutchinson, *Memorials of the Life of Colonel Hutchinson*, ed. C. H. Firth (1906), 20, 41; Markham, 'Muster-master', 71–2; C. H. Firth (ed.), *The Memoirs of Edmund Ludlow*, 2 vols. (1894), i. 38–9.

There was always a strong religious dimension to the artillery-garden movement. Chaplains and preachers to the HAC not only stressed that the martial tradition of London reached back to the time of Sir John Walworth (who would have been familiar to Londoners through the dramatic tableaux of the annual lord mayor's procession), but also invoked current military practice in the armies of Sweden and the Netherlands. *The Swedish Discipline* (1632) was aimed at members of artillery companies in 'the cities and corporations' of England. Following the example of Gustavus Adolphus in combining piety with martial practice, the anonymous author provided prayers for militia companies which had been read publicly in the Swedish army. It was the practice of Gustavus to compose prayers which he would say aloud on the eve of battle. *The Swedish Discipline* also printed an English translation of the Swedish Articles of War made from a copy furnished to the author by Sir Donald Mackay, first Lord Rheay. In another sermon to the HAC, a preacher told his audience that although commerce was their calling, they still had a special duty to practice arms and defend the cause of Protestantism both at home and abroad. If London merchants were diligent in their martial exercises, this would build a reputation which would make enemies less likely to prey upon them.[63] When the Coventry Military Garden was dedicated in 1622, King James I was actually present. The preacher, Samuel Buggs, reminded the company that mainland Europe was aflame with war, and their honour required that they should be ready without exception to defend their country and religion from all danger.[64]

Royalist propagandists would later charge that during the time since its refounding the HAC had become a nest of Puritans who used the Artillery Garden as a forum for airing their views—especially during the personal rule of Charles I. According to *Mercurius Civicus*, the Puritans who previously were uninterested in military matters gained control of the HAC when they realized that the realm could be reformed after their fashion by wielding the sword. Another royalist pamphleteer dated this Puritan incursion to the moment when the first Lord Brooke and his son Fulke Greville began exercising arms at the HAC.[65] King Charles and the Privy Council, alarmed by the infiltration of the HAC by Puritans, attempted to regain control over the company by reserving the patronage of all important offices in it to the king. However, in practice, the lord mayor and the Court of Aldermen were allowed to appoint all officers except the captain-general.

---

[63] *The Swedish Discipline, Religious, Civile and Military* (1632), sig. A2r, pp. 3–29, 69; Jeremy Leech, *The Trayne Souldier* (1619), sig. A3r & v, pp. 18, 24–5, 28, 45, 63–4; Thomas Adams, *The Souldier's Honour . . . Preached to the Worthy Companie of Gentlemen that exercise in the Artillerie Garden* (1617), sigs. A3v, B1r; John Stow, *The Survey of London*, rev. Anthony Munday (1633), 764–5.

[64] Samuel Buggs, *Miles Mediterraneus, or the Mid-land Souldier* (1622), sigs. A2–3, pp. 6–7, 11, 15, 17, 38–9. Cf. also John Davenport, *A Royal Edict for Military Exercises* (1629), 2, 6.

[65] V. Pearl, *London and the Outbreak of the Puritan Revolution: City Government and National Politics, 1625–43* (1961), 170–3; *A Letter from Mercurius Civicus to Mercurius Rusticus* (1643), 4–5; *Persecutio Undecima* (1648; repr. 1682), 59–60.

When this office fell vacant in 1631, Charles appointed Marmaduke Rawdon, lieutenant-colonel of the Red Regiment of the London trained bands, which precipitated a minor mutiny within the HAC. After the outbreak of the civil wars, Rawdon, a wealthy merchant with extensive overseas and colonial interests, chose to serve the king and raised his own regiment; he was knighted for gallantry after helping to defend Basing House. When Rawdon's term as captain-general of the HAC expired in 1639, Captain Foster, a vintner, was commissioned by the dominant Puritan faction of the HAC to go to the Netherlands and offer employment to Philip Skippon, a veteran of thirteen years in the Dutch army and the author of several devotional tracts. Why the king yielded up command of the HAC to a known Puritan is not clear. Skippon would later serve as major-general under the earl of Essex, and became the major-general of the foot in the New Model Army. In September of 1639 Calybute Downing preached his sermon to the HAC, declaring 'that for defense of religion and reformation of the Church, it was lawful to take up arms against the king'. Under the leadership of officers trained in the HAC and commanded by Skippon, the London trained bands were the first in England to rebel against their monarch, and during the early days of the English civil wars constituted the most well trained infantry of the Parliamentary armies.[66]

The martial spectacles involving musters, parades and historic re-enactments of battles and sieges which were performed at the London Artillery Garden attracted large and admiring audiences. These military displays were widely imitated elsewhere in the metropolis and in provincial towns from the 1620s, and furnish evidence of the remilitarization of urban elites in English society. This phenomenon of civic bellicism is separate and distinct from, and owes little to, the example of court and aristocracy. When Sir Simonds D'Ewes was studying at the Inns of Court, he frequently visited the London Artillery Garden to watch members practice with their pikes. On at least one occasion, in May 1622, D'Ewes stayed long enough to hear a sermon preached to members of the HAC. He and his fellow students eagerly sought news of how the king and queen of Bohemia fared, as well as news of Mansfeld's expedition. In January of 1623 D'Ewes and fellow revellers at the Middle Temple drank a toast to the queen of Bohemia—each with a drawn sword in his hand.[67] In May 1638 an elaborate military pageant and mock siege were performed by the Artillery Company of Great Yarmouth. After a parade through the town of two cornets of horse, several companies of foot, two cannons and a baggage train, the Yarmouth militia men staged a siege demonstrating modern fortifications and methods of siege warfare. John Roberts, formerly a soldier in the Dutch army, who watched the spectacle said that it was as plausible

[66] Emberton, *Skippon's Brave Boys*, 39–44, 49; *Persecutio Undecima*, 59–60; R. Ashton, *The City and the Court, 1603–1643* (1979), 174–5; P. S. Seaver, *The Puritan Lectureships: The Politics of Religious Dissent, 1560–1662* (1970), 69, 264; Hunt, 'Civic Chivalry', 231–2; Walker, *HAC* 51–2.

[67] Hunt, 'Civic Chivalry', 218; E. Bourcier (ed.), *The Diary of Sir Simonds D'Ewes, 1622–1624* (1974), 75–6, 87–8, 99, 102, 106, 112, 190.

an exercise as he had ever seen. The day's festivities concluded with a supper featuring 'great store of diversity of dishes' and 'plenty of wine'.[68]

The Puritans generally disapproved of games, but since they believed that effeminacy and degenerate pastimes invariably led to sin, they did approve of military exercises and remained attached to 'antique military values'. This certainly did not extend to an approbation of Robert Dover's Cotswold Games of 1636, although those exercises played a role in the revival of the martial values and exercises associated with the *campus martius*. Prince Rupert of the Rhine, then 18 years of age, is reputed to have attended the Cotswold Games in that year with his friend Endymion Porter, who was a gentleman of the bedchamber to the king and a close friend of Dover. Rupert would have been drawn by the martial content of many of the games, as were members of the gentry. When Rupert returned to England five years later to fight with the royalist forces, one of his cavalry captains was Robert Dover's son John.[69] There was, of course, the danger that military spectacles might feed a popular interest in the continental wars of religion and a desire to participate in a holy war. At the Restoration, William Cavendish, duke of Newcastle, blamed the civil wars and the social unrest of the Interregnum on popular curiosity about foreign and domestic political affairs. His cure for this popular political discourse was to encourage a revival of traditional games appropriate for the commonalty, and to have aristocrats busy themselves with hunting. He thought that royal patronage of racing, tilting and jousting would also encourage aristocrats to practise their equestrian skills and breed good horses.[70] However, outside of corporate towns and below the level of the gentry, there is little evidence to show that martial spectacles and games helped to revive a popular martial culture.

The spirit of the Roman *campus martius* appears not to have taken root among the members of the county trained bands. The concept of a 'perfect militia' was never pursued with enough vigour to transform the militia, except in the City of London. The historian Sir Charles Firth was persuaded that the Bishops' Wars of 1639 and 1640 demonstrated the failure of the Stuart military system in England and contributed significantly to bringing down the monarchy. Firth thought that the lack of training of the English militia proved to be a more serious defect than the lack of money or the disaffection of the king's subjects. Yet, for all of its defects, the Caroline militia was potentially the most powerful armed force in the Three Kingdoms, but it was never really put to the test because most of the county trained bands were never mobilized. Even a couple of well drilled regiments of trained bands, properly supported with artillery, could have turned back or

---

[68] John Roberts of Weston, *Great Yarmouth's Exercise* (1638), sig. A2r.

[69] P. Collinson, *The Birthpangs of Protestant England: Religious and Cultural Change in Sixteenth and Seventeenth Century England* (1988), 130; C. Whitfield, *Robert Dover and the Cotswold Games* (1962), 48–9.

[70] T. P. Slaughter (ed.), *Ideology and Politics on the Eve of the Restoration: Newcastle's Advice to Charles II*, APSM 159 (1984), 56, 60–1.

defeated the Scots Covenanting Army at the one and only battle of the Second Bishops' War, which was fought at Newburn on the banks of the River Tyne. They were never given the chance. The London trained bands would certainly have been capable of this, as they would later demonstrate during the English civil war.[71] As for Scotland, the long years of domestic peace had led to greater neglect of the militia in that kingdom than was the case in England. Edinburgh and Dublin both had military companies, but they were hardly comparable to the HAC and the London trained bands, although a couple of enterprising Scots had written military manuals designed for a Scottish militia in the 1620s. Sir Thomas Wentworth, Viscount Strafford, had built up a small standing army in Ireland and had offered to raise 8,000 troops to defeat the Covenanters, but the fear that Charles would employ an army made up largely of papists did Charles's cause more harm than good among his Protestant subjects.[72]

There were weaknesses in the Scots Covenanting Army which the English royalist forces could have exploited during the Bishops' Wars of 1638–40, but the fact remains that such opportunities were missed. There were also serious deficiencies in the Caroline military system which prevented the Royalist forces or the militia from maximizing their strengths. Prominent among these weaknesses was the king himself. Charles I never did understand the distinction between high noble rank and military competence. The leaders of the Scottish Covenanters understood this distinction when they appointed Sir Alexander Leslie, an experienced general officer with long and distinguished service in the Swedish army, to command the Covenanting Army. They also issued an invitation to Scots serving in foreign armies to come home and accept commissions. Although the colonels of regiments in the Covenanting Army were usually high-ranking noblemen (who, in a country where feudal relationships were far from dead, were good at recruiting), the lieutenant-colonels, who actually commanded in the field, were almost invariably experienced veterans. Charles I, on the other hand, drew his military commanders in the First Bishops' War of 1639 from among the great officers of the royal household. Thus, Thomas Howard, second earl of Arundel and Surrey, the earl marshal, was made lord general, and the third earl of Essex became the lieutenant-general, while Henry Rich, earl of Holland, commanded the horse. At least Arundel and Holland made good scapegoats for Charles when he dismissed them in 1639 for failing to achieve a victory. Charles had been forced to abandon

[71] Firth, *Cromwell's Army*, 12–13; M. C. Fissel, *The Bishops' Wars: Charles I's Campaigns Against Scotland* (1994), 295–6; Walker, *HAC* 50–1.

[72] E. M. Furgol, 'Scotland Turned Sweden: The Scottish Covenanters and the Military Revolution, 1638–1651', in J. Morrill (ed.), *The Scottish National Covenant in its British National Context* (1990), 135–6; Sir Thomas Craig, *De Unione Regnorum Britanniae Tractatus*, ed. C. S. Terry, SHS 60 (1909), 4701; P. Somerville-Large, *Dublin* (1979), 85; [Sir Thomas Kellie], *Pallas Armata, or Militarie Instructions for the Learned* (1627); James Achesone, *The Military Garden, or Instructions for All Young Soldiers* (1629); Adam Ferguson, *An Essay on the History of Civil Society* (1767), ed. D. Forbes (repr. 1966), 23–4; H. F. Kearney, *Strafford in Ireland, 1633–41: A Study in Absolutism* (1959), 188.

his planned assault on Scotland because of the poor state of the northern trained bands. Henry, Lord Clifford, who was a northern peer and had served as governor of Carlisle Castle, on the other hand, was slighted by Charles and insulted by Arundel, yet he put together a loyal group of Royalists, many of whom later played important roles as military commanders in the English civil wars.[73]

At the local level, the deputy lieutenants in many English and Welsh counties were reluctant to perform their duties on behalf of the king; they knew that efforts to impress men, collect militia rates and other exactions and appropriate arms and armour belonging to the counties would incur popular hostility, so many simply ceased to perform their duties.[74] Sir Hugh Cholmeley, a deputy lieutenant in North Yorkshire, busied himself during the Bishops' Wars mustering trained bands; he also commanded a regiment under the earl of Northumberland. When Sir Thomas Wentworth, Viscount Strafford, returned to Yorkshire from Ireland to exercise his duties as president of the Council in the North, he insulted and alienated Cholmeley, who had been well affected to the king but who had refused to pay Ship Money as a matter of principle, by accusing him of sedition and summoning him before the Council. Cholmeley would subsequently refuse to accept a commission to raise another regiment for the king. Cholmeley adds that Strafford treated many other Yorkshire gentlemen in the same way. In May 1642 Sir Henry Slingsby, another Yorkshire gentleman, was given a commission to command a foot regiment drawn from the trained bands. When he was later called upon to select a detachment of eighty men from his regiment to guard the king, 'few or none appeared'.[75] The dependence of the Caroline military system on the counties for administration, military leadership and financial support clearly was a weakness. Although the lieutenants and their deputies were willing enough to defend their counties, they were reluctant to contribute to a Royalist war effort against Scotland. Localism almost always prevailed, and during his reign Charles had acquiesced in this to a considerable extent. At the same time, the Scots Covenanting Army was raised by private means, that is, by feudal summons of the tenants of the Scots nobility. In this regard, the English militia, although raised by the counties, was at least provided for at public expense, and thus can be said to have risen slightly above the horizon of modern warfare. There certainly were deficiencies in the Caroline military system, but they derived as much from poor leadership as from underdeveloped military institutions.[76]

This spirit of localism was also compounded with political disaffection among the peers and gentry. The so-called Bishops' Wars were precipitated by Charles's unwise attempt to force the Anglican Book of Common Prayer on his Scottish

[73] R. T. Spence, 'Henry, Lord Clifford and the First Bishops' War, 1639', *NH* 31 (1995), 139–41, 154.

[74] F. Heal and C. Holmes, *The Gentry in England and Wales, 1500–1700* (1994), 213; Barnes, *Somerset*, 277–8.

[75] Sir Hugh Cholmeley, *Memoirs* (1787), 59–60; *Original Memoirs during the Great Civil War, Being the Life of Sir Henry Slingsby* (1806), 36.

[76] C. Russell, *The Fall of the British Monarchies, 1637–1642* (1991), 72–3.

subjects. This policy alienated subjects in all of the Three Kingdoms and exacerbated a situation where many of his subjects already distrusted him. He began a
war which he could not win, and he had to resort to negotiation because of his
inability to bring sufficient force to bear upon the Scottish Covenanters. Charles
could not possibly prosecute such a war as long as his English subjects remained
divided. His failure to consult with Parliament during the eleven years of personal
rule, his unpopular advocacy of Arminian prelates and policies and his general
political obtuseness ensured that he would never unite the English, and without
the cooperation of Parliament he could not finance a war with the Covenanters.
Charles had been warned by his chief advisor on Scottish affairs, James, third marquis of Hamilton, that he should pursue a political solution and negotiate with
the more moderate Covenanters. Hamilton had been sent to the Firth of Forth
with an expeditionary force of 5,000 men aboard thirty-eight ships to lie off of
Leith while another force was gathering in Yorkshire in preparation for an
invasion of the Scottish Borders. Hamilton's force was intended to blockade and
threaten Edinburgh. After the 15,000 or so troops under Charles and Arundel
deployed to the Scottish Border, two confrontations between Royalist forces and
Covenanters at Kelso and Duns Law helped persuade Charles that his forces had
been outmanoeuvred by Leslie; he backed down and negotiated the Pacification
of Berwick of 1639. While encamped with his army in the north, Charles had discovered that there was extensive disaffection in his camp, and some of his nobility
were in secret communication with the Scots. On 21 April 1639, at York, William
Fiennes, first Viscount Saye and Sele, and Robert Greville, second Lord Brooke,
publicly refused to swear the military oath. Lack of money had forced Charles to
raise military forces by ordering the nobility to call out their tenants by means of
commissions of array, a feudal prerogative which put the financial burden for the
war effort on the shoulders of the nobility. Out of approximately 123 English
peers in 1639–40, only forty-four were willing to attend upon the king, and only
thirty-three were willing to contribute men and money to the Royalist war effort.
Nathaniel Fiennes, son of Viscount Saye and Sele, had been in communication
with the Scots, and encouraged the Covenanters to persist in their opposition to
episcopacy and alterations in the liturgy of the Scottish Kirk. The Covenanters
also learned that nine of Charles's regimental commanders were prepared to join
the Scots with their regiments if the Scots invaded England and a fight ensued.
The Scots also learned of the poor state of the English army.[77]

Charles still pursued a military solution to a political problem, although his
military position in 1640 was weaker than it had been before he agreed to the

[77] Fissel, *Bishops' Wars*, 4–60; J. Scally, 'Counsel in Crisis: James, Third Marquis of Hamilton and
the Bishops' Wars, 1638–1640', in J. R. Young (ed.), *Celtic Dimensions of the British Civil Wars*
(1997), 18–21, 24–5; J. P. Cooper, 'Retainers in Tudor England', in G. E. Aylmer and J. S. Morrill
(eds.), *Land, Men and Beliefs: Studies in Early Modern History* (1983), 96; M. Schwarz, 'Viscount Saye
and Sele, Lord Brooke and the Aristocratic Protest to the First Bishops' War', *CJH* 7.1 (1972), 17–24;
P. H. Donald, 'New Light on the Anglo-Scottish Contacts of 1640', *HR* 62 (1989), 223–4.

Pacification of Berwick of 1639. The meeting of the Short Parliament in May 1640 brought no financial support to the Royalist war effort, and merely allowed Parliament an opportunity to publicize grievances. In the Second Bishops' War of 1640, the Scots invaded England and headed for Newcastle, which ought to have given the king a claim upon the allegiance of his subjects. An attempt to prevent Leslie and the Covenanters from crossing the River Tyne at Newburn turned into a rout of the king's army. The setback was more psychological than real, and was blamed on Edward, Viscount Conway, the commander in the field, by Charles and his courtiers, who remained in London for this campaign. Conway might have recovered from a single setback, but the lack of troops, supplies and money effectively ended the conflict. Almost half of the Royalist forces in this war had consisted of 13,000 members of the Yorkshire trained bands. The support of the Yorkshire gentry, who led the train-soldiers, could have made a difference for Charles's cause, but in fact, the Yorkshire Puritans were in communication with the Scots, so the militia system in this case seems to have been subverted from within. The troops who had been impressed in the south of England and sent north rioted, pillaged and murdered, and the trained bands were not called out until it was too late. The Scots were then able to occupy northern England and compel Charles to summon another English Parliament to pay them for their expenses incurred in the invasion and occupation of northern England.[78]

The idea of the Roman *campus martius* carried with it an admiration for amateur citizen-soldiers who exercised arms regularly. It also encouraged a Tacitean dislike of professional soldiers. The evidence examined in this chapter suggests that the English assimilated the prejudice against mercenary soldiers more readily than they accepted the lesson that members of the county militias could function well only if they trained regularly and to exacting standards. That veteran professional soldiers, serving as muster-masters, would be the instruments by which modern military theory and practice was to be imparted to the trained-bands was resented by the country gentry and the ratepayers.

The reception of mainland-European military innovations and the martial culture which accompanied them seems to have been largely limited to the soldiers from the British Isles who served in or had served in foreign armies and to the members of the artillery companies of London and provincial towns. The members of these military companies belonged to an urban society and culture which was more open to the concept of advancement based upon merit and a businesslike way of doing things, so they could appreciate the need for competence in military matters as well as commercial endeavours. The emphasis upon competence and efficiency which was gradually emerging in continental European military theory and practice was not yet fully appreciated at the courts

---

[78] Fissel, *Bishops' Wars*, 34–60; Russell, *Fall of the British Monarchies*, 89–90; D. Scott, ' "Hannibal at our Gates": Loyalists and Fifth Columnists during the Bishops' Wars—the Case of Yorkshire', *HR* 70 (1997), 269–75, 277, 281; C. Hibbard, *Charles I and the Popish Plot* (1983), 112–14.

of the early Stuart monarchs nor in the county communities, where high social rank remained the primary requisite for military command; displays of individual virtue and the attainment of indivisible honour continued to be the goals of battles rather than rational strategy and clear military objectives. Although the distinctions between court and country have often been cited as contributing to political divisions in pre-civil-war England, in fact, both cultures rated the preservation of social hierarchies more highly than the kind of military professionalism which it took to make effective use of modern military theory and methods to spell out a strategy which could bring victory. The Scots Covenanters were much quicker to grasp the importance of experience and professionalism when appointing leaders of their army, even though Scotland lacked the institutions and resources for keeping an army standing or deployed in the field for any length of time.

The concept of a 'perfect' or 'exact militia' was one which could have worked, but it would have required better leadership, the cooperation of Parliament and more revenue than either Parliament or subsidymen were willing to contribute. The failure of both James VI and I and Charles I to heed the old political rule inherited from the medieval world that a successful monarch must project the image of being a soldier-king and a military leader was unwise. The lack of an effective standing army or at least a well drilled militia denied credibility to their diplomatic efforts in a world of endemic warfare, and the emergence of a small professional naval force in the 1630s only partially alleviated this situation. Yet, given the unpopular policies which led to the failure of James VI and I to go to the aid of the Palatines in a timely manner, the disastrous military and naval expeditions of the 1620s, the eleven years personal rule and extra-parliamentary taxation—not to mention the unpopular policies of Arminianism—a more consistent and successful effort to turn the militia into an effective military force might well have aroused fears of royal tyranny. Gaining the necessary trust to rearm England in an age of religious warfare was essentially a political task and seemingly beyond the powers of Charles I's political imagination.

PART II

THE EXPERIENCE
OF CIVIL WAR
1640–1660

7

Mercenaries and gentlemen

It seems strange to me that men should conspire to believe all things more perplexed and difficult than indeed they are.... This mistake may well be compared to the conceit we had of soldiers in the beginning of the civil wars. None was thought worthy of that name, but he could show his wounds and allowed of his exploits in the Low Countries; whereas the whole business of fighting was afterwards chiefly performed by untravelled gentlemen, raw citizens and generals that had scarcely ever before seen a battle.

Thomas Sprat, *The History of the Royal Society of London for the Improving of Natural Knowledge* (1667), 73.

A complete cavalier is a child of honour, a gentleman well born and bred, that loves his king for conscience' sake.... He is the only reserve of English gentility and ancient valour, and hath rather chose to bury himself in the tomb of honour than to see the nobility of this nation vassalaged.

Edward Symmons, *A Military Sermon* (1644), 22–3.

The English and Scottish aristocracies had acquired a deep distrust of mercenary soldiers from reading Tacitus and Machiavelli and writers who followed in the classical humanist and republican tradition. Although those who fought in the States' Army were not considered in England to be mercenaries because, presumably, they had fought for the sake of conscience in a Protestant crusade, both Scottish and English aristocrats still believed that regardless of evidence of the experience and competence of others they still had the best claim to high command because of their superior social rank and the military exploits of their ancestors. The concept that military hierarchies were necessary for order and discipline still had not etched itself upon the English military mentality at home. It was thought that the king's honour required that his armies be commanded by men of high noble birth, and this emphasis upon social hierarchy made some sense as long as noblemen could recruit their tenants or kin to fill their regiments. The actual command of such units in the field could be entrusted to experienced professionals. This arrangement worked well enough in Scotland, parts of Ireland and in Wales and the north of England, but was a notable failure throughout most of England where rents rather than loyalty had become the nexus between lord and smallholder. There were other issues which divided competent and experienced professional soldiers from noble amateurs and gallants, and the New Model Army gained an advantage when the grandees, who mostly belonged to the peace party which advocated limited war aims and a negotiated settlement with the king, were purged from command in favour of generals and officers who gained promotion by merit or seniority. At the same time this latter group tended to advocate instrumental warfare rather than agonistic war and looked forward to total victory. This necessarily made the Wars of the Three Kingdoms more bitter and bloody.

Many officers and soldiers who fought in the British and Irish civil wars were veterans of the religious and dynastic wars of mainland Europe, but there is truth in Thomas Sprat's assertion that most officers began as amateurs, and through diligent perusal of the sizeable literature of military treatises, manuals on the exercise of arms and military memoirs, together with a willingness to learn from experience, acquired a degree of professionalization which is not often appreciated.

The ability to learn from experience is not a quality one would attribute to King Charles I. During the Second Bishops' War of 1640, a superior standing army was raised by the Scottish Covenanters and led by experienced Scottish professional soldiers who were veterans of the Swedish army's campaigns in Germany. The Scots Covenanting Army overwhelmed Charles's English army, which had been haphazardly raised and was commanded by incompetents and amateurs, and compelled the king to sue for peace, leaving the Scots in occupation of northern England until such time as the English Parliament should meet. At the end of the Bishops' Wars Charles had missed an opportunity to rid England of swordsmen when he turned down a request from the Dutch government and the English Parliament to enter into a Protestant alliance to assist his cousin Charles Louis, the elector palatine, with troops and financial aid. Sir Alexander Leslie, the commander of the Scots Covenanting Army, had expressed a willingness to lead an expedition to help the elector palatine, and there were those in the English Parliament who would have trusted Charles to command an army if he had been willing to commit himself to the Palatine cause.[1] Charles chose not to remember how foreign wars could unite divided nations, and instead threatened to use force against Parliament. In spite of being an island nation England was vulnerable to foreign invasion. The invasion of the Scots in 1640 precipitated the rebellion and civil wars of England, and, ultimately, the Wars of the Three Kingdoms led to the overthrow of the monarchy.[2]

Military expertise in the various armies in the early stages of the Wars of the Three Kingdoms derived principally from veterans of the Thirty Years War and other mainland European conflicts. Approximately 20,000 English soldiers had

[1] C. Hibbard, *Charles I and the Popish Plot* (1983), 132; The Nineteen Propositions, no. 17, printed in J. P. Kenyon (ed.), *The Stuart Constitution, 1603–1688: Documents and Commentary* (1966), 244–7.
[2] H. G. Koenigsberger, *Politicians and Virtuosi: Essays in Early Modern History* (1986), 21–2.

served abroad, probably more than 20,000 Irishmen, and at least 25,000 Scots. Between one-third and one-half of the Dutch field armies consisted of English and Scottish soldiers, while one-sixth of the Swedish armies in the time of Gustavus Adolphus was recruited in Scotland, and the numbers of soldiers in the fighting forces of Denmark-Norway drawn from the British Isles could not have been much inferior. Of course, the wastage rates of soldiers on campaign in the field were extremely high, but British military manpower came to be characterized by a constant two-way flow of officers and men between the British Isles and the European mainland after 1638.[3] Those who had served in the Dutch, Danish or Swedish armies were often strongly committed to the Protestant cause and usually chose to join the Covenanting or Parliamentary armies. English and Irish Catholics were particularly drawn to the Spanish Army of Flanders, and upon return home were likely to become Royalists or Confederates during the civil wars in England and Ireland. Of the political and military leaders of the opposing forces in England, probably a higher proportion of Royalists had foreign military experience because they tended to be younger and more widely travelled than Parliamentarians. The Royalist armies had more than sufficient numbers of officers and men, and always included numerous veterans of the Thirty Years War—especially from among the Welsh. One-third of the more than 500 English Royalist colonels studied by Dr P. R. Newman possessed sufficient knowledge and experience of military matters to be regarded as professionals. In Sir William Waller's Parliamentarian army more than half of the senior officers were Scottish veterans of continental European armies.[4] When the civil war broke out in England, Sir Henry Gage, who had commanded an English regiment in the Spanish Army of Flanders, came to the king at Oxford and offered his services. He had many years of experience as well as considerable theoretical knowledge of warfare. Not only was he able to bring several hundred veteran soldiers with him, he also diverted a shipment of arms coming from the Spanish Netherlands and intended for the Parliamentarians to use against the Royalist forces. His knowledge of fortification led the king to appoint him governor of Oxford. Gage immediately set about strengthening Oxford's defences and establishing lines of communication to the city and garrison's sources of provisions, but he served only three weeks before he was killed.[5] Another Catholic and veteran of the Low-Countries wars was Sir John Smith, a younger brother of Charles, first Lord Carrington. He had the reputation of being widely read in the military literature of the day, and proved to be a bold cavalry commander in the First Civil War and had risen to the rank of major-general of horse in the western army of Lord John

---

[3] Carlton, *GW* 19; I. Roy, 'England Turned Germany? The Aftermath of the Civil War and its European Context', *TRHS* 5th ser. 28 (1978), 130–1; *supra* Ch. 5.

[4] J. R. Jones, *Britain and Europe in the Seventeenth Century* (1967), 6–7; P. R. Newman, *The Old Service: Royalist Regimental Colonels and the Civil Wars, 1642–46* (1993), 126–7; Roy, 'England Turned Germany?', 130–1; R. Hutton, *The Royalist War Effort, 1642–46* (1982), 28–9.

[5] Edward Walsingham, *Alter Britanniae Heros: Or the Life of . . . Sir Henry Gage* (1645), 7–9, 19–21, 25.

Stewart before he was killed at the Battle of Bramdean, Hants., at the age of 30.[6] Sir Jacob Astley, later Lord Astley, trained in the Dutch army as a volunteer, was commissioned at the Battle of Nieuwpoort, served under Sir Horace Vere in the Palatinate, in the Swedish army under the marquis of Hamilton, and became a Royalist general in the English civil wars.[7]

In the Parliamentary armies, Sir Thomas Fairfax was an experienced officer who, like two previous generations of his family, had soldiered in the States' Army; he was an effective, calm and inspiring battlefield commander who became lord general of the New Model Army.[8] Colonel Christopher Potley, Sir William Waller's major-general, was a veteran of the Swedish army; he was highly regarded by Chancellor Axel Oxenstierna and the Swedish Senate, who conferred upon him a gold medal with the effigy of Gustavus Adolphus and a substantial pension for life. During his brief interlude as a Parliamentary officer, Sir Henry Rich, earl of Holland, showed great skill in deploying the London trained bands at the Battle of Turnham Green, which stopped the Royalist advance upon London. Like his commander at Turnham Green, the second earl of Essex, Holland had served in the States' Army. Essex's position as lord general owed more to the mantle which he had inherited from his father as leader of the swordsmen who had long advocated a strong and active alliance with mainland European Protestants against the Hapsburgs. His popularity with his soldiers, who cheered him with a 'Hey for Old Robin!', and his ability to recruit on the basis of that popularity outweighed his limited military competence.[9]

A military background and wide experience did not necessarily guarantee competence. Edward, second Viscount Conway, was born at The Brill, a Dutch cautionary town where his father was governor, and raised in a military garrison. He served his apprenticeship in arms under his uncle Sir Horace Vere and was commissioned in the States' Army. Clarendon said of him that 'there was no action of the English either at sea or land in which he had not a considerable reputation', although Sir Philip Warwick states that his behaviour at the Isle of Rhé did nothing to enhance that reputation. Since that expedition his principal area of expertise lay in 'eating and drinking'. A congenial and widely read man, he was a personal favourite of Algernon Percy, fourteenth earl of Northumberland, and the earl of Strafford, the lord general and lieutenant-general respectively, in the Second Bishops' War. Conway was appointed general of the horse through their patronage. Despite the fact that Conway and his troopers held the high ground and the strategic advantage at the Battle of Newburn, he failed to prevent the Scots Covenanters from crossing the River Tyne. His soldiers fled in panic, and Conway failed to rally them. Conway never again showed his face to the enemy and was disgraced.[10]

---

[6] Edward Walsingham, *Britannicae Virtatis Imago: or the Effigies of . . . Major-Generall Smith* (1644), 1–20.

[7] E. Warburton, *Memoirs of Prince Rupert and the Cavaliers*, 3 vols. (1849), i. 467–71.

[8] Gentles, *NMA* 60.

[9] Bulstrode Whitelocke, *Memorials of English Affairs*, 4 vols. (repr. 1853), i. 191, 211–12. SSNE, no. 6694. Potley later assisted Whitelock on his diplomatic missions to Sweden.

[10] Clarendon, *RCW* i. 185–6, 189–90; Sir Philip Warwick, *Memoirs of the Reign of King Charles I* (1813), 158.

The arrival of Prince Rupert of the Rhine in the Royalist camp at Nottingham in 1642 gave the king a commander with boldness and dash, which the Royalist armies had previously lacked. The personal courage and example of leaders such as Rupert still counted for a great deal in inspiring an army to fight. Rupert had made his first appearance on the battlefield in 1632 at age 13, when he accompanied the prince of Orange at the Siege of Rijnberg. In 1637, at the age of 18, he commanded a regiment of horse in the Thirty Years War in Germany and then spent three years as a prisoner of war. Rupert knew how to discipline an army, but not how to discipline himself or bridle his tongue. He would accept orders only from his uncle the king, and even then only on a selective basis. Rupert was also given to outbursts of temper and taciturnity which prevented him from getting along with the civilian counsellors on the king's council of war. In later life he grew to be an affable and courteous man, and he was always a hard-working officer. Rupert maintained an interest in the technical aspects of war which contrasted with the amateurism of many Royalist officers. When the king sent him to escort Queen Henrietta Maria to the Netherlands to raise money and buy arms, Rupert upon return brought with him experts in military engineering and ordnance.[11]

Martial values continued to permeate Scottish society, and the Scots served in the mainland European wars in large numbers—especially in the armies of Sweden, Denmark-Norway and the Netherlands. The Scottish Covenanters organized effectively for war from the beginning of the Bishops' Wars in 1638, and were able to recruit the cadre of a standing army from among experienced officers who had served in the armies of northern Europe. The commander of the Covenanting Army was Sir Alexander Leslie, later earl of Leven, who brought with him numerous veterans of the Swedish army. Leslie and his followers introduced techniques of the military revolution perfected in the Dutch and Swedish armies as well as bringing over a quantity of arms and munitions. Although the Scottish nobility recruited and nominally commanded most of the regiments of the Covenanting Army, the Scottish veterans of Swedish service actually led them in the field. Robert Munro, who became major-general of the foot and later led the Scots army in Ulster, had long commanded the proprietary regiment of Sir Donald Mackay, Lord Rheay, in Danish and Swedish service while the latter carried on his recruiting activities from northern Scotland or negotiated with government officials in Stockholm. Scottish veterans of the armies of northern Europe also contributed their expertise to the English Parliamentary forces in the early days. Sir James Dalrymple, later first Viscount Stair, for example, had fled Scotland after killing his father's murderer, and became a soldier overseas. He later returned and commanded a troop of Parliamentary dragoons.[12] Although the numbers have not

---

[11] Warwick, *Memoirs*, 248–51; [Thomas Malthus], *Historical Memoires of the Life and Death of... Rupert, Prince Palatine of the Rhine* (1683), 4–5; P. Morah, *Prince Rupert of the Rhine* (1976), 68–70; W. E. Knowles Middleton (ed. and trans.), *Lorenzo Magalotti at the Court of Charles II: His 'Relazione d'Inghilterra' of 1688* (1980), 38–9.

[12] J. Robertson, *The Scottish Enlightenment and the Militia Issue* (1985), 4–5; A. I. Macinnes, *Charles I and the Making of the Covenanting Movement, 1625–1641* (1991), 191; C. Rogers (ed.),

yet been worked out, a very high proportion of the general-officer and field-grade ranks in the Covenanting Army must have been professional soldiers, or what many English and Scottish aristocrats contemptuously called 'soldiers of fortune'. By contrast, of the 1630 officers who fall into these categories in the English Royalist armies, only 273 (or 17 per cent) can be classified as soldiers of fortune.[13]

The aristocracies of England and Scotland displayed a pronounced prejudice against the employment of soldiers of fortune or 'mercenary auxiliaries', as they were called in the Tacitean mode. Robert Greville, second Lord Brooke, believed that military commands should be given only to peers and expressed a distaste for professional officers who had served in the Thirty Years War. Brooke feared that they would introduce their plundering ways into England and, desiring to keep the war going and themselves in employment, would be enemies of a negotiated peace.[14] The belief that mercenary soldiers were easier to call in than to get rid of and likely to do more harm to those whom they served than the enemy was deep-seated in English thinking.[15] The professional soldiers who fought in the British civil wars were accused of not getting along with their fellow officers who were drawn from the gentry, of being harsh towards civilians and their own soldiers and of too readily changing sides to keep themselves gainfully employed. While the professional soldiers possessed military expertise and knowledge of the latest military technology, their presence in the Royalist and Parliamentarian armies always carried a cost, because it brought those causes into disrepute.[16] Lucy Hutchinson speaks disparagingly of Sir Thomas Ballard, the commander of the Parliamentary forces in Lincolnshire, whom she suspected had ties to some of the 'disaffected' gentry defending the Royalist garrison at Newark. Ballard, who came from a decayed gentry family, apparently secured his command because he 'had been bred up in the wars abroad'. Mrs Hutchinson thought that Ballard was lukewarm in leading the Parliamentary forces in their assault on Newark, and fellow officers complained of his 'sloth and outward carriage'.[17]

As a historian and political commentator, the earl of Clarendon was influenced by Machiavelli. He expressed a widespread English prejudice when he referred to Scottish soldiers as 'auxiliaries' or 'mere mercenaries'.[18] One of the reasons why

'Rehearsal of Events which occurred in the North of Scotland from 1635 to 1645 in Relation to the National Covenant', *TRHS* OS 5 (1877), 370–1; Sir John Dalrymple, *Memoirs of Great Britain and Ireland*, 2 vols. (1771–3), I. i. 216–17; SSNE, no. 5235.

[13] P. R. Newman, 'The Royalist Officer Corps, 1642–1660: Army Command as a Reflexion of Social Structure', *HJ* 26: 4 (1983), 953.

[14] Robert Greville, 2nd Lord Brooke, *A . . . Speech made by . . . Lord Brooke* (1643), 6–7.

[15] Sir Walter Raleigh, *The History of the World* (1614), ed. C. A. Patrides (repr. 1971), bk. V. ii. ii. 356–7; Thomas Fuller, *The Historie of the Holy Warre* (1639), 90; *The Earl of Castlehaven's Review: or His Memoires of . . . the Irish Wars* (1684), app., 19–20; D. Parrott, 'The Causes of the Franco-Spanish War of 1635–59', in J. Black (ed.), *The Origins of War in Early Modern Europe* (1987), 79.

[16] Roy, 'England Turned Germany?', 132–3; J. L. Malcolm, *Caesar's Due: Loyalty and King Charles, 1642–1646* (1983), 91–2.

[17] Lucy Hutchinson, *Memoirs of the Life of Colonel Hutchinson*, ed. C. H. Firth (1906), 114–17.

[18] Clarendon, *RCW* i. 99 n. 2, 149, 159, 214, 322; F. Raab, *The English Face of Machiavelli: A Changing Interpretation, 1500–1700* (1964), 149 and n.

English aristocrats regarded Scottish veterans of the Thirty Years War as soldiers of fortune was that so many of them chose their employers for reasons other than religious allegiance in what most observers regarded as a war of religion. The Swedes were dismayed when they captured two Scottish officers in the Imperialist army near Nuremburg who were Presbyterians. Colonel John Gordon commanded a regiment of Scots and Irish, and Walter Leslie was a major in the Imperial Guards. Leslie subsequently became a Catholic when he was made a count of the Holy Roman Empire. When Sir James Turner heard of the outbreak of the Bishops' Wars, he obtained his discharge from the Swedish army and went to Gothenburg to board a ship for home. Although his sentiments were Royalist, he admits that he chose the Covenanting side because the ship carrying Covenanters was the first that he came upon. Turner was distrusted by the Scottish nobility because he was a professional soldier. Later, after he became a Royalist, Charles II and Edward Hyde (later earl of Clarendon) proposed in 1654 sending Turner to the Highlands to communicate with William Cunningham, ninth earl of Glencairn, whom the king had commissioned to raise a rebellion against the Cromwellian regime. Turner demurred, saying that he would not make the best emissary because 'Glencairn and the other lords would look upon me as a soldier, and so one of those whom they thought had caballed together to suppress the nobility'. Turner candidly admitted that 'this was no excuse, but a certain and real truth'.[19]

Sir Alexander Leslie became the commander of the Covenanting Army through the influence of his clan chief, John Leslie, sixth earl of Rothes, one of the chief organizers of the Covenanting movement. Most contemporary observers made a point of noting his illegitimate birth, although he came of noble stock. Leslie was a successful professional soldier, who began his career in Sir Horace Vere's Regiment in the States' Army and, after fighting through most of the Thirty Years War, achieved the rank of field marshal in the Swedish army. He returned home with sufficient wealth to purchase two earldoms in Fife, and became known as the earl of Leven. Many in Scotland feared that an army which contained so many mercenaries and veterans of the Thirty Years War would rampage and plunder its way across the countryside, but Leslie proved quite capable of maintaining order and discipline in the Covenanting Army as well as providing invaluable advice on raising and equipping that army.[20]

The return home of professional soldiers was regarded with concern on both sides of the Border. Edward Somerset, sixth Lord Herbert of Raglan (later second marquis of Worcester), thought that Patrick Ruthven, earl of Forth and Brentford, who had been a lieutenant-general in the Swedish army and was appointed general-in-chief of the English Royalist army in 1642–3, was heedless of the well

---

[19] Sir James Turner, *Memoirs of his own Life and Times, 1632–1670*, BC 31 (1829), 13–16, 115.
[20] *Cal. S.P., Dom, 1640–1641*, 211–12; John Spalding, *The History of the Troubles and Memorable Transactions in Scotland and England, 1625–1645*, 2 vols., BC 25 (1828–9), i. 87–8; D. Laing (ed.), *The Letters and Journals of Robert Baillie*, 3 vols., BC, 76 (1841–2), i. 213–14; C. S. Terry, *The Life and Campaigns of Alexander Leslie, First Earl of Leven* (1899), 1, 11, 17–18, 20–1, 39–40.

being of noncombatants after long years of service in Germany. However, Ruthven's choice of serving in the Royalist rather than the Covenanting Army, which cut him off from so many of his old Scottish comrades from the Swedish army, was one based upon conscience.[21] The presence of Scottish professional soldiers in the Parliamentary armies was also a politically divisive issue. The Presbyterian Denzil Holles, in an anti-Cromwellian tirade, expressed a strong dislike for members of Parliament, such as Sir Arthur Hazelrig, who played at being soldiers, while stating a preference for experienced professional soldiers, who often happened to be Scots.[22] Members of Parliament also objected to the practice of subsidizing reformado officers (those who, temporarily without a command, served in the ranks) whether on full-pay or half-pay, because they were thought to be mercenaries and likely to foment tumults and mutinies when they were disbanded.[23] Amateur officers often thought that professional soldiers were too cautious about attacking or pursuing the enemy; the latter, through long experience, knew that they needed to weigh the risks of pursuing a fleeing enemy when their own troops were already exhausted by battle or when the possibility existed of a breakdown of order and discipline which would make an army unmanageable.[24]

The concept of selecting a military officer or commander on the basis of competence, experience or even seniority was still regarded as novel in England. Hobbes tells us that Henry Howard, third earl of Arundel, was chosen to command the king's army during the Second Bishops' War in 1640 because 'his ancestors had formerly given an overthrow to the Scots in their own country' and because of a 'foolish superstition' that he might enjoy the luck of his ancestors.[25] At the beginning of the English civil wars, Parliament appointed the third earl of Essex as lord general because he enjoyed popularity and could therefore attract volunteers; Essex had also commanded armies and had disassociated himself from the royal court. He was the son of his father, who was thought to have gained honour in the expedition to Cadiz and elsewhere, and had been the 'darling of the people'. Looking back on the Bishops' Wars, Clarendon remembered that a distinction could be discerned between courtiers and swordsmen. Essex had been favoured for command by the latter, while Arundel, whom the king preferred, merely looked martial.[26] Although the king passed Essex over for command of the Royalist forces in the Bishops' Wars, he would have agreed that it was appropriate for Essex to command the Parliamentary armies at the beginning of the civil wars since he regarded Essex as the 'chief rebel'. Perhaps Essex had the better claim to high command, but no one ever argued that he was competent, and he was removed from his command in 1645 by the Self-Denying Ordinance along with

[21] Newman, *Old Service*, 9–11; SSNE, no. 6696.

[22] *Memoirs of Denzil Lord Holles* (1699), 27.

[23] *Journals of the House of Commons* (1803), ii. 40b.

[24] R. Spalding (ed.), *The Diary of Bulstrode Whitelocke, 1605–1675*, BARSEH NS 13 (1990), 140–1.

[25] Thomas Hobbes, *Behemoth: The History of the Causes of the Civil Wars of England*, ed. William Molesworth (1682; repr. 1963), 39–40.   [26] Ibid. 140; Clarendon, *RCW* i. 150.

other aristocratic commanders. However, his funeral in 1646 afforded Parliament the opportunity to remind people that their first commander-in-chief had been a person of almost princely stature, and accordingly, he was given a lavish funeral at state expense.[27]

In Scotland on the eve of the Bishops' Wars, the crown had been conceded the right to exert force, but the nobility still retained the actual physical control of that force. When King Charles declared war on the Covenanters, the Scottish nobility combined these important manifestations of sovereignty in the Covenanting government. As late as 1644, when the Covenanting Army invaded England, almost all of the colonels of the thirty-one regiments of horse and foot were peers or sons of peers, and the military structures of this new government continued to be dominated by the nobility. Likewise, in the English Royalist forces the granting of commissions as colonels of regiments was closely related to their ability to raise soldiers, which preserved a certain advantage for landowners. But, once these regiments were raised, the English and Scottish aristocrats began to function as military officers, while the exercise of their seigneurial powers began to diminish.[28] Although the colonels of regiments in the English Royalist armies almost always came from peerage or gentry families, they might be younger brothers rather than heads of families or heirs. On the battlefield, a colonel who was a peer might find himself subordinated to a major-general who was of lesser social rank, and thus military competence and experience might in practice, if not by design, come to weigh more than social rank. In mainland European armies, in order to execute complex formations and manoeuvres on the battlefield, a new and more differentiated military hierarchy had come into existence ranging from corporals in companies to sergeant-major-generals or major-generals. Colonels, when drawn from the nobility, usually lacked the technical expertise to execute the new duties associated with modern warfare, although they remained useful for recruiting and other less demanding tasks. The rank of major-general was associated with the introduction of the military revolution, and since that officer issued the orders on the battlefield, he was invariably an experienced old soldier. It is the emergence of a clear and precise hierarchy of military rank as opposed to social rank which marks the emergence of a professional officer corps. Unfortunately, Charles I did not understand this development, and he continued to appoint military officers who were incompetent or whose brutal treatment of civilians damaged the Royalist cause.[29]

The increasing preference shown to professional soldiers in all of the armies during the Wars of the Three Kingdoms dismayed members of the aristocracy

---

[27] I. Gentles, 'Political Funerals During the English Revolution', in S. Porter (ed.), *London and the Civil War* (1996), 210.

[28] K. M. Browne, 'From Scottish Lords to British Officers: State Building, Elite Integration and the Army in the Seventeenth Century', in Macdougall, *S&W* 139–40; Newman, *Old Service*, 60–1.

[29] D. Eltis, *The Military Revolution in Sixteenth-Century Europe* (1995), 54–6, 58; Newman, *Old Service*, 660–1, 77–8; Malcolm, *Caesar's Due*, 94; Warwick, *Memoirs*, 27–8. On the French army, see D. Bitton, *The French Nobility in Crisis, 1560–1640* (1969), 40.

whose ideas about how to conduct warfare derived from their knowledge of earlier ages or from reading chivalric romances. That chivalric values still formed part of the vocabulary of a common language of honour at the beginning of the civil wars is now evident. The first battle of the Bishops' Wars began in 1640 with challenges and proclamations read by heralds. The initial battles of the English civil wars saw challenges to single combat issued by the earl of Essex, Lord Brooke and the earls of Lindsey and Newcastle in order to decide the outcome of the battle without a further effusion of blood.[30] Sir John Smith, while still a lieutenant during the Bishops' Wars, executed a feat of daring by leading a small party of horse behind enemy lines to punish a Scottish troop which had occupied and plundered the house of a local gentleman. He brought one Douglas, the sheriff of Teviotdale, back as a prisoner.[31] In a skirmish between Royalist and Parliamentarian cavalry in 1643, Sir Philip Stapleton rode up alone to Prince Rupert and fired his pistols at him (to no effect).[32] This somewhat archaic chivalric tradition embodied what John Adamson calls a 'rhetoric of ideas and values' not yet divided by ideological differences and shared by both sides. This rhetoric of chivalry was, however, employed by both Royalists and Parliamentarians in their propaganda justifying the resort to civil war. One recurrent theme of Parliamentarian propaganda was the depiction of the lord general, the third earl of Essex, as an exemplar of unwavering opposition to Spanish tyranny and popery, and the heir of a tradition of English chivalry which harked back to Sir Philip Sidney in the Netherlands and the second earl of Essex's raid on Cadiz in 1596.[33] Although Royalists such as Prince Rupert or the earl of Newcastle could identify with this tradition, the king could not. Clarendon believed that Charles I's army might have had a better chance of repulsing the Scottish invaders in 1640 if the earl of Essex had commanded it. But the fact that a courtier, the earl of Northumberland, had been appointed instead added to the slights which had alienated Essex from the king's party. Earlier, Essex had also been denied the keepership of Needwood Forest, which was practically at his own gate.[34]

    Chivalric culture was perhaps moribund, but those who still adhered to its values were doubtless pleased by the martial displays drawn up for a review by the king at York in the spring of 1639 in preparation for confronting the Scottish Covenanters on the Border. The better part of the English peerage and gentry were personally engaged and were expected to raise horsemen, who were organized in a manner more closely resembling feudal retinues than troops of cavalry. Sir Henry Slingsby was charged to raise two light horsemen from his estates in the West Riding, and he and his two horsemen joined the earl of Holland's troop of horse which was quartered at Slingsby's cousin's house at Twizel. After a stay of six weeks,

---

    [30] J. S. A. Adamson, 'Chivalry and Political Culture in Caroline England', in K. Sharpe and P. Lake (eds.), *Culture and Politics in Early Stuart England* (1993), 182–3.
    [31] Walsingham, *Britannicae Virtutis Imago*, 7–8.   [32] Whitelock, *Memorials*, i. 217.
    [33] Adamson, 'Chivalry and Political Culture', 164, 166–7, 185–7.
    [34] Clarendon, *RCW* i. 185.

during which the earl of Holland 'gave great entertainments to many of the commanders that frequented...him at that place', Slingsby decided that he liked the military life and thought that it was 'a commendable way of breeding gentlemen'. William Cavendish, first earl (and later first duke) of Newcastle, also raised a troop of horse that consisted entirely of '120 knights and gentlemen of quality', which marched to Berwick. A conflict arose between Newcastle and Holland, who was general of the horse, over the precedence of their troops. Newcastle was ordered to march with his troop in the rear of those belonging to the 'general officers of the field'. Newcastle's troop of horse had been designated Prince Charles's Troop, and rather than 'lessen his master's dignity by the command of any subject', he had furled the prince's colours. Subsequently, Newcastle complained to the king, who again subverted the military hierarchy by placing Newcastle and Prince Charles's Troop directly under his own command. When the army was disbanded, Newcastle challenged Holland to a duel to answer for the slight, but the king 'caused them both to be confined until they had made their peace'.[35]

Few of those brave gallants who marched to Berwick realized how fast the European military world was changing. One could no longer claim to be a warrior by being born noble; to assert military status one must now appear on the battlefield as part of a troop or a regiment of an army. Individual armorial bearings had disappeared from the battlefield, although individual company colours and troop pennants or guidons might still proclaim the identity of the captain. Soldiers were beginning to wear distinctive uniforms, and a man became an 'officer' because an office had been conveyed to him by a commission of the king or Parliament. Officers continued to resist the anonymity of modern military discipline and military uniforms by means of personal displays of valour on the battlefield, but it was a losing struggle as professionalization proceeded apace.[36] The practice of awarding captain's commissions on the basis of aristocratic privilege and royal patronage rather than promoting through the ranks offended and discouraged young gentlemen volunteers, although, as in every war, the increased rate of mortality tended to open up opportunities. Moreover, when a wealthy and high-ranking peer such as Edward Somerset, Lord Herbert of Raglan, the son and heir of the marquis of Worcester, proved to be an incompetent commander, his subordinates usually had to take the blame for his mistakes. After the disastrous campaigns of 1643, which seriously weakened the Royalist war effort in Herefordshire, a more experienced officer was appointed to become his second-in-command, although Herbert retained his rank and honour and was spared disgrace.[37] Prince

[35] *Original Memoirs Written during the Great Civil War, Being the Life of Sir Henry Slingsby* (1806), 26–8; Margaret Cavendish, duchess of Newcastle, *The Life of William Cavendish, Duke of Newcastle*, ed. C. H. Firth (1906), 6–7; see also Hutchinson, *Memoirs of the Life of Colonel Hutchinson*, 92.

[36] M. Keen, *Chivalry* (1984), 243; A. Giddens, *The Nation-State and Violence* (1985), 114–15; Bennett, 'The Officer Corps and Army Command', 301–2, 314–15.

[37] John Cruso, *Instructions for the Cavallrie* (1632), 8–9, 57–8, 112; Hutton, *Royalist War Effort*, 57–8, 112.

Rupert caused difficulties within the Royalist high command because his uncle the king, in recognition of his close relationship and royal dignity, had given him an independent command which stood outside the military hierarchy. Rupert not only refused to accept orders from the civilian secretary of state, Lucius Cary, second Viscount Falkland, but also would not obey a command from Robert Bertie, first earl of Lindsey, the commanding general, concerning the disposition of troops on the battlefield at the Battle of Edgehill. In a council of war convened on the eve of battle, Charles once again subverted the military hierarchy by ruling in favour of his nephew's desire to employ the more complicated Swedish system of battle squares rather than the more familiar and less complicated Dutch formation—contrary to the advice of Sir Jacob Astley, the sergeant-major-general of the foot, who was responsible for putting the battle plan into execution.[38] When the battle began, Rupert allowed his cavalry to pursue 'the chase, contrary to the discipline of war', and left the Royalist foot exposed to counter-attack by the Parliamentary commander, the earl of Essex, which 'gave Essex a title unto the victory of that day, which might have been his last day if they had done their parts and stood their ground'.[39]

Professional soldiers and amateur swordsmen from among the landed aristocracy also had different perceptions of what constituted military duty and martial reputation. Looking back on the English civil wars, in which he had spent a fortune raising soldiers for the late king, the second marquis of Worcester told Charles II that a soldier of fortune need 'not care for the love of people', but a nobleman had to be sensitive about such things lest the people hold a grudge against his posterity. Worcester said that his father had told him that the amount of money which he had spent in raising soldiers for the king would excite envy against him, and he had found this to be true.[40] Such sensitivity to public opinion within their own county communities may have been more characteristic of magnates than Royalist officers of lesser social stature. Most Royalist commanders and officers were thought to be indifferent to losses of soldiers other than persons of quality, to such an extent that it harmed the Royalist cause. Moreover, the losses through death in combat, sickness and desertion were so extensive that some Royalist regiments and troops came to be composed entirely of reformado officers.[41]

When the English civil wars began, the highest positions of command were given to grandees such as the third earl of Essex, Edward Montagu, Lord Mandeville (and soon to be the second earl of Manchester), and William Russell, sixth earl of Bedford. They had been important figures in parliamentary politics, and had support in the associational armies formed early in the war and among the county committees which tended to favour such worthies. From the beginning, the various Parliamentary armies had lacked military officers who were well-born gentlemen, and it was a common practice for regimental commanders such as Oliver Cromwell, when he raised a regiment in the fens, to appoint

---

[38] Morah, *Rupert of the Rhine*, 86–8. [39] Warwick, *Memoirs*, 252–4.
[40] Warburton, *Memoirs of Prince Rupert*, iii. 525. [41] Newman, *Old Service*, 67.

kinsmen as officers. However, the mediocre performance of the grandees and their lack of commitment to total military victory led to their replacement by men of lesser social rank but greater military ability.[42] Members of Parliament, such as Bulstrode Whitelocke, believed that their dignity required that they be given higher military rank than they actually received. Whitelocke was disappointed because he received no more than the command of a troop of horse when he had expected a regiment. He claimed that he had once commanded a troop in the French Royal Army, a commission which had indeed been offered to Whitelocke, but which, in fact, he had never taken up. The degree of Whitelocke's mastery of the strategy of modern warfare is revealed by the fact that he employed his troop to fortify and garrison his own seat at Fawley Court.[43]

The officer corps of the various Parliamentary armies became politicized over such issues as war aims, the role of peers in military command, the social status of junior officers as well as dislike of Scots and conflicts between Presbyterians and Independents. While the Parliamentary military forces were compelled to purge the grandees through a remodelling of the army in order to find commanders who were ideologically committed to achieving full victory, the king had no difficulty in recruiting commanders who were completely loyal to him and determined to win.[44]

The Self-Denying Ordinance, by excluding aristocratic officers such as the earls of Essex and Manchester, established an officer corps based on competence rather than birth, and it drew officers from the middling and mechanic classes. The criteria for promotion in the New Model Army were based partly upon seniority—especially at the troop and company level—but merit certainly counted for more at the higher ranks. This experiment was wholly without precedent in English military experience, and would never be repeated to the same extent—even in the twentieth century. When Sir Thomas Fairfax, the commander of the New Model Army, began to nominate officers, both Houses of Parliament, which retained the right to approve his nominations, objected to one-third of his nominees because they were religious and political radicals. The peers were undoubtedly offended by their own exclusion from command in the New Model Army, and also because the old leadership of the associational armies, including Manchester, Essex and other lords, had been effectively rusticated. The Peace Party were also defeated, and the role of Scottish professional officers diminished.[45] Furthermore, this was a highly politicized army which was determined to have a voice in the religious and political settlements which were being discussed in Parliament at the end of the First English Civil War. One of the army's leaders insisted that the New Model Army was no 'mere mercenary army, hired to serve

---

[42] I. Gentles, 'The Civil Wars in England', in J. Kenyon and J. Ohlmeyer (ed.), *The Civil Wars: A Military History of England, Scotland and Ireland, 1638–1660* (1998), 108; Carlton, GW 76, 182.

[43] Spalding (ed.), *Diary of Bulstrode Whitelocke*, 132–3; BL, Add. MS. 53,726, fo. 101.

[44] Gentles, *NMA* 4–5; Newman, *Old Service*, 2–3.

[45] Schwoerer, *NSA* 52–3; Firth, *CA* 49–50; Gentles, *NMA* 16–24.

any arbitrary power of a state, but had been authorized and raised by Parliament to preserve the liberties of Parliament and the people'.[46]

The Scots Army of the Solemn League and Covenant from the beginning followed a policy of requiring noble commanders without prior military experience to be assisted by professional soldiers with experience. In 1638–9 the Tables, as the interim and *de facto* governing body of the Covenanting movement were known, had decreed that in each regiment the colonel should employ a lieutenant-colonel and a major who were professional soldiers, while the ensign and sergeants of each company were also to be experienced soldiers. Otherwise, commissions, as might be expected, were awarded on the basis of patronage and kinship. Hugh Fraser, master of Lovat and heir of Hugh, seventh Lord Lovat, was made a lieutenant-colonel after marrying Sir Alexander Leslie's daughter. He may have accompanied James Graham, fifth earl of Montrose, in the occupation of Aberdeen, but died in 1643 without ever seeing a battle.[47] Andrew Melville obtained a commission in a cavalry regiment in the Covenanting Army commanded by Andrew, seventh Lord Gray, where his brother was a captain. Although Melville joined as a gentleman volunteer, Lord Gray very shortly found a cornetcy for him. When peace was concluded in 1647, Melville and his brother went to France to serve as mercenaries. Melville eventually served in the armies of France, Sweden and Brandenburg.[48]

Dr P. R. Newman's analysis of the social backgrounds of more than 500 Royalist colonels reveals that 90 per cent of them were peers or armigerous gentry. Thus, the Royalist armies were overwhelmingly recruited and led by the aristocracy. Of the 505 colonels examined, heads of families numbered 277 while 140 were younger sons or brothers. With regard to social status, 67.5 per cent of the Royalist colonels were gentry (including knights). Fifty-nine colonels were baronets and sixty-nine were peers or members of peerage families. Thirty-eight of these were members of the English peerage together with six Irish peers and three Scots. Dr Newman also believes that this aristocratic leadership of the Royalist forces represented to a considerable extent a class war on their social inferiors. That a third of these Royalist colonels had enough experience or knowledge of warfare to be regarded as professional soldiers does not invalidate this point, because knowledge of military affairs had become part of a gentleman's education.[49]

Denzil Holles and other Presbyterian enemies of the New Model Army thought that with the exception of their commander, Sir Thomas Fairfax, who was heir to a Scottish peerage, most of the officers of that army were sectarians and mechanics of low birth. However, Sir Charles Firth insisted that most were gentlemen by

---

[46] *A Declaration, or Representation of the Army* (1647), printed in W. Haller and G. Davies (eds.), *The Leveller Tracts, 1647–1653* (1944), 55.

[47] E. Furgol, *A Regimental History of the Covenanting Armies, 1639–1651* (1990), 4–5, 30–1; James Fraser, *Chronicles of the Frasers*, ed. W. Mackay, SHS 1ˢᵗ ser. 47 (1905), 276–80, 282.

[48] *Memoirs of Sir Andrew Melville*, trans. T. Ameer-Al (1918), 74–9; *DNB, sub* Andrew Melville (1624–1706).   [49] Newman, *Old Service*, 69–73, 126–7.

birth and nine came from noble families. Only seven colonels were not of gentle birth when the New Model Army was formed, although mortality opened up opportunities for the less well born, including London tradesmen. Cavalry officers tended to be drawn from higher social-status groups than infantry officers. As a whole, officers of the New Model Army had less experience of the mainland European wars than their Royalist counterparts—especially after the Scottish officers had been purged.[50]

Very few lawyers became officers, although there were some notable exceptions. One was Edward Littleton, first Lord Littleton, the lord keeper, who became a Royalist colonel and was regarded by Clarendon as a man of undoubted courage. He commanded a regiment raised for the defence of Oxford.[51] Bulstrode Whitelocke was another exception. He was for a time a Parliamentary officer, but proved to be more useful to the Cromwellian regime as a judge and a diplomat.[52]

Approximately one-tenth of the Royalist colonels were small gentry or parochial gentry or those who claimed to be gentlemen, and probably a large proportion of the company-grade officers would fit into this category. Some were of more marginal status—those who wished to become gentlemen and were attracted by cavalier culture. One such cavalier of marginal status was Sir Thomas Lunsford, a Royalist colonel who came from a decayed Sussex gentry family. In his younger days he was a notorious poacher, who had made a murderous assault on his neighbour, Sir Thomas Pelham of Laughton, who had prosecuted him in the Court of Star Chamber for unlawful hunting and assault on his gamekeepers. Lunsford avoided a sentence of three years' imprisonment by fleeing the realm and becoming a soldier in France. When he returned home, Charles I not only pardoned him, but made him lieutenant of the Tower of London. Before the English civil wars began, Lunsford alarmed members of Parliament by participating in a Royalist plot to seize the arsenal at Kingston-upon-Thames. An investigation by Parliament produced witnesses who testified that in France and the Low Countries Lunsford was known to be a drunkard and a quarreller, who once stole his company's payroll when he was an officer in the French army. Subsequently, as a Royalist officer, he shot mutineers without bothering to convene a court-martial and treated civilians in a brutal fashion. When Charles I gave commands to such men as Lunsford he alienated moderate opinion.[53] Another poacher who did well out of the war was Peter Bettsworth, variously described as a yeoman and a gentleman, who had made war on the deer belonging to Anthony Maria Browne, second Viscount Montague, a Catholic aristocrat, at Cowdray, near Midhurst,

[50] Firth, *CA*, 46–7.

[51] Newman, *Old Service*, 74–6; Clarendon, *RCW* ii. 106–10; *DNB*, *sub* Sir Edward Littleton, 1st Baron Littleton (1589–1645).   [52] Spalding (ed.), *Diary of Bulstrode Whitelock*, 86, 140.

[53] Clarendon, *RCW* i. 478; *The Journal of Sir Simonds D'Ewes from the First Recess of the Long Parliament to the Withdrawal of King Charles from London* (1942; repr. 1970), 345; W. H. Coates, A. S. Young and V. F. Snow (eds.), *The Private Journals of the Long Parliament, 3 January to 5 March 1642* (1982), 58, 172; Carlton, *GW* 43–4; *DNB*, *sub* Sir Thomas Lunsford (1610?–1653?); Manning, VR 291.

Sussex. It was difficult to persuade local juries to convict Bettsworth, but he was brought to heel by the Court of Star Chamber and heavily fined. During the Interregnum he became a justice of the peace, a member of the county committee and the Parliamentary governor of Calshot Castle, Hants.[54]

The presence of Catholic officers in the Royal army was another grievance of which Parliament had complained on the eve of the First English Civil War. In 1641 Parliament had enumerated seventy-one Catholics who held military commissions and called for their dismissal. It had been a policy of the king to exclude Catholics from his army, but he decided to make use of them when hostilities began. Understandably, this did little to enhance the popularity of the Royalist cause. High-ranking members of the Catholic nobility and gentry not only furnished much-needed support for the king's armies, but also provided castles, which served as garrisons. Basing House belonged to John Paulet, fifth marquis of Winchester, and withstood a long Roundhead siege; Raglan Castle was the seat of Edward, Lord Herbert of Raglan, later sixth earl of Worcester. Herbert was made lieutenant-general of South Wales and four other Catholic officers were given the same rank, contrary to the king's undertaking not to bestow high commands on any who were not Protestants. At the Battle of Edgehill, two of the five Royalist infantry brigades were commanded by Catholic officers. Although Catholics could hardly have exceeded 2 per cent of the population of England and Wales, possibly as many as one-third of the Royalist officer corps were Catholic, since we know that two-fifths of the Royalist officers killed in the English civil wars were Catholic.[55] Although the Royalist army may have looked like the pope's battalions to some, not all of the Puritans were to be found in the Parliamentary armies. Richard Atkyns, who had commanded a Royalist troop of horse at Chewton Fight in 1643, was Puritan enough to prefer taking communion with his troop on the day following the battle to sharing a venison dinner with his commander Prince Maurice.[56]

Veterans of the European religious and dynastic wars were to be found in all of the armies which fought in the Wars of the Three Kingdoms, but most officers acquired their introduction to military affairs from reading. Those who needed to learn about tactics and fortifications often started with Roman authors, but they very soon learned how the seventeenth-century mode of warfare differed from the past. This had the secondary effect of introducing them to the concept of historical change, thus initiating them into humanist culture and making them aware of the idea of progress. The emphasis on learning about war from experience tended to reinforce the empirical approach to the 'particularities' of war. This is connected to the explosion of military memoirs in the seventeenth century. Sir John Digby

---

[54] Manning, *VR* 294; id., *H&P* 224; A. Colby, *Central Government and the Localities: Hampshire, 1649–1689* (1987), 24.

[55] Malcolm, *Caesar's Due*, 94–6; J. Gillow, *A Literary and Biographical . . . Dictionary of English Catholics*, 5 vols. (1885–1902; repr. 1968), vol. i, p. x.

[56] *The Vindication of Richard Atkyns* (1669), in P. Young (ed.), *Military Memoirs: The Civil War* (1967), 16–17.

was an avid reader of books on 'martial affairs' in several languages. Although apparently he had no previous military experience, Digby commanded a troop of horse in the Second Bishops' War of 1640 which was well trained and disciplined and able to cover the retreat of the English infantry at the Battle of Newburn.[57] Roger Boyle, first earl of Orrery, could not forget witnessing the slaughter of a whole regiment in the Irish civil wars because the soldiers were unacquainted with the art of entrenching. His first important piece of writing before he achieved fame as a dramatist was his *A Treatise on the Art of War* (1677), which was written from notes based upon his reading and his experiences in the civil wars.[58]

The professionalization of officers serving in the English civil wars has been underestimated because very few of them chose to make lifelong careers of military service. However, there is much evidence that they had a good knowledge of professional codes of conduct derived from European military practice, and they were careful of their honour and reputation in negotiating terms of surrender and attempting to maintain discipline among their rank and file during the surrenders and to curb the natural propensity of their soldiers to plunder the defeated. Besides calling upon codes of honour which were widely dispersed throughout the European military world, Barbara Donagan believes that since most of these officers came from civilian backgrounds their sense of honour in their military careers was informed by concepts of gentlemanly honour which they had learned before taking up arms. This would have been reinforced by concepts of Christian duty that they had learned from sermons and reading.[59]

There seems to have been considerable unanimity of opinion concerning how officers were to behave upon the occasion of surrender. However, in armies where military hierarchies had not supplanted social hierarchies, considerable friction could arise in making military decisions about strategy and tactics. As a garrison or a field army prepared to engage the enemy, the usual practice in the European military world was for the commanding officer to convene a council or court of war customarily attended by all officers of the rank of colonel or higher. In the early stages of professionalization, where social hierarchies continued to intrude upon military hierarchies, high-ranking noblemen—even those without formal military rank—might also be invited. The members of the council of war, by custom, delivered their counsel candidly, but were supposed to yield to consensus when they were in the minority.[60] In actual practice, considerable factionalism surfaced in councils of war during the British and Irish civil wars from the very

---

[57] J. Dewald, *Aristocratic Experience and the Origins of Modern Culture: France, 1590–1715* (1993), 55–6; [Edward Walsingham], 'Life of Sir John Digby (1605–1645)', *CM XII*, CS 3rd ser. 18 (1910), 74–6.

[58] K. Lynch, *Roger Boyle, First Earl of Orrery* (1965), 221; *DNB*, *sub* Roger Boyle, Baron Broghill and 1st earl of Orrery (1621–1679).

[59] B. Donagan, 'The Web of Honour: Soldiers, Christians and Gentlemen in the English Civil War', *HJ* 44 (2001), 367–8.

[60] Henry Hexham, *The Second Parte of the Principles of the Art Militarie Practized in the Warres of the United Provinces* (1638), 6–7.

beginning, and it often arose from the different expectations of military amateurs and professional soldiers. Acting upon the advice of his council of war and veterans of the mainland European wars, the earl of Essex decided not to pursue the Royalists following the Battle of Turnham Green, although Bulstrode Whitelocke observed that it was later learned that the Royalists in retreat were particularly vulnerable. Experienced soldiers often feared that discipline would break down if soldiers, exhausted by battle and thirsting for plunder, pursued the enemy from the battlefield.[61] Whitelocke was also of the opinion that Essex later led his army into Cornwall for no good military reason except that one of his cavalry officers, John, second Lord Robartes, wished to collect his rents there. Finding themselves caught in a corner, Essex and Robartes embarked their cavalry and made their escape, leaving Major-General Sir Philip Skippon and his infantry without cavalry protection. Skippon wanted to fight his way out, but a majority of his council of war advised him to make terms with the Royalists.[62] Parliamentary army commanders such as Fairfax were usually scrupulous about consulting councils of war, because this was the accepted tradition in martial culture. Oliver Cromwell did likewise, except that he played a more dominant and leading role when he consulted them. His council of war also took on more of a political tone and became less important militarily. Fissures appeared in the command of the Parliamentary armies as early as the Battle of Marston Moor in 1644, between Cromwell and the Scottish officers in the Parliamentary forces. Cromwell had become the protector of the Independents against the Presbyterians, and Denzil Holles accused him of refusing to share the honours of victory with those Scots who had made important contributions to the victory over the Royalists, such as Major-General David Leslie, who commanded the Scottish horse, and Major-General Lawrence Crawford, who led the foot in the earl of Manchester's army. Cromwell's hatred of the Scots was not based upon a rational military assessment of their contribution but rather rested upon his belief that the Scots Presbyterian officers persecuted Independents in the Parliamentary armies. This proved to be disruptive to the army command structure.[63]

There were other ways in which non-military considerations worked against sound military strategy, good judgement and harmonious relations among allies. Noble commanders almost always placed their personal honour above such considerations. While James, duke of Hamilton was raising forces in Scotland for the Engager Army in July 1648 in order to intervene in England to restore Charles I, Sir Marmaduke Langdale, the English Royalist commander in the north, moved his army prematurely into Lancashire and desperately required assistance. Although Hamilton had not finished gathering his army together, to delay going to Langdale's assistance would have exposed Hamilton's honour as well as that of

61 Warwick, *Memoirs*, 158; Whitelock, *Memorials*, i. 192.

62 Whitelock, *Memorials*, i. 302; Firth, *Ludlow*, i. 100–1.

63 Firth, *CA* 57–8; id., *Oliver Cromwell and the Rule of the Puritans in England* (1900; repr. 1961), 102–8; *Memoirs of Denzil Lord Holles*, 15, 18; B. Coward, *Cromwell* (1991), 33–8.

the Royalist cause to injury. This is how Sir James Turner, one of Hamilton's lieutenants put the dilemma:

to march to his relief were to leave half of our forces in Scotland unlevied and an enemy behind our hand, ourselves in very bad condition, without money, meal or artillery or ammunition; to suffer him to perish was against honour, conscience and reason both of state and war. It would have given our enemies an occasion to insult; would have brought the duke's honour...to an everlasting loss, and would have given such apprehensions of jealousies to the Royalists in England, that never one of them would have joined with us, or owned us.[64]

In the event, when Hamilton finally joined Langdale, he failed to provide him with sufficient reinforcements to stand up to Cromwell and the New Model Army at the Battle of Preston in August 1648. Langdale put the blame for his defeat on what he called Hamilton's 'treachery and cowardice'.[65]

Differing perceptions of social rank versus military rank sometimes interfered with discipline and the carrying out of orders. When Charles I commanded Prince Rupert to go to the relief of the marquis of Newcastle's garrison at York and engage the armies of Fairfax and Manchester, Rupert, never known for tact, failed to consult with Newcastle before issuing commands to him in a very peremptory fashion. Rupert, it is true, was both a royal prince and an English peer (as duke of Cumberland), who outranked Newcastle socially and militarily at that time. But Newcastle was nearly twenty years Rupert's senior and a proud northern magnate, who had raised and paid for his own army and who had usually operated independently of the Royalist command structure. He was cooperating with Rupert more as an ally than a subordinate. By failing to follow protocol and consult with Newcastle and by neglecting to frame his commands as requests, Rupert alienated Newcastle on the eve of the Battle of Marston Moor. When Newcastle appeared to be dragging his feet, Rupert's usual display of confidence and initiative deserted him in what is regarded as the largest and most important battle of the First English Civil War. As a consequence of Marston Moor, Newcastle's army was shattered and Royalist resistance in the north withered.[66]

Rupert's presence in the Royalist high command continued to be divisive. After he surrendered the important port of Bristol, contrary to the king's express command, he was forbidden the royal presence. Rupert and his followers were convinced that George, Lord Digby, who variously served as secretary of state and lieutenant-general, had blackened their reputations, and, disobeying orders, Rupert entered Newark, where the governor, Sir Richard Willis, who was one of Rupert's supporters, provided a ceremonial welcome. Rupert then burst into the king's presence while he was at supper and demanded that the king convene a council of war to vindicate the prince's honour. The inquiry held by the council of

[64] Turner, *Memoirs*, 57–8.
[65] H. L. Rubinstein, *Captain Luckless: James, First Duke of Hamilton, 1606–1649* (1975), 206.
[66] Morah, *Rupert of the Rhine*, 152–4; Hutton, *Royalist War Effort*, 145–54.

war exonerated Rupert of the charges of treason and want of courage, but condemned him for indiscretion. This confrontation between Charles and Rupert
humiliated the latter, who replied by mounting what was little short of a mutiny.
Rupert assembled his horse (200 in number) in the market-place of Newark. The
king ordered John, Lord Belasyse, to draw up the Royal Life Guards to confront
them. Rupert asked for permission for him, his brother Prince Maurice and his
followers to leave England and enter foreign service. Charles replied that Rupert
and his followers could leave England, but he refused to give them permission to
enter a foreign army because they had 'dishonoured their swords'. Sir Richard
Willis, who departed with Rupert and the others, later sent Charles, Lord Gerard of
Brandon, back to Newark to challenge Belasyse to a duel. Belasyse was ordered by
the king not to accept the challenge, but he told the king that if he refused the
challenge, he would be dishonoured and could no longer serve the king.[67]

Most of the officers who fought in the British and Irish civil wars began as novices,
but were willing to learn the art of war from reading and their own experiences as
they plunged into the conflict. The war was sufficiently protracted and widespread to bestow upon most of them a degree of professional attainment.
However, they were less willing to learn from the veterans of the Thirty Years War
because of a deep-seated and persistent distrust of mercenary soldiers. It is difficult
to believe that this did not retard the reception of the theory and practice of the
military revolution, but it is difficult to assess to what extent this was true. To
mention only a few points, the Wars of the Three Kingdoms witnessed more
pitched battles and skirmishes and fewer prolonged sieges than was the case in the
mainland European wars, and cavalry certainly played a greater role in the British
and Irish civil wars than was the case in the Low-Countries wars.

At the same time, amateur swordsmen who commanded armies and regiments
were probably more willing to employ battlefield tactics learned from veteran professional soldiers than to be influenced by what the old soldiers had to say about
strategy. Long-term strategy and war aims remained matters of ideological dispute, which had to be fought out in the political rather than the military arena.
Certainly, many novices as well as professional soldiers continued to regard the
enemy as a worthy opponent in the earlier stages of the civil wars in England and
Scotland and continued to hope for a negotiated peace. However, it proved difficult to hold the king to past agreements at the end of the First English Civil War,
and the continuing desire for a negotiated settlement on the part of moderates
probably prolonged the wars. Unable to secure the kind of victory that would
assure a permanent peace, the moderates such as Essex and Manchester were
replaced by Cromwell and his kind, who were willing to put aside the rules of war
in order to pursue total victory. It is also clear that many swordsmen—whether

[67] HMC, '. . . Life and Memoirs of John Lord Belasyse, Written . . . by his Secretary, Joshua
Moone', *Ormonde MSS.*, NS 2 (1903), 388–90; Richard Symonds, *Diary of the Marches of the Royal
Army during the Great Civil War*, ed. C. E. Long, CS OS 74 (1859), 268–71.

amateurs or professionals—remained more focused on individual honour and reputation than on securing military objectives. Veterans of the mainland European conflicts, for all their military expertise, did not always obey orders from amateurs with higher military rank, and were not easy to integrate into officer corps made up mostly of military novices drawn from the landowning gentry.

Professionals and amateurs also disagreed about the application of discipline to soldiers in the ranks. Magnates and grandees depended upon popularity as a recruiting device, and always kept an eye upon how their tenants and the electorate would regard them and their posterity in more peaceful times. Magnates who possessed standing in their local communities were aware of the need not to offend local sentiment by allowing their soldiers to plunder civilian populations. The widespread phenomenon of armed neutralism testified to the difficulty of inculcating strong allegiance towards king or Parliament amongst the commonalty. Royalists who had been professional soldiers, such as Lord Goring, undoubtedly alienated many local communities. There were also many gentry among the Royalists who remained quite indifferent to the welfare of their soldiers, and saw their regiments waste away through disease and desertion. Some amateur swordsmen who still harboured chivalric notions about the superiority of mounted warfare also had difficulty becoming accustomed to the idea that modern warfare emphasized infantry tactics over cavalry, and they were dismayed by having to fill their regiments with lesser folk than gentlemen, often impressed, and lead them into battle.

An especially harmful legacy of the British and Irish civil wars was the degree to which military life and culture became politicized. Regimental commanders often achieved their military rank because of their social status as landlords, and their military and seigneurial functions might overlap and conflict. Many commanders were also members of the estates or parliaments of their respective kingdoms, and they arrived in camp with baggage trains laden with ideology and special interests. As landlords and magistrates who were used to wielding political influence in their local or national communities, acquiring and holding military office was a way of maintaining or extending political influence. Moreover, as the civil wars dragged on, questions of military competence, religious and political settlements, and social levelling heightened the conflict between social hierarchies and military hierarchies, and made aristocrats realize that measures had to be taken to preserve their privileged positions. These considerations must have troubled the minds of many aristocrats who found a military role thrust upon them, and it helps to explain the frequent changes of allegiance—especially among, but not limited to, English and Scottish officers. The Cromwellian regime would have appeared to be a stabilizing force after the suppression of the Levellers, but the Restoration would signify a return to sanity and hierarchical values.

8

Raising and organizing standing armies

We see the face of war and the forms of weapons alter almost daily; every nation striving to outwit each other in excellency of weapons.

Donald Lupton, *A Warre-like Treatise of the Pike* (1642), 131.

Another error may happen, especially where a free state is founded in arms, by conceding too great a power to the soldiery, who like the spirits of conjurers, do oftentimes tear their masters and raisers in pieces for want of employment.

Francis Osborne, *Advice to a Son* (1656), 112.

Whatever the constituent parts of a government are, if a strong army be in being, and it be headed by a Cromwell or a Lambert, the government may well be reckoned to consist of army as well as king, lords and commons; for brutish power will soon rank itself with reasonable and legal authority.

Sir Philip Warwick, *Memoirs of the Reign of King Charles I* (1813), 438.

The return of English, Irish and Scottish swordsmen from the mainland European armies upon the outbreak of the Wars of the Three Kingdoms introduced the influence of the military revolution, which necessitated more technically advanced weapons, larger and more permanent military forces as well as improved sources of finance and supply. There existed also by this time a large body of writings in English for those who wished to learn more about the increasingly technical aspects of war.[1] Experienced veterans and competent novices competed for positions of command and other military offices as the civil wars persisted; amateur gallants and grandees lost some of their briskness, and found it difficult to accept discipline and approach war as a corporate rather than an individual effort. Nostalgia for archaic weapons and individual displays of martial prowess persisted even among the military writers who were supposed to be advocating military innovation.[2] Officers who were willing to learn by experience and reading came to appreciate that an expert knowledge of military affairs and

---

[1] Carlton, *GW* 8; B. Donagan, 'Halcyon Days and the Literature of War: England's Military Education Before 1642', *P&P*, no. 147 (1995), 98–9. [2] Manning, *Swordsmen*, ch. 4.

proficiency obtained by training and drill were more valuable on the battlefield than valour and superior numbers. Gradually, commanders who had but recently been novices learned the importance of gathering intelligence, of developing lines of supply which freed their soldiers from foraging among local populations, and of concentrating their forces instead of scattering them among many small castles and fortified garrisons. Although there is evidence that many novice officers were developing a more professional attitude to the business of war, factionalism and a high degree of politicization among both officers and men continued to disrupt discipline and to contribute to political instability. This latter problem was especially evident in the English New Model Army.

On the eve of the British and Irish civil wars, England had no standing as a military power. The lack of administrative coherence among the three Stuart kingdoms was a source of weakness, and only the existence of a small navy prevented England from being totally insignificant. However, the British Isles had been a major source of military manpower for mainland European armies since the late sixteenth century. The Commonwealth and Protectorate would bring legislative and administrative unity, and Parliament began to meet annually in order to tap the potential wealth of the British Isles and pay for a standing army. Once the civil wars were ended, the Commonwealth of England, Ireland and Scotland began to lay claim to great-power status for a few short years by taking on the formidable naval forces of the Dutch Republic in the First Anglo-Dutch War and challenging Spain and other powers by pursuing a blue-water naval policy in the Mediterranean, the Carribean and elsewhere.[3]

In 1640 the threat of intervention in English affairs by Strafford's Irish army and the occupation of northern England by the Scottish Covenanting Army necessitated levying a military force in England, which raised the awkward question of who would command that army. Thomas Hobbes thought the crucial moment in the English Rebellion occurred when the Militia Bill was introduced into Parliament in March 1642, and was subsequently enacted as the Militia Ordinance without the king's assent: 'They had a bill in agitation to assert the power of levying and pressing soldiers to the two Houses of the Lords and the Commons; which was much as to take from the king the power of the militia, which is in effect the whole sovereign power. For he that hath the power of levying and commanding the soldiers, has all other rights of sovereignty which he shall please to claim.'[4] The question of who had the power to raise standing armies would bedevil relations between the executive and the legislature through the Interregnum and the Restoration until the Glorious Revolution, when the Bill of

---

[3] Firth, *CA* 1. See also J. S. Wheeler, *The Making of a Great Power: War and the Military Revolution in Seventeenth-Century England* (1999), esp. chs. 2–7; R. Hainsworth, *The Swordsmen in Power: War and Politics under the English Republic, 1649–1660* (1997), chs. 7–12; S. C. A. Pincus, *Protestantism and Patriotism: Ideologies and the Making of English Foreign Policy, 1650–1688* (1996), chs. 4–10.

[4] Thomas Hobbes, *Behemoth: The History of the Causes of the Civil Wars of England*, ed. William Molesworth (1682; repr. 1963), 102.

Rights of 1689 emphatically declared that it was illegal to levy an army in time of peace without the consent of Parliament. In June of 1642 Parliament went on to assert parliamentary control over all castles, fortresses and arsenals. Not only would Parliament not allow the king to raise and command a standing army, they were not even prepared to allow him a royal guard.[5]

One important aspect of command of an army was the selection of officers. Since patronage and clientage determined acquisition of civil office, this seemed a natural solution to the problem of choosing military officers. However, other tendencies had been at work in the European military world, and were beginning to exert a strong influence on English military thought. There was already a strong emphasis on merit, seniority and experience in the Anglo-Dutch Brigade of the States' Army, and most officers were promoted through the ranks—even though the purchase and sale of commissions was allowed. John Cruso merely reflected this tradition when he stated that the privileges of birth did not constitute a sufficient claim on military offices without knowledge and experience.[6] Such a policy was apparently already in effect as early as 1625 in Ireland and, presumably, also England, when military forces were raised. Edward, Lord Conway, the secretary of state who dealt with military matters and who had been a soldier himself, wrote to Henry Cary, Viscount Falkland, the lord deputy, in that year to secure a lieutenant's place in an Irish cavalry troop for a kinsman. Francis Annesley, Viscount Valentia, who commanded the troop, had already tried to give the lieutenancy to a candidate of his own. Conway had to remind both Valentia and the lord deputy that the king's policy was to prefer those with previous experience who had already served in the next lower rank, and his kinsman possessed these qualifications, and Valentia's candidate did not.[7] George Monck, duke of Albemarle, whose military career had begun in the Dutch army prior to the British and Irish civil wars, insisted that knowledge and experience were everything, and quoted a Roman precedent to make this point: 'For you may observe in all the Roman wars that they conquered more nations by their expert knowledge in martial affairs than they did either by their number or valour. It hath been the manner of all famous generals to bring their soldiers to perfection by exercise.'[8] Yet whether military officers acquired their military rank by purchase, patronage or promotion through the ranks based upon merit, seniority and experience, they came largely from aristocratic and gentry backgrounds.

During the English civil wars the king was able to recruit officers more readily than the Parliamentary armies. Although the Parliamentary cause attracted a number of high-ranking peers, a definite gentry bias in favour of the Royalist

---

[5] Schwoerer, *NSA* 33–4; 'The Nineteen Propositions', *The Lords Journal*, v. 97–9, printed in J. P. Kenyon (ed.), *The Stuart Constitution, 1603–1688: Documents and Commentary* (1966), 244–7.

[6] John Cruso, *Militarie Instructions for the Cavallrie* (1632), 2.

[7] BL, Add. MS. 11,133 (Correspondence of Henry Cary, Viscount Falkland, lord deputy of Ireland), fo. 56.

[8] George Monck, duke of Albemarle, *Observations upon Military and Political Affairs* (1671), 16–17.

cause can be detected. Consequently, the Royalist armies contained a disproportionate number of officers when compared to the Parliamentary forces, and there was always an abundance of peers, gentry and would-be gentlemen who wished to become officers. Royalist magnates raised their own troops and regiments—often at their own expense—but were not required to bring them up to full strength or to augment their numbers when reduced by battle casualties, disease or desertion. After a few months of fighting, Royalist colonels often commanded regiments whose strength was more comparable to a company or a troop. Nor could the king be dissuaded from issuing commissions to raise more regiments. Furthermore, it was not Royalist practice to merge decimated units as was done in the Parliamentary armies, where amalgamation was driven by a severe shortage of officers. In Royalist field armies, the ratio between officers and enlisted ranks was frequently as low as 1 : 4, and in garrisons which tended to fill up with reformados, that is, officers with neither men nor commands, the ratio was as low as 1 : 2.5. There always seemed to be an especially high proportion of gentlemen serving as commissioned officers in the cavalry. In 1645 General Monck described Prince Rupert's cavalry as a 'rabble of gentility'.[9]

Parliamentary infantry regiments, by contrast, often displayed ratios of officers to enlisted men of 1 : 18, and commanders of Roundhead regiments, out of desperation, frequently recruited Scots soldiers of fortune to serve as company- and field-grade officers.[10] Following the purge of the Scottish officers from the Parliamentary armies, many of the English officers who replaced them were regarded as being of low social status. Colonel Thomas Pride had been a butcher before the war, while Cornet George Joyce of Sir Thomas Fairfax's Regiment of Horse, who led the coup which seized the person of the king, had been a tailor. Members of Parliament thought that such officers were opposed to disbandment of the New Model Army because they were dependent on their pay for a livelihood. Their attempts to lobby against disbandment and to collect their arrears of pay drove them to intervene in politics. These are some of the reasons why the Parliamentary armies came to be regarded as mercenary or professional.[11]

Similar social trends can be observed among the Royalist officer corps as the war progressed. By 1643 the Royalist armies were changing from an organization based upon the trained-band system to volunteer regiments raised by members of the gentry who had been issued commissions for that purpose. Parochialism made it difficult to find commanders who would march their regiments far away from their estates, so the choice of command increasingly fell upon professional soldiers of lower social status who were willing to go anywhere. These were men who in

---

[9] J. L. Malcolm, *Caesar's Due: Loyalty and King Charles, 1642–1646* (1983), 96–7; Sir James Turner, *Pallas Armata: Military Essayes of the Ancient Grecian, Roman and Modern Art of War* (1683), 231; Firth, CA 26. [10] Malcolm, *Caesar's Due*, 97–8.

[11] C. M. Clode, *The Military Forces of the Crown: Their Administration and Government*, 2 vols. (1869), i. 28–9; Gentles, *NMA* 168, 196.

peacetime would not have had the opportunity to rise so high in the military hierarchy.[12]

The most important function of a military officer was leadership, the ability to inspire his men to give their utmost and persevere in the face of the enemy. Donald Lupton insisted that the English were brave and proved to be excellent soldiers when properly led and disciplined, as their service in mainland European armies testified. 'They fear not the face or force of the stoutest foe, and have one singular virtue beyond any other nation, for they are always willing to go on.'[13] However, in the early stages of the English civil wars many officers had not learned to exercise the kind of leadership which made their soldiers stand and fight. A petition from the officers of the Northern Horse to the king following the Battle of Marston Moor in 1645 complained that most of the troopers had deserted, leaving only officers and gentlemen volunteers together with their servants.[14] When the Army of the Solemn League and Covenant invaded England in 1640, the earls of Loudon, Lindsay and Rothes led their soldiers marching on foot while the other lords were mounted.[15] Sir Philip Monckton, a Royalist who commanded a company in Sir Thomas Metham's Regiment of Foot, led his men from the front. However, he did so mounted on horseback, and consequently lost contact with his men in the smoke of battle. His memoirs never mention any of his soldiers or companions and give the impression that he fought all battles single-handed.[16] Nathaniel Boteler, on the other hand, after a close study of Roman military history, thought that the best way to motivate soldiers was to recognize persons of merit individually and distribute spoil accordingly. Prior to the storming of the Royalist stronghold of Bristol in the late summer of 1645, Sir Thomas Fairfax and his council of war decided to distribute 6*s.* to each soldier to give him heart.[17] Sir Charles Cavendish, a Royalist colonel who had travelled widely and acquired military experience at an early age, was open and familiar with his men and won their loyalty to an unusual degree. John Aubrey quotes the elder Sir Robert Harley, a Parliamentarian officer, as saying that: 'generally, the commanders of the king's army would never be acquainted with their soldiers, which was an extraordinary prejudice to the king's cause. A captain's good look or a good word sometimes does infinitely win and oblige them; and he would say it was to admiration how soldiers will venture their lives for an obliging officer.'[18]

[12] P. R. Newman, 'The Royalist Officer Corps, 1642–1660: Army Command as a Reflexion of Social Structure', *HJ* 26 (1983), 947–8.

[13] Donald Lupton, *A Warre-like Treatise of the Pike* (1642), 36.

[14] E. Warburton, *Memoirs of Prince Rupert and the Cavaliers*, 3 vols. (1849), iii. 70–1.

[15] E. J. Cowan, *Montrose: For Covenant and King* (1977), 103.

[16] E. Peacock (ed.), *The Monckton Papers* (1884), 17–19. This memoir seems to have been written by Monckton to solicit a reward from Charles II for his services during the civil wars and in helping to effect the Restoration. He was rewarded with a captaincy in the Regiment of Foot Guards (*DNB, sub* Sir Philip Monckton (1620?–1679)).

[17] Nathaniel Boteler, *War Practically Performed* (1663), 200–1; Joshua Sprigge, *Anglia Rediviva: England's Recovery*, ed. H. T. Moore (1647; repr. 1960), 95.

[18] John Aubrey, *Brief Lives*, ed. O. L. Dick (1950), 59–60.

Joshua Sprigge thought that the Parliamentarian officers 'knew little of war', and were better Christians than soldiers, but learned from experience.[19] In the Parliamentarian armies, spiritual egalitarianism was often the foundation of morale. Officers shared the piety of their men and frequently led their units from the front. Chaplains played an important role in shaping that piety and morale. Chaplains in the New Model Army were appointed by the colonels of regiments and reflected their views; very few were Presbyterians. Rather than attempting to convert the rank and file, the function of the army chaplains was to provide a justification for fighting fellow Englishmen in a civil war and to exhort them to fight courageously. The New Model Army came to view themselves as an instrument of the Lord to punish the Anti-Christ, whom they came to identify with Charles I. This spiritual arrogance led the army leaders to ignore popular opinion and to behave ruthlessly in bringing the king to trial and execution, and subsequently in proceeding to undertake the conquest of Ireland.[20]

Because of high rates of wastage, recruiting was a continuing endeavour for all of the armies that fought in the Wars of the Three Kingdoms. Various methods were tried, ranging from persuasion to compulsion, and retention of troops once enlisted was difficult. The Scottish and Irish lords and chieftains were the most successful recruiters because those nations still retained more of their ancient martial traditions than was the case in England, and they could also exploit tenant loyalty and ties of kinship. Much neutralism was encountered in southern England and the West Midlands, and those Royalist magnates who were most successful at recruiting were largely confined to Wales and the north of England.

The Royalists did, of course, recruit successfully from among gentry and peerage families, but many of these aristocrats and their servants cherished antique notions of chivalry and wished to serve only in the cavalry. Because the Royalists were more successful at recruiting cavalry than infantry, they often fielded armies containing more of the former than the latter in pitched battles. The men-at-arms of the last days of feudalism had by this time given way to cuirassiers or heavy cavalry, who wore cuirasses consisting of breast- and back-plates, and were armed with pistols and sabres. Troops of cuirassiers were often composed entirely of noblemen and gentlemen. The light cavalry, usually drawn from yeomen and serving-men, were known as harquebusiers or carabineers, who carried a lighter and shorter version of the musket and a sword. The lowest in social status of all mounted troops were the dragoons, who were really mounted infantry and were so called after the light musket that they carried. They did not fight on horseback.[21]

The office of lord lieutenant and the control of the militias of the more populous south-eastern counties of England were mostly in the hands of Parliamentarians.

[19] Sprigge, *Anglia Rediviva*, 323.   [20] Gentles, *NMA* 96, 103–4, 107–8.

[21] 'A Brief Relation of the Life and Memoirs of John Lord Belasyse, Written and Collected by his Secretary, Joshua Moone', in HMC, *Ormonde MSS.*, NS 2 (1903), 376–80; Gervase Markham, *The Souldier's Accidence, or an Introduction into Military Discipline* (1635), 38–42.

Instead of issuing commissions of lieutenancy, which had been employed to raise a militia since the beginning of Elizabeth's reign, Charles I resorted to issuing commissions of array, which were based upon an unrepealed Statute of Henry IV, but which were regarded by many as antiquated and illegal. Clarendon was of the opinion that if the king had employed the more familiar commissions of lieutenancy, 'his service would have been better carried on' and less vulnerable to attack. Apparently, the purpose behind the commissions of array was to secure loyal counties and their militias.[22] When George Brydges, sixth Lord Chandos, attempted to raise Royalist forces in Cirencester by commission of array, he was threatened by 'the rude hand of the multitude', and barely escaped with his life. His house was then plundered by the crowd.[23] In the West Midlands and in the city of Chester and Cheshire, organized and militant neutralism prevented the king from securing those areas. The collapse of neutralism in the West Midlands forced the inhabitants to choose sides. In the event, most of the Royalist forces were raised in the more modern manner by issuing commissions to colonels to raise regiments, and this method commended itself because it was less public, more discreet and attracted less unfavourable attention.[24]

When the civil wars began the county militias were far from ready for battle, and the only reasonably well trained troops in England were the London trained bands, which were officered by members of the Honourable Artillery Company. Even the king understood that this was a valuable military asset and enrolled the prince of Wales, the duke of York and his nephew the elector palatine as members of the company on 1 June 1642. The original four regiments of the London trained bands were increased to 18,000 men in nine regular regiments and six auxiliary regiments by 1643. The London trained bands fell under the control of Parliament, and in the early days of the war were the chief source of infantry for the Parliamentary armies—especially those commanded by the earl of Essex and Sir William Waller. Although well drilled, they were not well disciplined. As Waller's army marched to the siege of Basing House, the men of the Red Regiment of the London trained bands were unused to walking so far and took three days to reach Brentford, and some began deserting before they were out of London. They had gotten no further than Farnham, Surrey, before the first mutiny occurred. Riots frequently broke out when Parliamentarian press-gangs sought to conscript Londoners into the army. The difficulties of impressing or recruiting men for the Parliamentary armies were such that by 1643 the metropolis had ceased to be the source of military manpower that it had been earlier.[25]

[22] R. Hutton, *The Royalist War Effort, 1642–1646* (1982), 6, 22–3; Clarendon, *RCW* ii. 205, 196 n.–197 n.

[23] *A True and Impartial History of the Military Government of the Citie of Gloucester*, 2nd edn. (1647), in Sir W. Scott (ed.), *Somers Tracts*, 13 vols. (1809–15), v. 303.

[24] Hutton, *Royalist War Effort*, 6–10, 22–3.

[25] Walker, *HAC* 49–50; Elias Archer, *A True Relation of the Red Trained Bands of Westminster . . . under the Command of Sir William Waller* (1643), 1–3; K. Lindley, *Popular Politics and Religion in Civil War London* (1997), 335–6.

Royalist regiments were mostly raised by their colonels with very little help or financial assistance from the king. Richard Atkyns raised a troop of eighty horse for a regiment commanded by Lord Chandos, but Atkyns had to pay his troop out of his own pocket. At least twenty of his troopers were armigerous gentry, and the remainder arrived well armed and mounted, so they were probably gentlemen or, at least, yeomen. Although Atkyns was a kinsman of Lord Chandos, he says that Chandos used his 'troop with such hardship that his gentlemen [troopers] unanimously desired me to go into another regiment'. Atkyns took his troop into Prince Maurice's Regiment of the Western Royalist Army. Atkyns himself had no previous military experience, but his Scots servant, Erwing, had served in the *gens d'armes* in France and undertook to train his troop. Erwing had been offered a commission as a lieutenant of horse by the Parliamentarians, but chose to stay with Atkyns out of personal loyalty. Whether Erwing was granted a commission in the Royalist army Atkyns does not bother to mention.[26] Sir Anthony Ashley Cooper was commissioned to raise a regiment of foot and a troop of horse by the Royalist lord-lieutenant of Dorset, William Seymour, marquis of Hertford, which he did at his own expense. In 1644 Cooper went over to the Parliamentarians and was given command of all the Parliamentary forces in Dorset, consisting of seven regiments of horse and foot.[27] After the Restoration, Henry Somerset, third marquis of Worcester, reminded Charles II of how he had raised 4,000 foot and 800 horse on his own credit at short notice for the Battle of Edgehill and the Siege of Gloucester. Moreover, he supplied his soldiers without making use of free-quarter—the practice of billeting troops upon innkeepers and householders—which he so detested in soldiers of fortune such as Patrick Ruthven, earl of Brentford, the Scottish commander of the English Royalist armies.[28] Richard Vaughan, second earl of Carbery, was the leading magnate of south-west Wales. His local power and reputation helped him to secure the towns of Haverfordwest and Tenby for the king and to raise Royalist troops. But his lack of military expertise and experience prevented him from effectively leading his soldiers. In 1644 he was unable to foresee and to resist a successful amphibious assault by Rowland Laugharne, a daring Parliamentary officer, who had once served overseas under the earl of Essex, and who captured Milford Haven and all the surrounding towns and fortifications with a few hundred soldiers. In North Wales the Royalist commander, Arthur, Lord Capel had difficulty raising soldiers because he was an outsider, and lacking military experience, he had no military reputation. In desperation he resorted to impressment, and in Shropshire he ordered the gentry to call up two tenants each in a kind of quasi-feudal levy. They came equipped only with clubs, and Capel failed to retain north-east Wales for the Royalist

---

[26] *The Vindication of Richard Atkyns* (1669), in P. Young (ed.), *Military Memoirs: The Civil War* (1967), 5, 7–8.

[27]. 'Autobiographical Sketch', in W. D. Christie, *A Life of Anthony Ashley Cooper, First Earl of Shaftesbury, 1621–1683*, 2 vols. (1871), vol. i, app. II, pp. xxviii–xxix.

[28] HMC, *Twelfth Report*, Appendix, Pt. IX (Beaufort MSS.) (1891), 60.

cause.[29] William Cavendish, earl of Newcastle, was one of the most successful of the Royalist grandees as a recruiter of men and a military leader. His numerous connections with the northern lords and gentry gave him the credit and reputation to raise a very large army, and he possessed the wealth to sustain it. Newcastle's army, clothed in their distinctive white coats, constituted an autonomous command, not subject to the Privy Council, and he had the power to confer knighthoods and coin money.[30]

After the Battle of Edgehill, which followed an unsuccessful campaign to march on London, the Royalist forces fell back on Oxford where they established their headquarters. Much of the manpower for the Royalist armies came from Wales and the Welsh Border, so a corridor of communications had to be maintained between Wales and Oxford, which required that the Royalists seize and maintain garrison towns such as Worcester in order to secure that corridor, which was a great drain on Royalist finances and manpower for field armies. The Royalist forces relied on voluntary contributions in this area, which was made easier by the revulsion of the local inhabitants against the Parliamentarian troops who had vandalized their churches and plundered their persons and property.[31] As the geographical base of Royalist recruiting narrowed, Royalist commanders began to draw upon the military manpower of Ireland. John, first Lord Byron, told the marquis of Ormonde that he preferred Irish soldiers to English because they were less mutinous and less influenced by the 'ill-affected people here'. Recruiting Irish soldiers for the king's armies won him few friends in England, but Byron reasoned that 'since the rebels call in the Scots, I know no reason why the king should make any scruple of calling in the Irish, or the Turks if they would serve him'. The marquis of Antrim was another Royalist military enterpriser who could raise mercenary soldiers from among his tenants and kinsmen in Ulster and the Western Isles of Scotland. Although he was a successful warlord, he had more of the courtier than the swordsman in him.[32]

When it disbanded the king's army, raised in 1640 to oppose the invasion of the Scots Covenanters, Parliament declared that it was illegal to impress subjects of the king to accompany a military expedition into a foreign country. Parliament then turned around and proceeded to raise another army, and declared that persons refusing impressment were to pay a fine of £10. Members of the trained bands were exempted, as well as subsidy-payers and their eldest sons, subject to minimum property qualifications. Thus, it was clear that it was the poor who were being singled out for military service. Parliament's justification for resorting to impressment was provided by the Irish Rebellion of 1641 and the threat that an Irish

    [29] Hutton, *Royalist War Effort*, 59–67, 68–75.

    [30] Margaret Cavendish, duchess of Newcastle, *The Life of William Cavendish, Duke of Newcastle* (1667), ed. C. H. Firth (1906), 83–5.   [31] Hutton, *Royalist War Effort*, 33–6.

    [32] Thomas Carte (ed.), *A Collection of Original Letters and Papers . . . found among the the Duke of Ormonde's Papers*, 2 vols. (1739), i. 39; J. H. Ohlmeyer, *Civil War and Restoration in the Three Kingdoms: The Career of Randall MacDonnell, Marquis of Antrim, 1609–1683* (1993), 204.

Catholic army might invade England.[33] Because the war remained unpopular with ordinary folk, recruiting continued to be a difficult task for the Parliamentarian authorities, and the use of press-masters was the ordinary method. Churchwardens and overseers of the poor were always glad to turn over vagrants and masterless men—especially in London. In the countryside, those conscripted were usually servants and apprentices and others who were too young or poor to be householders. Soldiers who had been impressed were often confined to bridewells or houses of correction to prevent their escape until such time as they could be conducted to a garrison or field army. Just before the Battle of Worcester in 1651, George Fox was finishing a gaol term of six months in the Derby house of correction. A group of men who had just been pressed for soldiers to reinforce the Commonwealth forces were also committed to the Derby bridewell to prevent their escape. After they came to know Fox, they elected him their captain. The Parliamentary commissioners decided to offer Fox a commission, but he pleaded his Quaker beliefs. Later, a justice of the peace decided to impress Fox as a common soldier, but he refused to accept the press money, so his confinement was extended indefinitely.[34] Parliamentary recruiting efforts went beyond cleansing local communities of social undesirables and troublesome adolescents. Gilbert Holles, second earl of Clare, complained to Lord General Sir Thomas Fairfax in 1644 that he was recruiting more soldiers in Derbyshire than the county could well bear.[35]

When the New Model Army was raised in 1645, Fairfax plundered the armies of the earls of Essex and Manchester and Sir William Waller for soldiers and junior officers, despite the fact that those armies had not yet been dissolved. Another significant source of recruits for the New Model Army and other Parliamentary armies was prisoners of war. There was a risk that ordinary soldiers faced in changing sides: they could be, and were, hanged as traitors and deserters if caught and recognized by their former commanders. Yet Royalist soldiers did defect to the Parliamentarian armies in large numbers and were valued as good soldiers. At the same time, a great many soldiers who had been pressed against their will and prisoners of war who had been pressured into changing their colours also deserted.[36]

As was the case with the Royalist armies, the New Model Army found it easier to raise troops for the cavalry than the foot. Although he was expected to furnish and feed his own mount, a cavalry trooper was paid three times what a private soldier in the foot received. Cavalry troopers in the New Model Army were volunteers—quite often old soldiers—and because their position was accorded higher status, they were not infrequently gentlemen. Gone were the days when Cromwell could accuse the troopers who had served in the earl of Essex's army of being 'most

[33] Clode, *Military Forces of the Crown*, i. 26–7.

[34] Roger Boyle, 1st earl of Orrery, *A Treatise of the Art of War* (1677), 19–20; J. L. Nickalls (ed.), *The Journal of George Fox* (1952), 65–7, 70.

[35] BL. Add. MS. 18,979 (Fairfax Correspondence), fo. 156r & v.

[36] Gentles, *NMA* 31–4; C. Carlton, 'The Face of Battle in the English Civil Wars', in Fissel, *W&G* 242–3.

of them old decayed serving-men and tapsters and such kind of fellows', in contrast to the gentlemen's sons who were to be found in the Royalist horse.[37]

Following the Battle of Preston in 1648, where the Parliamentarians defeated a Scots Royalist army under the command of the marquis of Hamilton, Captain John Hodgson remarked upon the ability of the Scots to raise army after army: 'The gentry of that nation have such influence over the commonalty, that they can lead them what way they please.'[38] While true, this is only part of the story. Scotland under the Covenant possessed unusual resources for raising military manpower. Although Lowland Scotland had not seen war in seventy years, Scotland could draw upon remarkable and varied resources of military manpower. Besides, of course, the tens of thousands of Scotsmen who had served in the armies of Scandinavia and northern Europe, and returned home to serve as the cadre of the Scots Covenanting armies of 1638 and thereafter, the Scottish lords, lairds and chieftains did retain a remarkable power to summon kinsmen and tenants to furnish military manpower. In addition, the Tables, or governing committees of the Solemn League and Covenant, undertook to explain the Covenanting cause to the new soldiers and potential recruits and to inculcate them with the Covenanting ideology. The Kirk provided chaplains for every regiment of the Covenanting armies, as it had for the mercenary regiments recruited for mainland European armies before 1638. Beyond that, the Covenanting government possessed something which England lacked—an administrative system organized at the parish level and coordinated with the shire committees of war, which recruited soldiers, relieved the distress of the families that they left behind and provided for the relief of wounded and maimed veterans. This administrative system, which was copied from the Sweden of Gustavus Adolphus, was carried on by shire committees of war and the presbyteries in each shire (not to be confused with the ecclesiastical courts), and instituted a national system of conscription characterized by effective local and national cooperation. The most prominent lairds were named parochial commissioners, and worked with the ministers to help recruit and collect contributions. These new local administrative institutions began to displace the heritable jurisdictions of the lairds, and facilitated regional mobilization and other responses to the war effort. From the beginning of the Bishops' Wars in 1638 until the English conquest of Scotland in 1651, the Covenanting government raised a dozen armies which campaigned and fought in each of the Three Kingdoms. In 1641 the Covenanting military forces probably totalled 30,000 men, or 3 per cent of Scotland's population.[39] This was a remarkable

[37] Firth, *CA* 39–40; S. C. Lomas (ed.), *The Letters and Speeches of Oliver Cromwell with Elucidations by Thomas Carlyle*, 3 vols. (1904), iii. 65.

[38] *Original Memoirs Written during the Great Civil War . . . Memoirs of Captain John Hodgson* (1806), 124.

[39] Cowan, *Montrose*, 61–3; A. C. Dow, *Ministers to the Soldiers of Scotland* (1962), 68–9; A. Macinnes, *Charles I and the Making of the Covenanting Movement, 1625–1641* (1991), 190; E. M. Furgol, 'Scotland Turned Sweden: The Scottish Covenanters and the Military Revolution, 1638–1651', in J. Morrill (ed.), *The Scottish National Covenant in its British Context* (1990), 137–9.

achievement, considering that Scotland suffered in excess of 2,000 war casualties leading up to 1649, and that the recruiting base was substantially diminished by bubonic plague in 1644–5 and famine in 1648–9. Within the Scottish armies, kirk sessions were established in every regiment to care for the sick and wounded.[40]

Scottish officers serving abroad remained in touch with and involved in Scottish domestic politics, because they served the Scandinavian monarchs as diplomats and military recruiters in the British Isles. Although they retained a sense of loyalty to the Stuart dynasty, in 1638 and thereafter many Scottish professional soldiers were unwilling to fight for Charles I against their own country. A national identity had superseded the personal loyalty to the Stuart monarchs.[41] Although the Royalist Sir Thomas Urquhart lauded the gallantry of those Scots 'martialists' who served in the armies of mainland Europe, at the same time he disliked the motives of those who came home to fight in the Covenanting Army, and condemned them as fanatical, mercenary and oppressive to their tenants. Those landlords who accepted commissions in the Covenanting Army without prior overseas experience he referred to as 'freshwater officers'. Urquhart was especially contemptuous of those stay-at-home colonels who raised regiments for the Covenanting cause, but accepted money from their tenants to be excused from service. Some colonels recruited soldiers by means of bounties and promises of plunder, but the cost of maintaining the armies of the Solemn League and Covenant fell hard upon the tenantry.[42] Probably the worst of these abuses by landlords turned proprietary colonels began to disappear as the new structures of local government replaced the heritable jurisdictions with parochial and shire committees of war and brought recruiting methods into the open. Although the recruiting was originally carried on by aristocratic colonels among their tenants to fill their regiments, these regiments always had a territorial base and the colonels became increasingly dependent upon lists of able-bodied men drawn up by the ministers of the Kirk and local committees. This helped to ensure victories over the Royalists, who relied on family connections and clientage alone to raise soldiers. Although their uniforms and clothing might differ, all soldiers, cavalry and infantry alike, wore the distinctive blue bonnet. The government of the Solemn League and Covenant, like the English Parliament, had created a distinctly national army.[43]

Once the various armies which were to fight in the Wars of the Three Kingdoms had been raised, it was necessary to train and discipline them. At this

[40] Furgol, 'Scotland Turned Sweden', 142; *Articles and Ordinances of War . . . of the Army of the Kingdom of Scotland* (1643), repr. in W. Oldys and T. Park (eds.), *HM*, 12 vols. (1808–11), v. 422–8, art. 1; Dow, *Ministers*, 85.

[41] S. Murdoch, 'The House of Stuart and the Scottish Professional Soldier', in B. Taithe and T. Thornton (eds.), *War: Identities in Conflict, 1300–2000* (1998), 49–50.

[42] Sir Thomas Urquhart of Cromarty, *ΕΚΣ ΚΥΒΑΛΑΥΡΟΝ [EKSKIBALAVON]: or, the Discovery of a Most Exquisite Jewel*, MC 30 (1834), 250–1.

[43] Macinnes, *Charles I and the Making of the Covenanting Movement*, 191; Rushworth, *HC* v. 604–5; Cowan, *Montrose*, 103.

point, military manuals and treatises became important. One of the most widely used was Henry Hexham's *The Principles of the Art Militarie*. Hexham had served as quartermaster in Lord Goring's Regiment in the States' Army. His manual was based on Dutch military practice, and was widely used in English armies. It was reprinted several times, and must be regarded as an important means of transmitting modern concepts of military discipline and usage to the British Isles. The appendix of Hexham's book contained the eighty-two articles of the Dutch *Krijgsrecht* of 1590, which was an amplification of the original 'Laws, Articles and Ordinances touching all Martial Discipline', as originally enacted by the States General in 1590. This had been a major step towards a code of articles of war and a system of military discipline in a property-conscious society which expected soldiers to be paid on time, to be content with their pay and to respect the rights and property of the Republic's citizens.[44] Another widely used military manual, by Robert Ward, drew upon both Netherlandish and Swedish military practices, and the author claimed to have consulted authorities on warfare in seven classical and modern languages. In the dedication to the king, Ward reminded Charles that wars had broken out in neighbouring kingdoms, and that the art of war had become very technical. There was also a dedication to the lords-lieutenant of Essex, Robert Rich, earl of Warwick, and William, second Lord Maynard, and to the deputy lieutenants and captains of the Essex trained bands, which suggests that Ward probably was employed as muster-master to the Essex militia. The inclusion of a poem dedicated to those who had served in mainland European armies also suggests that Ward himself had been a professional soldier. Muster-masters, through their training of the militia and through the medium of the manuals and treatises which they wrote, were important instruments for disseminating the ideas and practices of the military revolution from continental Europe to the British Isles.[45] Richard Elton, who was a former sergeant-major in the Parliamentary armies, published a military manual in 1650 intended for use by the London trained bands, which was commended by many Parliamentary officers such as Philip Skippon. These treatises attempted to teach close-order drill and battlefield tactics, but one is surprised to discover how often their authors cater to the aristocratic prejudice for edged weapons. Elton recommended a ratio of pikes to muskets of 1 : 2, although the usual ratio of pikes to shot in mainland European armies in 1650 was 1 : 3 or 4, and he still thought that the pike was the more honourable weapon.[46]

These military manuals were aimed at audiences who were predominantly gentlemen, and could not be insensitive to aristocratic prejudices against firearms. Blaise de Monluc, that exemplar of swordsmen, had once exclaimed: 'I wish to

---

[44] Henry Hexham, *The Principles of the Art Militarie Practiced in the Warres of the United Netherlands* (1637), app., pp. 9–15.

[45] Richard Ward, *Animadversions of Warre* (1639), title-page and dedications.

[46] Richard Elton, *The Compleat Body of the Art Military* (1650), title-page and p. 2; Parker, *MR* 18; Manning, *Swordsmen*, ch. 4.

God that they had never invented this cursed instrument! I wouldn't carry its marks, which still today leave me weak, and many brave men wouldn't be dead at the hands of those weaker and more cowardly than themselves.'[47] Donald Lupton personally preferred muskets, half-pikes and halberds as weapons for the foot, but he was certainly aware of the aristocratic prejudice in favour of pikes and against muskets.[48] The earl of Orrery, who had commanded the Cromwellian forces in Ireland in the early 1650s, persisted in believing that the pike was a more useful weapon than the musket. Orrery, who was the brother of Robert Boyle, one of the great leaders of the scientific revolution, asserted that persons of quality who volunteered to serve in the foot regarded the pike as a more noble weapon than the musket.[49] The actual proportion of pikes to muskets in English armies in the mid-1640s seems to have been 1 : 2, but in the Scots Covenanting armies during the same period it remained at a ratio of 2 : 3.[50] Writing in the 1630s, Nathaniel Boteler, although quite familiar with the Swedish military discipline, continued to advocate use of the longbow and argued that in certain circumstances it was superior to the musket.[51] This was not pure nostalgia, because all armies continued to employ archers to some extent during the civil wars.[52] Military manuals published on the eve of the civil wars also insisted upon a hierarchy and an order of precedence based upon chivalric values: 'Whenever horse and foot are mixed together, or whensoever they shall meet in public court or private council . . . the commander of the horse shall have priority of place before the commander of the foot.' Within the cavalry, by the same rules of precedence, cuirassiers always preceded carabineers and dragoons.[53]

Despite the persistence of antique chivalric notions among aristocratic officers, actual military practice in the mainland European wars of the sixteenth and seventeenth centuries enhanced the importance of infantry at the expense of the cavalry. Infantry tactics had become more aggressive as improved close-order drill made better use of the musket and increased the fire-power of infantry units. The mobility of the foot also increased as they abandoned armour. When the foot began to win more victories, the status of a command in the infantry gained more prestige in terms of honour.[54] By the standards of continental European military practice,

[47] Blaise de Monluc, *Commentaires, 1521–1576*, ed. P. Courteault (1964), 35, quoted in J. Dewald, *Aristocratic Experience and the Origins of Modern Culture: France, 1570–1715* (1993), 55–6.

[48] Lupton, *A Warre-like Treatise of the Pike*, 128–9, 142–3.

[49] Orrery, *Treatise of the Art of War*, 25–6. Although he was a cunning politician, Orrery was out of touch with modern military thought. In the preface to his *Treatise of the Art of War* (1677) he laments the lack of military treatises in English. What he seems to have meant by this amazing statement was that he was unaware of any English general who had left published observations on the art of war besides Sir Francis Vere. Those military treatises written by persons below the social and military rank of Vere apparently did not count in Orrery's view.

[50] C. S. Terry (ed.), *Papers Relating to the Army of the Solemn League and Covenant, 1643–1647*, 2 vols., SHS 2nd ser. 16, 17 (1917), vol. i, pp. xcv–xcvi.

[51] Boteler, *War Practically Performed*, 156–8.

[52] P. Edwards, *Dealing in Death: the Arms Trade and the British Civil Wars, 1638–52* (2000), 4.

[53] G[ervase] M[arkham], *The Souldier's Grammar* (1639), 63–4.   [54] Firth, *CA* 68–9.

this should have led to a higher proportion of shot to pikes in the infantry, and a higher proportion of foot to horse in field armies. However, even a commander as experienced as George Monck continued to advocate a ratio of infantrymen to cavalry troopers of 2 : 1 in field armies, although he was willing to concede that a besieging army should contain a ratio of 3 : 1 or 4 : 1, not counting dragoons.[55] The low ratios of foot to horse in armies of the English civil wars may have been attributable to the difficulties of recruiting, training and retaining foot soldiers. When James, first duke of Hamilton, was dispatched to Scotland with a Royalist naval force in 1639 during the Bishops' Wars, he carried with him 5,000 foot soldiers. Some idea of their level of training may be gathered from Hamilton's report stating that only 200 of them had ever fired a musket. Later, during the English civil wars, Royalist armies continued to encounter difficulties recruiting sufficient infantry because of weak popular support for the Royalist cause outside of Cornwall and Wales.[56]

In some ways, Scottish military practice was closer to that of the mainland European armies, which, because they had more to do with siege warfare, contained higher proportions of foot to horse. The Covenanting Army raised in 1643 to assist the parliamentary armies in England consisted of 18,000 foot, 2,000 horse and 1,000 dragoons—a ratio of 9 : 1 excluding the dragoons. Because the size of this army exceeded its capacity for logistical support, it had to move quickly into northern England to provision itself. The low proportion of horse to foot may well reflect problems of forage and provisions rather than any ideal ratio. That the Scots Covenanting armies contained any cavalry at all reminds us that they consisted predominantly of Lowlanders. Horses were foreign to Highland methods of warfare. A more distinctly Scottish military practice was the use of 'fire and sword' tactics against their opponents, that is, the destruction of crops, food stores and dwellings, and the slaughter of civilians upon whom the enemy might depend. This kind of Scottish warfare was usually directed against rebels or cateran bands by authority of a royal commission, and made no distinction between combatants and noncombatants.[57]

The discipline and performance of the Parliamentary foot improved with experience and time, although it is hard to imagine how it could have worsened since that October day in 1643 when the Red Regiment of the London trained bands marched towards Brentford. At the Battle of Edgehill, 22 October 1642, the Parliamentary infantry were so undisciplined and heedless of the rules of war, that their officers could not restrain them from slaughtering Royalists who had surrendered.[58] Parliamentary soldiers threw down their arms when they were left

[55] Albemarle, *Observations upon Military and Political Affairs*, 21–2.

[56] H. L. Rubinstein, *Captain Luckless: James, First Duke of Hamilton, 1606–1649* (1975), 98; Malcolm, *Caesar's Due*, 98–9.

[57] Furgol, 'Scotland Turned Sweden', 146; *Papers Relating to the Army of the Solemn League and Covenant*, vol. i, pp. lxxviii–lxxix.

[58] Archer, *True Relation of the Marchings of the Red Trained Bands*, 1–2; Carte (ed.), *Collection of Original Letters and Papers*, i. 10.

unprotected by their cavalry at the Battle of Roundway Down in 1643. On this occasion, Prince Maurice 'strictly commanded' his men to spare the prisoners, and when he learned that they had been impressed, he disarmed them and sent them home.[59] After the ranks of the New Model foot had been pruned by desertion, disease and hardship, their discipline and morale improved. At the Siege of Bristol in August 1645, the courage of the foot was such that they assaulted the walls and defences without waiting for them to be breached by artillery.[60]

Similarly, the Parliamentary horse were not the equals of the Royalists at the commencement of the war. Sir Arthur Haslerig's Regiment of Cuirassiers (called 'lobsters' because of their armour) were the first body of Parliamentary cavalry who could stand up to the Royalist horse. However, the Royalist cavalry troopers, many of whom had learned their cavalry tactics chasing the hart, pursued the enemy without regrouping, and headed straight for the enemy's baggage train. Cromwell, on the other hand, was an expert in training cavalry, and insisted that they regroup in order to be able charge again after he observed that the failure to do so was the chief weakness of Rupert's cavalry.[61] Both the Parliamentarian and Royalist horse were guilty of failing to exploit one of the chief functions of modern cavalry. They often failed to reconnoitre and gather intelligence. Also, at Cirencester, which was garrisoned by two regiments of Royalist horse, the commandant failed to post guards and was surprised by the earl of Essex in September 1643.[62]

At the beginning of the civil wars, the tendency of both sides was to fortify and garrison a multitude of small towns, castles and manor houses without regard to their military value. Bulstrode Whitelocke, when he entered upon his martial exploits for the Parliamentary cause, fortified one of his houses, Phyllis Court, at Henley-upon-Thames with bulwarks for guns and breastworks, and diverted the river into his moat. This private fortress was garrisoned with 300 foot and a troop of horse, and supplied with a great quantity of powder and match. This practice of maintaining numerous small garrisons had the effect of depriving both armies of badly needed manpower and munitions which could have been more effectively employed in augmenting field armies. Moreover, it was necessary for the soldiers of such small garrisons to spend much of their time foraging, thus sowing ill will in the neigbourhood. The Parliamentarians came to their senses before their Royalist counterparts, and after 1644 began ordering the fortifications of small and unnecessary houses and castles demolished and their garrisons more usefully employed. The failure of the Royalists to do likewise cost them much goodwill. Sir

---

[59] [Edward Walsingham], 'Life of Sir John Digby (1605)', ed. G. Bernard, *CM XII*, CS 3rd ser. 18 (1910), 85–6. [60] Gentles, *NMA* 75.

[61] *A True and Impartial History of the Militarie Government of the Citie of Gloucester*, in Scott (ed.), *Somers Tracts*, v. 316 n., 366, 369; Carte (ed.), *Original Letters and Papers*, i. 10; P. Morrah, *Prince Rupert of the Rhine* (1976), 143.

[62] Clarendon, *RCW* iii. 171–2; I. G. Philip (ed.), *The Journal of Sir Samuel Luke*, 3 vols., ORS 29, 31, 33 (1947–53), vol. i, pp. v–vii.

John Meldrum, who had defended Liverpool against a siege by Prince Rupert, also discovered that the confinement entailed by long sieges resulted in much factionalism among the local gentry. He advocated levelling the fortifications of cities and towns such as Liverpool unless they could be furnished with strong garrisons. Although a policy of abandoning fortified towns went against the received wisdom of the military revolution, Meldrum was of the opinion that it was 'both dangerous and unprofitable to this state . . . to keep up forts and garrisons, which may rather foment than finish a war'.[63] Besieging towns, such as Leicester, which Rupert sat down before in 1645, was much relished by that prince, who had learned his siege-craft in the Low Countries. Sir Edward Walker, the Royalist herald and antiquary, observed that Rupert's 'mastery and chiefest delight' was 'in attempts of this kind', but Walker saw a number of undesirable consequences which derived from long and costly sieges. Rupert's army suffered heavy casualties, and the sack of the town after its capitulation spared neither churches nor its hospital; such methods of war 'made the king and his army terrible . . . and the consequence thereof conduced to our destruction'. Besides the casualties which every siege cost the Royalist armies, the circumstances of sacking and occupying conquered towns provided opportunities for desertion 'occasioned by the breakdown in discipline'. Moreover, Rupert believed that once a fortified place had been summoned to surrender, his personal honour required following through with a siege even though the town or castle might have little military value and the manpower necessary for such an undertaking might be put to better use elsewhere. This disagreement about the value of fortified places and the desirability of reducing them with 'great ordnance' was part of a long-continuing debate concerning an integral feature of what is now called the 'military revolution'. Evidently, there were those who rejected such methods of warfare because they were incompatible with the classic military tactics of the ancient world.[64]

There could be no doubt about the military value of London. During the civil wars the Royalists viewed London as 'the inexhaustible magazine of both men and money with arms and other necessaries for keeping on foot those unnatural wars between the king's majesty and his liege people'.[65] London needed to be defended against Royalist attacks, but its inhabitants bore watching also. Like the civic militias of Holland, the London trained bands were brought into existence to preserve public order and to defend property, but like their Dutch counterparts, the London trained bands were highly politicized and sometimes became involved in public tumults and demonstrations themselves.[66] The possibility that the City

[63] R. Spalding (ed.), *The Diary of Bulstrode Whitelocke, 1605–1675*, BARSEH NS 13 (1990), 166, 186–9; Firth, *CA* 26–9; *Cal. S.P., Dom., 1644–1645*, 91. Articles of surrender for fortified places quite often required that castles and fortifications be demolished and no garrisons be kept there in future (BL, Add. MS. 18, 9979 (Fairfax Correspondence), fo. 160*r* & *v*).

[64] Sir Edward Walker, *Historical Discources* (1705), 127–9; John Bingham, *The Art of Embattailing an Army, or The Second Part of Aelian's Tacticks* (1629; repr. 1968), sig. A4*r*.

[65] [Walsingham], 'Life of Sir John Digby', 90.

[66] P. Knevel, *Burgers in het geweer: De Schutterijen in Holland, 1550–1700* (1994), 351–3, 414.

corporation might fall under the control of the Royalists meant that Parliament had to secure the seat of government by controlling the militia and guaranteeing their allegiance. The question of whether the king or Parliament would command the trained bands was tested when Parliament requested that they be placed under the command of the third earl of Essex. Essex and his family had always been popular in London where he, his father and his grandfather were viewed sympathetically as victims of 'court corruption'. The king, who came to view Essex as the chief rebel, refused. Parliament then instructed the lord mayor, a Royalist, to mobilize the trained bands. When the lord mayor declined, the Court of Aldermen appointed a committee of safety to assume control. This prompted the king to invade the House of Commons in January 1642.[67]

Parliament declared that Philip Skippon, a veteran of the Dutch army who had been employed in 1639 as captain leader of the Honourable Artillery Company, was to command the trained bands of London, Westminster and Middlesex with the rank of sergeant-major-general, rather than the lord-lieutenant or the mayor. The strength of the trained bands was augmented, and a grand muster in Finsbury Fields was staged on 10 May 1642 to demonstrate the London trained bands' martial resolve and support for the Parliamentary cause. The occasion would have been a complete military triumph but for one accident, when the colonel of the Red Regiment, an alderman appointed more for his political importance than his military expertise, had a sudden and uncontrollable 'yearning in his bowels' after being alarmed by an unexpected discharge of muskets. Like the aristocratic colonels of Royalist or Covenanting regiments, aldermanic colonels of the London trained bands were more useful for recruiting than actually leading men into battle.[68] The alderman-colonel's embarrassment notwithstanding, the martial displays in Finsbury Fields appear to have inspired some 8,000 London apprentices to volunteer their services for the Parliamentary armies. A pamphlet entitled *The Valiant Resolution of the Prentices of London* was published soon after the beginning of hostilities, and claimed to be expressing the sentiments of the young volunteers. The notable thing about this pamphlet is that their motivation is expressed in chivalric rather than Puritan values. The apprentices claim that they are to be distinguished from mere mercenaries swept up off the streets, are from good families and volunteered because of noble and generous sentiments.[69]

The Royalists had viewed London's importance in terms of financial resources and military supplies, and failed to appreciate its importance as a place where Parliament could raise substantial numbers of soldiers. Because the Royalists had such contempt for London's commercial society and bourgeois values, they

[67] I. Roy, ' "This Proud Unthankefull City": A Cavalier View of London in the Civil War', and L. Nagel, 'A Great Bouncing at Everyman's Door: The Struggle for London's Militia in 1642', in S. Porter (ed.), *London and the Civil War* (1996), 65–6, 69–71, 156.

[68] Nagel, 'A Great Bouncing at Everyman's Door', 78.

[69] W. Hunt, 'Civic Chivalry and the English Civil War', in A. Grafton and A. Blair (eds.), *The Transmission of Culture in Early Modern Europe* (1990), 204–5.

underestimated the military potential of the City trained bands. The London trained bands had not served in the Bishops' Wars, and the Royalists had conceived a poor opinion of the provincial militias which had gone north to the Scottish Border. Even Parliamentary spokesmen shared the view that pre-civil-war England was characterized by ignorance and neglect of martial discipline: 'the trained-bands . . . were effeminate in courage and incapable of discipline because their whole course of life was alienated from warlike employment.'[70] Whether the London trained bands were motivated by chivalric values, loyalty to Parliament or merely self-interest remains a matter of contention. Clarendon maintained that if the Royalist forces had shown more aggressiveness in the face of the London trained bands, and 'if the king had advanced and charged that massy body, it had presently given ground . . . The king had so great a party in every regiment that it would have made no resistance.'[71] While Major-General Skippon was very good at motivating his soldiers, giving them short, exhortative speeches in the manner of his mentor, Maurice of Nassau, we need not believe Bulstrode Whitelocke when he says that the London trained bands 'marched cheerfully' to meet the Royalists at the Battle of Turnham Green.[72] The strength of the London trained bands was that they were well drilled in formal infantry tactics by Skippon and their officers, who had their training in the London Artillery Garden, and they fought well in pitched battles. Their weaknesses were that they were not inured to the cold and dampness of camp life, and they did not perform well under Sir William Waller because of his practice of winter campaigning, rapid marches and skirmishing in woods and hedgerows in nasty weather. Waller had little respect for them, and regarded most of his men as hired substitutes who, in the midst of the assault on Basing House, mutinously cried out that they wished to go home, and forced him to break off the assault. The rate of desertion was very high among all of the London trained bands. The three regiments serving under Major-General Richard Browne were so depleted by desertion that they had to be amalgamated into one regiment. Because of their unreliability, the City trained bands were little used after 1644.[73]

With the king in custody at the end of the First English Civil War, factionalism surfaced in the New Model Army as the more radical officers and men became determined to participate in the making of any religious and political settlement. A mobilization of the trained bands was ordered as Sir Thomas Fairfax and the New Model Army approached the City, because of fears of a popular insurrection. All of the trained bands were ordered out 'on pain of death', but only the

[70] K. Roberts, 'Citizen Soldiers: The Military Power of the City of London', in Porter (ed.), *London and the Civil War*, 89, 90, 92; *A True and Impartial History of the Military Government of the Citie of Gloucester*, in Scott (ed.), *Somers Tracts*, v. 304.

[71] Nagel, 'A Great Bouncing at Everyman's Door', 85; Roberts, 'Citizen Soldiers', 102; Clarendon, *RCW* ii. 396.

[72] Nagel, 'A Great Bouncing at Everyman's Door', 85; Bulstrode Whitelocke, *Memorials of English Affairs*, 4 vols. (repr. 1853), i. 190–1.   [73] Roberts, 'Citizen Soldiers', 107–8.

Westminster Regiment stood to in strength, even though the lord mayor went in person to close up shops. Popular tumults erupted in Westminster, and Members of Parliament were menaced and abused by discharged soldiers clamouring for their arrears of pay. Guards were posted around the Palace of Westminster, and Parliament ordered Fairfax not to come within forty miles of London.[74] In July 1647 members of the City corporation and their Presbyterian allies attempted to stage an anti-army demonstration supported by reformadoes from disbanded regiments and deserters from the New Model Army. They attempted to induce more soldiers of the New Model to desert, and also sought to win support from the City militia. Another faction consisting of Royalist reformadoes and apprentices invaded Parliament in late July and sought to intimidate it into bringing the king back. This prompted the New Model Army to occupy London on 6 August. The soldiers were kept under strict discipline to avoid repeating the outrages of the reformadoes and disbanded soldiers.[75]

Numerous complaints about billeting and taxation and resentment against the New Model Army's political interference led to the enactment of the Militia Ordinance of 1648. The intent of this law was to create a militia based on the localities and commanded by Parliament and the lords-lieutenant, who would be drawn from Presbyterian aristocrats in order to counterbalance the New Model Army. The leaders of the New Model rightly perceived the Militia Ordinance as an attack upon the army. This challenge was met by Colonel Thomas Pride's purge of the Presbyterian members of the House of Commons. Following the purge, the Militia Ordinance was repealed.[76]

The purge of the Presbyterians by no means ended the factionalism in the army, in the London militia or in the political life of the City. Members of the militia were just as eager to participate in a constitutional settlement as the army, as became clear after the end of the Cromwellian regime. Hostility between the army and the citizens of London was increased in the late autumn of 1659, when the apprentices delivered a petition to the lord mayor for the privileges of Parliament and the preservation of civilian government by ministry and magistracy. The army was ordered into the City to suppress demonstrations by apprentices, and the soldiers killed several and 'cut and slashed' many more. The City continued to demand a free Parliament and control of their own militia, and army officers and soldiers were insulted by the populace.[77]

Many ordinary men were subjected to extended military service far from their homes during the civil wars; this widely shared experience could not help but

---

[74] C. H. Firth (ed.), *The Clarke Papers*, 4 vols., CS NS 49, 54, 61, 62 (1891–1901), i. 132–3, 136.

[75] R. Ashton, 'Insurgency, Counter-Insurgency and Inaction: Three Phases in the Role of the City in the Great Rebellion', in Porter (ed.), *London and the Civil War*, 54–5, 57; id., *Counter-Revolution: The Second Civil War and its Origins, 1646–1648* (1994), 379–80; M. A. Kishlansky, *The Rise of the New Model Army* (1979), 239–42, 247, 256–60; Gentles, *NMA* 143–4, 178–9, 185–90, 194.

[76] Schwoerer, *NSA* 56–7.

[77] Firth (ed.), *Clarke Papers*, iv. 91, 103, 112–13, 119, 166, 168–9, 187.

promote a precocious political awareness.[78] The various armies of the Three Kingdoms were all constituted before adequate systems of pay and supply came into existence. Raising armies came first; discipline and training came later. Every experienced officer of the seventeenth century knew that the greatest danger to an army was lack of discipline, and the chief cause of disorder was want of pay.[79] Although the soldiers of the Parliamentary armies were generally the best paid, it remained true that their pay was almost always in arrears; nor did they have complete confidence that Parliament meant to make good that debt. Prior to the founding of the New Model Army, when the associational armies were raised, loyalty to local officers was always stronger than allegiance to Parliament. Even when their officers were inexperienced, the men of the Army of the Eastern Association always preferred them to the experienced Scots professionals who had been hired by their commander, Robert Rich, second earl of Warwick.[80] One of the reasons why Oliver Cromwell wanted to new-model and get rid of the associational armies was because he hoped to break the ties of loyalty to peers such as the earl of Essex and the earl of Manchester. Cromwell maintained that 'his soldiers had learned to obey Parliament'. Denzil Holles, however, never a lover of Cromwell, insisted that Cromwell's own officers and soldiers were even more politicized and given to factionalism than the associational armies, and that Cromwell simply wished to get rid of rivals.[81]

The rank and file of the New Model Army had already become politicized over the issues of disbandment and arrears of pay, and certainly religious radicals were to be found within its ranks. The New Model Army's military successes enhanced the confidence of the officers and men by convincing them that Divine Providence favoured their cause. Their political and religious radicalism caused them to be feared not only by the Royalists, but also by those Parliamentarians who apprehended that the army would impose its will by force, and, for all their talk about liberty of conscience, crush all other religious opinions and practices. The army's challenge to the authority of Parliament especially offended Presbyterians such as Holles, who still hoped for a negotiated settlement with the king. The army also constituted an enormous expense to keep it standing, which Parliament and most taxpayers wished to reduce by disbandment. Talk of disbandment without making good arrears of pay provoked defiance from soldiers of the New Model Army, which had become a become a more cohesive corps through the shared experience of battle than Parliament realized. Parliament also demonstrated a disregard for legal niceties by proposing to conscript for service in Ireland (regarded as foreign service) soldiers who had voluntarily enlisted in the first place, and by ignoring their claims for pay. These issues, together with the question of legal indemnity for acts of war, served to politicize the rank and file

---

[78] Compare L. Colley, *Britons: Forging the Nation, 1707–1837* (1992), 312.
[79] Sir Robert Dallington, *Aphorismes Civill and Militarie* (1613), 184.
[80] C. Holmes, *The Eastern Association in the English Civil War* (1974), 39–40.
[81] *Memoirs of Denzil Lord Holles* (1699), 35.

and made them fearful of the Presbyterian party in Parliament. The Presbyterians for their part were ungenerous and short-sighted in dealing with the refusal of the soldiers to disband or go to Ireland, and the soldiers organized their resistance by circulating petitions. In June 1647 the officers assumed leadership of what became an army revolt; their organization provided for a system of representation on the army council of two officers and two 'adjutators' or 'agitators', representing the enlisted men, from each regiment. Although Lord General Fairfax disapproved of the factionalism which had appeared in the army since the end of the First English Civil War, he also could not condone what Parliament was trying to do. Attempting to assert the army's right to be consulted about the religious and political settlements of the kingdom, Fairfax and the army council stated that they 'were not a mere mercenary army hired to serve any arbitrary power of a state, but called forth and conjured by the several declarations of Parliament to the defence of our own and the people's just rights and liberties'. This declaration had probably been written by Ireton in an attempt to restrain the agitators.[82] After experiencing the political activism of the New Model Army, the English gentry began to insist upon the need to restrain military power and to confine it to a well-regulated militia. One writer, in 1648, went so far as to maintain that bridling the military power of the government was more important than the question of whether the militia should be placed under the command of Parliament or the king.[83]

The tension between the army and the Rump or Purged Parliament did not cease until Cromwell dismissed the Rump, and assumed the quasi-monarchical office of lord protector, effectively ending the Commonwealth. However, Cromwell's seizure of power did not end the discontent and turmoil within the army, nor bring stability to the British Isles.[84] In 1655, discovering that there were Royalist plots against his life, Cromwell sent orders to Ireland to return some part of the army to England. As they were drawn up upon the quay ready to embark for England, some of the soldiers refused to proceed, saying that they feared that they might be forced to fight against friends at home. General Fleetwood and some of his officers were present at the quayside, and held a court-martial on the spot. They hanged one of the leaders, and cashiered a whole company. In February 1658 Cromwell discovered extensive discontent among the officers of his own regiment concerning his assumption of personal power. When Cromwell sent for them, they expressed regret for the demise of the Commonwealth, although they indicated a willingness to continue in the army for the sake of the 'old cause', a term which they refused to define. Cromwell dismissed them, and later, Secretary Thurloe told General Monck that the cashiered officers were Anabaptists.[85] The dismissal was a futile gesture though, because the officers of the New Model Army

---

[82] Gentles, *NMA* 140–1, 147–50, 159–69, 178–9; *Cobbett's Parliamentary History of England*, 36 vols. (1806–20), vol. iii. cols. 582, 585–6; *Memoirs of Denzil Lord Holles*, 83–4; Thomas, Lord Fairfax, *Short Memorials* (1699), 119–20. [83] Schwoerer, *NSA* 55.

[84] Hainsworth, *Swordsmen in Power*, 137, 147.

[85] Firth, *Ludlow*, i. 402; Firth (ed.), *Clarke Papers*, iii. 140–1.

continued to meddle in politics. Upon the death of Cromwell, General John Lambert's party tried to dictate a constitutional settlement. The units of the army which had remained in England had been neglected by their officers, who spent their time playing political games in London, and the morale of their men had suffered accordingly. In Ireland, Lieutenant-General Edmund Ludlow, as commander-in-chief, assembled his officers who were in the Dublin area, and successfully persuaded them that it was wrong for the army to intervene in politics, that previous attempts to do so had miscarried and that it was their duty and best policy to submit to civilian control as represented in Parliament. General George Monck, who commanded the troops in Scotland, followed a parallel course, and refused to be drawn into army plots. He remained aloof from their conspiracies, and he told his own officers that the rule which he had learned in his years of service in the army of the Dutch Republic was that officers obeyed the civilian government and did not meddle in politics. Monck's officers obeyed, and discipline held. Monck had remained loyal to the Protectorate—even under Cromwell's son Richard— but now he could see no alternative to a restoration of the monarchy except continuing chaos. Monck's decision to work for the restoration of Charles II ended the intervention of the army as a body in English politics, and this conformed to a trend already observable in mainland Europe.[86]

The British civil wars presented the contending parties with major financial and logistical problems. There had been a tradition among English classical humanists, including Sir Francis Bacon, James Harrington and Marchamont Nedham, which held that valour and the possession of martial skill constituted the sinews of war. This tradition, which was more useful in motivating men to prepare for war than to prosecute it, exercised an important influence in the shaping of martial culture before the civil wars.[87] The realities of prolonged civil war altered this point of view, as Hobbes perceived when he stated that the king could have won the civil wars if he had possessed sufficient treasure, because 'very few of the common people . . . cared for either of the causes'.[88] The failure of the king's wartime government to develop a rational and efficient system of military and civil administration for raising troops and levying taxes resulted in these responsibilities, by default, devolving upon local military governors of garrisons. Their ruthless collection of taxes and contributions resembled nothing so much as the behaviour of warlords and robber-barons from the feudal past.[89] In the areas where Parliament was able to assume exclusive control of direct and indirect taxation, taxes rose to a level three times higher than that which had prevailed during the period of the king's personal

---

[86] Firth, *Ludlow*, ii. 118–20; Thomas Gumble, *The Life of General Monck, Duke of Albemarle* (1671), fos. 111–13, 116, 129v; *The Declaration of Sir Charles Coote . . . Lord President of the Province of Connaught* (1659), 1–8; Firth (ed.), *Clarke Papers*, iv. 22, 59, 87; Sir G. Clark, *War and Society in the Seventeenth Century* (1958), 75; Hainsworth, *Swordsmen in Power*, 250–71.

[87] M. Peltonen, *Classical Humanism and Republicanism in English Political Thought, 1570–1640* (1995), 202–13, 312; Manning, *Swordsmen*, ch. 2.   [88] Hobbes, *Behemoth* (1963 repr. edn.), 4.

[89] Hutton, *Royalist War Effort*, 103–4; Wheeler, *Making of a World Power*, 77–8.

rule in the 1630s, and remained at that level through the 1650s. Thus was asserted the principle that money was the sinews of war, and England and the conquered kingdoms of Ireland and Scotland took an important step towards becoming a military-fiscal state. The Commonwealth had borrowed the techniques of Dutch wartime finance, including the infamous 'Dutch Devil Excise', an excise tax which both the Royalists and the Parliamentarians made use of after 1643. Because parliamentary scrutiny was exercised over this system of wartime finance, the English fiscal-military state followed the Dutch model, and avoided the worst abuses of the French system with its venality and militarism.[90]

The New Model Army triumphed over all of its enemies, and was kept standing for fifteen years. This gave the English, the Irish and the Scots an unpleasant taste of a peacetime army in its latter days. Protector Cromwell's military prerogative powers came to be feared even more than those which had been exercised by Charles I in the late 1620s. For example, the billeting of the soldiers of the Parliamentary armies was a violation of the Petition of Right. There were, of course, no permanent military barracks at this time, so the soldiers were all billeted upon innkeepers and householders. The soldiers were supposed to pay for their food and lodging out of their pay, but since their pay was often in arrears, the landlords were offered certificates instead which might be redeemed at some later date—usually at a discounted rate. The legacy of the Interregnum was an aversion to standing armies and a fear of military rule. At the end of the seventeenth century John Trenchard said that the Cromwellian army was raised for a good cause and dedicated to liberty, yet it was corrupted and tempted to do violence to parliamentary liberties. This was not a mercenary army, but was raised from the people. How much more might Parliament and the people fear a standing army that was corrupt and dissolute.[91]

Nothing brought the impact of the military revolution and the changed European military world home so forcefully as the outbreak of the Wars of the Three Kingdoms, the return of the professional soldiers from the continental European wars and the creation of standing armies throughout the British Isles. More men and women had been exposed to the horrors of war and all of its accompanying disasters than at any time since the baronial chaos of the fifteenth century. The proportion of those who actually fought in the various armies of the British and Irish civil wars is certainly comparable to the levels of mobilization during the First and Second World Wars of the first half of the twentieth century. Learning new theories and methods of warfare and committing themselves to ideologies acquired from the shared experience of fighting religious wars enhanced the

---

[90] J. Brewer, *The Sinews of Power: War, Money and the English State, 1688–1783* (1989), 23–4; M. J. Braddick, *The Nerves of State: Taxation and the Financing of the English State, 1558–1714* (1996), 16–18, 28–9, 99–100, 221.

[91] Schwoerer, *NSA* 51; Gentles, *NMA* 132; Hutton, *Royalist War Effort*, 30; [John Trenchard], *A Short History of Standing Armies in England* (1698), 10.

political awareness of thousands of officers as well as many of the enlisted ranks, and this had the effect of permanently altering the political landscape. There would be no going back to the isolationist policies of the Jacobean peace or the supposedly 'halcyon days' of the 1630s. The Commonwealth of England, Scotland and Ireland had united the British Isles under one government for the first time; it had ended, at least momentarily, any threat of foreign interference or incursion, and had committed the new Republic to the Protestant cause. The Commonwealth navy had defeated the most formidable of sea powers in the First Anglo-Dutch War. Once again, the tempting prospect of being a major player in the affairs of mainland Europe presented itself, but this was tempered by the profoundly unsettling experience of paying the cost of standing armies which, as Tacitus and Machiavelli had warned, proved to be difficult to control and which refused to be content with their pay and to obey orders from the civilian authorities.

Nor was the question of who would command and control the military forces of the realm settled by the Restoration of the monarchy in 1660. It was no longer possible to survive without permanent military forces in the European diplomatic and military world in the latter part of the seventeenth century, but both the king and Parliament tried to pretend that the 'guards and garrisons' which Parliament did allow Charles II did not constitute a standing army, and that a militia would suffice. In the meantime, Charles II hid pieces of that permanent military force from Parliament's view in places such as Tangier and the Anglo-Dutch Brigade of the States' Army. Considering the heightened religious, ideological and political tensions of the Restoration period, conflict over the control of the army, as well as questions of who was qualified to hold a military commission in that army, were bound to be contentious.

9

Atrocity, plunder and discipline

There are two things that cause men to be desirous of this profession; the first is emulation of honour; the next is the hopes they have by licence to do evil. As the aims of the first are virtuous, so will they do good service. The other by strict discipline may be brought to do good service and to be obedient soldiers; but if that discipline be neglected, then they [will] prove the ruin of the army.

George Monck, duke of Albemarle, *Observations upon Military and Political Affairs* (1671), 2.

Soldiers...ought to stand more in awe of their generals than fear of their enemies.

Thomas Venn, *Military and Maritime Discipline* (1672), 3.

Professional soldiers and others who kept abreast of military innovations in mainland Europe understood the need to discipline their men and keep them focused on achieving military goals. Armies which foraged and plundered often became involved in secondary wars with local peasants, and forfeited the goodwill of those who might offer intelligence and assistance. Regular payment of troops and developed systems of supply obviated the need for plunder, improved discipline and reduced the incidence of mutiny. These goals, of course, first required a revolution in the way by which the state financed war. Those who were familiar with the Low-Countries wars were also aware of the important strides in reducing atrocities and promoting the more humane treatment of prisoners of war and noncombatants, as well as a more sensitive attitude towards churches and other sacred places and civilian property.

The articles of war in English and Scottish armies in the British Isles which attempted to regulate crimes and depredations by soldiers were derived from Dutch and Swedish military codes. Many officers attempted to prevent the plundering and massacre of enemy soldiers after their surrender and of noncombatants as well. It very much depended upon whether soldiers regarded the enemy as worthy opponents or as an evil menace, and armies sometimes became captives of their own propaganda. Efforts to restrain the destructiveness of war were distinctly less successful in Ireland, where Parliamentary forces gave vent to religious and ethnic hatreds, and pursued a policy of 'fire and sword'. Cromwell's massacre at Drogheda had the effect of poisoning the atmosphere in the Irish wars, and his actions were imitated by other armies. Even otherwise humane officers advocated slash-and-burn methods when dealing with the guerilla tactics of an elusive enemy in the difficult terrains of Ireland and Scotland.

The treatment of prisoners of war varied. Parliamentary commanders hanged Irish prisoners of war captured in England until Prince Rupert threatened a policy of retaliation. In England, officers were frequently released upon giving their parole not to take up arms against Parliament again; those who violated their parole were dealt with harshly. Victorious Parliamentary armies paraded Royalist prisoners of war through London as trophies of battle. English Royalist soldiers captured by Parliamentary armies were also induced to enlist by their captors. Irish and Scottish prisoners of war were sometimes allowed to enter foreign service, but many were also transported to the colonies as indentured servants.

From medieval times until the middle of the sixteenth century, the servants and subjects of a belligerent prince were viewed as belonging to the enemy. The consequence of this was that their property might be plundered because they were regarded as being parties to the feud between their liege lords. Thus, looting and booty was justified by the need to do maximum damage to the enemy, while the prospect of booty helped to attract mercenary soldiers to fight for the prince. Medieval writers had, at least, insisted that plundering the enemy was only permissible in just wars, but early modern writers, such as Hugo Grotius, held that the rules governing when booty could be taken and how prisoners of war were to be treated were independent of the question whether the war being fought was a just war. That being said, Grotius offered cold comfort to noncombatants. He stated that natural law, as testified to by Cicero, Polybius and Tacitus, permitted the devastation and pillage of enemy property, and, according to the law of nations, even sacred places were not excepted. The only exception that Grotius admits of is that the bodies of the dead may not be mistreated. Matthew Sutcliffe held that looting had two legitimate purposes: to diminish the enemy's capacity to make war, and to sustain an invading army when logistics and timely pay continued to be problematical.[1]

Thus, there was general agreement that looting and booty were legitimate under certain circumstances in a just war. Attempts to regulate plunder or even abolish the practice, along with attempts to limit the destructiveness of war by ensuring that noncombatants were not harmed, came about for practical reasons rather than from humanitarian considerations. Articles of war drawn up by military commanders in the late sixteenth and seventeenth centuries accepted the legitimacy of looting under certain circumstances, and sought only to curtail it under other circumstances in order to preserve military discipline, to prevent interference with military operations and to avoid provoking hostility among

---

[1] Redlich, *DPM* 2, 20; Hugo Grotius, *The Law of War and Peace* (1925; repr. 1962), III. v. 658–62; Matthew Sutcliffe, *The Practice, Proceedings and Lawes of Armes Described* (1595), 133.

civilian populations. Military commanders were especially concerned to prevent soldiers from turning to plunder at the moment when the enemy broke and fled, and to require them instead to pursue the enemy.[2] Thomas and Dudley Digges were more emphatic in their condemnation of contemporary practices of plunder and spoil, and showed how they undermined discipline and loyalty to the state. The ancient Roman practice, which they cited, was to bring all of the spoils of war to one public place, where a portion was equitably divided among all the soldiers, another portion was set aside for ransoming prisoners and remounting soldiers who had lost their horses, and a third portion was reserved for the public treasury to pay for future wars and keep taxes low. The modern practice of plunder and spoil, they asserted, was to allow unorganized pillaging without the supervision of officers (although they always collected their share), and if any of the soldiers were killed by hostile locals, then the captains and colonels would collect the pay of the dead soldiers until the muster-master discovered that the company's or regiment's strength had been depleted.[3]

Despite less than perfect success in the regulation of plunder, it remains true to say that in the seventeenth-century European military world the laws of war constituted an unwritten but widely accepted body of customs which touched upon terms of surrender, treatment and exchange of prisoners of war, passes and safe conducts, and the occasions when plunder was not permissible. The driving force behind observance of the laws of war was the reciprocal honour of adversaries, mutual self-interest and simple utility.[4] During the Wars of the Three Kingdoms, the customary rules of war were more frequently observed in England than in Scotland, and in Ireland they were barely observed at all.[5]

Looting and pillage had, of course, been part of English warfare in the past, but most of England had not experienced warfare since the fifteenth century, and Lowland Scotland had not seen a war since the latter part of the sixteenth century. Warfare in these parts was for most a new experience, and it was assumed that plunder, like the new methods of warfare, was a foreign contrivance and vice, introduced into the British Isles by soldiers of fortune returning from the mainland European wars. According to the *Oxford English Dictionary*, the word 'plunder' derives from the German and occurs no earlier than 1632.[6] James Gordon, parson of Rothiemay, thought that it had always been usual for Highlanders to plunder the countryside coming and going, but he believed that this kind of behaviour was

[2] Redlich, *DPM* 6–7; J. T. Johnson, *Just War Tradition and the Restraint of War: A Moral and Historical Inquiry* (1981), 47–8.

[3] Thomas Digges and Dudley Digges, *Foure Paradoxes of Politique Discourses concerning Militarie Discipline* (1604), 54–5.

[4] B. Donagan, 'Codes and Conduct in the English Civil War', *P&P* no. 118 (1994), 78–9.

[5] Ead., 'Atrocity, War Crime and Treason in the English Civil War', *AHR* 104 (1994), 1137–66; J. Morrill, 'Historical Introduction and Overview: The Un-English Civil War', in J. R. Young (ed.), *Celtic Dimensions of the British Civil Wars* (1997), 6.

[6] I. Roy, 'England Turned Germany? The Aftermath of the Civil War and its European Context', *TRHS* 5th ser. 28 (1978), 135–6; J. R. Hale, *War and Society in Renaissance Europe, 1450–1620* (1985), 44.

new among Lowlanders and dated from the Bishops' Wars. Another opinion held
that it was Argyll whose troops were 'the first plunderers in Scotland'.[7]

In the English civil wars, looting continued to be widespread and posed serious
problems of maintaining discipline; both Royalist and the Parliamentarian
authorities did try to limit the destructiveness of plundering soldiers. There was
little difference between the military codes of justice promulgated by the Royalist
and Parliamentarian armies. Both derived from the Dutch model, and the earl of
Essex's judge-advocate-general, the Dutch lawyer Isaac Dorislaus, had earlier
served in the same capacity in the king's armies. The enforcement of the articles of
war noticeably improved in both armies as officers gained experience and became
more professional in their attitudes regarding discipline. In the New Model Army
this task was assisted by more regular pay and the practice of supplementing its
general court martial with regimental courts for minor infractions. The Scottish
Articles and Ordinances of War (1641), published by General Sir Alexander Leslie,
were based upon the Swedish articles of war first promulgated by Gustavus
Adolphus. Irish Confederate Catholic commanders who had seen service in the
Army of Flanders drew upon the Spanish model. These were the codes of military
law which were actually enforced by councils of war or courts martial. They
reflected current practice in the European military world.[8]

A professional officer and a man of honour who valued his reputation would
also have been guided by standards of conduct which derived from religious or
moral principles which were essentially the same as natural law and the developing
law of nations. These principles were also widely accepted in the European
military world. Grotius insisted, for example, that natural law, the law of nations
and municipal law (that is, the particular law of one country or region) all forbade
a soldier to slay an enemy after the order for ceasefire had been given. Grotius
recognized that limitations on the destructiveness of warfare and the enforcement
of military discipline tended to the same purpose when he stated that a soldier
who failed to retreat when given the order to do so was a 'worthless soldier', while
a soldier who killed the enemy without orders (or military purpose) might be
punished by the laws of his country and obliged to make restitution.[9] Preachers,
divines and military chaplains also had much to say about codes of conduct for the
soldier. In this matter, the teachings of Protestant and Catholic divines did not
differ significantly in forbidding cruelty and the mistreatment of prisoners of war
and noncombatants. The moral guidelines which Richard Bernard laid down in
his *Bible-Battells* (1629) were succinct and unequivocal: commanders must deal
with prisoners and conquered peoples in a humane way. In the Old Testament

---

[7] James Gordon, parson of Rothiemay, *History of Scots Affairs*, 3 vols., SC 1, 2, 4 (1841), ii. 262;
C. Rogers (ed.), 'Rehearsal of Events which Occurred in the North of Scotland from 1635 to 1645 in
Relation to the National Covenant', *TRHS* os 5 (1877), 363.

[8] Redlich, *DPM* 22; Firth, *CA* 279–81, 283. The Swedish articles of war issued by Gustavus
Adolphus are printed in Robert Ward, *Animadversions of War* (1639), bk. II, pp. 42–54.

[9] Donagan, 'Atrocity, War Crime and Treason', 1142; ead., 'Codes and Conduct', 74–5; Grotius,
Law of War and Peace, II. xviii. 788–9.

subdued enemies were put to the sword only by the special commandment of God; generals should show mercy after victory; cruelty was the sign of a savage nature. The enemy dead must be decently buried. Churches must always be respected, as must clergymen. However, Bernard and most divines writing before the beginning of the civil wars emphasized that captured rebels were to be excepted from the requirement that soldiers be merciful to prisoners.[10] In order to preserve discipline, however, soldiers, after being admonished that certain acts were contrary to God's commandments and the laws of nature, were told that they still had to obey all orders, whether the command was lawful or not. Private soldiers were not to exercise independent judgement.[11]

Discipline was at the heart of modern military practice. It was difficult to gather together a field army sufficient in size to undertake long-range and large-scale operations if troops were dispersed for purposes of foraging (which was often accompanied by plundering). Consequently, many small and unplanned skirmishes resulted where modern military theory had limited application. These skirmishes often comprehended secondary conflicts with peasants—many of whom might possess military experience themselves. Military commanders also found it easier to obtain voluntary financial contributions from civilian leaders where they were able to keep order among their men and restrain them from plundering.[12] This kind of discipline could not be imposed upon mercenary soldiers without reasonably certain and regular pay, supply and provisioning. Thomas Raymond, who had briefly served as a gentleman volunteer in the States' Army in the early 1630s, remembered the misery of being a private in what was the best-paid army in Europe.

I cannot but think that the life of a private or common soldier is the most miserable in the world; and that not so much because his life is always in danger—that is little or nothing— but from the terrible miseries he endures in hunger and nakedness in hard marches and bad quarters, 30 stivers being his pay for eight days, of which they could not possibly subsist, but that they help themselves by foraging, stealing, furnishing wood in the field to the officers, straw; some are cobblers, tailors & c. . . . It is hardly to be thought the devastation that an army brings into the country. . . .[13]

Although Raymond liked and admired his colonel, he could not abide the cruelty of war, and he obtained his discharge from the Dutch army.

---

[10] Richard Bernard, *The Bible-Battells, or the Sacred Art Military* (1629), 246–52. See also *A Myrrour for English Soldiers* (1595), sig. D3*v*. *Bible-Battells* was compiled not only out of the Old Testament, but also from classical authors such as Thucydides.

[11] Donagan, 'Codes and Conduct', 77–8.

[12] J. Black, *A Military Revolution? Military Change and European Society, 1550–1800* (1991), 17; Sir G. Clark, *War and Society in the Seventeenth Century* (1958), 82–6; George Monck, duke of Albemarle, *Observations upon Military and Political Affairs* (1671), 107.

[13] G. Davies (ed.), *Autobiography of Thomas Raymond*, CS 3rd ser. 28 (1917), 43. See also M. Keen, *Chivalry* (1984), 228–30; *The Earl of Castlehaven's Review, or, his Memoirs of . . . the Irish Wars* (1684), app., 56–62.

Ralph, Lord Hopton, observed that during his campaigns in the west in 1643 the disorderliness and the appetite for plunder of the Royalist horse stood in the way of attempts to impose discipline in the Royalist armies. The town of Taunton had expressed a willingness to raise a contribution of £8,000 if the Royalist commanders could control their soldiers and prevent plunder. 'And the generals being fully advertised of the opportunity to begin a discipline in the army, and being themselves very desirous of it, were yet never able to repress the extravagant disorder of the horse to the ruin and discomposure of all.'[14] The rough methods of the Royalist governor of Worcester in raising money to pay his garrison drove many into the Parliamentary camp. Bulstrode Whitelocke says that the governor, one Colonel Bard, threatened the citizens with this warrant: 'Know, that unless you bring unto me ... the monthly contribution for six months, you are to expect an unsanctified troop of horse among you, from whom, if you do hide yourselves, they shall fire your houses without mercy, hang up your bodies wherever they may find them and scare your ghosts.'[15] According to a Royalist commissioner of array in Worcestershire, one of the reasons for the failure of the Royalist war effort in that county was that the Parliamentary committees kept control of their military forces and punished those guilty of plunder or atrocities. The Royalists had failed to respond to civilian complaints, and cut themselves off from popular support.[16] The ability to maintain order and discipline will go a long way in explaining how popular allegiance was bestowed. Sir William Brereton admitted to a friend that his Parliamentary troops had committed many acts of plunder in Wales and Cheshire, which made it difficult to obtain provisions from local inhabitants. Brereton had tried to curb such depredations by both persuasion and severe discipline, and he had been menaced by his own troops many times for doing so. He admitted, however, that his soldiers had suffered privation because of arrears of pay and lack of other necessities.[17]

The breakdown in discipline which resulted from the overwhelming desire of soldiers to pillage following a victory could destroy an army. Following the victory of James Graham, marquis of Montrose, at Kilsyth in August 1645 against a numerically superior and better-trained Covenanter army, his own Royalist army, flushed with victory, dissolved as officers and men gave themselves over to plunder and began to return home. The Covenanter nobles and chiefs fled or began cautiously switching their allegiances to King Charles. Montrose entered Glasgow and extorted as much money as he could from the city, and forfeited their goodwill. Sir David Leslie, sent by the Parliament-ary forces from England to help the Covenanters, took advantage of

---

[14] Sir Ralph Hopton, Lord Hopton, *Bellum Civile: Hopton's Narrative of his Campaign in the West, 1642–1644*, ed. C. E. H. Chadwyck Healey, SRS 18 (1902), 47.

[15] Bulstrode Whitelocke, *Memorials of the English Affairs*, 4 vols. (1682; repr. 1853), i. 540.

[16] R. Hutton, *The Royalist War Effort, 1642–1646* (1982), 77.

[17] *The Letterbooks of Sir William Brereton*, vol. 1: January 31st–May 29th, ed. R. N. Dore, RSLC 123 (1984), 320.

Montrose's weakened position, and defeated him at the Battle of Philiphaugh in September 1645.[18]

The pillaging of ill disciplined soldiers, who were not regularly paid and provisioned, quite often provoked violent and semi-organized reactions of peasants known as 'secondary wars'. In the southern and western counties of England, those who participated in loosely organized attempts to restrain plundering soldiers and maintain neutrality within their communities were known as 'clubmen', from the weapons they carried and the club law which they dispensed. These movements of clubmen first appeared in Somerset, Wiltshire and Dorset in the spring of 1645 in reaction to the brutal excesses of the Royalist armies—especially that commanded by George, Lord Goring—but subsequently spread eastwards into Berkshire, Hampshire and Sussex, and northwards to South Wales and the Welsh Border. Not all clubmen were strictly neutral. Royalist depredations could not avoid implanting a certain degree of sympathy for the Parliamentarians, but the Royalists themselves tried to win support from associations of clubmen by exercising some restraint. Although occasionally clergy and minor gentry might influence the clubmen, they preferred to select leaders from their own ranks, such as Humphry Willis, yeoman, of Woolavington, Somerset, who avoided being manipulated by Royalists and Parliamentarians, and did not hesitate to present petitions to the king or Parliament. Fairfax tried to conciliate the Somerset clubmen, but when a large force of clubmen obstructed the movement of Parliamentary troops, Cromwell, after unsuccessfully attempting to persuade them to disperse, ran them down with cavalry. Generally speaking, the clubmen favoured a negotiated peace and wished to retain the king: otherwise they were politically apathetic, wished to keep hostilities out of their local communities, and were determined to protect themselves from plundering soldiers.[19]

Scottish armies were notoriously poorly provisioned and paid during the civil wars. While campaigning in northern England in 1646, the Covenanting Army lived off the land, which generated secondary conflicts with the local inhabitants. As remnants of the Scots Engager Army retreated towards Scotland from their invasion of the north of England in 1648, many of them were massacred by the English countryfolk seeking revenge for the earlier plunder of the countryside when the Engager Army had marched south. Of those who were taken prisoner by the Parliamentary forces, those Scots who had been impressed were set free, but the volunteers were transported to Virginia and the West Indies as indentured servants.[20]

Problems of indiscipline often began with the officers themselves and gentlemen volunteers. Both the Royalists and the Parliamentarians were left with surpluses of

[18] James Fraser, *Chronicle of the Frasers*, ed. W. Mackay, SHS 1ˢᵗ ser. 47 (1905), 300–3.

[19] D. Underdown, *Somerset in the Civil War and Interregnum* (1973), 86–7, 98–9, 105–8, 112, 116–17; C. Carlton, 'Civilians', in J. Kenyon and J. Ohlmeyer (eds.), *The Civil Wars: A Military History of England, Scotland and Ireland, 1638–1660* (1998), 303–4.

[20] *Memoirs of Sir Andrew Melvill*, trans. T. Ameer-Ali (1918), 76; H. L. Rubinstein, *Captain Luckless: James, First Duke of Hamilton, 1616–1649* (1975), 219.

officers as the civil wars wore on, but the problem was especially acute among the former, whose armies contained whole units composed of reformadoes and volunteers. During the winter of 1643–4 Lord Belasyse was sent to York as governor and lieutenant-general during the absence of the marquis of Newcastle, who was then engaged against the Scots allies of the Parliamentarian forces. Discipline was less than satisfactory in Newcastle's army, and the York garrison was divided by 'factions and discontents'. Despite attempts by Belasyse to improve discipline, when he engaged Fairfax's army at Selby he found that all of his horse except the officers deserted in the face of the enemy.[21] In the early days of the First English Civil War, Lord Fairfax complained of guards at Wethersby near York being surprised because they were ignorant of their duties and asleep. Parliamentary officers had trouble controlling their men. At the Battle of Adwalton Moor, some of Fairfax's troopers stopped to strip the body of a dead Royalist colonel. Moments later, a cannonball killed two of the plunderers, and Fairfax told his troopers that this was divine punishment for their disobedience.[22] In 1644 Sir John Meldrum laid siege to Nottingham with an army of 7,000 men. One officer who was bringing up reinforcements stopped for a day which he spent drinking in a tavern. The besieging army was composed of military units from several counties. 'The commanders were so emulous of one another, and so refractory to commands, and so piquing in all punctilios of superiority that it galled' Meldrum, 'who having commanded abroad, and been used to deal with officers that understood the discipline of war, was confounded among those who knew not how to obey orders'. The consequence was that the assault on Nottingham failed.[23] In late 1642 Sir Ralph Hopton marched into Devonshire to augment his Cornish army with well affected gentry, who were summoned to Modbury as a *posse comitatus*. Unlike the Cornish gentry, the Devon gentry could not count on their tenants following them: 'there appeared a great concourse of people, yet it was rather like a great fair than a posse, there being none but the gentlemen that had any kind of arms or equipage for war.' Hopton, whose own army was exceptionally well disciplined, regarded the Devon gentry as a rabble. Their inability to mount an adequate guard around their camp led to the capture and defeat of many of them as a consequence of a surprise raid by the Parliamentary horse. Because of his failure to secure Devon, Hopton had to withdraw into Cornwall for the winter.[24]

George Monck thought good discipline in an army began with the officers themselves. Generals should beware of giving positions of command to officers who were 'covetous or given to pillaging'. Monck also believed that the prerequisite for good discipline among the rank and file was punctual payment of the soldiers; that being the case, one could 'with justice' maintain discipline by severe

[21] 'A Brief Relation of the Life and Memoirs of John Lord Belasyse, Written and Collected by his Secretary, Joshua Moone', HMC, *Ormonde MSS*, NS 2 (1903), 383–4.
[22] Thomas, 3rd Lord Fairfax, *Short Memorials* (1699), 5, 40–1.
[23] Lucy Hutchinson, *Memoirs of the Life of Colonel Hutchinson*, ed. C. H. Firth (1906), 175–7.
[24] Hopton, *Bellum Civile*, pp. xxv, 25–7; Clarendon, *RCW* iii. 79.

punishments.[25] While fighting in Ireland, Sir James Turner spoke with admiration and respect for his enemy, Owen Roe O'Neill, because O'Neill, who had gained experience in the Spanish Army of Flanders, had imposed upon the Confederate Army of Ulster a degree of discipline which was too often lacking in Ireland.[26] During the Royalist Siege of Gloucester in 1643, the besieging army found the Parliamentary garrison to be very loyal and well disciplined, and few sought to desert. However, when a raiding party sallied forth from the garrison, it was discovered that their bravery derived, in part, from the fact that they were fortified with 'as much wine and strong water as they desired to drink'. Whenever the soldiers from the Gloucester garrison were captured, they 'were always drunk'. When Gloucester was reduced, 'a very great licence' broke out in the Royalist army—both amongst officers and soldiers. The Royalist officers extorted protection money from the citizens of Gloucester. Generally speaking, the Royalist cavalry in the west under Prince Maurice and the marquis of Hertford were badly disciplined, and did not care about their reputations for plundering. This caused difficulty in collecting taxes for the Royalist war effort.[27]

The Parliamentary authorities could be very harsh in punishing desertion. At the Dorchester Quarter Sessions in April 1646, a panel of judges consisting of civilian justices of the peace and military officers enforced an ordinance of Parliament for soldiers who deserted by condemning three to hang, two to run the gauntlet and two 'to be tied neck and heels', and one to be pilloried with a rope around his neck. However, at the August 1646 Quarter Sessions, Anthony Ashley Cooper begged for the life of a condemned felon because he had been a Parliamentary soldier. Cooper, who always had an eye on his constituency, consistently supported such reprieves for former Parliamentary soldiers.[28]

Restraining plunder and atrocities was certainly important to enforcing discipline, but few commanders in the British and Irish civil wars possessed the authority, will or the resources to prevent these depredations entirely. The rules of war in the seventeenth century in any case allowed plunder when a town was taken by assault or storm. Plunder was necessary when pay was in arrears or an army was inadequately supplied. Moreover, soldiers might mutiny if denied plunder, unless the town offered a substantial gratuity in lieu thereof. In the early years of the civil wars, the failure of Parliament to pay the soldiers of Essex's army in a timely fashion made plunder likely; in the latter part of the wars the armies of Fairfax and Cromwell were more successful in punishing and restraining plunder.[29] Although George Monck was fond of inventing aphorisms about the evil effects of plunder on military discipline, his troops could have competed with

25 Monck, *Observations*, 14; R. E. Scouller, *The Armies of Queen Anne* (1966), 279.
26 Sir James Turner, *Memoirs of his own Life and Times*, BC 31 (1829), 26.
27 Clarendon, *RCW* iii. 79, 165–7.
28 'Autobiographical Sketch', in W. D. Christie, *A Life of Anthony Ashley Cooper, First Earl of Shaftesbury, 1621–1683*, 2 vols. (1871), vol. i, app. II, pp. xxxiv, xxxvii–xxxviii.
29 Firth, *CA* 191–3, 291–3; E. H[ogan]. (ed.), *The History of the Warr of Ireland from 1641 to 1653 by a British Officer of the Regiment of Sir John Clotworthy* (1873), 181–3.

the best (or worst) of Wallenstein's foragers in the Thirty Years War. When Monck was lieutenant-colonel of his cousin, Robert Sidney, earl of Leicester's Royalist regiment in Ireland, 'by his several expeditions into the country', his men 'returned with such booties that his regiment seemed to be purveyor of provisions for the whole city [of Dublin]; and any soldier, though sick [and] without shoes, would strive to go out with "honest George Monck", for so they familiarly called him'. Later Monck became the Parliamentary commander in Scotland. After his troops stormed Dundee in August 1651 they put some 8,000 soldiers and townspeople to the sword. Monck's men were then allowed to plunder the town for two weeks.[30]

Whether through necessity or an absence or failure of discipline, all armies that fought in the Wars of the Three Kingdoms were prone to plunder or commit atrocities at some point. The Royalists probably got the worst of it in popular estimation, because the term 'cavalier', in a pejorative sense, linked the king's party with the plundering excesses of soldiers who had served abroad. Being poorly and irregularly paid, Royalist armies were difficult to control—especially after they had obtained a victory or successfully assaulted a town. The prospect of plunder was often the only consideration that could keep them from deserting, and Royalist officers did not always set a good example themselves when it came to pillaging.[31] The earl of Newcastle's white coats had a fearful reputation for plundering: 'It was observed by some that the land was like Eden before him, and behind him was a barren wilderness.'[32] When Lord Goring's army marched through Essex, they stopped at the earl of Warwick's house at Leeze to confiscate the arms in the armoury. The soldiers who were assigned to carry the arms away, however, broke ranks and fell to hunting and havocking the deer in the earl's park. Having worked up a great thirst, they then consumed twenty hogsheads of beer and another hogshead of sack. Their officers were unable to restrain them.[33]

Both Royalists and Parliamentarians sometimes resorted to plunder and pillage as instruments of policy. In 1643 Prince Rupert threatened townspeople with plunder by his 'licensed and hungry' soldiers if they failed to furnish him provisions and labourers. On other occasions the threat of 'fire and sword' was levelled against villages which might furnish provisions for the Parliamentary garrison at Gloucester, and against the inhabitants of Oxfordshire, Buckinghamshire and Berkshire if they did not provision the Royalist garrison at Oxford.[34] In

[30] Thomas Gumble, *The Life of General Monck, Duke of Albemarle* (1671), fos. 15–16; Gentles, *NMA* 441, 551, n. 122.

[31] I. Roy, 'The English Civil War and English Society', in B. Bond and I. Roy (eds.), *War and Society: A Yearbook of Military History*, 2 vols. (1975), i. 37–40; id., 'England Turned Germany?', 128; Firth, *Ludlow*, i. 44.

[32] *Original Memoirs Written during the Great Civil War . . . Memoirs of Captain John Hodgson* (1806), 98.

[33] 'The Life of Mr Arthur Wilson the Historian . . . Written by Himself', in Francis Peck, *Desiderata Curiosa*, 2 vols. (1732–5), II. xii. 31–3.

[34] Whitelocke, *Memorials*, i. 225, 239, 253–4.

London, the Parliamentary authorities grew heedless of individual rights, and used general warrants to search the homes of suspected Royalist sympathizers in order to keep weapons and money from being sent to the king's assistance.[35]

There were numerous instances of soldiers plundering civilians because their officers could not or would not restrain them. During the Bishops' Wars, soldiers of the king's army pillaged Yorkshire, partly because they were not paid and partly because their officers made little effort to impose discipline. Victims who complained usually suffered retaliation. A witness to these acts of plunder told Ferdinando, second Lord Fairfax, that the officers of the king's army were responsible for the want of discipline because of their failure to keep their soldiers busy by training them.[36] Parliament had the opportunity to gather an abundance of evidence that the king and his military commanders were incapable of protecting his subjects from his own military forces. Many officers demonstrated a reluctance to push their authority too far for fear of provoking mutiny. Officers who had recently been justices of the peace in their county communities had difficulty delineating military and civilian jurisdictions. They were uncertain about how far martial law was legal in England, and afterwards were always fearful of the legal consequences of their actions as soldiers. Parliamentarian officers usually sought to obtain acts of indemnity to protect themselves against prosecution for their actions during the civil wars. Decisive officers, on the other hand, were not scrupulous about whether they possessed the authority to execute martial law, because they understood the very real potential for mutiny and plundering if their provisions ran out.[37] Yorkshire suffered much—not only from the various Royalist and Parliamentarian armies that foraged and pillaged their way across the countryside, but also from the Scots who campaigned extensively in Yorkshire. Denzil Holles also accused Cromwell of trying to discredit the Scots army garrisoned in northern England by withholding their pay in an attempt to provoke them to mutiny and plunder. Some estates and farms in Yorkshire were so depleted by marauding soldiers that the tenants and smallholders could not meet their tax assessments, and had to ask Parliament for relief. Yorkshire magistrates also complained of the difficulty in securing punishment of soldiers who had committed criminal acts. There was a riot at a market town in Yorkshire in which some men were killed, and a council of war executed a number of Scots soldiers and cashiered others. Holles says that this riot was engineered by the Cromwellians, although the Scots Covenanting Army, having been denied their pay by the English Parliament, had actually attempted to levy a local tax by their own authority.[38]

---

[35] K. Lindley, *Popular Politics and Religion in Civil War London* (1997), 324–7.

[36] BL, Add MS. 18,979 [Fairfax Correspondence], fos. 69–70; G. W. Johnston (ed.), *The Fairfax Correspondence*, 2 vols. (1848), ii. 203–4.

[37] *Fairfax Correspondence*, ii. 200–1; R. Bennett, 'War and Disorder: Policing the Soldiery in Civil War Yorkshire', in Fissel, *W&G* 259–60.

[38] Bennett, 'War and Disorder', 254–5; *Memoirs of Denzil Lord Holles* (1699), 46, 48; R. Bell (ed.), *Memoirs of the Civil War: The Correspondence of the Fairfax Family*, 2 vols. (1849), i. 209–12.

The London trained bands were especially destructive because they were not satisfied with mere plunder. They also gave vent to their religious zealotry by acts of iconoclasm directed at parish churches and acts of pillage and extortion visited upon the persons and households of papists as they marched west in 1642. The lieutenant-colonel of the regiment in which Nehemiah Wharton served as a sergeant attempted to restrain Wharton and his fellows, but they refused to obey him, and later obtained his removal. Wharton and the other plunderers raided a deer park belonging to a Royalist, and curried favour with their captain and other officers by feasting them on venison. The same officers condoned their actions.[39] Sergeant Wharton, being quite literate, fully documented his pillaging as if it were a game. He describes how the London trained bands continued to plunder until Lord Brooke threatened them with martial law. For a while, more stringent discipline was imposed. However, this did not deter Wharton and his merry band of deer-stealers. Wharton and his fellows continued to raid the deer parks of 'malignants'; he boasted that they made this 'their daily practice', and that he ate venison as often as he used to eat beef. In the long run, Lord Brooke's threat to execute martial law had little effect, and the soldiers continued to plunder the houses of recusants and Royalist malignants.[40] Sir William Waller had the reputation of being too lenient in the discipline of his soldiers, and allowing them to engage in pillage and spoil that exceeded the rules of war. Waller stood by silently, sword in hand, while his men vandalized Chichester Cathedral. When an old trooper, a veteran of the Low-Countries wars, asked 'with the permitted familiarity of the time', why he did not intervene, Waller replied that his sword was drawn to protect himself, and not to discipline his men. The old trooper said that in the Dutch-Spanish wars the commanders of the armies of the two opposing sides had agreed not to pillage and vandalize one another's churches. He added that his old colonel would have reacted to such an outrage by hanging a dozen pillagers as an example.[41]

Bulstrode Whitelocke, a Member of Parliament and sometime officer in the Parliamentary army, possessed houses that were plundered by both Royalist and Parliamentarian soldiers. When Richard Browne, an alderman and timber merchant of London as well as a major in the Parliamentary forces, accepted the surrender of Greenland House, which had been made into a Royalist stronghold, Whitelocke tried to obtain the return of some of his plundered property. Browne cited military law to the effect that Whitelocke's property interest had been forfeited, and that such goods were now lawful prizes for his soldiers, and he was 'loath . . . to displease the soldiers'.[42] It was dangerous to deny plunder to soldiers who had just

---

[39] *CSP Dom., 1641–1643*, 371–3.   [40] Ibid. 382.

[41] W. Webb (ed.), *Military Memoirs of Colonel John Birch . . . Written by Roe, his Secretary*, CS NS 7 (1873), 56, 163 n. James Gordon, parson of Rothiemay, said that the practice of using churches for barracks and stables was not usual in Scotland until the arrival of Cromwell and his army (*History of Scots Affairs*, 3 vols., SC 1, 2, 4 (1841), ii. 262).

[42] R. Spalding (ed.), *The Diary of Bulstrode Whitelocke, 1605–1615*, BARSEH NS 13 (1990), 150, 152.

won a victory. On another occasion, after the foot soldiers of the Parliamentary forces 'had done all the service, and run all the hazard' in the capture of a Royalist stronghold, their commander granted all the booty to the horse and excluded the foot. Since the infantry were without provisions, the Parliamentary commander realized that he had stirred up a hornets' nest, and was hard put to restore order.[43]

The observance of terms of surrender involved not only the enforcement of discipline, but also touched the personal honour of the officers who were the parties to the articles of surrender. Failure to honour such terms had far-reaching consequences. When the Parliamentary garrison at Reading agreed to surrender in April 1643 after a siege of two weeks, the terms were honourable and allowed the garrison to march out 'with flying colours, arms and four pieces of ordnance, ammunition, bag and baggage, light[ed] match, bullet in mouth, drums beating and trumpets sounding'.[44] The terms indicated that the honour of the officers and men of the garrison remained intact, and the retention of personal arms was intended to allow them to defend themselves against plunder and atrocity. The terms of surrender notwithstanding, the Parliamentary soldiers fell upon the Royalists as they marched out and 'reviled' and abused them and plundered their baggage train. The earl of Essex and his officers did try to restrain his men from pillaging the Royalist garrison of Reading by beating and slashing the soldiers with their swords, but they were unable to restore order. A few months later, when the Parliamentary garrison of Bristol surrendered in July, the Royalist soldiers remembered the behaviour of the enemy at Reading and were mutinously disinclined to honour the surrender agreement worked out by their commander. Although Rupert and his soldiers had a bad reputation in Parliamentary pamphlets for their plundering ways, the Parliamentary commander at the surrender of Bristol told the House of Commons that Prince Rupert and his officers did everything they could to restrain their soldiers—again, including slashing them with their swords.[45]

In 1644 Essex's army was cornered by Lord Goring's army. Fearing that he might have to fight both the Royalists and hostile countryfolk, Essex deserted his army with his chief officers and made his way to Plymouth. Sir Philip Skippon, whom Essex left in charge of the foot, proposed to fight the Royalists, but his council of war advised surrender. The terms granted were not the best, and only corporals and above were allowed to retain their arms. The Royalists pillaged those of Skippon's troops who had not enlisted in the Royalist army, and Skippon rode up to the king and reproved him to his face for breach of the terms of surrender, telling the king that 'it was against his honour and justice that his articles should not be performed'.[46]

---

[43] Hutchinson, *Memoirs of the Life of Colonel Hutchinson*, 218–19.

[44] Clarendon, *RCW* iii. 25.

[45] Ibid.; Donagan, 'Codes and Conduct', 94; *A Relation made to the House of Commons by Colonel Nat[haniel] Fiennes*, quoted in E. Warburton, *Memoirs of Prince Rupert*, 3 vols. (1849), ii. 267. At the surrender of the Royalist garrison of York in 1644, the Parliamentary soldiers also refused to honour the terms of surrender (*Original Memoirs Written during the Great Civil War, Being the Life of Sir Henry Slingsby* (1806), 49–54).   [46] Whitelocke, *Memorials*, i. 302.

When Cromwell sent Robert Venables with a military expedition to the West Indies in 1654, there was disagreement over the issue of how booty was to be distributed. Cromwell had ordered the proceeds from booty and pillage to go towards the costs of the expedition, but Venables argued that since his expedition was made up of the misfits from all of the regiments of the New Model Army, and poorly provisioned as well, that to deny his men legitimate plunder was to invite mutiny. It was also contrary to the practice at home, and their pay was in arrears. Venables did his best to keep his men under control. After his descent upon Santo Domingo, he proposed granting two weeks' pay in lieu of pillaging the town. His officers, who had not been paid in some time, demanded instead three months' pay, but both parties compromised on six weeks' pay in lieu of plunder.[47]

Sooner or later, most commanders in the British and Irish civil wars made the effort to restrain plunder. When Sir John Digby raised a cavalry regiment at the beginning of the First English Civil War, many of his troopers were attracted by his reputation and left other units to join his regiment. Digby would not tolerate his men taking advantage of innkeepers and plundering the countryside. Anyone who violated his orders was punished and dismissed from his regiment.[48] During the English civil wars, commanders of one side would sometimes provide written documents of protection for the property of persons on the opposite side. When a certain major named Humphreys violated such an order by breaking into a Royalist's strongbox in order to collect a contribution, he was punished by being sent, together with the regiment of which he had in the meantime become colonel, into Wales where it was hoped that he and his soldiers might become more civilized.[49] Basil Feilding, second earl of Denbigh, restrained his soldiers from plundering Oswestry, Shropshire, after he had captured the town because the townspeople had offered him a contribution of £500. However, when Prince Rupert's horse were quartered at Henley-on-Thames, Sir John Byron was unsuccessful in preventing the troopers from plundering Bulstrode Whitelocke's house at Fawley Court and havocking his deer park.[50] In response to a proclamation issued by Lord General Fairfax against theft by his soldiers, a recusant gentleman complained to Fairfax concerning abuse and plunder of his household by Fairfax's men. Fairfax was able to make a partial restitution of three of the five horses taken from his stables, but all the recusant gentleman could obtain for his cattle was a receipt. The problem was that there was little distinction between plundering and requisitioning.[51] Despite his well-known prejudice against Scots, Oliver Cromwell issued a proclamation strictly forbidding plunder before his army entered Scotland in 1648. Following the Battle of Preston in 1648, Cromwell had cashiered Colonel Wren and several of his officers for 'plundering with their

[47] Robert Venables, *The Narrative of General Venables . . . Relating to the Expedition to the West Indies and the Conquest of Jamaica, 1654–1655*, ed. C. S. Firth, CS NS 60 (1900), 5–7, 14.

[48] [Edward Walsingham], 'Life of Sir John Digby (1605–45)', ed. G. Bernard, *CM XII*, CS 3rd ser. 18 (1910), 83–4.   [49] Webb (ed.), *Military Memoirs of Colonel John Birch*, 144–9.

[50] Whitelocke, *Memorials*, i. 188–9, 271.   [51] BL, Add. MS. 18,979, fo.168 r & v.

soldiers'. After the Siege of Edinburgh, Cromwell hanged two troopers for the same offence 'in the view of our army'.[52] Both the Royalists and the Parliamentarians meted out summary justice for acts of plunder, and they also did not hesitate to execute mutineers after courts-martial had tried and condemned them. Such executions were carried out in such a way as to inspire terror as well as to punish.[53] In Ireland, at the surrender of Limerick Castle, whose garrison had been granted quarter, the earl of Castlehaven's Confederate soldiers broke discipline and plundered the garrison. Castlehaven's officers attempted to protect the garrison, and when Castlehaven returned from his hunting expedition he punished the mutineers by shooting two of them.[54]

Commanders and officers attempted to restrain plundering by their soldiers in order to preserve discipline and to keep those under their command focused on the military task at hand. However, 'fire and sword' could be visited upon a particularly recalcitrant enemy as an instrument of military policy and tactics. The town of Marlborough had refused to heed a call to surrender after being besieged in 1643 by a Royalist army led by George, second Lord Digby, Thomas, fourth Lord Wentworth of Nettlestead, William Villiers, second Lord Grandison, and Sir Daniel O'Neal. There was bad blood between the townsfolk of Marlborough and the Royalists as a result of an encounter the previous year, and the order was issued to set fire to the town and to take prisoner anyone trying to put out the fires.[55] George Monck, who had fought in Ireland and Scotland as well as the Low Countries, advocated use of 'slash and burn' tactics when an enemy pursued guerilla warfare. He also thought that an army should not abandon any part of its own country without first wasting and burning it: 'for it is better to preserve yourself in a ruined country than keep it for your enemy.'[56] While assisting in the Cromwellian conquest of Ireland, Lord Broghill resorted to terror and atrocity to frighten garrisons into surrendering. After the surrender of Castletown Castle, he had all of the officers of the defending garrison shot 'to affright those little castles for so persistently holding out'. At the Battle of Macroom, on 10 April 1650, Broghill hanged the bishop of Ross within sight of Carrigdrohid Castle after the commander had refused a summons to surrender.[57] In 1643 the utter spoliation of the Ulster countryside by the Scots and Royalist armies denied grain to the Confederate army, who were forced to buy it 'at very dear rates' from the Scots and the English.[58]

The Parliamentary armies demonstrated little regard for the rules of war when fighting in Ireland. In England, when armies or garrisons of fortified places surrendered, the commanders of the two parties engaged in what Barbara Donagan

---

[52] Rushworth, *HC* viii. 1274.   [53] Donagan, 'Codes and Conduct', 87.

[54] *Castlehaven's Review*, 108–10.

[55] *Extracts of Some Letters from Some Gentlemen of Quality in his Excellencie's Army, Concerning the State of the King's Army* (1642), 2–3; *Marleborowe's Miseries, or England turned Ireland* (1643) [BL, TT E245. (8)], 3, 6.   [56] Monck, *Observations*, 7–8.

[57] K. M. Lynch, *Roger Boyle, First Earl of Orrery* (1965), 77–8.

[58] H[ogan]. (ed.), *Warre of Ireland*, 34–5.

calls 'an etiquette of negotiation and surrender', which engaged the honour of the officers of both parties, and led to a contractual agreement specifying the actual terms of surrender. The officers of the victorious army were obliged to protect the defeated soldiers, and those who surrendered always attempted to retain sufficient personal weapons to protect themselves from abuse and pillage.[59] With numerous breaches in the walls and one day's supply of provisions remaining, Edmund Ludlow was obliged to surrender Wardour Castle in 1644. When discussing terms of surrender, Ludlow asked first that the garrison be allowed to march out, but that was a mere bargaining ploy. Then he asked for 'quarter without distinction for every one', which was granted. Subsequently, the Royalists brought to Ludlow's attention the fact that two of his men had been recognized as deserters from the Royalist army. Ludlow reminded the Royalists that the terms were 'quarter without distinction', and that the two had been impressed against their will and obliged to fight for a cause that offended their consciences. The Royalist reply was that this should have been made known to them at the time of the negotiations, and that their consciences would not permit them to allow deserters to escape justice.[60] When the Royalist defenders of Sheffield Castle surrendered in August 1644, they agreed to pay a gratuity of £500 to the Parliamentary soldiers for not plundering their persons and the castle. They were allowed to carry with them 100 muskets to defend themselves from plunderers and marauders.[61] The storming of the Royalist fortifications at Bridgwater in July 1645 began with two sermons—one by Hugh Peters. After an artillery bombardment and an assault by the Parliamentary forlorn hope, Sir Thomas Fairfax summoned the Royalist governor to yield. The governor refused, and the next day Fairfax instructed him to send out the women and children. After further bombardment, the Royalist governor asked for terms. Fairfax replied that 'they within had destroyed so fine a town [and], should have no conditions, but should submit to mercy'. When the governor persisted in asking for terms, Fairfax agreed to spare all lives; the inhabitants were to be spared plunder upon the payment of a gratuity to the Parliamentary soldiers; the officers and soldiers of the garrison were not to be stripped of their clothes.[62]

At the surrender of Colchester in 1648 Fairfax refused to negotiate with Sir Charles Lucas because he had broken his 'parole of honour' in taking up arms against Parliament in the Second Civil War, 'contrary to the rules of war'. The Siege of Colchester had lasted for four months and required several assaults before the Royalist garrison of 3,000–4,000 men surrendered. Those officers and men under the rank of captain were allowed to surrender with 'fair quarter'; the 'lords, all captains, and superior officers' were granted 'mercy'. When pressed by the Royalist commissioners exactly what he meant by these terms, Fairfax replied: 'By fair quarter we understand that with quarter for their lives, they shall be free from

---

[59] Donagan, 'Codes and Conduct', 87–91.   [60] Firth, *Ludlow*, i. 77–80.

[61] BL, Add. MS. 18,979, fo. 158.

[62] Joshua Sprigge, *Anglia Rediviva: England's Recovery*, ed. H. T. Moore (repr. 1960), 70–3.

wounding and beating, shall enjoy warm clothes…shall be maintained with victuals fit for prisoners while they shall be kept prisoners.' As for the officers of and above the rank of captain who surrendered upon 'mercy', they 'were without certain assurance of quarter; so as the lord general may be free to put some immediately to the sword if he see cause'. However, he intended to spare the lives of all except a few of the highest in social and military rank. Arthur, first Lord Capel, Sir Thomas Lucas, and Sir George Lisle were, in the event, executed. Fairfax made a distinction between the last two, whom he considered to be 'mere soldiers of fortune' and whom he had shot after a hurried court-martial, and Lord Capel, who was 'considerable for estate and fortune', and was condemned by a Parliamentary commission. Margaret, duchess of Newcastle, who was Lucas's sister, states that he had argued that he did not break his parole because he had purchased his freedom and estates at the end of the First Civil War, but she neglects to mention that when her brother compounded for his freedom, he also took an oath not to fight against Parliament.[63] The other Royalist leaders of the Second Civil War, the duke of Hamilton and the earl of Holland, were also tried by Parliamentary commission and condemned and executed for treason. Six officers of the Royalist garrison at Pontefract Castle, which had held out until 1649, were subsequently tried at the assizes and hanged, protesting that they should have been tried by a military court. Their commanding officer, Colonel John Morris, told his captors that they were establishing a dangerous precedent in allowing a civilian court to try them for acts committed as soldiers. Many thought that the justice meted out by Fairfax had been too harsh; Lucas and Lisle, in particular, came to be regarded as Royalist martyrs. The Army Council tried to blame it all on 'Charles Stuart, that man of blood'.[64]

Most Parliamentary officers and not a few Irish Royalists felt no obligation to honour the protocols and terms of surrender with members of the Irish Catholic Confederate army. By contrast, Ulick de Burgh, fifth earl of Clanricarde, who was acting as a Royalist commissioner to treat with the Confederates, felt obliged to reprimand a subordinate officer who had burnt the town of Ballymore, co. Sligo, which belonged to Theobald, second Viscount Taaffe, and hanged Taaffe's messenger, while Clanricarde was in the process of negotiating with Taaffe.[65] On another occasion, when Murrough O'Brien, seventh Lord Inchiquin's Parliamentary army engaged Lord Taaffe's Confederate forces at the Battle of Knockanauss, co. Cork in 1647, the Scots Catholic Highlanders of Alasdair MacColla, who had once served under Montrose, were run down by the Parliamentary horse. MacColla and the remnant of his men, armed with only target and broadsword, surrendered to a cornet named O'Grady. A certain Major Purdon demanded of Cornet O'Grady why he had granted quarter. Purdon shot

[63] B. Donagan, 'The Web of Honour: Soldiers, Christians and Gentlemen in the English Civil War', *HJ* 44 (2001), 379; ead., 'Atrocity, War Crime and Treason in the English Civil War', 1150; Rushworth, *HC* vii. 1274, 1303; Fairfax, *Short Memorials*, 121–4; Nathaniel Boteler, *War Practically Performed* (1663), 206–8; Cavendish, *Life of… Duke of Newcastle*, app. X, 212–13.

[64] Donagan, 'Atrocity, War Crime and Treason', 1159–62; Carlton, *GW* 328–9.

[65] J. Lowe (ed.), *Letter-book of the Earl of Clanricarde*, IMC (1983), 10–11.

MacColla in the head while he was a prisoner. O'Grady told his superior that it was murder 'to kill him', and challenged Purdon to a duel every year thereafter for the next seven years.[66]

Such atrocities cannot be blamed solely on lack of discipline or the bloody example of officers such as Purdon. They derive, at least in part, from official policy. In 1644 the English Parliament enacted an ordinance denying quarter to Irish prisoners of war. When Parliamentary commanders carried out executions in obedience to this ordinance, Royalist commanders almost invariably retaliated, although one Royalist general, Sir Ralph Hopton, discouraged such retribution. In 1649 Prince Rupert told the third earl of Essex that the Irish soldiers whom Essex had executed had fought the Catholic rebels in Ireland, and so were presumably Protestant. Rupert also told him that he would have assumed that Essex was aware of natural law and the law of nations, and thus would have expected him not to obey the ordinance. However, Rupert's awareness of these legal and moral principles had not prevented him from retaliating by executing a like number of prisoners.[67] Edward Symmons, the chaplain to the Life Guard of the prince of Wales, told his audience that although soldiers were messengers of God sent to execute justice, yet they were not to kill wantonly and indiscriminately, because God was a merciful God.[68] Parliamentarians were much outraged by the reports of atrocities committed against Protestants during the Irish Rebellion of 1641 by Catholics and were disposed to seek revenge, although it is now generally accepted that these reports—especially those compiled by Sir John Temple—were much exaggerated. However, the third earl of Castlehaven, an English Catholic who held an Irish peerage and command in the Confederate army, admits that there were atrocities on both sides.[69] Sir James Turner, who was sent as a major in Lord Sinclair's Regiment to Ireland to help restore order in 1642, was not as inclined to be sceptical of the reports as was Castlehaven, but he still expressed strong disapproval of the vengeance visited upon Irish prisoners: 'Those who were taken got bad quarter, being all shot dead. This was much used by both English and Scots all along during that war, a thing inhumane and disfavourable, for the cruelty of one enemy cannot excuse the inhumanity of another. And herein their revenge overmatched their discretion, which should have taught them to save the lives of those they took, that the rebels might do the like to their prisoners.'[70]

Sir Michael Woodhouse, the sergeant-major-general of the Royalist army and a veteran of the Irish wars, was regarded as a particularly brutal commander. It was assumed that he had learned his bad habits fighting in Ireland. Following the Siege

[66] H[ogan]. (ed.), *Warre of Ireland*, 71–3.

[67] C. H. Firth and R. S. Rait (eds.), *Acts and Ordinances of the Interregnum, 1642–1660*, 3 vols. (1911), i. 554–5; Donagan, 'Atrocity, War Crime and Treason', 1148; BL, Add. MS. 11,331, fos. 75v–76v.   [68] Edward Symmons, *A Militarie Sermon* (1644) [BL, TT, E.53 (19)], 24–5.

[69] *Castlehaven's Review*, 28–9.

[70] Turner, *Memoirs*, 19–20. The duke of Newcastle was also strongly opposed to killing prisoners in cold blood (Cavendish, *Life of . . . Duke of Newcastle*, 23–4).

of Hopton Castle in 1643, he had the entire garrison of thirty-one men put to the sword. It is true that the commander of this small castle had obstinately refused to surrender when called upon to do so, but he apparently was quite ignorant of the rules of war. While Woodhouse could claim that he was justified by the rules of war in exacting the full penalty, few commanders were prepared to go quite so far.[71] Woodhouse was under the command of Prince Rupert, and this was not the only time that Rupert failed to control his subordinates. Colonel Edward Massey reported that at the taking of Leicester the Royalists 'put men, women and children to the sword', and killed 200 Scottish prisoners of war before Prince Rupert arrived at the scene and restored order.[72] Scottish prisoners of war in the hands of the Parliamentary armies were treated no better than the Irish. After the defeat of Montrose's army at Philiphaugh in September 1645, 'a great number' of the Scots who were not killed during or after the battle were carried to Newark Castle, where, according to James Somerville, they were massacred in the castle courtyard. They probably included some of MacColla's Highlanders.[73]

King Charles I had given Prince Rupert strict orders not to surrender Bristol when it came under siege by Fairfax's army in 1645, because it was the last port remaining in Royalist hands. For that reason, Rupert delayed giving an answer to Fairfax's terms. After a spirited defence of an outlying fort at Priors Hill, the Parliamentary soldiers could not be restrained from putting the Royalist officers and men to the sword. Four hours later Rupert asked for a parley, which was granted, and by evening had secured honourable terms of surrender. The king, who ignored the fact that the plague was raging inside the city and many of Rupert's men had deserted, never forgave Rupert for surrendering Bristol.[74] Charles remained insensitive to the predicaments of his servants and subjects. In April 1643 Colonel Richard Feilding, the acting Royalist governor of Reading, being short of powder and unaware that a relief column was approaching, negotiated terms for surrender with the earl of Essex. A messenger arrived and told him that there could be no negotiations since the king was approaching. Feilding did not think that his honour would permit him to break off negotiations, and apparently this position was supported by his council of war. After the surrender, a court-martial sentenced Feilding to death, but Rupert persuaded the king to pardon him. However, Feilding was deprived of his regiment, and reduced to serving as a volunteer.[75]

While it is true that the methods of warfare employed in Ireland had long differed from those of the European military world, as a consequence of the experience of Irishmen who had served in mainland European armies the practices pursued in warfare and in the protocols of surrender by the Catholic Confederate

---

[71] J. and T. W. Webb, *Memorials of the Civil War between King Charles I and the Parliament of England as it affected Herefordshire*, 2 vols. (1879), i. 387–90.

[72] H. G. Tibbutt (ed.), *The Letter Books, 1644–45, of Sir Samuel Luke*, BHS 42 (1963), 298.

[73] James [by right 11th Lord] Somerville, *Memorie of the Somervilles* [ed. Sir W. Scott], 2 vols. (1815), ii. 360 and n.   [74] Sprigge, *Anglia Rediviva*, 107.

[75] P. Morah, *Prince Rupert of the Rhine* (1976), 114–15.

army commanders had begun to narrow the gap between continental and Irish practice. However, Oliver Cromwell's massacre of the garrison and townspeople of Drogheda poisoned the atmosphere in the Irish civil wars ever thereafter. Knowledge of what happened at Drogheda stiffened the resistance of the Irish Royalists and Confederates. On 12 September 1647 the Parliamentary forces attacked Cashel. After Chair Castle had been taken and Roche Castle stormed, the garrison of Cashel retreated to the great rock where the Cathedral of St Patrick was located, and fortified the churchyard. The Parliamentary soldiers had already put to the sword the fifty warders of Roche Castle. Six companies of infantry defended the churchyard, and besides the women and children, they numbered 800. They were called upon to surrender and told that if they did so within an hour they could have quarter 'with bag and baggage'. Otherwise, all would die. The defenders of the churchyard offered to negotiate, but that was refused, and the assault began. Just before going into action, the Parliamentary soldiers were reminded of Catholic massacres. All of the Confederate officers and soldiers died except one, as well as all of the clergy and some of the women. Fewer than 100 remained alive, and the bodies were stacked five and six deep in the churchyard. This was followed by extensive pillaging and acts of iconoclasm.[76] When the Scots Royalists led by Sir George Munro took Temple Patrick, it was reported that no quarter was allowed to any member of the New Model Army. Cromwell failed to take the Confederate stronghold of Clonmel by siege with a loss of 1,500 soldiers—the worst reverse that the Parliamentary armies suffered in Ireland. Cromwell was forced to allow Major-General Hugh Duff O'Neill and his soldiers quarter and to give them permission to leave Ireland for Spanish service. Hugh Duff was the son of Owen Roe O'Neill, and when Cromwell learned that he had been born in Spain and had served in the Spanish army, he started to renegue on his grant of quarter until the mayor of Clonmel shamed him into keeping his promise. Cromwell never willingly showed mercy to Catholic Confederate troops. Apparently, Cromwell had issued the order to put the garrison and townspeople of Drogheda to the sword under the mistaken impression that the garrison contained Confederate Catholics. Although the Royalist commander was an English Catholic, most of the garrison were Protestant Irish and English Royalists. Again, when the earl of Castlehaven had released the Parliamentary garrison to Cromwell after the Confederates had taken the town of Athy by storm, but found that they could not hold it, he had hoped that Cromwell might in future return the courtesy. But Cromwell 'little valued civility', and soon after returned the favour by executing the officers of the garrison at Gowran.[77]

Evidence exists that at least some of Cromwell's officers and men thought his vindictive behaviour towards the Irish was excessive. At Drogheda, despite Cromwell's orders to put the whole garrison to the sword, his men were more merciful and chose to take prisoners rather than kill defenceless men. When

---

[76] Alexander Piggot, *The Taking of Roche Castle* (1647), 3–8.
[77] H[ogan]. (ed.), *Warre of Ireland*, 87; Gentles, *NMA* 357–8; *Earl of Castlehaven's Review*, 155.

Cromwell departed Ireland, he left his son-in-law Henry Ireton in command. Ireton was nearly as ruthless as Cromwell, and his terms for the surrender of Limerick were very harsh and caused Henry O'Neill, the Confederate commander, to hold out longer. When O'Neill drove the civilians out—most of whom desired to leave in any case—Ireton slaughtered forty of them beneath the walls by way of example. However, Ireton did court-martial and cashier a colonel who killed fourteen prisoners who had earlier been granted quarter by a subaltern officer. After Limerick was taken, Ireton tried to persuade his council of war to condemn O'Neill, but Edmund Ludlow and a number of other officers opposed Ireton's harshness and he relented.[78]

The breakdown of the alliance between the Irish Royalists and the Catholic Confederates facilitated the victory of the Parliamentarians in Ireland. After the Confederates drove out Owen Roe O'Neill and the duke of Ormonde withdrew his support, many of the officers of the Irish Royalist army reasserted their Confederation allegiances and elected Ever MacMahon, bishop of Clogher, as their general. That a Catholic bishop was now leading the Confederate Army of Ulster incensed the Parliamentary forces. After this army was defeated by Sir Charles Coote at the Battle of Letterkenny (or Scarrifhollis) in co. Donegal in June 1650, there occurred an atrocity that from a legal point of view was worse than the massacre at Drogheda. Coote's 'officers and private soldiers of horse and foot had more mercy than he had', and accepted the surrender of groups of Confederate soldiers. Coote ignored the terms of surrender of his subordinate officers, and put all of the Confederate prisoners to the sword, including a major-general and three colonels. The bishop-general was kept in prison until his broken leg healed, and then was hanged at Inniskillen. Again, Coote's reputation for not honouring terms of surrender made it difficult to secure the surrender of garrisons. At Charlemont, Sir Phelim O'Neill demanded hostages from Coote before he would negotiate terms of surrender. The terms that O'Neill obtained were that he and his men would march out with bag and baggage after their wounds had healed, and proceed to a port where Coote would have ships waiting to carry them overseas.[79]

An important cause of contention between officers of the Parliamentary army and the Rump Parliament was the failure of the latter to enact a new ordinance extending and renewing the Act of Articles of 1649. This ordinance had used the authority of Parliament and the courts to validate articles of surrender negotiated by Parliamentary army commanders, and involved the principle that a soldier and a gentleman would always keep his word as given in terms of surrender. These officers had developed a sense of military honour which was more important to their sense of self-respect than vindictiveness or Puritan ideology.[80]

The development of this code of conduct was incomplete and came too late. The Cromwellian conquest of Ireland and Irish losses from battlefield casualties,

---

[78] Gentles, *NMA* 361–2, 379; Firth, *CA* 302–3.
[79] H[ogan]. (ed.), *Warre of Ireland,* 113, 124–30.   [80] Gentles, *NMA* 421–2.

atrocity and disease constitute one of the greatest wartime demographic disasters of modern history. Sir William Petty estimated that out of a population of 1,466,000 people in 1641, 616,000 died as a direct result of the rebellion and civil wars between 1641 and 1652. During the same period Petty also calculated that 34,000 soldiers were transported into Spain, Flanders and France together with 6,000 boys, women and priests, making a total of 40,000 banished. Also, during this eleven-year period, 87,000 people died of famine and exposure to the cold or during transportation to Barbados and elsewhere, and another like sum were put to the sword by English and Scottish armies which never numbered more than 40,000. The consequence of such demographic devastation was that tillage nearly ceased, and cattle had to be imported. But the most lasting legacy was enduring bitterness. By comparison, England and Wales, with more than double the population of Ireland, lost between 100,000 and 125,000 people.[81]

Like their Puritan adversaries, many Anglican and Catholic Royalists assumed that the outcome of battles or preservation of an individual in dangerous circumstances was in the hands of Divine Providence. But when an individual was killed in battle there was still wounded honour to be avenged—especially when the fatal wound was caused by someone of base birth. Sir John Digby led his cavalry regiment in a charge at the second Battle of Newbury during which two of his men were killed by a cannon shot. One of them was a former servant of his brother Kenelm. The gunner who fired the shot was singled out for special abuse even after he had been killed. When Digby's troopers returned the next day to bury their dead, they found that the body of the gunner who fired the fatal shot bore seventeen wounds, which act Edward Walsingham recorded with great satisfaction.[82] Personal animosities and family vendettas always get mixed in with civil wars. In Somerset on the eve of the English civil wars, the Royalists and the Parliamentarians were contending for control of the militia, and personal quarrels preceded the outbreak of the First Civil War. Robert Blake commanded a regiment of foot in which his brother Samuel was captain of a company. Samuel Blake was lured into an ambush at a tavern near Bridgwater by a Royalist rival and killed. Apparently the vindictiveness of this incident contributed to sharper divisions in the county community, although Robert Blake thought that his younger brother 'had no business' at the tavern.[83] Ever sensitive to affronts to honour—his own and that of friends—Sir John Smith, who became a major-general in the Royalist army, made his way into enemy territory in Lincolnshire to punish a Parliamentary officer who had abused a Royalist officer while he was a prisoner of war.[84] Acts

---

[81] Sir William Petty, *The Political Anatomy of Ireland* (1691), 17–20; T. W. Moody, F. X. Martin and F. J. Byrne (eds.), *A New History of Ireland*, 9 vols. (1976–86), iii. 357; C. Carlton, 'The Face of Battle in the English Civil Wars', Fissel, *W&G* 240–1.

[82] [Edward Walsingham], 'Life of Sir John Digby (1605–1645)', *CM XII*, CS 3rd ser. 18 (1910), 89–90.   [83] [John Oldmixon], *The History and Life of Robert Blake* [c.1740], 10–12.

[84] Edward Walsingham, *Britannicae Virtutis Imago, or the Effigies of . . . that Incomparable Knight, Major Generall Smith* (1644), 10.

of personal revenge could be carried out in the midst of battle. At a skirmish in Dorchester, Major Sydenham 'of Poole' spied the Royalist cavalry officer, Major Williams, who had killed his mother. With the help of his troopers, Sydenham exacted his vengeance and slew the Royalist major.[85] In 1649 an Irish Parliamentary colonel named O'Connelly, who had surrendered to John Hamilton's troop of Irish horse, was slain by a member of that troop while attempting to escape. This man, whose name was also Hamilton, was the brother of Captain Hamilton, whom O'Connelly had killed in a duel the previous year. Hamilton revenged himself upon O'Connelly by kicking the latter to death, 'which by the law of arms he might do in regard he [O'Connelly] had broken his quarter [i.e., given his parole not to escape]'.[86] The Royalists sought revenge upon diplomatic agents of Parliament following the execution of Charles I in 1649. In The Hague, a dozen Cavaliers burst into the chamber of Isaac Dorislaus, the civil lawyer who had helped to draft the charges against the king, and assassinated him. Not long afterwards, Royalists also killed Anthony Ascham, the Parliamentary diplomatic agent in Madrid.[87]

These individual acts of revenge and vindictiveness contrast sharply with the chivalric gestures which noblemen in both the Parliamentarian and Royalist armies offered one another in the earlier phases of the civil wars. When Henry Clifford, fifth earl of Cumberland, died at York in December 1643, preparations for his funeral required his household servants to cross the lines. Although Cumberland's sympathies were Royalist, Ferdinando, second Lord Fairfax, the Parliamentary commander in Yorkshire, readily granted permission and provided letters of safe conduct for the late earl's servants to go to London and Hull in order to buy food and cloth for the mourners, and to make all aware of the earl's funeral.[88]

The treatment of prisoners of war improved somewhat during the course of the civil wars—if one ignores the behaviour of Cromwell and his lieutenants and the experience of war in Ireland. But being a prisoner of war during the Wars of the Three Kingdoms was at best a humiliating experience and frequently led to banishment and impressment in foreign armies or indentured servitude in West Indian hells—especially for non-English soldiers who fell into the hands of the Parliamentarians. In the late spring of 1645, following the Battle of Naseby, Sir Thomas Fairfax sent up to London 4,500 Royalist prisoners, who were marched from Northampton to the outskirts of London. Eighty captured colours, including fifty-five taken at Naseby, were 'carried in triumph in the faces of the prisoners'. Behind the captured colours came the senior officers mounted on horseback in order to avoid any suggestion that the social hierarchy had been subverted. At the end of St Martin's Lane the senior officers were sent to Peterhouse in

---

[85] Whitelocke, *Memorials*, i. 342. [86] H[ogan]. (ed.), *Warre of Ireland*, 92–4.
[87] Thomas Hobbes, *Behemoth: The History of the Causes of the Civil Warrs of England*, ed. William Molesworth (1682; repr. 1963), 206.
[88] R. T. Spence, 'A Noble Funeral in the Great Civil War', *YAJ* 65 (1993), 115–17.

Aldersgate and the junior officers were confined to the Mews in Charing Cross. From there the Green and Yellow Regiments of the London trained bands escorted the prisoners along the Strand into the City past gibbets which had been erected for the instantaneous punishment of any among the prisoners or in the crowds who became disorderly, for London was apparently under proclamation of martial law at that time. The prisoners were then confined to the Artillery Ground near Tothill Fields, where, exposed to the elements, they were subjected to pressure to enlist for service in Ireland or to give their word to live in peace. Some who did neither were pressed and sold to the Spanish ambassador for service in the Spanish Army of Flanders. The remainder were confined until the end of the First Civil War.[89] John Vicars says that a Parliamentary committee allocated £200 to buy the prisoners bread and beer, which he regarded as an act of charity rather than a moral and legal obligation. He contrasted this with the treatment of Parliamentarian prisoners by the Royalists in Oxford and Cornwall.[90]

The last engagement of the Wars of the Three Kingdoms in England was the Battle of Worcester in September 1651. Between 2,000 and 3,000 Royalists died at Worcester, and as many as 10,000 were taken prisoner. Four thousand prisoners were displayed as trophies of war when Cromwell made his triumphant entry into the City of London nine days later. Cromwell and many of his subordinates had no pity to waste upon Irish, Scots and Welsh captured in England, and most of them were sold into indentured servitude in the West Indies or the North American colonies—officers as well as soldiers. Among the Scottish soldiers taken prisoner at Worcester was Andrew Melvill. Already wounded, he was captured by Parliamentary troopers who began to strip him of his belongings. Melvill saw a cornet and asked to be treated as a prisoner of war. The officer ordered the pillagers to cease, but one of the troopers, angry that he was deprived of his booty, declared that he was determined that no one else would get it, and shot Melvill in the stomach. Subsequently, another Parliamentary officer and some Royalist ladies nursed Melvill back to health, but his brother was one of those transported to the West Indies.[91]

One of Cromwell's motives in mounting the military and naval expedition to the West Indies in 1654 under the command of William Penn and Robert Venables, according to Edmund Ludlow, was to provide employment for reformado officers so as to keep them away from anti-Cromwellian intrigues and factions. Part of the manpower for this expedition was found in Barbados where a

[89] *The Manner how the Prisoners are to be brought into the City of London* (1645) [BL, TT E. 228 (48)], 1–2; John Vicars, *The Burning Bush Not Consumed* (1646), 173; Firth, *Ludlow*, i. 123; Donagan, 'Web of Honor', 386; S. R. Gardiner, *History of the Great Civil War, 1642–1649*, 4 vols. (1901), ii. 256–7.   [90] Vicars, *Burning Bush*, 173.

[91] Gentles, *NMA* 409: *Memoirs of Sir Andrew Melvill*, ed. and trans. Ameer-Ali, 122–9; W. C. Abbott (ed.), *The Writings and Speeches of Oliver Cromwell*, 4 vols. (1945; repr. 1970), iii. 305, 368, 290, 720, 821–2; iv. 628. On the transportation of Irish prisoners of war and their forced impressment into mainland European armies, see also J. P. Prendergast, *The Cromwellian Settlement of Ireland*, 3rd edn. (1922), 80–1, 88–93; Firth, *Ludlow*, i. 284, 322–3; C. McNeill (ed.), *The Tanner Letters: Original Documents and Notices of Irish Affairs in the Sixteenth and Seventeenth Centuries*, IMC (1943), 361, 371.

proclamation was made granting freedom to those indentured servants who enlisted. 'Two thousand servants listed themselves to the great damage of the planters.' Ludlow also states that one of the pretexts for declaring war on Spain in the West Indies was that Cromwell and 'one Major Walters' were involved in a contract to deliver Irish prisoners of war to the Spanish army for £30,000, but the king of Spain had never settled this debt with Cromwell and Walters.[92]

In the early stages of the English civil wars both the Royalist and Parliamentarian armies were difficult to control because those in the ranks were often impressed, rarely paid and looked to plunder for their reward.[93] Of the two opposing forces, the Royalists were the more undisciplined, because many of the commanders and officers little valued popular opinion or how it affected popular allegiance. Although the evidence is sparse, it is clear enough that Scottish armies were obliged to live off of the land because the resources of both Covenanters and Royalists were never adequate to sustain their military forces, and their presence in England provoked hostility among the civilian population and the Cromwellian faction in the army. Although the state of discipline among the Irish Royalist and Confederate armies warrants more investigation, we do know that Irish officers with mainland European military experience made commendable efforts to control their forces.

By the end of the English civil wars, it was generally agreed—even by Royalists—that the New Model Army had achieved a high standard of discipline. It required a lot of effort to achieve that level of discipline, considering that some of the first regiments raised by Parliament, as Sergeant Nehemiah Wharton's letters make clear, were little better than plundering expeditions. At first the Parliamentary commanders lacked the legal authority to punish plunderers and mutineers, and John Hampden and five other colonels in Essex's army asked their commander to obtain from Parliament the necessary authority to employ martial law. Royalist commanders, perhaps less concerned about legal niceties, had issued articles of war as a matter of course and relied upon the king's prerogative to do so. Both Parliamentarian and Royalist articles of war derived from continental models. As discipline and conditions of service improved, desertion became less of a problem in the New Model Army. Conscription ceased after 1651, and thereafter the ranks of the New Model were filled with volunteers—many of them former Royalist prisoners of war.[94]

Yet the New Model Army was a far from perfect military instrument. It was highly politicized and riven by ideological disputes. Indiscipline spread in the

---

[92] Firth, *Ludlow*, i. 384–5. Scottish prisoners of war were also impressed into regiments being raised for service in the West Indies. Masterless men, women and children were also transported to the West Indies on the orders of Cromwell. Some of them may have been camp-followers from the Royalist insurrections, because Cromwell told the Council of State of Scotland that they were potentially seditious (John Thurloe, *Collection of State Papers*, 7 vols. (1742), iii. 497–8; iv. 129).

[93] Roy, 'English Civil War and English Society', i. 137.   [94] Firth, *CA* 36, 37, 276–9.

army following the end of the monarchy in 1649 over the issue of arrears of pay and the prospect of being posted to Ireland without first being paid. The army's presence in London brought the enlistment of numerous radicals which heightened the unrest, and radicalism in the army was also fostered by the printing of subversive pamphlets and joint meetings between soldiers and civilians. It is interesting that Leveller propaganda attempted to depict the Irish as victims of the greed and ambition of the New Model officers, who wished to carve out estates in Ireland and were willing to sacrifice the lives of their soldiers to do so.[95]

This points to another problem which goes beyond the greed of the officers or the discontent of the soldiers over arrears of pay. The massacres which were perpetrated in Ireland reveal an army which was out of control and had lost sight of military goals, and which made the English conquest of Ireland immensely more difficult and bloody than it should have been. This bloody-mindedness was not the result of a failure of discipline. The blame for this should be laid upon Parliament, which first inaugurated the policy of denying Irish soldiers captured in England the customary status of prisoners of war, as it was applied in the European military world, and which later undermined discipline in the army by failure to recognize its obligation to pay its soldiers in full.[96] Next the blame should be assigned to Oliver Cromwell, who, although he is usually proclaimed a military genius and great war leader by the authors of the 'great man' biographies, allowed his own religious fanaticism and hatred of Celtic peoples to cloud his military judgement when he went to Ireland to secure that unhappy isle from the interference of mainland European powers.

[95] Gentles, *NMA* 315–17, 326–49.
[96] J. S. Wheeler, *The Making of a World Power: War and the Military Revolution in Seventeenth-Century England* (1999), 189.

10

The Civil Wars in Ireland and Scotland

... Every nation no matter how barbaric, has the right to defend itself against a more civilized one that wants to conquer it and take away its freedom. And, moreover, it can lawfully punish with death the more civilized as a savage and cruel aggressor against the law of nature.

Bartolomé de Las Casas, *In Defense of the Indians*, trans. S. Poole (1992), 47.

'Tis not the least misfortune of this country that the younger sons of the nobility and gentry have in all times had their inclinations debauched to an idle, for the most part criminal, and almost always unprofitable sort of life; I mean that of a soldier of fortune. Their talents might have been better employed in trade and husbandry to the improvement of their county, and increase of their patrimony.

Andrew Fletcher of Saltoun, *Two Discourses concerning the Affairs of Scotland* (1698), in *Political Works*, ed. J. Robertson (1997), 46.

... Through the whole country there were daily musters; and young soldiers, who lately had been accustomed with the plough, were now called out and taught every day to handle their arms, with no little noise and quarter-keeping....

John Gordon, parson of Rothiemay, *History of Scots Affairs*, 3 vols., SC 1, 2, 4 (1841), ii. 207–8.

The Wars of the Three Kingdoms were a complicated mixture of civil wars, wars of conquest or colonial wars, and wars of national liberation.[1] The wars in Ireland and Scotland also demonstrated how the affairs of the Three Kingdoms had become inextricably linked together. The first standing army in the British Isles was raised in Ireland by Sir Thomas Wentworth, first earl of Strafford, as lord deputy. Although many of the soldiers were veterans of the Spanish Army of Flanders and other armies of Catholic Europe, Strafford maintained good discipline while he remained in Ireland. When Strafford was called to England, the Irish

---

[1] B. Donagan, 'Atrocity, War Crime and Treason in the English Civil War', *AHR* 99 (1994), 1139.

army disintegrated, and many of the soldiers joined the Irish Rebellion of 1641. The Spanish and French armies were denuded of Irish soldiers, who returned home seeking opportunity and employment. On several occasions during the civil wars the New English settlers were left undefended as Irish Royalist troops were used to defend Dublin or to reinforce the king's armies in England. At the same time, Charles's conciliation of the Irish Catholic Confederates tended to drive many New English into the ranks of the Parliamentarians. The civil wars in Ireland were complicated by the presence of four different armies contending for supremacy, including forces from Scotland as well as England. The harsh tactics employed by Cromwell and the Parliamentarian armies caused the Confederates and the Royalists to resist more strongly and prolonged the conflict. Defeat in the field did not end the resistance of the Confederates, and many subsequently became tories and rapparees and resorted to guerilla warfare. By labelling such fighters as outlaws, the Parliamentarians justified sending Irish soldiers (along with their women and children) into exile to fight in mainland European armies or banishing them to the colonies as indentured servants.

The Scots Covenanting Army was the second standing army raised in the Three Kingdoms, and it succeeded in compelling Charles I to recognize the Presbyterian religious settlement in Scotland and to call a Parliament in England. The successful example of the Scots Covenanters was not lost on the Irish.[2] The Wars of the Three Kingdoms also militarized Scottish society to an extent unknown since the fourteenth century.[3] The colonels of the regiments of the Covenanting Army were almost invariably noblemen, who were successful in recruiting their own tenants, but many of the field and general officers were professional soldiers and veterans of the Swedish army. The commander-in-chief, Sir Alexander Leslie (later first earl of Leven), a professional soldier, was chosen because the Scottish nobility could not agree upon one of their own. Although the Covenanters gave a good account of themselves, they could not defeat the New Model Army. Scottish Royalist resistance revived under the leadership of the marquis of Montrose, and later, the earls of Glencairn and Middleton, who made effective use of Highland soldiers, joined by English Royalists, mosstroopers from the Border and Irish tories. The Cromwellian conquest of Scotland led to a more generous peace settlement than was the case in Ireland, because the Parliamentarians did not regard the mostly Protestant Lowlanders as being as alien as the Catholic Irish and the Highlanders from the Isles, and also because the peace settlement in Scotland was administered by the more moderate General Monck. However, many of the rank and file who participated in Glencairn's Rebellion were, like the Irish, banished to serve as mercenary soldiers in mainland European armies or transported as indentured servants to the colonies.

---

[2] J. Kenyon and J. Ohlmeyer, 'The Background to the Civil Wars in the Three Stuart Kingdoms', in Kenyon and Ohlmeyer (eds.), *The Civil Wars: A Military History of England, Scotland and Ireland, 1638–1660* (Oxford, 1998), 30.

[3] K. M. Brown, 'From Scottish Lords to British Officers: State Building, Elite Integration and the Army in the Seventeenth Century', in Macdougall, *S&W* 137–8.

The Civil Wars and Conquest of Ireland

The English government to which the lord deputy and the Irish administration were answerable never possessed sufficient manpower to conquer Ireland in the sixteenth century and maintain the ascendancy of the New English. During Tyrone's Rebellion, or the Nine Years War as the Irish call it, as many as three-quarters of the English forces in Ireland were Irish Catholics. The allegiances of these hired soldiers, insofar as they possessed any, probably did not differ greatly from those in the rebellious Irish forces, and the lord deputy Lord Mountjoy's solution to this problem after the rebellion had ended was to encourage these swordsmen to join mainland European armies in the belief that 'three parts in four of these countrymen do never return'.[4] Although it had been Lord Mountjoy's intention to conciliate rather than drive out the great Irish lords, the flight of the earls in 1607 opened the lands of the earls of Tyrone and Tyrconnell in Ulster to colonizing by Scots and English planters. This ended the trade in mercenary soldiers or redshanks between the western seaboard and Isles of Scotland and the province of Ulster. Also, the accession of James VI to the English throne had altered the relationship between the two main parts of Gaeldom, which began to drift apart culturally and linguistically. The politically aware Catholic Irish landowners had no choice but to recognize James VI and I as their monarch. James accepted the Irish as subjects, which Elizabeth had never done, and they in turn hoped for a measure of toleration from James. Irish clerics, reflecting a reception of Jesuit theology during their continental exile, told Catholics that they could give their allegiance to a Protestant king, and this helped to promote loyalty to the Stuarts. The bardic poets who remained behind also adapted to the patronage of Irish nobles who were loyal to the English crown.[5]

The task of defending the Protestant ascendancy in the plantations of Ireland increasingly fell upon English, Welsh and Scots captains who were veterans of the Dutch and other mainland European armies who brought their soldiers (who had rarely received their full pay) along with them as tenants holding lands under military obligations. These men were dependably Protestant and could be counted upon to assist the provost-marshals in maintaining order among the dispossessed native Irish. By 1620 there were some 50,000 English and Scots colonists in Ireland, and since many of them were former soldiers, this was

---

[4] R. Loeber and G. Parker, 'The Military Revolution in Seventeenth-Century Ireland', in J. H. Ohlmeyer (ed.), *Ireland from Independence to Occupation, 1641–1660* (1995), 72.

[5] J. Dawson, 'The Gaidhealtachd and the Emergence of the of the Scottish Highlands', in B. Bradshaw and P. Roberts (eds.), *British Consciousness and Identity: The Making of Britain, 1537–1707* (1998), 266; B. Ó Buachalla, 'James Our True King: The Ideology of Irish Royalism in the Seventeenth Century', in G. Boyce, R. Eccleshall and V. Geoghan (eds.), *Political Thought in Ireland Since the Seventeenth Century* (1993), 9–15; M. Caball, *Poets and Politics: Continuity and Reaction in Irish Poetry, 1558–1625* (1998), 115.

thought to be sufficient to dissuade the Spanish from another invasion of Ireland.[6]

Protestantism failed to take root among the Old English of Munster and much of southern Ireland. Both the Catholic Old English and the Old Irish were disenfranchised by the Irish Parliament of 1613–15, and it had also become difficult for Irish lords and tenants to secure title to their own lands. The persecution of the Catholic Old English and Old Irish drove these two communities together and they began to intermarry. This was also paralleled by the integration of soldiers and clerics from these two groups who lived in the Irish communities of mainland Europe. This led to the emergence of a new Irish identity which would become the basis of political allegiance of the Catholic Confederation of Kilkenny in the 1640s.[7]

When Charles I went to war with Spain in 1625, the opportunity presented itself for Spain or other continental powers to stir up trouble at England's back-door, and it was known that dissident groups, such as the Gaelic Irish of Ulster, were willing to cooperate with Spanish efforts to foment rebellion. This focused attention on the need to have more effective military forces in Ireland, and opened a debate about whether to return to the traditional hosting of tenants of the Old English lords, institute a trained-band system among the New English or to augment the small standing army. The fear and distrust among the Protestant New English precluded any military role for Catholics, and caused the king to reject the first two alternatives; instead, he ordered the Irish standing army increased in size to 5,000 foot and 500 horse.[8] The decision to increase the size of the Irish army was contentious and disgruntled both the Catholics and the New English. The cost of the augmented Irish army was to be born by Irish landowners, and the nobility were to work out the exact financial details. In exchange, Charles was prepared to yield some 'matters of grace and bounty', such as modifying the oath of supremacy to make it more acceptable to Catholics, suspending recusancy fines, curtailing the operation of martial law and halting the plantation of Catholic lands. The 'Graces', in effect, also constituted an invitation to discuss the administration of the army. This concession, together with allowing the Old English Catholics to petition Charles for the 'Graces' in the first place, was a major political blunder because the members of the Protestant ascendancy were opposed to any relaxation of the Penal Laws or suspension of colonization. Charles had expanded the Irish army before he had the means to pay for it. The Irish Parliament never ratified the 'Graces'. Dublin Castle was consequently forced to resort to the levying of forced loans, the use of soldiers to collect rents and taxes (a practice not unlike the 'dragooning' of peasants in France) and the billeting of

---

[6] V. Treadwell, *Buckingham and Ireland, 1616–1628* (1998), 32, 36, 152; [T. Fortescue], Lord Clermont (ed.), *An Account of the Rt. Honourable Sir Arthur Chichester, Lord Belfast, Lord Deputy of Ireland, by Sir Faithful Fortescue* (1858), 7–13; [Edmund Borlase], *The History of the Irish Rebellion* (1743), 108.　　　　　[7] P. Lenihan, *Confederate Catholics at War, 1641–49* (2001), 2–8.
[8] A. Clarke, *The Old English in Ireland, 1625–42* (1966), 28–35.

soldiers upon civilians, thus breaking an earlier agreement by the Irish government not to engage in such practices. Because of the failure to pay the Irish army on time, troops had to be widely dispersed in order to live off the land, which, in the opinion of Lord Deputy Falkland, made the Irish soldiers more dangerous than an invading army.[9] When Sir Thomas Wentworth, Viscount Wentworth (later earl of Strafford), became lord deputy in 1632, he found the money to pay for the Irish army at a time when England could not afford to pay for a standing army. However, the Irish army was in a sorry state: it was scattered in many small garrisons; it did not train; military offices had been granted to court favourites; and the officers were negligent and spent their time quarrelling and duelling with one another.[10] In his capacity as lord general of the Irish army, Lord Deputy Wentworth took special care to see that the troops of the establishment were well trained and ready to fight. He summoned all of the companies and troops to Dublin in rotation, and would sometimes drill them himself. During these month-long inspections he caused the officers to give an account of the discharge of their duties, and reprimanded or cashiered them for their absenteeism or negligence. Wentworth also insisted that the officers reside in garrison and not on their estates, and he caused the enlisted men to be put to labour when they were not training or standing guard.[11] Both Catholics and New English were intimidated by Wentworth's standing army, but he did have a sense of political reality. Although he did not enforce the Penal Laws rigourously, he did open Connaught to plantation, and advised Charles I against allowing Randall MacDonnell, second earl of Antrim, a courtier and warlord, to raise troops from amongst his own kinsmen for use against the Covenanters in 1638, because Antrim was a Catholic and this would displease the New English settlers in Ulster. This policy was reversed in 1640, and Wentworth (now earl of Strafford and lord-lieutenant) urged the king to allow him to raise a new Irish army of 8,000 foot and 1,000 horse for use against the Scots. They were recruited from mostly Catholic veterans of the armies of Spain, Spanish Flanders and France.[12] Because of the presence of these mostly Catholic veterans of the French and Spanish armies—Lord Mountjoy would have had trouble imagining so many returning home—Ireland

[9] M. Perceval-Maxwell, *The Outbreak of the Irish Rebellion* (1994), 16–17; Lenihan, *Confederate Catholics*, 8–11; Clarke, *Old English in Ireland*, 36–7, 47–8; J. H. Ohlmeyer, 'The Wars of Religion, 1603–1660', *MHI* 161.

[10] Sir Philip Warwick, *Memoirs of the Reign of King Charles I* (1813), 123; BL, Add. MS. 11,033 [Correspondence of Henry Carey, Viscount Falkland, lord deputy of Ireland], fo. 113; William Knowler (comp.), *The Earl of Strafforde's Letters and Dispatches*, 2 vols. (1739), i. 144.

[11] BL, Add. MS. 18,979 [Fairfax Correspondence], fos. 40r & v; Knowler, *Earl of Strafforde's Letters and Dispatches*, i. 144, 195, ii. 203–4.

[12] Knowler, *Earl of Strafforde's Letters and Dispatches*, ii. 203–4; J. H. Ohlmeyer, *Civil War and Restoration in the Three Kingdoms: The Career of Randall MacDonnell, Marquis of Antrim, 1609–1683* (1993), 280; *The Earl of Castlehaven's Review* (1684), 18–19. Castlehaven states that while these men were veterans of the Spanish and French armies, not one in twenty of them were Irish. Most modern historians appear to assume that Strafford's New Irish Army was almost entirely composed of Irish veterans of the Spanish and French armies.

had, in one sense, been remilitarized to a significant degree. However, the Protestant settlers in Ulster had grown less martial. Few of them owned muskets, and they had ceased living in fortified dwelling-places. When the Irish Rebellion began in 1641, the Dublin government had sent out the contents of its arsenals to the Old English landowners in Leinster, but not to the Protestants of Ulster.[13]

When the English government perceived that the declaration of war against Spain and then France in the 1620s also invited incursions by the governments of those belligerent states in Ireland, it was decided to strengthen the fortifications of Irish towns—especially along the coast. During the late sixteenth-century wars in Ireland, the native Irish had avoided pitched battles and favoured guerilla-type warfare, which was characterized by ambushes and small skirmishes. The English preferred to operate out of fortified towns, which could dominate the country-side. Irish towns built during the Elizabethan conquest of Ireland were invariably walled and the streets were laid out in a grid pattern to make control easier. Some fifty-six towns in seventeenth-century Ireland were walled compared to 108 in England and twenty-one in Wales. New walls were constructed around Derry in 1613–18. They were 1,700 yards in circumference and cost £10,357. The many walled towns and castles in England required numerous garrisons which depleted the manpower resources from which field armies were constituted, and came increasingly to be seen as irrelevant. The same was true in Ireland, but the revival of guerilla war and banditry during and after the Irish civil wars and the need to protect supply lines meant that urban fortifications continued to be seen as neces-sary. In 1642 few places in Ireland possessed the more modern Italian-style fortifica-tions which had become widespread in mainland Europe, and most of these were along the coast and defended ports. Most Irish towns retained medieval-style curtain walls reinforced with earthen ramparts hastily thrown up. Away from the coast this did not much matter, because it was too difficult to drag artillery trains through the interior. In Ireland, as in England, until the very last days of the civil wars, most fortified places were taken by assault without prior artillery bombard-ment. Urban fortifications continued to be seen as necessary in Ireland until the end of the Williamite wars.[14]

In order to help Charles I subdue the Scots Covenanters and overawe the English Parliament, Strafford had concentrated his mostly Catholic New Irish Army, led by Protestant officers, at Carrickfergus. The previous March, Sir Henry Vane, principal secretary of state to Charles, had told the lords justices of Ireland that the English Privy Council had received reports that four Irish colonels from the Spanish army together with a number of priests were in Ireland upon the pretext of recruiting for Spanish service, but in actuality were there to foment rebellion. The existence of Strafford's New Irish Army in 1640–1 was used by John Pym and others to whip up fear of a popish plot in the English Parliament.

[13] Loeber and Parker, 'Military Revolution in Seventeenth-Century Ireland', 72–3.
[14] Ibid. 67–9, 82–3, 87; S. M. Jack, *Towns in Tudor and Stuart Britain* (1996), 5–8.

The Scottish Covenanters also apprehended that such a force could descend upon the western seaboard of Scotland. Because of their fear of this Irish army, Pym and the opposition in the English Parliament refused to negotiate with the king until it was disbanded. It is far from certain that Charles I intended to bring the Irish army into England at this time. There was the problem of where to find the money to pay off the army after the order was given to disband it. With Strafford in England, the political situation had begun to deteriorate in Ireland, and the Old English were no longer willing to pay for the army. While making plans to disband Strafford's army and send it to Spain, Charles was rumoured to be plotting to keep it in existence and use it to seize Dublin Castle. The plot failed because the Protestant authorities in Dublin had been forewarned. However, credence was lent to rumours of this plot by the king's delay in disbanding the army while he found the money to pay it off. Part of the New Irish Army did actually go to Spain, but many of the Irish soldiers would later return home to fight for the army of the Catholic Confederation; the remainder, their pay in arrears, were drawn into the Irish Rebellion when it broke out in October 1641.[15]

As a consequence of the determination of both Catholics and Protestants to depict the Irish civil war as a war of religion, new identities emerged in Ireland based upon religious differences. A Protestant who was of Old Irish descent, such as Murrough O'Brien, first earl of Inchiquin, was reckoned to be an Englishman; a Catholic of English descent, such as James Touchet, third earl of Castlehaven, was considered to be an Irishman.[16] In retaliation for the alleged atrocities committed by the rebels during the Irish Rebellion of 1641, the two lords justices who assumed power after the execution of Strafford ordered the army not to grant quarter to prisoners and did everything possible to animate the soldiers against Catholics. They issued commissions of martial law, and provost-marshals summarily executed Catholics and 'mere Irish', and were especially harsh towards priests and those who were captured in arms. Irish Protestants assumed that the priests who accompanied the rebels were there to stir up trouble rather than to act as chaplains.[17]

The leaders of the Irish Rebellion of 1641, such as Sir Phelim O'Neill, did not intend a massacre nor did they believe that they could reverse the policy of plantation, but they did intend to assert liberty of Catholic worship and to recover the lands seized from them by New English and Scots planters. However, their example led the populace to attack the property (though not the persons) of the planters, to plunder them and to extort money from them. Although Catholic landowners tried to restrain such attacks, their intervention was little heeded by

[15] Perceval-Maxwell, *Outbreak of the Irish Rebellion*, 179–82, 240; [Borlase], *Irish Rebellion*, 8–9; Lenihan, *Confederate Catholics*, 15–18.
[16] Sir Richard Cox, *Hibernia Anglicana: or, the History of Ireland*, 2 vols., 2nd edn. (1692), vol. i, preface, unpaginated.
[17] Edward Hyde, earl of Clarendon, *The History of the Rebellion and Civil Wars in Ireland* (1719–20), 153–4, 156; [Borlase], *Irish Rebellion*, 42–3, 224–9; J. Hogan (ed.), *Letters and Papers Relating to the Irish Rebellion*, IMC (1936), 688–9.

the people. Most provincial areas of Ireland were stripped bare of all troops in order to defend Dublin. Munster, for example, was left with but one troop of horse for defence, and Protestant landlords such as Roger Boyle, Lord Broghill, had to fall back on their own resources to raise men for the protection of themselves and their tenants. Violent deaths among Protestant settlers typically occurred when they offered resistance. When Protestants banded together to recover their properties, the casualties on both sides increased. Deaths and injuries suffered by Catholics in these encounters provoked revenge against the settlers, which in a few instances, such as the incident at Portadown, co. Armagh, when 100 men, women and children were drowned in the River Bann, could credibly be called massacres. But such incidents were rare. At the same time, there were instances where bands of armed settlers retreated to fortified castles and churches, offered resistance and refused to surrender. When such places were taken, the defenders were put to the sword. Since this practice was permitted by the rules of war, technically it cannot be considered a massacre. However one looks at it, the Irish Rebellion of 1641 did take a bloody toll of the New English and Scots settlers. Out of a population of some 5,000 in co. Antrim, between 11 and 25 per cent perished in the violence.[18]

Rumours and hearsay evidence have posited the existence of a number of plots preceding the outbreak of the Irish Rebellion in late October 1641. One plot appears to have involved the Old English and the king in a scheme to get rid of the Irish government under the lords justices and replace it with one more to the king's liking. A counter-plot was attributed to Robert Sidney, Viscount Lisle (later second earl of Leicester), and his supporters among the New English, who had purportedly reached a compromise with the Old English in the south of Ireland in which all agreed that the disposition of Irish estates should be decided by the Irish rather than the English Parliament—thus ignoring Poyning's Law, which had long subordinated the former to the latter. If true, the sincerity of Lord Lisle and his circle is to be doubted, because when he was appointed lord deputy of Ireland in 1641, he advocated a draconian reconquest of Ireland which would obliterate Catholicism and redistribute the land of Catholics. Lisle's determination not to allow the Scots to participate in the reconquest of Ireland alerted the Scots to the Anglocentric imperialism of the Independents in the English Parliament, and such hostility to all Gaels further alienated the Protestant supporters of James Butler, first marquis of Ormonde. Some Scots also began to realize that the preservation of their autonomy could be better promoted by supporting the monarchy rather than the English Parliament. Lisle had overplayed his hand even before he had taken up residence in Dublin Castle, and the earl of Inchiquin effectively

---

[18] [Borlase], *Irish Rebellion*, 47; K. M. Lynch, *Roger Boyle, First Earl of Orrery* (1965), 39–45; N. K. Maguire, 'Regicide and Reparation: The Autobiographical Drama of Roger Boyle, Earl of Orrery', *English Literary Renaissance*, 21 (1991), 262–3; N. Canny, 'What Really happened in Ireland in 1641?', in J. H. Ohlmeyer (ed.), *Ireland from Independence to Occupation* (1995), 30–5; *Castlehaven's Review*, 28–9; Ohlmeyer, 'Wars of Religion, 1603–1660', 163.

mobilized opposition to Lisle in the English Parliament by depicting him as a dangerous Independent to the Presbyterians. However, the New Model Army's occupation of London in 1648 ended Inchiquin's influence, and in the event, Lisle's policies for the reconquest of Ireland carried the day.[19]

Except for the members of the English aristocracy and their followers who had served in mainland European armies or in the ill fated expeditions of the 1620s, the commonalty of England were, for the most part, demilitarized on the eve of the Wars of the Three Kingdoms. The Parliamentary army had to rely upon the London trained bands in the early stages of the First English Civil War, but they proved increasingly intractable. The king had to look outside of England for infantry. In the long run, Wales was one important source of foot. The king was also advised that Ireland was a likely place to recruit, where he could not only find men who were willing to fight, but also the military enterprisers who were able to recruit them, something entirely lacking in England. It was James, duke of Hamilton, who suggested to King Charles that he employ Randal MacDonnell, second earl of Antrim, to find the men he needed. Antrim possessed an unusual amount of land and power in eastern Ulster, because his father, the first earl, had assisted the Elizabethan consolidation of power in Ireland. The first earl had also grabbed lands in Antrim and on Rathlin Island, and had effectively defended his claim to them against the challenge of George Crawford, a Scottish landowner, before the lord deputy. He also employed poets from the bardic family of Ó Gnímh to validate his claim against his older brother. Like his father, the second earl (and later first marquis) of Antrim was a skilled courtier. At first Strafford was unwilling to recruit Catholic soldiers, but Charles persisted, and Antrim began to raise 200 horse and 5,000 foot without waiting for a formal commission of array. Although he had no actual military experience, because of his numerous kin and the blessings of the bardic poets Antrim was perceived as an authentic Gaelic warlord, and his Scottish allies and cousins the Catholic MacDonalds had promised to raise 4,000 men to wrest Kintyre and the Isles out of the hands of Archibald, eighth earl of Argyll, and the Campbells, who had sided with the Covenanters after learning of Antrim's preparations for war. Antrim's attempt to send his military force to aid the king during the Bishop's Wars failed because of a lack of money, the failure of Strafford to cooperate and problems of logistics and communication with the king as he took to the field. Five years later, in 1644, Antrim would become a successful military entrepreneur raising troops for the king.[20]

Charles I's decision to recruit soldiers in Ireland for use in England was to have unfortunate consequences, which reverberated throughout the Three Kingdoms.

---

[19] Perceval-Maxwell, *Outbreak of the Irish Rebellion*, 192–3, 203; J. Adamson, 'Strafford's Ghost: The British Context of Viscount Lisle's Lieutenancy of Ireland', in Ohlmeyer (ed.), *Ireland from Independence to Occupation*, 138–58.

[20] Ohlmeyer, *Civil War and Restoration*, 27–8, 42–3, 80, 82, 86–91; Caball, *Poets and Politics*, 126–7; Macinnes, *CC* 99–100.

In England, the Royalist party was depicted as the party of popery, while in Ireland a number of Irish Royalists deserted the king's party and joined the Parliamentarians. Montrose's use of Irish and West Highland soldiers, whom Scottish Lowlanders regarded as indistinguishable, cost the king potential allies among his Scottish subjects because of their propensity to plunder. In 1643 Charles signed a peace treaty with the Irish Confederates which granted Catholics concessions in order to facilitate the recruiting of soldiers in Ireland to use in the English civil wars, and also to enable the king to withdraw English troops from Ireland. Large areas of Ireland, such as the province of Munster, were stripped bare of English soldiers. Roger Boyle, Lord Broghill, and Murrough O'Brien, earl of Inchiquin, chose to remain in arms and appealed to Parliament for protection. Antrim, besides supplying soldiers to the king, demanded high rank in the combined Confederate and Royalist forces, and similar concessions had to be made to other Confederate commanders. The presidency of Munster was given to an Irish rebel, Donough Maccarty, second Viscount Muskerry (later first earl of Clancarty); the denial of this same office to the earl of Inchiquin caused that nobleman to switch his allegiance to Parliament, which conferred the Parliamentary office of president of Munster upon him.[21]

The Cessation, as the peace treaty between the king and the Confederates was known, not only embittered Irish Protestants, but made for unstable allegiances. Inchiquin had declared that he and other Protestants of Munster could not accept the Royalist concord with the Confederates, because they feared that Protestantism would be extirpated. Inchiquin also stated that he could not recognize the Cessation unless the king first made peace with Parliament. The Cessation not only increased Protestant fears, but also made men such as Inchiquin more bloody-minded. As president of Munster, Inchiquin committed atrocities and was responsible for the massacre of the priests and gentry who had sought refuge in the cathedral at Cashell in co. Tipperary in 1647. Inchiquin, whose brother was a Confederate, changed sides again in 1648, and concluded a truce with the Catholic Confederation. Inchiquin's negotiations with the Confederation of Kilkenny proved to be as divisive for the Confederates as his defection from the Royalist cause had been earlier in 1643, when the two lords justices had joined him in defecting. The Cessation had also alienated Sir Robert Monro, the commander of the Scottish forces in Ulster, who, despite Confederate assurances that the Scots in Ulster would not be molested, refused to be drawn in because no money was provided to pay off his army, and because he feared that Protestants would be persecuted.[22]

---

[21] Ohlmeyer, *Civil War and Restoration*, 135–7, 140–2; Lynch, *Roger Boyle, First Earl of Orrery*, 49–52; Firth, *Ludlow*, i. 185.

[22] Firth, *Ludlow*, i. 185; [Murrough O'Brien, 1st earl of Inchiquin], *A Letter from... Lord Inchiquin and the other Commanders in Munster* (1644), 1–12; [Edmund Borlase], *The Reduction of Ireland to the Crown of England* (1675), 237–8, 244–5; J. S. Wheeler, *Cromwell in Ireland* (1999), 41–2.

Another notable defector from the Irish Royalists was Roger Boyle, Lord Broghill (and later first earl of Orrery). Broghill was in London in 1649, intending to go into exile to join the Royalists, when Cromwell summoned him, showed the evidence of treason he had against him, and offered him the choice of serving Parliament by fighting the native Irish without having to take an oath of allegiance or being confined to the Tower. Although Broghill served Cromwell faithfully, he was horrified by the king's execution and remained in touch with the Irish Royalists, and Henry Ireton and Edmund Ludlow never trusted him. Broghill was an effective military commander, but unlike most soldiers he admitted that he enjoyed the heat of battle and killing the enemy. It was his practice not to take prisoners, except 'persons of good quality' whom he could ransom. According to his chaplain, Thomas Morrice, it was Broghill who first proposed the plan to remove the Catholic gentry of Ireland to Connaught and to give their lands to Cromwellian officers and soldiers.[23]

The Catholic Confederation of Kilkenny came about when a number of Old English lords from the south and Gaelic chiefs from Ulster met with representatives of the Catholic clergy in Kilkenny in May 1647 and drew up a government which was intended to confer legitimacy upon their alliance, restore law and order and bring the popular tumults under control. Whether the new Confederation of Kilkenny ever succeeded in achieving the latter objective is debatable, but they established an administration and raised military forces comprising an army for each of the four provinces, together with a more mobile force called a 'running army'. These armies were at first poorly armed and supplied, but the situation improved when the port towns of Waterford, Limerick and Wexford declared for the Confederation. The General Assembly of the Confederation also insisted upon the recognition of the new Irish identity, which was intended to join together Old Irish and Old and New English, and townsmen and countryfolk.[24]

The nucleus of the Confederate armies came from Strafford's disbanded New Irish Army, which in 1641 was incorporated into the Army of Ulster commanded by Sir Phelim O'Neill, who represented what remained of the Tyrone interest in that province. This army mustered between 8,000 and 10,000 men. Their level of training was reflected in their ability to deploy rapidly and seize objectives. They were soon reinforced by perhaps as many as eight or nine regiments recruited for or serving in the Spanish Army of Flanders or the French army, who were persuaded to join the Confederates by Conor, second Lord Maguire. Most of these units had been raised in Leinster, Munster and Connaught by Colonels John and Garret Barry, kinsmen of the earls of Barrymore, Thomas Preston and Colonels Taaffe and Porter. These forces were strongly Old English.[25] In Ulster,

[23] Lynch, *Roger Boyle, First Earl of Orrery*, 70–3, 75; Roger Boyle, 1st earl of Orrery, *A Letter from the Lord Broghill to ... William Lenthall* (1651) [BL, TT, E. 640 (10)], 1, 4–5.

[24] J. Ohlmeyer, 'The Civil Wars in Ireland', in Kenyon and Ohlmeyer (eds.), *The Civil Wars*, 77; Wheeler, *Cromwell in Ireland*, 15–16; Lenihan, *Confederate Catholics*, 24–6; Perceval-Maxwell, *Outbreak of the Irish Rebellion*, 258–9.

[25] Perceval-Maxwell, *Outbreak of the Irish Rebellion*, 205–8, 214–17; Loeber and Parker, 'Military Revolution in Seventeenth-Century Ireland', 71–2; [Borlase], *Irish Rebellion*, 8–9, 41.

Old Irish gentry were able to raise hostings of regimental size. These military units were not drawn from their tenants, because the Ulster Old Irish gentry were seldom substantial landlords and did not command their tenants' support. Indeed, Sir Phelim O'Neill had recently evicted his own Irish tenants and given the tenancies to New English settlers from whom he could extract higher rents. Rather, the source of military support was to be found among the *derbh fine*, or true kin, who shared a common descent. For example, one of O'Neill's followers, Cormac O'Hagan, raised a hosting approximating the size of a regiment in which five of his twelve captains were O'Hagans and four were O'Neills. One cannot speak of an O'Hagan clan or sept still existing because the New English authorities had deliberately tried to disperse such kinship groupings, but the O'Hagans still maintained strong kinship ties through the custom of fosterage, or sending sons to be raised by other members of the kinship group. To be a foster-brother constituted a strong claim to loyalty, and at the beginning of the Ulster Rebellion these ties of kinship were important in recruiting followers. That, however, did not constitute a claim on the loyalty of Catholic tenants, who were no part of this kinship group. Thus, when the rebellion broke out, the tenantry attacked Protestants rather than following military leaders such as Sir Phelim O'Neill, who never intended to murder Protestants. At the same time, the close kinship ties of the O'Neills made it difficult for Sir Phelim to enforce discipline on his followers, and some of them were also guilty of committing atrocities.[26]

By contrast, Antrim was able to recruit from among his tenants as well as kinsmen when he raised an army in 1644. His recruiting base also extended beyond Ulster to the Old Irish who lived in the Pale, where he found discontented officers who previously had been unable to obtain commissions in the Confederate armies which tended to be dominated by the Old English outside of Ulster. Some of these officers had experience of the continental wars and others were veterans of earlier campaigns of the Irish and Scottish civil wars. There is good reason for thinking that their knowledge of war was quite up-to-date, since most of the soldiers of Antrim's regiments were equipped with muskets rather than bows and pikes, but most other Confederate soldiers were not as well armed. However, contrary to what used to be thought, the West Highlanders who were led by Antrim's cousin and major-general, Alasdair MacColla, also appear to have been armed with muskets and half-pikes when they launched the 'Highland charge' against their enemies. A few of them were also armed with swords and targets, in the manner of the sword-and-buckler men of Spanish infantry companies who had been retained for close encounters with the enemy.[27]

---

[26] Lenihan, *Confederate Catholics, 1641–49*, 29–32.

[27] Ohlmeyer, *Civil War and Restoration*, 138–40, 154–62; E. H[ogan]. (ed.), *History of the Warre of Ireland* (1873), 71–3. Also compare Lenihan, *Catholic Confederates*, 193–4, with J. M. Hill, *Celtic Warfare, 1595–1763* (1986), 1–6, 173–81. By 1644, Antrim's activities as a military enterpriser had extended beyond raising soldiers for the Confederation to supplying troops to the Spanish Army of

Between 1642 and 1649 the Confederate forces controlled as much as two-thirds of the Irish countryside and fielded an army of 20,000–25,000 men before they were absorbed into the Royalist forces. For a time they possessed the strategic advantage which could have enabled them to defeat the Parliamentary forces in Ireland, as they had defeated Sir Robert Monro's Scottish army at Benburb in June 1646. Antrim's recommendation to send MacColla to assist Montrose in Scotland was a brilliant piece of strategy, and prevented the Covenanters from reinforcing Monro's army in Ulster. However, the Confederate forces were divided in their leadership, because inexperienced noblemen such as the earl of Castlehaven were preferred to the highest commands over experienced professionals such as Owen Roe O'Neill and Thomas Preston, and because the Confederation's attempt to integrate Old English lords from the south and Gaelic chiefs from Ulster did not work out well. Moreover, the arrival of the papal nuncio to the Confederation of Kilkenny, Giovanni Battista Rinuccini, archbishop of Fermo, in 1645 complicated the attempts to work out a permanent political and religious settlement between the Confederates and the Royalists. The Confederates never again regained the initiative in the field, and the king was denied the Irish soldiers that he needed so badly to pursue the civil war in England. Furthermore, the Confederate field forces were always at a tactical disadvantage because they never had sufficient cavalry when they faced the Parliamentary forces on the battlefield, and after the arrival of the New Model Army they never had the numbers to defeat the English. When the alliance between the Royalists and the Confederates broke down, James Butler, marquis (and later first duke) of Ormonde, as the king's lieutenant, surrendered Dublin to the Parliamentary commander, Michael Jones. Jones's very effective campaigning and his victory at Dungan's Hill in August 1647 allowed him to clear the Confederates out of most of Leinster and establish a base for the Cromwellian conquest. Dublin was for a time besieged by a Royalist–Confederate army led by Inchiquin after he defected from the Parliamentarians in 1648. He abandoned that siege and marched south. Jones and the Parliamentarians might have been contained within Dublin if the advice of Owen Roe O'Neill, an experienced soldier, had been followed about constructing defences at the gates of Dublin in order to obstruct Parliamentarian sallies. But the ranks of the Confederates had become badly divided, and the Confederate Council in Kilkenny, dominated by the papal nuncio, was effectively at war with Owen Roe O'Neill. O'Neill was an ultramontane Catholic, but he was also Gaelic to the core and he did not work well with the Old English. Irish identity, which the Confederation had tried to promote, was disintegrating.[28]

Flanders. He also had acquired a couple of frigates and manned them with Dunkirk privateers in order to transport and equip his soldiers and protect his lines of communication from Parliamentary ships.

[28] J. S. Wheeler, 'Four Armies in Ireland', in Ohlmeyer (ed.), *Ireland from Independence to Occupation*, 43–65; P. Lenihan, ' "Celtic" Warfare in the 1640s', in J. R. Young (ed.), *Celtic Dimensions of the British Civil Wars* (1997), 116–18, 121–2, 133–5.

Upon the departure from Ireland of the Royalist lord-lieutenant, the marquis of Ormonde, in 1650, Ulick de Burgh, first marquis of Clanricarde, remained as lord deputy. He attempted to reconcile the Irish to Charles II and to improve relations between the Irish and the New English. Despite his reputation for possessing an 'even temper', he was never quite trusted by the Irish, perhaps because as the Royalist governor of Galway he was too close to Sir Charles Coote, the brutal Parliamentarian commander in the west, and had punished Irish marauders and bandits—including his own Bourke kinsmen—very severely. His routine use of martial law could not have made him very popular, and while he promoted the Royalist–Confederate alliance, he persisted in opposing the papal nuncio Rinuccini, and later laid siege to the Confederates in Galway. Clanricarde also had a hand in the abortive scheme to bring Charles IV, duke of Lorraine, a supplier of mercenary soldiers, into Ireland as the Catholic protector. Clanricarde, a Catholic himself, always had trouble remembering which side he was on.[29]

There was little debate among the leaders of the new Commonwealth of England concerning the need to subdue Ireland. It was agreed that honour required revenge for the massacre of the New English planters in 1641, and even the Levellers, who were not enthusiastic about military adventures in Ireland, could not dispute the likelihood that an unconquered Ireland would provide a base from which the Royalists could invade England and Wales. Since Fairfax could not be brought to participate in the trial and execution of the king, and refused to signify his loyalty to the Commonwealth, Cromwell was the person looked to in order to lead an expedition to Ireland. Parliamentary confusion over war aims probably prolonged the conquest. George Monck, who commanded the Parliamentary forces at Dundalk, came to an agreement with Owen Roe O'Neill, the commander of the Irish forces in Ulster and Connaught, which resulted in a truce of three months. This agreement, had it been prolonged, could have shortened the war. O'Neill asked for liberty of conscience for Catholics, an act of indemnity for all acts since the beginning of the Irish Rebellion in 1641 and a commission for himself in the Parliamentary army. Agreement by the Council of State and the Rump Parliament would have destroyed the fragile Royalist coalition with the Confederates. But the Rump Parliament could not be diverted from exacting revenge for the 1641 Rebellion, so the proposed agreement was repudiated when Monck's truce with O'Neill expired.[30]

Cromwell left Ireland in late May 1650, having been called back by Parliament. He had been in Ireland for nine months, during which time he had taken every port on the eastern and southern coasts by siege except Waterford, which held out for some time longer. Although he had been able to augment his army with

---

[29] [Borlase], *Irish Rebellion*, 100–1, 254–5; J. Lowe (ed.), *Letter-Book of the Earl of Clanricarde, 1643–7*, IMC (1983), 18–19; [Ulick de Burgh, marquis of Clanricarde], *Memoirs of the . . . Marquis of Clanricarde, Lord Deputy of Ireland* (1744), 78–83; Wheeler, *Cromwell in Ireland*, 5, 10, 202–5.
[30] Gentles, *NMA* 351–6; Wheeler, *Cromwell in Ireland*, 50–1, 55–7.

Royalist prisoners of war, he lost so many soldiers to disease and left so many behind to garrison captured towns that almost none of his original army of 12,000 survived, although he never once fought a pitched battle in the field. The discharged Cromwellian soldiers who did survive the conquest of Ireland never received their arrears of pay. They were supposed to receive Irish land instead if they became settlers, but this seldom happened, and their officers often cheated them when they came over to Ireland or sold their claims to land. At home, Parliament was unable to make a peace settlement without the active participation of the army. Cromwell also failed to impose a permanent peace settlement by taking upon himself the quasi-regal title of lord protector and attempting to establish a dynasty. As Hobbes explained it, Cromwell could not call himself a king, because in a republic he had to share the honour and glory of the army's victories with his officers, and Richard Cromwell could not succeed his father because he was 'without any military glory'.[31]

By the spring of 1652 the Cromwellian army had obtained the surrender of more than 350 ports, forts, castles and fortified garrison towns in Ireland. However, the countryside was so infested with tories that supporters of Parliament could not safely travel without cavalry escorts. These were not always available, because the English army believed that it was necessary to establish another 100 garrisons and fortified places to protect their lines of communication. As the English army became more dispersed they became more vulnerable to the guerilla warfare pursued by the numerous marauding bands who lived by cattle-raiding. These tories were not mere bandits, but rather consisted of peasants and soldiers who had eluded capture, and were led by gentlemen and officers from the Confederate armies. They knew the terrain, and retreated into the seemingly trackless bogs, forests and mountains, such as the Wicklow Mountains south of Dublin, where cavalry could not pursue. So free were the tories to roam the countryside that the English had all but become captives in their own fortified garrisons. This was the price of refusing to grant the Irish freedom of religion and security of land titles, and the consequence was total economic collapse. The English response was to proclaim martial law and summarily try and execute all captured guerilla fighters. The tories retaliated by murdering Cromwellian soldiers. Bounties were posted for the heads of tories, and the price varied from 40s. for a common tory to £30 for a bandit captain. That the system produced so many heads was due to the numbers of Irish who were willing to act as informers. The problem of tory bands persisted until the end of the Williamite wars.[32]

[31] Gentles, *NMA* 375; J. P. Prendergast, *The Cromwellian Settlement of Ireland*, 3rd edn. (1922), 234–5; Thomas Hobbes, *Behemoth: The History of the Causes of the Civil Wars of England*, ed. William Molesworth (1682; repr. 1963), 136–7.

[32] Gentles, *NMA* 380; Prendergast, *Cromwellian Settlement*, 79, 340–6; [Orrery], *Letter from Lord Broghill*, 1, 5; É. ó Ciardha, 'Tories and Mosstroopers in Scotland and Ireland in the Interregnum: A Political Dimension', in Young (ed.), *Celtic Dimensions*, 141–63.

The Civil Wars and Conquest of Scotland

The disastrous military expeditions of the 1620s and the withdrawal from mainland European affairs during the 1630s exposed the weaknesses of Stuart government in England and Scotland. The Stuart monarchs appeared to be incapable of raising effective military forces for use at home or abroad. James VI and I had reduced the power of the greater nobility on the Scottish Privy Council, but they continued to retain extensive judicial and administrative power in the localities. Charles I began his reign by alienating many of his Scottish subjects through an increase in teinds (or church tithes). As part of an attempt to bring religious uniformity to the Three Kingdoms he sought to impose Arminian theology, Laudian ritual and stronger episcopal government upon the Kirk of Scotland; this angered the Presbyterians who were in the majority in Lowland Scotland south of the Tay Valley, and provided the opportunity for the Lowland Scots nobility to rebuild leadership among the people and protest the growing influence of an alien government which ruled from London. The introduction of the new liturgy into the kirks of Edinburgh and Glasgow provoked rioting, and royal authority in Scotland began to collapse as noblemen, lairds and ministers forged a new alliance and drew up the National Covenant. The Covenanters proposed to take charge and reverse the trend towards domination by London in matters of church and state. When Charles I agreed to the first meeting of the General Assembly of the Kirk of Scotland since 1618, the Royalists and Scottish Episcopalians who came to Glasgow to attend it were disorganized and were greeted by armed Covenanters in the streets.[33]

The Covenanting movement led to the emergence of a national identity together with a strong centralized state that was without precedent in Scottish history. The Covenanting government demanded ideological conformity, financial support and conscription for its army. Although neutralism was widespread, the Covenanters were remarkably successful in the Lowland parishes in purging hostile moderators from the presbyteries, compelling the remaining moderators and householders to sign the Covenant and persuading parishioners to support and join the Covenanting Army. Many of the general officers, as well as field-grade and company officers were recruited from among Scots serving in the Swedish army who were veterans of the Baltic and Thirty Years Wars. Also borrowed from the Swedish state was an administrative machine based upon shire and parish which raised money, conscripted soldiers, relieved their dependants and cared for maimed soldiers returning from the wars. The Covenanting movement provided a model for revolution in the other kingdoms, but the English and the Irish

---

[33] K. M. Brown, *Kingdom or Province? Scotland and the Regal Union, 1603–1715* (1992), 99–105, 108–17; E. J. Cowan, 'The Making of the National Covenant', and P. Donald, 'The Scottish National Covenant and British Politics 1638–1640', in J. Morrill (ed.), *The Scottish National Covenant in British Context* (1990), 72–4, 90–5.

governments were slower to follow the example of the Scots Covenanters in providing a welfare system for widows, orphans and disabled veterans.[34]

The leaders of the Covenanting moment not only intended to carry through a revolution in church and state; they also meant to intervene in the affairs of England and Ireland. The Covenanting Army's occupation of northern England prevented Charles from crushing the rebellion in Scotland, and allowed the English Parliament to meet and give voice to pro-Scottish propaganda from the Presbyterian faction of that body. Subsequently, a Scottish army fought alongside the Parliamentarians in the First English Civil War, and another army was dispatched under Major-General Robert Munro to Ulster to protect the Scots settlers in Ireland and prevent an Irish army from intervening in the west of Scotland.[35] With a considerable part of the Covenanting forces deployed outside Scotland, the Lowlands, especially the east coast, became vulnerable to invasion by the Royalists. The Covenanters began to rebuild the defences of Edinburgh in anticipation of a Royalist expedition, and the nobles who led the Covenanting movement provided a patriotic example by carrying the first buckets of dirt to rebuild the fortifications of Leith, which had been constructed by the French in the time of Queen Mary. The citizens of Edinburgh joined this effort, while the Covenanting Army drilled every day. That the Scottish Rebellion brought home many bellicose swordsmen is illustrated by the 'Incident' plot of October 1641, when a group of Royalist swordsmen conspired to kidnap the earl of Argyll and the duke of Hamilton. Although this conspiracy never got beyond drunken boasts in taverns, Hamilton, fearing for his life, deserted the king and denounced his sovereign for failing to protect himself and Argyll. Hamilton and Argyll emerged as heroes who had escaped a papist and Royalist conspiracy, the king was made to appear a villain, and this rendered it impossible to raise military support in Scotland for the Royalist cause for some time.[36]

Charles I had alienated Archibald Campbell, eighth earl of Argyll, perhaps the most powerful of the Scots nobility, by intriguing against him with the earl of Antrim, the Irish chief of ClanDonald South and the rival whom Argyll particularly feared because of the threat that Antrim posed to the former MacDonald lands in the West Highlands and the Isles. Argyll and the other Campbell chiefs declared allegiance to the Covenanting movement in 1638 so that they might start

[34] A. I. Macinnes, 'Gaelic Culture in the Seventeenth Century: Polarization and Assimilation', in S. G. Ellis and S. Barber (eds.), *Conquest and Union: Fashioning a British State, 1485–1625* (1995), 169; Macinnes, *CC* 88; Brown, *Kingdom or Province?*, 116–17; E. Furgol, 'The Civil Wars in Scotland', in Kenyon and Ohlmeyer (eds.), *Civil Wars*, 42–8; id., *A Regimental History of the Covenanting Armies, 1639–1651* (1990), 2–3; S. Murdoch, 'The House of Stuart and the Scottish Professional Soldier, 1618–1640: A Conflict of Nationality and Identities', in B. Taithe and T. Thornton (eds.), *War: Identities in Conflict, 1300–2000* (1998), 50.

[35] Furgol, 'Civil Wars in Scotland', 48–9.

[36] James Gordon, parson of Rothiemay, *History of Scots Affairs*, 3 vols., SC 1, 2, 4 (1841), ii. 207–8; H. L. Rubinstein, *Captain Luckless: James, First Duke of Hamilton, 1606–1643* (1975), 132–7. See also J. Scally, 'Counsel in Crisis: James, Third Marquis of Hamilton and the Bishops' Wars, 1638–1640', in Young (ed.), *Celtic Dimensions*, 19–20.

immediately upon the task of recruiting armies from among their tenants and clansmen. This had the effect of polarizing clan politics. One of the first acts of hostility on the part of the committee of the Scottish Estates was to give Argyll a commission of fire and sword to pursue his rivals, John Murray, first earl of Atholl, James, seventh Lord Ogilvy, who was the heir of the first earl of Airlie, the Farquharsons of Braemar and other loyal Highlanders in Lochaber and Badenoch. This led Airlie to appeal to James Graham, fifth earl (and later first marquis) of Montrose, for help; Montrose occupied Airlie Castle in order to keep it out of the hands of Argyll and the Campbells. Although Montrose had entered the civil wars on the side of the Covenanters, he would later lead the Royalist war effort against the Covenanters.[37] Whereas the Covenanting movement had raised a nationally conscripted army that was committed to an ideology and financed by the state, Charles I's Royalist forces in Scotland depended upon the family connections of territorial magnates, who recruited tenants and kinsmen, as well as the hosts summoned by the Highland chieftains. These Royalist lords, lairds and chieftains resented the centralizing tendencies of the Covenanting government, distrusted the territorial ambitions of magnates such as Argyll, and in the Highlands and north of the River Tay were more likely to be Episcopalians and Catholics rather than Presbyterians. Of the fifty major clans studied by Professor Macinnes with regard to their allegiance during the Scottish civil wars, twenty-one were Royalist, fourteen were Covenanters, five were neutral, six changed allegiance and one remained divided. Only six gave the Covenanters their undivided loyalty.[38]

The key to organizing Royalist resistance to the Covenanter regime was engaging the leading members of the nobility, who, in the absence of a Scottish Royalist war machine for raising and paying an army, were best equipped to gather recruits together. Many of the Lowland nobility had become demilitarized, many were elderly, and many did their best to straddle the fence and remain neutral. The Covenanters went after those who were neutral or equivocal and applied strong pressure to conform, and a number of peers succumbed to these pressures who later reverted to Royalism. However, almost all of those who held court offices remained loyal to Charles. Keith Brown has determined that of some twenty-eight Scottish Royalist peers, nineteen heads of families or sons or brothers fought for the king during the civil wars. Three brothers of James Stewart, fourth duke of Lennox, were killed fighting for their sovereign; William Douglas, third earl of Morton, who had been a soldier and had grown too old for war, sent two sons to serve the king, one of whom was killed.[39] The allegiance of the many was a matter

---

[37] P. Hopkins, *Glencoe and the End of the Highland Wars* (1986), 20–1; Macinnes, *CC* 95–7; E. J. Cowan, *Montrose: For Covenant and King* (1977), 94–5.

[38] Macinnes, *CC* 98–9, 242, 248–9; E. M. Furgol, 'The Northern Highlander Covenanter Clans, 1639–1651', *NS* 7 (1987), 119–31.

[39] J. Goodare, 'The Nobility and the Absolutist State in Scotland, 1564–1638', *History*, 78(1993), 180–1; K. M. Brown, 'Courtiers and Cavaliers: Service, Anglicisation and Loyalty Amongst Royalist Nobility', in Morrill (ed.), *Scottish National Covenant in its British Context*, 158–78.

largely determined by lords or clan chieftains. Scotland remained a feudal society in the seventeenth century, and Scots peers and Highland chieftains retained great control over their tenants and followers. Below the Lowland peers, there were few lairds who were substantial enough to be comparable to the English gentry, and many actually worked their own land. In the Highlands, clan rivalries and individual lords and chieftains often decided the allegiance of large numbers of followers. Archibald, eighth earl and first marquis of Argyll, bestowed his allegiance in order to protect and advance his territorial interests in both the West Highlands and in Badenoch, Lochaber, Atholl and Angus. Although Scottish Episcopalians and Catholics opposed the Covenanters, probably the most important reason why so many clans were Royalist was because of their fear of the territorial ambitions of Argyll and the Campbells. The Mackays of Strathnaver became Royalists because they apprehended the territorial ambitions of John Gordon, fourteenth earl of Sutherland, a leading Covenanter in the north. Dislike of the Royalist George Gordon, second marquis of Huntly, caused the Frasers and the Mackintoshes of ClanChattan to declare for the Covenanters.[40]

The decline of ClanDonald South in western Scotland had assisted the ascendancy of Argyll and the Campbells. The MacDonalds were among the important sources of the trade in redshanks or mercenary soldiers between Ireland and the western seaboard of Scotland. The Irish of Ulster and the Gaels of western Scotland had formerly shared one language, one culture and one religion. The coast of Antrim and the Kintyre Peninsula are separated by only thirteen miles, but the plantation of Ulster had driven a wedge between these two parts of Gaeldom, the languages began to diverge and Protestant evangelization of the Highlands further weakened the links. The rallying of many Highland clans to the Royalist cause—especially those of the West Highlands and the Isles—represented an attempt to restore these broken links. A number of vernacular Gaelic poets, such as Iain Lom *alias* John MacDonald of Brae Lochaber, gave vent to the MacDonalds' traditional hatred of the Campbells for their depredations dating back to the fifteenth century. Iain Lom regarded the Lowland settlers whom Argyll was importing into the West Highlands as being culturally and racially inferior. Since he spoke primarily from a MacDonald point of view, Iain Lom praised Alasdair MacColla for importing Irish soldiers to help the Royalist cause in Scotland, and in this manner promoted a pan-Gaelic consciousness. Since MacColla's Irish soldiers, who came almost exclusively from the estates of the earl of Antrim, spent most of their time plundering and killing Campbells in the West Highlands before proceeding to the assistance of Montrose in eastern Scotland, most West Highland clan chieftains were less enthusiastic about Iain Lom's polemic verses.[41]

[40] Macinnes, *CC* 94–5; G. Holmes, *The Making of a Great Power: Later Stuart and Early Georgian Britain, 1660–1722* (1993), 22–3; D. Szechi and D. Hayton, 'John Bull's Other Kingdoms: The English Government of Scotland and Ireland', in C. James (ed.), *Britain in the First Age of Party, 1680–1750: Essays Presented to Geoffrey Holmes* (1987), 243–4.

[41] Macinnes, 'Gaelic Culture in the Seventeenth Century', 163–4; id., *CC* 99–100; B. P. Lenman, *England's Colonial Wars, 1550–1688* (2001), 152–6, 167–8.

In the north-east, one of the leading peers, George Gordon, second marquis of Huntly, although a Royalist in sympathy, held off declaring for the king and was imprisoned in Edinburgh Castle. His son James, Viscount Aboyne, made his way to the king and had himself declared king's lieutenant in his father's place. The marquis of Hamilton, who in June 1639 was anchored in the Firth of Forth with 2,000 soldiers, not trusting Aboyne, sent them back to England to avoid turning them over to him. Aboyne returned to his father's ancestral castle of Strathbogie, where he began to raise forces that included both Lowlanders and Highlanders. He was criticized by the Covenanters for accepting into his army men who had been declared outlaws and robbers. Another of Huntly's sons, Lord Ludowick Gordon, donned Highland attire and was adopted as leader by the Highlanders. The Gordons and other allies, who numbered 500 horse and 3,000 foot, were undisciplined volunteers who were not paid and lived by plunder. When they descended upon Aberdeen, they lived at free quarter and soon wore out their welcome. The second-in-command under Aboyne was William Gunn, a veteran of the German wars whom Aboyne had acquired from Hamilton's entourage. When Aboyne and Gunn confronted the Covenanting Army at the Battle of Megray Hill on 15 June 1639, Gunn sat down to breakfast without bothering to issue orders to Aboyne's army. The contingent of Highlanders was very raw and was exposed to savage cannon fire because of his thoughtless leadership, and very quickly deserted.[42]

A third of the population of Scotland still lived in the Highlands in the seventeenth century, and the cultures and societies of Highland and Lowland Scotland had diverged since the medieval period. The clan system, although by no means confined to the Highlands, seemed alien to many Lowlanders, and they associated it with private warfare and plunder—usually directed at other clans—and assumed that this was a normal state of affairs. The Lowlanders no longer spoke Gaelic and assumed that the poetry of that language was largely an incitement to bloodletting. That the Lowlanders often referred to Highlanders as 'Irish' merely demonstrates the contempt they felt towards the Gaelic-speaking Highlanders. The Highlanders of eastern Scotland were perceived as being more peaceful, and eastern Highlanders regarded those from the West Highlands as ferocious and savage. This derived from their poverty and the pastoral nature of their economy, but there is no denying that the western Highlanders were also much given to feuding, cattle-raiding and, in the case of a few clans such as the MacGregors, banditry. At the same time, the *fine*, or clan gentry of the eastern Highlands, and the Campbells and their dependants in the western Highlands were being drawn more and more into Lowland Scottish elite culture, which was also tinged with Protestantism. Although James VI and I and Charles I took little interest in the Highlands except to order the extermination of those whom they regarded as broken men and bandits, those clans which feared the expansionism of the Campbells

[42] Gordon, *Scots Affairs*, ii. 260–1, 265–9, 272–4.

and the House of Argyll were anxious to give their allegiance to the Royalists during the Scottish civil wars. Highland soldiers were used to advantage against the Covenanters by Montrose, but because they were difficult to control they were distrusted by many on both sides.[43]

From the beginning of the Bishops' Wars until well into the Scottish civil wars, the Highlanders—whether they fought for the Covenanters or the Royalists— were usually armed with bow and arrow, broadsword and target. When Gael fought Gael these weapons usually sufficed, although they had become obsolete in Ireland when West Highlanders were brought to Ulster by the earl of Antrim in 1641. Lowlanders were always astonished to see Highlanders with their plaids slung over their shoulders and their bare legs—after which they were called 'redshanks'.[44] Despite the slowness of the Highlanders in adopting firearms, they enjoyed for a period of time a tactical advantage over Lowland soldiers. As Lowlanders came to rely upon firearms they neglected the skills required for wielding blade weapons, which put them at a disadvantage when required to repulse a Highland charge, which supposedly was first employed by Alasdair MacColla and his redshanks in Ireland in 1642. The musket remained very much a defensive weapon until well after the invention of the socket bayonet at the end of the seventeenth century, unless the musketeers were well drilled in the rapid-fire-and-advance tactics of the Swedes. The Lowland soldiers that the Covenanters employed against Montrose and MacColla had not made the full transition to modern infantry tactics, were not well drilled and were not especially martial. Whereas Highland chieftains were expected to lead their men into battle from the front, Lowland commanders, following more recent continental prac- tice, remained behind the front lines to coordinate their troops. Nor had the Covenanters developed effective light field artillery, or learned how to coordinate infantry, cavalry and artillery in the field. Consequently, the shock tactics of MacColla's Highlanders, after first firing and then flinging away their bows or muskets as well as plaids, would instil terror in their enemy.[45]

When Montrose led a revolt of the Scottish nobility against the Covenanters and declared for the king, it was discovered that the Covenanting ministers so completely controlled the Lowland districts that he was unable to recruit fol- lowers. He could not even raise soldiers among his own Graham kinsfolk. His first campaign as a Royalist commander depended upon English troops borrowed from the earl of Newcastle, who numbered no more than 1,200 men, reinforced by a troop of horse led by the improbable figure of Captain Frances Dalzell, the illegitimate daughter of Robert, first earl of Carnwath. Montrose's best source of soldiers were the followers of Alasdair MacColla, who consisted of exiled Scottish

---

[43] Hopkins, *Glencoe*, 11–12; Macinnes, *CC* 1–2, 30–1, 58–64, 81.

[44] D. Stevenson, *Alasdair MacColla and the Highland Problem in the Seventeenth Century* (1980), 68, 79; C. S. Terry (ed.), *Papers Relating to the Army of the Solemn League and Covenant, 1643–1647*, 2 vols., SHS 2nd ser. 16, 17 (1917), vol. i, p. xcvi.

[45] J. M. Hill, *Celtic Warfare, 1595–1763* (1986), 47–8; id., 'The Distinctiveness of Gaelic Warfare, 1400–1750', *EHQ* 22 (1992), 323–45.

Catholics and their Irish kin from the Glinns or glens of Antrim. The Gaelic Irish of Antrim and the Highland Scots of Kintyre were practically indistinguishable. The conversion of the captain of the MacDonalds of ClanRanald by Gaelic-speaking Irish Franciscans stiffened the resistance of many Highland chiefs to Lowland Protestantism, and tended to re-establish and strengthen the ties between the West Highlands and the Isles and Gaelic Ulster. The regimental commanders under MacColla were all kinsmen; many of his soldiers had fought in the Thirty Years War and under Owen Roe O'Neill in the armies of the Catholic Confederation of Kilkenny. MacColla was not a traditional Gaelic warlord, but rather came from the lower ranks of the gentry of the Clan Ian Mor (ClanDonald South), and was known as a mercenary soldier. However, he enjoyed the support of vernacular Gaelic poets. MacColla's men fought for religious reasons, and were determined to settle scores with Argyll and the Campbells and to re-establish Clan Ian Mor in the Isles and along the western seaboard of Scotland. Because of their determination to seek revenge, it was at first difficult to persuade other clans to join them until MacColla became allied with Montrose, who was able to rise above clan rivalries and restrain MacColla from fighting a purely religious war.[46]

Alasdair MacColla, *alias* Alexander MacDonald, was possessed of legendary valour and became an epic hero among the Royalist Highlanders as a result of a year-long campaign culminating in the Battle of Kilsyth in 1645. However, at the beginning of the campaign he lacked the social standing necessary to persuade the Scottish Royalist clans to follow him, and he was also viewed as an outsider. In any case, the Highlanders would only follow a member of the ancient nobility.[47] Although he was a Lowlander, Montrose appeared in Highland dress to lead MacColla's host and the Highlanders whom he gathered together in Atholl. Subsequently, he was also joined by John Graham, Lord Kilpont, son and heir of

---

[46] George Wishart, *The Memoirs of James Marquis of Montrose, 1639–1650*, trans. A. D. Murdoch and H. F. M. Simpson (1893), 37, 45, 47–8, 50, 54–6; Cowan, *Montrose*, 144–8, 152–7; J. Ohlmeyer, ' "Civilizing of those Rude Partes": Colonization within Britain and Ireland, 1580s–1640s', in N. Canny (ed.), *The Origins of Empire: British Overseas Enterprise to the Close of the Seventeenth Century*, (1998), i. 126–7; Stevenson, *Alasdair MacColla*, 54; Macinnes, 'Gaelic Culture in the Seventeenth Century', 176–7; John Spalding, *Memorialls of the Trubles in Scotland and England, A.D. 1624–A.D. 1645*, 2 vols., SC 21, 23 (1850–1), ii. 407; *ODNB, sub* Alasdair MacColla [Sir Alexander MacDonald] (d. 1647).

[47] Those who lived in the Highlands and its peripheries did not recognize military rank. Following his defeat and capture at Carbisdale, Montrose was carried prisoner to Edinburgh for trial. On the way, his captor, Maj.-Gen. Holburn, a Covenanting officer, stopped at Skibo Castle in Sutherland and asked the Dowager Lady Grey of Skibo for entertainment for the night. Lady Skibo strictly upheld social rank and precedence. Before she had a chance to seat Montrose at her right hand at the dinner table, Holburn presumed to seat him according to the military order which he had observed on the march. Lady Skibo was highly offended, grabbed a roasted leg of mutton off the table 'by the shank, and hit Holburn such a notable blow on the head with the flank part of the hot juicy mutton as she knocked him off his seat, and completely spoiled his uniform'. Fearing an attempt to rescue the prisoner, the other officers present apparently reached for their swords, but Lady Skibo, still brandishing the leg of mutton reminded them that they were guests in her house and that she would determine the precedence in seating them (Wishart, *Memoirs of James Marquis of Montrose*, app., 314–15).

William, seventh earl of Menteith, and 500 more men. Montrose's army then descended the Tay Valley to the outskirts of Perth, where they engaged a Covenanter army commanded by David Weymss, Lord Elcho, son and heir of John, first earl of Weymss and James Murray, second earl of Tullibardine, at Tippermuir, or St Johnston, on 1 September 1644. This was the first encounter between a Highland and a Covenanter army, and the latter lost nearly one-third of a force consisting of 700 horse and 6,000 foot. The Covenanter army was made up of 'untried men and freshwater soldiers', who were unable to stand up to the Highland charge mounted by Montrose's much smaller force of perhaps 1,700 men. Short of powder, the Highlanders lined up in three ranks and fired all at once, then used their short muskets as clubs or discarded them. Descending from higher ground upon Elcho's men, they then assailed the Lowlanders with stones, clubs and broadswords (although the Irish had no swords). Despite their lack of pikes, Montrose's men were able to withstand Elcho's cavalry. Two weeks later, at the Battle of Aberdeen, the Highlanders again demonstrated that they could maintain discipline on the battlefield and neutralize a cavalry charge.[48]

Montrose could win battles with the help of his Highlanders, but he could not win the support of the Scots nobility, and he alienated many other potential supporters in Scotland. The city of Aberdeen is a good case in point. Aberdeen had harboured Catholic sympathizers at the beginning of the Wars of the Three Kingdoms. Montrose had been there in 1639 as a Covenanter commander, when his soldiers were billeted upon the city and lived at free quarter. The people of Aberdeen could not help but notice that Argyll maintained better control of his men. When Montrose returned in September 1644 with an army made up mostly of Royalist Highlanders, he called upon the Covenanter garrison to surrender. Women, children and the elderly were to be sent out, and those remaining would have no quarter. When a drummer accompanying Montrose's envoys was shot in violation of the truce, Montrose gave orders to spare no one. Montrose was not a bloodthirsty man, but he believed that the Covenanters needed to be punished for not observing the conventions of war. Montrose's soldiers raped and slaughtered for three days before he could restore order. Aberdeen was not a Covenanting town, but this rampage cost him potential support.[49]

However effective MacColla's men were on the battlefield, they remained an undisciplined rabble at other times. They had to be kept on the move or they would desert; they refused to continue fighting in the Lowlands, and they resented being denied plunder for political reasons or because military objectives had to be pursued. The behaviour of MacColla's soldiers led Lowlanders to view

---

[48] Macinnes, *CC* 99–104; Wishart, *Memoirs of James Marquis of Montrose*, 54–62; Patrick Gordon of Ruthven, *A Short Abridgement of Britane's Distemper from the Yeare of God 1639 to 1649*, ed. J. Dunn, SC 10 (1844), 73–5, 82–3; Hill, *Celtic Warfare*, 45–8; id., 'The Distinctiveness of Gaelic Warfare', 335; Furgol, 'Civil Wars in Scotland', 58.

[49] Gordon, *Scots Affairs*, ii. 228–9; S. Reid, *The Campaigns of Montrose: A Military History of the Civil War in Scotland, 1639–1646* (1990), 174; Cowan, *Montrose*, 164–8.

Highland troops as bloodthirsty savages and tended to widen the cultural and religious divisions between themselves and Highlanders. Montrose's campaigns failed to destroy the Covenanters militarily or the power of Argyll and the Campbells, and MacColla failed to re-establish the Clan Ian Mor in the Isles. Montrose and MacColla drifted apart, and the former was deserted by the Gordons. After defeat, Montrose went into exile in an attempt to find arms and munitions and to raise more troops. He returned to Scotland by way of the Orkneys in March 1650, having lost part of his force of German and Danish mercenaries at sea, and was defeated at Carbisdale in April 1650. He was then taken to Edinburgh by the Covenanters and executed.[50]

Charles I's cousin, James, duke of Hamilton, although a less inspiring figure than Montrose, was more successful in bringing together members of the Scottish nobility, Royalists and moderate Covenanters than Montrose. In late September 1647 Hamilton, taking advantage of growing disenchantment with the authoritarian tendencies of the Covenanter government, fear of the English Parliamentarians and especially the growing power of the Independents in the Parliamentarian party and army, entered into the 'Engagement' with Charles I during his escape to the Isle of Wight, to introduce Presbyterianism into England for a three-year trial period in return for military assistance to the king. Although the Scottish Estates sanctioned the Engagement, the General Assembly of the Kirk opposed it, and obstructed recruiting efforts to such an extent that when Hamilton marched south into north-western England, he lacked the men and materiel to defeat the Parliamentary forces. His army and their English Royalist allies suffered two crushing defeats at Winwick and Preston in August 1648.[51]

Following the execution of Charles I in January 1649, the Scots indicated a preference for continuing the monarchy by proclaiming Charles II king of Scotland, England, Ireland and France even before the Rump Parliament had formally abolished it and inaugurated the Commonwealth. Thus did the Covenanters announce their intention of imposing Presbyterianism and monarchy on the Three Kingdoms. The Scots had invaded England three times within the previous ten years, but now the Commonwealth government sent Cromwell and the New Model Army northwards to invade Scotland. Beginning with the Battle of Dunbar in September 1650, the conquest of Scotland was set in motion. Cromwell had hoped for a negotiated peace, but Scottish resistance caused the war to drag on, exhausting Scottish resources and decimating the manpower of the realm. Although the Battle of Worcester, where Charles II and the English and Scottish Royalists were defeated in September 1650, is often considered the last major battle of the Wars of the Three Kingdoms, the

[50] Stevenson, *Alasdair MacColla*, 267–8; Cowan, *Montrose*, 164–8, 173–87, 213, 229–30, 257–9, 261–79; Macinnes, *CC* 92–4; Furgol, 'Civil Wars in Scotland', 65.

[51] Brown, *Kingdom or Province?*, 134–6; Furgol, 'Civil Wars in Scotland', 63–4; D. Stevenson, *Revolution and Counter-Revolution in Scotland, 1644–1651* (1977), 94–114.

Cromwellian conquest of Scotland remained tenuous, and resistance continued for several more years.[52]

Despite the several incursions of Scottish armies into England, the Cromwellian conquest of Scotland was far more restrained than that of Ireland. When Cromwell invaded Scotland in 1650–1 he made sure that his troops, who eventually totalled 20,000, were well supplied and provisioned, so that his army did not have to waste time and manpower foraging. This made the task of maintaining discipline easier, and he was able to concentrate his forces for the task of subduing David Leslie's army. John Nicoll says that pillaging, drunkenness and mutiny were punished very severely by officers of the New Model Army in Scotland, but adds that he thought the English army commanders were interested only in making a few examples in order to maintain discipline and to make a statement to the Scots rather than in doing justice in the case of every complaint received from the civilian population. The men of the New Model Army still had to be rewarded, and when they stormed Dundee on 1 September 1651 the English soldiers, having killed some 700 or 800 Scots in the assault, grew 'rich and gallant' from the plunder. However, standing orders for the pacification of Scotland limited the plundering to a period of twenty-four hours.[53]

Resistance to the English occupation continued until 1655 in the Highlands and the eastern peripheries, the Borders and the western shires. The English land forces were stretched thin, and the outbreak of the First Anglo-Dutch War in 1652 raised the possibility that the pro-Stuart Dutch navy might occupy the Shetlands or the Orkneys. In any case, the English navy could not effectively patrol the whole coast of Scotland and prevent the landing of Royalist reinforcements. It was William Cunningham, ninth earl of Glencairn, who kept the resistance to the English occupation alive. Glencairn was a courageous and respected officer who led the retreat of those Scots who had survived the Battle of Worcester and escaped capture. The army that Glencairn raised was diverse, although the largest contingent consisted of Highlanders. Both Sir Ewen Cameron of Lochiell and John Graham of Deuchrie later claimed to have been the first to join Glencairn's Rebellion.[54] Locheill brought 700 Highlanders—about half of them armed with bows and arrows—but most Highland chiefs hosted fewer than 100 men. Archibald Campbell, Lord Lorne (and later ninth earl of Argyll), was accompanied by 1,000 foot and fifty horse, but grew discontented and remained only two weeks before deserting to the English. The Campbell foot

[52] Brown, *Kingdom or Province?*, 134–6; Macinnes, *CC* 108–10; Stevenson, *Revolution and Counter-Revolution*, 165–210.

[53] Gentles, *NMA* 387–8, 391–8; John Nicoll, *A Diary of Public Transactions and other Occurrences*, ed. D. Laing, BC 52 (1836), 33; Bulstrode Whitelocke, *Memorials of English Affairs*, 4 vols. (1682; repr. 1853), iii. 351; C. H. Firth (ed.), *Scotland and the Commonwealth: Letters and Papers Relating to the Military Government of Scotland, 1651–1653*, SHS 18 (1895), pp. xxxiii, 15–16.

[54] J. Macknight (ed.), *Memoirs of Sir Ewen Cameron of Lochiell*, MC 59 (1842), 97–8; John Graham of Deuchrie, *The Expedition of William, Ninth Earl of Glencairn*, Miscellanea Scotica, 4 (1819), 61.

chose to remain, but were widely distrusted. Glencairn allowed them to re-enlist after swearing another oath of allegiance. Other notable adherents of Glencairn included John Murray, second earl (and later first marquis) of Atholl, who raised a regiment of 1,200 foot and 100 horse, and Major-General William Drummond (later fourth Lord Maderty and first Viscount Strathallan) and Thomas Dalyell, who had both served in the Russian army as lieutenant-generals. One of the most colourful of Glencairn's volunteers was an Irish colonel, Edward Wogan, who, although he came from an Old English Catholic family of the Pale, was probably a Protestant. He had served in Okey's Dragoons in the Parliamentary army earlier in the civil wars, before becoming a Royalist. When he defected from the Parliamentary army during the Second English Civil War, he led his whole troop from southern England through hostile territory, stormed Carlisle Castle and freed 200 Royalist prisoners, before making his way to Scotland where he commanded a Royalist cavalry regiment. He then returned to Ireland to serve under Ormonde. Subsequently, he joined Glencairn's Rebellion, and was killed at the age of 28 in a skirmish with a regiment of Cromwellian cavalry.[55] James Graham, second marquis and son of the great Montrose, also served under Glencairn, as did James Somerville of Drum and Cambusnethan, a former lieutenant-colonel in the Covenanting Army, who converted to Royalism after he had become disenchanted with the feuding and backbiting in the Covenanting movement. He was commissioned by Glencairn to raise a regiment in Clydesdale, his home district, but was unable to do so because of the English occupation. After Glencairn's defeat at Dunbarton, Somerville's family was surprised to see him return home in Highland dress.[56]

Gradually, Glencairn's army grew large enough for him to advance into the Lowlands, and taking advantage of the fact that General Monck had been confined to his sickbed, he fought a successful battle with Colonel Kidd, the Cromwellian governor of Stirling Castle at Aberfoyle Pass, and successfully repulsed at Cromar Major-General Thomas Morgan's men from the English garrison at Aberdeen. More Highland chiefs now joined Glencairn: the laird of Glengarry came with 300 men, Locheill raised another 400 Lochaber men, and the tutor of MacGregor 200. However, Glencairn's army, made up of Lowlanders, mosstroopers and Highlanders from clans that had often been rivals in the past, was rent by factionalism and defections. King Charles II had designated John Middleton (later first earl of Middleton) to command the Royalist forces in Scotland. Charles later explained that he was merely following the precedent of the Covenanting Army in assigning the nobility to recruiting duties, but employing

[55] Macknight (ed.), *Memoirs of Sir Ewen Cameron*, 97–9; Graham, *Expedition of William . . . Earl of Glencairn*, 63–7; *DNB*, *sub* Thomas Dalyell *or* Dalzell (1599?–1685) and William Drummond, 1st viscount of Strathallan (1617?–1688); SSNE, no. 6632; D. Murtagh, 'Colonel Edward Wogan', *IS* 2 (1954–6), 45–53.

[56] *DNB*, *sub* James Graham, 2nd marquis of Montrose (1631?–1669); James [by right 11th Lord] Somerville, *Memorie of the Somervilles* [ed. Sir W. Scott], 2 vols. (1815), ii. 361–5, 466–7.

professional soldiers as general officers. Glencairn met up with Middleton in Sutherland in March 1654. Middleton had been a Covenanter, but became a firm Royalist after the execution of the Charles I. He commanded Charles II's cavalry at the Battle of Worcester, but was captured and imprisoned in the Tower of London, whence he escaped disguised in his wife's clothing, before making his way into exile and joining the court of Charles II in France. After turning command of the Royalist forces over to Middleton, Glencairn sought to fight a duel with Sir George Munro, who had insulted Glencairn and his Highlanders the previous evening, calling them 'nothing but a number of thieves and robbers'. Middleton tried to compose the quarrel, and Glencairn agreed to pledge friendship to Munro with a cup of wine, but Munro sullenly refused to do the like. They fought their duel before dawn, and Glencairn gave Munro two bad wounds before the former's manservant stopped the fight. Middleton took away Glencairn's sword and placed him under arrest. Glencairn then departed Middleton's camp with his troop of horse, although he continued to recruit for his army. Middleton's army began to disintegrate after another encounter with Morgan's forces at Lochgarie.[57]

Cromwell had left George Monck in Scotland in 1651 as commander-in-chief, and charged him with cleaning up the ragged ends of the English conquest— especially in the Highlands. English soldiers found it very difficult to fight in the Highlands. They were not only intimidated by the ruggedness of the terrain and the changeable weather, but also by their awareness that they were constantly followed by Highlanders who knew how to use the terrain to their advantage, and who sniped at them from time to time. Logistical support was also a problem, because Lowland teamsters were reluctant to go where their fathers had never gone before. The Parliamentary army lacked sufficient cavalry even in the Lowlands to prevent the plundering raids of mosstroopers. Although eleven regiments of foot would have been sufficient to defeat any Royalist army in a pitched battle, in actuality that army was dispersed, as in Ireland, among many small garrisons.[58] General Monck established magazines and garrisons in the Highlands and then ordered two expeditionary forces to follow under the command of Thomas Morgan and himself in an attempt to prevent Glencairn and Middleton from joining together. Monck was always prepared to offer generous terms to those Scots who were willing to submit, but in those districts which offered resistance he employed fire and sword. Monck had at first wished to use special courts martial to try the chief leaders of the rebellion and to punish mosstroopers, who continued to be active in the Border region, but Cromwell

[57] Macknight (ed.), *Memoirs of Sir Ewen Cameron*, 97–101; Graham, *Expedition of William...
Earl of Glencairn*, 67–75; *Scotland and the Commonwealth*, ed. Firth, 204–5, 230–1; G. H. Jones,
Charles Middleton: The Life and Times of a Restoration Politician (1967), 3–4; C. H. Firth (ed.),
Scotland and the Protectorate: Letters and Papers Relating to the Military Government of Scotland, SHS
31 (1899), 28–9.
[58] Firth (ed.), *Scotland and the Commonwealth*, pp. xlviii–lii, 204–5, 230–1, 361.

reserved the death penalty for spies, English deserters and those prisoners of war who broke their parole. In 1655 Cromwell, fearing that the Royalist rebellion in Scotland would spread to England, offered Middleton and the Scottish Royalists generous terms. Middleton, who had retreated to Dunvegan on the Isle of Skye, advised the Highland chiefs to accept Cromwell's offer, but some of his other followers joined the mosstroopers in their continuing guerilla war on the Borders.[59] Before accepting the terms of surrender, Locheill sought to give himself a more advantageous position for negotiation. This he did by ambushing and slaughtering several hunting parties from the English garrison at Inverlochy. The governor of the garrison lost most of the officers of two regiments as a consequence. He then kidnapped three English colonels, treated them with great courtesy and allowed them to act as the emissaries of one of the last Highland chiefs from Glencairn's Rebellion to hold out. One of the colonels negotiated Locheill's terms of surrender directly with Monck. Monck granted Locheill a full indemnity, his soldiers were allowed to retain their arms and he was also awarded reparations for damages done to his lands by Monck's soldiers—surely extraordinarily generous for terms granted to the losing side![60]

This was the price that Monck had to pay for achieving a greater degree of peace than perhaps the Highlands had ever known. He and Cromwell also sought to dampen down feuds within Scottish society which could rekindle the flames. When an enemy of Sir Thomas Urquhart of Cromarty procured the quartering of a troop of horse upon Urquhart's tenants and the use of his house as a garrison while he was imprisoned in the Tower of London, the English government intervened and countermanded the order. Monck also discouraged James Livingstone, first earl of Callendar, from attempting to prosecute Locheill for an alleged riot committed in 1651. Monck cited a well established Scottish legal precedent, 'to give indemnity to all thefts and robberies committed in time of war that such things, being in oblivion, the public peace might be the better preserved'.[61]

William Douglas, first earl of Selkirk (and afterwards third duke of Hamilton), had also participated in Glencairn's rising, and submitted to Monck in 1655. He was required to enter into a bond of English £4,000 to remain at peace with the protector and the Commonwealth, and also received an indemnity. In addition he was granted a licence to raise a regiment for French service and was to be allowed to replenish it every two years. The same privilege was granted to William, third Lord Cranstoun, a military enterpriser for the king of Sweden, and to four other peers and a number of gentlemen to levy regiments of 1,200 men each for foreign service in France or Sweden. Charles II regarded the exile of so many swordsmen as prejudicial to his service and mischievous to the kingdom, and he

[59] Firth (ed.), *Scotland and the Commonwealth*, pp. xxx–xxxi, 268, 361; George Monck, duke of Albemarle, *Observations upon Military and Political Affairs* (1671), 4–5; Nicoll, *Diary of Public Transactions*, 175; Macknight (ed.), *Memoirs of Sir Ewen Cameron*, 109–10, 137–9.

[60] Macknight (ed.), *Memoir of Sir Ewen Cameron*, 137–9, 149–50, 160.

[61] Hopkins, *Glencoe*, 28–9; Sir Thomas Urquhart of Cromarty, *Logopandecteision* (1653), in *Works*, MC 30 (1834), 380–1; Macknight (ed.), *Memoirs of Sir Ewen Cameron*, 160.

attempted to dissuade some of these peers and gentlemen from exercising their licences to levy troops. Although Cromwell and Monck were willing to come to terms with individual lords, lairds and chieftains who had joined Glencairn's Rebellion, it remained their policy either to send their followers into exile as mercenary soldiers or to transport them as indentured servants to the colonies. Monck was persuaded that many people in Scotland were so poor and idle that they did not know how to live except by arms, and that only by banishing them would Scotland acquire peaceful habits.[62]

The tendency to view the British and Irish civil wars as wars of religion seems first to have manifested itself in Ireland, where Protestant propagandists exaggerated the extent of the massacres that occurred during the Irish Rebellion of 1641. So strongly did the distorted recollection of these events penetrate the collective memory of Irish and English Protestants that, for years to come, no amount of rational argument and empirical evidence could dispel these myths.[63] This had the effect of making the conflict more bitter; it led to atrocities during the Cromwellian conquest by commanders who ought to have been familiar with the received rules of war, and consequently, by stiffening the resistance of the Confederate Irish, prolonged the conflict, unnecessarily wasted English and Irish lives and poisoned the memory of future generations. Although the biographers of Cromwell often proclaim that the protector's aim was to bring peace and stability to the British Isles and make Ireland safe from foreign invasion, his efforts to pursue such a policy were often counter-productive. It was not the only time that Cromwell and his party allowed desire for revenge and satisfaction of honour to cloud their judgement and defeat their political and military objectives. Moreover, the Anglocentric policies of officials such as Lord Deputy Leicester, Protector Cromwell and the Independents alerted the Scots to the danger that English imperialism posed to the constitution, the Presbyterian religious settlement and the autonomy of Scotland. Again, this had the effect of driving more and more Scots into the hands of the Royalists, and made the conquest of Scotland more prolonged and bloody.

Because of the perennial shortages of military manpower in England, the English conquest of Ireland in the late Elizabethan period necessitated the use of Old Irish and Old English soldiers, despite official limits on the use of such individuals. Following the end of the Irish Nine Years War, these swordsmen were sent into exile by Lord Deputy Mountjoy, who assumed that they would never return. (The same assumption was made by the Scottish Privy Council when they licensed the raising of mercenary soldiers for the armies of northern Europe.) But return they

[62] Firth (ed.), *Scotland and the Protectorate*, pp. xxxii, 44, 80–2, 99–100, 153–4, 159, 164, 167, 178, 189, 272, 276, 286–9, 321, 352; John Thurloe, *A Collection of State Papers*, ed. Thomas Birch, 7 vols. (1742), iv. 41; Nicoll, *Diary of Public Transactions*, 175.

[63] D. Woolff, *The Social Circulation of the Past: English Historical Culture, 1500–1730* (2003), 362 n.; L. Colley, *Britons: Forging the Nation, 1707–1837* (1992), 330–1.

did in the early 1640s, when they or their descendants found their way into Strafford's New Irish Army. When Strafford's recall caused that force to disintegrate, many of those soldiers participated in the Irish Rebellion of 1641, just as the Covenanting Army recruited its cadre from veterans of the armies of northern Europe in 1638–40. As a consequence, Irish society was militarized in ways never intended by the English governors. The Covenanter system of national conscription also had the effect of remilitarizing the Lowlands, and because both the Covenanters and the Royalists turned to the Highlanders as a source of military manpower, the clansmen were increasingly brought into contact with the European military world to a degree that could not have been predicted in the early 1640s. The use of Irish soldiers by Strafford and Charles I in both Ireland and England and later in Scotland cost the Royalists much popular support, and as a result, limited the areas in which the Royalists could recruit. The Covenanters were also more successful in forging a national identity that enjoyed popular support than were the Irish Confederates.

Beyond provoking widespread fear and dislike of popery, the extensive recruiting of Irish soldiers did little to win popular support for the Royalists, and many areas of England displayed neutralist sentiments. The Royalist armies recruited a disproportionate number of their soldiers in Wales and the north, but many Royalist soldiers who subsequently became prisoners of war were persuaded to enlist in the Parliamentary forces. Both Royalist and Parliamentarian armies also relied upon Scottish swordsmen for officers at all levels of command. Until Cromwell's purge of Scots and Presbyterians from the Parliamentary armies and the rise of the Independents, popular support for fighting the civil wars remained weak, while Royalist regiments sometimes consisted disproportionately of gentlemen volunteers and reformado officers. In the long run, the reliance of English armies during the earlier civil wars on officers and soldiers from Ireland and Scotland continued a process of integration of soldiers from the Three Kingdoms, which had begun during the Dutch war of independence in the late sixteenth and early seventeenth centuries when they served together in the States' Army in large numbers, and was to continue in the English standing army after the Restoration of Charles II. When the Act of Union was enacted in 1707, this process of assimilating Scots and Irish soldiers into a truly British army had been going on for several generations. During the late eighteenth century, as the manpower needs of the British army increased under the stress of global warfare, the Whiggish objection to employing Catholic officers and soldiers from Ireland and the Highlands diminished and finally disappeared. A great military power with imperialist ambitions cannot be too fussy about the religion of the soldiers it employs.

PART III

THE DECAY OF A MILITARY TRADITION
1660–1688

11

Standing armies in the Three Kingdoms

War is no longer an accident but a trade, and they that will be anything in it must serve a long apprenticeship to it. Human wit and industry has raised it to such a perfection, and it is grown to such a piece of manage that it requires people to make it their whole employment.

> [Daniel Defoe], *A Brief Reply to the History of Standing Armies in England* (1698), 14.

Nothing makes the king's power to be so adored as the evidence that in a moment he can raise a favourite from the lowest condition to far above what ancient nobles have arrived unto, or what their ancestors in many ages have purchased by their services or their blood. Our court way to it is easy and pleasant; the way of rising by war is with difficulty and danger.

> Algernon Sidney, *Court Maxims*, ed. H. W. Blom, E. H. Mulier and R. Janse (1996), 68.

The politically articulate classes in Restoration England generally regarded standing armies as odious, and were anxious to see the New Model Army disbanded. Charles II was allowed by Parliament to retain guards and garrisons as long as he paid for them. However, there were Royalist swordsmen who needed to be rewarded with military offices, and General Monck's regiment was retained from the Cromwellian forces as a reward for his part in effecting the Restoration of the Stuart monarchy. Those Cromwellian soldiers who were not content to return to their pre-war occupations were encouraged to seek employment in mainland European armies. Although the term 'standing army' would gradually lose some of the connotations of a mercenary band and come to mean a professional and long-service force which was loyal to and paid by the state, the events surrounding the Second and Third Anglo-Dutch Wars and the suppression of Monmouth's Rebellion revived the fear of an expanded standing army as a tool of absolutism and popery in the French manner. Moreover, the need to buy or reward the support of the aristocracy wiped out whatever progress towards a merit system of awarding military office had been achieved in the Parliamentarian and Royalist armies during the civil wars, and reasserted the distinction between gentlemen and career officers. A purchase system for commissions took root and enjoyed official sanction, and many experienced officers and soldiers were driven into destitution or military service abroad. Some of the king's military forces were loaned or leased to mainland European armies or hidden away in Tangier, Ireland or other colonies. In the absence of barracks, and prior to the Mutiny Act of 1689, maintaining discipline remained problematical. Factionalism and the political intrigues of the officers undermined the loyalty of the army and bred discord. The expansion of the armies of the Three Kingdoms under Charles II and James VII and II only exacerbated these problems.

Most old Cromwellians were turned out of military office in England, but the Cromwellian adventurers in Ireland were deemed necessary for preserving the Stuart regime. This was especially true of Roger Boyle, earl of Orrery, who had been instrumental in the Restoration of Charles II in Ireland. Although he never held an Irish office of higher rank than president of Munster, Orrery was powerful enough to have James Butler, first duke of Ormonde, removed as viceroy. Under Orrery's influence the Irish army was highly politicized, and he built up a party which was later hostile to Richard Talbot, duke of Tyrconnell's attempt to Catholicize the officer ranks of James II's Irish army. Failure to pay the Irish army left it in a perpetual state of mutiny. The Irish army had been scattered in small garrisons so that the officers might live on their own estates, until the independent companies were regimented under James II. The Irish army was useless for suppressing banditry in the countryside, and would have been incapable of repelling a French invasion. Tyrconnell's control of the Irish army diminished the powers of the lord-lieutenant, alienated moderate supporters of the regime and infuriated Protestants.

In Scotland, military patronage was also an important source of support for the later Stuarts during the Restoration, but there were never enough offices in the Scots army or the Scots regiments of the English army to go around. The small Scottish army was employed to enforce religious uniformity and to crush Covenanter rebellions as well as the Argyll Rebellion of 1685. The use of Highlanders to assist the army in this task was disruptive and unpopular. The allegedly cruel tactics of officers such as Thomas Dalzell did much to make the Scots army unpopular, and the English Parliament feared that James VII and II might employ it against them, or use it to help the French fight Protestants in mainland Europe.

The bravery which Charles II had shown in leading cavalry charges through the streets of Worcester in September 1651 helped to restore some prestige to the Stuart monarchy among swordsmen during the king's exile following his remarkable escape to the continent. Many of the Royalist soldiers who had not been killed or captured at the Battle of Worcester or sold into indentured servitude in the plantations followed Charles to France and, later, the Low Countries. Their circumstances were unhappy, many took service in mainland European armies and factionalism divided their ranks. The division between the courtier faction, led by George, Lord Digby (subsequently second earl of Bristol), and the 'soldiers of fortune', who gathered around Prince Rupert, continued to fester: when Digby landed in France in 1649, he was challenged to a duel by Henry, Lord Wilmot (later first earl of Rochester). Digby became a lieutenant-general in the French Royal Army, but was later banished after becoming involved in an intrigue against Cardinal Mazarin. Most Royalists would have preferred to have taken service with the French Royal Army, but Cromwell's treaty with France forced them to leave and seek refuge in the Spanish Netherlands, where they formed an English brigade in the Spanish Army of Flanders which engaged them in a war with France. The earl of Rochester commanded a regiment of English guards in that brigade, and John, first earl of Middleton, commanded a Scots regiment which was, in part, recruited from among former Royalist officers and Scottish deserters from the Swedish army. An Irish regiment was led by James, first duke of Ormonde.[1] These Royalist troops, fighting under the Spanish flag, engaged a contingent of the New Model Army sent by Cromwell to fight alongside the French army at the Battle of the Dunes in June 1658 in an attempt to seize Dunkirk from the Spaniards. This small Royalist army, still in the service of Spain, was abandoned by Charles when he returned to England at the Restoration.[2]

A large standing army was out of the question when Charles returned to England in May 1660. The memory of the rule of the major-generals ensured that, and many also remembered the depredations of Royalist armies during the civil wars. The cost of maintaining a large standing army had also been a great burden during the Commonwealth and Protectorate. In 1665 the Venetian ambassador told the Grand Council of Venice that the cost of keeping a standing army absorbed most of the revenues that the government raised. No king had 'ever squeezed so much money out of the people as he [Cromwell] now gathers in'. Because Cromwell believed that he could not trust the nobility, he made it a policy to give military commissions to men of humble birth so as to give them a vested interest in maintaining the Protectorate. This interest made it difficult for Charles to gain support for a return of the monarchy. Despite the brave and sensible efforts of the new lord protector, Richard Cromwell, who succeeded in winning support from many of the grandees and senior officers, he failed to gain the backing of the junior officers and the rank and file of the New Model Army, who had grown used to having their say in the affairs of the Commonwealth. The Protectorate began to disintegrate, and with Parliament dissolved, there was no way of paying the army off. General Monck returned from Coldstream on the Scottish Border with a well disciplined force, declaring that the lesson he had learned as a career officer in the Dutch army was that military officers took their orders from the civilian government rather than giving them; he recalled the Long

---

[1] I. Gentles, *NMA* 409; E. Warburton, *Memoirs of Prince Rupert and the Cavaliers*, 3 vols. (1849), iii. 220–1; W. Blundell, *Crosby Records: A Cavalier's Notebook*, ed. T. E. Gibson (1880), 154–5; *DNB*, *sub* George Digby, 2nd earl of Bristol (1612–1677); G. H. Jones, *Charles Middleton: The Life and Times of a Restoration Politician* (1967), 3–4; SSNE, no. 6698.
[2] A. Woolrych, *Britain in Revolution, 1625–1660* (Oxford, 2003), 678–81; Childs, *AC* 2–4.

Parliament, including the excluded members, and thus set the stage for the Restoration of Charles II.[3]

The English distaste for standing military forces was acquired from reading Machiavelli and also from the actual experience of the disorders resulting from martial law, billeting and extra-parliamentary taxation associated with the ineptly managed military expeditions of the 1620s. Similar complaints arose from the existence of the Parliamentary armies during the Interregnum and from the political interference in the affairs of Parliament by the New Model Army. The Presbyterian faction in Parliament were able to enact the Militia Ordinance of 1648, which was intended to create a local militia commanded by the aristocracy and which could be used to counterbalance the standing military forces. Four days after the passage of this ordinance Colonel Pride excluded the Presbyterians from Parliament, and the Militia Ordinance was repealed and never implemented, but the fear that its enactment reflected of standing armies did much to shape the political attitudes later associated with the Whig or anti-court party. John Trenchard, who later became a spokesman for that point of view, said of the Cromwellian army that it was raised for a good cause and dedicated to liberty, and yet it was corrupted and tempted to violence against Parliamentary liberties. If this army, which was raised from the people and 'composed for the most part of men of religion and sobriety', could be corrupted, how much more would they have to fear 'a dissolute and debauched army' raised by 'an ambitious prince'.[4]

Despite the strong prejudice against standing armies, the Disbanding Act of 1660, enacted by the Convention Parliament, allowed the king to raise and maintain an unspecified number of guards and garrisons as long as he paid for them. The Cavalier Parliament enacted another statute in 1661 which granted command of the navy and the militia to the king, but Parliament never authorized a further enlargement of the military forces. No previous English monarch had ever possessed control over so sizeable a force in peacetime. The various Republican plots and rebellions that occurred in the early 1660s seemed to justify an enlarged royal guard for the king. However, the expansion of the army during the Third Anglo-Dutch War was a different matter, and thereafter military affairs became a constant source of contention in the king's relations with Parliament.[5] Although Charles II's army was not illegal, the English army cannot be said to have possessed a constitutional foundation until the enactment of the first Mutiny Act

---

[3] Giovanni Sagredo's *Relazione* of 1656, in E. and P. Razzell (eds.), *The English Civil War: A Contemporary Account*, 5 vols. (1996), v. 9–10; J. S. Wheeler, *The Making of a World Power: War and the Military Revolution in Seventeenth-Century England* (1999), 207–9, 213; R. Hainsworth, *The Swordsmen in Power: War and Politics in the English Republic, 1649–1660* (1997), 242–6, 250–68.

[4] Schwoerer, *NSA* 56–7; [John Trenchard], *A Short History of Standing Armies in England* (1698), 10.

[5] F. W. Maitland, *The Constitutional History of England* (1909), 326–7; Schwoerer, *NSA* 72–3; Razzell and Razzell (eds.), *English Civil War*, v. 20–1; James Macpherson (ed.), *Original Papers Containing the Secret History of Great Britain from the Restoration to the Accession of the House of Hannover*, 2 vols. (1775), i. 17–19.

of April 1689 provided full parliamentary recognition of an English standing army, and provided a legal basis for the use of military law and courts martial for enforcing discipline within the realm of England. Until that time military offences were legally determinable only by civil magistrates.[6]

Until the expansion of the army began during the Third Anglo-Dutch War, Charles II's army was adequate only for guarding his person and quelling minor popular disturbances. It certainly would not have been equal to repelling an invasion or deploying an expeditionary force. Its main reason for existence was to reward place-seekers and restless and unemployed soldiers at the time of the Restoration. Except for Monck's Regiment, which became the Coldstream (or Second Foot) Guards, all of the regiments of the Cromwellian army were designated for disbandment. The remainder of the English Royalist Brigade in the garrison of Dunkirk and Mardyke was retrieved to form the First Foot Guards, and Dunkirk was sold to Louis XIV. Together with two bodies of horse, the Life Guards and the Royal Horse Guards, these units constituted the whole of the English army quartered in England in 1660–2. Many Cavalier reformadoes were unable to secure commissions in the armies of the Three Kingdoms, and instead sought places in the ranks of the Life Guards and the Horse Guards. In accommodating them as troopers, they were paid considerably more than private soldiers in the regiments of foot, and, to prevent their officers from exploiting them, the sale of places and promotions in the enlisted ranks was prohibited.[7]

The continuing existence of Cromwell's army had posed a threat to Charles II, and disbandment began with the Restoration. Discharged soldiers were not given their full arrears of pay unless they had been under General Monck's command. They were, however, granted liberty to ply a trade within any municipal corporation. Those soldiers who had been issued debentures in lieu of full pay in 1647, and had sold them to their officers, were not compensated. Cromwellian officers who had purchased estates in England with such debentures lost their lands, but those who had acquired estates in Ireland retained them. Edmund Ludlow thought that the officers who had helped to restore the king had betrayed their oaths of loyalty to Parliament. The disbandment of Cromwell's army was not carried out completely. After his marriage to Catherine of Braganza, Charles sent four regiments of English troops, mostly from the garrison of Leith, purged of their Cromwellian officers and replaced with Royalists, to Portugal to help maintain that kingdom's independence from Spain. Some of the officers and men of the English Brigade in Portugal later returned to the English army when the Third Anglo-Dutch War brought expansion. Another 3,000 men, organized into four regiments of English and Irish troops, were dispatched to garrison England's new colony of Tangier, which was part of the dowry of Queen Catherine. They

---

[6] C. Walton, *History of the British Standing Army, 1660–1700* (1894), 529, 531.

[7] Childs, *AC* 17–19, 233; id., 'The Restoration Army, 1660–1702', in D. Chandler (ed.), *The Oxford Illustrated History of the British Army* (1994), 489, 52; R. E. Scouller, 'Purchase of Commissions and Promotions', *JSAHR* 62 (1984), 217.

came from recently discharged Cromwellian soldiers and from a regiment which had been in Dunkirk.[8]

It was not easy integrating the old Cromwellians into the army and navy or government during the Restoration period, because old allegiances were not soon forgotten. On the eve of the Restoration, the duke of Newcastle reminded Charles II that it was not the clergy or lawyers who provided his father with men and money during the civil wars but the peerage and the gentry. Therefore the king would do well to remember that they were the principal bulwark of the monarchy. At the beginning of the Second Anglo-Dutch War in 1665, Lieutenant Mansell of the *Rainbow* was tried before a court-martial aboard the *Royal Charles* presided over by the Lord Admiral James, duke of York, Prince Rupert and Edward Montagu, first earl of Sandwich, for reproaching his captain and a major of marines with having served as rebels with Cromwell's commission. He was convicted of disobedience and unruliness and cashiered from the navy. The duke of York afterwards made a speech stating that the king and he did not wish to have reference made to past allegiances, and that they regarded all of their officers as good subjects.[9] Algernon Sidney was conscious of following the example of his grand-uncle, Sir Philip Sidney, whom he viewed as a martyr to the cause of Dutch independence and Protestant liberty. During the exclusion crisis of 1678–83 Sidney adapted these principles to the cause of a republican ideology which he put to use in trying to revive the English civil wars.[10] The dangers posed by the conspiracies and rebellions of republicans and religious radicals early in the Restoration provoked a search for arms by soldiers, but few people were persuaded that Quakers and Fifth-Monarchy Men constituted any real threat. The Second Anglo-Dutch War of 1665 provided the excuse again to search private homes for weapons, and Parliament demanded that Catholics as well as Protestant dissenters be disarmed. The officers of the militia, however, showed a reluctance to confiscate private property, and it was thought reasonable to allow even Catholics to retain sufficient weapons to defend their persons and their households. Although the militia had been purged of politically suspicious officers, the royal government had come to distrust it and preferred to employ the regular army for maintaining order. This was a politically divisive issue, and after *c*.1675 the followers of Anthony Ashley Cooper, first earl of Shaftesbury, equated standing armies with corruption and the militia with the liberties of the subject.[11]

---

[8] Firth, *CA* 201–7; id., *Ludlow*, ii. 325–6; P. H. Hardacre, 'The English Contingent in Portugal, 1662–1668', *JSAHR* 38 (1960), 112–16.

[9] T. P. Slaughter (ed.), *Ideology and Politics on the Eve of the Restoration: Newcastle's Advice to Charles II*, APSM 159 (1984), 46–7; R. C. Anderson (ed.), *The Journal of Edward Montagu, First Earl of Sandwich, 1659–1665*, NRS 64 (1929), 173.

[10] J. Scott, 'The Laws of War: Grotius, Sidney, Locke and the Political Thought of Rebellion', *History of Political Thought*, 13 (1992), 568, 574.

[11] J. T. Malcolm, *To Keep and Bear Arms: The Origins of an Anglo-American Right* (1994), 78–9; J. G. A. Pocock, *The Machiavellian Moment: Florentine Political Thought and the Atlantic Republican Tradition* (1975), 410.

Scotland was also troubled by difficulties in reconciling old foes. Although General Monck had granted an indemnity to Sir Ewen Cameron of Locheill upon his surrender, such was the terror that Locheill had visited upon his rivals and enemies that there were attempts to settle scores with him after the Restoration. He had incurred the enmity of John Maitland, first duke of Lauderdale, whose faction held sway on the Scottish Privy Council. When Locheill was summoned before the Privy Council and failed to appear, letters of fire and sword were issued against him to a number of peers together with his old rival, Sir Lauchlan Macintosh. The other commissioners refused to help Macintosh execute the commission, and urged him to accept the composition that Locheill had offered. Macintosh's own clansmen were reluctant to follow him, but he was able to host 1,500 followers, of whom 300 were armed with bow and arrow—the last time that a considerable number of soldiers so armed appeared in the Highlands. The two clans were ready to do battle on the banks of Loch Lochy when John Campbell, first earl of Breadalbane, arrived with 300 of his men, and being a kinsman of both chiefs, insisted upon mediating an end to the quarrel.[12] One of the rebels who fought in Argyll's Rebellion of 1685 was an Englishman, Richard Rumbold, described as a 'maltster'. He had also been implicated in the Rye House Plot of 1683, although he denied that accusation. However, he did admit to fighting as a colonel with Argyll's forces, and, upon interrogation, it also came out that he had been present at Charles I's execution as a trooper in Cromwell's Regiment of Horse. He admitted to being a republican, and thought that it was no sin to pull down the monarchy.[13]

Fortunately for Charles II, most of the old Cromwellians and former Parliamentary soldiers were content to go back to their peacetime occupations and live quietly at the Restoration. Pepys contrasted their meek acceptance of the hand of Providence with the swaggering of the Cavaliers:

... of all the old army now, you cannot see a man begging in the street. ... Every man in his apron and frock &c., as if they had never done anything else—whereas the other [the Cavaliers] go with their belts and swords, swearing and cursing and stealing. ... And this is the difference between the temper of one and the other. ... The spirits of the old Parliament soldiers are so quiet and content with God's providences that the king is safer from any evil meant him by them, a thousand times more than from his own discontented Cavaliers.[14]

In order to obtain a commission in Charles II's army, one had to be a former Royalist officer or the son of one, and enjoy the patronage of either George Monck, who was made duke of Albemarle and captain-general, or of James, duke of York. Commissions were obtained by purchase or, more rarely, by gift, and

[12] J. Macknight (ed.), *Memoirs of Sir Ewen Cameron of Locheill*, MC 59 (1842), 182–93.

[13] Sir John Lauder of Fountainhall, *Historical Notices of Scottish Affairs*, ed. D. Laing, 2 vols., BC 87 (1848), ii. 651–2.

[14] R. Latham and W. Matthews (eds.), *The Diary of Samuel Pepys*, 11 vols. (1971), iv. 373–4 (9 Nov. 1663).

many of the higher ranks were held by courtiers, who also served as gentlemen of the wardrobe or bedchamber, or who held some other royal office. For the most part, they remained gentlemen officers and amateurs with no professional training and a diminishing pool of military experience as the old Cavalier officers died off. The garrisons were also commanded by amateurs such as Sir John Reresby, who was governor of York; he was bellicose and frequently challenged others to fight duels, but otherwise never used his sword in battle. Like most garrison officers he regarded his office as a part-time position, and he lacked both experience and professional expertise. Those career or professional officers who wished to learn the exercise of arms and gain actual military experience continued to serve in the Dutch or French armies or in the Tangier garrison and the English Brigade of the Portuguese army. In the standing regiments of the English home army, old Cromwellians were almost entirely confined to the Coldstream Guards, and they had little prospect of advancement unless they served overseas. The English home army was inferior to practically every army of northern Europe, and could not possibly have provided a field force.[15]

The gentlemen officers and the garrison commanders were also highly politicized. They held their military offices because of their social rank, as a reward for services rendered to the crown or because they belonged to a political faction. Essentially they were courtiers—certainly not professional soldiers. Of a sample of 188 who held commissioned rank between 1661 and 1685, John Childs has found that thirty-nine were peers or sons of noblemen, seventy-three were knights or baronets or the sons of the same, while fifty-three came from the ranks of esquires and gentlemen. Only eighteen were of more humble birth. Thus, the officer class was overwhelmingly aristocratic. Social rank carried more weight than one's place in the military hierarchy, and a military career was not a means of social advancement in the standing regiments of the English home army. The professional officers who served overseas were younger sons of gentlemen for the most part or from even more humble backgrounds. Most tellingly, of the 188 officers in Professor Childs's sample, eighty-nine gentlemen officers at some time held seats in the House of Commons, and sixty-one were members of the House of Lords. The professional officers were also highly politicized; fifty-four of them sat in the Commons, and fourteen belonged to the House of Lords.[16]

The idea that swordsmen possessed special inherent gifts that gownsmen and courtiers lacked was fading in the England of Charles II. Although many aristocrats sought places in the Restoration army, they did not feel as compelled to authenticate their honour on the battlefield as earlier generations had. Standing armies existed in the Three Kingdoms in the Restoration period less from military necessity than to provide employment for the aristocracy. Charles II's court had become much more militarized than that of his grandfather James VI and I, but

[15] Childs, *AC* 30–1; J. Carswell, *The Descent on England: A Study of the English Revolution of 1688 and its European Background* (1969), 23; BL, Lansdowne MS. 805 ['Biographical and Highly Sarcastic List'], fos. 83–9; Manning, *Swordsmen*, 150, 201, 213.   [16] Childs, *AC* 37–8.

most of his military officers cannot be said to have undergone the process of professionalization. They did not constitute an officer corps, but merely an officer class.[17] Edmund Verney, having obtained a commission in the Guards in about 1677, represents the attitude of country gentlemen and aristocrats who were not ready to accept the anonymity and discipline of wearing the king's uniform, which they regarded as livery and therefore a mark of servile status. Verney thought it sufficient to wear a habit that was 'soldier-like'. In any case, he did not think that his tailor was equal to duplicating the uniform of an officer of the guards. His father, Sir Ralph Verney, told him that a baronet of Suffolk had appeared at Whitehall in the uniform of an officer, and was laughed out of court. Sir Ralph thought that a suit of armour or a buff coat was a more fitting costume. This attitude was not peculiar to the English aristocracy at this time. Pascal thought that the robe and the sword lived in two different worlds. The gownsmen needed to dress up in elaborate costumes to perform their duties because their authority rested, in part, upon illusion; soldiers did not need to don costumes or uniforms, because their authority was based upon force.[18]

Professional soldiers in the Three Kingdoms and throughout Europe continued to advocate that young gentlemen serve an apprenticeship in arms in the ranks before accepting a commission. In order to build up a political following Charles II ignored this custom, which Roger Boyle, first earl of Orrery, claimed derived from Roman practice. A man might now be made a colonel the first day of his military career, 'so that the necessity of being capable to command before men actually do it being not imposed, it takes away one of the greatest motives to become a soldier. For few will go about and by a rough way when there is a short and smooth one.'[19] The anonymous author of *Advice to a Soldier* (1680) observed that the practice of granting officers preferment without regard to merit discouraged gentlemen of more humble birth who were particularly useful in time of war; he advised the young gentleman to obtain experience as a 'private gentleman' or gentleman volunteer before accepting or purchasing a commission. Honour does not consist in the possession of great offices, but in how one discharges those offices so that the prince is served and the public good advanced, he insisted.[20] Although there were some half-hearted attempts to prohibit the sale of commissions, the practice became regularized and flourished during the Restoration. Charles II not only purchased commissions for his bastard sons, but began levying a tax of 5 per cent on the sale price to support the Royal Hospital, Chelsea. James VII and II also permitted and sanctioned the sale of military commissions. Under the purchase system, the colonel was the proprietor as well as the commander of

---

[17] Ibid. 30–1; A. Vagts, *A History of Militarism*, rev. edn. (1959), 49–50.

[18] F. P. and M. M. Verney, *Memoirs of the Verney Family during the Seventeenth Century*, 2 vols. (1907), ii. 327; Blaise Pascal, *Pensées*, trans. A. J. Krailsheimer (1966; repr. 1986), 39–41.

[19] Roger Boyle, 1st earl of Orrery, *A Treatise of the Art of War* (1677), 15.

[20] *Advice to a Soldier... Written by an Officer in the English Army* (1680), repr. in J. Malham (ed.), *HM*, 12 vols. (1808–11), viii. 353–5.

the regiment, and the captain had the same relationship to his company. Consequently it was difficult to discipline such officers for absence from their units provided those units were where they were supposed to be.[21]

Those former Royalist officers who wished to pursue a military career at the Restoration found that places were hard to come by in the English home army. Since commissions were rarely awarded on the basis of merit, without the recommendation of high birth, the patronage of the dukes of York or Albemarle or the cultivation of the arts of the courtier, the prospects for place or promotion were meagre. John Gwyn was a Royalist from a minor gentry family in Wales. Before the civil wars he had been employed to instruct the royal princes in military exercises. At the time of the Restoration he was a major in the Royal Regiment of Guards, but as the son of a plain gentleman he lacked the social status to retain that rank in peacetime. In 1663 he was listed as an indigent officer and was reduced to serving as a trooper in the Royal Horse Guards. Of the two bodies of Household Cavalry, the Royal Horse Guards were distinctly inferior to the Life Guards. Originally, many of the men of the Royal Horse Guards came from the troopers of Cromwell's Life Guard when it was disbanded, whereas Charles II's Life Guards was mostly made up of Cavalier gentlemen. They were paid 4s. per diem, whereas the Royal Horse Guards received only 2s. 6d. As the old Royalist reformadoes faded away and died off, the Life Guards became a kind of school 'for young gentlemen of very considerable families, who are there made fit for military commands'. They were also more privileged than the Royal Horse Guards: unlike them, they did not perform police duties, and were not detached for foreign service. How effective the Life Guards was as a school of war is debatable. Algernon Sidney accused Charles II of endeavouring 'to corrupt, ruin, and effeminate the nobility which ought to be the leaders of the people for redress of grievances and against foreign enemies'.[22]

Daniel Defoe, who entered into the standing-army controversy in the 1690s with John Trenchard and other enemies of permanent military forces, thought that the long period of peace since the end of the civil wars had produced a large degree of ignorance and inexperience among the officers of the English army, and that they had failed to keep pace with the rapid changes in the art of war in the second half of the seventeenth century.[23] This is also reflected in the military literature of the Restoration period. The early seventeenth century saw the publication of a rich literature of military treatises, memoirs and drill manuals by writers from

[21] Scouller, 'Purchase of Commissions and Promotion', 217–20; id., *The Armies of Queen Anne* (Oxford, 1966), 278–9; Walton, *British Standing Army*, 451–2.

[22] Edward Ward, *Mars Stript of his Armour: Or, the Army Displayed in all its True Colours* (1709), 8–9; N. Tucker (ed.), *The Military Memoirs of Captain John Gwyn* (1822), in P. Young (ed.), *Military Memoirs: The Civil War* (1967), 39–40; *DNB, sub* John Gwynne (*fl.* 1660); Childs, *AC* 21–2, 34–5, 257–8; Algernon Sidney, *Court Maxims*, ed. H. W. Blom, E. H. Mulier and P. Janse (1996), 78.

[23] Daniel Defoe, *A Brief Reply to the History of Standing Armies in England* (1698), 14; id., *An Essay upon Projects* (1697), 254–6. See also G. Hanlon, *The Twilight of a Military Tradition: Italian Aristocrats and European Conflicts, 1560–1800* (1998), 350–1.

the Three Kingdoms which recorded their observations on the significant changes occurring in military theory and practice based upon their experience in the mainland European armies during the Eighty Years War, the Thirty Years War and the Northern Wars of Scandinavia and Russia. Perhaps because so many people were war-weary, military theorists were thinner on the ground in the Restoration period. Sir James Turner was the author of an important military treatise which reflected his extensive experience in the Thirty Years War and the Wars of the Three Kingdoms, but which must have been dated when it was published in 1683.[24] The earl of Orrery also wrote a military treatise, but his experience was limited to the Irish civil wars.[25]

During this same period, the monarchs of mainland Europe developed military academies and promoted the professionalization of their officer corps, but England neglected such developments, and when the Three Kingdoms were drawn into the continental wars after 1689, the officers who served William II and III were mostly foreigners or English and Scots who had served in the Dutch or other mainland European armies.[26] Charles II's government was presented with a proposal for a professional military academy patterned after similar schools operating in Italy and France. This scheme, put forward in the late 1670s by Solomon de Foubert, a Huguenot who had operated an academy in Paris, failed to attract support from the king and his courtiers who were at the time distracted by the Popish Plot, but encouragement was offered to Foubert to establish a riding academy which he opened in Piccadilly. Foubert's academy continued to operate for the remainder of the century, and taught fencing, riding, mathematics and the exercise of arms. However, there was no official support for putting Foubert's academy on a more permanent and professional footing.[27] Daniel Defoe came up with another proposal to establish a royal military academy in 1697. One part of his proposed 'Royal Academy for Military Exercises' would have trained officers for the artillery and the engineers. Defoe thought that a faculty of twenty-six officers to teach 2,000 cadets in a building four times the size of the Royal Hospital, Chelsea, would be adequate for his military academy. It would be another half-century before the first Royal Military College was established at Woolwich.[28]

Except for regiments detached for foreign service, the English home army never deployed in battle before William III's descent on England in 1688. Under Charles II, it was rare for a unit larger than a company to drill or train together.

[24] Sir James Turner, *Pallas Armata: Military Essayes of the Ancient Grecian, Roman and Modern Art of War, Written in the Years 1670 and 1671* (1683); Childs, *AC* 63–4. Turner's valuable memoir, *Memoirs of his Own Life and Times (1632–1670)*, BC 28 (1829), was published only in the 19th century. Although Turner had risen to the rank of major-general in the civil wars, he was reduced to serving as a major in the Foot Guards and later the Regiment of Dragoons in the Scots Army of the Restoration.   [25] Roger Boyle, 1st earl of Orrery, *A Treatise of the Art of War* (1677).
[26] Vagts, *History of Militarism*, 56.
[27] W. H. Manchée, 'The Fouberts and their Royal Academy', *PHSL* 16 (1938–41), 77–97; Childs, *AC* 65–6.   [28] Defoe, *Essay upon Projects*, 260–77.

Because the concept of a military hierarchy had not supplanted social hierarchies in Charles II's army, it was not possible to establish a chain of command, and it is difficult to imagine what would have held such an army together in the heat of battle—nor does the performance of James VII and II's army of 1688 offer a compelling reason to think otherwise. The failure of James's English army to offer substantial resistance to William's invading force can be blamed on James's indecisiveness and the shifting allegiances of his officers, but attention should also be paid to the deficiency of training and discipline which was characteristic of the military culture of Charles II's home army.[29] Discipline had been weak among the officers of the army. In November 1678, when war with France seemed likely after England had realigned herself with the Netherlands and Spain, a captain in Sir Henry Gooderick's Regiment, which was raised for service in Flanders, resigned his commission in order to challenge his colonel to a duel. Gooderick accepted the challenge and recruited a second for a multiple combat. Gooderick's second killed the captain with a thrust through the body, but Gooderick was also wounded. Experienced military commanders recognized that duelling was subversive of military hierarchies and discipline, but this evil practice continued in the English army throughout the seventeenth century.[30]

The manuals of drill of the late seventeenth century reveal that colonels had limited contact with soldiers of their regiments. Colonels were often absent recruiting soldiers, and rarely went into the field with their men. The colonel was also responsible for paying, provisioning, clothing and supplying his regiment. Discipline too was his responsibility, but this was a duty that was usually delegated. Colonelcies and other military commissions were given out to members of Parliament to buy votes during the expansion of the army in 1678 when war with France was expected. A regiment was essentially a recruiting device rather than a tactical unit; it might consist of one or more battalions. Battalions were commanded in the field by lieutenant-colonels who were more likely to be experienced soldiers. The sergeant-major, by now usually shortened to major, was the source of orders and commands and was the officer primarily responsible for drilling the battalion, although some of his duties devolved upon the adjutant.[31] However, an official drill manual of 1682 stated that the major and the adjutant were always to be present when the companies were drilled in order to issue commands. Soldiers were to be instructed by the subaltern officers of the company.[32]

English military treatises of this period tended to be preoccupied with place, order and precedence on the parade ground and the battlefield as a tableau of hierarchy. Pikemen always marched onto the parade ground before the musketeers because the pike was the more ancient weapon, and pikemen were often gentlemen volunteers. The earl of Orrery, perceiving the obsession with the precedence

---

[29] Cf. Childs, *AC* 44; id., *AJGR* 185–90.

[30] A. Browning (ed.), *Memoirs of Sir John Reresby* (1936), 160; Childs, *AC* 235; Manning, *Swordsmen*, 226–8, 231–2, 234–44.   [31] Walton, *British Standing Army*, 404–8.

[32] *An Abridgement of the English Military Discipline* (1682), 3, 7, 38.

of regiments and how they reflected hierarchy and order, advocated that on the battlefield 'all regiments should in course take their turns to be in the van, the rear and other parts of the army'. In the foot, only the commander of a battalion might ride a horse when the troops were marching or drilling. If advancing onto the battlefield, he was to dismount and march pike in hand in the midst of the battalion with the colours. The precedence of the captains determined the placing of the companies, the eldest captain's company being on the right, the second captain's company on the left, and the youngest in the centre. Lieutenants marched at the rear or on the flanks of the battalion in order to deter desertion and to strike down cowards. In the cavalry, the officers were to stand and ride close to their troopers. Only the commanding officer was to ride ahead of the ranks. It was, however, thought to be unseemly for officers to be too great a distance from their men.[33]

Military treatises published otherwise than by authority show more concern with the duty of officers to maintain morale and motivate their soldiers. Thomas Venn, who had trained with the Honourable Artillery Company of London and had commanded a cavalry troop, provides a refreshing alternative to the concern with hierarchy that characterizes the Restoration military establishment. Venn implicitly criticizes the Cavalier officers of the Restoration home army by insisting that discipline and morale were undermined by commanders who were careless about their reputations, who failed to recognize honour in their subordinates and who promoted on the basis of favour rather than merit. Commanders and paymasters must be careful to pay on time, because failure to do so undermined discipline and led to mutiny, desertion, theft and pillage. Venn also asserted that the failure to encourage Christian worship and to punish blasphemy encouraged lax discipline. He was especially emphatic about the need to oppose duelling and to compose quarrels before they become fatal.[34]

Another unofficially published military treatise, the anonymous *Advice to a Soldier* (1680), was authored by a professional English soldier with experience in overseas expeditions or mainland European armies—most likely the French army. He states that a good commander treats his soldiers as he would his own children: he combines kindness with strictness of discipline. The young officer was reminded that whatever he achieves in the army will be due to the affection and courage of his soldiers. His duties extend well beyond presenting an example of bravery to his men; he must also look to their pay, provisions and quarters, and see that they receive medical attention. Officers must know their soldiers well, but not be too familiar. The subaltern officer or captain also had an obligation to promote the careers of non-commissioned officers when they performed well. Officers should avoid being absent more than was necessary, and should keep

---

[33] Orrery, *Treatise of the Art of War*, 59; Manning, *Swordsmen*, 135; *The Exercise of the Foot: With Evolutions according to the Words of Command* (1690), 222; *Abridgement of English Military Discipline*, 87–8, 92, 95–6, 114, 119–23, 128.

[34] Thomas Venn, *Military and Maritime Discipline* (1672), 3–4.

their men busy, so that they do not become involved in mutinies or other mischief.[35]

The anonymous author of *Advice to a Soldier* was also concerned to instruct officers on how to motivate soldiers before a battle. The justness of the cause should be explained to them, and chaplains should be employed to provide a moral justification. Their officers might also relate to them the deeds that their ancestors had performed in France; they must be careful not to teach soldiers to despise the enemy, but rather to regard him as a worthy foe, so as not to be caught off guard. However, soldiers can be taught to hold the enemy in contempt in order to enhance their courage: 'The contempt of a crafty enemy is one of the greatest advantages you can give him, and he who commands valiant men, as the English are, need not be afraid to make them sensible of danger. It will rather serve to inflame than abate their natural courage; whereas if they be taught to slight the enemy, they will be apt to think of a victory without labour, without danger: such an imagination will teach them to be careless, and carelessness will lay them open to inevitable ruin and destruction.'[36]

It was difficult for commanding officers to maintain discipline in Charles II's home army, because the only legal means of punishing soldiers was in civil courts under the common law. The Tudor kings had exercised the power to proclaim martial law within the realm in time of rebellion when the king's banner was unfurled, but that had not been done since 1569. It should be noted that there was a legal distinction between martial law, which could be applied to civilians in times of emergency, and military law, which was employed for disciplining soldiers. In 1601 the royal judges had ruled in the *Case of Soldiers* that unruly soldiers or deserters were to be tried by justices of oyer and terminer in the counties in which the offences were committed.[37] Articles of war had long been routinely issued for overseas expeditions and garrisons where the common law did not reach, but no articles of war to establish military courts were issued by royal authority for the English home army until 1666. The Articles of War of 1666 provided for capital penalties and forbade civil magistrates to try any soldier for any offence except treason. However, lawyers and magistrates hotly disputed the legality of the Articles, and continued to insist that only the common law applied within the realm. Evidence suggests that officers of the home army hesitated to risk their necks by applying the Articles of 1666 in capital cases, but they did constitute courts martial to deal with lesser breaches of discipline. Nonetheless, there were confrontations between military commanders and magistrates. Sometime in the early 1660s Sir John Bramston quarrelled with Aubrey de Vere, twentieth earl of Oxford, over the question of whether one of the troopers in Oxford's Regiment of Royal Horse Guards could be tried under the civil jurisdiction in a case of rape. Oxford, whose understanding of the law was meagre, could not comprehend how

---

[35] *Advice to a Soldier... Written by an Officer in the English Army* (1680), repr. *HM*, ed. Malham, viii. 356–7, 360.   [36] Ibid. 359–60.

[37] Manning, *VR* 178–85, ch. 9, esp. 233–4.

a guardsman charged with protecting the king could possibly be tried by gownsmen in a civil court. When Oxford complained to the king, the lord chancellor, the earl of Clarendon, had to tell him that the matter was not triable by court martial, but was to be determined in the common-law courts.[38] The English home army continued to operate without articles of war sanctioned by Parliament until the Mutiny Act of 1689. This made it difficult to suppress mutinies such as occurred in 1674, when two companies of the second duke of Buckingham's regiment of marines mutinied because their company commanders, Hugh Montgomery, second earl of Mount-Alexander, and Captain Swiftnan, the former highwayman, cheated them of their pay.[39]

For the most part, Charles II was content to be guided by the opinions of his legal advisers concerning the legality of military courts, and he avoided open conflict with Parliament on this question. James VII and II, however, constituted courts martial on the basis of the royal prerogative. At the beginning of James's reign, commanding officers were told by William Blathwayt, the secretary-at-war, to refer serious crimes involving civilians and soldiers to the common-law courts. Courts martial could be resorted to only when one soldier committed a crime against another soldier, but not when a civilian was involved. George Clarke, the judge-advocate-general, stated that James altered this policy by referring all legal business, including that involving civilians, to a standing court martial which met weekly at the Horse Guards. This effectively removed the army from any scrutiny or review by judges, Parliament or other civilian officials, and made it wholly dependent upon the exercise of the royal prerogative. Army officers disliked being subject to the common-law courts because they thought that judges encouraged deserters. During the encampment of the army on Hounslow Heath in the summer of 1688, the governing council of war established a court martial to maintain discipline within the bounds of the camp.[40]

Soldiers accused of capital crimes were still tried by the common-law courts during the reign of James VII and II, but the king did not tolerate judges who were lenient. The question arose during a trial at the Old Bailey in London in 1686 whether a soldier who deserted was guilty of felony since the king was not at war. The recorder of London, who presided at the soldier's trial, refused to give judgment, and referred the case to the royal judges. James ordered the judges to execute the soldier, and the order was carried out by the recorder's deputy.[41] In 1687 and 1688 a number of soldiers were executed in view of their regiments for running from their colours. Two were executed at Covent Garden and Tower Hill—presumably condemned by common-law judges coerced by King James. James had also ordered the execution of a third at Plymouth after his conviction at

[38] Maitland, *Constitutional History*, 326–7; Childs, *AC* 78–81; *The Autobiography of Sir John Bramston*, CS os 32 (1845), 126–7.

[39] Walton, *British Standing Army*, 529; O. Airy (ed.), *Essex Papers*, vol. 1: *1672–1679*, CS ns 47 (1890), i. 208.   [40] Childs, *AJGR* 91–2.

[41] *Autobiography of Sir John Bramston*, 245–6.

the Berkshire Assizes, but Lord Chief Justice Herbert and a colleague doubted the legality of James's order, so Herbert was demoted to puisne judge, and the soldier was conducted to Plymouth to be executed.[42]

James did not declare martial law during the duke of Monmouth's Rebellion of 1685, and used a variety of methods for punishing deserters which managed to alienate those who cared for legal procedure. Deserters from the army were punished with death by both assizes and summary courts martial. Pressure was applied to common-law judges and justices of oyer and terminer to construe desertion in peacetime as felony, and the recorder of London was dismissed for refusing to do so. The crown had become concerned about the number of deserters who were making their way to London. It became more difficult to maintain the fiction that military law and authority were subordinate to civilian authority and the common law; they were now wholly dependent upon the royal prerogative.[43] Colonel Percy Kirke, a professional soldier and one of the last governors of Tangier before the colony was abandoned, commanded a detachment of dragoons which provided an escort for Lord Chief Justice Jeffreys during the holding of the 'Bloody Assizes' in the aftermath of the Monmouth Rebellion. He and his men did much to discredit James's government during the Bloody Assizes by their unruly behaviour. Thomas Bruce, earl of Ailesbury and Elgin, who later became a Jacobite, insisted that Kirke deliberately tried 'to render the king odious in the eyes of his subjects'.[44]

In the overseas garrisons, such as Tangier, punishments for infractions of discipline were especially harsh, and fell unevenly on enlisted men and officers. The judge advocate of the Tangier garrison, John Luke, a civil lawyer by training, kept a record in his journal of courts martial during three of his twelve years in that forlorn imperial outpost. Soldiers were routinely flogged for theft or disrespect to officers, or sentenced to ride the wooden horse for three days at a time. Executions for murder or mutiny were not infrequent, and one soldier who had defected to the Moors was 'condemned to be hanged and to remain at the brow of the hill just without Charles Fort'. An enlisted man was tried at a court martial for killing another man in a duel. The majority of the court did not think that it was murder, but he was found guilty and shot. Another man was convicted of stealing a cup and sentenced to hang, but the governor pardoned him. A major who slashed his sergeant with his sword for impudence apparently went unpunished. However, an ensign who had verbally abused a sergeant whom the lieutenant-colonel thought was an exemplary soldier was himself publicly rebuked in front of the sergeant.[45]

Tangier was acquired as an English colony along with Bombay in 1661 as part of the marriage dowry that came from Portugal at the time of Charles II's marriage

---

[42] Luttrell, *RSA* i. 400–1, 442.   [43] Childs, *AJGR* 93–4.

[44] Thomas Bruce, 2nd earl of Ailesbury and 3rd earl of Elgin, *Memoirs*, 2 vols., RC (1890), i. 121–3.

[45] H. A. Kaufman (ed.), *Tangier at High Tide: The Journal of John Luke, 1670–1673* (1958), 61, 64, 100, 102–3, 159, 192.

to Catherine of Braganza. In its day it was the largest garrison outside of the British Isles prior to the acquisition of Gibraltar and Minorca during the War of Spanish Succession. Soon after the English arrived the garrison was built up to four regiments of foot comprising 4,000 English, Welsh, Scots and Irish veterans of the civil wars who had been packed off to Tangier to help pacify the Three Kingdoms. Put down in the midst of hostile territory on the Atlantic coast of Morocco, the officers proved too restless to endure the tedium of garrison life and a diet of salt meat without a bit of sport and adventure. When they ventured outside the walls to hunt, they were set upon by the Moors, and reprisals were undertaken in order to avenge the honour of the English army. One such punitive expedition, consisting of 500 officers and men, was cut to pieces. The first governor, Henry Mordaunt, second earl of Peterborough, was forced to spend most of his time in England pleading for supplies and provisions. In 1663 Peterborough was replaced as governor by Andrew Rutherford, earl of Teviot, a Scottish professional soldier who had served in the French army, but not in the Wars of the Three Kingdoms. When Teviot arrived in Tangier he discovered that the common soldiers did not share their officers' taste for adventure. They were demoralized and unwilling to venture outside of the walls. In order to persuade the soldiers that they might open the gates again, Teviot improved the outer defences so effectively that the Moors asked for a truce. As governor of Tangier, Teviot restored the morale of the enlisted ranks and instilled confidence and stability. Teviot also reduced the garrison to two regiments of 2,000 men, because with the great expense of maintaining Tangier and the shortage of military manpower, four regiments could not be kept up to strength.[46]

The earl of Teviot was regarded as a successful colonial governor. When he arrived in Tangier he found the soldiers of the garrison half-starved, and immediately began procuring provisions in order to forestall a mutiny. Under the previous governor the troops had been idle. Teviot put them to work to improve Tangier's defences. The governor also composed differences between town and garrison, and he was careful 'to carry an even hand in all controversies that happened betwixt the Christians and those Jews that were there residing. . . . Both by nature and religion, he was inclined to impartial justice.' Teviot was sensitive and tactful too in his dealings with the Moorish rulers, but also knew when to be forceful, and hostilities were kept to a minimum. However, even with improved fortifications and the construction of a huge and expensive fortified mole to protect the harbour and provide a safe anchorage for naval and merchant ships, Teviot still regarded Tangier as an undefendable base. Unfortunately, he was killed in 1664 in a sally against the Moors along with more than 400 officers and men.[47]

---

[46] Childs, *AC* 115–18; L. Colley, *Captives* (2002), 23–41; Sir Hugh Cholmley, *An Account of Tangier* (1787), 39–40, 63–4.

[47] Lancelot Addison, *A Discourse of Tangier under the Government of the Earl of Teviot*, 2nd edn. (1685), 20–1; id., *The Moores Baffled: Being a Discourse concerning Tang[i]er, Especially when it was under the Earl of Teviot* (1681), 3–4, 6–7, 17, 23, 26.

Service in Tangier was hardship duty, but it was also a place where young gentlemen of limited means could begin their careers or gain experience. Commissions could be obtained in regiments of the Tangier garrison without purchase, whereas a commission in the Holland Regiment, when it was part of the home army, cost £400–600. Although no purchase was required for a commission in the Tangier Regiment, one of two in the garrison, the help of a patron was always necessary. Those who were successful in obtaining commissions usually had prior service in the French or other European armies, and there were always gentlemen volunteers in the Tangier garrison awaiting commissions. Tangier was a place where an officer could obtain battle experience; the future colonial governor, Francis Nicholson, also gained diplomatic experience when his commandant, Percy Kirke, sent him on a diplomatic mission to Mulay Ismaïl, the sultan of Morocco. However, pay was irregular and usually in arrears, provisions frequently rotten and always meagre; bad diet contributed to unusually high rates of sickness and death, and consequently, mutiny often lurked in the background. One of the Regiments posted to Tangier was Dumbarton's, or the Royal Scots. This regiment had served in the French army, and was stationed at Cork just prior to being ordered to Tangier in 1680. The soldiers were reluctant to board ship at Kinsale, because their pay was sixteen months in arrears, and there were insufficient officers present to prevent desertion. Eventually the regiment was paid their arrears plus three months, and two battalions of sixteen companies proceeded to Tangier, where in one single skirmish twenty-four officers and 250 men were killed. Unable to obtain money from Parliament to maintain Tangier unless he agreed to the exclusion of his brother James, duke of York, from the throne, Charles II decided to abandon it in 1683. George Legge, first Lord Dartmouth, a relative of Buckingham, was sent out to accomplish this task. He demolished the mole, ransomed some forty officers and men kept as slaves by the sultan of Morocco, and, along with a garrison of 2,800, carried home 114 invalid soldiers who were among the first inmates of the Royal Hospital, Chelsea.[48]

At the Restoration, each of the Three Kingdoms possessed its own separate standing army. However, soldiers from Scotland and Ireland were increasingly recruited to serve in the English home army; they also constituted a significant part of the English forces detached for service in overseas garrisons or foreign armies—especially when it was difficult to recruit volunteers from England. These Irish and Scottish regiments eventually were integrated into the English military establishment. The Scottish and Irish standing armies were barely able to maintain order at home, and were not organized to form field forces. The Irish army was certainly not equal to defending Ireland against foreign invaders.

[48] B. T. McCully, 'From the North Riding to Morocco: The Early Years of Governor Francis Nicholson, 1655–1686', *WMQ* 3ʳᵈ ser. 19 (1962), 538–9; H. M. McCance (ed.), 'The Diary of Sir James Halket', *JSAHR* 1 (1922), 3–4, 6, 18, 21; N. T. S. Williams, *Redcoats and Courtesans: The Birth of the British Army (1660–1690)* (1994), 50–6.

The Irish standing army was also riven by factionalism. Control of the armed forces was disputed between Roger Boyle, Lord Broghill, like George Monck an old Cromwellian of shifting allegiances, and James Butler, first duke of Ormonde, who had been the king's lieutenant in Ireland during the civil wars and had served Charles II in exile during the Interregnum. Ormonde was reappointed lord-lieutenant in 1661, and was nominally the commander of the Irish army, but Broghill, who was created earl of Orrery and made president of Munster, was the one who, along with Sir Charles Coote, had persuaded the Cromwellian forces in Ireland to accept the Restoration. Through his tight control of military patronage Ormonde tried to please the king and buy support among the Irish aristocracy by bestowing upon them the choicest military commissions—especially in the thirty independent cavalry troops. Many of these were concentrated around Dublin, and their officers were expected to support Ormonde in the elections for and in the proceedings of the Irish Parliament. Ormonde himself took in almost £6,000 per year from the various military offices that he held, and it goes without saying that the purchase system was well established in the Irish army. It was also necessary to come to terms with the old Cromwellians in Ireland, many of whom had fought or bought their way into the landed aristocracy. Orrery was able to help many Cromwellian officers at the lower grades retain their commissions, and he had great influence with this group, who came to be identified with maintaining the Protestant interest. The distribution of commissions to buy political support resulted in garrisons and forts being established close to the estates of local notables rather than where sound military strategy and doctrine might dictate, and the consequence was that the Irish army, which consisted almost entirely of unregimented independent troops and companies before 1672, lacked the structure and organization necessary to resist any invaders, or even deal effectively with banditry.[49]

The duke of Ormonde was jealous of the powers that the earl of Orrery possessed because they were nearly as extensive as his own as lord-lieutenant of Ireland. The president of Munster's authority comprehended civil and military powers, the authority to dub knights, to be attended by guards and the power of life and death in punishing crimes. One way that he had of undercutting support for Ormonde, to whom Catholics were more likely to look for protection, was to encourage the recruitment of Catholics for service in mainland European armies or to serve in the king's forces abroad. Ormonde looked to undermine Orrery's power in Munster by refusing his requests for money to rebuild forts or pay and equip soldiers in that province during the Second Anglo-Dutch and French Wars. Orrery was a dangerous man to have as an enemy, and with the help of the second

---

[49] T. C. Barnard, 'Aristocratic Values in the Careers of the Dukes of Ormonde', in T. C. Barnard and J. Fenlon (eds.), *The Dukes of Ormonde, 1610–1745* (2000), 167–9; Barnard, 'Scotland and Ireland in the Later Stewart Monarchy', in S. Ellis and S. Barber (eds.), *Conquest and Union: Fashioning a British State, 1485–1725* (1995), 271; HMC, *Report on the Manuscripts of the Marquis of Ormonde*, ed. J. S. Gilbert, 2 vols., OS (1895, 1899), ii. 265; S. J. Connolly, 'The Defence of Protestant Ireland, 1660–1760', *MHI* (1996), 232–4.

duke of Buckingham, he was able to persuade the king to recall Ormonde as lord-lieutenant in 1669. In November of that year Ormonde and Henry Bennet, first earl of Arlington, retaliated by organizing the impeachment of Orrery in the English Parliament on the pretext that he had raised money from the king's subjects by his own authority. Among the witnesses against Orrery were men who had been active in the Irish Rebellion and whose land had been given to Cromwellian soldiers. Orrery insisted on defending himself before the House of Commons, where he argued that the Cromwellian adventurers were necessary for keeping the Old Irish under control. Orrery also came into conflict with successive viceroys in Ireland. He clashed with John, first Lord Berkeley of Stratton, over the latter's leniency towards Catholics, and told Berkeley that the command of garrisons in Munster belonged to him. Orrery purged these garrisons of papists who had crept in while he was absent in England, and he called upon the king in asserting his right to appoint his son, Henry Boyle, a lieutenant in his own troop of horse, against Berkeley's attempt to insert another in that post. In April 1672 Berkeley was recalled and replaced as lord-lieutenant by Arthur Capel, earl of Essex. Orrery at first welcomed Essex's appointment until the lord-lieutenant's announcement in June 1672 that he was suppressing the office of president and the military courts in the provinces of Munster and Connaught and replacing them with common-law courts. Essex also told Orrery not to meddle with the militia in Munster. Orrery resigned his offices, and moved from his official residence at Charleville to his private castle at Ballymartin, near Cork. He took with him five cannon, which he fired when drinking healths to the king, but Essex ordered Orrery to return the pieces because he permitted no 'private man to have possession of a regular fortified place'.[50]

With a strength of 2,500 horse and 5,000 foot the Irish army was the largest in the Three Kingdoms in 1661, but its discipline and effectiveness was undermined by a lack of funds which resulted from the Irish Exchequer's failure to pay its soldiers in a timely fashion. New recruits in the Irish army, many of whom were raised in England so as to keep the Irish army Protestant, were usually not paid for the first six months, and yet were responsible for their diet. The pay of the old soldiers—many of them remaining from Cromwellian days—was usually nine months in arrears. They were used to labouring to supplement their pay, but the new recruits, Orrery reported, refused to do so, and were on the verge of mutiny. Many townsmen and merchants refused credit to the soldiers and officers because they were already deeply in debt. Orrery often dipped into his own pocket to relieve them. When it was proposed to eliminate the office of quartermaster in troops of horse, Orrery told Ormonde that there was already a shortage of officers, because most cavalry troops were commanded by peers and gentlemen who were almost invariably absent. The quartermasters were generally former senior officers

---

[50] *The State Letters of Roger Boyle, 1ˢᵗ Earl of Orrery*, comp. Thomas Morrice (1742), pp. vii, 55; K. M. Lynch, *Roger Boyle, First Earl of Orrery* (1965), 135–41; *Essex Papers*, ed. Airy, i. 250–2.

who had been reduced in grade with the reorganization of the Irish army at the Restoration, and paying their arrears of pay at discharge would cost more than maintaining them for life. The new senior officers of the Irish army were often corrupt. Orrery reprimanded one colonel for returning false musters for his company. The colonel sought Orrery's pardon, but then repeated the offence in the most egregious manner.[51]

The Irish army was poorly equipped to fight at the beginning of the Second Anglo-Dutch War. Several garrisons were abandoned because they were inadequately manned, and there was a continuing shortage of powder and shot. The few large garrisons, such as Cork, Limerick and Waterford, lacked sufficient provisions and munitions in their magazines to withstand sieges. Orrery told Ormonde that a field army would be necessary if invaded, but without a regimental and staff system, it is difficult to see how the widely dispersed independent troops and companies would have been coordinated. When Louis XIV declared war, Orrery was able to extract more money to repair some of the forts of Munster, and pay the army more regularly. This seems not to have been adequate though, and in 1678 the garrison of Waterford began employing soldiers to collect 'contributions' for quartering soldiers, and then forcing householders to accept soldiers without their consent—both practices of dubious legality. Because the army was less than effective, Orrery proposed forming a militia, but Ormonde so distrusted Orrery that he was reluctant to give him so much military power even when the possibility of invasion became evident. However, once Ormonde relented he was appalled when Orrery was quickly able to raise a militia in Munster of 2,000 horse and 3,500 foot, and then to muster it and flaunt it in Ormonde's face when the lord-lieutenant undertook a progress through the province.[52]

The Irish army was in a sorry state when Essex assumed power as lord-lieutenant. The pay of the army was nine months in arrears, and the soldiers were impoverished. Not only were the independent troops and companies widely dispersed, the soldiers within those units were also scattered since they had to work for their subsistence wherever they could find employment. Some had returned home to live with their families. The castle guard at Carrickfergus, a place of considerable importance, consisted in 1673 of a company of four men and two boys, but 'never an officer that attended'. Captains of horse grumbled when their troops were not stationed near their estates. Many soldiers were deeply in debt, reported Essex, and their companies could not be deployed until their debts were discharged. A mutiny broke out at Drogheda, which resulted from disrespectful words spoken by a soldier to a company officer who had refused to lend him money to buy shoes. The other soldiers in the company would not allow the accused to be punished. Essex feared that the whole army was on the verge of

---

[51] A. J. Guy, 'The Irish Military Establishment, 1660–1776', *MHI* 212; *State Letters of... Earl of Orrery*, comp. Morrice, 26–7, 87, 168; Childs, *AC* 204–6.

[52] *State Letters of... Earl of Orrery*, comp. Morrice, 26–7, 136–7, 140–1, 317–18; *Essex Papers*, ed. Airy, i. 1–5; Lynch, *Roger Boyle, First Earl of Orrery*, 125–6.

mutiny because of the failure to pay them. He thought that the discipline of the soldiers who had been sent to Ireland from England was particularly lax. One of the officers who had come over with them was Captain 'Swift' Nix, a former highwayman pardoned by King Charles and allowed to purchase a commission. Essex began to insist that officers of the Irish army sell their commissions only to men who had his prior approval. In 1677 Essex reported that the Irish army contained many 'old and decayed men', who had to ride in wagons when the army made long marches. He proposed that deductions be made from the soldiers' pay for pensions and for the maintenance of a hospital for old soldiers. Essex thought that if it were known that the Irish government had a policy of not turning old soldiers out to starve, it would aid recruiting.[53]

At the beginning of the Wars of the Three Kingdoms, only those Scots peers and gentlemen who had served in continental European armies had any experience of war. The civil wars also brought about a remilitarization of the stay-at-home nobility, and consequently the Restoration government displayed what Keith Brown calls a 'quasi-military flavour'. Not only military peers, but also the sons of gownsmen competed for the few military offices, which were dispensed by official patronage. Those with court connections were better rewarded than experienced professional soldiers. The wielding of royal patronage in the Scots army, as in the case of England, allowed the later Stuart monarchs to manipulate noblemen who desired military commissions as well as officers who were ambitious to be created peers. To a greater extent than was the case in Ireland, the patronage of military offices in the Scottish army was brokered in London and was mostly controlled by English politicians or Scots sitting on the English Privy Council, which tended to make Scottish officers increasingly dependent upon the English political and military establishments. John Maitland, first duke of Lauderdale, was given the task of making Charles II's government in church and state absolute in Scotland, and this involved the small Scots army and the militia in the brutal suppression of conventicles and popular rebellions of dissenters and Covenanters.[54]

The Scots nobility had been compelled to pay for the Cromwellian occupation until 1662, when the two remaining regiments in the Leith Citadel were sent into Portuguese service. Upon being relieved of this financial burden they had no wish to see the crown raise another standing army. Ever since 1638 they had learned to associate standing armies with religious radicalism, governmental absolutism, high taxation and loss of local autonomy. Therefore, the Scottish military establishment began in a modest way with raising the Troop of Guards in 1661. It consisted of noblemen and noblemen's sons, and was commanded by Sir James

---

[53] *Essex Papers*, ed. Airy, i. 86–7, 213–14; C. E. Pike (ed.), *Selections from the Correspondence of Arthur Capel, Earl of Essex, 1675–1677*, CS 3rd ser. 24 (1913), 53–6, 70–1, 115–16. The Royal Hospital, Kilmainham, was built in Dublin in 1681. It preceded the Royal Hospital, Chelsea, which was not begun until 1684 (Childs, *AC* 55).

[54] K. M. Brown, 'From Scottish Lords to British Officers: State Building, Elite Integration and the British Army in the Seventeenth Century', in Macdougall, *S&W* 145–7; Sir John Lauder of Fountainhall, *Historical Observations, 1680–1686*, ed. A. Urquhart and D. Laing, BC 66 (1837), 122.

Livingston, first earl of Newburgh, who had shared Charles II's exile and commanded a Scottish regiment in Flanders. To this was added a regiment of Foot Guards, raised in 1662 and initially consisting of only five companies. This regiment was commanded by George Livingston, third earl of Linlithgow, as lieutenant-colonel; the second-in-command was Sir James Turner as captain and major. Otherwise, there were only a few independent companies garrisoning Edinburgh, Stirling and Dumbarton Castles, and a few independent troops of horse raised and commanded by peers or old warhorses, such as Lieutenant-General Sir Thomas Dalzell, who held high rank in a very small army. A few of these units were later expanded into regiments during the Anglo-Dutch Wars or in time of rebellion. To a greater extent than in England or Ireland, the Restoration political and military settlement in Scotland rested upon the understanding that the crown would draw its military forces primarily from fencible men embodied in a militia.[55]

The officers and enlisted ranks of the small Scottish standing army in the early 1660s included former Covenanters who had fought with Montrose and 'Engagers' who rode with the duke of Hamilton into Lancashire; others were Cavaliers who had fought at Worcester and Dunbar as well as those who had participated in Glencairn's Rebellion. There were professional soldiers who had long served in the armies of Sweden, Denmark-Norway, Russia, the Dutch Republic and France. Most were reformadoes, reduced in rank and down on their luck. Bishop Burnet was not very sympathetic to their plight, and doubted the boasts of the earls of Glencairn and Middleton and other Scottish Cavaliers about their exploits in the civil wars: 'They were followed by the herd of the Cavalier party, who were now fierce and full of courage over their cups, though they had been very discreet managers of it in the field and in time of action. But now every one of them boasted that he had killed his thousands. And all were full of merit and as full of high pretensions; far beyond what all the wealth and revenues could answer.'[56] Although Sir James Turner had been a major-general in the civil wars, and had been knighted by Charles II, he did not enjoy the necessary patronage of the earl of Middleton after the Restoration. During the Second Anglo-Dutch War he briefly held the rank of lieutenant-colonel of the Scottish Foot Guards, but when the army was reduced in size in 1667, the peers attempted to force the professional soldiers out and grab their commissions. In 1668 Turner was obliged to resign his military commission on the pretext of arbitrary and brutal treatment of people during the Pentland Rebellion of 1666. His commission as lieutenant-colonel was given to Alexander Erskine, third earl of Kellie, who had been a devoted Royalist while Turner was still an officer in the Covenanting Army in

[55] B. P. Lenman, 'Militia, Fencible Men and Home Defence, 1660–1797', in Macdougall, *S&W* 172–3; C. Dalton, *The Scots Army, 1661–1688* (1909; repr. 1989), pt. i, pp. 3,13, 37.

[56] Gilbert Burnet, bishop of Salisbury, *Bishop Burnet's History of his own Time*, 4 vols. (1742), i. 104.

Ireland.[57] When Lieutenant-General William Drummond's Regiment of Horse was raised in 1666, one troop was given to John Murray, second earl (and later marquis) of Atholl, who had taken up arms in 1650 in an attempt to free Charles II from the influence of the Covenanters. His sixty troopers were all gentlemen. When the troop was disbanded in 1667, all of the officers were kinsmen, but two of his three corporals were reformed captains. Lieutenant-General John Drummond's troop, also disbanded at the same time, included two majors serving as corporals. The gentlemen-troopers were mostly long-service veterans who obviously were beyond the cadet stage.[58] Another cavalry officer was Colin Lindsay, third earl of Balcarres, who had been presented to Charles II at court in 1682. At the age of 16 he was given command of a troop of horse consisting of 'one hundred gentlemen, who had been reduced to poverty during the troubles'.[59]

During the Second Anglo-Dutch War it was feared that the Scots Covenanters and the Dutch might join forces in promoting war and rebellion against the three Stuart kingdoms, so the Scottish government decided to collect fines against the Covenanters which had been levied earlier. Payment was forced by quartering troops upon those who owed fines until they were ready to pay. Sir James Turner led the Scottish Foot Guards into south-western Scotland, where the Covenanters were thick upon the ground. His officers, like himself, were often veterans of the German wars, and some had served the czar of Russia, whose methods were none too delicate. James Sharp, archbishop of St Andrews, took advantage of this opportunity to press for greater compliance with episcopal government. The Covenanters resisted, took Turner prisoner at Dumfries and precipitated the Pentland Rising of 1666. The Pentland rebels marched to within a few miles of Edinburgh in an attempt to gain the support of the citizens of that city. At this point, Thomas Dalzell, whose military experience reached back to the Isle of Rhé expedition of 1628 and whose expertise extended to service in the Russian army fighting Turks and Poles, was put in charge of the regular and militia forces to run down the Covenanters. Turner later reported that many of the Covenanters were veteran soldiers who knew how to handle their weapons and drill expertly, although only a couple of their officers were experienced soldiers. Otherwise, they were led by their ministers. The rebel force of 1,000 was defeated at Rullion Green and their leaders—thirty-six in all—were executed; of the rank and file who survived, most were sent in chains to Barbados, Virginia and New England. Under the leadership of Dalzell, Major-General William Drummond, another veteran of Russian service, and Turner, the soldiers continued to be quartered upon the Covenanters until they conformed, but the cruelties of Dalzell, Drummond and Turner were much exaggerated and based upon hearsay evidence.

---

[57] Sir James Turner, *Memoirs of his own Life and Times, 1632–1670*, BC 31 (1829), 189–90, 200, 219; Dalton, *Scots Army*, pt. i, pp. 34–5. The charge of brutality against Turner may be specious, since he was a more humane man than most officers.

[58] Dalton, *Scots Army*, pt. i, p. 14; pt. ii, pp. 61–2; K. Murray, duchess of Atholl, *A Military History of Perthshire, 1660–1902* (1908), 4–6, 8–18.

[59] Colin Lindsay, 3rd earl of Balcarres, *Memoirs touching the Revolution, 1688–1690*, BC 71 (1841), pp. xi, xiv; Dalton, *Scots Army*, pt. i, pp. 135–6.

Probably, such tales were circulated to help the courtiers drive the professionals out of the officer ranks.[60]

In 1673 the duke of Lauderdale prodded the Scottish Parliament to enact a statute authorizing the king to raise an army of up to 2,000 horse and 20,000 foot, and order it march to any part of the king's dominions. The English Parliament viewed this Scottish Act for Settling the Militia with alarm, because they feared such an army might well threaten the parliamentary independence of England or Ireland. The English Parliament also objected to the king sending parts of his forces to France to be maintained by the king of France. The English Parliament feared that contingents of the army seconded to the French army might be brought back to coerce them.[61]

Lauderdale was determined to force episcopacy upon the Scots, but he also understood that diehard Presbyterians might well rebel. In 1677 he issued the so-called 'Bond', which made heritors and masters responsible for the good behaviour of their tenants and servants. To compel acceptance of the Bond, Lauderdale mobilized a force of regulars, militia and Highlanders, the latter known as the 'Highland Host', to live at free quarter in the disaffected areas which now began to extend outside of the south-west. Bishop Burnet thought that Charles II was trying to precipitate a rebellion as an excuse to raise a larger standing army. The Highland Host of 1678 failed to provoke the Presbyterian 'Whigs', as they had come to be called, to rebel, so the Highlanders were sent home. Because they had plundered as they marched south, the country people sometimes sought revenge by ambushing and attacking the Highlanders as they marched north again. The depredations of the Highlanders in Lanarkshire and Ayrshire caused much ill feeling, and led some of the inhabitants to emigrate to Ulster.[62] Although Lauderdale failed to provoke a general rising of the Covenanters by the employment of the Highland Host in 1678, the Covenanters turned out the following year to seek revenge at Bothwell Bridge on the River Clyde near Hamilton. This time the rebels, who called themselves 'the Covenanted Army in Scotland now in arms', led by one Robert Hamilton, gathered nine miles from the encampment of the Scots army under the command of the king's natural son, James Scott, duke of Buccleuch and Monmouth, who had the title of captain-general of the forces in England and Scotland. They barricaded Bothwell Bridge, but were driven off by artillery and then cut down by horse and dragoons reinforced by 300 foot and the marquis of Atholl's Highlanders. Seven or eight hundred Covenanters were killed and 1,200 taken prisoner out of as many as 11,000 who had risen up in the first place. Again, some of the rebels escaped to Ulster.[63]

[60] Childs, *AC* 198–9; Dalton, *Scots Army*, pt. i, pp. 18–28.
[61] C. M. Clode, *The Military Forces of the Crown: Their Administration and Government*, 2 vols. (1869), i. 62–3.
[62] J. R. Elder, *The Highland Host of 1678* (1914), 2–4, 9, 15, 17–19, 45–6, 97–8, 100, 128.
[63] Ibid. 138; *The Defeat of the Rebels at Bothwell-Bridge* (1679), 3, 5–7; *News from Ireland* (1679), 3.

The promulgation of military law and the establishment of military courts did not present the legal problems in Scotland that they did in England. The 'Laws and Articles of War' of 1666 for the Scots army were issued and ratified by the authority of the king, and many infractions were punishable by death. We also know that these articles of war were strictly enforced in the regiment raised in 1678 by Lord James Douglas, the younger brother of George, first earl of Dumbarton. In 1684 a soldier was shot on Leith Links for striking a sergeant. Within the regiment, a regular and demanding regime of drill and training was carried out on a daily basis. Soldiers were required to keep their beards short, and to tie their hair back in queues so as not to obstruct their vision when firing their muskets. Officers were forbidden to keep cellars for drinking where the men were separated from their money. Not that they could have had much money, for their pay was always in arrears, although that did not prevent the colonel from deducting the cost of their clothing and the ribbons to tie back their queues from what little pay they did receive.[64]

Standing armies were necessary in the Three Kingdoms at the time of the Restoration because the civil wars and the regimes of the Interregnum bequeathed a legacy of instability and unrest. Also, the Cromwellian military forces had yet to be disbanded. Each of the Three Kingdoms would experience threats to the Restoration settlements in church and state, and it could not be denied that these posed possible threats to the person of the monarch. Moreover, the foreign policies of the Commonwealth and Protectorate governments had re-engaged the Three Kingdoms, dominated by England, in mainland European affairs and established vulnerable colonial outposts in the West Indies and the Mediterranean, and it was not in England's naval, maritime and trading interests to withdraw from these theatres. The Commonwealth and Protectorate regimes had also fought a naval war with the Dutch Republic and laid the basis for a continuing challenge to Dutch naval and maritime power which would require two more wars over the next two decades to resolve. The likelihood of the conflict continuing with the Dutch was increased by James, duke of York's hostility to the Dutch for being republicans and aggressive competitors for trade and colonies, but these wars also provided the pretext for expanding the standing armies of the Three Kingdoms, and putting the military manpower resources of Ireland and Scotland at the disposal of the English forces.

The officer classes of the armies of the Three Kingdoms as they were reconstituted at the Restoration revealed the decay of a proud military tradition which had been built up in the various armies of the civil wars even as they were at one another's throats. This common military tradition had been largely formed by the shared experiences of swordsmen from the British Isles who had served their apprenticeship in the exercise of arms in the European military world prior to the

---

[64] Dalton, *Scots Army*, pt. i, pp. 84–94; Lauder, *Scottish Affairs*, i. 580; ii. 561.

civil wars. These old soldiers who had risen up in the military hierarchy by merit and competence were sent packing by well born cavaliers whose claim to military office was based upon high birth and court connections, and whose ranks were increasingly filled by persons whom the Scots called 'freshwater soldiers'. Most of the professional soldiers once again had to seek employment in mainland European armies and distant garrisons, or accept reduced status in the home armies in order to allow Charles II and James, duke of York, to reward the most intimate of their followers or to appease turncoat Cromwellians. This was a poor foundation upon which to develop effective military forces, and the lack of conscientious and experienced officers, joint training of large units and a legal basis for discipline made these home armies useless for much beyond suppressing rebellions and conspiracies. Discipline was also undermined by the lack of sufficient funds to pay the soldiers in a timely fashion and by dishonest captains.

Nor was the English Parliament disposed to provide Charles II with the funds to raise a more effective military force. Recent and unpleasant memories of the standing armies of the Protectorate only reinforced an older political tradition that had long been positively hostile to the very concept of standing armies and professional soldiers (usually referred to as soldiers of fortune). That the militia did not provide a realistic alternative to raising trained, effective and disciplined military forces which could protect property and lives, preserve public order and be deployed overseas did not signify. The members of that political faction devoted to asserting the liberties of Parliament in England and guarding against popery, who came to be known in the 1670s as Whigs, made opposition to standing armies part of the core of their political ideology. They had come to distrust Charles II for his dissembling ways and ties to France, and James, duke of York, because of his Catholicism and his absolutist tendencies. The Whigs would entrust command of a more effective standing army only to a monarch, such as William II and III, who could discipline it and employ it in the defence of Protestant liberties in a way that did not constitute a threat to Parliament.

12

The decay of the militia

The Romans, who understood the art of war beyond all the world, did not make soldiery a refuge of poverty and idleness; for none but men of fortune and property, whose private interest firmly engaged them to the public good, had the honour of serving in their armies.

[John Toland], *The Militia Reformed: Or an Easy Scheme of Furnishing England with a Constant Land Force* (1698), 19.

As to the militia, I suppose every man is now satisfied that we must never expect to see it made useful till we have disbanded the army.

[John Trenchard], *A Short History of Standing Armies in England* (1698), 40.

Our security is the militia; that will defend us and never conquer us.

Sir Henry Capel, speaking to the House of Commons, 1673, in Anchitell Grey (comp.), *Debates of the House of Commons, from the year 1667 to the Year 1694*, 10 vols. (1769), i. 218.

Many landowners and political leaders of the Three Kingdoms opposed standing armies, although they did pay lip service to the exercise of arms and advocated or participated in the militia. These beliefs and prejudices were acquired from reading Machiavelli or his disciples, such as James Harrington and Andrew Fletcher of Saltoun. Machiavelli was the chief source of the civic tradition and the concept of a citizen militia. Only in the British Isles did politically articulate people still seriously view a citizen militia as an alternative to a standing army in the latter part of the seventeenth century. The experiences of the civil wars had confirmed their hatred and mistrust of standing armies as instruments of absolutism and tyranny. Yet it could not be denied that the county militias of England were in decline as effective military forces for the defence of the realm, while the militias of Ireland and Scotland were only sporadically activated and lacked continuity. James VII and II denigrated the militia of England for being ineffective and disloyal. Those who feared standing armies, especially when commanded by Catholic monarchs, assumed that the militia could never flourish until the army was disbanded. They assumed that a militia would be more loyal, because an officer in the militia of high social standing and property would fight for religion, king and country, whereas the mercenary fought only for pay. Also, a militia promised more political stability than standing armies, which had caused so much discord in the 1650s and looked like they would do so again in the 1670s and 1680s. The 'country' faction, which evolved into the Whigs in the 1670s, wanted a militia that was commanded by peers and gentry in the county communities and not by courtiers or professional soldiers or foreigners. Such a militia would supposedly be immune to royal absolutism since the chain of command went through lords-lieutenant, deputy lieutenants and militia officers who were chosen from among the most eminent county families, and valued their reputations in the county community. By contrast, before the Glorious Revolution the army was solely dependent on the crown, and the king controlled all commissions and promotions.

As the militia ceased to be a tactical military arm, it continued to function as a kind of constabulary, and was employed for breaking conventicles of religious dissenters; during the Popish Plot, it was used for disarming papists and also for keeping order in urban areas. Although militia companies and troops continued to muster and drill in most areas, militia regiments mustered infrequently and received little training. The militia's loyalty was conditional, and James II found them unreliable or positively disloyal during the suppression of the Monmouth Rebellion in 1685. Both Charles II and James II thought that it was important to control the trained bands of London and the Honourable Artillery Company, which seem to have maintained a higher state of proficiency. However, Thomas Venn, a military writer, thought that the militia officers spent most of their time at musters engaging in Bacchanalian feasts.

The Irish militia contained many who were old Cromwellians and nonconformists. Viceroys of Ireland, such as James Butler, first duke of Ormonde, and Arthur Capel, first earl of Essex, were at pains to diminish the influence of Roger Boyle, earl of Orrery, president of Munster and a major-general in the Irish army, among the members of the Irish militia in Munster, which was that part of Ireland most vulnerable to foreign invasion. Irish landowners were anxious to maintain a functioning militia in order to suppress the tories or Irish bandits, who drew their strength from among dispossessed landowners, tenants and disbanded soldiers. They viewed the Irish militia as the first line of defence of the Protestant interest.

In Scotland, the concept of a militia was originally viewed as an English idea, and had very little support until the time of the Second Anglo-Dutch War and the Pentland Rising when the militia was employed to ride down religious dissidents. Although Charles II tried to limit the Scottish militia to well affected areas, it became clear that it had come to be dominated by Presbyterian interests. Because of the lack of discipline among the militia men and a desire to destroy the military power of the nobility, James VII and II persuaded the Scots Parliament to abolish the militia in 1685, and then attempted to revive it again at the time of the Williamite invasion of England in 1688.

As a consequence of reading Machiavelli and living through the civil wars, many of the politically articulate acquired an abiding distaste for entrusting command of military forces—whether standing armies or militia forces—to a single ruler. Republicans especially feared military forces under centralized control, and as the years passed during the Restoration period, this view came to be shared by those who were called Whigs. In January 1654/5, following Colonel Pride's purge of the Presbyterians in the Long Parliament, the remainder of the MPs, known as the Rump, passed an ordinance giving Cromwell the command of the militia during the intervals when Parliament was not sitting. This 'standing militia' was to be paid for by a decimation tax on Royalists, and was intended to quell Royalist uprisings, which remained a problem until the end of the Protectorate. This standing militia was to be commanded by Cromwell's major-generals, each of whom ruled one of the eleven military districts into which England and Wales were divided, rather than by the office-holding gentry of the counties. The Cromwellian militia was a volunteer force consisting mostly of horse-bands who were to muster four times a year, and could also be called up at will. The individual troopers were paid £8 per year out of the decimation tax on Royalists—the same people whom they were supposed to ferret out from among those of dissolute lives who lived like gentlemen without visible means of support. The appointment of officers of the militia to the county commissions of the peace was also widely resented. The standing militia, which functioned as a kind of military police, was deemed to be necessary as the disbandment of the Parliamentary armies continued. The members of the militia were required to swear allegiance to the lord protector, and to be ready to march upon forty-eight hours notice. Such a force was regarded as hardly less obnoxious than a standing army. Both were seen as tools of absolutism, and the memory of the abuses of standing armies and standing militias branded itself upon the collective memory of Royalists and Whigs alike.[1]

Ad hoc military expeditions were from time to time raised prior to the Wars of the Three Kingdoms and deployed overseas. They were usually commanded by military amateurs of high social rank, but always employed at least some professional officers who had gained experience in mainland European armies. Nevertheless, in the absence of a standing army, the militia had always been thought of as the main military force of England. With the emergence of a standing army during the civil wars, the militia came to be viewed as an auxiliary home-defence force exercising the powers of a kind of constabulary. However, in the minds of Republican and, later, Whiggish political theorists, the militia continued to offer the model of an alternative military force to a standing army, which they regarded as an odious institution long after amateur military organizations could be regarded as serious contenders in the European military world. An argument

---

[1] C. H. Firth (ed.), *The Clarke Papers*, 4 vols., CS NS 49, 54, 61, 62 (1891–1901), iii. 19, 65–6; J. R. Western, *The English Militia in the Eighteenth Century: The Story of a Political Issue, 1660–1802* (1965), 5–8; A. Coleby, 'Military–Civilian Relations on the Solent, 1651–1689', *HJ* 29 (1986), 954.

could be made that in the Roman or Ottoman or mainland European theatres of politics, mercenary and standing military forces were often instruments of arbitrary government, but the alternative forms of military organization, such as feudal retinues, hostings of clan chieftains or part-time militias composed of amateurs did not promise a better outcome.[2]

The Restoration military settlement as enacted by the Cavalier Parliament was, however, shaped by political necessity rather than military theory and practice. The English people had learned to dislike standing armies during the Interregnum, and the Machiavellian arguments as to why a militia was to be preferred to a standing army would be endlessly reiterated by articulate and persuasive politicians and political theorists. During the civil wars the extensive domestic manufacture and importation of firearms and other weapons left a huge surplus of weapons of war, not to mention already existing hunting-weapons, in the hands of ordinary people as declining prices made them easily affordable. Many English and Welsh people possessed arms, and it was thought preferable to arm the friends of the Restoration government and to counterbalance the malcontents among Republicans, old Cromwellians and religious 'fanatics'.[3]

The Restoration settlement of the militia recognized that a militia was necessary for the preservation of order, and was a politically preferable alternative to a large standing army. It cleared up those legal ambiguities about the obligations of householders to support a militia and to serve in it that had existed since the repeal of the Elizabethan Militia Act of 1558 in 1604. The statutory obligations of those with annual incomes above a certain level to pay militia rates, to find weapons and to attend musters were established, and penalties provided for disobedience. The cost of the militia was to be borne by annual assessments payable by the month, and was not dependent upon parliamentary subsidies. The militia was authorized to exercise police powers, and continuity was ensured by the appointment of clerks to keep records, make disbursements and issue orders authorized by the lieutenants and deputies. Considering the lack of trust in Charles I to raise and command an 'exact militia', it is remarkable that Parliament gave Charles II command of the militia. Actually, the question of who controlled the militia, which had caused so much trouble in 1642, was still not resolved in 1661. The Restoration militia settlement rested upon the understanding that the king could command only if the lieutenants and deputies of the county militias cooperated and the power of the gentry was preserved. Some of those in Parliament who supported the enactment of the Restoration Militia Statutes had hoped that a standing militia could be created which would preclude the establishment of the kind of standing army led by professional officers that mainland European states took for granted. In any case, the king was unsuccessful in

---

[2] Western, *English Militia*, pp. xiv, 3.

[3] P. Edwards, *Dealing in Death: The Arms Trade and the British Civil Wars, 1638–52* (2000), 237–41; J. L. Malcolm, *Guns and Violence: The English Experience* (2002), 49–53: Manning, *H&P* 39, 45–7; id., *Swordsmen*, 142, 146–7.

attempting to re-establish the prerogatives of raising men and money for military purposes, and local officials often refused to cooperate with the crown.[4]

The Militia Acts of 1661 and 1663 thus gave the prerogative of command to the king, but more power devolved upon the lords-lieutenant and deputy lieutenants of the county militias as leaders of the county communities than was the case before the civil wars. The number of deputy lieutenants per county was increased, and the lords-lieutenant spent much more time consulting with and socializing with their deputies. The hierarchy of command within each county militia reinforced the ties of kinship and clientage and patronage within the landed classes of the county community. The lieutenant, who was invariably a peer after the Restoration, spent more time visiting different parts of the county, and his progresses and receptions came to be attended with the same ceremony and spectacle that was lavished upon formal musters. The trained bands were now clothed in uniforms which might be yellow, red, blue or white according to their regiment; they were given new colours, and the drummers were often decked out in coats adorned with silver lace. Older deputy lieutenants might regard this as an expensive affectation—the more to be resented and opposed because the cost was paid by an assessment of doubtful legality—but such obstructionists were usually dropped from the commission of lieutenancy. For his part, the lord-lieutenant felt obliged to provide hospitality and gifts for his deputies.[5]

At the time of the Restoration, William Cavendish, first duke of Newcastle, told Charles II that without a sizeable standing army he must be certain that he controlled the militia and London: 'Without an army in your hands, you are but a king on the courtesy of others.'[6] Republicans and old Cromwellians remained entrenched in county governments in England and Wales. Not only were many households in possession of surplus weapons of war; numerous veterans of the civil wars knew how to handle those weapons and remained unreconciled to the Restoration settlement. For a decade after 1660 royal proclamations were issued at regular intervals ordering disbanded soldiers to leave London. In Wales, Roundheads continued to pervade the magistracy, and remained a political force for some time. They were united by their membership in nonconformist congregations, and later, in the 1670s, came to enjoy the patronage of Whig politicians and courtiers. Thus, the Royalists had good reason to fear them following the Restoration—especially since so many of them had previously held high military command. A number of the Roundheads were arrested and gaoled at the time of the Restoration, and some went into exile, but plots continued in several Welsh counties until the end of the Second Anglo-Dutch War. The Welsh Republican plots mirrored those in England, and made Charles II's government nervous

[4] A. Fletcher, *Reform in the Provinces: The Government of Stuart England* (1986), 319–23; Western, *English Militia*, 9; I. F. W. Beckett, *The Amateur Military Tradition, 1558–1945* (1991), 50.

[5] Western, *English Militia*, 48; Fletcher, *Reform in the Provinces*, 329–32.

[6] T. P. Slaughter (ed.), *Ideology and Politics on the Eve of the Restoration: Newcastle's Advice to Charles II*, APSM 159 (1984), p. xiv.

about maintaining political stability. The militia may have declined as a military force, but it performed a much-needed function by helping to maintain order and stability—especially when the army was too small to police the countryside or deal with large-scale disorder.[7]

The urgent situation, many thought, justified Charles II's assumption of command over the militia in 1660 without statutory authority to do so. In early 1661 Thomas Venner, a cooper and a Fifth-Monarchist, outraged by the execution of some of the regicides, led an uprising in London. The Militia Act of 1661 indemnified those who had participated in the suppression of Venner's Rising, and it also confirmed the assumption of command of the militia by the king. Although there were those who grumbled about the legality of paying militia rates or serving in the militia until the Act of 1663 was passed, most of the governing classes seemed to agree that the maintenance of public order and stability was a high priority. For his part, Charles II appointed lords-lieutenant and deputy lieutenants without paying too much attention to the civil-war allegiances of their families. The main criterion for appointment was their standing in the local community, and thus Charles and his Privy Council avoided introducing the taint of partisanship into the county militias. This helped to restore unity to the upper ranks of the county militia officers, so that they were able to maintain order during the alarms that accompanied Venner's Rising.[8]

Between the Restoration of Charles II and the end of the Second Anglo-Dutch War the militia settlement appears to have worked well. Andrew Coleby's study of the relations between the crown and the leaders of the Hampshire militia shows that the Restoration government was more successful than its Interregnum predecessors in involving local inhabitants enrolled in the militia in discharging police duties in the county. Although the Restoration militia forces were smaller than the Caroline trained bands, they were better organized. Weaponry had been brought up to date, and the militia regiments and companies were equipped with flags, ensigns, trumpets, drums and uniforms in order to improve morale. The militia legislation was well received in Hampshire, because there was more local control over the militia than there had been in Cromwell's time. The Hampshire militia willingly cooperated in the surveillance and disarming of those thought to be disaffected. Because of a royal dockyard and fortifications along the Solent and on the Isle of Wight, Hampshire was a strategically sensitive area and was open to foreign incursion. The militia of the Isle of Wight and Hampshire mustered during the Second Anglo-Dutch War and were placed under the command of experienced officers from the Guards regiments in London. Troops of the Royal Horse Guards were dispatched to reinforce the militia and the fortifications were

---

[7] P. Jenkins, ' "The Old Leaven": Welsh Roundheads After 1660', *HJ* 24 (1981), 809–12; Western, *English Militia*, 4–5.

[8] Fletcher, *Reform in the Provinces*, 316–19; J. P. Kenyon (ed.), *The Stuart Constitution, 1603–1688: Documents and Commentary* (1966), 374; Henry Neville, *Plato Redivivus* (c. 1681), repr. in C. Robbins (ed.), *Two English Republican Tracts* (1969), 125.

inspected. The presence of regular army officers was not resented, but apparently welcomed by the local government officials of Portsmouth and the Isle of Wight, who were concerned about strengthening the defences of these areas. Such preparations probably deterred the Dutch from inflicting the humiliations on the Solent that were inflicted upon Chatham and Sheerness.[9]

As the tactical military role of the Restoration militia diminished, it became more politicized—much more so than had been the case with the Caroline militia. Besides harrying nonconformists, who were especially strong in corporate towns, the lords-lieutenant and lesser militia officers began to meddle in partisan politics and parliamentary elections. Parliament trusted the militia because it was under the influence of peers and gentry in the county communities, and the militia officers were men of substance. They gave their allegiance to the Church of England, Parliament and local communities, unlike courtiers whose primary allegiance was to the king or professional officers who were dependent on their pay. The militia, unlike the standing army, could not effectively be used for imposing the royal will if it went against the interests of Parliament or the local communities, because the chain of command went through the lords-lieutenant and their deputies.[10]

The use of the militia to harass dissenters began to diminish following the end of the Second Anglo-Dutch War, as the possibility of Republican uprisings faded. Indeed, Horatio, first Viscount Townshend, used his office of lord-lieutenant to his advantage in electoral politics against the cavalier gentry while, at the same time, promoting a more tolerant attitude towards nonconformists in the municipal corporations which offended strict Anglicans. In the borough of Yarmouth, Townshend actually commissioned a dissenter as a captain in the town militia. He also employed his militia officers to seize the city of Norwich's principal inn and to disrupt the hustings during the parliamentary elections of 1675—one of the first instances of the influence of Whiggery in a parliamentary election. This behaviour led to Townshend's replacement as lord-lieutenant by a cavalier, Robert Paston, first Viscount Yarmouth, but the local resentment about Townshend being turned out of his office had the effect of creating a powerful Whig interest in the county of Norfolk. In Wales and along the Welsh Border, Charles Paulet, first duke of Bolton, also used his powers as lord-lieutenant to consolidate his political control over parliamentary constituencies and municipal corporations.[11]

What little professional training in the exercise of arms that was available to the county militias came from the muster-master, who was supposed to be a professional soldier. He was paid a salary which came out of the militia rates rather than the special assessment which had caused so much trouble before the civil wars. The Militia Act of 1663 also specified that the muster-master was to be a resident

[9] A. Coleby, *Central Government and the Localities: Hampshire, 1649–1689* (1987), 104–11.

[10] C. M. Clode, *The Military Forces of the Crown: Their Administration and Government*, 2 vols. (1869), i. 36–7; Fletcher, *Reform in the Provinces*, 333.

[11] Fletcher, *Reform in the Provinces*, 335–7: D. Ogg, *England in the Reign of Charles II*, 2 vols., 2nd edn. (1963), i. 253–4; ii. 474–6.

of the county, because the local gentry did not welcome outsiders, and this probably had the effect of preferring the local amateur over the experienced professional. In any case, musters were infrequent, and training and equipment insufficient for anything but keeping order amongst the populace. Much of the blame for this state of affairs fell upon the lords-lieutenant, who failed to collect sufficient funds from the ratepayers to maintain the militia. Although the rank and file of the trained bands were supposed to be made up of property-owners and household-ers, it became usual for such persons to hire substitutes from among the servant and artisan classes. The militia companies began to fall apart after the Second Anglo-Dutch War, because funds intended for the militia were diverted by the crown to other military uses such as improved fortifications and ordnance.[12]

The Second and Third Anglo-Dutch Wars focused attention on a number of political and military problems. The Second Dutch War revealed that the English Republicans and dissenters no longer posed a threat to political stability. At the same time the Dutch invasion of the Medway revealed weaknesses in the defences of England and southern Ireland, and provided the crown with the pretext for expanding the standing military forces beyond the guards and garrisons allowed in the original Restoration military settlement. The expansion of the army was temporarily halted at the end of the Second Dutch War, but resumed with the Third Dutch War and continued through the reigns of James VII and II and William III. The existence of an enlarged army and the evident decline in the military usefulness of the militia prompted a renewal of the theoretical debate concerning the danger of standing armies and the possible role of a reformed militia. As a Whig faction emerged in the 1670s, they became the main but not the only proponents of the concept of a reinvigorated militia as an alternative model to a standing army led by professional officers.

Machiavelli, whose works began to be read in the early seventeenth century in the British Isles, was the main source of the civic tradition and its concept of a citizen militia. Machiavelli had stressed the important connection between citizenship and the willingness of citizens to serve as soldiers. These ideas were further developed and reinforced by his principal Anglophone disciples, James Harrington and Andrew Fletcher of Saltoun, but the politically articulate of the Three Kingdoms had in the meantime also become familiar with some of the sources of Machiavelli's ideas through their own reading of Roman authors—especially Cornelius Tacitus. Central to the concept of the civic tradition was the belief that participation in a militia was as much an expression of civic virtue as participation in the governing of the political community; this shared military experience also served to bind citizens together and to overcome, to a certain extent, differences in social status. Fletcher thought that a well regulated militia was the 'chief part of the constitution of any free government'. Roman liberty had

---

[12] Western, *English Militia*, 26–30; Fletcher, *Reform in the Provinces*, 322; Beckett, *Amateur Military Tradition*, 50; Andrew Fletcher of Saltoun, *A Discourse of Government with Relation to Militias* (1698), in *Political Works*, ed. J. Robertson (1997), 23.

perished when a permanent military force of paid professional soldiers replaced the earlier citizen army of the Republic. Harrington's adaptation of the Machiavellian civic tradition to English practice argued that in a well ordered commonwealth it was morally and politically necessary for military power to be in the hands of a yeomanry—the English equivalent of the Roman citizen-soldier— who would constitute a militia. Unless citizens maintained martial virtue by regularly exercising arms, they would become exposed to the vagaries of fortune. Thus, political institutions needed to be activated by a moral will and a public spirit called *virtù*. The Machiavellian meaning of *virtù* was a manifestation of 'manly energy' in pursuit of glory in uncertain circumstances in order to preserve the political community. The ability and willingness to serve as citizen-soldiers was the test of a political community's attachment to *virtù* and liberty.[13]

The political usefulness of these ideas in late seventeenth-century England was emphasized by Walter Moyle, an MP from Cornwall, and other Whig enemies of standing armies, such as John Trenchard, who gathered in the 1690s at Will's Coffee House and the Grecian Tavern. Moyle, drawing upon his considerable knowledge of Roman history, argued that the Romans kept the martial spirit alive by maintaining a militia composed of men of property who exercised arms. Such people were unlikely to submit to the rule of one person, and would always be enemies of tyranny.[14] The problem with the concept of a militia as it derived from the Florentine civic tradition was that it did not accord with the reality of late seventeenth-century war and politics. It is fair to say that Machiavelli and his English disciples had a better understanding of Roman than of modern European history. Machiavelli, who was attached to the practice of the Roman Republic of relying upon a citizen-army or militia, did not explain why so many European states, republics as well as monarchies, had preferred to raise standing armies. James Harrington, in his *Oceana* (1656), could not imagine a society in which the state could afford to raise and maintain an army by levying taxes, and his concept of a standing army derived from the example of the voracious hordes such as those commanded by Wallenstein, Mansfeld or Charles of Lorraine during the Thirty Years War and which lived by plunder, rather than by the example of the New Model Army of the Commonwealth and Protectorate. The latter may have been a comparatively well disciplined army, but Harrington did not believe that the English government was sufficiently well endowed with treasure to keep it standing indefinitely. Even the regents of the Dutch Republic at the end of the Eighty Years War concluded that the States' Army would have to be disbanded. Like Machiavelli, Harrington denied that money provided the sinews of war. The advocates of the militia, from late fifteenth-century Italy to the Three Kingdoms

[13] J. Robertson, *The Scottish Enlightenment and the Militia Issue* (1985), 9–10, 12–14; J. G. A. Pocock (ed.), *The Political Works of James Harrington* (1977), 58–9; Fletcher of Saltoun, 'Introduction' and *Discourse of Government*, in *Political Works*, ed. Robertson, pp. x, xix, 21–2.

[14] Walter Moyle, *An Essay on the Constitution and Government of the Roman State* (1796), in Robbins (ed.), *Two English Republican Tracts*, 229.

in the late seventeenth century, adhered to the belief that 'the true sinews of war were to be found in the martial valour of an armed citizenry'.[15] By the mid-1670s the term 'standing army in time of peace' in the political language of the radical Whigs had become associated with the notions of prerogative and corruption. This was as much the fault of Protector Oliver as Charles II, because it was Cromwell who had abolished feudal tenures, and thus made a militia or a standing army solely dependent upon him. For James Harrington, the basic concept of a 'standing army in time of peace' was that it depended upon a solitary ruler, and this, more than the soldiers who comprised that army, was what made such a force so obnoxious, because the king might govern by means of that army.[16]

However politically useful the concept of a well regulated militia was for attacking Stuart absolutism and standing armies, the fact remained, as the English disciples of Machiavelli had to admit, that the militia had become a useless military instrument. John Trenchard confessed that the actual state of the English militia was so bad that it discredited the whole concept of a militia. James Harrington admitted that whereas the ancients expected free men of property to serve as soldiers as part of their political obligations, the English nobility, gentry and freeholders, having lost the martial spirit, ceased to exercise arms and hired substitutes to serve in the militia from among servants and artificers. Harrington complained that the English aristocracy could not understand that by entrusting their sons to 'common soldiers' for their education, they would be able to acquire martial virtue, protect their liberties and emulate the Romans as 'lords of the earth'. Some forty years later, in 1698, Andrew Fletcher and John Toland made the same complaint in so many words.[17] While Toland admitted that the militia as constituted in the 1690s was useless, he claimed that history demonstrated that such a situation was not inevitable. Standing armies were so pernicious that a way had to be found to inculcate the martial spirit in men of property. Thomas Venn's *Military and Maritime Discipline* (1672), a drill manual intended for use by the militia, declared that soldiers must be regarded as necessary and desirable in England, and that to bear arms or to honour those who did so was the patriotic duty of Englishmen and loyal subjects. A chaplain who preached to the Honourable Artillery Company of London in 1680 insisted that Christianity did not turn men into cowards who were reluctant to undertake dangerous enterprises. The two essential qualities of a

[15] Fletcher of Saltoun, *Political Works*, ed. Robertson, 'Introduction', pp. xix–xx; Pocock (ed.), *Political Works of James Harrington*, 58–9; Manning, *Swordsmen*, 74–5.

[16] J. G. A. Pocock, *The Machiavellian Moment: Florentine Political Thought and the Atlantic Republican Tradition* (1975), 410–11.

[17] [John Trenchard], *A Short History of Standing Armies in England* (1698), 40–1; *The Model of the Commonwealth of Oceana* (1656), in Pocock (ed.), *Political Works of James Harrington*, 312; Fletcher of Saltoun, *Discourse of Government*, 21–2; [John Toland], *The Militia Reformed: Or an Easy Scheme of Furnishing England with a Constant Land Force* (1698), 17–19. Fletcher's comments were intended to include Lowland Scotland. Harrington's reference to 'common soldiers' means professional soldiers, including officers. The education that he refers to is the traditional 'apprenticeship in arms' whereby gentlemen volunteers served in the ranks of permanent armies before accepting military commissions (Manning, *Swordsmen*, ch. 4).

soldier, he maintained, were courage and good conduct—thus placing the emphasis upon the possession of moral virtues rather than professional knowledge and competence.[18]

The advocates of reforming the militia asserted the need to revive martial virtue among the propertied classes, but had few ideas about how to make the militia an effective military instrument. Their rhetoric was primarily directed towards depicting standing armies as instruments of despotism and the political necessity of resuscitating the militia. Despots were reliant upon mercenary soldiers who, because they were not men of property, lacked independence and civic virtue and were isolated from the civic tradition. Despotism became established by conquest or corruption, that is, by citizens putting private selfish interests ahead of the public good. There was no more certain evidence of such corruption than the widespread acceptance of mercenary soldiers. Evidence of such corruption, according to Andrew Marvell, poet and MP, could be found in the practice of naval and military officers sitting in Parliament as royal placemen. Such men were unlikely to criticize the wars with the Netherlands or vote to reduce or abolish the army. Henry Neville, the English translator of Machiavelli, insisted that the appetites of mercenary soldiers were so insatiable that the despots who hired them could not long continue to satisfy them, and would inevitably be overthrown. Thus, mercenary armies also contributed to political instability. Andrew Fletcher, who supposedly served as a volunteer in the crusade to drive the Turks out of Europe, was careful when commenting upon the abuses in standing armies which arose when officers failed to pay their men their full wages, because he did not want to provoke challenges from those same officers—although Fletcher himself was a dueller and was quick to take offence.[19]

Proposals to reform the militia were almost invariably linked to schemes for educating youth. Roger Boyle, first earl of Orrery, observed that the training of the militia fell short of what the Greeks did, and failed to inure men to hardship. The Greek way was to give military training to men when they were young, rather than in middle age as was the case in the English system, which excluded apprentices and servants and included only husbandmen and masters of households.[20] The education of youth was also the key element in John Toland's scheme for substituting a militia for a standing army. To insure the participation of the propertied classes, he proposed that anyone who wished to qualify for any civil or military office for profit or honour be required to serve 'two campaigns [campaigning seasons, presumably] by land or sea'. Toland felt that this would fit in

[18] Thomas Venn, *Military and Maritime Discipline* (1672), sigs. C*r* & *v*, C1*v*; John Scott, *A Sermon Preached before the Artillery Company of London* (1680), sig. A2*r*, pp. 1, 6.
[19] Robertson, *Militia Issue*, 10–11; *An Account of the Growth of Popery and Arbitrary Government in England* (1678), in A. Grosart (ed.), *The Complete Works of Andrew Marvell, MP*, 4 vols. (1875; repr. 1966), iv. 323; Pocock (ed.), *Political Works of James Harrington*, 135; Neville, *Plato Redivivus*, 177–81; Algernon Sidney, *Discourses concerning Government* (1698; repr. 1979), 120; Fletcher, *Discourse of Government*, 16–17.
[20] Roger Boyle, 1ˢᵗ earl of Orrery, *A Treatise of the Art of War* (1677), 4–5.

with the grand tour if England were not at war, and if a state of war existed the prospective officers could serve as volunteers on the continent with the armies of England's allies. Toland also thought that this practice would bridge the cultural gap between swordsmen and gownsmen: 'Thus men of arts and arms will be the very same species among us, whereas now they are extremely different in most parts of the world; for the former are generally cowards and the latter barbarous and rude.' Although Toland would make freeholders the basis of the militia, he also proposed to give military training to 'auxiliaries', as he called servants, since some of them would someday become 'freemen' and masters of households. Toland answers those who objected that training servants in the use of arms would conflict with the Game Laws by remarking that the defence of the kingdom is to be preferred to the loss of a few birds, which in any case could easily be destroyed without firearms. He did not wish 'to see the nation disarmed a second time under pretense of preserving game'.[21] Although not a member of the Radical Whig circle of Neville, Moyle, Toland and Trenchard, Daniel Defoe was aware that standing armies were politically objectionable and that the county militias were poorly trained in the use of firearms. He stated that the glory of England had once been the skill of her longbow-men, whose proficiency in the use of this military weapon had provided them with diversion in peacetime. He urged that marksmanship with the musket be encouraged by having the gentry offer prizes in competitions. He hoped that marksmanship could become a recreation comparable to archery in medieval times. It would be a more wholesome sport, he thought, than cockfighting, cricket or tippling.[22]

It was the end of the Nine Years War in 1697 that prompted the Standing Army Controversy of 1697–8. The Radical Whigs saw the opportunity to disband the army, and this prompted the most extensive, if not most candid, discussion in early modern Europe concerning the meaning of the civic tradition and the relative merits of standing armies and militias. Ultimately, the debate was not really about the military effectiveness of the two alternative models of military organization. It is quite doubtful whether the Whigs really wanted to see an efficient military organization established in England. Henry Neville argued that the Whiggism of the Restoration period came into being because of the fear that the king would enforce his prerogative power by military means, while Parliament lacked the means of preventing this abuse of power short of a resort to civil war. This tended to distort the politics of the time, and had the effect of exaggerating religious policies and prejudices which otherwise would have been less divisive.[23]

The opponents of a standing army asserted that it would be sufficient for England to rely for its defences upon its navy and a well regulated militia. Daniel Defoe had no trouble demolishing this argument. He pointed out that the navy

21 Toland, *Militia Reformed*, 56, 74–5, 88–9.
22 [Daniel Defoe], *An Essay upon Projects* (1697), 278–80.
23 Robertson, *Militia Issue*, 14–15; Pocock (ed.), *Political Works of James Harrington*, 135.

had, in the recent past, been unable to prevent the invasions of the duke of Monmouth and William of Orange. As for land forces, a well regulated militia was like a black swan—an 'unheard of thing'. In arguing for a standing army, Defoe said that war had become a trade that necessitated a long apprenticeship and required experience as well as courage. Members of the militia must necessarily remain amateurs. Nor could a standing army be raised, trained and shipped to Flanders in time to stop the French army, which had demonstrated that it could move very quickly. Defoe insisted that the only time within his memory that soldiers had openly defied the law was in an election of the two sheriffs of London, when soldiers of the London trained bands—not those of the regular army—sought to influence the election results.[24] John, first Lord Somers, wanted to maintain a 'land-force' from year to year subject to an annual review by Parliament as long as Louis XIV continued to pose a threat to peace, but he studiously avoided calling that force a standing army. Although he avoided disparaging the English militia, Lord Somers insisted that the best of militias could never be as proficient as a permanent military force, because the latter trained continuously.[25]

As the militia lost its relevance as a tactical defence force during the Restoration period, it was kept in existence by Parliament because the Whigs saw it possessing a role as the defender of Protestant liberties against arbitrary royal government, and because most members of Parliament were militia officers. For a time it had found a useful role as a constabulary, but that also met with a mixed reaction. Following the Second Anglo-Dutch War, dissenters came to be regarded as less of a threat, and as old Cromwellians grew older the government generally became less concerned about security and stability. The Declaration of Indulgence of 1672 sought to defuse disaffection at home by granting toleration to dissenters and recusants. The arbitrary and sometimes illegal use of the trained bands to crush religious dissent by searching houses for arms and committing people to the custody of provost-marshals, not to mention the use of the militia to interfere in elections, brought complaints about the abrogation of liberties of the subject, and rendered the militia obnoxious in the eyes of many. In the City of London, large crowds obstructed the work of the City trained bands in trying to break up the meetings of dissenters and to destroy their meeting-houses. The Whigs continued to hope that the militia might be reformed, and in 1678 a committee of the House of Commons chaired by one Colonel Kirkby began to investigate how the militia might be made more militarily effective, and a major debate took place on the subject in the autumn. A bill to reform the militia was introduced which proposed having one-third of the militia on active duty at any one time. Charles II vetoed

---

[24] [Daniel Defoe], *A Brief Reply to the History of Standing Armies in England* (1698), 10–14; id., *An Argument Shewing that a Standing Army, with the Consent of Parliament, is not Inconsistent with a Free Government* (1698), 22–3.

[25] John, 1ˢᵗ Lord Somers, *A Letter Ballancing the Necessity of Keeping a Land-Force in Times of Peace* (1697), 3–7, 12.

the bill because he thought he would not be able to control such a force, and it would pose a threat to his sovereignty. The bill was a reaction to the threat perceived to have been caused by the Popish Plot; otherwise Parliament rarely showed an inclination to make the militia a more effective military force. Crown officials instead preferred to build up the standing army.[26]

Parliament had already demonstrated that it wished to disarm the populace. By the Game Act of 1671, only landowners who were armigerous, lords of manors or possessors of hunting franchises might own weapons—whether guns or bows. Moreover, gamekeepers were empowered to search houses for such unlawful weapons. It was not necessary to show that the weapons had ever been used for unlawful hunting. Mere possession of them justified confiscation, and the enforcement of the statute was placed in the hands of a single magistrate. Joyce Malcolm argues that this law gave the Protestant gentry the authority to disarm Catholic tenants where the crown failed to do so, and it could be justified by their lack of hunting privileges and low economic status rather than religion.[27]

There is good reason to believe that the number of men who were trained in the use of firearms diminished during the Restoration period, and there is evidence that the total numbers enrolled in the county militias declined from pre-civil war days. The frequency of annual musters of the whole county militia certainly fell, and furnishes abundant evidence of the decay of the militia as a tactical military force. Few counties held annual musters outside of the years when there were emergencies such as the threat of invasion by the Dutch. Musters were more likely to take place by hundreds, because so much of the four days allotted by Parliamentary legislation would have been spent assembling units from the more remote parts of the county. Training does seem to have occurred more frequently at the company level, which would have been more consistent with use of the militia as a constabulary. In Suffolk in 1671, militia companies mustered for two days of small-arms and close-order drill, and this was followed by four days of training at the regimental level after the harvest had been gathered. However, in Buckinghamshire the militia units mustered only at the troop and company level in 1677, and only for two days in a year. The Buckinghamshire militia consisted of a single regiment of foot made up of companies of eighty to eighty-five men and three troops of horse comprising fifty-six to sixty-one men each. In only one case were two whole companies of foot mustered and drilled on the same days. Otherwise, only one company drilled at a time.[28] The horse-bands probably

---

[26] Coleby, *Central Government and the Localities*, 111; Western, *English Militia*, 27–30, 48–9; D. P. Carter, 'The Lancashire Militia, 1660–1688', in J. L. Kermode and C. B. Phillips (eds.), *Seventeenth-Century Lancashire: Essays Presented to J.H. Bagley*, THSLC 82 (1982), 170, 176; J. Miller, 'The Militia and the Army in the Reign of James II', *HJ* 16 (1973), 660–1; Ogg, *Reign of Charles II*, ii. 574.

[27] Kenyon, *Stuart Constitution*, 494, 502; J. L. Malcolm, *To Keep and Bear Arms: The Origins of an Anglo-American Right* (1994), 75–6.

[28] Western, *English Militia*, 26; Fletcher, *Reform in the Provinces*, 325–6; HEH, Ellesmere MSS., EL 8527; Carter, 'Lancashire Militia, 1660–1688', 170–1.

assumed greater importance in police activities than the foot companies, and because of their greater mobility were probably more effective. Before the civil wars, the horse-bands were made up exclusively of the servants and retainers of aristocratic households, but at the Restoration these were integrated into the county militia, and the cost of maintaining them and providing the personnel was spread more equitably among the lesser gentry and yeomanry. Although the amount of time available for drilling the militia companies and troops was limited, there were many complaints that much of this time was wasted in drinking and feasting in taverns. Certainly, Thomas Venn took this as an indication of decline among the county militias.[29] One can only wonder how much the Wiltshire militia drilled, since at the time of the Monmouth Rebellion in 1685 most of the locks on their muskets were rusted out, and they lacked moulds to make bullets. In many of the western counties the lords-lieutenant were nowhere to be found, or were negligent. Nevertheless, the militia did obstruct the movement of the rebels by getting in their way and containing efforts by Monmouth's captains to recruit more followers. It was, however, made abundantly clear that the militia was tactically useless, undisciplined and lacking in courage.[30]

When Parliament assembled in the autumn following the suppression of Monmouth's Rebellion, James II made a speech from the throne in which he stated that the desertions by members of the militia and their lack of training demonstrated that the militia possessed no military value and could not be relied upon. At the same time James made an argument for enlarging the standing army, and asked Parliament to double the subsidy to pay for that expansion. The members expressed their dislike of the proposed expansion of the regular army, and with the failure of the king to observe the Test Act with regard to the appointment and commissioning of Catholic civil and military officers. The House of Commons did agree to give the king more money, but at the same time proposed to draw up a bill to reform the militia, which the king took to be a vote against the expansion of the army. From this time onwards, an opposition party began to organize to oppose the court faction in Parliament. For his part, James began diverting funds intended for the militia to pay for the expansion of the army.[31]

It is clear that Charles II was losing control of the county militias in the 1670s, and James deliberately neglected them after their poor performance during Monmouth's Rebellion. But both monarchs heeded the duke of Newcastle's advice that, without a large standing army, they needed to maintain royal influence over the trained bands of the City of London. Newcastle had also added that

---

[29] Fletcher, *Reform in the Provinces*, 325–6; Venn, *Military and Maritime Discipline*, 6–7; Carter, 'Lancashire Militia, 1660–1688', 168.

[30] P. Earle, *Monmouth's Rebels: The Road to Sedgemoor, 1685* (1977), 61–3, 83–6; R. Clifton, *The Last Popular Rebellion: The Western Rising of 1685* (1984), 192–5; G. Davies, 'The Militia in 1685', *EHR* 43 (1928), 604–5; *The Autobiography of Sir John Bramston*, CS os 32 (1845), 184–5, 205; Miller, 'Militia and the Army', 61–2.

[31] T. B. Macaulay, *The History of England from the Accession of James II*, 6 vols. (1856), ii. 14, 17–18; *Autobiography of Sir John Bramston*, 211–12; Ogg, *Reign of Charles II*, i. 253–4.

at the same time they needed to respect the rights and privileges of the City, but this sound advice James and Charles apparently did not hear. The City trained bands were better-drilled and disciplined than those of the provincial militias, because their officers received good instruction through their membership in the Honourable Artillery Company of London. The City trained bands drilled every two weeks in the Artillery Ground and mounted spectacles and martial displays for festive occasions. All of the officers of the trained bands appear to have been members of the HAC, and from 1662 all sergeants were ordered to join the company as well. Membership appears to have been limited to those who were free of the City, and servants and apprentices were specifically excluded, while those whose behaviour was unseemly could be expelled. Altogether, the criteria for membership in the HAC accorded well with the notions of the civic tradition and the exercise of arms which were taught by the English disciples of Machiavelli.[32]

Prior to the civil wars, the HAC, along with provincial artillery companies, had played a significant role in the revival of a civic martial culture, but in the Restoration period the Company became politicized and membership appears to have fallen off. James, duke of York, made it his business to become involved in the affairs of the HAC, and was chosen 'commander-in-chief' of the company. He also meddled in the company elections. Thus, Charles II felt comfortable in relying primarily upon the City trained bands to preserve order during the Exclusion Crisis and other popular tumults, rather than sending in the royal guards. The outbreak of the plague in 1665 severely curtailed the activities of the HAC and reduced membership. In the City trained bands, as in the county militias, the practice of employing substitutes became widespread. The lieutenancy of the City was purged after the Test Act of 1673, and the six regiments of the trained bands remained loyal. The crown's interference in HAC affairs is certainly not unconnected with the Company becoming embroiled with national politics during the Exclusion Crisis in 1679. Factionalism surfaced during the annual feast of the Company, which turned into a demonstration of loyalty to the duke of York, and the Company's stewards were chosen from among his followers. The opposing faction boycotted the annual feast, or gave their tickets to their servants. Following the banquet, James encountered popular hostility as he returned through the streets of London to Westminster. Membership of the HAC declined further in the last years of the reign of Charles II, when he suspended Company elections and retained the old Tory officers until his death. There were warning signs that the London trained bands, along with the county militias, were becoming politically unreliable. In 1681 nine officers were put out of their commissions in the London trained bands. On 26 June 1684, the occasion of the Midsummer Marching Watch, the duke of York attempted to re-establish good relations with the HAC by leaving his coach and mounting a horse to lead the company through the City of London. At the Artillery Ground the duke

---

[32] Slaughter (ed.), *Newcastle's Advice*, p. xiv; Walker, *HAC* 76–7; D. Allen, 'The Role of the London Trained Bands in the Exclusion Crisis, 1678–1681', *EHR* 87 (1972), 293.

dismounted and led the regiments in a review, carrying a pike. Afterwards, he was entertained at a banquet in the tent of one of the regimental colonels.[33]

When James became king he dispensed with the county militias, but he continued to regard the London trained bands as important and necessary for maintaining order because of the long history of popular disturbances in the City. In October 1688 James restored the City charter and the old Tory lieutenants. During the Monmouth Rebellion when the City trained bands had been slow in mounting guards to protect a Catholic chapel, the king threatened to bring in the royal guards if the mayor did not act. William III restored the HAC's privileges in 1689, including the right to elect their own officers. However, membership in the HAC continued at a low level during the years of William and Mary, and officers of the London trained bands often neglected to join the HAC for military instruction. The staging of martial spectacles during the war years of the 1690s appears to have fallen into other hands. In June 1691 the Artillery Company of Westminster re-enacted the Siege of Mons in Tothill Fields. In July 1693 the artillery train from the Tower of London provided a spectacle of blowing up forts with mines, 'to the great satisfaction of the spectators', although two people were badly injured by accidents. During the 1690s the trained bands of Westminster appear to have been manned and officered by tradesmen and mechanics, and fit only to be caricatured by the low satires of Ned Ward.[34]

During James's brief reign neglect of the militia went hand-in-hand with expansion of the army. James also purged the commissions of the peace and lieutenancy, and appointed Catholics and dissenters who lacked the experience and the social standing necessary for executing those offices. After dispensing with the county militias and purging the commissions, though, James had to reappoint some of those individuals when he finally awakened and realized that William of Orange was indeed preparing an invasion of England. The militia had decayed so far that he was unable to revive it in many counties. Although the militia did function in a few areas during William's invasion, James failed to secure the cooperation of those lieutenants and deputies whom he had earlier purged. Their interest was in maintaining local control, not in cooperating with James. The populace were especially disaffected in the south-west of England where William landed, and the militia was not equal to policing the disaffected areas. The army was also less than reliable because of the turmoil over the presence of Catholic officers and Irish regiments in England, which bred hostility and violence. The army was, for the most part, never put to the test, because so many officers were disloyal or had deserted. The rank and file were probably more loyal than the officers.[35]

---

[33] Walker, *HAC* 76–7, 81, 87–9; Allen, 'London Trained Bands', 287–8, 290, 295–8, 302; Luttrell, *RSA* i. 92, 312.

[34] Miller, 'Militia and the Army', 664–6; Walker, *HAC* 93–9; Luttrell, *RSA* ii. 242; iii. 129; Edward Ward, *The London Spy*, ed. P. Hyland, 4th edn. (1709; repr. 1993), 143.

[35] J. Miller, *Popery and Politics in England, 1660–1688* (1973), 219–20, 272; id., 'The Militia and the Army', 659, 667–71; Fletcher, *Reform in the Provinces*, 346–7; J. R. Western, *Monarchy and Revolution: The English State in the 1680s* (1972), 273–4, 277.

The loyalty of the Irish militia was also suspect. Sir William Petty estimated that in 1672 the military forces of the kingdom of Ireland included a standing army of 6,000 and a militia of 24,000 or 25,000, many of whom were veterans of the civil wars and nonconformists. All of them were Protestants, and Petty further estimated that these Protestant militia men possessed three-quarters of the horses 'serviceable for war'.[36] Roger Boyle, Lord Broghill and soon to become earl of Orrery, had served as one of the lords justices of Ireland along with Sir Charles Coote, and was instrumental in effecting the Restoration of Charles II in his other kingdom. He continued in that post for three years before James Butler, first duke of Ormonde, was appointed lord-lieutenant of Ireland. Orrery was then made president of Munster, where he served until the presidency of Munster was suppressed in 1672 and he was removed. Besides the powerful presidency of Munster, which gave him authority over almost all of the substantial Irish militia, Orrery was a major-general in the Irish army, and had held high command in the Cromwellian forces in Ireland. Orrery had come to resemble nothing so much as an over-mighty subject. He took special pride in the militia, which he drilled to a degree of competence that was unknown in England. He built a magnificent house at Charleville where he lived in splendour and held the presidential courts, which excited much envy. When the duke of Ormonde, as lord-lieutenant, made a progress through Ireland, the well-organized display of the militia and Orrery's popularity among the Protestants made Ormonde fear that Orrery was a man who might take independent action, and a coolness developed between them. Orrery claimed that his carefully prepared defences had deterred the French and the Dutch from invading southern Ireland during the Third Anglo-Dutch War. Ormonde feared that Orrery's determination to exclude Catholics from the militia might provoke rebellion—a fear that Sir William Petty shared. Petty thought that the Protestant landowners hoped to exploit a Catholic rising in order to dispossess more Catholic landowners and consolidate their hold on the land. Consequently, Orrery's plans to turn his militia into a permanent auxiliary military force were frustrated by the refusal of Ormonde to authorize payment for the time that Orrery's militia had spent on active service.[37]

Orrery's attempts to establish a permanent militia grew out of his determination to protect the Protestant interest from what he perceived to be a revival of Catholicism. He wished to disarm everyone in Ireland except soldiers, members of the militia, peers and civil officers of the crown. Orrery's 'well regulated militia', however, proved unreliable during the Third Anglo-Dutch War: many individuals in the militia failed to muster when they were called upon, and the force had to be reinforced by regulars. This Orrery blamed upon Ormonde's failure to pay

---

[36] Sir William Petty, *The Political Anatomy of Ireland* (1691), 43, 46–7.

[37] *The State Letters of . . . Roger Boyle, 1ˢᵗ Earl of Orrery*, comp. Thomas Morrice (1742), 35–6; O. Airy (ed.), *Essex Papers*, vol. 1: *1672–1679*, CS NS 47 (1890), i. 9–11; S. J. Connolly, 'The Defence of Protestant Ireland, 1660–1760', in *MHI* 233–6; L. Irvin, 'The Earl of Orrery and the Military Problems of Munster', *IS* 13 (1977–9), 10–19.

the members of the militia. The regular soldiers turned out to be a distinct liability, because their pay was often more than a year in arrears and some, out of desperation, turned to crime when local merchants refused to extend credit to them. Ormonde was removed as lord-lieutenant in 1669. In 1672 Arthur Capel, first earl of Essex, was sent to Dublin in his place; although he was an uncompromising Protestant and Whig, Essex too grew alarmed at Orrery's ambitions. Charles II reassured Essex that he was right in denying Orrery a licence to fortify his castle of Ballymartin or Ballymartyr, near Cork. Essex was also opposed to allowing Orrery to continue to command the militia, because he and his followers represented the old Cromwellian faction who already possessed too much power in Ireland, and because such a policy would effectively privatize the use of force. Indeed, some of them had already been disarmed by Ormonde for that very reason. The Protestant landowners grew alarmed at this and complained that the failure to maintain the militia had led to an increase in the bands of tories, who committed numerous robberies, and was detrimental to the Protestant interest. Essex preferred to use the army to keep order, but he conceded that there were compelling political reasons for making concessions to the Protestant landowners by maintaining the militia.[38]

Essex was recalled as lord-lieutenant in 1677, and Ormonde reinstated. The Popish Plot and threat of possible French invasion of Ireland made it appear politic to Ormonde to revive the militia. Orrery exploited the circumstances to increase his own power at the expense of the lord-lieutenant. By the mid-1670s the Irish Protestant aristocracy had come to distrust the Stuarts and their religious policies to such a degree that cooperation was no longer possible. When James VII and II came to the throne, he disarmed and disbanded the Irish militia because he regarded it as a preserve of the Protestant interest, and he began the process of catholicizing the Irish army. Richard Talbot, duke of Tyrconnell, the new commander of the Irish army, believed that a reliable alliance between the crown and the Protestant interest could not be constructed, because the Protestant landed aristocracy were still permeated by Republican and old Cromwellian sentiments. It would be better to form an alliance with Catholic aristocrats, whom he regarded as the natural leaders of Irish society.[39]

In Scotland, as in Ireland, the great danger of maintaining a militia was that it would be controlled by the nobility and used for their own purposes. In 1663 the Scottish Parliament authorized a fencible force of 2,000 horse and 20,000 foot, most of which would be raised at the expense of the nobility. As in the other two kingdoms of the Stuart monarchy, the Scots nobility and gentry disliked standing armies, and preferred militias or fencible forces, in which they would serve as

[38] Airy (ed.), *Essex Papers*, i. 9–11, 147–9, 238–40; *State Letters of . . . Roger Boyle, 1ˢᵗ Earl of Orrery*, comp. Morrice, 243; K. M. Lynch, *Roger Boyle, First Earl of Orrery* (1965), 226–7.

[39] Lynch, *Roger Boyle*, 226–7; T. Barnard, 'Scotland and Ireland in the Later Stewart Monarchy', in S. G. Ellis and S. Barber (eds.), *Conquest and Union: Fashioning a British State, 1485–1725* (1995), 264–5, 272–3.

officers. Charles rejected this offer because he felt more comfortable retaining a small contingent of Cromwellian soldiers to guard against his enemies both at home and abroad. Like the English and Irish armies at the beginning of the Restoration period, the Scots army, which was the smallest of the three, consisted only of guards and garrisons, and could not constitute a field army. However, in 1666 Scotland was disturbed by discontent among the remnant of the Covenanters in the south-west of the country, and when soldiers were sent there to break up illegal conventicles, the Scottish Privy Council realized how exposed the country was to invasion during the Second Anglo-Dutch War. The Scots were a major trading partner of the Netherlands, and there were rumours of collusion between the Scots Presbyterians and the Dutch. The heavy-handed intervention of the army provoked the Pentland Rising, which was made to appear more formidable than it actually was by the incompetence of the commanders of the army. It was realized that Scotland needed a militia to suppress popular disorders.[40]

The small Scots army, having proved itself useless for dealing with popular disturbances, was largely disbanded in 1667. The idea of a militia was an English concept, and an organized military force called by that name did not appear until after the Second Anglo-Dutch War and the Pentland Rising. The Scottish archbishops on the Privy Council disliked the idea because they assumed that the common people, of which the rank and file of the militia would have been composed, were 'generally ill affected' to the Kirk, and could not be counted upon to carry out acts such as the suppression of the Pentland Rising. The compromise agreed upon was not to raise infantry in the disaffected areas but only some horse. The Scottish Estates designated a number of men as being subject to military obligations; they did not actually propose to raise and pay for such forces, so the Privy Council had to take the initiative. The militia was to be levied only in well affected shires and placed under the command of selected noblemen. The militia companies were to be armed with the older style matchlock muskets and pikes, and more modern weapons were specifically prohibited. The new militia was to be organized only into companies rather than regiments, because Charles II did not entirely trust even the most Royalist of the members of the Scots nobility, and disloyal persons such as the earl of Argyll were excluded. A few companies of militia were actually raised and maintained on active service, but because their pay was not current, the militia men were ill disciplined. These militia companies were largely employed against religious dissenters. This arbitrary use of military power during the Restoration period began to discredit Scotland's strong martial tradition.[41]

---

[40] Ibid. 270–1; B. P. Lenman, 'Militia, Fencible Men and Home Defence, 1660–1797', Macdougall, *S&W* 174; Lenman, *Jacobite Risings in Britain, 1689–1746* (1980), 283–4; K. M. Brown, *Kingdom or Province? Scotland and the Regal Union, 1603–1715* (1992), 152–3. On the Pentland Rising see above, pp. 285–6.

[41] *Bishop Burnet's History of his own Time*, 2 vols. (1724, 1734), i. 243; Lenman, 'Militia, Fencible Men and Home Defence' (1756), 183; Brown, *Kingdom or Province?*, 32, 156; Robertson, *Militia Issue*, 6.

John Maitland, first duke of Lauderdale, the main proponent of absolutism on Charles II's Scottish Privy Council, found himself pushed by the Scottish archbishops into taking a stronger stand against the dissenting Covenanters. There was increasing resistance to such a policy from landowners, members of the militia and the common people. This opposition found a voice in the faction led by William, third duke of Hamilton, which had ties to the circle of James, duke of Monmouth, who was the protector of English nonconformists. Because of the failure of the Scottish crown to make the nobility, lairds and heritors responsible for the behaviour of their tenants in religious matters, the Privy Council resorted to raising a mixed force of regulars and fencible men to quarter upon dissident tenants and householders in the south-western shires. A standing army of 5,000 foot and 500 horse was raised from amongst militiamen. The official strength of the militia was again set at 20,000 foot and 2,000 horse. The occupying force, which was posted to the south-west, became known as the 'Highland Host', although only about one-third of them were Highlanders. They remained quartered upon the houses of the Covenanters for a little more than five weeks, but their behaviour gave the militia a bad name for many years to come, although accounts by historians sympathetic to the Covenanters, such as Robert Wodrow, undoubtedly exaggerated the depredations of the 'Highland Host'. In the Highlands, independent companies in the service of Archibald Campbell, ninth earl of Argyll, and Sir John Campbell of Glenorchy, which were used to gather taxes, also exploited the opportunity to pursue private quarrels.[42]

The Scots army and the militia or fencible units did not work well together: conflicts arose between the officers of each, and duels were fought. During the reign of Charles II, the militia and the army were both subordinated to the authority of the commander-in-chief of the army and were subject to military law, although doubt existed among lawyers concerning whether the militia should be subject to army command and law. In 1680 the Scottish judges ruled that the militia was not under the command of army officers or the jurisdiction of courts martial. The Scots nobility found the idea of taking orders from professional military officers repugnant. Needless to say, discipline was a problem in the Scottish militia. During his residence in Scotland from 1679 to 1682, James, duke of York and Albany (the latter was his Scottish title), found much wrong with the Scottish militia, which had a poor record for preserving order. James probably was thinking of the militia muster and review, held in Edinburgh in May 1677 on the anniversary of Charles II's birthday and Restoration, which was the occasion of a riot and a violent confrontation between the prentice boys and the merchant youth that required that a troop of Life Guards and a squadron of cavalry be brought in to quell the disorder. James compelled the City of Edinburgh to raise a full-time town guard to suppress tumults. Sir John Lauder thought that this was a

---

[42] Brown, *Kingdom or Province?*, 32, 159; Lenman, 'Militia, Fencible Men and Home Defence', 179–80; *The Method of Turning the Militia of Scotland into a Standing Army* (1678) [HEH 133860, no. 5]; Sir John Lauder of Fountainhall, *Historical Notices of Scottish Affairs*, 2 vols., BC 87 (1848), i. 191.

great invasion of Edinburgh's liberties and privileges, and asserted that James would have liked to have done the same to London. Moreover, complained Lauder, the officers of the town watch were not even burgesses or townsmen, and the captain of the Edinburgh watch had more power than the provost of Edinburgh. Apparently on the instructions of the duke of York and Albany, certain officers of the militia of the western shires had their commissions cancelled, were disarmed and discharged from the legal obligation to maintain horses worth at least Scots £5. Then, in May 1683, they were called to active duty again, but found it difficult to gather together the necessary accoutrements in time to muster. During the earl of Argyll's Rebellion in 1685, many militia men committed acts of indiscipline. The militia commanders were ordered to select for active duty only 'the prettiest [most valiant] men and best armed'. These men were to be paid for twenty days' service, and their pay was to be collected from those members of the militia who were not called up. At Aberdeen, the fencible men commanded by John Hay, twelfth earl of Errol, mutinied when told that they were not chosen to serve; they said that 'they had hearts to fight as well as they that were chosen and would neither return nor quit their pay'. Lauder says that their real motive was 'the hope of robbing and spoiling'. The mutineers opened fire with their muskets, and were in turn fired upon, after which order was restored. Many members of the militia of the southern Scottish shires deserted rather than be placed on active service.[43]

When James, duke of York and Albany, succeeded his brother as James VII and II, he dismantled the security system based upon the militia and fencible men. He persuaded the Scottish Parliament in 1685 to abolish the militia because he wished to destroy the military power of the nobility. When faced by invasion from William of Orange, James tried to revive the militia, but he was unable to create a strong enough force to prevent the descent into chaos during the Glorious Revolution. Scotland had been left completely undefended, because the small Scots standing army had been transferred to England. When William II and III was made king of England, he trusted his Scottish subjects as little as James had, and the militia sank into a slough of neglect along with the Irish and English militias.[44]

The thinkers of the Scottish Enlightenment were keenly interested in debating the issue of a militia, because of Scotland's strong martial culture. Scotland's national identity had been bound up with a continuing tradition of martial prowess that was shared by both the nobility and the common people. The feudal method of raising armies from among tenants and kinsmen, however, was also associated with weak political institutions. Scotland's experience with standing armies during the civil wars and the Restoration period had left a bitter taste in the mouths of many Scots, and that is why the leading thinkers continued to hope

---

[43] C. Walton, *History of the British Standing Army, 1660–1700* (1894), 475; Sir John Lauder of Fountainhall, *Historical Observations, 1680–1686*, vol. I, ed. A. Urquhart and D. Laing, BC 66 (1857), 169; id., *Scottish Affairs*, i. 151, 357–8.
[44] Lenman, 'Militia, Fencible Men and Home Defence', 184–5.

that some sort of national militia based upon the Roman model might help
Scotland to make the transition to the modern world while retaining some degree
of autonomy in the regal union with England. Andrew Fletcher was one of those
Scots who had hoped that a plan for a national militia could be agreed and implemented. Fletcher was a well travelled man with a good grasp of European affairs.
He had also briefly served as a soldier, and understood that the decay of militias
was a European-wide phenomenon. By the end of the seventeenth century
European states had all come to depend upon mercenary armies, and the most
powerful and successful ones paid for these armies by means of a system of
taxation and extensive trade. In the late 1690s Scotland had access to neither.[45]

If the standing armies of the Commonwealth, Protectorate and Restoration periods were highly politicized, the militias of the Three Kingdoms were more so. This
made the provincial and the London and Edinburgh militias unreliable and
potentially disloyal unless the crown could maintain tight control. This may have
been feasible with regard to the City of London trained bands, but became nearly
impossible in the case of the English county militias as well as those of Ireland and
Scotland, because their officers were drawn from the local aristocracies and were
heavily engaged politically. During the 1660s, when both the crown and the
provincial elites, speaking through the Parliament of England and the Estates of
Scotland, feared uprisings by Republicans, old Cromwellians and religious
'fanatics', it was agreed that maintaining political stability justified breaking conventicles and destroying nonconformist meeting-houses. This joint effort covered
over fissures which would become apparent only later. In Scotland and Ireland,
the actual or potential disloyalty of militias and fencible forces was more evident
because of the non-Anglican leanings of those members of the aristocracies whose
Royalist allegiance was opportunistic and weak at best.

However useful the trained bands and horse-bands were for performing
constabulary duties, they possessed little tactical military value. They did little to
help prevent the humiliating incursions of the Second Anglo-Dutch War or to
suppress uprisings such as the Monmouth Rebellion. While the possibility must
be admitted that the political stupidity of James VII and II contributed to William
II and III's invasion in 1688, it is also difficult to argue that the officers of the militias of the Three Kingdoms had not violated their oaths of loyalty by defecting to
William in the middle of what Whig historians have refused to recognize as a civil
war. The earlier instances of negligence and disloyalty of the militias forces had
provided Charles II and James VII and II with the pretext for expanding the
standing army of England. At the same time, it appears that the English
Parliament might not have opposed a limited expansion of the army if Charles
had not been so devious and disposed to arbitrary rule. The political and

[45] Robertson, *Militia Issue*, 1–3, 25–6, 50–1; Fletcher of Saltoun, *Two Discourses*, 37; Lenman,
Jacobite Risings, 283–4.

diplomatic circumstances surrounding the Third Anglo-Dutch War suggested to many that popery and French influence, together with the possible future succession of a Catholic heir to the throne, posed a greater threat to the safety of the realm than Republicanism, Protestant nonconformism or even an invasion by William of Orange. The fear that an enlarged standing army could become an instrument of royal tyranny prompted a revival of the debate about a reinvigorated militia as an alternative military force. The English and Scottish disciples of Machiavelli drew upon a great fund of useful political theory, strongly republican in content, to oppose the expansion of the army and other Stuart policies. This was expedient for defending parliamentary liberties, but from a military perspective, by inculcating a distaste for standing armies and professional soldiers, the pursuit of political ideology by military, naval and militia officers contributed to the growing and continuing problem of the deprofessionalization of the officer class of the armies of the Three Kingdoms in the Restoration period, and made the British Isles vulnerable to foreign invasion.

The argument that the English Parliament wanted a reformed militia consisting of citizen-soldiers who exercised arms and cultivated martial virtue in Roman fashion was also specious, since Parliament no more desired a proficient militia than a standing army. Parliament was more interested in disarming the populace in order to counteract unlawful hunting and fowling than in promoting the use of firearms in a reformed militia. The existence of county militias commanded by the aristocracy was as politically useful for manipulating parliamentary elections for the benefit of the Whig camp as the presence of military and naval officers sitting and voting as royal placemen in Parliament was to the supporters of the royal court and government. From the perspective of the later Stuart monarchs, the training and arming of a proficient militia would have been tantamount to arming factions of the aristocracies of the Three Kingdoms that had recently been in arms against Charles I and Charles II. In the Celtic parts of the Stuart kingdoms especially, a proclivity for private warfare had not entirely disappeared.[46]

---

[46] Manning, *Swordsmen*, ch. 5.

13

English, Irish and Scots in mainland European armies

I intend to continue in Russia somewhat longer albeit God knoweth the pay there yields us but a bare existence as things go now. Even in Scotland soldiers of fortune can attain no honourable employment for nobles and persons of great quality; in England aliens are seldom employed, so that necessity (who was never yet a good pilot) constrained us to serve foreign princes when notwithstanding, if with honour we be any ways steadable[1] to our native country, it would be some comfort.

Patrick Gordon of Auchleuchries, 'Sixteen Further Letters of General Patrick Gordon', ed. S. Konovalov, *Oxford Slavonic Papers*, 13 (1967), 81–2.

Many swordsmen from the British Isles serving in the mainland European wars had returned home to participate in the Wars of the Three Kingdoms. As the Cromwellian regime conquered Ireland and Scotland and concluded the Third English Civil War, it pursued a policy of banishing captured swordsmen and, sometimes, their dependants and followers to the West Indies and Virginia or encouraging friendly or allied powers to raise military manpower in those conquered countries. At the Restoration there were limited places for the Cromwellian soldiers and returning Cavaliers in the standing armies of the Three Kingdoms. Consequently, there was a considerable exodus of professional soldiers or men who had grown up knowing none other than the military life. Once again, they served in the same armies they had before the civil wars, including those of Sweden, Denmark-Norway, Poland, Imperial Austria, France, Spain, Venice and, especially, the Dutch Republic. They also served in the armies of the newly independent kingdom of Portugal and Muscovite Russia. Those who wished to pursue careers as officers continued to serve a military apprenticeship in the ranks as gentlemen volunteers, and volunteers who desired adventure were especially attracted to the campaigns and sieges of the Imperialist and Venetian forces in their struggle to drive the Ottoman Turks from Europe and the Mediterranean islands.[2]

---

[1] Useful in a military capacity.

[2] Manning, *Swordsmen*, ch. 4; J. W. Stoye, *English Travellers Abroad, 1604–1667: Their Influence in English Society and Politics* (1952; repr. 1968), 239–76.

Until William of Orange's invasion of England and conquest of Scotland and Ireland, which, together with England's involvement in the Nine Years War, brought an expansion of the English/British armies, the British Isles continued to be an important source of manpower for continental European armies. The Scottish and Irish governments cooperated with foreign recruiting officers in exiling unemployed swordsmen, sweeping up vagrants and even impressing prisoners from gaols. The recruiting officers of mainland European armies performed their work quite openly in taverns and inns, and Charles II provided Louis XIV of France with a number of regiments of the English army on loan. James VII and II curtailed the activities of foreign recruiting officers when he began to build up his own armies in the Three Kingdoms. And, since William II and III viewed the British Isles as a valuable source of military manpower for the Anglo-Dutch forces during the Nine Years War, those who continued to make careers in continental European armies after he became king came largely from the Catholic populations of the British Isles.

Some of the English and Scots regiments of the Dutch army had been allowed to run down following the end of the Eighty Years War, the death of William II and the suspension of the offices of stadholder and captain-general by the States General. William III built them up again after the stadholdership was restored, and turned the Scots and Anglo-Dutch Brigades into superior fighting forces that later would constitute the core of the Dutch army that descended upon England in 1688. These regiments, as well as the Dutch navy, had provided a refuge for many swordsmen from the British Isles who could not give their allegiance to the Stuarts.

George Monck believed that an important way of preventing civil war or a reoccurrence of the late civil conflict was to send masterless men to the plantations or to fight in foreign wars. It was understood that prisoners of war, unemployed swordsmen and discharged veterans fell into that category.[3] The governments of the Three Kingdoms had been following such a policy off and on since the late sixteenth century, and it was revived again in the 1650s under the Commonwealth and Protectorate. The Irish had maintained a continuous presence in the Spanish Army of Flanders since 1586, when Sir William Stanley and his regiment had changed their allegiance from the Dutch States General to the Spanish crown. The Irish had the reputation of being brave and sturdy soldiers who could endure astonishingly long marches. Prior to the Wars of the Three Kingdoms, there were usually two Irish regiments in the Army of Flanders, peaking at four regiments with a strength of 7,000 men in 1635–6. Thereafter, two regiments were posted to Spain, and smaller detachments fought in Lorraine with Duke Francis or the prince of Condé. Between 1643 and 1660 military enterprisers were awarded contracts to raise another fourteen regiments, although perhaps five of these never

---

[3] George Monck, duke of Albemarle, *Observations upon Military and Political Affairs* (1671), 145–6.

formally mustered. The various Spanish armies absorbed a large part of the surplus manpower during the Irish civil wars, when fewer economic opportunities were open to Irishmen. A further three Irish regiments were raised for the Army of Flanders between 1667 and 1673, and one continued in Spanish employ as late as 1686.[4]

Between 1634 and 1660 more than 30,000 Irish soldiers served in the French royal army. The arrival of Thomas Wentworth, earl of Strafford, as viceroy of Ireland was the occasion for a renewed official campaign to send Irish swordsmen into foreign service. They were raised by Old English military enterprisers from the south-western counties, and recruitment continued at a high level until the outbreak of the civil wars. Recruitment of new regiments for French service resumed in 1644, and Old English families such as the Butlers preferred to raise soldiers for the French army because the Irish regiments of the Spanish Army of Flanders were controlled by officers from Ulster, and they also hoped for French intervention in the Irish civil wars on the side of the Catholic Confederation of Kilkenny.[5]

Sir William Petty, in his calculations of the demographic disaster resulting from the Cromwellian conquest of Ireland, estimated that more than one-third of the Irish population of 1641 perished in the civil wars or were banished. Petty stated that Cromwell sent 34,000 adult males to serve as soldiers in the armies of Spain and France between 1651 and 1654. It is not unreasonable to suppose that perhaps 10,000 or 11,000 women, children and camp-followers accompanied them into exile. The surviving muster rolls of Irish regiments demonstrate how close family ties were among the Irish military community abroad. By this date the focus of the Spanish war effort had shifted from Flanders to Portugal, Catalonia and the Basque provinces, and the swordsmen who were banished were transported in ships under conditions comparable to those endured by African slaves during the Atlantic Middle Passage, although the voyage to Spain usually took two weeks rather than two months. Many died on their way to the war zones, where the Spanish army was fighting Portuguese and Catalan rebels and French troops. Of the 34,000 who were put aboard ship for military service in Spain between 1651 and 1654, only 18,000 survived to be enlisted in the Spanish army. After 1653 the Spanish government ceased recruiting Irish soldiers, and many discharged soldiers and their dependants became beggars and vagrants.[6]

The Irish military migration to mainland European countries was driven not only by military defeat, but also by a conjuncture of disasters—famine, plague

---

[4] B. Jennings, *Wild Geese in Spanish Flanders, 1582–1700*, IMC (1964), 3–21. As late as 1642, two of the Irish regiments in Spanish Flanders were commanded by the descendants of the earls of Tyrone and Tyrconnell (J. Hogan (ed.), *Letters and Papers Relating to the Irish Rebellion between 1642–46*, IMC (1936), pp. ix–x, 12).

[5] É. Ó Ciosáin, 'A Hundred Years of Irish Migration to France, 1590 to 1688', in T. O'Connor (ed.), *The Irish in Europe, 1580–1815* (2001), 99–100.

[6] R. A. Stradling, *The Spanish Monarchy and Irish Mercenaries: The Wild Geese in Spain, 1648–1668* (1994), 115–16, 141–3, 159–60, 163; Ó Ciosáin, 'Irish Migration to France', 101–2.

and religious persecution—that often accompanied war in the in the seventeenth century. One of the consequences of the traffic in mercenaries between the Irish ports and those in Catalonia in the 1650s was the introduction of the plague, which had taken a heavy toll in the Mediterranean, into Ireland. Although the Spanish army desperately needed the manpower, the Spanish people did not welcome the Irish soldiers and their camp-followers, whom they viewed as beggars, vagrants, carriers of disease and potential bandits, and local officials sometimes refused to allow ships carrying recruits to land or even take on provisions. Perhaps as many 4,000 Irish disembarked in 1652 alone in the ports of Cantabria and the Basque provinces, and the populace sometimes attacked them. Small wonder that the Irish frequently mutinied and deserted, to protest the appalling conditions of life in the Spanish army. If the Spanish people did not welcome the presence of Irish men and women in their midst, the Spanish government preferred them to other mercenaries because they were not heretics.[7]

Another 18,000 Irish swordsmen went into exile in France during the 1650s, following military commanders such as James Butler, first marquis of Ormonde, Murrough O'Brien, first earl of Inchiquin, and the O'Sullivan Beare. The Irish mostly fought for the French Royalist cause during the Fronde, but some followed the *frondeurs*. Another Irish regiment in the service of Charles IV, duke of Lorraine, was captured, and the soldiers offered to serve the king of France in the regiment commanded by James, duke of York. The proportion of Irish troops in the French royal army rose from perhaps 2 per cent during the Thirty Years War to as much as 8 per cent at the peak of the Franco-Spanish War that ended in 1659. The Irish regiments in the French army were disbanded after the Peace of the Pyrenees, and the Irish companies were dispersed among German, English and native French regiments. Many Irish soldiers spent a lifetime in the French army before retiring to the Invalides. At times, Irish soldiers in the French army may have been as numerous as the Swiss.[8]

France was a favoured place of exile for many Royalists in the 1650s. Justin MacCarthy, later Viscount Mountcashel and commander of the Irish Brigade in France under James II, accompanied his family as a boy to France after the collapse of the Catholic Confederation of Kilkenny, where he became fluent in French. His father, Donough, second Viscount Muskerry (and later first earl of Clancarty), became a military enterpriser and raised troops for the armies of Venice and Poland, while his brother Cormac commanded a regiment in French service composed of Lord Muskerry's tenants and dependants in Munster. Justin began his military career in the French *Regiment d'Hamilton*, which was commanded by his cousin George Hamilton. He was James, duke of Monmouth's second-in-command in the *Regiment royal anglais*, and later served in the Danish army before being called home by James II to command a regiment of the Irish

---

[7] Stradling, *Irish Mercenaries*, 70, 78–9, 95–7, 117, 127–32.

[8] Ó Ciosáin, 'Irish Migration to France', 101–2; *The Memoirs of James II: His Campaigns as Duke of York, 1652–1660*, trans. A. L. Sells (1962), 122.

army.[9] Gervase Holles, the English antiquary and lawyer, after his capture while serving as a Royalist colonel at Colchester, was allowed to go into exile when he indicated a desire to enter Venetian service, but he chose instead to accept a commission as a colonel in the French army. Thomas Culpeper, later engineer-general to James II, began his military career in the French army in 1654 at the Siege of Arras. He was a careful student of the fortifications of Vauban, and compiled a notebook of observations on military engineering, gunnery and logistics. This compilation included notes on every important European siege from the 1640s to the Siege of Vienna of 1683.[10]

Under the Cromwellian Protectorate, recruiting for foreign service was subjected to more careful control so that the banishment of swordsmen and the levying of troops accorded with Cromwellian foreign and military policy and did not disoblige allies. Cromwell especially cultivated close relations with Sweden because, as the Venetian ambassador stated in his report of 1656, Sweden was 'the strongest bulwark for resisting the House of Austria'. Cromwell allowed William Vavasour, a veteran of the Thirty Years War and a former colonel in the English Royalist army, to raise a regiment of 1,200 foot for service in the Swedish army. One thousand of these men were persons previously designated for transportation to Jamaica, and 200 were volunteers raised in England by beat of the drum.[11] The Cromwellian government was so determined to rid Scotland of swordsmen that they not only allowed recruiting officers for the king of Sweden to operate in Scotland and England but also paid them subsidies. From the perspective of the Scots Royalists who joined William, third Lord Cranstoun's Regiment in 1656, one stated that 'the Royalists chose rather to go abroad, though in mean condition, than live at home under a yoke of slavery'. One contingent recruited for Cranstoun's Regiment consisted of forty-three Frasers, including six of Hugh Fraser, seventh Lord Lovat's sons and at least twenty-two gentlemen. The forty-three Frasers marched out of Inverness before being embarked for service in Poland, and only four ever came home.[12] Cromwell had allowed Lord Cranstoun to raise his regiment only after the government was assured that Scottish soldiers recruited for Swedish service would not assist a Stuart restoration. Those who were not recruited in Scotland were drawn from among prisoners of war captured at the Battle of Worcester and intended to be sent as indentured servants to Barbados. Although the close relationship between Scotland and Sweden that existed before 1640 was weakened as England under Cromwell became a military and diplomatic

[9] J. A. Murphy, *Justin MacCarthy, Lord Mountcashel, Commander of the First Irish Brigade in France* (1959), 1–2, 4–12.

[10] P. R. Newman, *The Old Service: Royalist Regimental Colonels and the Civil War, 1642–46* (1993), 155; BL, Harley MS. 945 ['Maxims and Observations of War', by Col. Thomas Culpeper, Engineer General to James II], pp. 3–4, 11–14, 50, 117.

[11] E. and P. Razzell (eds.), *The English Civil War: A Contemporary Account*, 5 vols. (1996), v. 13; A. Grosjean, 'Royalist Soldiers *and* Cromwellian Allies? The Cranstoun Regiment in Sweden, 1655–58', in S. Murdoch and A. MacKillop (eds.), *Fighting for Identity: Scottish Military Experience, c. 1550–1900* (2002), 66.

[12] James Fraser, *Chronicles of the Frasers*, ed. W. Mackay, SHS 1st ser. 47 (1905), 417.

ally of the Swedes, some Scottish Royalists were willing to fight for Sweden, which was bound by treaty not to assist a Royalist restoration, because they were offended by Charles II's betrayal of Montrose, and preferred Swedish military service to indentured servitude in the West Indies. Yet there was a risk that Cromwell took in allowing Scottish Royalists to enlist in the Swedish army. When Charles II issued a letter calling upon his subjects serving in foreign armies to return to their allegiance, 300 soldiers of the Cranstoun Regiment deserted before they reached Swedish territory and chose instead to join the army of Denmark-Norway which kingdom was then at war with the Cromwellian Protectorate's ally, Sweden.[13]

The more steadfast Royalists from the British Isles found service in the army of the kingdom of Denmark and Norway less objectionable than fighting for an ally of Cromwell. The king of Denmark-Norway was driven to recruit foreigners into his army because he regarded his own subjects as untrustworthy. Except in a few cases, such as the mixed Irish and Scottish regiment raised by Philip O'Sullivan Mor in 1657, most recruiting for the Danish army during the Interregnum was carried on in third countries such as the Netherlands or Russia. Sir James Turner was raising a regiment for Danish service in the Netherlands, where unemployed soldiers were plentiful in 1657, when Sweden inflicted a decisive defeat on the king of Denmark-Norway. Thereafter, the market for mercenary soldiers in Scandinavia collapsed. Whereas Scottish officers in the army of Denmark-Norway had once constituted 22 per cent of the officer corps during the Danish phase of the Thirty Years War, that proportion dropped to under 5 per cent during the Torstensson War with Sweden of 1643–5 and the Danish-Swedish war of 1657–60. Opportunities for soldiers from the British Isles diminished after 1660 because of a lull in the Baltic wars and as a consequence of the exhaustion of Swedish and Danish financial resources. Sweden and Denmark could no longer recruit whole regiments from the British Isles, although individual Scots continued to join the Swedish army as before, and of course there remained a sizeable Scottish military community in Sweden from the earlier migration.[14]

As opportunities for Scots martialists in the armies of the Scandinavian kingdoms began to close off in the 1650s, they were obliged to look further afield. Among the Royalists who fled Scotland to avoid imprisonment by the Cromwellian regime were Thomas Dalyell of Binns, William Drummond of Cromlix and William Johnston. They went to Muscovy in 1655, carrying with them a letter from the exiled Charles II to Czar Alexis. Dalyell and Drummond both fought in the Russo-Polish wars. Dalyell had been a general officer in the Scottish Royalist army at Worcester, and was given the rank of general in the Russian forces. Drummond (later fourth Lord Maderty and first Viscount

[13] Grosjean, 'Royalist Soldiers *and* Cromwellian Allies?', 62–3, 66–7, 76–7; M. E. Ailes, *Military Migration and State Formation: The British Military Community in Seventeenth-Century Sweden* (2002), 18–19.

[14] Sir James Turner, *Memoirs of his own Life and Times, 1632–1670*, BC 31 (1829), 126–30; SSNE, no. 78; Ailes, *Military Migration*, 18–20; S. Murdoch, *Britain, Denmark-Norway and the House of Stuart, 1603–1660: A Diplomatic and Military Analysis* (2000), 226–30.

Strathallan) was commissioned a major-general. However, it was easier to achieve high rank in the Muscovite forces than to resign. It required the personal intervention of Charles II to obtain the release of Dalyell and Drummond, who returned to Scotland in 1665. Both, in turn, commanded the Scots standing army, and were known for their severity of discipline and cruelty in crushing the Covenanter rebellions. One Covenanter called Dalyell 'a Muscovite beast'.[15]

The most well-known Scot who went to Muscovy was General Patrick Gordon of Auchleuchries. Gordon wrote perhaps the most extensive and detailed military memoir of the seventeenth century—even today only partially translated and published in English—and, after long and distinguished service in the Russian army and navy, became a confidant and friend of Peter the Great, and left numerous descendants in Russia. Gordon's father ranked as the Scots equivalent of a yeoman, and his mother was a Catholic. As a Catholic himself (and he remained devout all his life), he could not attend a Scottish university, so he 'resolved to go to some foreign country'. When Gordon made his way to the Baltic, he took advantage of an extensive network of Scottish merchants and encountered Scots priests and numerous Catholics. He attended a Jesuit College near Königsberg, but while he valued the education, he did not like the sedentary life of a scholar. For a time he joined the household of a Polish nobleman and travelled. In 1655 he happened to be in Hamburg, where some Swedish recruiting officers persuaded him to join a Scottish cavalry troop in the Swedish army. Like Dalyell and Drummond, Gordon fought in the Russo-Polish wars. He found Swedish discipline to be severe, and remarked that soldiers were hanged for trivial offences.[16]

Another Scots soldier who wrote a full autobiography was Andrew Melville, who began his military career in Lord Grey's regiment of the Scots Covenanting Army. When his regiment was disbanded in 1647, Melville and his brother went to France to seek employment. His brother, not caring for French life, went to Venice, while Andrew obtained a commission as an ensign in a French regiment of foot guards. He fought in Flanders under Marshal Jean de Grassion until made a prisoner of war. Since his fellow officers did not ransom him, he entered the service of the duke of Lorraine, who was raising soldiers for Charles, prince of Wales, to carry to England to assist the king. Melville, who was now a captain-lieutenant, was given command of a company consisting of a mixture of Germans, French, English, Scots and Irish who were to train in the Netherlands before embarking for England. When his men heard a rumour that the duke of Lorraine, instead, intended to sell them to Spain, they mutinied. With difficulty, Melville and his fellow officers restored order. When news was received that the First Civil War had ended in England, the duke of Lorraine sold the regiment to Spain a

[15] *Passages from the Diary of General Patrick Gordon of Auchleuchries, 1635–1699*, SC 20 (1849), 78 n.–79 n.; P. Dukes, 'Scottish Soldiers in Muscovy', *The Caledonian Phalanx: Scots in Russia* (1987), 16–18; D. Fedosov, *The Caledonian Connection: Scotland–Russia Ties—Middle-Ages to Early Twentieth Century: A Concise Biographical List* (1996), 28, 32–3, 59; SSNE, no. 3863.
[16] *Diary of General Patrick Gordon*, 4–21.

second time. Melville and the officers of his company were outraged, and conspired with their men, of whom only the English and Irish remained, to refuse to embark for Spain. Since the duke of Lorraine had already been paid by Spain, he merely assigned them to winter quarters and did not force them to go, but he did not pay them either. In desperation, Melville and his company accepted service in the Spanish Army of Flanders, where at least they were paid.[17] During the Fronde, Melville served in Cardinal de Retz's Scottish Guard, rising to the rank of captain. The cardinal preferred Scots because he felt that he could not trust Frenchmen. When the cardinal's Scottish Guard was disbanded at the end of the Fronde, Melville was taken into the Scottish *gens d'armes* commanded by Frederick von Schomberg (later duke of Schomberg in the English peerage and William II and III's commander-in-chief in Ireland). Here he campaigned in Champagne and Picardy with James, duke of York's company, which consisted of sixty gentlemen—all reformadoes—each accompanied by one or two servants. Subsequently, Melville served under Marshal Turenne in Flanders.[18]

Because the Royalists were perceived as a continuing threat to the Protectorate, Cromwell in 1655 signed a treaty with France—then emerging as the dominant European power—expelling Charles II and his followers from that country. Since the war between Spain and France continued, the Spanish were glad to give assistance to Charles, who crossed into Spanish Flanders where he raised six regiments of Royalist followers, many of whom left French service to follow him. These included a regiment commanded by Henry Wilmot, first earl of Rochester, and a Scottish regiment belonging to Lieutenant-General John Middleton (later first earl of Middleton), but actually commanded by James Livingstone, first earl of Newburgh. James, duke of York, led an Irish regiment whose proprietary colonel was Donough MacCarthy, second Viscount Muskerry. Muskerry had resigned his commission in the French army, and told his men (whom Cardinal Mazarin had refused to release to Muskerry) to meet him in Flanders. Eight hundred of them—many of them Muskerry's tenants—deserted with their arms *en masse*. Two more Irish regiments were commanded by Theobald, second Viscount Taaffe (and later first earl of Carlingford), and George Digby, second earl of Bristol. To these were added, in 1656, another Irish regiment commanded by James Butler, first marquis (and later first duke) of Ormonde. None of these units was up to strength, and altogether the seven regiments consisted of no more than 3,000 men.[19] Under the provisions of the treaty of 1655 with Cardinal Mazarin, Cromwell agreed to send 6,000 men under the command of Major-General Thomas Morgan to assist the French army at the Siege of Dunkirk and Mardyke. They fought against the Royalists at the Battle of the Dunes in May 1658. The battle was won by Marshal Turenne's Anglo-French

[17] *Memoirs of Sir Andrew Melvill*, trans. T. Ameer-Al (1918), 79–8, 83, 92–109. I have used the *DNB*'s spelling of his surname (*sub* Andrew Melville (1624–1706)).   [18] Ibid. 144–7.
[19] C. H. Firth, 'Royalist and Cromwellian Armies in Flanders', *TRHS* NS 17 (1903), 67–74. Another source adds an eighth regiment led by Thomas, 5th Lord Wentworth of Nettlestead (*Some Account of the Family of the Butlers* (1716), 89–92).

force; as many as two-thirds of the British and Irish Royalists in the Spanish Army of Flanders died in the battle. The Cromwellian troops remained in occupation of Dunkirk and Mardyke until after the Restoration.[20]

One Royalist soldier who began his career in exile, but who prospered at the Restoration, was Sir Edmund Andros. His first military service was as a gentleman volunteer in a troop of cuirassiers commanded by his uncle, Sir Robert Stone, who was a member of the court of Elizabeth, queen of Bohemia, at The Hague—always a haven for swordsmen from England and Scotland. Between 1656 and 1659 he fought with the combined forces of the Netherlands and Denmark in the war against Cromwell's ally Sweden. At the Restoration, Andros became gentleman-in-ordinary to the widowed queen of Bohemia, whose court had migrated to London. In 1662 he was commissioned ensign in the Coldstream Guards, and five years later was a major in the Barbados Regiment, which served as a marine regiment with the Royal Navy in the Carribean, where he saw action in the Battle of St Pierre with the French navy. He did as well in marriage as in war, marrying a cousin of William, earl of Craven, colonel of the Coldstream Guards and a favourite of the queen of Bohemia. In 1674 he was sent to New York as captain of a company of foot, and after a few months became its governor.[21]

The British Isles were left with a surfeit of military officers after the Restoration; more of the Royalist exiles would have been welcomed home had there been more places in the standing armies of the Three Kingdoms. Whether those who had changed their allegiance during the civil wars would be forgiven and made welcome at court depended on their social rank and political influence. George Monck, duke of Albemarle, and Roger Boyle, earl of Orrery, having played pivotal roles in bringing about the Restoration of the Stuarts, were accepted at court and rewarded. It would have been impolitic for Charles II to have done otherwise. But turncoats of middle and lower rank were not welcome. Joseph Bampfield had risen through the ranks of the Royalist armies from ensign to command a brigade under Lord Hopton. Prince Rupert had made him governor of Malmesbury. After the execution of Charles I he went into exile in the Netherlands and contracted with the French government to raise a regiment, and evidently got permission from the Commonwealth government to do so, before he and his papers were seized. Thereafter, Bampfield appears to have functioned as a double-agent for both Charles II and Cromwell. At the Restoration he was imprisoned in the Tower. Although later released, he was told that he would be unwelcome at court. Bampfield went into exile in the Netherlands, where he commanded a Frisian regiment in the Dutch army.[22]

[20] Firth, 'Royalist and Cromwellian Armies in Flanders', 75–87.

[21] E. F. Carey, 'Amias Andros and Sir Edmund his Son', *Trans. of the Guernsey Soc. of Nat. Sci. and Local Research*, 7 (1913–16), 45–8.

[22] J. Childs, 'The British Brigade in France, 1672–78', *History*, 69 (1984), 384–5; *Colonel Joseph Bampfield's Apologie* (1685), 5, 58, 60–1; *DNB, sub* Joseph Bampfield (*fl.* 1639–1685); F. J. S. ten Raa and F. de Bas, *Het Staatsche Leger*, 8 vols. (1911–80), vi. 142, 221. The fact that numerous swordsmen had to go into exile to find employment after the Wars of the Three Kingdoms was sufficiently famil-iar to theatre audiences to permit Aphra Behn to locate her play, *The Rover: Or, the Banish't Cavaliers*

The decision of Charles II's government to send troops to Portugal in 1662 resulted from the need to find employment for Cromwellian and Royalist veterans of the civil wars, and was authorized by the commercial and marriage treaty with Portugal. The dispatch of an English military force suited the needs of both the houses of Stuart and Braganza. Portugal had been fighting for its independence from Spain since 1640 and needed military manpower, while the Scots wanted England to remove the three Cromwellian regiments that continued to garrison the Citadel of Leith at the Restoration. Such was the need for experienced soldiers in the Portuguese army that the king of Portugal wanted to raise 12,000 foot in England. He did not want Irish soldiers, because they were seen as being too closely tied to Spain and might well end up fighting Irish soldiers in the Spanish army. Charles agreed to raise two regiments of foot from the three regiments at Leith, and 2,200 volunteered for this service then proceeded to Portugal under the command of Sir Thomas Morgan, formerly a Cromwellian major-general. Among the volunteers was Charles Croke, the author of *Fortune's Uncertainty*, a semi-autobiographical picaresque novel of the Restoration period, and a younger brother of Colonel Unton Croke of the Parliamentary army, who had joined his brother's regiment and troop as a gentleman volunteer, but was prevented from obtaining a commission by the reduction of the army. He and his elder brother Unton went to Portugal in 1663 as members of the earl of Inchiquin's Regiment of Horse. Four hundred of the 600 troopers of Inchiquin's Regiment were gentlemen's sons and reformadoes. At the Battle of Evora between Spain and Portugal, the English made up nearly one-fifth of the Portuguese army. Croke served as a cornet in his brother's troop, but was cashiered by Frederick von Schomberg, his commanding officer in the Portuguese army, for neglect of duty. He then appears to have gone over to the Spaniards.[23]

Having served abroad in the Swedish and Polish armies during the Protectorate, Patrick Gordon wished to return home when he heard that Charles II had been restored to the throne, but his father told him that there were no opportunities in Scotland because military commissions would go to the nobility and old Royalist soldiers who had been close to Charles II in exile. Gordon had already secured a discharge from the Polish army, and he needed to look about for employment; he was lured to Moscow by Russian diplomats with whom he had dealt in the exchange of Russian prisoners. The Russians promised to keep him in their army for no more than three years and to promote him to colonel within that time. He, of course, stayed a lifetime.[24]

(1677), in Naples, in which she states that her English cavaliers had earlier fought at the Siege of Pamplona in Navarre.

[23] P. H. Hardacre, 'The English Contingent in Portugal, 1662–1668', *JSAHR* 38 (1960), 114–16, 118–23; Charles Croke, *Fortune's Uncertainty, or Youth's Unconstancy* (1667), Luttrell Soc. Reprints, 19 (1959), intro., pp. v–viii, 51–3, 61–3. When the earl of Sandwich, as ambassador to Spain, crossed the frontier into Portugal to help negotiate an end to the war between Spain and Portugal, he was greeted by 11 squadrons of Portuguese horse, of which three were English (R. Ollard, *Cromwell's Earl: A Life of Edward Mountagu, 1st Earl of Sandwich* (1994), 195).

[24] *Diary of General Patrick Gordon*, 33–4.

Hugh Mackay came from the kind of background that enabled him to obtain a commission in Dumbarton's Regiment, a Scots regiment in the English army on loan to King Louis XIV. Mackay was related to the Lords Reay, the proprietary colonels of Mackay's Regiment, and to the Munros, who supplied so many of the officers for the regiments raised by the Lords Reay for the kings of Denmark and Sweden. His father had been colonel of a Scots Royalist regiment in the civil wars. In France Mackay was a companion of the young John Churchill, later duke of Marlborough. He became acquainted with the prince of Condé and Marshal Turenne, two of the greatest generals of the age. In 1669 Mackay served as a gentleman volunteer in a small force of 100 young French officers that Louis XIV sent to aid the Venetian Republic and to gain foreign military experience. Mackay and his fellow French officers participated in an expedition against the Turks on the island of Candia. Here he distinguished himself, and was awarded a medal by the Venetian Republic. Long service abroad had weakened Mackay's ties to Scotland, and he became alienated from Charles II's Scottish government which failed to bring to justice the murderers of his two elder brothers. In 1672, as a captain in Dumbarton's Regiment, still in French service, Mackay fought in the Second Dutch War. While garrisoned in the town of Bommel in Gelderland, he attracted the attention of a Dutch lady whom he later married. In order to win the approval of her parents, Mackay accepted a commission in the Scots Brigade of the Dutch army. He sold his estates in Scotland and acquired lands in Holland. His Calvinist piety tended to reinforce ties to his wife's family, and he was made welcome at the Orange court by the young stadholder William III. He accompanied William in the descent on England, and became commander-in-chief of the Scottish army.[25]

Another wave of Scots emigrants went into exile following the Monmouth and Argyll rebellions of 1685. In Scotland, followers of Archibald, ninth earl of Argyll, were not pursued as relentlessly as those of the duke of Monmouth were in England. There were only two executions in Scotland following Argyll's failed rebellion, because 'there had been no battle', but some 200 persons were attainted, and many of them sought refuge in the Netherlands 'and afterwards returned with the prince of Orange at the Revolution'.[26] One of those was William Maxwell of Cardoness, who was born posthumously to the wife of a Scots Covenanting minister who had been deprived of his living in the Kirk. Maxwell was imprisoned in the Tolbooth Prison while a student at the University of Edinburgh for attending illegal conventicles. He decided to continue his medical studies at Leyden, where a sermon preached by William Carstairs persuaded him that he needed to take up the cause of Protestantism in a more militant fashion. He joined the Dutch army and accompanied William III in the invasion of England. Later he fought with William in the Nine Years

---

[25] J. Mackay, *The Life of Lieut.-General Hugh Mackay, Commander in Chief of the Forces in Scotland, 1689 and 1690*, BC 53 (1836), 1–8: ten Raa and de Bas, *Staatsche Leger*, vi. 252–3.

[26] Sir John Dalrymple, *Memoirs of Great Britain and Ireland*, 2 vols., 2nd edn. (1771–3), i. 80–1.

War.[27] Another son of a Covenanting clergyman was Samuel Vetch. His father William had participated in the Pentland Hills Rebellion as the captain of a rebel cavalry troop. Hearing that he had been condemned to death, William escaped to England and lived under an assumed name. After the discovery of the Rye House Plot of 1683, William Vetch followed the earl of Argyll into exile in the Netherlands, where he became involved in the plots that preceded the Argyll and Monmouth Rebellions of 1685. Their mother sent Samuel and his brother William to join their father in the Netherlands and to study at Utrecht. The two brothers accompanied William of Orange in his descent on England—probably as volunteers in the Scots or Anglo-Dutch Brigades. Both Samuel and his brother were subsequently commissioned as officers in Scottish regiments of the English army, and fought in the Nine Years War. Samuel participated as a captain in the failed Scots colony of Darien in Panama in 1698, and was later employed as an Indian agent and a colonel of colonial troops in North America.[28]

Members of the gentry who had been military officers or who aspired to become officers were not easily assimilated into civilian pursuits at the end of the civil wars, and consequently, shortages of military officers occurred less frequently. The more humble orders of society, on the other hand, were reluctant to serve in foreign armies when peace returned to the Three Kingdoms. The small standing army of England during the reign of Charles II encountered few problems in recruiting for the home army, but impressment was resorted to for filling quotas for overseas expeditions during the war years of 1673 and 1678.[29] Recruiting officers for foreign armies were only allowed to enlist volunteers in England. In Ireland, the king allowed Sir George Hamilton to recruit 600 men for his *Regiment d'Hamilton* of the French army. Hamilton was also permitted to select additional recruits from among convicted felons who had been sentenced to transportation to 'our foreign plantations'.[30] Recruiting officers of the Dutch army and their agents were especially active in London and Edinburgh, where they made their headquarters at taverns, and offered bonuses for enlistment and entertained their new recruits until enough had been gathered together to convey to Holland or Zeeland aboard a troopship. When the Irishman Peter Drake enquired about enlisting in the States' Army in London in 1701, he was guided by a Gaelic-speaking Irish sergeant of the Foot Guards acting as a recruiting agent for the Dutch army to a French officer in the Dutch army who used a public house to recruit for his regiment. The Irish sergeant was paid a guinea a head for each recruit that he brought in, and Drake was offered an enlistment bounty of four guineas.[31] Although he spent many years in the ranks before obtaining a commission,

---

[27] H. M. B. Reid (ed.), *One of King William's Men: Being Leaves from the Diary of Col. William Maxwell of Cardoness, 1685–1697* (1898), 8–20, 25, 134, 153, 162.

[28] G. M. Waller, *Samuel Vetch: Colonial Enterpriser* (1960), 4–5, 8–13; *DNB, sub* Samuel Vetch (1668–1732). [29] Childs, *AC* 21, 184–6.

[30] BL, Stowe MS. 204, fo. 28.

[31] A. Corvisier, *Armies and Societies in Europe, 1494–1789*, trans. A. T. Siddall (1979), 44–5; *The Memoirs of Capt. Peter Drake* (1755), 39–44.

Drake was an inveterate dueller. His family in Dublin had once given him 20 guineas to establish himself in a useful occupation, but Drake spent the money on fencing lessons. When he was put aboard ship at Gravesend to be carried to Holland, he managed to get into a fight the very first day with a sergeant who turned out to be his company sergeant, and who was ever thereafter Drake's enemy.[32]

The generous enlistment bounty paid to Peter Drake may reflect a growing shortage of military manpower in the British Isles on the eve of the War of Spanish Succession. A severe shortage of manpower also existed in the one Scottish and three English regiments which formed part of William III's leaguer at the Siege of Maastricht in the summer of 1676. In London, the Dutch ambassadors were handing out commissions in the States' Army to gentlemen volunteers who could recruit ten men or more. This haphazard method of recruiting resulted in companies of fifteen to twenty men arriving in the field, where the excess of officers was paid off and the companies consolidated. Although the Dutch troops were paid promptly, there was a problem obtaining sufficient provisions, and men deserted to forage for food. When some of the English officers asked the prince-stadholder for permission to hang deserters, William—ever mindful of the shortage of soldiers in the Dutch forces—replied that he would not permit such a harsh sentence for men 'that ran away to get bread to preserve life'.[33]

Recruiting efforts by foreign officers in Edinburgh in the 1680s encountered considerable difficulties. In May 1682 some Dutch officers were in Edinburgh recruiting for the Scots Brigade. One of the officers was the son of the town major who commanded the Edinburgh watch, and his efforts to enlist apprentices went beyond the bounds of lawful persuasion and provoked a riot among the trades apprentices—many of whom were subsequently imprisoned. Continuing demonstrations by the apprentices sought to pressure the magistrates into setting the impressed men free, but instead they summoned regular troops from outside the city to suppress the riots and carry the prisoners to Leith to be embarked. The regular troops fired upon the Edinburgh crowd as rioting continued, and killed a dozen people. When King James VII and II called home the three regiments of the Scots Brigade in 1685 to assist in the suppression of the Monmouth Rebellion, many of the soldiers deserted and made their way back to Edinburgh, where the Scottish Privy Council ordered the deserters rounded up and returned to their commanders. In January 1688 King James sent a letter to the Scottish Privy Council withdrawing permission from officers of the States' Army to recruit in Scotland. Sir John Lauder thought this looked like a portent of war, but James's excuse was that he wanted to recruit men for his own armies. Proclamations were also issued in Scotland and England calling home English and Scots soldiers and sailors from Dutch service.[34]

---

[32] *Memoirs of Capt. Peter Drake*, 29–30, 47.

[33] William Carr, *A Particular Account of the Present Siege of Mastricht* (1676), 2–3, 22–3.

[34] Sir John Lauder of Fountainhall, *Historical Notices of Scottish Affairs*, ed. D. Laing, 2 vols., BC 87 (1847), ii. 657, 847, 860; id., *Historical Observations of Memorable Occurrents in Church and State, from*

The presence of James, duke of York and Albany, in Scotland in August 1681 seems to have led the Scottish Privy Council to allow Colonel Henry Gage to recruit for his regiment of the Spanish Army of Flanders, which was known as the duke of York's Regiment. At first Gage and his officers were told that they could only recruit privately without beating the drum. Then, only a few days later, they were allowed to recruit to the beat of the drum and to forcibly compel those who had accepted recruiting money to carry through their contract. They were empowered to take up recruits who deserted, but could not enlist any soldiers of the regular army in Scotland. By October of 1681 Colonel Gage still had not met his quota, and the Scottish Privy Council gave him permission to enlist some of the rebels who still remained in prison after the suppression of the Bothwell Bridge Rebellion of 1679. Only one of the Covenanters consented to enlist, while five defied James and the Privy Council with treasonable words, and were hanged for their pains. Several days later four more prisoners were brought before the duke of York and the Council and also refused to join Colonel Gage's regiment, but this time the duke of York had them removed from the Council Chamber in order 'that they might not also hang themselves with their own tongue'.[35] Colonel Gage was in Edinburgh again in February 1684. Complaint was made to the Privy Council that Gage's officers were impressing men by a combination of drink and physical force. It would appear that some of the recruits were accepting enlistment money with the intention to desert immediately afterwards. The Privy Council stopped the Spanish troopship from sailing in order to investigate the complaints. Sir John Lauder, lord of session and a contemporaneous witness, explained that Scottish law allowed the forcible impressment of prisoners, beggars, vagrants and foreigners, but not apprentices—even if they consented. The bailly of Leith ordered the impressed men released from the Leith Tolbooth, but soldiers of the Leith garrison intervened and took the part of Gage's officers. Presumably, the recruits were sent to Flanders.[36]

Peter Drake was a military confidence man—a latter-day Falstaff—who made a career of collecting enlistment bounties and then deserting. Drake considered himself to be a gentleman, and was very prickly about injuries to his honour—such as when he was serving in an Irish regiment of the French army and he and his fellow cadets were reduced to the rank of private at the end of the Nine Years War. He deserted, and indeed he deserted from more regiments of the English, Dutch and French armies than can be precisely counted. Moreover, he was such a persuasive and charming rogue that he often brought half-a-dozen or more deserters with him to his new regiment, and was rewarded with multiple enlistment bounties by recruiting officers anxious to meet quotas. Apparently, on the principle that former poachers make the best gamekeepers, he became a recruiting officer

---

October 1680 to April 1686, ed. A. Urquhart and D. Laing, BC 66 (1840), 66–7; H. Paton (ed.), *RPCS, 1686–1689* (1932), 3rd ser., vol. xiii, p. viii.

[35] P. H. Brown (ed.), *RPCS, 1681–1682* (1915), 3rd ser., vii. 174, 181, 210: Lauder, *Scottish Affairs*, i. 330–3.   [36] Lauder, *Scottish Affairs*, ii. 495–6; *RPCS, 1683–1684*, 3rd ser., viii. 315.

himself in the Chevalier's Guards (a newly raised Irish Jacobite regiment), and began soliciting and enlisting English and Irish deserters from the English, Dutch and Spanish armies of the Confederate forces. It had taken him ten years to achieve commissioned rank. His reputation as a chronic deserter was such that he had been banned from joining any regiments of the British forces in the Low Countries after fomenting several mutinies and mass desertions.[37]

The Wars of the Three Kingdoms heightened the political awareness of soldiers from the British Isles, whether they returned home to fight or remained in foreign service. This process of politicization sharpened national and religious identities and promoted a fastidiousness in matters of allegiance which gave rise to factional struggles among British and Irish swordsmen in foreign armies. The Dutch army offers a good case study of this phenomenon. At the end of the Eighty Years War in 1648 and after the death of the stadholder William II in 1650, the Dutch Republic went through a period of crisis during which there was no stadholder or captain-general. The Scots Brigade appears to have lost its privileged status and exclusively Scottish character. A number of Dutchmen, Germans and French refugees obtained commissions in the brigade and morale declined among the soldiers and younger officers. The Scots Brigade acquired the reputation of being composed of deserters and outcasts of all nations, and the younger Scots officers and cadets looked elsewhere for opportunity while the native Scots in the ranks simply deserted. The young William III began to rebuild the Dutch army after he was made captain-general in 1672, and when Hugh Mackay came into Dutch service William asked him to reorganize the Scots Brigade and made him colonel of one of the regiments. That Mackay was promoted over more senior officers caused much resentment.[38]

With the outbreak of the Second Anglo-Dutch War in 1665, the allegiances of the English and Scottish officers and men in the States' Army had been severely tested. The Dutch feared an invasion of coastal districts, and the Zeeland government proposed that all English and Scottish soldiers in Dutch service should be required to take a more solemn and explicit oath of allegiance to the States General or be dismissed. Johan de Witt and the Holland government wanted all English and Scots troops cashiered. At the same time, Charles II issued a proclamation ordering the Anglo-Dutch and Scots Brigades home. However, the Dutch government seems to have realized that the army would be seriously weakened if it could not continue to draw upon the manpower of the British Isles. Most of the field-grade officers obeyed Charles II and returned home; many were incorporated into the new Holland Regiment of the English army and the Lord Admiral's Regiment. A notable exception was Colonel Thomas Dolman, whose regiment, serving as

---

[37] *Memoirs of Capt. Peter Drake*, 39–60.

[38] Francis Grose, *Military Antiquities Respecting a History of the British Army*, 2 vols. (1786–8), vol. ii, app., pp. 25–6; ten Raa and de Bas, *Staatsche Leger*, vi. 252–3; *A Short History of the Life of John Bernardi* (1729), 18. There were actually four Scots regiments in the States' Army, but the fourth, the Erskine Regiment, did not belong to the Scots Brigade.

marines aboard the Dutch fleet, led the landings at Sheerness and Landguard Fort in 1665. An unknown number of English officers of lesser rank continued in Dutch service during the remainder of the war. It also appears that nearly all Scots were willing to remain in Dutch service during the war. The English and Scots regiments were broken up and the officers and soldiers dispersed among other units of the Dutch army. At the end of the war, the English and Scottish units were reconstituted as one Irish, three English and four Scottish regiments.[39]

The Dutch army became increasingly politicized during the second and third quarters of the seventeenth century. The States General had long meddled in military and naval affairs, and the princes of Orange, for their part, had built up their own party in the Orange court and the officer corps to preserve a degree of independence in their military decisions. The stadholders and their supporters had at times resorted to murder and assassination to preserve their position. This ideological contentiousness affected the foreign officers in the States' Army in complex and different ways which, in turn, could not but shape their allegiance to the Stuart and Orange dynasties. Aubrey de Vere, twentieth earl of Oxford, was the son of Robert, the nineteenth earl, who commanded a Dutch regiment and was killed at the siege of Maastricht in 1632. Aubrey's mother was a Frisian noblewoman. He remained in the Netherlands at the beginning of the Wars of the Three Kingdoms and entered the Dutch army at an early age. He commanded his own regiment between 1646 and 1654. By 1654 he was in England, participating in Royalist plots, and was imprisoned in the Tower of London by the Protectorate regime. However, he was freed in time to help negotiate the return of Charles II, and was rewarded with the colonelcy of the Royal Horse Guards. His lieutenant-colonel in the Oxford Regiment of the Anglo-Dutch Brigade was Robert Sidney, brother of Algernon, that uncompromising republican. Robert Sidney and the earl of Oxford had a falling-out—quite possibly over politics—and proposed to fight a duel, which was prevented by mutual friends. The earl of Oxford later became a Whig, sided with William III against James II and fought at the Battle of the Boyne.[40]

The Netherlands was a haven for political and religious refugees, and the Dutch protected such persons and refused to cooperate with the English government in requests for extradition. It became a place where opponents of the Stuart regime could gather in preparation for launching revolts against the Stuart kingdoms. Although the States General had agreed to banish the supporters of the duke of Monmouth and the earl of Argyll, the Dutch authorities dragged their feet until the rebel leaders had already sailed in 1685. When Sir William Temple was sent as

[39] PRO, Holland State Papers, SP 84/173, fos. 102, 109, 118; 84/174, fos. 33, 96, 144; Childs, *AC* 171–2, 240–2; ten Raa and de Bas, *Staatsche Leger*, vi. 141–2, 221, 231, 252–5, 257, 287; Sir William Temple, *Observations upon the United Provinces of the Netherlands* (1673; repr. 1932), 16. Again, one of the English regiments was not part of the Anglo-Dutch Brigade.

[40] Arthur Collins, *Historical Collection of the Noble Families of Cavindishe, Holles, Vere, Harley and Ogle* (1752), 276–7; ten Raa and de Bas, *Staatsche Leger*, vi. 481–2; *DNB, sub* Aubrey de Vere, 20th earl of Oxford (1626–1703).

envoy to Brussels, he visited The Hague, where Secretary of State Joseph Williamson's spies reported that he sowed dissension among English officers in the Dutch army and promoted disloyalty to Charles II.[41]

In May 1674 William III moved south into the Spanish Netherlands in preparation for a major campaign against Louis XIV. Although England was formally allied to France and still engaged in the Third Dutch War, Charles II's new ambassador to the court at Brussels, Sir Richard Bulstrode, visited the prince of Orange's camp near Nivelle and came away with the impression that most of the officers in the Dutch field army were English and Scots. The Dutch forces massing in Flanders were growing quite large—approaching 35,000 men—and the Dutch were hungry for manpower. A draft of soldiers intended for Lord George Douglas's (later the Dumbarton) Regiment of the French army were on their way to France when a privateer captured their transport and carried them to a port near William's camp. The recruits were willing to serve under William, and were taken into the regiment of Colonel Walter Scott of Balwheary.[42] One of the English volunteers who went to the prince-stadholder's leaguer that summer was George Carleton, who had previously served as a volunteer with the English navy against the Dutch. He arrived with a letter of introduction to Major-General Walter Vane, who took Carleton under his wing and found a place for him in the prince of Orange's own company of guards, where he served alongside two Scots who later became famous, John Graham of Claverhouse (later first Viscount Dundee) and David Colyear (later first earl of Portmore). Graham and Colyear would later fight on opposite sides in the Williamite Wars.[43]

The Dutch army was usually well disciplined and paid in a timely fashion. William III was always careful to avoid conflicts with peasants by restraining his soldiers from foraging or plundering. However, his attempt to build up a sufficient mass of troops to obstruct Louis XIV's advance into the Low Countries strained Dutch resources to the utmost. The previous summer captains of the Scots Brigade had complained that they had not been reimbursed by the States General for paying the companies that they had brought into the field, and had been compelled to take out loans which had brought them to the brink of financial ruin. Other officers made complaints about the low rates of pay which made it difficult to recruit.[44] The campaigning season of 1674 was late in starting, the soldiers were restless and the Imperialist troops arrived late and were ill disciplined, despite almost daily executions by their generals. The unrest began to spread to the Dutch

[41] J. Walker, 'The English Exiles in Holland During the Reigns of Charles II and James II', *TRHS* 4th ser. 30 (1948), 119–20; PRO, SP 84/164, fo. 229r & v.

[42] Sir Richard Bulstrode, *Original Letters Written to the Earl of Arlington* (1712), 17–21; ten Raa and de Bas, *Staatsche Leger*, vi. 252–3.

[43] *The Military Memoirs of Capt. George Carleton* (1728), 10–13; J. Childs, *Nobles, Gentlemen and the Profession of Arms in Restoration Britain, 1660–1688: A Biographical Dictionary of British Army Officers on Foreign Service*, SAHR, Spec. Publication, 13 (1987), 19, 38. For a brief discussion of the authenticity of Carleton's *Memoirs*, cf. Manning, *Swordsmen*, 133 n.

[44] PRO, SP 84/114, fo. 174r & v.

army. The campaign did not go well, and the Dutch lost a third of their field army through attrition and battlefield casualties. Sir Walter Vane was killed at the Battle of Seneffe, and Sir Richard Bulstrode reported that the English and Scottish officers were very dispirited.[45] Two years later, in the campaign of 1676 which focused on the siege of the French-held Fortress of Maastricht, the Dutch army still had not made up its losses from 1674. The armies of the allied powers amounted to no more than 24,000–26,000 men, and the three regiments of the Anglo-Dutch Brigade could muster no more than 2,500 men plus 100 volunteers and reformadoes. The siege was rendered especially difficult because a drought had made the River Maas too dry to transport the siege artillery to Maastricht. William gave the English the honour of attacking the first bastion (without sufficient artillery bombardment), and all but 300 of the Anglo-Dutch Brigade were killed or wounded in the siege, including many officers. So desperate was the prince of Orange for manpower that he declared a 'free leaguer' by suspending the excise tax on food and drink in order to attract volunteers as well as boors to work on the fortifications.[46] The terrible slaughter at Maastricht did open up opportunities for promotion, and George Carleton finally obtained a post as an ensign in Sir John Fenwick's Regiment. Carleton's new commission was wetted, not with the customary debauch, but with his own blood after he was wounded. Later, in garrison at Grave, Carleton learned fortification and military engineering.[47]

William III was seen as the defender of their liberties by the Protestants of the British Isles and elsewhere in northern Europe. Service in the States' Army still continued to be perceived as a Protestant crusade among many swordsmen. The prince-stadholder was often less fastidious. His army included Catholic officers, and one of the regiments of the Anglo-Dutch Brigade—the Clare Regiment—contained many Catholics. The first colonel of the regiment was Daniel O'Brien, Viscount Clare, who was a Catholic, as was a later colonel, Patrick Wisely. When the Protestant Thomas Butler, earl of Ossory, son of the first duke of Ormonde, took command of the regiment in 1678, he found that most of the soldiers, who were recruited from among the Old English of Munster, were Catholics, as were most of the officers, and they were not happy with his appointment. Ossory introduced a Protestant chaplain into the regiment, and declared that it was his intention not to commission any more papists. When Ossory lay dying in 1680, Charles II proposed to replace him as commander of the Anglo-Dutch Brigade with George Douglas, earl of Dumbarton, a Catholic. William III would have none of it, and gave command of the brigade to Henry Sidney, afterwards earl of Romney.[48] The States' Army continued to recruit Irish Catholic soldiers well into

---

[45] Bulstrode, *Original Letters*, 56–7, 97.   [46] [Carr], *Siege of Mastricht*, 1–2, 11–12, 21–5.

[47] *Military Memoirs of Capt. George Carleton*, 25, 31–7.

[48] Ten Raa and de Bas, *Staatsche Leger*, vi. 254–6; C. McNeill (ed.), *The Tanner Letters: Original Documents and Notices of Irish Affairs in the Sixteenth and Seventeenth Centuries*, IMC (1943), 419–20; [Carr], *Siege of Mastricht*, 27; *An Historical Account of the British Regiments Employed Since the Reign of Queen Elizabeth and James I in the Formation and Defence of the Dutch Republic* (1794), 55; Childs, *Profession of Arms*, 5, 7, 14, 17, 22, 29, 31, 34, 57, 59, 60, 79, 96, 100.

the eighteenth century, but maintained a policy that their officers should be Protestant. The princes of Orange appreciated the scarcity of military manpower, but were also concerned that the presence of Catholics in the Dutch army might prove embarrassing.[49]

Catholic officers had been common enough in the Anglo-Dutch Brigade in the 1670s. One who left a memoir was John Bernardi. Bernardi's father Francis, who had been born in England, was sent by the Republic of Genoa as an agent to the English Commonwealth in 1651. John thought that his father was too strict and ran away from home with the help of Jane Lane, a Catholic lady of Worcestershire, who had helped Charles II make his escape from England following the Battle of Worcester. Mrs Lane arranged for John Bernardi to enlist in a garrison company at Portsmouth which was commanded by a relative. At the end of the Third Anglo-Dutch War, Bernardi's company was disbanded. With the help of his godfather, William Anselme, who was the lieutenant-colonel of the Clare Regiment of the Anglo-Dutch Brigade, Bernardi joined the States' Army as a cadet. After receiving praise for bravery at the Battle of Seneffe, he was commissioned as an ensign in the Clare Regiment. At the Siege of Maastricht the prince of Orange promoted him to lieutenant, and by 1685, when he was 27 years of age, he had his own company and had married a wealthy lady of Utrecht. His godfather, William Anselme, did not fare well towards the end of his life. He had been forced out of the lieutenant-colonelcies of two Dutch regiments—perhaps because of his religion—and subsequently became a colonel and major-general in Spanish service. But with the end of the wars and his fortunes reduced, Anselme returned to the Dutch army as a private sentinel in his godson's company.[50]

After the Restoration the English government attempted to control the migration of English soldiers from the Three Kingdoms in a way that would be compatible with diplomatic policy. Unfortunately, the governments of Charles II and James VII and II never were able to prevent the unseemly spectacle of having soldiers from the British Isles fighting one another in the armies of both England's allies and foes. This was partly explained by a growing divergence between Stuart foreign policy and public opinion which became evident in the 1670s and 1680s. The dispatch of the British Brigade to fight with the French army against the Dutch in 1672 represented an attempt to bring this traffic in mercenary soldiers under control. Although the officers of the English, Irish and Scots regiments seconded to the French army hoped that actual battle experience would bring promotion in the English home army, the rank and file resented being sent to France, and took every opportunity to desert. Within two months of being raised, Thomas Dongan's Regiment lost half of its strength by desertion. Sir William Lockhart's Regiment was troubled by successive mutinies as they marched through Kent to a port of embarkation. At Canterbury, the troops killed one of

---

[49] BL, Add. MS. 15,872, fo. 112.

[50] *Life of Major John Bernardi*, 1–15, 21–2, 28–31, 36, 44; ten Raa and de Bas, *Staatsche Leger*, vi. 254–6; Childs, *Profession of Arms*, 7.

their ensigns. Many of the soldiers of the British Brigade arrived in France in rags and lacking equipment. Upon disembarkation, they were dismayed to find a want of food and shelter.[51]

In order to preserve the appearance of neutrality in the continuing wars between the Netherlands and France and to counterbalance the presence of the many officers from the Three Kingdoms in the Dutch army, Charles II encouraged his subjects to volunteer to serve with the French. Although the duke of Monmouth had been made a captain in the Life Guards in 1668 at the age of 19, his active military career began in 1672, when he led 'a great train of gentry' and 'a complete band of stout English soldiers' to the French camp at Charleroi. The purpose was to enable Monmouth to acquire martial glory. Exactly what his achievements were on this campaign is unclear, but when he returned to France the next year he commanded a regiment and came home a major-general. His companions in the French campaigns included John Sheffield, third earl of Mulgrave; Louis de Duras, earl of Feversham; Richard, first Viscount Lumley; Robert Constable, third Viscount Dunbar; William, third Lord Alington; and Charles, second earl of Middleton. These courtier-soldiers apparently went to France with the intention of observing rather than participating in the French military effort. Since men such as Middleton did not lack courage, the explanation for his studied indolence seems to be that he and some of his companions sympathized with the prince of Orange.[52]

There were other subjects of Charles II who were glad of the opportunity to serve in the French army. One was Sir George Hamilton, an Irish Catholic of recent Scots descent, who had been a page to Charles in exile and later served in Charles's Life Guards, but was cashiered along with other Catholics in 1667. A new troop of *gens d'armes*, composed entirely of cashiered English Catholic officers and soldiers, was added to the French army soon thereafter. In 1675 Hamilton returned home to Ireland to recruit an Irish regiment for the French army, one of four that Charles allowed to be levied despite the terms of the peace treaty with the Netherlands and the express prohibition of the English Parliament. The king instructed Sir George's brother Anthony, who went to Ireland as the recruiting officer, to enlist the soldiers quietly and to embark them from a port where there was no garrison. The duke of York suggested Dingle, but the French transports arrived at Kinsale, so the recruiting effort did not go unnoticed. The officers of the regiment included a number of Hamilton brothers and kinsmen, as well as Thomas Dongan, who was the lieutenant-colonel. Other Irish officers who later became prominent in the forces of James VII and II also gained experience in

[51] J. Childs, 'The British Brigade in France, 1672–1678', *History*, 69 (1984), 386–8; id., *AC* 54, 80, 175–9, 196; id., *Profession of Arms*, 26; M. Glozier, *Scottish Soldiers in France in the Reign of the Sun King: Nursery for Men of Honour* (2004), ch. 7; W. D. Christie (ed.), *Letters Addressed from London to Sir Joseph Williamson*, CS NS 8, 9 (1874), ii. 81.

[52] *An Historical Account of . . . James, Duke of Monmouth* (1683), 20, 31, 37, 41, 56; G. H. Jones, *Charles Middleton: The Life and Times of a Restoration Politician* (1967), 34–5.

the British Brigade of the French army in the 1670s including Justin MacCarthy, Viscount Mountcashel, and Patrick Sarsfield, Lord Kilmallock.[53]

The original four regiments of the British Brigade, raised under the terms of the Secret Treaty of Dover, eventually grew to six, and were employed in the land campaign against the Dutch in the Third Anglo-Dutch War. They accompanied the prince of Condé and Marshal Turenne into Westphalia, the Duchy of Cleves and the province of Gelderland. One English officer who left an account of his participation in this campaign was Henry Herbert (who succeeded as fourth Lord Herbert of Cherbury in 1678). Herbert pursued a career as a professional soldier from the time he participated in Booth's Rebellion in 1659 until he left the army in 1689. Despite his high social rank, he made his way slowly in the English army. At the Restoration he secured a commission as an ensign in the Irish Foot Guards. By 1665 he was a lieutenant in an independent garrison company in Ludlow Castle, and in 1667 he became a captain in the duke of York's regiment of marines. In 1671 he was seconded to Sir Henry Jones's Regiment of Light Horse in the British Brigade of the French army. He probably went to France to gain battle experience, but he had also incurred the duke of York's displeasure for wounding John Churchill in a duel while on active duty during the Second Anglo-Dutch War. That this assignment and exile was a form of punishment is suggested by the fact that Herbert despised his colonel as an Old Cromwellian who lacked the qualities of a gentleman. Many of the officers and troopers whom Herbert encountered in Sir Henry Jones's Regiment of Light Horse had served in Portugal, and they included a number of Scots and Scots-Irish. Like his Scottish cornet, David Dunbar, who claimed to be 28 but who could remember battles fought thirty years earlier, they were officers whose careers were not advancing. Herbert's fellow officers had grown accustomed to perpetual campaigning, and knew how to entertain themselves with hunting, carousing, dancing and making fun of their colonel. The English officers traded substitutes between different regiments to cover losses incurred in battle in order to collect dead-pays. The troopers fared better in the field where they could plunder, but suffered privation when they returned to garrison in Nancy during the winter of 1672–3. Here their pay was inadequate for the cost of living and they were restrained from supplementing their rations by foraging. When Herbert learned that the colonel was cheating his troopers by withholding part of their pay he challenged him to a duel, but Jones refused. During the campaigning season of 1673 Herbert returned to the duke of York's marine regiment aboard the fleet, because he wanted to gain experience fighting at sea.[54]

---

[53] R. Clark, *Anthony Hamilton* (1921), 1–6, 29–33, 42–9, 53–6, 60–9, 74–5; Murphy, *Justin MacCarthy*, 29–30; J. G. Simms, 'A Jacobite Colonel: Lord Sarsfield of Kilmallock', *IS* 2 (1955), 205; Childs, *AC* 25–9.

[54] C. T. Atkinson, 'Charles II's Regiments in France, 1672–78, part I', *JSAHR* 24 (1946), 54–6; J. Childs (ed.), 'Captain Henry Herbert's Narrative of his Journey through France with his Regiment, 1671–3, and Ane Account of Our Regiments March from their Winter Quarters to their Entrance in France', *CM XXX*, CS 4th ser. 39 (1990), 289–357; id., *Profession of Arms*, 29.

Another cause that attracted volunteers and mercenary soldiers from the British Isles was the crusade to drive the Turks out of Europe and the islands of the Mediterranean. This war was led by the Venetian Republic, but Imperial Austria was increasingly drawn into the conflict as the Turks advanced up the Danube Valley from the Balkans towards Vienna in the latter part of the seventeenth century. As Vincenzo Gussoni, the Venetian ambassador to the Stuart court, wrote in 1635, the people of the Three Kingdoms had a natural aptitude for war which they acquired by experience in foreign conflicts. Although volunteers came from all of the Three Kingdoms, Irish Catholics seem always to have predominated, perhaps because their religion helped to gain them more acceptance. In the period after 1660, when so many swordsmen were banished from Ireland and Scotland, they probably were also attracted by the fact that Venetians were paying a premium of 20 to 50 per cent more in wages to northern European soldiers than the going rate for mercenaries in Italy. One soldier of fortune who led his regiment from Germany to Candia (modern Crete—a Venetian colony since the thirteenth century) in the last days of the Thirty Years War was Colonel Brereton, who was born in Ireland, but probably was descended from the Cheshire family of that name. The Candians thought so highly of Brereton that they made him a sergeant-major-general, and placed him in charge of their land forces. He died of a fever in Crete. Thomas Middleton was an English privateer who hired himself out to the Venetian-Candian naval forces. He was dismissed for cowardice for moving his ship to another position in the battle line without permission. However, Middleton subsequently redeemed himself by engaging a Turkish squadron of twenty-five ships and inflicting heavy damage. Middleton then returned to Candia and presented the general who had dismissed him with 'a whole tun of salted heads of those he had killed' in boarding the Turkish gallies. Middleton was given a gold medal and reinstated. Another privateer who fought in the Candian navy was George Scott of Fife, who was highly skilled in gunnery. He was the chief advisor to the Candian council of war on matters of gunnery and engineering. He also had a son who was especially skilled as a military engineer. Both died in the service of Candia.[55]

Undoubtedly the most famous Irish soldier to fight in the Imperialist army against the Turks was Francis Taaffe, later third earl of Carlingford, who became a general officer and a diplomat in Hapsburg service. Taaffe had been involved in negotiations with Charles IV, duke of Lorraine, a military enterpriser, about intervening in the civil wars in Ireland as protector of the Catholic Confederation of Kilkenny. Later, Taaffe and Duke Charles both served together in the latter's regiment of cuirassiers, which Taaffe himself later commanded. In July 1683, while camped at Passau, Taaffe wrote letters to his elder brother, the second earl of Carlingford, mentioning that an Imperialist army of 23,000 men was anticipating

[55] E. and P. Razzell (eds.), *The English Civil War: A Contemporary Account*, 5 vols. (1996), i. 18–19; Roger Palmer, 1st earl of Castlemain, *An Account of the Present War between the Venetians and the Turk* (1666), 19, 37–41, 45–6.

an attack by an Ottoman army of 160,000 plus another 40,000 Tatar and Hungarian auxiliaries, who were camped 'within cannon-shot of us'. Carlingford published his brother's letters in London, and helped to promote an awareness among swordsmen of the Three Kingdoms of the significance of the Imperialist war against the Turks and how desperate their situation was.[56] The writer of the preface to Taaffe's published letters held him up as 'an example to awake the virtue of the English nation and make all gentlemen sensible how much more it would be both for their interest and honour to employ their swords in this occasion for the defence of Christendom than to waste their fortunes in gaming houses and taverns and kill one another, as they do, in senseless and brutal quarrels'.[57] The Turks laid siege to Vienna that summer, and all of the countryside around Vienna was 'in flames'. English volunteers, such as John Grenville, Lord Lansdowne (and later second earl of Bath), responded, but it was the arrival of the armies of the king of Poland and several German princes that lifted the Siege of Vienna in September. King James VII and II was so impressed with Taaffe that he entrusted his illegitimate son, James Fitzjames, duke of Berwick, to Taaffe's care to serve his apprenticeship in arms. In 1694 Taaffe, who had succeeded as third earl of Carlingford, was promoted to field marshal and made a member of the Order of the Golden Fleece.[58]

The publication of Francis Taaffe's letters came too late to permit many volunteers to reach the Imperialist camp before the Siege of Vienna was lifted. However, Sir George Etherege, the English resident at the Imperial Diet in Ratisbon (Regensberg), noted a stream of aristocratic volunteers from the Three Kingdoms passing through in 1686 on their way to participate in the Siege of Budapest. Following Taaffe's example, they attached themselves to the Imperialist army commanded by Charles IV, duke of Lorraine. The volunteers included Lord George Savile, son of the first earl of Halifax; William Herbert, later second marquis of Powis; and William Stewart, first Viscount Mountjoy, a high-ranking officer in the Irish army, together with his son and heir William. Savile was wounded, while the son of the seventh earl of Clanricarde was killed as was Lord Mountjoy's brother-in-law, a volunteer named Forbes, who was the son of the first earl of Granard. Sir John Bramston's godson, Richard Wiseman, who had no hope of inheriting an estate because his father had encumbered it with debts, had resolved to make a career as a soldier. He had already served as a volunteer in the Dutch army and perhaps attended the military academy at Saumur. Wiseman's motive for going to Budapest, where he lost his life, was to gain 'esteem and favour with the king [James II], who indulged soldiers above all others'. The next

[56] H. Murtagh, 'Two Irish Officers and the Campaign to Relieve Vienna, 1683', *IS* 15 (1982–3), 255–6; 'The Correspondence of Francis Taaffe, Earl of Carlingford', *Memoirs of the Family of Taaffe* (1856), 225–8.

[57] *Count Taaffe's Letters from the Imperial Camp, to his Brother the Earl of Carlingford* (1684), preface.

[58] Murtagh, 'Two Irish Officers', 255–6; 'Correspondence of Francis Taaffe, Earl of Carlingford', 232–3; *Count Taaffe's Letters*, 1, 3, 15.

summer Etherege saw more volunteers making their way to Hungary to fight the Turks. They included Lord Charles Hamilton, son of the fifth earl of Abercorn; Walter, Lord Dungan, son of the first earl of Limerick; George Hay, fifth earl of Kinnoull; and 'Mr Fitzjames', that is, the duke of Berwick. Hamilton and the others fought in the Battle of Mohács, and Kinnoull died there.[59]

While these volunteers undoubtedly wished to help liberate Christian lands from the rule of the Turk, another motive seems to have been a desire to win favour and promotion in the armies of James VII and II, which were undergoing expansion. Another volunteer who was present at the Siege of Budapest was Jacob Richards, a young Irish engineer officer attached to the English Ordnance Office, who was sent by King James to observe the campaign. Jacobs took careful notes of what he saw, and subsequently visited Greece. Upon his return to England he was promoted and put in charge of modernizing the defences of Hull. Jacob Richards was an officer in the train of artillery in 1688, but transferred his allegiance to William III. He was a Protestant and the son of an Irish Cromwellian colonel, Solomon Richards of co. Wexford. Jacob fought with King William in Flanders in the Nine Years War. He was highly regarded, and was to be retained in the peacetime army with the rank of colonel. However, in 1697 Jacob Richards left England to enter the service of the Venetian Republic. One can only speculate concerning the reason: he seems to have wished to be with his younger brother John, who as a Catholic had been disinherited by their father and excluded from the British army. Jacob had made contact with the Venetians a decade earlier, and in 1697 both Jacob and John entered Venetian service and proceeded to Corinth and other places in Greece to strengthen the fortifications of this newly acquired Venetian territory. There was also a plan to establish a colony of Irish Catholic soldiers in Greece to serve the Venetians. At the end of the war in Greece, Jacob entered the service of Frederick Augustus, elector of Saxony and king of Poland, while John Richards went to Portugal. The king of Portugal had requested the loan of some British officers. As a Catholic, John could not qualify for a commission under Queen Anne, so he was commissioned in the Portuguese army, but with a pension from the queen upon the recommendation of her ministers (who apparently included the duke of Marlborough).[60]

Before 1689 Irish soldiers recruited for the Imperial Austrian army had been assigned to existing regiments, but in that year the Holy Roman emperor and William III of England entered into an agreement to raise an Irish regiment for Imperial service. The men were drawn from Irish regiments in the English army at

---

[59] F. Bracher (ed.), *Letters of Sir George Etherege* (1974), 30–1, 37, 49, 56, 123, 128; *The Autobiography of Sir John Bramston*, CS OS 32 (1845), 235–8.

[60] Jacob Richards, *A Journal of the Siege and Taking of Buda by the Imperial Army* (1687), 5–6, 10–12, 15, 18, 22, 30–1, 38; F. J. Hebbert, 'The Richards Brothers', *IS* 12 (1975), 200–5; Childs, *Profession of Arms*, 77; BL, Stowe MS. 459 [Diary of John Richards' Travel from Dublin to Venice], fos. 16*v*–19*v*, 20*r*; Stowe MS. 466 [Letterbook of John Richards, 1703–4], fos. 5*v*–9*r*,17*v*–18*v*, 21*r* & *v*. In April 1703 John Richards wrote to his brother Michael, also a military engineer, to tell him that their brother Jacob had died of alcoholism just after the two of them had joined the king of Poland's army.

the time of James II's flight to France, and had been interred on the Isle of Wight because of their known loyalty to King James. The 1,800 Irish soldiers were offered no choice in the matter and were sold to the emperor, who had failed to support James. Since the emperor was opposed to Louis XIV of France, he had entered into an alliance with William III of England and the Netherlands. Half of the regiment deserted as soon as they landed in Germany. The remaining Irish soldiers were destined for Hungary, where they were to fight the Turks. Another 100 deserted as they marched through Silesia and Moravia. When they finally arrived in Hungary, it was decided to assign them to other Imperialist regiments because their continuing loyalty to James II made them suspect. Indeed, Jacobite agents actually tried to foment disloyalty among Irish soldiers in the Imperial Austrian army. When the Irish army of James II was disbanded following the end of the Williamite wars in 1691, another regiment was raised for Imperial service by Georg von Hessen-Darmstadt, but most Irish soldiers chose to enter the French army. This regiment, consisting of 2,400 men, was reduced by a third through illness, and it was difficult to maintain discipline because the Irish troops engaged in faction-fights with the Imperialist troops with whom they were quartered. Again, this second Irish regiment was disbanded and the soldiers reassigned to other units. Plans to raise a third Irish regiment were abandoned.[61]

As opportunities for military employment dried up in the Three Kingdoms, the Netherlands and Scandinavia in the 1650s and 1660s, soldiers of fortune from the British Isles were driven to look further afield. As Muscovy opened a window on the west and sought to modernize, Scottish and other foreign officers were useful in importing and introducing western European weapons, tactics and discipline. They were also frequently employed as diplomats, as they had been earlier in Sweden and Denmark-Norway. Patrick Gordon of Auchleuchries and Paul Menzies, both Catholics, were especially useful in this regard. The latter was sent on a diplomatic mission to the pope in 1672 to improve relations with Rome and to attempt to secure papal approbation for a crusade against the Crimean Tatars and the Ottoman Turks. Patrick Gordon was successful in persuading Czars Ivan and Peter to grant permission to build a Catholic Church in Moscow, staffed with priests, where they allowed freedom of worship to soldiers from western Europe. At the same time, soldiers of fortune serving abroad were useful sources of information and constituted a kind of informal intelligence network for the rulers of their native countries. Patrick Gordon, who served in the armies of Sweden, Poland and Russia, kept up a correspondence with the second earl of Middleton and Sir Joseph Williamson, who was secretary to the earl of Arlington. Thus, the English government was kept informed about military and foreign affairs in Russia, Ukraine, Poland and on the borders of the Ottoman empire.[62]

---

[61] J. O'Neill, 'Conflicting Loyalties: Irish Regiments in the Imperial Service', *IS* 17 (1987–90), 116–18.

[62] P. Dukes, 'Scottish Soldiers in Muscovy', 18–22; S. Konovalov, 'Sixteen Further Letters of General Patrick Gordon', *Oxford Slavonic Papers*, 13 (1967), 72–95.

Patrick Gordon was a well travelled soldier of considerable experience. He was articulate, observant and left a most valuable memoir. Soon after joining the Swedish army in 1655 he was captured by the Poles; a Scots Franciscan named Innes obtained his release on condition that he joined the Polish army. Gordon was then recaptured by the Swedes. He was taken before a fellow Scot, Lieutenant Field Marshal Robert Douglas, who accepted Gordon's explanation of how he came to be in the Polish force, and enlisted him for three years service in the Swedish army. Gordon was assigned to Douglas's own company of Scottish cadets and sent back to Warsaw to recruit Scottish prisoners of war for Douglas's company. He returned with twenty-four recruits. The captain-lieutenant of Gordon's company was John Meldrum, and the troops were employed in cattle-raiding. Since they were very good at this (being Scots), Gordon had soon earned 100 Reichsthalers and acquired a pair of good horses. He was bothered by these practices, but remembered that the Swedish army lived off the land, and this was what one had to do to survive. After being taken prisoner by the Imperial Austrian army, Gordon escaped and made his way back to the Swedish camp. He demanded to be discharged, on the pretext that he had never been paid or reimbursed for his equipment. Soldiers in the Swedish army at this time were expected to live by plunder. For a time Gordon joined a band of Scottish freebooters, who specialized in capturing Austrians and selling them to the Swedish army. In 1658 he once again joined the Swedish army as an ensign, and was assigned to Colonel Anderson's regiment. Captured again by the Poles, he was assigned to a cavalry regiment. Gordon was by now an experienced soldier with the rank of captain-lieutenant, and found himself courted by the Poles, the Muscovites and the Imperialists. He was about to join an Austrian cavalry regiment commanded by a distant kinsman, Colonel Patrick Gordon of the Steelhand, but the regiment was never raised. With the conclusion of peace between the Holy Roman Empire and Ottoman Turkey, he was persuaded to join the Russian army.[63]

The Scots abroad maintained a kind of freemasonry among themselves, whatever army they served in. While travelling to Prague with a group of fellow Scots, Gordon learned that Scots were being discharged from the Swedish army and that better opportunities were to be found in Russian service. He and seven fellow Scots decided to set out for Moscow. He was commissioned a major, but had trouble getting the scribe to deliver his commission until he paid a large bribe. Gordon was always troubled by the bribery and extortion, which were part of the fabric of Russian life. He was posted to a regiment commanded by Daniel Crawford and officered entirely by Scots, but made up of 700 mutinous Russians, all deserters from other regiments. As the major, Gordon was expected to drill and discipline them. Since foreign officers were not permitted to marry Russian women unless they converted to the Russian Orthodox Church, Gordon fixed upon Katharine von Bockhoven, the 16-year-old Catholic daughter of a colonel in the Russian army.[64]

---

[63] *Diary of General Patrick Gordon*, 22–35.   [64] Ibid. 38–40, 46–50.

Service under the czars always raised the problem of conflicting allegiances. Gordon did well in the Russian army, and by 1686 was a lieutenant-general and commander of the Kiev garrison. However, he was homesick and sought release from Russian service. Despite the personal intervention of James VII and II, arranged by his friend the earl of Middleton, he was unable to secure a discharge. He was allowed to return to Scotland for a period of three months to settle family business, but was obliged to leave his wife and family behind as pledges for his return. Indeed, he was in temporary disgrace for attempting to resign, and was threatened with demotion to the rank of ensign and banishment to some remote place. Gordon redeemed himself only by admitting his error and craving pardon. He regarded all of these histrionics as a 'stage play'. Most Scots found it difficult to leave the czar's service, and left numerous descendants who subsequently became russified.[65]

The banishment of unemployed soldiers from the British Isles was a policy pursued by the Cromwellian government in order to preserve the hard-won peace and to maintain political stability. This policy was continued by Charles II at the Restoration for much the same reason, but Charles, like Cromwell, attempted— not always successfully—to control the traffic in mercenary soldiers to mainland Europe in a way that would be compatible with English diplomatic and military policy. Charles loaned officers and soldiers to Portugal and France, and this allowed them to obtain actual experience of battle before returning home. He also retained nominal control over units which had been seconded to those armies. Charles probably would have preferred to have curtailed or ended the service of his subjects in the Dutch army. James VII and II later tried, unsuccessfully, to gain control over the officers and men of the Anglo-Dutch and Scots Brigades of the States' Army. The Netherlands had become a place of refuge for Radicals and Republicans from the Three Kingdoms who were unhappy with the Stuart dynasty, and they were invariably protected by Dutch authorities when extradition was requested. Some of these dissidents participated in the incursions into the Thames estuary during the Second Anglo-Dutch War, and William III could not have contemplated his invasion of England in 1688 without the military manpower of the Anglo-Dutch and Scots Brigades. In the short run, James VII and II was able to draw upon the services of English, Irish and Scots officers who had gained battlefield experience serving with a variety of mainland European armies, but many of these swordsmen, after long years in exile, had become men of divided allegiance. William III was careful to cultivate bonds of friendship with the officers from the British Isles who served under his command in the wars with Louis XIV, a cause more to their liking, and they proved willing to help in his invasion of England and conquest of Scotland and Ireland, or subsequently to defect to his cause.

---

[65] *Diary of General Patrick Gordon*, 158–62; Konovalov, 'Letters of General Patrick Gordon', 74–5; Dukes, 'Scottish Soldiers in Muscovy', 22.

One notable difference in the attitudes of swordsmen from the British Isles serving abroad may be noted. Prior to the Wars of the Three Kingdoms, soldiers of fortune who joined mainland European armies were more likely to attach themselves to a particular person, such as a proprietary colonel who raised his regiment on the basis of kinship ties (as in Scotland and Ireland) or a person who inspired personal loyalty (such as Elizabeth, queen of Bohemia). This could lead, for example, to Catholic soldiers like Sir John Hepburn fighting under the banners of Protestant monarchs such as Gustavus Adolphus. In the more remote parts of England and Wales before and during the civil wars it was still possible to raise smaller units, such as cavalry troops, on the basis of kinship and retinue, but most regiments levied in England for service in foreign armies were impressed and could be counted upon to desert at the first opportunity, unless they were reasonably well paid, as in the Dutch army. The impact of the British and Irish civil wars as well as the mainland European wars such as the Thirty Years War was to heighten political awareness and to make officers and volunteers, and private soldiers as well, more careful and discriminating in how they bestowed their allegiances. Immediately following the Restoration most career soldiers were probably glad to be employed no matter where, but by the 1670s, when the revival of the mainland European wars offered more choices of employment, religious and political loyalties seem to play a greater role in choice of employment. Protestant officers and volunteers, when pressured by Charles II to volunteer for service with the French army fighting the Dutch, were more disposed to observe the fighting than to participate. At the end of the Williamite Wars in Ireland, Irish soldiers resisted being compelled to fight in the Imperial Austrian army because the Holy Roman emperor had failed to support James VII and II during the Williamite Wars and was allied to their arch-enemy, William III. They were happy enough to join the French army because of Louis XIV's assistance (however limited) to their own monarch.

The Stuart monarchs awakened late to the potential value of the military manpower of the Three Kingdoms. When James VII and II called home the English and Scottish regiments of the Dutch army during the Monmouth Rebellion in 1685, he began to understand that the prince of Orange had built the Scots and Anglo-Dutch Brigades into superb corps, and attempted to retain many of the officers in his own armies and to gain control of the military commissions issued to Englishmen and Scots in the States' Army, but it was too late. William had already suborned the loyalties of most of the officers, and that would cost James his kingdoms.

PART IV

THE RECOVERY OF A MILITARY TRADITION 1688–1702

14

The descent on England

To convince how jealous the king [James VII and II] was of the prince [of Orange], he considered for some time whether he should demand of the States General the six British regiments in their pay, which regiments by stipulation they were obliged to send over on the king's demand in case of invasion. The regiments landed, and I saw them march to Hyde Park to a review, and one seldom saw such a fine body of men, and for experienced officers the same; but what the king apprehended was the officers all preferred and raised by the prince of Orange.

Thomas Bruce, 3rd earl of Elgin and 2nd earl of Ailesbury, *Memoirs*, 2 vols., RC 21 (1890), i. 114 (the date is 1685).

Among the other blessings which we his [William III's] subjects shall enjoy from him, this is not one of the least, that as he is a valiant and warlike monarch, so he will raise again among us the ancient genius of true British valour, which was so very much decayed to our great dishonour under the luxury and easiness of the last two reigns.

William Sawle, *An Impartial relation of . . . Last Summer's Campaign in Flanders* (1691), 20.

William Sawle, a chaplain with the English army in Flanders during the Nine Years War, was not fond of the Dutch, but he praised William III as 'a valiant and warlike monarch', who had come to the throne following a long period of military decay which he believed characterized the reigns of Charles II and James VII and II. As a result of three years of war in Ireland and Flanders, Sawle thought that the English army was well furnished with experienced officers, and that an ancient martial tradition had been revived. This profound alteration in the military and foreign policies of England and, subsequently, the kingdoms of Ireland and Scotland as well, led Great Britain and Ireland into a long century of global wars with France that ended only in 1815 at Waterloo. This reorientation of British priorities was accomplished not by the Glorious or bloodless Revolution of Whig mythology, but by the invasion of England resulting from the largest and most successful joint military and naval amphibious operation ever launched in early modern Europe. The decision to declare the throne of England vacant and to offer the crown to the prince of Orange, and thus to commit England to a mainland war, was taken by the Convention Parliament while London was under Dutch military occupation. This transfer of allegiance was accomplished less peacefully in Scotland and Ireland, which were incorporated into the Williamite monarchy by military conquest.

The officers of the six English and Scots regiments in the States' Army who accompanied William, prince of Orange in his descent on England in November 1688, as well as the officers of James's English army, were highly politicized, and the allegiance of the latter had been weakened by conspiracies within the army organized by officers who had been suborned by William and his Whig agents. John, Lord Churchill, Edward Hyde, Viscount Cornbury, Charles Trelawny and other key officers in the English army during the confrontation between the English and the Dutch armies ran from their colours, and James II, whose courage had been so resolute on earlier occasions, lost heart as his officers deserted, and he never offered battle. The loyalty of the English, Irish and Scottish regiments of the English army was never tested on the field of battle; William advanced on London as James fell back. James abandoned the realm of England, but attempted to recover his three thrones with French aid, by making a stand against William in Ireland. Although the desertion of military and naval officers and aristocrats of the Three Kingdoms had helped to consolidate support for the prince of Orange's rule, William never trusted officers from the British Isles who had not served with him in the Dutch army. He had little liking or respect for English peers, because he thought that they were not amenable to military discipline. William's preferential treatment of Dutch officers and disdain for English officers and magnates led some of the latter to correspond with James VII and II in exile and to defect to the Jacobite cause. This weakened the authority of the officers of the English army, and necessitated the passing of the Mutiny Act of 1689 by Parliament in order to restore discipline following a series of mutinies among regiments in England. Moreover, despite William's stated intention of protecting the Protestant religion from the threat of popery, his Dutch invasion force probably contained almost as many Catholic officers and soldiers as James II's English army.

By securing the entry of the Three Kingdoms into the Nine Years War against Louis XIV of France, William III re-established contact between the military worlds of mainland Europe and the British Isles, fostered the growth of a fiscal-military state on the Dutch model and, through a shared military experience, presided over the emergence of a British state and an integrated army that went on to acquire great-power status.

At the beginning of James VII and II's reign in February 1685, the English army totalled fewer than 9,000 men, of whom 1,400 were garrison troops not available for field armies. The Irish army could muster 7,500 men; the Scots army a mere 2,200. The Monmouth Rebellion of 1685 gave James the excuse to expand the English army, and thanks to unwonted subsidies from the English Parliament to meet the imminent threat to security, he was able to increase the size of the

English army to nearly 20,000 men by December 1685. Peers and substantial gentry were pressured to raise regiments of foot and troops of horse for James's expanding army, and Thomas Bruce, soon to be the second earl of Ailesbury and third earl of Elgin, with no previous military experience, was given command of a troop of horse in Henry Mordaunt, second earl of Peterborough's new cavalry regiment. He was made senior captain of the regiment and given one week to drill his men before they were to be reviewed by the king.[1] The regiments which had been raised to suppress the Monmouth Rebellion were afterwards kept standing, and soldiers who thought that they had joined for temporary service began to desert in large numbers. Desertion was also a serious problem in the Scots army, where low pay caused discontent. The Scottish Foot Guards, a long-established corps, lost almost 7 per cent of their number within the space of two months.[2]

The threat of a Dutch invasion provided the pretext in the spring of 1688 for a further expansion of the army, and James's attempt to recall the officers and men of the Anglo-Dutch and Scots Brigades of the States' Army furnished enough experienced officers for James to add one regiment of 700 men to each of the armies of the three Kingdoms. A further seven regiments of foot and five of horse were added to the English establishment, but probably only two-thirds of the projected strength of 34,000 men could be mustered by the time that William's invasion force landed at Torbay in November 1688. When reinforced by troops from Ireland and Scotland, James probably was able to assemble a field army of 30,000.[3]

At the beginning of his reign James inaugurated the practice of having the better part of his army assemble for six weeks every summer on Hounslow Heath. The purpose of this encampment was to drill and train the army in large tactical units and to increase its proficiency, but it also served, thought the citizens of London, to intimidate the populace. Each summer a mock battle was staged after constructing large and elaborate earthen ramparts; in 1687 the Siege of Buda was re-enacted. Such events constituted a tourist attraction, and courtiers brought their ladies out to observe the spectacle, but Dutch propaganda depicted the Hounslow Heath mock battles as 'shooting at butterflies in the air', which was much resented by James and the court. The great confluence of troops was bound to cause some disorder, considering how raw some of the soldiers were. Although the king had forbidden it, some soldiers lived at free quarter and extorted money from innkeepers and merchants. The summer encampments were also disturbed by conflict between Irish Catholic officers and members of the Association of Protestant Officers. The Bill of Rights of 1689 would later charge that James II had unlawfully raised and maintained a standing army in peacetime without the consent of Parliament, and had allowed his soldiers to live upon free quarter.[4]

---

[1] Childs, *AJGR* 1–2, 31; Thomas Bruce, 2nd earl of Ailesbury and 3rd earl of Elgin, *Memoirs*, 2 vols., RC 21 (1890), i. 108–9.   [2] Childs, *AJGR* 92–3.

[3] Ibid., pp. xi–xiii, 3–4; *The Military Memoirs of Capt. George Carleton* (1728), 38.

[4] Childs, *AJGR* 96–9; *Memoirs of... George Carleton*, 38–9; C. Jackson (ed.), *The Diary of Abraham de la Pryme, the Yorkshire Antiquary*, SS 54 (1870), 8; F. W. Maitland, *The Constitutional History of England* (1909), 328.

James VII and II worked hard promoting professionalism in the English army, and one of the ways he did this was by commissioning officers with extensive experience in the mainland European wars. These officers had fought in conflicts from the wars of northern Europe to the Venetian and Imperial Austrian campaigns against the Turks. Regiments such as the Royal Scots, the Royal Regiment of Foot and the Holland Regiment were led entirely by officers who had fought in the Dutch and French armies. Another policy that James followed which was meant to integrate his armies and promote loyalty to the monarchy was the exchanging of regiments between the Three Kingdoms. The Royal Scots had always been part of the English army since they transferred from French to English service in 1678. Other English regiments were stationed in parts of the kingdom remote from where they had been raised. Another regiment was raised in England in 1685 and sent to the Irish establishment. The whole of the Scots army was transferred south in 1688, and four Irish regiments crossed St George's Channel in the same year to help defeat William of Orange. These exchanges anticipated the integration of the armies of the Three Kingdoms into the British army after 1707. Without being able to draw upon the military manpower of Ireland and Scotland at a time when population growth was static, Great Britain could hardly have acquired great-power status. Unfortunately, the political nation and some of the officers of the English army were less receptive to these exchanges. The presence of Irish Catholic soldiers in England summoned up memories of 1641, and the removal of the whole Scots army from the northern kingdom made it possible for William of Orange's friends to carry out a change of regime in Scotland.[5]

Both as lord admiral, before the Test Act required him to resign that position, and later as king, James VII and II sought to inspire personal loyalty and to reward officers who were loyal to him. Those officers who responded to his call to return home from service in the Anglo-Dutch and Scots Brigades were provided with places in three new regiments in the armies of the Three Kingdoms. James did much to promote professionalism in the officer class, but he never succeeded in overriding their religious and political sympathies. A few Protestant officers were deprived of their offices to make room for Catholic gentlemen, but outside of the Irish army, James never succeeded in building up more than a small core of loyal Catholic officers in the English army. If James failed to eradicate the religious and political sympathies that undermined loyalty to him, it has to be said that other armies in Europe also failed to achieve the same objective in the seventeenth century. And James had not quite four years in which to impose more professional standards. James's detractors accused him of intending to purge Protestant officers from the English army as he had done in the Irish army, of violating the Test Act and the Recusancy Statutes by using the suspending and dispensing powers of the royal prerogative, and generally intending to use a popish army to subdue the English Parliament and impose absolutism on his subjects. James certainly did

    [5] J. R. Western, *Monarchy and Revolution: The English State in the 1680s* (1972), 136–9; Glozier, *Scottish Soldiers in France*, ch. 10.

commission Catholic officers in the English army, but there were hardly sufficient Catholics with military experience to displace its Protestant officers. James was sensitive to the problems of Catholic military officers, who had few opportunities for employment in the armies of mainland Europe in the 1680s except in the war against the Turks. He did constitute a fourth troop of the Life Guards in 1686 to provide employment for Catholic reformadoes, but Henry Jermyn, first Lord Dover, its Catholic commanding officer, sold places in the troop, and many of the troopers were actually French Huguenots. James did offer commissions to Catholics when the English army expanded in 1685 and 1688, but as Professor Childs has conclusively demonstrated, the number of Catholic officers never exceeded slightly more than 200, or 11 per cent of the total number of army officers. James's desire to open opportunities for Catholics was always secondary to the military need of inculcating professionalism and a degree of detachment from ideology. Moreover, Catholic officers were widely dispersed throughout the army. The English army remained overwhelmingly Protestant. James thought that there were no more than a thousand Catholics in the rank and file (although the number was probably greater than that), whereas Sir John Reresby estimated that William of Orange's invasion force may have contained 4,000 Catholic officers and men. The small Scottish establishment was even more solidly Protestant, and very few Catholic officers obtained commissions.[6]

The Irish army was much in need of reform at the beginning of James II's reign. The army consisted mostly of independent companies quartered on the estates of their captains. The pay of the soldiers was much in arrears, and when they were paid, the deductions for clothing and equipment were so excessive that the soldiers were left with only about 2*d.* per diem to live upon out of a daily rate of 6*d.*, where it was estimated that they could barely subsist on 4*d.* per day. To make matters worse, the officers of the Irish army routinely defrauded their men, and this practice reached to the very top of the command structure. The cavalry were more mobile only because they had to move at regular intervals in order to find sufficient fodder for the horses. James wished to impose a regimental command structure on the independent companies so that they could be drilled in larger units, but the lack of sufficient inns or permanent barracks for winter quarters hindered this process.[7]

One of James II's motives in remodelling the Irish army was to provide relief to Catholics who had suffered persecution under the Protestant minority by opening opportunities in civil and military offices from which they had been totally excluded. The king entrusted this task to Richard Talbot (later earl of Tyrconnell and lord deputy after 1687) as commander-in-chief of the army. Talbot convinced James that the officers of the Irish army included numerous Old Cromwellians

---

[6] Childs, *AJGR* 18–21, 23, 27, 29, 150–1; Ailesbury, *Memoirs*, i. 130–1; A. Browning (ed.), *Memoirs of Sir John Reresby* (1936; repr. 1991), 553.

[7] S. W. Singer (comp.), *The State Letters of Henry, Earl of Clarendon, Lord Lieutenant of Ireland*, 2 vols. (1763), i. 164–6, 169, 292–3; R. Clark, *Anthony Hamilton* (1921), 76–8.

and crypto-Republicans, although such persons had long since been replaced by Anglicans. On the night of 23 October 1685 a group of Protestants in the garrison town of Athlone lit bonfires to commemorate the Irish Rebellion of 1641 and the alleged massacres in order to intimidate Catholics. Talbot seized upon this incident, allegedly perpetrated by Old Cromwellians, to demonstrate the connection between Whiggism and sedition, to justify his suppression of the Protestant militia and to help persuade James of the need to purge the Irish army. Knowing little of Ireland and ignoring the advice of his own nephew Henry Hyde, second earl of Clarendon, the lord-lieutenant, James was dependent on Talbot, an Old English Catholic, who was remarkably effective in purging some 7,000 Protestant officers and soldiers between 1685 and 1688. They were replaced with Old English officers and Catholic Old Irish soldiers. Little wonder that the perception of Protestants throughout the Three Kingdoms was that the king meant to use a remodelled Irish army to impose Catholicism and absolutism in England and Scotland, but there is no convincing evidence that this really was James's intention or that of Talbot, now earl of Tyrconnell, who wanted an Ireland less dependent on England. Tyrconnell clearly exceeded his orders from the king, and did much to drive leaders of the Protestant ascendancy, such as James, second duke of Ormonde, and his clients into the arms of William of Orange. Some of the Protestant officers who were dismissed had invested all of their financial resources in the purchase of their commissions, and they often came from families noted for their loyalty to Charles I. They were not compensated for the cost. Although some of Tyrconnell's new colonels, such as Justin Maccarty (later Viscount Mountcashel) and Richard Hamilton, were competent and experienced officers, many of the newly commissioned officers were not. Probably no more than one-eighth of the new officers were professional soldiers.[8]

Tyrconnell and his officers were given a free hand in reforming the Irish army. They turned out as many as 500 men in a single day, and administered savage corporal punishments without regard to whether these accorded with army regulations and past usage. When a Scottish regiment was sent to Ireland to replace Irish regiments posted to England, it contained many soldiers who were old and of different height. James ordered them discharged and replaced by young men of the same stature. The lord-lieutenant, the earl of Clarendon, was anxious that provision be made for the soldiers who had been discharged at the new Royal Hospital, Kilmainham, since deductions from their pay had been made for that purpose. Tyrconnell would not hear of it because the hospital lacked the funds to accommodate them; he said that the soldiers had already enjoyed the king's pay for many years. As a consequence of the purges, many of the soldiers in the Irish army were young and inexperienced. They received little training, and were

---

[8] Childs, *AJGR* 57–67, 71; T. C. Barnard, 'Athlone, 1685; Limerick, 1710: Religious Riots or Charivaris?', *Studia Hibernica*, 27 (1993), 61, 63, 66–7; J. G. Simms, *Jacobite Ireland, 1685–91* (1969; repr. 2000), 22–5; HEH, Hastings MSS., HA (Military Box), 2 (3); Singer (comp.), *State Letters of . . . Earl of Clarendon*, i. 285.

mostly used to fight tories. James II's goals of reforming the Irish army, of improving training and discipline and equipping it with more modern arms were lost sight of as Tyrconnell carried out the purge of Protestant officers. By emphasizing religious and political loyalty, James and Tyrconnell succeeded in making the Irish army less militarily effective. As a result, it made a poor showing in the Williamite war against the more experienced and better-trained troops of the prince of Orange. Only the assistance of French troops allowed the Jacobite army to hold out as long as it did.[9]

The purge of the Irish army also had a deleterious effect on the English army. The Irish troops brought over from Ireland in August and September 1688 were mostly posted to Portsmouth to help protect the dockyards and to work on the new fortifications. The garrison of Portsmouth had remained quite loyal to King James until the moment when he asked the officers to endorse his religious policy and to accept Irish soldiers into their units. The king's natural son, James Fitzjames, duke of Berwick, was governor of Portsmouth and colonel of Princess Anne of Denmark's Regiment of Foot. When he ordered the lieutenant-colonel, John Beaumont, to take in forty Irish soldiers and to dismiss as many of the regiment's soldiers to make room, Beaumont, the brother of an Irish peer, and five other senior officers, who became notorious as the 'six Portsmouth captains', refused to obey—thereby setting in motion a mutiny that spread to the subaltern officers of the regiment. When James learned of this indiscipline, he ordered the six officers to be brought to Windsor Castle and tried by court martial for disobeying orders. They refused to back down and were cashiered. A week later, seven junior officers in the same regiment refused to obey the order and were dismissed from the army without trial. Following the Williamite invasion of England, five of the six 'Portsmouth captains' were reinstated, and Beaumont was promoted colonel.[10]

As opportunities for military careers in Scandinavia dried up in the latter part of the seventeenth century, Scottish aristocrats who wished to become officers became increasingly dependent upon the Stuart monarchs in London for patronage. Since the number of commissions in the Scots army was always limited, ambitious Scots martialists looked to the English army, which incorporated Scottish regiments from the 1670s. This phenomenon promoted the integration of English and Scots officers in the English army before a British army formally came into existence as a consequence of the Act of Union of 1707. Prior to the Glorious Revolution, this had made the Scots officers more loyal to James VII and II and the Jacobite cause. This was true not only of the officer class; manifestations of loyalty to the Stuarts in the rank and file helped to precipitate mutinies against

---

[9] Singer (comp.), *State Letter of . . . Clarendon*, i. 169, 215, 285–7, 336–7; ii. 89–90; Childs, *AJGR* 57; J. McGuire, 'James II and Ireland, 1685–90', in W. A. Maguire (ed.), *Kings in Conflict: The Revolutionary War in Ireland and its Aftermath, 1689–1750* (1990), 45–7; Simms, *Jacobite Ireland*, 37–8.
[10] A. Coleby, 'Military-Civilian Relations on the Solent, 1657–1689', *HJ* 29: 4 (1986), 949–52; E. J. Priestley, 'The Portsmouth Captains', *JSAHR* 55 (1977), 153–64; Childs, *AJGR* 99.

William II and III among Scottish regiments in 1689. However, the pursuit of careerism and the need to obtain military patronage could cut both ways, and this dependency also attached other Scots to William of Orange—especially those whose religious principles caused them to pursue careers in the Dutch army.[11]

In the small Scottish home army, officers were employed in suppressing domestic rebellions—when they were not engaged in violent disputes concerning whose regiment had precedence in the order of marching. This happened in 1685 when two militia regiments—one from Edinburgh and the other from Fife—violently and publicly disputed who should march on the right hand as they headed westward in pursuit of the earl of Argyll's rebel followers. Only the presence of General Thomas Dalzell prevented the two regiments from fighting one another. Some of Ewen Cameron of Lochiel's Highlanders, when called upon to help suppress the Argyll Rebellion, attacked a party of gentlemen volunteers and murdered several of them. Sir John Lauder wondered whether they could not understand English or whether they simply intended to rob the gentlemen. George Douglas, earl of Dumbarton, led the Scots army in pursuit of Argyll's forces from Glasgow to near Stirling. From there the chase continued all night until the earl of Argyll and his followers were run down as they crossed the River Clyde at the Ford of Inchenann. Argyll's feudal power had declined to such an extent that many Campbells had refused to follow him in the Rebellion of 1685. Argyll was executed, his heir Archibald, Lord Lorne (later tenth earl and first duke of Argyll), forced into exile, and his castles and forts in western Scotland, nine in number, were demolished.[12]

The most formidable and well organized military opposition to King James VII and II came not from the officers in the armies of the Three Kingdoms—most of whom were slow in declaring themselves for the prince of Orange—but from the English, Irish and Scots officers in the States' Army. The Orangist officer corps stood apart from the bourgeois life and culture of the Dutch Republic; they were aristocratic and, more than any other comparable military class in Europe, they could claim, on the basis of their expertise and experience, to be a body of professional officers. They were excluded from political office in all of the Dutch provinces except Friesland and Zeeland. Except for William's cousin Henry, count of Ouwerkerk, who was descended from the bachelor Maurice of Nassau, none of William of Orange's closest companions had great estates to distract them from the life of court and camp; many, such as Willem van Bentenck (William's military advisor in later life and subsequently earl of Portland), had shared the straitened circumstances of William's boyhood. Focused as they were upon the military life and dedicated to the struggle against Louis XIV, this small coterie

---

[11] K. M. Brown, 'From Scottish Lords to British Officers: State Building, Elite Integration and the Army in the Seventeenth Century', in Macdougall, *S&W* 145–7.

[12] Sir John Lauder of Fountainhall, *Historical Observations . . . October 1680 to April 1686*, vol. i, ed. A. Urquhart and D. Laing, BC 66 (1837), 176–7; id., *Historical Notices of Scottish Affairs*, ed. D. Laing, 2 vols., BC 87 (1848), ii. 629; *An Account of the taking of the Late Earl of Argyll* (1685), 1; D. Szechi and D. Hayton, 'John Bull's Other Kingdoms: The English Government of Scotland and Ireland', in C. Jones (ed.), *Britain in the First Age of Party: Essays Presented to Geoffrey Holmes* (1987), 244.

dominated the Orange court and officer corps, which still retained the reputation of being the best nursery of arms in Europe.[13]

The court of William of Orange was also a very cosmopolitan circle. Willem Friederich van Nassau-Zuylestein, William's illegitimate uncle, was the son of William's tutor, and a cavalry commander. He had learned English from his mother, Anne Killegrew. Perhaps the most distinguished military figure among those who accompanied the prince of Orange in the descent on England was Frederick Henry, vicomte de Schomberg (and later first duke of Schomberg in the English peerage). He too was half-English and was related to the Dudley family. His own family had lost their ancestral estates in the Palatinate, and Schomberg grew up in exile in the Netherlands. He began his military career in the Scottish Guards of the French Royal Army and served under Marshal Turenne. After reorganizing the Portuguese army, where he would have met a number of English officers, and upon his return to France, Schomberg was made a duke and a marshal of France by Louis XIV. He left France following the Revocation of the Edicts of Nantes, which abolished freedom of worship for French Protestants, and went to the Netherlands, where he reorganized the Huguenot regiments of the Dutch army. Although he was past the age of 70 when he accompanied the prince of Orange to England in 1688, Schomberg was probably the best general in Europe at the time.[14]

When William of Orange's invasion force landed at Brixham on Torbay in November 1688, the six regiments of the Anglo-Dutch and Scots Brigades formed the vanguard. Reformed and reorganized on more than one occasion, some of these corps dated back to the late sixteenth century. They had often borne the brunt of the fighting in Dutch field armies. Although paid by the States General, they took their orders from and gave their loyalty to the House of Orange. Since the time of Charles II they were theoretically on loan to the States General, and could be recalled by the king of England, as happened at the time of the Monmouth Rebellion in 1685. William of Orange was also supposed to consult with the Stuart monarchs about the commissioning of officers—especially since the commander of the Anglo-Dutch Brigade often functioned as the English ambassador to The Hague. These conventions contained much ambiguity and were the source of misunderstanding and tension between the prince of Orange and Charles II and James VII and II. The case of Henry Sidney (whom William of Orange later created earl of Romney) is a good example of the problems presented by this situation. In 1665, when he was 25 years of age, Sidney had been dismissed as groom of the bedchamber to James, duke of York, after he had become enamoured of Anne, duchess of York. In 1678 Charles II gave him command of a regiment and sent him as envoy to the States General, where he remained for

---

[13] J. Carswell, *The Descent on England: A Study of the English Revolution of 1688 and its European Background* (1969), 20–1.

[14] Ibid. 19–20; *The Memoirs of James II: His Campaigns as Duke of York*, trans. A. L. Sells (1962), 74 n.–75 n.

approximately two years. During this time he became a favourite of William of Orange. When James Butler, earl of Ossory and commandant of the Anglo-Dutch Brigade, died in 1680, William ignored Charles II's nominee for the post and made Sidney commanding officer, a position which he continued to hold until deprived by James II in 1685. Sidney became an important channel of communication between William and the Whigs in England. He signed the declaration of the five Whigs urging William to seize the English throne, and he accompanied William's invasion force to England.[15]

Given the example set by Sidney, it is little wonder that the officers of the six regiments of the Anglo-Dutch and Scots Brigades of the States' Army also developed the habit of engaging in partisan politics. While one faction remained in touch with the Whigs who had fled England and Scotland after the failure of Monmouth's and Argyll's Rebellions of 1685 and sought refuge in the Netherlands, another faction attempted to kidnap one of the Whig exiles, Sir Robert Peyton, and return him to James II for trial. This incident brought protests from Dutch officials, but William of Orange, out of deference to James II, intervened to save these officers from punishment, and he actually dismissed a few of Monmouth's supporters from the six regiments. This was merely a token concession on William's part; James was generally unsuccessful in securing his cooperation in removing supporters of Monmouth, and those who were discharged from the British regiments in the Dutch army were hidden away in the service of German princes until William needed them. Generally speaking, William and the States General were very uncooperative in expelling political refugees from the Netherlands.[16]

During the Third Anglo-Dutch War, the Anglo-Dutch Brigade had been disbanded and the officers and men remaining in Dutch service reassigned to other units of the of the States' Army; the officers of the Scots Brigade did not think that a war between their king and the States General touched their allegiance. The business of rebuilding the Anglo-Dutch Brigade following the end of that war was difficult, and William III was young and inexperienced when the stadholderate was restored and he was given command of the States' Army as captain-general. When the States' Army met the French at the Battle of Seneffe in 1674, more than half of the officers and men of the Anglo-Dutch Brigade were killed along with their commander, Major-General Sir Walter Vane. The rapid turnover in officers opened up opportunities, and it was at this time that John Bernardi, an Englishman of Genoese descent, obtained a commission in the Anglo-Dutch Brigade through the intercession of Lieutenant-Colonel Anselme, his godfather. Many of the English and Scottish generals of the reigns of William III and Queen Anne served in the Anglo-Dutch and Scots Brigades and gained

    [15] Henry Sidney, earl of Romney, *Diary of the Times of Charles the Second*, ed. R. W. Blencoe, 2 vols. (1843), vol. i, pp. xv–xvii, xix–xxiv, 130–1; Carswell, *Descent*, 21–3; Childs, *AJGR* 120–3.
    [16] J. R. Jones, *The Revolution of 1688 in England* (1972), 180–1; Sir John Dalrymple, *Memoirs of Great Britain and Ireland*, 2 vols., 2nd edn. (1771–3), I. i. 53, 55.

experience during the period that followed the Battle of Seneffe down to the Williamite invasion of England. George Ramsay and Thomas Livingstone later became major-generals; Sir Henry Bellasise and Thomas Tollemache became lieutenant-generals; David Colyear became commanding general in Portugal in 1710 and later governor-general of Gibraltar as well as a peer.[17]

If William of Orange inspired friendship and loyalty in some, he bred loathing in others. The Anglo-Dutch Brigade suffered very heavy losses in the 1670s, and because of shortages of military manpower, the regimental commanders found it difficult to make these up. Most of the men of Sir John Fenwick's Regiment deserted during the Siege of Maastricht—not once, but two years (1676–7) in a row. Fenwick attributed this to the fact that at this time the pay of French soldiers was higher than in the Dutch army, and he urged William to persuade the States General to increase the rate of pay for his soldiers. William told Fenwick 'in a very cold way that he was a man of interest in his country' and could easily recruit replacements. William dealt very harshly with Fenwick on this occasion, and told him 'I care not whether you and all your nation were under water'. William also gave out that he never had a high opinion of Fenwick's courage. This reached Sir John's ears, and ever thereafter he always held William 'in aversion'. Ultimately, Sir John Fenwick became a Jacobite.[18] James Graham of Claverhouse, an officer in the Scots Brigade, was also driven to leave the States' Army by William's ingratitude. He had saved the prince's life at the Battle of Seneffe in 1674, and apparently William promised him the colonelcy of one of the three regiments in the Scots Brigade. Instead the gave the command of that regiment to Hugh Mackay, whom William considered to be more pious, and Claverhouse resigned his commission, saying 'he would not serve a prince who had broken his word'. Claverhouse returned to Scotland, where Charles II gave him command of an independent troop of horse. Upon his accession to the throne, James VII and II made him colonel of the Royal Regiment of Horse. Later he was promoted major-general, created Viscount Dundee and given command of the Scottish army in 1688. Dundee and Mackay would meet again at the Battle of Killiecrankie, where the former, commanding the Jacobite Scottish army, defeated the latter's Williamite forces. However, 'Bonnie Dundee' was killed, and the Jacobite forces left leaderless.[19]

When the six regiments of the Anglo-Dutch and Scots Brigades were recalled at James's request in 1685 to assist in the suppression of the Monmouth Rebellion, James was taken aback to discover the extent of personal loyalty on the part of the officers to William of Orange. Some of the soldiers in the Scots Brigade drank the

---

[17] John Bernardi, *A Short History of the Life of Major John Bernardi* (1729), 15, 17–18, 21; Carswell, *Descent*, 228–9; J. Childs, *Nobles, Gentlemen and the Profession of Arms in Restoration Britain, 1660–1688: A Biographical Dictionary of British Officers on Foreign Service*, SAHR, Spec. Publication, 13 (1987), 7, 19, 76, 90.

[18] Ailesbury, *Memoirs*, ii. 390; Childs, *Profession of Arms*, 31.

[19] J. Ferguson, *Two Scottish Soldiers: A Soldier of 1688 and Blenheim and a Soldier of the American Revolution* (1888), 4–5; Dalrymple, *Memoirs*, I. i. 46; J. Mackay, *The Life of Lieut. General Hugh Mackay, Commander in Chief of the Forces in Scotland, 1689 and 1690*, BC 56 (1836), 10–11.

duke of Monmouth's health, and two were condemned to be shot. For this reason, the king hesitated to send them to the west until the suppression of the rebellion was well in hand. The next three years saw a contest between James and William for the loyalties of the officers and men of the six regiments. James gave Hugh Mackay the rank of major-general in the English army, and upon the return of the six regiments to the Netherlands, he recommended that William grant Mackay the same rank in the Dutch army. William refused, although Mackay was effectively the commanding officer of the Scots Brigade with the pay of a major-general. Mackay began telling his officers that he intended to leave the Dutch army, and invited them to follow his example. However, when he went to The Hague to take leave of William III, the prince told him of the 'secret designs then hatching in England against the king' and that he and his officers might soon be unemployed if they returned home. Mackay then returned to his garrison and told his officers that James VII and II had deceived them, and that they should remain in the pay of the States General. Meanwhile, James tried to influence the appointment of the senior officers of the six regiments; William resisted the appointment of Catholics to positions of command, and the Whigs in the Dutch army were able to undermine loyalty to James.[20]

William of Orange began dismissing Catholic officers from positions of command in the six regiments, and accommodating Huguenots driven from the French army by the Revocation of the Edicts of Nantes and Irish officers purged by Tyrconnell from the Irish army. The latter became a focus of discontent in the Anglo-Dutch Brigade. Émigrés from the Three Kingdoms made their way to the Netherlands, and William began organizing two more British regiments commanded by Sir Robert Peyton and David Leslie, fifth earl of Leven and second earl of Melville. By the time that William's expedition set sail in November 1688, one-quarter of his invasion force consisted of soldiers from the British Isles.[21]

The action that finally polarized allegiances in the six regiments was James's proclamation recalling them in March 1688. William would not permit enlisted men to return home, but he allowed officers to follow their consciences. Some of the officers feared retribution from James if they returned, and they devised an assassination plot against the naval commander sent to convey them to England. James expected only Catholics and loyalists to come home, but the number of officers who actually did return probably exceeded his expectations. Contemporaneous and present-day estimates vary widely, but Professor Childs puts the number at a minimum of 104 out of the 234 officers of the six regiments, including three colonels and a fair proportion of the other senior officers of the rank of captain or above. John Bernardi, who was among those who returned home and were recommissioned by James, thought that more would have returned, but they remembered that when Charles II had recalled the Anglo-Dutch Brigade earlier many of

---

[20] Ailesbury, *Memoirs*, i. 114; Bernardi, *Life*, 62–3; Childs, *AJGR* 123–7; G. H. Jones, 'The Recall of the British from the Dutch Service', *HJ* 25: 2 (1982), 423.

[21] Jones, *Revolution of 1688*, 181–2; Carswell, *Descent*, 158.

the officers had ended up begging in the streets of London when lack of funds forced the king to disband much of the army. Service under the prince of Orange guaranteed certainty of employment. William did not allow non-commissioned officers and private soldiers to leave Dutch service, and their officers intimidated them and even hanged a couple of would-be deserters. Nevertheless, forty-four soldiers did manage to escape and, with the help of priests and the English ambassador in Brussels, made their way back to England. Some sergeants who left Dutch service were subsequently commissioned by James upon their return home, which may somewhat inflate the number of officers who obeyed James's proclamation to return.[22]

The prince of Orange would bring a formidable army to England in November 1688, but the English army mustered a sizeable field force and might have beaten off the Anglo-Dutch invaders if it had been properly led. However, the English army failed to offer battle, because of conspiracies and desertions among officers which left James II disheartened. While evidence is lacking concerning when the army conspiracies began, they certainly were under way before the end of 1687. The discovery of Dutch spies, persistent rumours about conspiracies within the army and, finally, incontrovertible evidence of invasion preparations in September 1688 were all ignored by James. Like his failure that autumn to lead his army in the field against William's invasion force, no satisfactory explanation of James's inaction has been provided.[23]

There were several nuclei of conspiracies in James II's English army. One was the aptly named Treason Club, which met at the Rose Tavern in Russell Street, Covent Garden. It had a distinct Whiggish cast and appears to have been led by Richard Savage, Viscount Colchester (and later fourth Earl Rivers), who was one of the first officers to desert James and whose military career prospered under William III and Queen Anne. A number of the military officers who belonged to the Treason Club had served in France with the duke of Monmouth in the Royal English Regiment, and at least two of them had lost their commissions because they remained too close to Monmouth at the time of his rebellion in 1685. Another member of the Treason Club was Thomas Tollemache, who gave up his commission as lieutenant-colonel of the Royal Fusiliers to become a colonel in the Anglo-Dutch Brigade, and who accompanied the prince of Orange in his invasion of England.[24] Tollemache was also a member of the 'Tangerines', a tightly knit group of military and naval officers who had served together in Tangier and the Mediterranean before that colony was abandoned. At the centre of this conspiracy were Charles Trelawny, a younger brother of the bishop of Bristol, and Percy Kirke, both of whom commanded regiments after 1684. Like John, Lord Churchill, a major-general under James and another Tangerine, they were all professional soldiers who had

---

[22] Childs, *AJGR* 133; Jones, 'Recall of the British', 428–30; Bernardi, *Life*, 49–51.
[23] Childs, *AJGR* 141–7.
[24] Ibid. 155–6; id., *Profession of Arms*, 81, 90; E. D. H. Tollemache, *The Tollemaches of Helmingham and Ham* (1949), 72–5.

seen extensive experience in mainland European armies and depended upon their salaries and continuous employment. Being Protestants, they feared that James's policy of finding commissions for Catholics might deprive them of the prospect of future promotion, and so they kept their options open by corresponding with the prince of Orange. The naval officers were especially important in serving as liaisons with William. The Tangerines also included John Churchill's younger brother George, Matthew Aylmer (later first Baron Aylmer) and Georg Byng (later first Viscount Torrington). All of these naval officers had served under Arthur Herbert (later third earl of Torrington) at Tangier and in the Mediterranean. Herbert had been cashiered in 1687 for refusing to support the repeal of the Test Act, which required all commissioned officers to take communion in the Anglican rite. In November 1688 Herbert was the nominal commander of the Dutch naval fleet that carried William to Torbay. Another group of dissidents was the Association of Protestant Officers, who came together when James II's army camped on Hounslow Heath in the summer of 1688. That autumn the Association of Protestant Officers would coordinate the desertions of some of the individual officers, but failed to deliver the bulk of the English army. The core of the conspirators who were naval and military officers probably numbered no more than thirty men, but they did succeed in destroying the confidence of King James in his army and navy. The civilian leaders of the Orangist conspiracy, such as George Savile, first marquis of Halifax, Charles Talbot, twelfth earl of Shrewsbury, and William Cavendish, fourth earl of Devonshire, likewise constituted only a small part of the political nation, but they were well placed and powerful men. Devonshire took £12,000 to the Netherlands to contribute to William's cause, and accompanied the prince of Orange to Torbay.[25]

Thus William of Orange was assured of the political support of a small group of well-placed members of Parliament and military and naval officers. William's overriding concern was to prevent James VII and II from forming an alliance with Louis XIV against the Dutch Republic and its Confederate allies. That outweighed his interest in Protestant liberties and the constitutional position of Parliament, and explains why he interfered in English domestic affairs beyond his concern to preserve the inheritance of his consort Mary, the second daughter of James II. It was apparently when James refused to enter into an alliance against Louis XIV that William decided to invade England. While William's decision to mount this invasion was based partly upon personal dynastic interests, the States General of the Dutch Republic lent their support to the venture because his diplomatic and military position as head of the Confederate alliance against Louis XIV was tied to the survival of the Dutch Republic.[26]

[25] Carswell, *Descent*, 167–8; Childs, *AJGR* 143, 156, 162, 186; E. B. Powley, *The English Navy in the Revolution of 1688* (1928), 13–14, 79–80; W. A. Speck, 'The Orangist Conspiracy Against James II', *HJ* 30 (1987), 453.

[26] Powley, *English Navy*, 2–4; J. I. Israel, 'General Introduction', Israel (ed.), *The Anglo-Dutch Moment: Essays on the Glorious Revolution and its World Impact* (1991), 21–3.

Over the last two millenia England has been successfully invaded by foreign
princes and powers only four or five times. Other hostile powers have planned or
actually mounted invasions without success. The Williamite descent on England,
like the Spanish Armada of a century earlier, was meant to be a pre-emptive strike
dependent upon stealth. The Spanish Armada of 1588 had consisted of an invasion
fleet of 130 ships carrying 25,000 soldiers and mariners. The Armada failed to land
in England and, upon attempting to return to Spain by way of the North Sea, lost
half of its ships and a third of its personnel. A century later, in November 1688, the
Dutch invasion fleet of 463 ships (including fifty-three warships) carrying 40,000
men and 5,000 horses succeeded in landing at Torbay in south-western England.
William's invasion force consisted of 14,352 foot soldiers and 3,660 cavalry troopers, plus an artillery train and perhaps as many as 5,000 volunteers. The Dutch ships
were manned by 9,154 sailors of different nationalities, including English and Scots.
The six regiments of the Anglo-Dutch and Scots Brigades constituted the vanguard
of the force that landed at Torbay. Although the Radical Whig lords and gentlemen
did not flinch at the prospect of civil war, many of the English and Scots soldiers
were horrified at the prospect of fighting their own countrymen.[27]

The Williamite invasion of the British Isles in November 1688 was viewed as a
very risky venture and a bold strategic move for a small country that had always
fought defensive wars. William was only 38. By his own admission, his military
education had been deficient, and he always regretted not having served an
apprenticeship in arms under some great general such as the prince of Condé. He
held the offices of captain-general and admiral-general, and yet he was more ignorant of naval warfare than he was of military strategy. William may have possessed
native qualities of military leadership, but when his expedition set sail from
Holland and endured weather as foul as that encountered by the Spanish Armada
a hundred years earlier, he knew as much about naval operations and amphibious
warfare as had the duke of Medina Sidonia. He was, however, a convinced
Calvinist, and believed that he had benefited from Divine Providence. That the
House of Orange had led the Netherlands to many victories was viewed as
evidence of his Providential mission which, in the opinion of John Whittle, an
English chaplain who accompanied William in his descent on England, made him
a latter-day Constantine. That William of Orange had frequently exposed himself
to danger on the battlefield without serious injury was taken by Whittle to be
further evidence of Divine intervention. Moreover, William had restored unity to
the faction-ridden Dutch Republic.[28]

---

[27] J. I. Israel and G. Parker, 'Of Providence and Protestant Winds: The Spanish Armada of 1588
and the Dutch Armada of 1688', in Israel (ed.), *Anglo-Dutch Moment*, 335–8; Israel, 'Dutch Role',
105–9. The Dutch invasion fleet included three shiploads of 'English lords' (Carswell, *Descent*, 170).

[28] Powley, *English Navy*, 95–6; Israel, 'Dutch Role', 105; S. Groenveld, ' "J'equippe une flotte tres
considerable": The Dutch Side of the Glorious Revolution', in R. Beddard (ed.), *The Revolutions of
1688* (1991), 236–42; John Whittle, *Constantius Redivivius: or... the Wonderful Providences and
Unparalleled Successes... of... William the 3ʳᵈ* (1693), 2–5, 47, 69–70.

Raising, equipping and supplying William of Orange's invasion fleet of 1688 and the army it carried was a logistical task of herculean proportions, but it was accomplished with speed and efficiency. The principal contributors to this effort were the States of Holland, the Amsterdam Admiralty College and, to a lesser extent, the Rotterdam Admiralty. Besides the cavalry mounts and draught animals, fodder and provisions, William also carried printing presses, paper and propaganda leaflets intended to persuade the subjects of James VII and II that they were being liberated rather than conquered. At the same time, he commissioned Romeyn de Hooghe to make etchings and to engrave newsprints in suitable baroque splendour for popular consumption. In order to make up for the soldiers withdrawn from Dutch garrisons and fortresses, the States General hired 14,000 troops from Brandenburg and other German principalities, plus another 6,000 from Sweden. All in all, the size of the States' Army had increased from 40,000 to 80,000 on the eve of the Dutch invasion. The Dutch government had taken a great risk and invested heavily in the invasion of England.[29]

William's military power derived from his offices of stadholder, captain-general and admiral-general of five of the seven Dutch provinces. However, it was his position as prince of Orange, a small territory in southern France which had been occupied by Louis XIV, that gave him the legal authority to make war on the Three Kingdoms without being regarded in international law as a privateer. Although most jurists did not recognize the right of subjects to rebel against their sovereigns, they did allow that other sovereign princes might come to the aid of oppressed subjects. This had helped to legitimate the position of William's ancestor William the Silent when he led the Dutch in their rebellion against Philip II of Spain. William of Orange mustered his army at Nijmegen, where he chose those aristocratic volunteers who were to accompany him. These included, besides his Dutch and French Huguenot officers and companions, the earl of Shrewsbury; Charles, Viscount Mordaunt (and later third earl of Peterborough), who had been at Tangier; Charles Gerard, first earl of Macclesfield; Archibald, tenth earl of Argyll; and Sir James Dalrymple (later Viscount Stair). The latter had commanded a troop of Parliamentary dragoons and had been made a judge by Cromwell; at the age of 70 he became a soldier again. The invasion forces embarked at Helvoetsluis at the mouth of the River Maas and set sail on 11 November (1 November, o.s.). After being beaten back by storms, they made their way into the English Channel. Because of the foul weather (which was normal at this time of year), the Dutch armada was escorted only by smaller warships because the top-heavy first- and second-raters had been left behind. As soon as the armada entered the English Channel (3 November, o.s.), the prince of Orange struck the

Dutch colours and hoisted his own standard. He sailed close to Dover so that the invasion fleet could make a 'bravado', the Dutch ships firing their guns in a mock salute. Warning beacons were lit all the way to London, signifying that William's armada had been sighted.[30]

The Dutch armada needed an east southeasterly wind to carry it from Holland to the coast of Devonshire, but at just the right moment a westerly blew the fleet into Torbay, where the troops disembarked at Brixham. Only a westerly wind could have made this difficult manoeuvre possible. The concept of a Protestant wind such as this which, by Divine Providence, wafted the prince of Orange's armada safely to its landing while preventing James II's navy, anchored at the Gunfleet Sand off Harwich, from pursuing and intercepting the Dutch invasion fleet, dated back a century to the late-summer gales of 1588 which had scattered the Spanish Armada as it sought to beat its way along the coast of Spanish Flanders to pick up an invasion force to transport to the coast of England. Although naval men did not place much confidence in providential winds, the concept helped to justify the overthrow of an anointed sovereign ruler in an age when many still believed in divine-right monarchy.[31]

William of Orange was able to land his invasion force only because the English navy failed to pursue and intercept the Dutch armada. Had the navy been successful in doing so, the Glorious Revolution might have gone down in history as the 'Fourth Anglo-Dutch War'. As David Davies points out, the conspiracies in the English army would have come to naught had William failed to establish a foothold on English soil. James II had been poorly supplied with intelligence about the plans and strategy of the Dutch fleet, while the renegade Admiral Herbert was able to supply William with excellent intelligence and advice. James expected a landing on the North Sea coast, which, along with the Thames Estuary, was well defended, but Herbert had advised establishing a beachhead in the southwest. The final decision was, of course, determined by the prevailing winds. The Dutch admirals had also been instructed to avoid a naval engagement, because William did not want to destroy the illusion that he had come to liberate the English people. Although the officers of the Royal Navy were factious and engaged in conspiracies to the same degree as their army counterparts, in the event the navy did not defect. Overcome by caution, they simply did not fight. By contrast, in 1588 the navy and its merchantmen auxiliaries had engaged and harried the Spanish invasion fleet so effectively that the Spaniards were never able to convey the Army of Flanders to the coast of England as planned. In 1688 the Royal Navy, despite many advantages over the Elizabethan navy, never engaged the Dutch fleet. Besides the unfavourable winds which worked against the English

---

[30] Western, *Monarchy and Revolution*, 239; [John Whittle], *An Exact Diary of the Late Expedition of . . . the Prince of Orange* (1689), 9, 16–17, 23, 30–2; C. James (ed.), 'Journal of the Voyage of William of Orange from Holland to Torbay, 1688', *JSAHR* 51 (1973), 17; Dalrymple, *Memoirs*, i. 216.

[31] [Whittle], *Exact Diary*, 33–4; C. James, 'The Protestant Wind of 1688: Myth and Reality', *ESR* 3 (1973), 201–21.

navy's ability to manoeuvre, the Dutch transports of 1688 were more modern in design and were able to sail at top speed and keep up with the naval vessels, unlike the slower transports of 1588. As well as positioning the English fleet at the Gunfleet, James had also wanted to station part of the English fleet off the Dutch coast where the invasion convoy could have been intercepted, but his admiral, George Legge, first earl of Dartmouth, who meant to fight William, feared the consequences of keeping ships on station there in such foul weather.[32]

It probably did not make sense to divide the fleet and risk ships in dangerous waters, since so few English naval vessels were sent to sea. Between the Restoration and the Third Anglo-Dutch War, the Royal Navy had nearly doubled in size under the leadership of Charles II and James, duke of York, as lord admiral. However, these extra ships were of little use when the prince of Orange invaded England because most of them were laid up for want of money and manpower. James could not be persuaded that William's activities presented a danger until it was too late, and in any case, he thought that the cost of outfitting a larger fleet would have been too great. Only twelve third- and fourth-rate ships were prepared for service, along with some guard-ships and fire-ships, and the coastal forts were strengthened. When James made a visit to Chatham and the Medway fortifications, he expressed disappointment at the meagerness of the salutes fired and the healths proposed in honour of his visit; Pepys worried that the guns in the forts were not securely mounted.[33]

When the prince of Orange landed, he unfurled his standard which bore the motto 'For the Protestant Religion and Liberty'. Sir John Reresby caught the irony of this: 'The prince declared that he had no design for the crown, and yet sought it all he could. He came to settle the Protestant religion, and yet brought over 4,000 papists in his army, which was near as many as the king had English of that religion in his.'[34] John Whittle, one of William's English chaplains, whose chief task, by his own account, was to preach and write propaganda, stated that the prince's white standard declared 'peace unto all such as would live peaceably'. Lest there be confusion, under the white standard was set up 'the red or bloody flag ... signifying war unto all such as did oppose his just designs'. By a coincidence that did not escape Whittle's notice, the day the prince of Orange's force landed at Torbay was 5 November, o.s.—Gunpowder Treason Day—'and the bells were ringing as we were sailing toward the bay and as we landed, which many judged to be a good omen...'. William's soldiers had strict orders not to plunder, and generally they were well received, although a few of the local inhabitants wondered if William would not end up like the duke of Monmouth. Those of his twenty-six or so regiments which did not have full complements were recruited up to strength.[35]

[32] D. Davies, 'James II, William of Orange, and the Admirals', in E. Cruickshanks (ed.), *By Force or By Default: The Revolution of 1688–89* (1989), 82–5, 95–9; Israel and Parker, 'Providence and Protestant Winds', 342–3.

[33] D. Ogg, *England in the Reign of Charles II*, 2 vols., 2nd edn. (1963), i. 280–2.

[34] A. Browning (ed.), *Memoirs of Sir John Reresby* (1936; repr. 1991), 553–4.

[35] [Whittle], *Exact Diary*, 30, 33–4, 39–40.

James II had expected William's invasion force to land on the North Sea coast of Yorkshire or East Anglia or, perhaps, in Kent or the Thames Estuary, and had dispersed his troops accordingly. London also had to be garrisoned strongly because of its past history of popular tumults and the presence of the young prince of Wales. James's field army was not the equal of William's in strength and certainly not in terms of quality and experience. William, however, upon disembarking his troops and horses (of which 600 had died on the voyage), had to allow time for rest and regrouping, and this gave James the opportunity to march reinforcements to the south-west—although continuing heavy rains slowed the progress of both opposing armies. As James concentrated his field forces on Salisbury Plain, Sir John Lanier and six regiments of cavalry preceded them to reconnoitre William's movements and screen the advance of the English army. The most experienced English regiments followed and were reinforced by Irish and Scots regiments. The latter undertook a forced march from the north in bad weather, and were much fatigued when they reached Salisbury Plain.[36] The first skirmish between the Williamite and Jacobite forces occurred at Wincanton, Somerset. A Scottish lieutenant of Major-General Mackay's Regiment and twenty-four musketeers were hidden behind a hedgerow leading into the town when a squadron of 150 English horse approached. The lieutenant challenged the officer in charge of the English cavalry, and when the latter declared himself for King James, the Scots lieutenant shot him through the head and the musketeers opened fire. Whittle regarded this as a very bloody skirmish and said that the Williamite musketeers would have been annihilated had not the townspeople swarmed into the streets to see what was going on. The prince of Orange advanced on Exeter where his artillery train had landed, and continued beating the drum for recruits. The chaplain John Whittle seized St Kerrian's Parish Church by military force and preached a sermon there.[37]

When James II arrived to join the encampment of his army on Salisbury Plain, he learned that many of his officers had stated an unwillingness to fight the prince of Orange. Louis Duras, earl of Feversham, a Huguenot soldier who served as James's commander-in-chief, recommended dismissing these officers and replacing them with sergeants. Feversham thought the rank and file were loyal. George Douglas, earl of Dumbarton, asked for permission to attack with his 3,000 Royal Scots. Among the other officers who pressed James to attack were John, Lord Churchill—'in order to wipe off the suspicions which had been suggested against him'—and James's illegitimate nephew, Henry Fitzroy, duke of Grafton. James refused to authorize the attack on William's army, saying 'he would not throw away the lives of so many brave men upon an action which could not be decisive'. Apparently, James never formally unfurled the royal standard. The following day, Churchill, Grafton, Colonels Kirke and Trelawny and a number of other high-ranking officers including Prince George of Denmark, slipped

---

[36] Israel, 'Dutch Role', 124–30; Childs, *AJGR* 183–90.
[37] [Whittle], *Exact Diary*, 50, 52, 57–8.

out of camp and went over to William. James Butler, earl of Ossory, who would shortly succeed as second duke of Ormonde, and who was a second cousin of the prince of Orange, also defected with Churchill. He later became general of the horse under William, and fought with him in Ireland and Flanders.[38]

The desertion of John Churchill did not elicit admiration among the officers of the prince of Orange's army. When he arrived in William's camp, Schomberg told Churchill to his face 'that he was the first lieutenant-general he had ever heard that deserted from his colours', and even after he became duke of Marlborough and captain-general under Queen Anne, he was remembered for changing his colours in the midst of a battle.[39] The duke of Grafton had asked for command of the fleet in place of Lord Dartmouth and had been refused by James. Sir John Dalrymple accused Grafton of spreading disaffection among naval commanders and persuading them not to oppose the prince of Orange. John Churchill's brother George 'was the first sea officer who deserted'. John Granvill, first earl of Bath and governor of Plymouth, brought that garrison over to William. During the six days that James was at Salisbury Camp, the king also received news that Henry Booth, second Lord Delamere, 'had raised the people of Cheshire'; the earl of Devonshire had delivered the counties of Derbyshire and Nottinghamshire to the prince of Orange; while Thomas Osborne, first earl of Danby, had seized York and neutralized its garrison. Before the defections from the army began, James II's army had been a sufficiently formidable force to deter the nobility and gentry of England and Wales from committing themselves to William's cause. It was only the presence on English soil of William's undefeated army that caused them to put aside their fears of popular disorder and to commit themselves. William was annoyed at the slowness of the English aristocrats in declaring themselves for his cause, but at the same time, he made it clear that he did not need their military assistance.[40]

The prince of Orange's invasion of England was a heavy blow to the prestige of the English army. The desertions of officers from his army further disheartened James II. At the same time, William had expected mass desertions, but Lord Cornbury's defection to the prince of Orange with his regiment of dragoons is one of the very few instances of these. The total number of desertions from James's army by private soldiers was perhaps no more than 1,000. Approximately three-quarters of the senior officers (captains and above) went over to William, together with four-fifths of the subaltern officers. Thus, the army was deprived of its leadership. Although there is good reason for believing that the rank and file

---

[38] Dalrymple, *Memoirs*, i. 164–6; James Macpherson (ed.), *Original Papers Containing the Secret History of Great Britain from the Restoration to the Accession of the House of Hannover*, 2 vols. (1775), i. 157–9; T.B., *The Life and Character of James Butler, Late Duke ... of Ormond* (1729), sigs. A2r, C4v–D4v; [Whittle], *Exact Diary*, 52, 56.

[39] Macpherson (ed.), *Original Papers*, i. 162–3; M. Foot, *The Pen and the Sword: A Year in the Life of Jonathan Swift* (1966), 36–7, 39–40, 150–2.

[40] Dalrymple, *Memoirs*, I. i. 136, 165–6; Macpherson (ed.), *Original Papers*, i. 162–3; Israel, 'Dutch Role', 124–30.

remained loyal and would have fought if properly led, James decided that the army would likely have been defeated in a pitched battle, and so he ordered it to follow him back to London. Dalrymple says that 'most of the private men shed tears when they heard of his retreat'. Without the presence of their officers, that retreat was somewhat disorderly.[41]

William's main purpose in invading England was to secure the manpower and military resources of the Three Kingdoms for the Confederate war against Louis XIV. Yet William's forcible incursion and subornation of most of the officers not surprisingly contributed to a process of disintegration within the English army. A case in point is that of Charles Gerard, Viscount Brandon's Regiment of Horse, raised in October 1688. James II had earlier pardoned Brandon for his part in the conspiracy behind Monmouth's Rebellion. His trust in Brandon and his decision to give him a commission to raise a regiment was rewarded by Brandon's loyalty during the Glorious Revolution—even though his father, Charles, first earl of Macclesfield, went over to the prince of Orange. John Churchill, now holding command under the prince, disbanded Brandon's Regiment because Brandon did not display sufficient zeal for William by delivering his troops. Churchill's decision to disband the regiment much offended Brandon's father, who said that he may have been a rebel in acting against the king, but implied that Churchill, being a serving officer holding high command under James, was a traitor.[42] William's agents and supporters also contributed to the indiscipline and disorder in the English army by spreading false rumours among its soldiers to whip up hatred of the Irish troops who had recently joined it. After most of James's Irish regiments had been disbanded by order of William and confined to the Isle of Wight, rumours spread that the Irish soldiers had made their way to Uxbridge to cut the throats of Protestants. In fact the only Irish soldiers near Uxbridge were those of Arthur, Viscount Forbes's Regiment, which having been purged of Catholics, was retained in William's service. As a consequence of this false rumour, panic spread across much of England. There is evidence that the dissemination of these rumours was organized to help William secure control over the localities— perhaps by someone in the Post Office. Another rumour insinuated that the Irish had burnt Kingston-upon-Thames. Apparently skirmishes occurred near Reading and Maidenhead, and some twenty Irish soldiers were killed. From Preston, Lancs., Thomas Bellingham reported that news had been received 'by express' that 8,000 Scots and Irish 'were ravaging the kingdom', and had massacred people in Birmingham and Stafford.[43]

When the prince of Orange reached London, he was deaf to advice not to arouse anti-Dutch feeling by deploying Dutch troops in a conspicuous fashion. Instead,

[41] Childs, *BAW* 7–8; id., *AJGR* 183–90; Speck, 'Orangist Conspiracy', 461; Israel, 'Dutch Role', 124–5; Western, *Monarchy and Revolution*, 142; Dalrymple, *Memoirs*, I. i. 165–6; [Whittle], *Exact Diary*, 52.   [42] Ailesbury, *Memoirs*, i. 132–3.
[43] G. H. Jones, 'The Irish Fright of 1688: Real Violence and Imagined Massacre', *BIHR* 55 (1982), 148–53; [Whittle], *Exact Diary*, 68–70; A. Hewitson (ed.), *Diary of Thomas Bellingham, an Officer under William III* (1908), 36–7.

he ordered the English guards regiments out of the London area, dispersed them in small units across the countryside and replaced them with his Dutch Blue Guards. Despite the treason of so many highly placed officers, William still regarded the English army as loyal enough to James to pose a threat. In order to lessen that threat, the king was escorted out of London by Dutch mounted guards. London remained under military occupation until 1690—something that Whig historians have preferred not to dwell upon. The choices made by the Convention Parliament in the making of the revolution settlement, Professor Israel reminds us, were constrained to some degree by this foreign military presence.[44]

William of Orange had his own personal and dynastic reasons for invading England, but his Whig supporters gave out that they supported his invasion in order to preserve the Church of England from the threat of popery and to restore the ancient constitution by overthrowing Stuart absolutism. The reasons why the States General and the States of Holland underwrote the invasion had nothing to do with religion, and aimed simply at destroying James VII and II's political and military power by neutralizing or destroying the English army. They aimed at imposing a parliamentary monarchy in England that would reverse James's foreign and military policies, prevent a joint attack by France and England on the Netherlands and generally favour the diplomatic, military and commercial aims of the Dutch Republic. The degree of involvement of the Dutch government in the invasion was deliberately and cynically suppressed, and the leadership of William as the sovereign prince of Orange was depicted as a response to pleas for assistance from the English people.[45] As long as England remained disengaged from mainland Europe, France did not pose a threat to English security. That the Revolution of 1688–9 committed England and, subsequently, the other two kingdoms to a long century of warfare with France, at such a cost of treasure and men's lives, mostly benefited the Dutch Republic and William of Orange. However, many of James II's critics in the English Parliament did view with increasing alarm Louis XIV's expansionist policies and his abolition of freedom of worship, and in their view the French had replaced the Spanish and the Dutch as potential enemies of England.[46]

William of Orange could assert a dynastic claim to the throne based on the fact that his consort was the younger daughter of James VII and II, but by itself such a claim was very weak. He could also claim that he responded to a plea for assistance

[44] Israel, 'Dutch Role', 125–30. When James II had earlier attempted to flee England on 18 December 1688, he was intercepted at Rochester by a troop of Dutch cuirassiers, who, their captain admitted, were mostly Catholics. Indeed, an elderly lieutenant confessed that he had formerly served in the Spanish Army of Flanders, and had once fought alongside James as duke of York at the Battle of Dunkirk (Ailesbury, *Memoirs*, i. 220).

[45] Israel, 'Dutch Role', 120–3; id., 'England, the Dutch, and the Mastery of World Trade', in D. Hoak and M. Feingold (eds.), *The World of William and Mary: Anglo-Dutch Perspectives on the Revolution of 1688–89* (1996), 76–7, 79.

[46] J. Black, 'The Revolution and the Development of English Foreign Policy', in Cruickshanks (ed.), *By Force or By Default*, 136; J. G. A. Pocock, 'Standing Army and Public Credit: The Institutions of Leviathan', in Hoak and Feingold (eds.), *William and Mary*, 88.

from Whigs and Protestants, and was offered the crown by the Convention Parliament. However, his elaborate preparations for striking medals, erecting triumphal arches and his provision for graphic artists to accompany his invasion force all suggest that he also wished to base his claim to the throne upon the right of conquest. Such an interpretation accords well with the mentality of a soldier-king, who had lived much of his life in military camps surrounded by soldiers.[47] This might also help to explain why James II avoided a pitched battle with William, knowing that he had little chance of prevailing. The crown of England was offered to William and Mary while London was under Dutch military occupation; the vote in the Convention Parliament was very close, and was obtained under circumstances that offended even the Radical Whigs. William III's first speech from the throne to the Convention Parliament insisted on the urgent need to send troops to reinforce Coalition armies in Flanders and the Netherlands, and to contribute substantially to the costs of the Nine Years War. William also decided that the English government should pay for the 12,000 Dutch troops still stationed in England, and send substantial forces to deal with the Jacobite Rebellion that had broken out in Ireland. Thus, the involvement of England and, later, Scotland and Ireland in the War of the League of Augsburg, otherwise known as the Nine Years War, together with the creation of an enormously expensive fiscal-military state on the Dutch model, with its increasingly heavy burden of taxation, was the price that the people of England (and later the United Kingdom) had to pay for the establishment of a parliamentary monarchy.[48]

In 1689 William III and his Dutch backers found themselves in a military mess that was largely of their own making. Half of the Dutch forces had been used to invade England at the same time that the Dutch Republic and other Coalition members found themselves at war with France. William had contributed to the disintegration of the English army by suborning the officer class, destroying morale and promoting indiscipline. Quite understandably, he did not trust that army to garrison London, and he was making arrangements to send some regiments to the Netherlands and Flanders to protect the Republic from French incursion. Scotland remained unconquered, and Ireland had rebelled. While undertaking the conquest of Ireland and Scotland, William also needed to recruit military manpower for the war against Louis XIV, and because of this urgent need William could not disband James II's army and build a new one as Charles II had done in 1660. He had to make do with the one he found. And he also had to persuade the English Parliament to give legal existence to an army that they had regarded as unconstitutional, and to

[47] Nicolaus Chevalier, *Histoire de Guillaume III, Roy d'Angleterre, d'Ecosse, et d'Irlande, Prince d'Orange &c.: Contenant ses Actions le plus memorables, depuis sa Naissance jusques à son Elevation sur le Trône, & ce que s'est passe depuis jusques à l'entière Reduction d'Irlande. Par Medailles, Inscriptions, Arcs de Triomphe & autres Monumens Publiques* (1692), *passim*.

[48] Israel, 'Dutch Role', 132–5; id., 'General Introduction', 21–3; J. Scott, 'England's Troubles', in R. M. Smuts (ed.), *The Stuart Court and Europe: Essays in Politics and Political Culture* (1996), 29, 32–3; J. Brewer, *The Sinews of Power: War, Money and the English State, 1688–1783* (1989), 23–4, 28–31.

pay for the same.[49] The remnant of James II's army gave only a nominal allegiance to William III, and so a lawful authority was needed by which order and discipline could be maintained and wrongdoers punished. This obvious need led to the enactment of the First Mutiny Act of 1689. The Mutiny Act had been hurriedly passed after certain troops remaining from James II's army mutinied. It allowed the army to constitute courts martial to punish mutiny, desertion and sedition with sentences of death. All other crimes were to be heard and determined by the common-law courts as long as the military units were present in England. One consideration that helped to make the use of martial law more acceptable in England was that William III's Dutch soldiers, when marching towards London in 1688, had behaved better than James's English troops.[50]

The enactment of the Mutiny Act was also prompted by the mutiny of several corps of the English army in March 1689. Two units were Scottish regiments carried on the English establishment or recently attached. William III had planned to send them to the Netherlands, but the soldiers objected that submitting to such orders was equivalent to suffering 'transportation like felons', and 'was unworthy of their own character or that of their nation'. The first to mutiny was the Royal Regiment of Foot (more familiarly known as the Royal Scots, and formerly known as Douglas's or Dumbarton's Regiment). They were at Ipswich preparing to embark for the Netherlands, when they seized the money intended for their pay, purged officers who did not share their sentiments and prepared to march north to Scotland. The Royal Scots had served in the French army since the 1630s, when their colonel, Sir John Hepburn, had left the service of Gustavus Adolphus, until 1679, when Charles II called them home, and many of the regiment's officers and men would have been reluctant to fight Louis XIV. There was also unrest in other regiments: some had been sent to new quarters after William ordered them out of London; their ranks had been partially purged of suspected loyalists and Catholics; and the earl of Feversham, James's army commander, had attempted to discharge the soldiers without their back pay. When Prince George of Denmark's Regiment of Foot was ordered from Brentford to Greenwich to be embarked for service in the Netherlands, several of the companies mutinied, and many soldiers deserted on the way. At Croydon they encountered the Royal Regiment of Horse (the Scots Greys), commanded by John Graham of Claverhouse and recently detached from the Scots army, and when the two regiments met the Scots urged the English soldiers to mutiny. The two Scottish regiments were strongly loyal to James VII and II, and took the position that their allegiance was owed to the king of Scots and the government of Scotland. The deployment of

[49] Childs, *BAW* 7–8; Browning (ed.), *Memoirs of Sir John Reresby*, 553–4; Maitland, *Constitutional History*, 328.

[50] Maitland, *Constitutional History*, 328–9; C. M. Clode, *The Military Forces of the Crown: Their Administration and Government*, 2 vols. (1869), i. 142–3; C. Walton, *History of the British Standing Army, 1660 to 1700* (1894), 529, 531, 539–41. The Mutiny Act has been re-enacted every year, and continues to give the army the legal authority to maintain discipline by courts martial sitting in the United Kingdom.

both Dutch and English cavalry who were loyal to William II and III was necessary to subdue the mutinies, but William treated the Scottish mutineers leniently because he 'respected their spirit'. All were pardoned, a few officers removed, and the two regiments were sent to the Netherlands. The other disaffected soldiers in the English army were transported to Flanders to turn their 'animosity of spirit against the enemies of Britain'. Sir John Dalrymple wondered at the number of Englishmen who still did not understand how vulnerable England would be to invasion without a standing army or a militia.[51]

William II and III found it difficult to ascertain allegiance in the English army, which remained highly politicized. He really trusted only those officers from the Three Kingdoms who had served under him in Anglo-Dutch and Scots Brigades. Some officers opposed him in the wars of conquest in Scotland and Ireland, some retired from military life, but many, including John Churchill, kept their options open by maintaining contact with James VII and II while serving William in a less than whole-hearted manner, because William lacked sufficient officers from the Dutch army to displace all of the officers of the English army. William particularly disliked using English peers as officers; he had little respect for them, because he thought that they were not amenable to military discipline and could not be relied upon to obey orders. He took command away from those peers who had already raised regiments. One way in which William promoted loyalty and professionalism was by continuing James VII and II's policy of integrating the officers and men of the armies of the Three Kingdoms into one British army. Although nominally a separate military establishment continued to exist in England, Scotland and Ireland, in practice the individual regiments were posted to each of the Three Kingdoms without regard to national identity.[52]

The term 'Glorious Revolution' seems inappropriate for an alteration of government that could not have happened without a large-scale armed invasion of England. Edmund Burke, a little more than a century later, said that it was a civil war, and Professor Pocock calls it the 'Fourth English Civil War'. There was little bloodshed in this Fourth English Civil War because James II, dismayed by the mass desertion of his officers who had sworn loyalty to him, chose not to plunge the nation into a bloodbath, but it was still a civil conflict, because there was no legal and constitutional way of removing a king. It was, 'invariably and necessarily, an act of war, of armed rebellion and civil war'.[53] That the Whigs regarded it as a just and necessary alteration of government does not obviate the fact that it remained an armed conflict as long as the Dutch expeditionary force, including British troops, remained on English soil while the purged regiments of what had been James II's English

[51] Dalrymple, *Memoirs*, i. 211–13; C. D. Ellestad, 'The Mutinies of 1689', *JSAHR* 53 (1975), 4–16.
[52] Childs, *BAW* 13–14; W. C. Foxcroft, *The Life and Letters of Sir George Savile, Bart., First Marquis of Halifax*, 2 vols. (1898), ii. 205–8; C. Dalton, *The Scots Army, 1661–1688* (1909), p. xxvii.
[53] J. G. A. Pocock, 'The Fourth English Civil War: Dissolution, Desertion, and Alternative Histories in the Glorious Revolution', in Schwoerer (ed.), *Revolution of 1688–1689*, 52–8.

army were sent to the Netherlands and Flanders. This 'Fourth English Civil War' also had a fratricidal element that is often overlooked. The European military world of the seventeenth century was small enough that many officers of the English army and the Anglo-Dutch invasion force would have served together in the schools of war of that period—the States' Army and the English Brigade of the French army or the garrison of Tangier. Unlike the generation of their fathers who fought in the Wars of the Three Kingdoms, most of them were professional soldiers dependent upon salaries and continuing employment. Through long service in foreign armies, their allegiances had become flexible and ambivalent. But clearly, the change of colours in the middle of a campaign by such officers as Churchill, Cornbury, Trelawny and Kirke violated the shared code of conduct of seventeenth-century soldiers, and William of Orange and Marshal Schomberg could never bring themselves to trust such men.

It is better to view the Revolution of 1688–9 within a British context, since the chief feature of the strategy of William of Orange and the regents of the Dutch Republic was to prevent James VII and II from forming an alliance with Louis XIV and allowing the latter access to the military manpower of the Three Kingdoms. In order for William to deny such access and to deploy the military resources of the British Isles against the French, he had first to conquer Scotland and Ireland as well as England, as Cromwell had done a generation earlier. There can be no doubt that the Revolution of 1688–9, seen in this context, was a bloody and complicated civil war as well, because in both Scotland and Ireland there were Jacobite armies prepared to offer resistance to conquest by the prince of Orange.

15

The Williamite conquest of Scotland and Ireland

Scotland is an inexhaustible treasure of men, as may be demonstrated by the vast numbers they have in our armies and navy, and in the armies of the Swede, the Pole, the Muscovite, the Emperor, Holland and France. What might not England do, had she in her pay all the Scots actually in the service of these princes, where they are daily cutting one another's throats, and, at the expense of their country's impoverishment, gain the empty reputation of being the best soldiers in the world? This is a treasure beyond the Indies....

[Daniel Defoe], *An Essay at Removing National Prejudices against a Union with Scotland*, Part I (1706), 28, quoted in S. H. F. Johnston, 'The Scots Army in the Reign of Queen Anne', *TRHS* 5th ser. 3 (1953), 1–2.

It has been observed by many that that part of the growth of an oak which faces north is more hardy and tougher to the axe than other parts. Indeed, where it is necessary to undergo fatigue it is impossible for those who live delicately and luxuriously to vie with those limbs that are inured to hunting in rough and mountainous country; for hunting trains body and character and checks effeminacy.

Sir Thomas Craig, *De Unione Regnorum Britanniae Tractatus*, ed. C. S. Terry, SHS 60 (1909), 456–7.

Because of widespread disaffection among officers of the English army and navy and the political elite, the Williamite invasion of England was relatively bloodless. The political allegiances of James VII and II's Scottish and Irish kingdoms were more divided, and those realms had to be conquered by military force. The conquest of Ireland was especially protracted and bloody. Scotland was conquered more easily, and eventually provided a seemingly endless supply of manpower for the Dutch and British armies during the following century. The Irish Jacobite army, because it comprised mostly Catholics, passed into French service with very few exceptions. The relatively quick collapse of James's regime in Scotland, despite initial military successes, was facilitated by the failure of the Stuarts to cultivate and reward allegiance among Highlanders, as well as the Scottish tradition of having members of a house on both sides of a civil war to ensure survival. James had called the small Scots army into England at the time of the prince of Orange's landing in England, thus denuding the Lowlands of military forces. The Lowlands also appear to have been undergoing a process of demilitarization since the end of the Wars of the Three Kingdoms. John Graham of Claverhouse, Viscount Dundee, like Montrose a generation earlier, was to demonstrate how effective use might be made of Highland soldiers, but his death in battle deprived the Jacobite forces of his valuable leadership.

William of Orange did not trust the officers of James II's English army which he now controlled, and all but two of his generals in the war in Ireland were foreigners. Also, more than half of the soldiers in the Williamite army in Ireland were from lands other than the British Isles. The Williamite army suffered large-scale wastage during their first winter in Ireland, because the English soldiers were neither well trained nor inured to hardship, and were not well disciplined. James's Irish army, which had been largely purged of Protestants by Tyrconnell but not trained and modernized, needed to be reinforced by French troops, but the inability of James to pay his troops caused widespread plunder and desertion. The Williamite wars in Ireland witnessed a number of drawn-out sieges, which exacerbated mutual hostility among the inhabitants of that unhappy isle. Many of William of Orange's soldiers were tied down fighting rapparees, who, taking advantage of their knowledge of the terrain, fought a guerilla campaign that revived much of the nastiness of traditional Irish warfare and which, in turn, perpetuated the bitterness between Protestants and Catholics. The terms of the Treaty of Limerick, which ended the Williamite war of conquest, as drawn up by the Dutch General Godart van Reede, Baron Ginkel (and subsequently first earl of Athlone), and allowing certain rights to Catholic landowners, were not honoured by the Irish government, and the penal laws against Catholics were partially revived. As in the Cromwellian conquest of Ireland, the Williamite conquest, in terms of deaths related to the war and the forced emigration of the defeated Jacobite soldiers and their families, brought demographic disaster—albeit on a smaller scale.

The Conquest of Scotland

Whereas the Stuart kingdoms of Ireland and Scotland had been a source of weakness to Charles I at the beginning of the Wars of the Three Kingdoms, in the reign of James VII and II they were, if anything, a source of strength thanks to the thoroughness of the Cromwellian conquest of them, of which the restored Stuart monarchy was a beneficiary. It was easier for James to raise taxes in the other two kingdoms than in England, and they also provided military manpower for the king's forces. The wielding of the royal patronage in the armies of England and Scotland helped the later Stuart monarchs to manipulate noblemen who desired commissions as well as officers who were ambitious to be created peers. For both the Scottish and the English armies, this patronage was based in London and was controlled by English politicians, which tended to make Scottish officers increasingly dependent upon the English political and military establishments. Scottish military officers of aristocratic background were mostly loyal to James, and two Scottish regiments played a prominent role in the mutinies of 1689. Consequently, William II and III could not expect to establish his authority in Scotland as easily as he did in England.[1]

King James had considered John Graham, Viscount Dundee, and Colin Lindsay, third earl of Balcarres, to be the most loyal lords among the Scottish peerage, and at the time of the prince of Orange's invasion the king entrusted the civil government of Scotland to Balcarres and command of the army to Dundee. Balcarres's father, the first earl, had died at Breda a year before the Restoration. Balcarres presented himself to Charles II at court, and at the age of 16 was given 'command of a select troop of horse, composed of one hundred gentlemen who had been reduced to poverty during the troubles'. Later he sailed with James, duke of York and lord admiral, at the Battle of Solebay. Since Balcarres was related to William of Orange through his first marriage to Mauritia van Nassau van Beverwaert, he could have done well under the new regime, but he remained loyal to James and subsequently spent ten years in exile with him. He and Dundee made their way to Edinburgh in February 1689. In his memoirs, Balcarres says that the Scots Privy Council had called the militia to active duty in 1688, and kept a quarter of them standing. The gentry of the western shires vied for positions of command. After he arrived in Edinburgh, Balcarres learned that they had already committed themselves to the prince of Orange. Archibald Campbell, tenth earl of Argyll (and later first duke), although still attainted, returned from exile, and 'prepared his own tribe to fight against a family which had put the father and the grandfather of their chieftain to death'. James Douglas, the second son of the second marquis of Queensberry, who was commander-in-chief of the Scots army until replaced by Dundee, had worked to undermine loyalty to James VII, and later joined William of Orange in Ireland. Ultimately, after the known supporters of James were purged, the remaining officers of the small Scottish army opted for military careers under William rather than exile with James.[2]

John Graham of Claverhouse in Angus was related to James Graham, marquis of Montrose. He began his military career as a gentleman volunteer in the French army, and then joined William of Orange as a cornet in one of his troops of horse guards. At the Battle of Seneffe in 1674 William lost his horse, and was in danger of being captured when Claverhouse dismounted, helped him onto his own horse and

---

[1] J. R. Western, *Monarchy and Revolution: The English State in the 1680s* (1972), 146–7; K. M. Brown, 'From Scottish Lords to British Officers: State Building, Elite Integration and the British Army in the Seventeenth Century', in Macdougal, *S&W* 145–6.

[2] Colin Lindsay, 3rd earl of Balcarres, *Memoirs touching the Revolution in Scotland, 1688–1690*, BC 71 (1841), pp. xviii–xix, 6–8; Sir John Dalrymple, *Memoirs of Great Britain and Ireland*, 2 vols., 2nd edn. (1771–3), I. i. 133–4; Childs, *Profession of Arms*, 27.

carried him to safety. William rewarded Claverhouse with a captaincy in a troop of guards and encouraged him to become a candidate for the next available colonelcy in a Scots regiment of foot. Some time later, Claverhouse believed that both Hugh Mackay and David Colyear had been promoted colonel ahead of him, and when he encountered Colyear in the courtyard of the palace of Het Loo, he exchanged angry words with him and struck him with a cane. The officer of the guard arrested Claverhouse, who was summoned before William to explain why he had presumed to strike a person within the verge of the palace. Claverhouse started to apologize for his behaviour, but then objected that he was more injured than Colyear, to whom William had given the regiment that Claverhouse thought was promised to him. William, reminding Claverhouse of the customary penalty for striking someone within the verge of the court, said he was giving him something 'more valuable than a regiment... your right arm'. This was the occasion when Claverhouse resigned from the Dutch army and returned to Scotland with a commission in the Scots army. Claverhouse, or Viscount Dundee as he became, was always impetuous and something of a romantic. Dalrymple says of him: 'Dundee had inflamed his mind from his earliest youth by the perusal of ancient poets, historians and orators with the love of the great actions they praise and describe. He is reported to have inflamed it still more by listening to the ancient songs of the Highland bards.'[3] Although he was a Lowlander like his kinsman Montrose, this knowledge of Highland culture and Gaelic literature helps to explain Dundee's ability to recruit and lead Highland soldiers who would only rarely accept as their leader someone other than one of their own chieftains. In the Convention Parliament that met in Edinburgh in early 1689, Dundee was from the beginning an intransigent Jacobite—above the usual factionalism and jockeying for place and position that characterized Scottish politics—and was driven only by ideology. By the spring, the Scots Privy Council had lost control of the Convention Parliament, which had become the *de facto* government. From that point of view, when Dundee raised James VII's royal standard on Dundee Law in April, he had become a rebel.[4]

The commander of the government forces and Dundee's chief enemy in the short amount of time remaining to him was his old rival in the Scots Brigade of the Dutch army, Hugh Mackay of Scourie. Mackay had been close to William of Orange ever since he undertook the reorganization of the Scots Brigade following its disastrous losses at the Battle of Seneffe. William had preferred Mackay over Dundee when handing out promotions, and the latter had accompanied William in the descent on England. Upon landing, William sent Mackay north to assume command of the government forces in Scotland. He arrived in Edinburgh in March 1689—essentially a stranger in the land he had left when quite young.

    [3] H. Jenner (ed.), *Memoirs of Viscount Dundee... by an Officer of the Army* (1714; repr. 1903), 3–4; [John Drummond of Balhaldy], *Memoirs of Sir Ewen Cameron of Locheill*, MC 61 (1842), 274–5; Dalrymple, *Memoirs*, I. ii. 46.
    [4] B. Lenman, *The Jacobite Risings in Britain, 1689–1746* (1980), 30–1; D. Szechi, *The Jacobites: Britain and Europe, 1688–1788* (1994), 44; M. Lynch, *Scotland: A New History*, rev. edn. (1992), 301.

Most of the military units that Mackay was compelled to rely upon, apart from a few Dutch troops, were commanded by Scots noblemen, who could raise soldiers easily enough but were without military experience. As had been the case in 1638–42, in 1689–90 military talent and experienced officers were not easy to come by at home, and were more likely to be found among Scots military communities overseas. Even fewer officers in the Scots army had experience of fighting in the Highlands, where Dundee, like later Jacobite leaders, was to recruit his army and make his stand. Although Scotland would be conquered more easily than Ireland, Mackay, although born a Gael, and his officers would have to relearn the lesson that a Lowland army could not operate in the Highlands without a string of forts and good lines of supply.[5]

Before 1689 it had been easier to raise soldiers in the Lowlands than in the Highlands of Scotland. Although Dundee's most remarkable military feat was raising a Highland army that defeated Hugh Mackay's government forces at the Battle of Killiecrankie in July 1689, it is well to remember that his army consisted of fewer than 2,000 Highlanders and 500 Irish. In 1689 Scotland's reputation for providing a seemingly inexhaustible source of soldiers derived largely from the past. Patrick Abercromby was a Jacobite writer who thought that martial culture was the dominant theme of Scottish political expression. His *Martial Achievements of the Scots Nation* was meant to be a history of Scotland from earliest times to the end of the seventeenth century, but his two enormous volumes never got beyond the end of the fifteenth century. Like a good Scots Jacobite, Abercromby believed that Scottish identity could be maintained only by reviving the 'Auld Alliance' with France. John Hamilton, second Lord Bellhaven, in a speech to the Scottish Estates when the Act of Union of 1707 was under consideration, argued that Scotland's martial heritage was the best evidence of a 'common moral purpose'. However, since Scotland lacked the treasure to harness that military potential on its own, it needed to secure trade advantages in a union of the two kingdoms in order to foster economic development in Scotland. Those who spoke of Scotland's treasure of military manpower, such as Daniel Defoe and Andrew Fletcher of Saltoun, exaggerated the size of its population, which was little more than 1 million at the end of the seventeenth century. The Lowlands was no longer a predominantly martial society after 1688, and the military potential of the Highlands had yet to be realized.[6] During the Restoration, Scotland ceased to be independent in a military sense: members of the Scots aristocracy were being absorbed into the officer class of the English establishment, while the Scottish

---

[5] J. Mackay, *The Life of Lieut.-General Hugh Mackay, Commander in Chief of the Forces in Scotland, 1689 and 1690*, BC 56 (1836), 10–13, 15, 42; *The Military Memoirs of Capt. George Carleton* (1728), 38–42.

[6] Mackay, *Life... Hugh Mackay*, 45; Patrick Abercromby, *The Martial Achievements of the Scots Nation*, 2 vols. (1711, 1715), vol. i, sig. B1r & v; J. Robertson, *The Scottish Enlightenment and the Militia Issue* (1985), 5, 42–5; [Daniel Defoe], *An Essay at Removing National Prejudices against a Union with Scotland* (1706), 28, quoted in S. H. F. Johnston, 'The Scots Army in the Reign of Queen Anne', *TRHS* 5th ser. 3 (1953), 1–2.

militia fell into disuse during the reign of James VII and II. Charles II had neglected to adequately reward Highlanders for their assistance in effecting the Restoration, and their allegiances remained divided. Moreover, since the centre of court life and the source of military patronage came to be located in London, Highland lords and chiefs were at a disadvantage.[7]

In Scots Highland societies, the individual members of clans claimed a common descent and shared a communal sense of honour, so that an affront to one was an affront to the honour of all. The clansman was always welcome in the tower or castle of his chieftain, where he was entertained according to his station, but was always accorded the status of a gentleman when he followed his chieftain into war. As gentlemen, they were sensitive about points of honour. Since their methods of agriculture were not as demanding of labour as those of Lowlanders, Highlanders had more leisure to spend upon war and the chase which they loved equally well. Their practice of feuding or private war was habitual, and when they committed plunder and rapine upon Lowlanders, they termed it 'right and justice'. From their habit of spending the winter months hunting, they learned to endure hardship and privation—under Montrose they were capable of marching sixty miles in a day without stopping, and their plaids provided adequate protection in all elements without the need to carry tents. However, Highlanders were difficult to control, and although they obeyed their chieftains, they were not amenable to military discipline. In Highland methods of warfare, victory was important for the honour and reputation it brought rather than its political or military consequences. They served without regular pay, and had a not unreasonable expectation of plunder, which could destroy discipline at the peak of battle. Highlanders had their limitations as fighters; their campaigning season could not conflict with planting and harvest; they could not cross a river if it meant swimming; they lacked artillery and transport, and had no knowledge of siegecraft. As long as they spoke only Gaelic, they found modern military manuals inaccessible.[8]

The war that Dundee declared in the name of James VII against the government forces is called the First Jacobite Rebellion, and the army of mostly Highlanders that he gathered together came not from the larger clans and magnates, but from smaller marginal clans such as the Macdonalds of Keppoch, Clanranald and Glencoe, the Stewarts of Appin and the MacGregors—although the latter adhered too late to participate in the Battle of Killiecrankie. The Keppoch and Glencoe Macdonalds and the MacGregors were regarded as little better than cateran bands, but in their defence it has to be said that previous Stuart kings in alliance with some of the Campbells had marginalized them by unremitting persecution earlier in the seventeenth century. A more respectable ally and a valuable lieutenant was Sir Ewen Cameron of Locheill, who was 60 years of age

---

[7] P. Hopkins, *Glencoe and the End of the Highland War* (1986), 22–3; Robertson, *Militia Issue*, 6–7.
[8] Mackay, *Life...Hugh Mackay*, 45–6; Dalrymple, *Memoirs*, I. i. 47–55; Sir Thomas Craig, *De Unione Regnorum Britanniae Tractatus*, ed. C. S. Terry, SHS 60 (1909), 456–7; Manning, *Swordsmen*, 168.

and had fought in the Glencairn Rebellion of the 1650s. Dundee found him to be a valuable advisor.[9]

Dundee was an experienced soldier, well versed in modern warfare, and had studied the culture of the Highlanders enough to know that their methods of warfare were comparatively primitive. He had an extraordinary ability to make the best use of the Highland warriors, but he had to adapt himself to their expectations, habits and limitations, as well as strengths. To this he added his own flair for histrionics in leading troops in battle. He had feared that the Highlanders might have grown less alert during the years of relative peace preceding Killiecrankie. When Dundee proposed to impose modern military discipline upon them, the Lowland officers and the younger Highland chiefs (some of whom were mere boys) supported the idea, but Sir Ewen Cameron of Locheill advised that the Highlanders would make more effective fighters if they retained their own methods of warfare and were commanded by their own leaders. This, Locheill observed, had proved the best course of action under Montrose. He also thought that the Highlanders would lose their courage if reduced to a state of servitude like other European soldiers. In any case, the introduction of modern discipline would be time-consuming, and Locheill assumed that Dundee's army would not be in existence for very long.[10]

Dundee had no easy time holding together his army of clansmen, and he was unable to assemble all of them in time to fight at Killiecrankie. One of the clan chieftains who had joined Dundee, Macdonald of Keppoch, took the opportunity of settling some scores with an old enemy, Sir Lauchlan Macintosh, who had remained neutral in the war. Keppoch slipped away with his followers and ravaged the Macintosh country. Upon hearing of this, Dundee delivered a stinging rebuke to Keppoch, and told him he did not want him serving under him. Keppoch begged Dundee to keep him on, and said he would not have attacked Macintosh had he not thought him the king's enemy, and promised strict obedience thereafter. When members of the Clan Cameron sought to revenge themselves on the Grants for hanging one of their kinsmen, they killed a Macdonald. When Macdonald of Glengary complained of this to Dundee, the latter refused to punish the Camerons because, as the Highlanders were not regularly paid and subject to discipline, and were expected to live on their own resources, he did not regard them as being strictly under his command. Moreover, they were ignorant of military law. Dundee also told Glengary that the provocation had been great because the Macdonald who had been hanged together with the Grants were adherents of the king's enemies. If he were to punish those accused by Glengary, the Highlanders would cease to fight for the king's cause. The duplicitous John, Lord Murray, heir of John, first marquis of Atholl, attempted to deceive his 1,200 followers during his father's absence and make them think that they were going to

[9] Lenman, *Jacobite Risings*, 44–7.
[10] Hugh Mackay, *Memoirs of the War Carried on in Scotland and Ireland, 1689–1691*, BC 48 (1833), 20; [Drummond], *Cameron of Locheill*, 250–1; Balcarres, *Memoirs*, 46.

fight for King James, when he was actually in communication with General Mackay and intended to support William II and III. When his followers pressed Murray for a straight answer about his allegiance, he refused to reply. They deserted him *en masse*, and declared their loyalty to James.[11]

General Mackay had very little confidence in the army that the Scottish Convention Parliament of 1689 had authorized. Ten regiments of foot consisting of 6,000 men, one regiment of dragoons of 300 men and twelve troops of horse containing 600 men were to be raised. Command of these units was entrusted to peers and gentlemen with no military experience. Furthermore, the commanders of these units, Mackay complained, were allowed to choose all of their own officers upon the basis of popularity and ability to raise soldiers rather than competence and experience. The only reliable units in the Scots force were the three regiments from the Scots Brigade of the Dutch army, but they were much reduced in strength. One new regiment that did stand out was that raised by the 20-year-old James Douglas, earl of Angus, son and heir of James, second marquis of Douglas, which came to be known as the Cameronians and who later gave a good account of themselves fighting the remnants of Dundee's army in the Highlands. The Cameronian Regiment was originally comprised of members of the Cameronian sect which had separated from the Kirk in 1680. They were all raised in a single day without beat of the drum or payment of a bounty, for the purpose of guarding the Scottish Estates.[12]

Both the Jacobite and Williamite armies suffered from serious disadvantages prior to the Battle of Killiecrankie. Dundee was short of cavalry, and was not very successful in raising more horse in the eastern Highlands. He had also hoped to be reinforced by King James from Ireland, but then he got news that English ships had captured a shipment of arms, munitions and provisions being sent to him by way of the Isle of Mull. His Highlanders and the Irishmen led by General Alexander Cannon were already half-starved, but they followed Dundee cheerfully. This compelled him to forage in the Lowlands at the foot of Glenlivet. It was not much easier for Mackay to raise cavalry. He did not trust his dragoons, and the core of his horse consisted of 100 English troopers from Lord Colchester's Regiment who, with their horses, found it very fatiguing negotiating the mountainous terrain. They were short of fodder, and of little use for gathering intelligence. At Edenglassy, Dundee came upon a store of provisions intended for Mackay, but also learned that Mackay's reinforced army was marching towards him. Not wishing to expose his Highlanders to cavalry, which was the one thing they feared, Dundee decided to withdraw to the Grampian Highlands on the pretext that they were joining other clans. He conducted an orderly retreat along the banks of the River Spey and its tributary the River Garry into Badenoch. Dundee's men did not complain of their hunger, because their general shared the same diet

[11] [Drummond], *Cameron of Locheill*, 242–3, 254–7.

[12] Mackay, *Memoirs*, 7; A. Crichton, *The Life and Diary of Lieut. Col. J. Blackader of the Cameronian Regiment* (1824), 32–49.

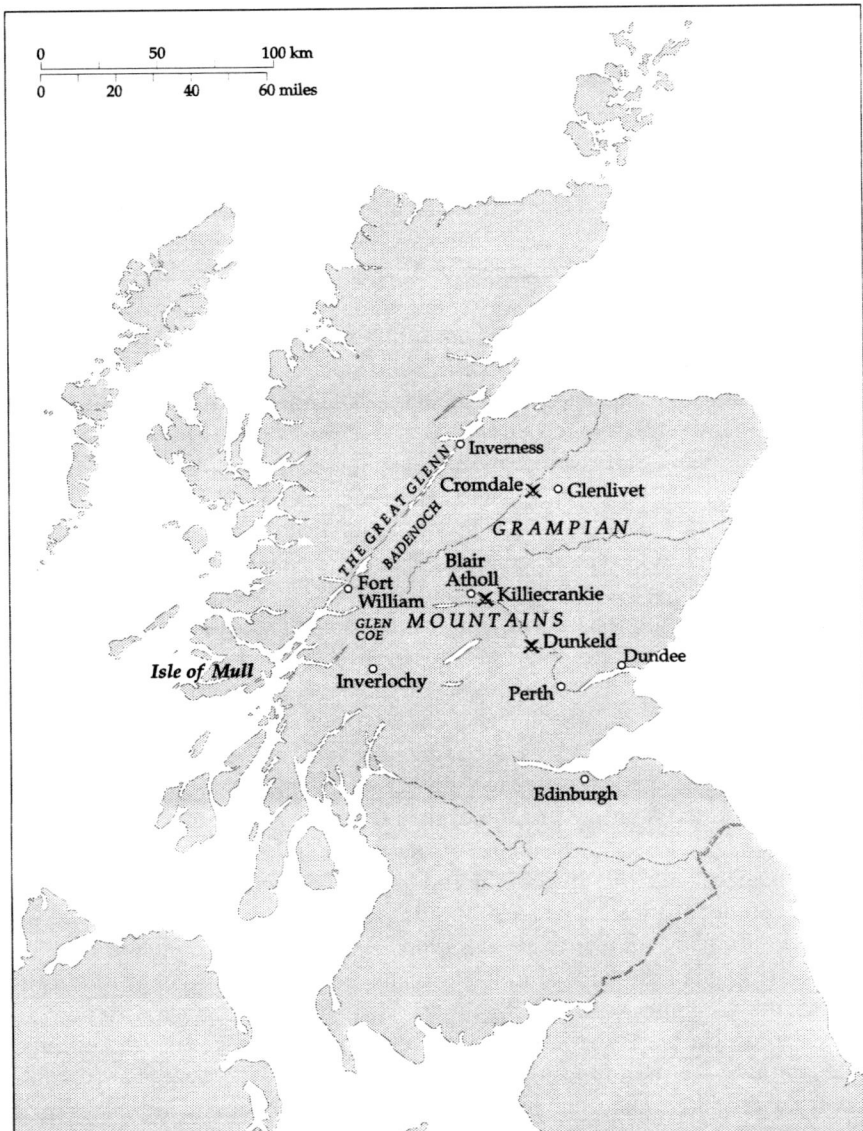

Map 15.1. The First Jacobite Rebellion, 1689

and walked beside them. The decision was taken to fight at the pass of Killiecrankie, before Mackay, whose army was already half as large again as Dundee's, could bring up reinforcements. The Highlanders were on the heights above the pass, and fell upon Mackay's dragoons and infantry as they came through it. This was ideal terrain for a classic Highland charge—casting aside their plaids, they charged down the hillside, fired their muskets and pistols and fell upon Mackay's men with broadsword and target. They fought, not in rank and file, but as clans. Mackay's forces were defeated, but it was a pyrrhic victory, because one-third of Dundee's army was killed, another third wounded and the remainder dispersed by going after Mackay's baggage train or were too exhausted to pursue the retreating army. Worst of all for the Jacobites, Dundee, who did not heed the wishes of his officers to remain behind cover, was killed at the end of the battle. William's government in Scotland was safe, and Mackay still had an army with which to pursue the Highlanders.[13]

Killiecrankie may have been a costly victory, but having become part of Jacobite legend, it was enough to encourage continuing resistance in the Highlands. In August 1689 the Cameronian Regiment, which was garrisoned at Perth, marched to Dunkeld at the entrance to the Highlands and fought a battle in which a much smaller Williamite force, numbering 800 and consisting mostly of the inexperienced Cameronians, blocked the advance of a much larger Jacobite force of at least 3,000 men led by the Irish general, Alexander Cannon. The Jacobite army included remnants of Dundee's army and the Atholl Highlanders who had deserted their colonel, James, Lord Murray. The Jacobites were still able to field an army the next spring led by Major-General Thomas Buchan, but their resistance to the Williamite conquest of Scotland was ended by the Battle of Cromdale, near the modern Grantown-on-Spey, on 1 May 1690.[14]

Following the Battle of Killiecrankie, Hugh Mackay went to Ireland where he fought alongside William of Orange at the Battle of the Boyne. William praised Mackay's gallantry and conduct on that occasion, and asked him why he had not displayed the same characteristics at Killiecrankie. Mackay said that he had much underestimated the fighting qualities of the Highlanders, and that if William had faced Highland soldiers at the Battle of the Boyne he might well have found it more difficult to cross the river. At the end of the First Jacobite Rebellion William allowed Dundee's officers, some 150 in number, to enter the French army. They formed a company of reformadoes serving as gentlemen volunteers, and saw action at Perpignan on the Spanish border, and later on the Rhine. Most of them died of wounds or disease. After 1689 the Highland charge lost much of its power of shock, because the firepower of the British infantry doubled with the replacement of firelock muskets with flintlocks, and the widespread use of socket bayonets which had replaced pikes and plug bayonets and which provided a more adequate defence against cavalry charges.[15]

[13] [Drummond], *Cameron of Locheill*, 243–5, 257–8, 264–5; Dalrymple, *Memoirs*, I. i. 46–7, 53–4, 55–6; Mackay, *Memoirs*, 51–2; Mackay, *Life... Hugh Mackay*, 44–53, 57–60; Hopkins, *Glencoe*, 157–61; J. M. Hill, 'The Distinctiveness of Gaelic Warfare, 1400–1750', *EHQ* 22 (1992), 337–8.

[14] Crichton, *Blackader*, 88, 93, 95; Szechi, *Jacobites*, 44–5; Lynch, *Scotland*, 301; Hopkins, *Glencoe*, 178–89.

[15] Jenner (ed.), *Dundee*, 73–104; [Drummond], *Cameron of Locheill*, 297; Hill, 'Distinctiveness of Gaelic Warfare', 337–8.

The conquest of Scotland gave William control only of the Lowlands. He did establish a military presence at Inverness and Fort William (Inverlochy) in the Great Glen, but because of his lack of interest in Scotland and his overriding concern with the prosecution of the Nine Years War, he neglected to follow up his military victories, and no Scottish or British government really governed the Highlands, where Jacobitism remained active as a protest against the Edinburgh and London regimes, until after the defeat of the Rebellion of 1745. The reimposition of Presbyterian rule in the Kirk alienated Scottish Episcopalians, who were numerous in the Highlands, while the revulsion against the Glencoe Massacre of 1692 and the revival of feuding in the Highlands all provide evidence of the instability of that region.

Behind the Glencoe Massacre lay the government in Edinburgh's attempt to appease the Highland chiefs and secure their loyalty, but negotiations failed because of bad blood between rival clans such as the Macdonalds and the Campbells. Sir John Dalrymple, master of Stair and secretary of state (and later first earl of Stair), attempted to bait the Catholic Macdonalds by calling upon all clan chieftains to swear an oath of allegiance to King William. He expected some of the chiefs to drag their feet, and when Alexander MacIan of Glencoe, chief of one of the smaller Macdonald septs, delayed giving his submission by the deadline of 1 January 1692 (n.s.), Stair commissioned a Campbell chief, Robert Campbell of Glenlyon, to punish the Macdonalds of Glencoe with 'fire and sword'. Glencoe had intended ultimately to sign, and indeed attempted to do so at Fort William, but was refused. On the night of 13 February 1692, after accepting his host's hospitality, Glenlyon and his Campbell levies massacred many of the 200 Glencoe families, plundered and burnt their dwellings and drove the remainder into the snows, where more died of exposure.[16]

Jacobite loyalties remained strong in Scotland and subverted the allegiances of many Scots aristocrats and even army officers. In 1694 John, Lord Murray (later earl of Tullibardine, second marquis and first duke of Atholl), was given a commission to raise a regiment of foot for William II and III. His own tenants, who were mostly Stewarts and Robinsons of Atholl, were all Jacobites and looked upon Murray as a 'tyrant'. In desperation, he conceived of a dishonest scheme to recruit Frasers for his regiment by telling them that he was actually raising soldiers for the exiled James VII. Hugh Fraser, ninth Lord Lovat, a man of 'feeble understanding', and his cousin Simon Fraser, laird of Beaufort (and later eleventh Lord Lovat), were duped into raising companies of Frasers, believing that they would assist King James upon his landing in Scotland. Simon Fraser, who also had his own store of deviousness, discovered that he was commissioned as a lieutenant and only promoted captain after he had raised 300 men. Even then, he had to purchase his commission. When Lord Murray became principal secretary of state, he

[16] Lenman, *Jacobite Risings*, 53–4; Hopkins, *Glencoe*, 310–38; Szechi, *Jacobites*, 66–8; Lynch, *Scotland*, 305–7.

tried to compel the officers of his regiment, which was then guarding Holyrood Palace, to swear an oath of loyalty to William II and III, and abjure their allegiance to King James. The officers were all Jacobites and grumbled, but swore the oath in order to retain their salaries. Simon Fraser subsequently resigned and obtained a commission as captain of the grenadier company in Macgill's Regiment. Murray, now earl of Tullibardine, continued his vendetta with Simon Fraser in his capacity as secretary of state, and in 1698 he raised a force of some 1,500–2,000 Highlanders as well as regulars from Inverness and Fort William to punish the Frasers. Although Simon Fraser could raise only 200–300 Frasers, he attacked the Atholl Highlanders at the Pass of Autnagoire. Many fled, but those who were captured threw down their arms and asked for quarter. The Fraser women, who accompanied their husbands into battle, screamed for vengeance, but the Fraser tacksmen or gentlemen told Fraser that it would be murder not to grant quarter. This suggests that restraints upon war were coming to be accepted even in the Highlands. However, Simon Fraser, now Lord Lovat (his father died on this campaign running through the Highlands at the age of 68), imposed upon the Atholl Highlanders, led by Lords James and Mungo Murray, a humiliating ceremony of surrender that he had read about in a Roman history book. He 'made these miserable cowards march, like so many criminals, between the ranks of his men, and obliged them immediately to quit his territories by the same road they had entered them'.[17]

The Conquest of Ireland

It was especially evident in the Williamite wars in Ireland how little confidence William II and III had in English and Scots commanders. Besides Godart van Reede, Baron Ginkel, and Meinhard Schomberg, the son of the duke of Schomberg (and later duke of Leinster and third duke of Schomberg), Hugh Mackay found himself serving under Henri de Massue de Ruvigny, second marquis de Ruvigny (and later earl of Galway), a French Huguenot; Heinrich Maastricht, count of Solms, a German in Dutch service; and Ernst von Tettau, a Dane. Tollemache and Mackay were the only generals from the British Isles. Two other British generals, Percy Kirke and James Douglas of Cavers, were withdrawn from Ireland and sent to Flanders because of disagreements with the other members of William's corps of commanders. Douglas, of the Scots army, 'was charged with mutinying because he spoke freely about the soldiers being abused for want of pay and other necessaries'.[18]

According to Dalrymple, the various expeditionary forces that William sent to Ireland totalled 36,000 men. 'Distrusting English soldiers to fight against one

[17] Simon [Fraser, 11th] Lord Lovat, *Memoirs*, trans. W. Godwin (1797), 6–19, 37–8, 76–83, 90–7; Hopkins, *Glencoe*, 443–62.

[18] Mackay, *Life ... Hugh Mackay*, 111–12; Hewitson, (ed.), *Diary of Thomas Bellingham*, 94; E. S. de Beer (ed.), *The Diary of John Evelyn*, 6 vols. (1955), v. 7.

who had been lately king of England, he took care that more than half of his army should consist of foreigners.' The foreign troops included 10,000 Danish soldiers, 7,000 from the Dutch and Brandenburg armies, and 2,000 Huguenots—the latter organized into a brigade of three regiments of foot and one of horse that was part of the English military establishment. The first group sent to Ireland consisted of some 15,000 troops who sailed from Hoylake, near Chester, during August and September 1689, and landed near Carrickfergus. Together with Williamite forces from Enniskillen and Kirke's three regiments from Derry, the army could not have exceeded 20,000 men.[19] William wanted to land this force near Dublin, but Schomberg advised going ashore in Belfast Lough. Before putting ashore, it was necessary to clear three French warships out of the lough in an engagement that lasted three hours. Upon landing, Schomberg laid siege to the Norman fortress of Carrickfergus, which was garrisoned by two Jacobite regiments under the command of MacCarty Moor, in order to secure the neighbourhood. The siege lasted seven days. Schomberg allowed the defenders to keep their sidearms, and provided them with a cavalry escort to protect them from the country-people; the latter were Scots-Irish, and they so abused the Catholic soldiers that they fled back to Schomberg for protection.[20]

Many of the Irish Protestants were at first ambiguous in their allegiances because of William of Orange's apparent inactivity. However, when they saw James II raising an army, and heard rumours that the Jacobite soldiers were not to be paid but were to live off of the land, this ended any ambiguity they might have felt. George Story, a chaplain with William's army and the author of a full and remarkably accurate (if not completely impartial) account of the war, says that William exercised great care to keep his soldiers from plundering so as not to alienate either his Protestant or Catholic subjects, and would summarily execute soldiers caught taking property. He also issued orders that no soldier was to stray beyond the lines of encampments upon pain of death. Despite frequent executions and the sight of comrades' bodies hanging by the side of the road on marches, William's generals found it difficult to restrain their soldiers from straggling and plundering. Stragglers were easy prey for rapparees. Story insists that 'sickness and hard marching' and stragglers lost to rapparees took a greater toll on William's army than sieges and battles. The Williamite war, or the 'War of the Two Kings' as it is called in Gaelic, was also a messy civil war: numerous desertions and changes of allegiance led to frequent executions of soldiers in both armies as examples to their comrades. Another chaplain, Rowland Davies, who was attached to Lord Cavendish's Regiment of Horse, provides an example of a cleric who offered small

---

[19] Dalrymple, *Memoirs*, I. ii. 124; Mackay, *Life... Hugh Mackay*, 111; J. G. Simms, *Jacobite Ireland, 1685–91* (1969; repr. 2000), 122; id., 'Schomberg at Dundalk, 1689', repr. in Simms, *War and Politics in Ireland, 1649–1730*, ed. D. W. Hayton and G. O'Brien (1986), 93.

[20] Simms, 'Schomberg at Dundalk', 92; *An Exact Account of the Duke of Schomberg's Happy Voyage from Highlake... to Carrickfergus* (1689), 1–2; [George Story], *A True and Impartial history of... the Kingdom of Ireland during the Last Two Years with the present State of Both Armies* (1691), 10.

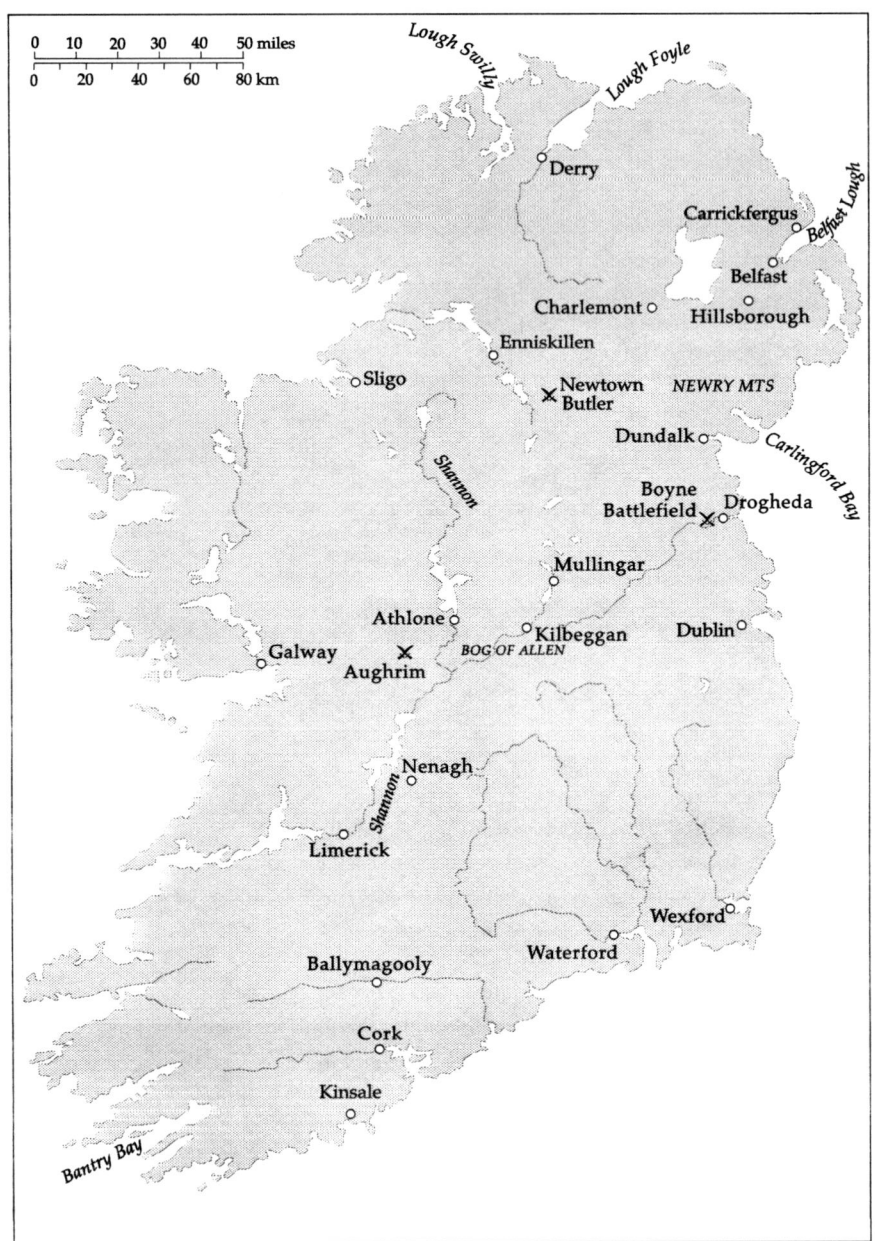

Map 15.2. The Williamite war in Ireland

consolation to the soldiers. He appears to have acted primarily as a quartermaster; he hunted with the officers, and was armed with a sabre and a carbine. On one occasion Davies preached a sermon against swearing on Sundays while soldiers from his own regiment were being led away to execution.[21]

Not long after William III sailed for Ireland, a French fleet under Admiral Tourville defeated a combined Anglo-Dutch fleet off Beachy Head on the coast of Sussex on 30 June 1690. This was a major setback for William, but he exerted himself to impress upon his soldiers the assurance that they faced no threat from the French. He staged a military review among his assembled troops on the shores of Belfast Lough to restore confidence and exhort his soldiers to victory. As each regiment passed in review, William rode in amongst them 'to encourage the soldiers and to satisfy himself of the state of every regiment'. When an order was 'brought to him to sign for wine for his table, he said aloud, "No, he would drink water with his soldiers"'. His campaigning histrionics also extended to sleeping amongst his troops—albeit in a portable house allegedly designed by Sir Christopher Wren. He marched with his soldiers by day, declaring that 'he came not to Ireland to give leave to the grass to grow under his feet', and he had the fleet sail slowly along the coast 'to elevate their spirits by the grandeur of the spectacle, and to confirm them by the idea of security which it conveyed'. Although William did not take time to reform the English army, he did occasionally make an example of officers who abused their soldiers. He cashiered Sir John Edgeworth for equipping his regiment with cast-off and inadequate uniforms.[22]

William of Orange had need to encourage his men, because the expeditionary force under the command of the duke of Schomberg that had landed the previous year at Carrickfergus fared poorly. After the successful siege of Carrickfergus Castle, the duke's army of 15,000 moved south to Dundalk at the foot of the Newry Mountains, where they went into winter quarters in the autumn of 1689. Schomberg's force was unable to campaign because they were logistically unprepared. The Danish troops did not disembark until late September; the transports from Hoylake had not brought enough horses for the artillery, and the cavalry had not arrived; there were inadequate shoes and clothing; the magazines were not stocked with sufficient provisions; and few of the English soldiers, who were mostly untrained and ill disciplined recruits, had ever fired a musket or had any knowledge of field hygiene. Moreover, their officers lacked the knowledge, experience and inclination to train their men. Lacking tents, Schonberg gave the order to build barracks (which were simply huts in the seventeenth century) out of wood and turf; the Dutch and French Huguenot soldiers knew what to do, but

---

[21] Dalrymple, *Memoirs*, I. i. 230; [Story], *True and Impartial History*, 104, 107; R. Caulfield (ed.), *Journal of... Rowland Davies*, CS OS 68 (1857; repr. 1968), 83, 102, 112–14, 127–8, 132–3.

[22] Dalrymple, *Memoirs*, I. ii. 135; J. Ehrman, *The Navy in the War of William III, 1689–1697* (1953), 341–66; E. B. Powley, *The Naval Side of King William's War* (1972), 134–43; Simms, *Jacobite Ireland*, 143; Robert Parker, *Memoirs of the Most Remarkable Military Transactions from the year 1683 to 1718... in Ireland and Flanders* (1747), 13–14.

the English, being raw soldiers, neglected to obey the duke's orders until it was too late. The original campsite proved to be wet and boggy, and part of the camp had to be moved to higher ground. The consequence was that more than half of Schomberg's army died of disease that winter—mostly from dysentery.[23]

After the army went into winter quarters at Dundalk, Schomberg put on his best display of paternal regard for his soldiers in order to restore their morale. As wagons bearing the sick and wounded left the camp,

Schomberg ordered his colonels and brigadiers to attend like corporals and sergeants upon the wagons, the ships and hospitals. He stood himself during many hours in the cold and rain, leaning upon a bridge along which the long line of carriages, filled with disabled soldiers passed in sight of the army, to thank them for their services, to lament their distresses, and to cherish their spirits, and to reprimand every officer who showed not the same attention with himself, shaking with age, but more with the strength of his affection.... Touched with the same generous sensibility of their general, the soldiers repented their clamours they had raised against him, and attentive only to his anguish, forgot their own.[24]

Schomberg had his hands full during the winter of 1689–90. An Irish army commanded by James II's natural son, James Fitzjames, duke of Berwick, put on vaunting displays within full view of Dundalk camp. Schomberg ignored them because, although the Irish had fired on his men, he observed that they were not very proficient in the use of their arms, and were not likely to attack across the dangerous bog that separated the two armies, while his forces were well protected behind entrenched positions. Schomberg also had other problems: he discovered 200 Catholic soldiers in the three Huguenot regiments who had to be disarmed and returned to England. Six of them were *agents provocateurs* who apparently had been planted to sow dissension. They were hanged. The army remained short of provisions, and had to forage, but because of proximity to rapparees, foraging had to be done by large, well armed parties. Bread had to be rationed, so Schomberg issued it only to the enlisted men because he thought that the officers could shift for themselves. King William's order that the officers were to pay their men promptly was read out to the whole army; the officers were also ordered to see that their sick were attended, and they were also to keep a strict accounting of the number of sick and effective soldiers and where they were located, as well as an inventory of weapons. By June, new arrivals of troops had built the Williamite army at Dundalk up to 30,000.[25]

[23] [Story], *True and Impartial History*, 15, 22–3; Parker, *Memoirs*, 15–16; Dalrymple, *Memoirs*, I. ii. 87–8, 90–3; BL, Add. MS. 41,141 (Richard Kane, 'Account of the Most Remarkable Transactions which happened in the Campaigns made from the Year 1689 to the Conclusion of the Peace of Ryswick in 1697'), fos. 24r & v, 25r & v; Richard Kane, *Campaigns of King William and the Duke of Marlborough*, 2nd edn. (1747), 1–2; *The Autobiography of Sir John Bramston*, CS OS 32 (1845), 347.

[24] Dalrymple, *Memoirs*, I. ii. 94.

[25] [Story], *True and Impartial History*, 16, 22–5, 27–8, 72; BL, Add. MS. 41,141, fos. 24r & v, 25v; Kane, *Campaigns of King William*, 3–4; M. Glozier, *The Huguenot Soldiers of William of Orange and the 'Glorious Revolution' of 1688: The Lions of Judah* (2002), 119–24.

The English navy had been able to maintain control of St George's Channel, but William had reduced naval expenditures in order to divert funds to the land war in Flanders, and the English fleet could not patrol the south-west coast of Ireland effectively. King James was able to sail from Brest and land his forces at Kinsale and Bantry Bay in March 1690. In two separate French naval convoys he carried with him his two illegitimate sons, James, duke of Berwick, and Henry Fitzjames, known as the Grand Prior, as well as many English, Welsh, Irish and Scots Jacobite officers. Among them were John Bernardi, sometime an officer in the Anglo-Dutch Brigade, who had obeyed James's recall of the officers of that corps in 1685; John Stevens, an ardent English Catholic Jacobite, whose father had been a page to Catharine of Braganza; and Thomas Buchan, who had commanded the Jacobite army in the Scottish Highlands following the death of Viscount Dundee. Perhaps as many as 50,000 Irishmen had volunteered to fight under King James, most of whom were armed with clubs and half-pikes, and who proposed to serve under local gentlemen and kinsmen. They generally lacked uniforms, shoes and muskets. John Stevens, who obtained a commission as a lieutenant in the Grand Prior's Regiment, found the Jacobite army to be 'very raw and undisciplined, and the generality almost naked, or at least ragged and ill shod'. He thought the horse were well mounted and equipped, but they were not very numerous. Stevens also complained of the poor quality of the Irish officers, and said that well qualified English Jacobite officers were denied suitable rank on the excuse that the Irish soldiers would follow only their own leaders. Because it was doubted that James could pay, provision and equip an army of that size, Patrick Sarsfield (later titular earl of Lucan), who had graduated from a French military academy, was made a brigadier and authorized to visit camps and garrisons and reduce the Jacobite army to a more manageable size of 35,000 men.[26] In actuality, the Jacobite army probably levelled out at 25,000, and was continually plagued by desertions. By contrast, William III calculated that his forces in 1690 included 34,560 foot and 9,300 horse—one of the few occasions in his military career when he fielded an army superior in size to that of the enemy.[27]

It is difficult to avoid the conclusion that the Jacobite forces simply lacked the administrative apparatus to keep an army intact in the field. Edmund Nugent was the colonel of a regiment of foot and a regiment of horse. He had difficulty paying his soldiers and securing provisions, forage and mounts for his cavalry regiment at Mullingar. The local magistrates were uncooperative, the country folk unforthcoming and Nugent had to requisition what he needed. For this he was reprimanded by Sir Ignatius White, the duke of Berwick's secretary at Dublin Castle, for alienating the

[26] Ehrman, *Navy in the War of William III*, 245–6; P. Wauchope, *Patrick Sarsfield and the Williamite War* (1992), 46–50; John Bernardi, *A Short History of the Life of Major John Bernardi* (1729), 52–4; R. H. Murrray (ed.), *The Journal of John Stevens Containing a Brief Account of the War in Ireland, 1689–1691* (1912), pp. ix–x, 8–9, 14, 21–3, 28, 32–3, 59, 64–7, 74, 216; J. G. Simms, 'A Jacobite Colonel: Lord Sarsfield of Kilmallock', *IS* 2 (1955), 205.
[27] S. B. Baxter, *William III and the Defense of European Liberty, 1650–1702* (1966), 263.

local magistrates, and by James II for not showing more initiative.[28] In July 1690 another Jacobite regiment that two weeks earlier had consisted of 800 men was reduced to 300, of whom only 150 were armed, by desertion. The Grand Prior's Regiment was never recruited up to strength, and because of continuing desertions had to be collapsed from twenty-two to thirteen companies. According to John Stevens, when the soldiers were removed from officers to whom they owed personal loyalty, they would often desert rather than serve under another—with the connivance of 'their own idol officers' who had been reduced to the status of reformadoes because of inexperience or incompetence, and who had laid aside 'the public good for private malice'. Stevens asserts that most of the men recruited for the Jacobite regiments were ignorant and could barely understand English, and had never fired their weapons. Stevens himself seems not to have spoken Gaelic. They were amenable only to discipline resting on brute force, but an officer could not punish a non-commissioned officer or private soldier who was his own kinsman. Such officers were nearly as ignorant of military matters as their men, and could only drill them by rote memorization of drill manuals. Following the Battle of Newtownbutler, when a Jacobite army retreated from the battlefield, a subordinate officer, misunderstanding an order issued by Major-General Justin MacCarty, Viscount Mountcashel, led a large number of men to their deaths by drowning in bogs and loughs as they were pursued by the enemy. George Story attributed this to Divine Providence rather than mere incompetence. It is perhaps no wonder that the widespread resort to hanging as a punishment failed to deter desertions, since Daniel O'Brien, third Viscount Clare, who recruited a number of regiments for the Jacobites, scoured the prisons for condemned felons and other prisoners who were 'fit for military service'.[29]

It was important for the Jacobite army to gain control of Ulster if James was to make his way back to Scotland. However, the Protestants controlled a number of key points in Ulster that dominated the main communications routes—Derry, Enniskillen, Sligo and Hillsborough. Derry had been nominally under the governance of James's lord-lieutenant Tyrconnell, and was garrisoned by Sir William Stewart, first Viscount Mountjoy's Regiment, purged of Catholics and commanded by Colonel Robert Lundy, a Protestant Scot. The clouds of war gathering on the horizon had driven as many as 30,000 Protestants into the narrow confines of Derry's fortifications. Tyrconnell had wanted to replace the Mountjoy Regiment with the Irish and Highland Scots soldiers of Alexander MacDonnell, third earl of Antrim's Regiment, which the inhabitants of Derry refused to accept because they believed that they were all papists six feet tall and more, and relatives of those who had spilled Protestant blood in the Rebellion of 1641. By 14 April 1689 a combined French and Jacobite army had advanced to within sight of Derry, and the suburbs were burnt or pulled down to clear a field of fire. Colonel

[28] HEH, Stowe-Nugent MSS. (Spec. Subjects, War of 1689–91), 1 (nos. 5–6, 19, 21, 30–2, 47).
[29] Murray (ed.), *Journal of John Stevens*, 62–4, 105, 142–3; [Story], *True and Impartial History*, 5; Wauchope, *Sarsfield*, 71–2; Simms, *Jacobite Ireland*, 69–71; J. Ainsworth (ed.), *The Inchiquin Manuscripts*, IMC (1961), 17.

Lundy, the governor of the city, who had changed allegiance without enthusiasm, regarded Derry as indefensible because of the lack of provisions, and was in favour of abandoning Derry and retreating back to England. The common soldiers were enraged at their officers, some of whom had fled already, and they did violence to those who remained behind. A cavalry captain who enjoyed the confidence of both the soldiers and the people relieved Lundy (who was ever thereafter regarded as a traitor) of his governorship, but refused to accept the office himself. The soldiers of Lundy's regiment chose new officers to replace those who had fled. George Walker, a Church-of-Ireland cleric, took over the governorship, but as an Episcopalian in a sea of Presbyterians, he was not popular. He made matters worse by helping Lundy to escape and allegedly hoarding provisions. Walker was also viewed as a defeatist, distrusted by the people and was faced with a mutiny. The decision to defend Derry against the French-Jacobite siege was made when the apprentice boys snatched the keys from the guardhouse and locked all of the gates to keep out Antrim's soldiers.[30]

On 30 July 1689 a relief expedition commanded by Major-General Percy Kirke was sighted in Lough Foyle. The combined French-Irish Jacobite force besieging Derry had bombarded the city, but had not assaulted its defences. Other than a few sallies, the defenders of Derry had done little to resist the siege except to hold out as provisions diminished. The frigate and the two merchant ships with provisions brought by Kirke broke the boom laid across Lough Foyle by the French; the merchant ships proceeded to the quay in Derry, and the siege was over. Derry had held out for 105 days, during which a third of the garrison had perished from disease, malnutrition and wounds—especially the former. The defenders of Derry comprised some eight regiments—mostly militia and irregulars raised by the local Protestant gentry. When Kirke entered Derry the inhabitants and defenders had reason to wonder if they had been liberated or conquered. He confiscated cattle from the local farmers without compensation; his soldiers plundered the refugees, whom Kirke forced to return to their homes; he denied the defenders full pay for their services, tried to impress some of them, and seized their saddles and weapons; sick and disabled soldiers were simply turned out on the highways to beg. Those who complained were threatened with hanging on the newly erected gallows. Percy Kirke was a brute and an autocrat, but he may also have been punishing the inhabitants and defenders of Derry for participating in a mutiny and mob rule.[31]

Both the Jacobite and Williamite forces had their peculiar weaknesses when engaging in siege warfare. When the duke of Schomberg was able to resume

[30] George Walker, *A True Account of the Siege of London-Derry* (1689), 11–16, 19–20; John Mackenzie, *A Narrative of the Siege of London-Derry* (1690), 7, 23, 28–30, 33, 35; Simms, *Jacobite Ireland*, 95–6. Mackenzie was a military chaplain who was present at the siege of Derry, and wrote his pamphlet to correct the mistakes and omissions of Walker's account. Mackenzie viewed the successful defence of Derry as an act of Providence.

[31] Walker, *Siege of London-Derry*, 17, 35, 38, 40–1; Mackenzie, *Siege of London-Derry*, 45–7; Simms, *Jacobite Ireland*, 95–113.

campaigning in May 1690 following the disastrous winter spent at Dundalk camp, he set out for Charlemont Fort in co. Armagh, which had been constructed by the Elizabethan general Charles Blount, eighth Lord Mountjoy, to house a garrison. Charlemont was not a large fortress, but it did contain artillery and ammunition, and threatened an important supply route as long as the Jacobites possessed it. The governor of the garrison, Teague O'Reagan, was an experienced soldier who had fought in France, and his first reply to Schomberg's summons to surrender was a burst of bravado. The braving words were only meant to preserve O'Reagan's honour; he lacked the provisions to hold out because, besides a garrison of 400, he also had to feed 200 women and children. This was a weakness in resisting a siege, as O'Reagan admitted to Schomberg when he finally accepted the latter's honourable terms of surrender, because 'the soldiers would not stay in the garrison without their wives and mistresses'. As Schomberg later reported, when he surrendered, 'Teague's horse was very mad and himself very drunk'.[32]

Sligo was another stronghold that Robert Lundy had abandoned to the Jacobites. It was the key to the route between Connaught and Ulster, because, at that time, it was better fortified than Enniskillen. Patrick Sarsfield was sent to occupy Sligo, but after he marched north to besiege Enniskillen, Sir Teague O'Reagan, recently knighted, was given the governorship by King James as reward for his spirited, if futile, defence of Charlemont. Although retaken by the Williamite forces, Sarsfield took Sligo again by siege. The Jacobites were still in control in the early summer of 1691, when Colonel John Michelbourne, who commanded the Williamite forces in Ulster, called upon O'Reagan to surrender. Godart de Ginkel, Michelbourne's commander, actually offered to take O'Reagan into his own service if he would surrender, and Michelbourne, who had served with O'Reagan in France, sent him a present of whiskey. Michelbourne was much blamed for having twice failed to take Sligo, but he was obliged to undertake this task with only a few companies of regular troops and some companies of Ulster militia, who were more interested in cattle-raiding than the tedious work of siege warfare. Altogether, Michelbourne had no more than 800 men. When he held a council of war with the militia captains about plans to attempt another siege and swore them to secrecy, they broadcast his plans within two hours and he resolved never to trust them again. O'Reagan was a wily old fox who knew how to drag his feet. He was allowed first to consult with his superior Tyrconnell, then he entered into negotiations with Michelbourne in August 1691 for terms of surrender. He was, as before, allowed generous terms, but then broke off negotiations on the excuse that Michelbourne could not control the Ulster militia who continued to plunder the countryside. This disorder in Michelbourne's camp attracted rapparees posing as camp-followers, who began to steal back the horses and cattle plundered by the Ulster militiamen. O'Reagan's delaying tactics allowed the

---

[32] [Story], *True and Impartial History*, 60–4; Wauchope, *Sarsfield*, 96–7; Simms, *Jacobite Ireland*, 137–8.

Jacobites to reinforce his garrison. However, on 14 September 1691, realizing that his situation was beyond hope, Sir Teague O'Reagan surrendered Sligo.[33]

The failure to take Derry and Enniskillen had made it difficult for James II to hold on to Ulster, which he had planned to use as a bridgehead to Scotland. William of Orange was determined to take Dublin, and James equally determined to retain it. Because they did not control St George's Channel, the French could see no point in holding on to Dublin, and wanted to burn it and withdraw behind the River Shannon, which constituted a more formidable physical barrier. Both James and William seemed intent upon meeting one another in a pitched battle. James moved north to Drogheda, and was able to select his position on Donore Hill on the south side of Boyne Water, two miles west of the town. His army did not have time to entrench, and he failed to take into account the fact that the River Boyne could be crossed at a number of points. James could bring only a little more than 23,000 men into the field against William's 36,000, and through a failure of intelligence and strategy, he had only one-third of his army to withstand the better part of the Williamite force. On a very hot 1 July 1690, after an artillery bombardment, the Williamite foot forced the river and threatened to corner the Jacobites in a bend in the River Boyne. James had to withdraw his forces towards Dublin; the retreat was orderly enough at first, and neither side suffered losses that were not sustainable, but James—blaming his army for his defeat—lost heart, fled to France and never again appeared on a battlefield. Thomas Bellingham, who was an aide-de-camp to the prince of Orange, says that William led a pursuit of the Jacobites at the head of a contingent of Enniskillen horse. William had earlier been slightly wounded, and the brave old duke of Schomberg was killed while rallying his Huguenot regiments. Bellingham also paid tribute to the courage of the Jacobite horse of Tyrconnell's Regiment, but George Story claimed that all of James's Irish cavalry troopers had been issued a half-pint of brandy, and most were drunk when they charged 'so desperately'.[34]

The military significance of William of Orange's victory at the Boyne has been much exaggerated. However, William knew how to turn it into a propaganda victory, and he had at hand army chaplains whose task it was to record his triumphs, as well as Dutch printers and engravers who were the best satirists in Europe. The defenders of William of Orange felt the need to justify his claim to rule the Three Kingdoms on the basis of providential intervention. Not only was his victory over James II at the Battle of the Boyne attributed to Divine Providence, but the story about him being grazed by a bullet while riding his horse within musket-shot of the enemy was frequently repeated in the same vein.

[33] John Michelbourne, *An Account of the Transactions in the North of Ireland... with a Particular Relation of the Manner of Besieging and Taking the Town of Sligoe* (1692), 1–6, 8–9, 19–41, 49, 54–60, 63, 66, 88–9; Luttrell, *RSA* ii. 275.

[34] Hewitson (ed.), *Diary of Thomas Bellingham*, 130–1; J. Childs, 'The Williamite War, 1689–1691', *MHI* 201; Wauchope, *Sarsfield*, 99–113; H. Murtagh, 'The War in Ireland, 1689–91', W. A. Maguire (ed.), *Kings in Conflict: The Revolutionary War in Ireland and its Aftermath, 1689–1750* (1990), 72–9; [Story], *True and Impartial History*, 85.

In Flanders, the Dutch and English armies were commanded to celebrate the victory at the Boyne with sermons, toasts, festive dinners and a ceremonial 'triumph of the field', featuring reviews, cannonades and a grand tattoo. Further evidence that William had a divine mission was furnished by his survival of an assassination plot in 1692 in Flanders, and by the fact that the Confederate armies were almost always outnumbered by the French, and yet withstood Louis XIV. Again, he was exposed to continuous fire at the Battle of Steenkirk in 1692 and survived.[35]

The retreat of the Jacobites from the Boyne began in a reasonably orderly fashion, but as the Irish army moved south much of it began to disintegrate. Dublin was abandoned, and the Williamites sacked Catholic houses. In the retreat from the battlefield the Jacobite army had left behind much of its baggage, including tents, and when the remnants of the army reached Limerick two weeks later the soldiers had to build huts. John Stevens reported that the Irish dragoons appointed to guard the baggage train plundered that which they were appointed to guard. Stevens lost all of his clothes and money. The Irish army, now under the command of Tyrconnell, prepared to make a stand south of the River Shannon at Limerick, while the French, except for one general officer, withdrew to Galway, where they had uninterrupted communication with Brest. Tyrconnell, who was one of the few survivors of the Cromwellian siege of Drogheda, proposed treating with William of Orange while he still had an army in the field and could hope to obtain decent terms of surrender. The proposal provoked outrage among most of the senior Irish officers, who were led by Patrick Sarsfield, the man who had twice taken Sligo. Sarsfield had emerged as a hero in the eyes of his fellow officers, and because of his many ties of kinship he possessed the ability to unite the Old English of Munster and the Old Irish of Ulster and continue to resist the Williamites.[36]

Like every war, the Williamite war in Ireland has its tales of atrocity committed by both sides. At the same time, it must be said that the conquest was not nearly as brutal as the Cromwellian conquest of Ireland forty years earlier. Officers of both the Jacobite and Williamite forces had served in mainland European armies, and contact with the European military world increasingly introduced into Ireland, as into the Scottish Highlands, a concern with limiting the cruelty and destructiveness of warfare. George Story says that the Irish Jacobite army had on one occasion captured some prisoners in the midst of a battle, 'but not being able to carry them off, they killed Col. Herbert and one or two more'. Story said that this was permissible in certain circumstances, citing the precedent of the Battle of Agincourt of 1414, when Henry V, spying fresh enemy troops about to enter battle, ordered his

---

[35]   D. Hayton, 'The Propaganda War', in Maguire (ed.), *Kings in Conflict*, 106–21; [John Whittle], *A Short Review of the Remarkable Providences attending Our Gracious Sovereign William III* (1699), 78–80, 82, 86; William Sawle, *An Impartial Relation of... Last Summer's Campaign in Flanders* (1691), 13–14.

[36]   Childs, 'Williamite War', 201–3; Murray (ed.), *Journal of John Stephens*, 142; Wauchope, *Sarsfield*, 114–20.

men to slay their prisoners. At the same time, Story also tells of some foreign mercenaries in the Williamite army who killed a Jacobite officer, Ulick Bourke, third Viscount Galway, after he had surrendered on quarter.[37] The duke of Berwick told Count Solms that there was a rumour that he was sending Irish and French prisoners of war to the American plantations to be sold as slaves. Berwick told Solms that he would retaliate by sending Williamite prisoners to the French galleys. Solms sent a letter to Berwick denying the rumour, but at the same time warning that any severity towards prisoners from the Williamite armies would meet with appropriate retaliation. Jacobite officers used this rumour to deter their men from deserting. The justification for selling prisoners of war into slavery, a practice in which Cromwell and his lieutenants had engaged, derived from Roman legal thinking which held that a soldier became a slave 'by the very fact of his capture', but was rarely seen in European wars of the late seventeenth century, although the Dutch did still sell North African, non-Christian prisoners to the Spanish.[38] Early in the Williamite war the Irish had burned towns as they were forced to withdraw from them. When, in June 1690, William of Orange's army came within four miles of the Jacobite encampment at Newry, William sent a trumpeter to warn the Irish army that if they continued this practice he would no longer grant quarter to Irish and French prisoners when they were captured. The Jacobite army gave up the tactic, and when James II gave his farewell speech to the lord mayor and notables of the city of Dublin he stated that he did not intend to put the torch to Dublin because he thought such an act would be barbarous.[39]

William of Orange appears to have issued threats of severity as part of a campaign of psychological warfare, although his generals were less likely to act upon those threats. On his return journey from the failed attempt to take Limerick, William warned the Irish governors of Waterford and Drogheda that they must surrender immediately or be denied quarter. At the Siege of Limerick the Williamite besiegers practised 'germ warfare' by catapulting bodies and the carcasses of horses into the town.[40] The war in Ireland harshly impacted on civilians because the Jacobite forces mainly lived off of the land, as did William of Orange's soldiers to a lesser extent. Nevertheless, the violence against civilians was directed largely against their property rather than their persons. The victims of choice, when the Jacobite army foraged, were Protestants. However, even Catholics could become victims if they did not cooperate. John Stevens tells of an encounter with a Catholic innkeeper in the Naas, who refused to accept billets issued by King James. Stevens and his fellow officers of the Grand Prior's Regiment forced their way in to obtain beds, food and wine. Stevens claims that this was the first

---

[37] George Story, *A Continuation of the Impartial History of the Wars in Ireland* (1693), 135–6; Wauchope, *Sarsfield*, 234.

[38] Story, *Continuation of the Impartial History*, 42–3; Redlich, *DPM* (1956), 30–1.

[39] W. Griffyth, *Villare Hibernicum: Being an Exact Account of all the… Towns… Reduc'd by his Majestie's Army since his First Landing in Ireland* (1690) [HEH, Bridgewater Pamphlets, vol. 8/C12], sigs. B1r, B3r; [Story], *True and Impartial History*, 5–6.

[40] Griffyth, *Villare Hibernicum*, sigs. B2v, D2r, F1r.

time that he ever employed violence against a non-combatant. He says that King James backed them up, and he paid for that to which he was not entitled by his billet.[41] William and his lieutenants knew how important the New English landed interest was to his cause. When Thomas Bellingham was campaigning with the duke of Schomberg in Ulster in September 1689, he persuaded the duke to send a cavalry detachment to protect Bellingham's tenants and estates at Germonstown, co. Kildare. The protection offered by the troopers did not, however, prevent Bellingham's house from being burnt. Again, in June 1690 General Ginkel allowed Bellingham six dragoons to guard his tenants and cattle. Bellingham's diary also records how they plundered Jacobite granaries and wine cellars. Both sides depended very much on foraging, and conducted scorch-and-burn campaigns against one another. The Williamite author of *A Faithful History* admits that the Protestants of Ulster exaggerated their own strength, and terrorized their Catholic neighbours.[42]

A notable feature of the Williamite war in Ireland was the increasing prevalence of guerilla warfare carried on by bands of irregular fighters called rapparees. How one distinguishes rapparees from tories or bandits is not perfectly clear, except that the former operated in larger bands, often cooperated with the Jacobite forces and enjoyed the support of priests and the Catholic populace. As Protestant and Williamite authorities disarmed Catholics and drove them out of towns to tramp the highways, there was no difficulty recruiting men to become rapparees. Their name comes from the half-pike that they carried. Today, such bands of irregular soldiers would be regarded as fighting a war of national liberation, but contemporary observers saw them as bandits, or at best as being related to the partisans, or light troops, employed in the mainland European wars to forage or to harass the enemy in highly mobile operations. As such, they were useful to regular military forces, but were nevertheless despised by them. Edward Ward thought that the professions of partisan fighter and highwayman were exactly interchangeable.[43]

The prominence of rapparees increased as order began to break down following the Battle of the Boyne and dissension developed in the Jacobite forces between French and Irish officers and soldiers, and among the Irish between the adherents of Tyrconnell and the more numerous followers of Sarsfield. The involvement of rapparees in the resistance to Protestant rule was also a direct consequence of the occupation of more and more towns by the Williamite forces of General Ginkel and the harsh measures against Catholics. However, the rapparees had constituted a threat to law and order even before King James landed at Kinsale, since he issued

---

[41] *A ... History of the Northern Affairs of Ireland* (1690), 4–5; Murray (ed.), *Journal of John Stevens*, 50–1.

[42] Hewitson (ed.), *Diary of Thomas Bellingham*, 9, 82–3, 86–7, 129; *Northern Affairs of Ireland*, 6–7, 9.

[43] Story, *Continuation of the Impartial History*, 49–50; *An Exact Journal of the... Progress of their Majesties' Forces under the Command of Gen. Ginkel* (1691), 8; Griffyth, *Villare Hibernicum*, sig. D2v; [Edward Ward], *Mars Stript of his Armour: Or, the Army displayed in all its True Colours* (1709), 10–11.

a proclamation against rapparees who had been plundering his English subjects in Munster. This suggests that highwaymen or tories made up the core of rapparee bands in 1689, and they were also a problem when the duke of Schomberg arrived in Antrim in 1689. Their numbers swelled even more as soldiers deserted from the Jacobite army, which found it increasingly difficult to pay and feed its troops.[44]

The rapparees were particularly troublesome to the Williamite forces when they went into winter quarters in 1690–1. The dispersal of Ginkel's field army into garrisons in small towns and villages made them vulnerable to raids by rapparees, who would at the very least steal the Williamites' horses and cattle. They also provided useful intelligence to the Jacobite army, and, making use of the cover of woods and bogs, were able to maintain a good communications system and disappear at will. If pursuers were too close, the rapparees would lie down in brooks with only their noses sticking out, and they knew how to hide their weapons by submerging their muskets, first removing the firelocks and stopping up the muzzle and touch-hole. In this way the rapparees tied down more and more of Ginkel's forces. Hitherto, the rapparees had operated in small bands, but during the winter of 1690–1 they formed larger groups and maintained permanent base camps. One camp near Kilbeggan sheltered more than 2,000 rapparees, who lived in cabins and huts. As members of the partisans increased, they would gather on the hills within sight of the Williamite forces and perform acts of bravado then flee into the bogs and woods. On one occasion English forces pursued them to their camp, killed fifty of them and burnt their huts. The huge Bog of Allen also provided fortified island hiding-places for the rapparees. This bog was the largest in Ireland; it was forty miles in length, beginning only twelve miles west of Dublin and extending as far west as Athlone. Irish regulars and partisan troops sometimes operated together when raiding Williamite garrisons and camps. On one occasion, Brigadier 'Long Anthony' Carroll, leading a force of 240 horse and dragoons and 250 'volunteers' or rapparees, fell upon English reinforcements approaching the garrison town of Ballymagooly, and fought a skirmish that lasted several hours and involved three attacks on the English column. Story says that Carroll was based at the 'strong castle' of Nenagh, co. Tipperary, and could summon as many as 2,000 men when needed.[45]

The commander of the Williamite forces, General Ginkel, appears to have offered an amnesty to those rapparees who were willing to surrender. They refused, and were told that thereafter they could expect to be dealt with by martial law. Because the rapparees often mixed in with the camp-followers of the Williamite forces, all Irish, both Catholic and Protestant, were ordered to stay in their homes and all camp-followers were forbidden to follow the army, except

[44] *The Landing and Reception of the Late King James at Kinsale* (1689) [BL, 816.m. 23, no. 98], 1–2; [Story], *True and Impartial History*, 16; Wauchope, *Sarsfield*, 183–5.
[45] *Forces under... Ginkel*, 8–9; *The Taking by Storm of the English Town of Athlone* (1691), 1–2; [Story], *True and Impartial History*, 156–7; Story, *Continuation of the Impartial History*, 49–50, 58–9, 64.

licensed sutlers. Irish Catholics were put under curfew during evening hours, and
those in possession of arms were to be deemed rebels. Their cattle and horses were
confiscated, and bounties were proclaimed on the heads of priests who were
thought to be stirring up the rapparees. The lords justices and the Council in
Dublin issued a proclamation to the effect that Catholics living in districts where
rapparees operated would be deemed rebels and dealt with by martial law unless
they discovered the same to the authorities. The Williamite army began fighting
the Irish rapparees with irregular forces of their own. They employed Protestant
rapparees from the north, who had picked up their weapons on battlefields, and
members of the Protestant militia who disguised themselves and infiltrated the
Catholic rapparees. The Protestant militiamen were more severe against the rapparees than the Williamite regulars. The militiamen revived the practice of bringing in the heads of rebels, which was encouraged by the law, and was 'a custom in
that country'. The Williamite regulars also began hanging rebels after trying them
by courts martial. By contrast, when the rapparees took prisoners they preferred to
ransom the officers and keep the enlisted men in custody. When some partisans
stole some horses from a Danish cavalry regiment, the colonel threatened to hang
several villagers if the horses were not returned along with the culprits. As a result,
some of the rapparees who had taken the horses were delivered up. When captured and threatened with death, turncoat partisans would sometimes reveal the
hiding-places of their companions. In August 1691 John McCabe, 'the notorious
rapparee who ... infested the Bog of Allen', was brought to Dublin along with the
'white sergeant' and several other companions, 'where they were hanged up in
chains at the Naas'. Since McCabe and the 'white sergeant' had been dismissed
from the Jacobite army 'for some rogueries', they were considered to be under no
military discipline and therefore could be punished as common bandits. The
Treaty of Limerick of 1691 did not end the rapparee problem. Regular government forces were still employed in hunting them down as late as 1695. They were
punished under military law when caught.[46]

The campaigning season resumed in the spring of 1691. The French had
withdrawn their forces from Galway because they regarded the war as lost, although
they did send a few more ships to Limerick carrying money, provisions, clothing and
generals, but no troops. Several more sieges and battles at Athlone, Aughrim and
Galway were necessary before Ginkel could invest the main Jacobite stronghold at
Limerick on the River Shannon. The Irish officers became more disenchanted with
the French generals, who were removed, and Sarsfield, as the senior Irish general,
found himself in command. Ginkel had made several offers of generous terms in an
attempt to induce the Jacobites to surrender, and Sarsfield now realized that nothing
more could be accomplished in Ireland except to spill more blood. He believed that
Ireland could never be free of William of Orange until the remaining Jacobite forces

[46] *Forces under... Ginkel,* 3–9, 13–14; [Story], *True and Impartial History,* 152, 156–7, 161;
Story, *Continuation of the Impartial History,* 55, 58–9, 61–2, 67, 175, 229, 231; Luttrell, *RSA* iii. 423,
426, 439.

joined the French in fighting William and the members of the Grand Alliance in mainland Europe. In any case, in their present position the Irish Jacobites were becoming divided among themselves, and their army suffered numerous desertions. From Ginkel's point of view, the war effort in Flanders was not going well for William and the Confederate allies, and too many of William's soldiers were tied down in Ireland who could be better employed in the war against the French.[47]

The negotiations between Ginkel and Sarsfield led to the treaty of Limerick, signed on 3 October 1691. The main points insisted on by Sarsfield were granted. The Jacobite army would be evacuated to France, and Catholics would retain the same liberties that they enjoyed under Charles II, including freedom of worship, security of estates and the right to hold civil and military offices. William and Mary accepted the terms of the Treaty of Limerick, knowing full well that the Protestant establishment and the Irish Parliament would disallow them. Indeed, William had intended to use confiscated Irish estates to reward followers—the grant of indemnity to Jacobite combatants and the other terms of the treaty notwithstanding. Not only did the Irish Parliament disallow most of the terms of the Treaty of Limerick; something very like the Penal Laws of 1641 were revived in 1704, which curtailed freedom of worship, barred Catholics from all offices and professions, denied their children access to an education in Ireland, and prevented them from bequeathing their estates to Catholic heirs or purchasing property or even owning a horse. Jacobite combatants could retain their estates only if they abjured their religion and allegiance and swore loyalty to William and Mary. Colonel Edmund Nugent changed his allegiance to retain his estate at Carolanstown, but that did not prevent the Williamite troops who were quartered at Carolanstown from plundering his house and property, although restitution was ordered.[48]

The military articles of the Treaty of Limerick were put into effect almost immediately—thus beginning the flight of the 'Wild Geese'. English ships began providing free passage for the officers and soldiers of King James's army almost immediately, and French ships completed the process in December 1691. Rapparees who had surrendered to Ginkel were also included. The most recent estimates of those who went to France place the number at 19,000, and with women and children the total is in excess of 20,000, or approximately 1 per cent of a population of 2,200,000. George Story estimated that the total number of people who died by the sword, sickness and famine in the Williamite conquest of Ireland was 100,000 (or 4.5 per cent of the population). Story also insists that many of the Jacobite soldiers had to be constrained to board the transports when they learned that they were to be drafted into the French army; rumours also circulated that some were destined to fight the Turks in Hungary, like the soldiers from the Irish regiments disbanded at Portsmouth in 1688. Most of the soldiers who were exiled

[47] Simms, *Jacobite Ireland*, 201–49; Wauchope, *Sarsfield*, 200–62; Kane, *Campaigns of King William*, 13–14.
[48] F. McLynn, *The Jacobites* (1985), 18–19; Simms, *Jacobite Ireland*, 249–65; HEH, Stowe-Nugent MSS., 1 (57, 60).

to France were unable to contact their families, and so thousands of women and children must have been left behind in Ireland without any means of support. Some of those families that reached Cork and tried to accompany their husbands and fathers were brutally beaten back from the boats. There were more desertions from the Jacobite army at this point which the Williamite authorities did nothing to discourage, and Story observed that many of the regiments marching from Limerick to the port of embarkation at Cork were under strength.[49]

William of Orange and the Dutch Republic achieved part of their strategic aims in preventing James II's English army from going to the assistance of Louis XIV by the relatively bloodless invasion of England. The conquest of Scotland was a fairly minor diversion, although conceivably that campaign could have been more pro-tracted and difficult if Dundee had survived the Battle of Killiecrankie and recruited more Highland soldiers. The Williamite war in Ireland, however, was a major diversion of badly needed troops from the war effort of the Grand Coalition in mainland Europe; the Williamite forces were tied down in Ireland for more than two years and did not become available for the Flanders campaign or the manning of garrisons in the Netherlands until the campaigning season of 1692 was under way. William and the regents of the Dutch Republic viewed the British Isles as an important source of military manpower, yet certain policies pursued by William and the Dutch government worked against making full use of that potential

Table 15.1. George Story's estimate of military and civilian casualties in the Williamite conquest of Ireland

Irish Jacobite officers killed or died	617
Irish soldiers killed or died	12,676
Rapparees killed by Williamite army and militia	1,928
Rapparees hanged after court martial or legal process	112
Rapparees killed and summarily hanged by soldiers and others	600
Officers in the Williamite army killed in battle	140
Williamite soldiers killed in the field	2,037
Williamite soldiers killed by rapparees	800
English and foreign officers who died during the Williamite conquest	320
Soldiers of the Williamite army who died of disease and other natural causes since the landing in Ireland	7,000
Number of people who died in Ireland during the Williamite war by the sword, sickness and famine	100,000

Source: George Story, A Continuation of the Impartial History of the Wars in Ireland (1693), 317.

[49] Childs, 'Williamite War', 209; N. G. Rouffiac, 'The Irish Jacobite Exiles in France, 1692–1715', T. Barnard and J. Fenlon (eds.), The Dukes of Ormonde, 1610–1745 (2000), 195–7; Story, Continuation of the Impartial History, 237–8, 262, 264; Wauchope, Sarsfield, 277–81. For a summary of George Story's quantitative analysis of military and civilian casualties in the Williamite war, see Table 15.1.

for recruiting soldiers. Although Dutch governmental policy had favoured religious toleration in the Netherlands for military and mercantile reasons, and William had allowed at various times the presence of Catholics in the Dutch army (and, apparently, even in the force that invaded England in 1688), he became a captive of his own propaganda, depicting himself as a protector of Protestant liberties in the Three Kingdoms. This obliged him to purge Catholic officers and soldiers from his armies, many of whom would have been willing to fight for him in return for steady pay and employment. William's Protestant subjects in the Three Kingdoms rejected such a policy which had worked well enough in the States' Army. The English army had to rely heavily on the press-gang for recruitment during the Williamite and Nine Years Wars. It was only because England had a larger population than the Netherlands that it appeared attractive as a source for military manpower. At the end of the seventeenth century the English government recruited a smaller portion of its population base for military service than did the Dutch—a significant change in Dutch recruiting polices and practices since the time of Maurice of Nassau, when the Republic had preferred to recruit most of the men in its field armies from abroad. Moreover, discipline and retention of military personnel were hampered by the English government's inability to pay its soldiers in a timely fashion. The fiscal-military state may have its origins in the 1690s, but the state apparatus for making war still remained underdeveloped, and the long delays in paying the soldiers continued to cause high rates of desertion.[50]

The Williamite war and the ensuing peace settlement alienated most of the Irish population by excluding them from the political nation and declaring them unfit to render military service, and the English and Scottish governments failed to recognize the potential for recruiting soldiers in the Highlands well into the eighteenth century. The military talents of Catholic Ireland benefited only continental European armies until the nineteenth century. Moreover, William of Orange's ham-fisted personal diplomacy and his lack of interest in his British and Irish kingdoms except as sources of money and military manpower helped to encourage the Jacobite ideology of protest in those realms. Some of William's personal followers—mostly from the Anglo-Dutch and Scots Brigades—did eventually achieve high rank in the English army, but this was perhaps more due to high attrition among general officers than to William's patronage and personal encouragement. The perception among the officer class of the Three Kingdoms was that he always favoured Dutch, German and Huguenot commanders.

[50] Childs, *BAW* 102, 127–8, 144–53.

16

The Nine Years War

It is mightily to the honour of old England to hear what valiant sons she brings forth, when all foreign nations expected her past bearing courageous men.

C. Jackson (ed.), *The Diary of Abraham de la Pryme, The Yorkshire Antiquarian*, SS 54 (1870), 66.

The conduct of war thus became a true game, in which the cards were dealt by time and accident. In its effect it was a somewhat stronger form of diplomacy, a more forceful method of negotiation, in which battles and sieges were the principal notes exchanged. Even the most ambitious ruler had no greater aims than to gain a number of advantages that could be exploited at the peace conference.

Carl von Clausewitz, *On War*, trans. and ed. M. Howard and P. Paret (1976; repr. 1993), 713.

Abraham de la Pryme thought that participation in the Nine Years War restored England's martial honour. Similar pride in military success could be found throughout the British Isles among supporters of William II and III, who viewed the war as a conflict fought in defence of Protestant liberties. By 1694 the combined armies of the Three Kingdoms were approximately five times larger than Charles II's land forces had been ten years earlier. The integration of these land forces was promoted by the common experience of serving together in campaigns in Flanders and on the Rhine, and they made a substantial contribution to the victories of the armies of the Grand Alliance against King Louis XIV, such as the recapture of the fortress of Namur in 1695—the first time that a marshal of France had ever yielded territory. The English government's participation in the Nine Years War signified that English diplomatic and military priorities had shifted from preventing mainland European powers from interfering in Ireland or Scotland to obstructing the ambitions of hostile major powers on the European mainland. The English navy, which had formerly concentrated on guarding the Narrow Seas and St George's Channel, was now deployed under a blue-water strategy to the Mediterranean, the Atlantic and the Caribbean. This new strategy indicated that England had become a great power, but it required revolutionary methods of war finance and heavier taxation, caused a drain upon the economies of the British Isles and severely disrupted trade. William II and III's Confederate forces relied extensively upon British manpower and English finances. Whereas the generals of the Williamite army in Ireland were almost all foreigners, attrition among the allied general officers in the Nine Years War opened up opportunities and the experience of war bred British commanders of repute.

Despite official attempts by William's ministers to manipulate public opinion through the publication of books and pamphlets depicting the exploits of British arms, there was serious opposition to participation in the Nine Years War. Soldiers in England and Scotland were raised by impressment from a limited pool of manpower. Recruiting officers and press-gangs resorted to desperate measures, which encountered violent popular resistance and obstruction by the English Parliament and municipal authorities in both England and Scotland. Desertion rates by impressed soldiers whose pay was increasingly in arrears were high. Disapproval of both the king and the war led to Jacobite riots in London, while expressions of loyalty to the exiled king were detected among both army and navy officers. Even at the end of the Nine Years War, the purge of Catholics and Irish from the guards regiments was still less than complete. The English Parliament continued to disapprove of standing armies, and undertook a massive disbandment at the end of the Nine Years War that caused problems of lawlessness when some colonels attempted to disband their regiments without paying off their soldiers. The parliamentary move to disband occasioned a revival of the controversy about standing armies.

King William II and III saw himself as a soldier-king, and he wished others to accept him in that role in order to emphasize the significance of the wars that he was fighting on behalf of Protestant liberties. Except for the summer that he spent in Ireland, it was his habit to go into the field in Spanish Flanders at the start of every campaigning season in order to be seen by his troops and to raise their morale, even though this meant neglecting political problems in the Three Kingdoms. Because the French armies almost always outnumbered the forces of the Grand Alliance, he started the campaigning season as early as possible, before the French forces were fully provisioned and supplied, in an attempt to gain a slight advantage. This meant that he was usually absent from England from spring until early autumn. Because of the position of military command that he had assumed, he could hardly have done otherwise, since Louis XIV himself had been present in 1692 to lead the French army at the investing of Namur. The honour of each monarch was therefore at stake. William usually departed London for the Netherlands between late January and early May, and, affecting an air of nonchalance, he often allowed some time for hunting before he proceeded to his camp in the Spanish Netherlands.[1]

William exploited the opportunities for propaganda, and the War of the Grand Alliance against Louis XIV was depicted as 'a holy war by sea and land' fought to

---

[1] Edward D'Auvergne, *A Relation of . . . the Last Campaigne . . . in the Spanish Netherlands, 1692* (1693), 1; *An . . . Account of the Siege of Namur* (1695), 2.

determine 'the liberty or slavery of Europe', and a war that restored martial honour to England after a long dormancy. William himself was portrayed as a 'valiant and warlike monarch' and the 'model of a brave commander', who derived his legitimacy from his role as the 'deliverer' of the 'Reformed Church'. Books and pamphlets were published in London and Edinburgh as well as Amsterdam to rally public support for William's wars, and to remind the king's subjects that other nations would respect a country only if it had 'the best swords'.[2] Army chaplains in particular, such as John Whittel, Edward D'Auvergne and William Sawle, were among the principal propagandists who wrote on William's behalf, but not all military chaplains joined in this effort with the same enthusiasm. One anonymous wag, who claimed to be an army chaplain, gathered together what purported to be a collection of petitions from a number of chaplains claiming their right to 'brandy good store', but begging to be excused 'from preaching and fighting'. He also printed a satirical 'Proposal of the Poets to raise their Majesties a Sum of Money' by erecting 'a glory office in all the principal corporations and towns in the kingdom', in order to allow those 'ambitious of glory' to purchase it for a price, with the proceeds going to support the war effort.[3]

William's self-glorification may seem excessive, but he had need to appeal for support for his cause. A number of assassination plots were mounted against him by the marquis de Louvois, secretary of state to Louis XIV, and the duke of Berwick. The first, in 1692, was discovered in his camp in Flanders, and a French nobleman, evidently posing as a Huguenot officer, was executed after a court martial. The second, in 1696, involved disaffected soldiers in the home army, and was planned to be a signal for a Jacobite uprising and an invasion of England.[4] Certainly, one purpose of the sermons and pamphlets preached and published by military and naval chaplains was to make soldiers and sailors aware 'of disaffected persons and traitors' within their own ranks. On 11 June 1695, 'being the birthday of the pretended prince of Wales', a number of Jacobite leaders, including Sir John Fenwick and some army officers, met 'at the Dog Tavern in Drury Lane, where, with kettle drums and trumpets, &c.', they lit a bonfire and tried to force spectators to drink the prince's health. Their refusal to do so occasioned a riot. The inquiry into this tumult, together with the discovery that Fenwick was also involved in an assassination plot, later led to his trial for treason, subsequent condemnation by act of attainder and execution after the two-witness rule was dispensed with during the proceedings. That Jacobite sympathies were widespread in London is suggested by the fact that although the royal judges determined that the Jacobite rioters who participated in the tumults in Drury Lane and the

---

[2] John Whittel, *Safety in War* (1692), sig. A2, p. 10; C. Jackson (ed.), *The Diary of Abraham de la Pryme*, SS 54 (1870), 66; William Sawle, *An Impartial Relation of . . . Last Summer's Campaign in Flanders* (1691), 20–1; *An Account of the Siege of Mons* (1691), 1.

[3] *The Chaplains' Petition to the Honourable House for Redress of Grievances* (1693), 3.

[4] *A True Account of the . . . Conspiracy against the Life of his Sacred Majesty William III* (1692) [BL, 816.m.23, no. 99], 5–6; S. B. Baxter, *William III and the Defense of European Liberty, 1650–1702* (1966), 336–7; Childs, *NYW* 309–10.

Haymarket should be tried for high treason, the grand jury of Middlesex chose to indict them for misdemeanour riot. The trial jury found some of the defendants guilty, and the judge fined them, but some of the rioters, such as Sir John Fenwick, were actually acquitted of the misdemeanour charges.[5] In 1693 there were similar displays of disaffection when 'some officers of the fleet at Portsmouth drank King James's health'. In July 1697 a general muster of the army was held on Blackheath, when all 'papists and Irish' were supposed to be discharged. 'Some days since two bailiffs went thither to arrest a captain; the soldiers cut off their ears, and sent them home without their prisoner.' As late as January 1697/8, Henry Sidney, earl of Romney, and John, Lord Cutts, were commanded to turn out all of the Irish and Catholics in the First and Second Regiments of Foot Guards.[6]

During the Nine Years War the officer corps of the armies of the Three Kingdoms expanded fivefold from the last days of the reign of Charles II, and thus opened up opportunities for military careers that had not existed in the British Isles since the Wars of the Three Kingdoms. In 1684 there were 442 commissioned officers on the English establishment, 175 in the Scots army and 406 in the Irish army. The expansion of the English army under James VII and II increased that establishment to 1,869 officers, but did not significantly alter the number of officers in the Scots and Irish armies. However, by 1693–4 the number of officers in all three armies had risen to 5,000. Opportunities increased, and Robert Parker, who had joined the Williamite forces before they embarked for Ireland in 1689, finally gained a commission in the Royal Regiment of Foot of Ireland after half of his regiment died in the storming of Sulfine Abbey in Flanders during the Siege of Namur. Parker himself was wounded and spent six months recuperating.[7] It was still possible to rise through the ranks and obtain a commission in the British armies and the corps serving in mainland European armies in the late seventeenth century, but gentlemen volunteers and cadets found that it took much longer to do so—even when large-scale conflicts such as the Nine Years War furnished new opportunities. Increasingly, the choicest military offices went to those with court connections and patronage. This was a consequence of the remilitarization of the aristocracies of the Three Kingdoms—especially that of England.[8]

Of all officer ranks that of colonel was perhaps the most highly politicized, because one needed a powerful patron to purchase a colonelcy, and the office was often used as a stepping-stone to a seat in Parliament. Each needed a constituency, and the distinction between an enlistment bounty and a thinly disguised bribe or political favour was largely metaphysical. The most important difference was that voters were freeholders, and recruits were usually propertyless, young unmarried men. Ned Ward's sardonic opinion was that a colonel was 'a very good man'

---

[5] Whittle, *Safety in War*, 12; Luttrell, *RSA* iii. 483–4, 486–7, 489; J. Garrett, *The Triumphs of Providence: The Assassination Plot, 1696* (1980), 72–3, 250–5; D. Szechi, *The Jacobites: Britain and Europe, 1688–1788* (1994), 55–6.   [6] Luttrell, *RSA* iii. 178; iv. 250, 600.

[7] Childs, *BAW* 37; Robert Parker, *Memoirs of the Most Remarkable Military Transactions* (1747), 55–6.

[8] Manning, *Swordsmen*, 117, 132–3.

because he set the idle and poor to work, clothed and fed them, and shielded them from creditors.[9] Certainly, a colonel was nothing if not a political animal. His primary job was recruiting, and his understanding of political issues was necessary to recruit and motivate his men. There survives the complete text of a speech given by a colonel to his regiment just before they sailed for Flanders. If the speech was addressed not just to the officers but to the soldiers as well, which seems to have been the case, the colonel assumes a considerable degree of political sophistication on the part of his rank and file, and further assumes that they will be familiar with many political and economic issues such as excise taxes and the nature of individual liberties, which he discusses. He also takes for granted that they will have a fairly detailed knowledge of Jacobite propaganda, which he must try to counteract with reasonable arguments. The colonel appeals to both their sense of sacrifice and their desire for gain: 'To us is granted the inestimable advantages of being taught and continually practising the military discipline of marching, watching, fasting, nay, and starving too, which is the perfection and consummation of the utmost art of war. To us is given to divide the rich and heavy spoils of our enemies by means of those constant victories to which we have, and . . . still hope to be led on by the courage and conduct of our invincible monarch.'[10]

James Butler, second duke of Ormonde, did not have to spend long years in the ranks to become an officer. He was a cousin of William of Orange by reason of his descent from Maurice of Nassau, and had accompanied John Churchill in deserting James II in November 1688. Ormonde was a cavalry officer and commanded the Second Troop of Life Guards. William made him general of the horse in Flanders and, for a time, brought him over to Ireland to help raise troops. He gave a good account of himself at the Battle of Landen in 1693, where he commanded from the front. Ormonde was captured by the French, but was exchanged for the duke of Berwick. While in Flanders, Ormonde maintained a lavish table, and his quarters became a place of resort for British officers. This princely hospitality was more appropriate to the social rank of duke than his military rank of general, and exceeded the level of entertainment provided by King William, who regarded such lavishness as effeminate, but tolerated it in Ormonde despite complaints and warnings by jealous rivals. Ormonde's motive for this hospitality seems to have been a desire to increase the prestige of the British army. He probably spent £4,500 a year on such entertainments, while his duchess, Emelia van Beverwart, who was also descended from the House of Nassau, was spending approximately the same amount in London. Although Ormonde later became a Jacobite during the reign of Queen Anne, he remained loyal to William, who always trusted him.[11]

---

[9] [Edward Ward], *Mars strip't of his Armour: Or, the Army displayed in all its True Colours* (1709), 7.
[10] *A . . . Speech made by an English Colonel to his Regiment* (1691), 8–9.
[11] T.B., *The Life . . . of James Butler, Late Duke . . . of Ormond* (1729), sigs. C4v–D1r, D3v–D4v, pp. 25–8; *Memoirs of the Life of . . . James, late Duke of Ormond* (1738), 47–9, 85; [Daniel Defoe], *An Account of . . . James Butler (late Duke of Ormond)* (1715), 35–6; T. C. Barnard, 'Aristocratic Values in

Ormonde tried to win respect for British officers by hospitality and diplomacy, but others were less circumspect in their criticism of King William because of the preference shown to foreign officers. Sir Charles O'Hara (later Lord Tyrawley), a lieutenant-colonel in the First Foot Guards, complained that the Dutch Blue Guards were treated preferentially and received higher pay than the English guards. William Sawle, an army chaplain, repeated a rumour current in the English camps in Flanders that the Dutch cavalry troopers were cowards, and that the Dutch would not dare fight the French without help from England.[12] Thomas Tollmache was also favoured by William because he was well born (his mother was Elizabeth Murray, countess of Dysart and duchess of Lauderdale), and he had served briefly in the Anglo-Dutch Brigade and accompanied William in his descent on England. William rewarded him with the colonelcy of the Coldstream Guards and also made him a major-general in Flanders. Tollemache also came to believe that William treated foreign officers preferentially. He threatened to resign his commission, and it required a two-hour session with Tollemache and a promotion to lieutenant-general before William could persuade him to rescind his resignation. Tollemache's dislike of foreign officers was only increased by his perception of mismanagement by William's cousins and favourites, Count Solms and the prince of Waldeck, at the Battle of Steenkirk (Steenkerke) in 1692.[13]

The campaign of 1693 in Flanders had gone badly, and William suffered major defeats at Landen and Charleroi. Public opinion began to question the competence not only of the Dutch generals but of William himself. 'King William's War' disrupted the English economy, soldiers and sailors remained unpaid for months at a time and privateers from Dunkirk and Brest raided English commerce. Tollemache sensed that a number of high-ranking military and naval officers wished to demonstrate that they could manage without Dutch William. Moreover, the English Parliament tended to favour a blue-water naval strategy rather than continuing to pour money into the bottomless pit of William's Grand Coalition in the Spanish Netherlands. The idea was that if the Royal Navy made 'descents' on the long coast of France, Louis XIV would be obliged to withdraw troops from Flanders to fortify and defend that coastline. Tollemache suggested a raid on the port of Brest. This was the first military operation mounted during the reign of King William III where English general officers outnumbered foreigners. Tollemache was to command the land forces and Peregrine Osborne, marquis of Carmarthen, admiral of the Blue, would be responsible for the naval side of this amphibious operation. The raid was meant to be a surprise attack, but the French knew about it two months in advance, and so Vauban, the great French military engineer, had time to improve the harbour defences of Brest. Consequently, the landing party could not hold the

the Careers of the Dukes of Ormonde', T. Barnard and J. Fenlon (eds.), *The Dukes of Ormonde, 1610–1745* (2000), 161, 170.

[12] BL, Add. MS. 9,723 [Blathwayt Papers], fos. 93–4; Sawle, *Impartial Relation*, preface, p. 2.

[13] Childs, *Profession of Arms*, 90; E. P. H. Tollemache, *The Tollemaches of Helmingham and Ham* (1949), 72–8.

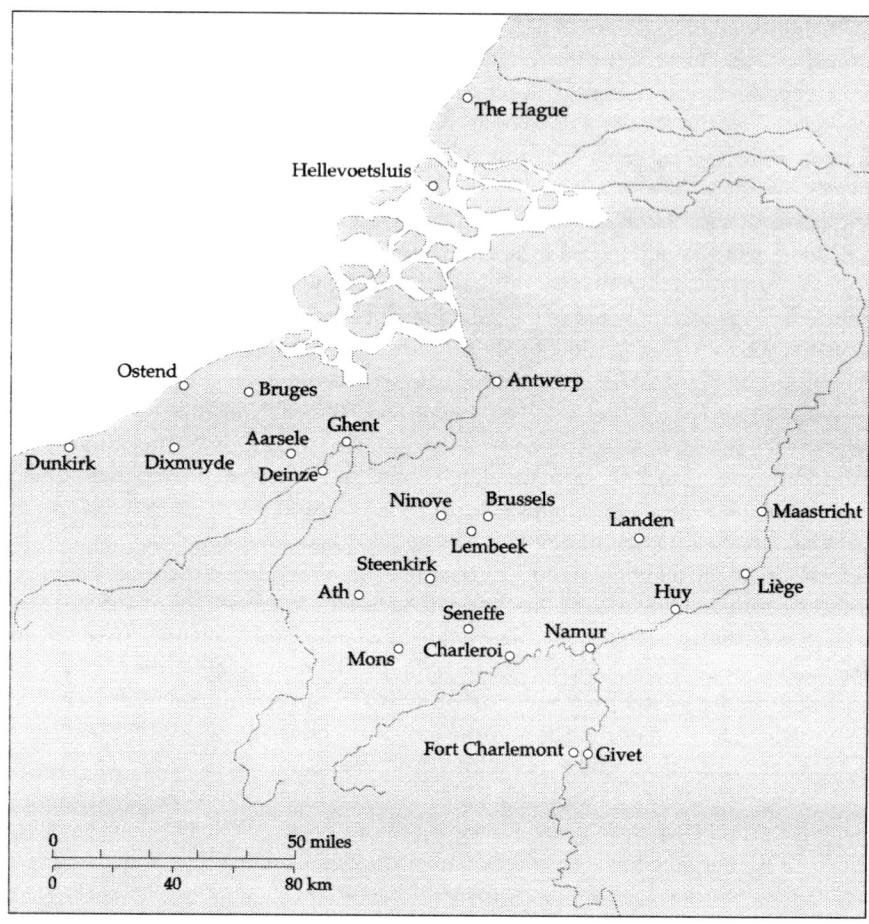

Map 16.1. The Spanish Netherlands during the Nine Years War

beachhead; Tollemache was fatally wounded, and the soldiers had to withdraw. Tollemache was blamed by some for the failure, but this was a difficult amphibious operation, and the earl of Romney as master-general of the ordnance, failed to dispatch the bomb vessels and store ships in a timely fashion.[14]

The most ambitious of the English general officers was John Churchill, earl of Marlborough. He had led a successful expedition that captured Kinsale and Cork in 1690. He was already the highest-ranking officer in the English army, but he wanted more. He demanded the rank of captain-general, command of the English

[14] Childs, *NYW* 246; id., *BAW* 209–37; Tollemache, *Tollemaches of Helmingham and Ham*, 77–82; Peregrine Osborne, marquis of Carmarthen and duke of Leeds, *A Journal of the Brest Expedition* (1694), sig. A2, pp. 6, 15, 18–19, 35–6, 42, 46.

forces in Flanders and a dukedom as well as a knighthood of the garter. Marlborough's insistence that English troops should be commanded only by English officers was politically popular, but also self-serving. King William regarded him as a person of inferior social status who could not possibly talk to such exalted princes as the electors of Bavaria and Hanover or the duke of Württemberg, and they certainly would not have spoken to him. William chose to exercise the office of captain-general of the English army himself, and he did not trust Marlborough and kept him at arm's length. Marlborough may not have been a great general, but his extraordinary diplomatic skills held the allied coalition together in the next reign. Ailesbury thought that had any other general presided over the Grand Alliance, the Dutch and English armies would have come to blows.[15] The political sentiment that British soldiers should be commanded only by British officers was widely shared. In March 1700/1 the House of Commons resolved that no person, not born in the British Isles or not born of English, Irish or Scottish parents, could hold a military office or be granted lands in the Three Kingdoms.[16]

By joining the Grand Alliance during the Nine Years War, England committed itself to a 'double-forward policy' of deploying most of the military forces of the Three Kingdoms to Flanders, the main but not the only theatre of war, and its navy to the Mediterranean, the Atlantic and the Caribbean, which made some very nervous about the vulnerability of the British Isles to invasion. This policy was thought to be damaging to English trade, and no European country except perhaps the Netherlands had ever attempted such risky strategy. English armies and navies had to be supplied from contractors overseas rather than from home, and English trade overseas was not yet sufficient to cover the cost of food and supplies purchased outside England. Beginning in 1689, the English Parliament was asked not only to subsidize allied armies in the Low Countries, but also to repay the loan of £600,000 made by the Dutch States General to finance William of Orange's invasion of England. Six Scottish regiments were sent to Flanders as soon as the First Jacobite Rebellion was crushed in the Highlands, and at least two English regiments were posted to the Rhine to assist the Confederate forces besieging the French-held citadel of Mainz. The build-up of British troops in Flanders began as early as 1691, while the Williamite war continued in Ireland. The campaigning season of 1691 began with the French siege of Mons en Hainault (Bergen or Berg Henow) close to the French border, and the English government sent nine guards and line battalions (or fewer than 10,000 men)— less than a quarter of the Allied forces—which was increased to three squadrons of horse and perhaps fourteen battalions of foot by the end of the campaigning season. However, the French had increased their field forces at Mons to 70,000 by the time that the city surrendered at the end of March. That discipline in the English

---

[15] Baxter, *William III*, 298–300; Thomas Bruce, earl of Ailesbury and Elgin, *Memoirs*, 2 vols., RC 21 (1890), ii. 541.   [16] Luttrell, *RSA* v. 24.

army was not all it could have been is revealed by Edward D'Auvergne's description of the practice of 'pickering' by individual gentlemen volunteers from the English and French horse, who broke formation, rode to the front line and fired pistols at one another.[17]

The completion of the Williamite conquest of Ireland freed all of the British forces for deployment in the Low Countries except for a small home army. The British army in Flanders grew to 21,000 during the 1692 campaigning season, and the English Parliament was asked to subsidize an additional contingent of 19,000 foreign troops—mainly from Denmark, Hanover and Wolfenbüttel. Smaller subsidies went to Saxony, Hesse-Cassel, Bavaria, Brandenburg-Prussia and Imperial Austria. William hoped to be able to field an army of 100,000 men in Brabant and Flanders. The French possessed an army of nearly 84,000 men in Flanders, but they could easily reinforce that army from other parts of the Spanish Netherlands, France and Lorraine, including a corps of 12,000 Irish and 12,000 French reserved for the invasion of England. Altogether, the French possessed 120,000 men in the Low Countries. William was able to concentrate 78,000 troops to defend Namur, a citadel built in 1679 at the confluence of the Sambre and Meuse (Maas) rivers by the famed Dutch military engineer Menno, baron van Coehoorn. Although William enjoyed a slight numerical superiority over the French force of 60,000 at Namur, his camp was stretched out over a considerable distance, and both sides were plagued by heavy rains, which turned the boggy grounds along the rivers into a sea of mud. The French Siege of Namur prevailed, and the citadel surrendered. The French had the advantage of being able to supply their troops more conveniently by means of the Rivers Sambre and Meuse, which flowed out of France past Namur. Warfare in the late seventeenth century had become a kind of game where important fortified towns were besieged and captured to reduce the possibility of marauding enemy parties destroying the other army's foraging area or, later, to present as bargaining-chips at a peace conference. At the same time, the loss of a fortress such as Namur was a severe blow to William's prestige.[18]

William's strategic aims were to keep Louis XIV out of the Spanish Netherlands so that it could continue to function as a buffer zone between the Dutch Republic and France, and to compel Louis to recognize his claim to the Three Kingdoms. The subordinate military strategy was defensive: to keep Louis from advancing on the Netherlands and to bleed France white in terms of manpower and treasure—in other words, a war of attrition. Other than that, William's generals were remarkably devoid of strategic imagination. The huge armies were difficult to manoeuvre because of the many rivers, streams and boggy land to be crossed.

---

[17] D. W. Jones, *War and Economy in the Age of William III and Marlborough* (1988), 7–8, 16, 28, 30, 32–5, 64–5; A. Crichton, *The Life and Diary of Lieut.-Col. J. Blackader of the Cameronian Regiment* (1824), 107–9; *An Exact Diary of the Siege of Ments* [Mainz] (1689), 12; Edward D'Auvergne, *The History of the Campagne in Flanders for the Year 1691* (1735), 28, 32, 42–7, 50, 58, 115.

[18] Jones, *War and Economy*, 7–8; Childs, *BAW* 243–68; id., *NYW* 178–92.

The rival armies mostly remained in semi-permanent camps that were very difficult to keep provisioned and supplied. In 1691, while camped at Lembeek, George Frederick, prince of Waldeck, who commanded the Confederate army while William III was in Ireland, refused a challenge to do battle from the French commander, François-Henri de Montmorency, duc de Luxembourg and marshal of France, because he knew that the latter had destroyed all of the fodder in the area, and he would therefore have to do without cavalry and artillery and would have difficulty sustaining an army on the plain of Cambron in the Somme Valley. The Allied generals were also divided in their councils—not only with regard to strategy, but also concerning who would have the posts of honour in such a battle. Moreover, the Confederate army of 56,000, which had found their encampment a 'garden' when they arrived, had, after three weeks, 'made the country like a desert', so they had to move to another encampment. The opposing armies did not engage in battle without mutual consent, and very soon both had to retire to their winter quarters because they had consumed everything in the district.[19]

In the campaigning season of 1693 William's field army consisted of fifty-two battalions of foot, of which twenty-five were British, but only four of the thirteen general officers were British. William had chosen a campsite on the banks of Landen Beek or Brook, a tributary of the River Demer near Liège, where fodder was readily available. It was also William's policy to bring fodder from Holland, because he did not wish to arouse the hostility of the peasants by sending out foraging parties. Moreover, his army was much troubled by desertions, and executions of those caught occurred daily. However, the site of William's camp at Neerlanden was unsuitable for him to manoeuvre his army for defensive purposes, and Marshal Luxembourg attacked him on 18/28 July. Although he had been advised to retire to a more defensible position, William refused. The Allied army came off badly and lost 12,000 men—one-fifth of its strength—while the French army suffered as many as 15,000 casualties. The French could make up the losses more readily than the Confederates, and William failed to relieve Charleroi, which the French captured. This enabled the French army to straighten out a salient and strengthen their lines of defence.[20] The following summer James Drummond, fourth earl of Perth, visited the battlefield at Landen and found the site still strewn with 'heads and bones of limbs, skeletons of horses, old hats, shoes, holsters and saddles...'. He also found that the red poppies of Flanders crowded out the grain in cultivated fields, while the uncultivated ground appeared to be carpeted with a 'scarlet sheet' well fertilized by the blood spilled the previous year.[21]

[19] Sawle, *Impartial Relation*, 16–17.

[20] Edward D'Auvergne, *The History of the Last Campagne in the Spanish Netherlands, 1693* (1693), 19–21, 28; *A Relation of the Battel of Landen* (1693) [BL, 816.m.23, no. 100], 1–2; Childs, *NYW* 233–46.

[21] W. Jerden (ed.), *Letters from James Earl of Perth ... to his Sister, the Countess of Errol*, CS OS 33 (1845), 28.

Having suffered severe defeats at Landen and Charleroi in 1693, the allies began the campaign of 1694 with larger forces. It was agreed that the armies of the Grand Alliance would raise 93,635 men. The armies of the Three Kingdoms would furnish 29,100 and the English Parliament would subsidize another 27,209. This obliged Louis XIV to increase the size of his army for reasons of prestige, but it put a heavy strain on the French economy, and there were severe shortages of food not only in France and the Spanish Netherlands, but in England and the Dutch Republic as well. The productive farmlands of the Spanish Netherlands—especially Brabant—had been pillaged and spoiled for five years by the Confederate and French armies, and the peasants had given up in despair. William II and III issued an order forbidding, upon pain of death, any marauding of the countryside or molesting of any victuallers, provision merchants or sutlers. There was little to be gained from foraging, and William's armies lost too many troops by desertion or capture by the enemy. The French could not afford to be as fastidious, because they lacked provisions and their soldiers were not adequately paid, so they sent out foraging parties as large as 1,200 cavalry accompanied by horse artillery. Many French soldiers took the opportunity to desert and become prisoners of the Allies. Louis XIV put out peace-feelers, but since he remained unwilling to recognize William II and III's title to the crowns of the Three Kingdoms, the English government was uninterested in negotiating. The shortage of provisions and fodder restricted the campaigning of the Allies, and only one major action was undertaken. The castle of Huy was recaptured from the French, but the British forces took no part in this operation.[22]

When the campaigning season of 1695 began in May, food shortages and economic distress obliged the French army to assume a defensive posture. Louis continued peace negotiations, and expressed a willingness to recognize William's title to the Three Kingdoms, but at the same time continued to encourage the Jacobites. The Allied armies in the Spanish Netherlands established three great camps at Aarsele, Dixmuide and Ninove with a view to reducing the town and citadel of Namur, and thus damaging the reputation of French arms. Louis XIV did not believe that the Allies could succeed, even though they had concentrated 110,000 troops for that purpose. Louis staked his honour on the outcome, and appointed Louis-François, duc de Boufflers and marshal of France, to command at Namur. The Allied armies could not expect to defeat the French army because of its size and quality, and could hope for no more than to try and hold the line in Spanish Flanders until Louis XIV sued for peace. If successful, the reduction of Namur would produce a symbolic victory in this stalemate war, and would keep Louis tied down and thus limit the mischief he could do elsewhere.[23]

[22] Edward D'Auvergne, *The History of the Campagne in the Spanish Netherlands, 1694* (1694), 2, 26–31, 35–43, 52, 83–4; Jones, *War and Economy*, 30; Childs, *NYW* 250–2, 259–61; id., *BAW* 268.
[23] Edward D'Auvergne, *The History of the Campaign in Flanders for the Year, 1695* (1696), 11–18, 26, 40.

The investment of Namur began 1 June 1695 (n.s.), when 40,000 pioneers recruited in Brabant began to construct lines of circumvallation and contravallation, and to build pontoon bridges across the Sambre and Meuse. The siege was directed by Baron van Coehoorn, the Dutch engineer-general, whose skill in directing the operations was thought by some to exceed that of the great French military engineer Sebastien le Prestre de Vauban. The French garrison of Namur consisted of twenty-one battalions of foot and eight regiments of dragoons. The Allied forces, when assembled, mustered ninety battalions of infantry, and could call upon 149 squadrons of horse and dragoons. The British contingent at Namur included seventeen battalions of English and Scots infantry. A French relief column was making its way slowly towards Namur, but was distracted by the desire to exact vengeance on the countryside—even 'without having any regard to the religious houses'. By 18 July the Allied armies had fought their way through Vauban's outer fortifications, and five battalions of English and Dutch guards attacked the Brussels Gate of Namur. On this occasion, the French suffered 1,600 casualties. The general assault on Namur began on 3 August, and after enduring a terrible bombardment and a siege lasting two weeks, the French surrendered the town the following day. Most of the terms that the French asked for were granted, but at the formal yielding of the citadel on 1 September, Marshal Boufflers was arrested by order of William III because the Allied soldiers at Deinze and Dixmuide had been detained and ill-treated by the French, contrary to the terms of surrender of those camps when they capitulated. Boufflers was not released until the Allied prisoners at Deinze and Dixmuide were freed and a number of Allied prisoners of war who had been compelled to take service in the French army were discharged.[24]

The Allied reduction of Namur in 1695 brought much credit and glory to the armies of the Grand Alliance, and William III did not miss the opportunity to claim most of the credit. The lords justices, his deputies in London, were told to proclaim a day of public celebration. William still regarded the senior officers of the British forces with contempt, and it must be admitted that many of them were corrupt and mediocre. However, Bishop Burnet thought that 'the subaltern officers and soldiers gave hopes of a better race that was growing up, and supplied the errors and defects of their senior officers'.[25] Louis XIV was in no position to retake the fortress of Namur, nor could he make up his losses in Piedmont, and his Mediterranean fleet at Toulon could not put to sea because of a British blockade. Yet he was still determined to compel the Allied powers to make peace on his own terms, and so, in 1696, in order 'to keep up the glory of his arms', he increased the size of his army by nearly fifty regiments. The French government also started circulating rumours that they were preparing to invade England, and to lend credibility to that threat they began building transports and floating batteries and

---

[24] *Siege of Namur*, 10, 12, 14–15, 17–18, 21–2, 24, 44, 51, 56; Childs, *NYW* 282–96; Gilbert Burnet, bishop of Salisbury, *History of His Own Time*, ed. M. J. Routh, 6 vols. (1833; repr. 1969), iv. 274–5. [25] Burnet, *History*, iv. 274–5.

organizing assassination plots against William. The English generals and admirals gave little credence to these rumours because the French navy was short of warships, but the fear of invasion coupled with the possibility of a Jacobite rising did oblige William to return twenty regiments to England as insurance against a French descent. Ten of them were subsequently returned to Spanish Flanders, when the French invasion and a Jacobite rebellion failed to materialize. During the campaigning season of 1696 the Allies did mount a daring raid deep into French territory, where they attacked an important French magazine at Givet near Fort Charlemont on the River Meuse. Here the Allied troops destroyed all of the hay and straw, making it very difficult for the French army to operate with cavalry and artillery. The French had to dissipate time and effort foraging, which decreased their effective troop strength, while the Allies could obtain fodder locally or from Holland by water. This constituted another severe blow to Louis XIV's prestige.[26]

Despite the symbolic victories at Namur and Givet, the forces of the Grand Alliance were usually overwhelmed in the field, and the Allies did no better than to hold the line in the Spanish Netherlands. The duke of Savoy had signed a separate peace, and German troops had to be withdrawn from the Low Countries to reinforce the Rhine defences. The Spanish resistance to the French advance on Barcelona would have collapsed had it not been for the timely arrival of an English naval expedition. The Imperialists still had the Turks to contend with on their southern flank. Just as the German princes began to withdraw from the Low Countries, Marshal Nicholas Catinat, one of France's best generals, was enabled by peace on the Italian front to bring his army of 40,000 men to the Spanish Netherlands. The three French armies that Louis XIV planned to deploy in the Spanish Netherlands totalled almost 145,000 men, while William III could barely hope to field more than 104,000. Even that number would be very difficult to sustain in the field, because England and the Dutch Republic had been reduced to a state of financial exhaustion. William was determined to be the first in the field in order to occupy the best of a limited number of campsites with access to water and fodder and deny them to the French, but this imposed great hardship on the British troops since they lacked adequate clothing. Despite the fact that William had pawned his jewels to pay his soldiers, they were receiving only half-pay at best. Although Louis XIV was in the stronger position, he was concerned about the declining health of the childless King Charles II of Spain, as he intended to put forward a claim for a Bourbon succession to the Spanish throne and possession of the Spanish Netherlands. He calculated that pressing such a claim would be easier in time of peace than war. Thus, Louis XIV was willing to negotiate a peace settlement, but desired at least one more bargaining-chip. Since Namur was too well defended, the French military leadership decided to lay siege to the Castle of Ath on the River Dender, even as the peace commissioners were beginning their

---

[26] Edward D'Auvergne, *The History of the Campagne in Flanders . . . 1696* (1696), 2–4, 10, 13, 16–17, 20, 29–30, 34–6, 42–5; Childs, *NYW* 310–11.

negotiations at the Palace of Rijswijk near The Hague. Vauban had strengthened the defences of Ath when the castle had been in French hands, and it was he who directed the siege in 1697. Vauban began bombarding Ath with heavy batteries on 17/27 May, and Ath capitulated in less than a month. William had decided not to go to the relief of Ath, but rather to position his troops to hold the line against a possible French advance on Brussels. A peace treaty was finally agreed that recognized William II and III as king of England, Ireland and Scotland, but left his German and Spanish allies to their own devices. No territory changed hands, but the Allies kept everything they had fought to defend except Strasbourg. The fruits of victory largely accrued to William, and were no more tangible then the personal prestige that he had gained. France's position as the dominant power had not been diminished. The recognition of William's title to the Three Kingdoms turned out to be nearly worthless, and the Peace of Rijswijk provided only a brief truce before the War of Spanish Succession began four years later. The Nine Years War may have resulted in a draw, but William was the winner in terms of martial prestige. His reputation as a soldier-king spread throughout Europe, and England had achieved great-power status during his reign.[27]

The outcome of wars, battles and sieges had long been thought to depend upon Divine Providence, or, at least, victorious rulers and generals such as William of Orange and Cromwell had promoted a providential explanation of historical events. However, as Carl von Clausewitz pointed out, by the end of the seventeenth century war had come to be viewed as a kind of game, and the outcome was determined by accident or chance. Certainly, the intellectual currents of the late seventeenth century promoted a more rational analysis of war. War had been regarded as an art by Renaissance writers such Machiavelli, but it was coming to be studied as a science by the time of Nine Years War. War, as it was practised during the late sixteenth and seventeenth centuries, consisted of numerous sieges of fortified places, while pitched battles occurred less frequently. The admirers of military engineers liked to think that they could build impregnable fortresses, but there really was no such thing, as the two sieges of Namur demonstrated after the citadel and its outlying fortifications had been built and rebuilt by the two best military engineers in the world—Coehoorn and Vauban. No modern professional commander would undertake a siege of a fortified place unless there was an excellent chance of carrying it through in one campaigning season. Public opinion, informed by the detailed reports of battles and sieges by the likes of William Sawle and Edward D'Auvergne, came to recognize this, and as Daniel Defoe noted, wagering on the length and outcome of sieges became a popular craze in the 1690s. There were, of course, plenty of confidence-tricksters who took advantage of this betting fever, but as Defoe remarked, a more respectable form of wagering on sieges appeared when it became 'a branch of assurances', as the insurance business was called in the 1690s. More than £200,000 was thought to have been

[27] Edward D'Auvergne, *The History of the Campagne in Flanders . . . 1697* (1698), 2, 13, 22–5, 35–42, 58–9, 71; Childs, *NYW* 331–41; Baxter, *William III*, 354–60.

wagered on the outcome of the second Siege of Limerick. Jacobites recognized that the wagering craze also presented opportunities for subversive propaganda. In March 1691 a trooper from the earl of Oxford's Regiment, masquerading as a Dutch officer, rode through the streets of London spreading the rumour that 'Mons was relieved by King William; 'tis said he was employed by some of the Jacobites to encourage the Williamites to lay wagers that Mons was not taken'. This was regarded by the government as seditious, and in April 1691 the attorney-general prosecuted wagerers for spreading rumours that the Jacobites were likely to recapture Cork, and that James II would be restored. In December 1692 the lord mayor of London forbade wagering on the outcome of sieges, and prohibited assurance offices from accepting such wagers. This came after considerable amounts of money had been bet on the French Siege of Namur during the previous campaigning season.[28]

As England was drawn into the Grand Alliance and the first of a long series of wars with France lasting a century-and-a-quarter, the English government was called upon to make larger and larger contributions of military manpower and money. The financial and material effort required in the 1690s came close to overwhelming the economy, and required the government to develop an administrative and financial apparatus for making war on a large scale and for prolonged periods of time. This was a difficult task, because the responsibility for organizing and administering the war effort was divided and dispersed among a war secretary, who was responsible for the infantry and cavalry and took his orders directly from the sovereign, who acted as his own captain-general; the master-general of the ordnance; the paymaster-general; the Treasury, which organized provisioning; and of course the Admiralty Board. The English Parliament was asked to pay for the costs of the Nine Years War, and understandably the MPs had an interest in ascertaining how their subsidies were being spent. William III never had the time or inclination to promote army reforms, although he knew that they were badly needed. The reports of the parliamentary accounts commissioners reveal their frustration in trying to hold these various military administrators accountable for how they spent the monies appropriated by Parliament. The accounts were not presented in the form prescribed by Parliament, the pay warrants always seemed to exceed the number of effective soldiers revealed by the muster rolls, regiments were transferred from the Scottish military establishment to that of England, and regiments that were supposed to be disbanded turned up in Ireland in ways which mocked parliamentary authorization, and the paymaster-general and the regimental agents were guilty of corrupt practices and extorted exorbitant profits from their offices. From time to time Parliament tried to impose reforms on the military administration. In 1691 legislation was introduced to prevent false musters and dead-pays—practices long tolerated in the military forces of the

---

[28] Carl von Clausewitz, *On War*, trans. and ed. M. Howard and P. Paret (1976; repr. 1993), 713; [Daniel Defoe], *An Essay on Projects* (1697), 171–2, 175–7; Luttrell, *RSA* ii. 202, 207, 473, 633; Garrett, *Triumphs of Providence*, 73–4.

Three Kingdoms. Another provision would have exempted from military punishment privates and non-commissioned officers who deserted the army if they could prove that their pay was more than forty days in arrears. This amendment was later dropped—presumably after someone explained to the members of the Upper House how quickly this provision could destroy an army. Members of Parliament wanted very much to gain some control over William III's army, but they did not know which end of the beast to grab.[29]

The population of England in the 1690s was not yet large enough to yield a pool of military manpower that could be exploited without resorting to violent, illegal and unpopular methods of recruiting. Out of a population of approximately 5½ million in the 1690s, England and Wales probably possessed something like 462,000 physically fit men between the ages of 16 and 40 who could be persuaded to volunteer for military service or who could be impressed without raising the ire of a family head of sufficient wealth and status to appeal to the authorities. Although Ireland and Scotland provided additional reservoirs of military manpower, the main burden of finding soldiers for the British forces continued to fall upon England, because Irish Catholics were officially excluded, and Irish Protestant regiments and Scottish Highlanders were regarded as being susceptible to Jacobite propaganda. The peoples of the British Isles remained insular in outlook, and it was difficult to persuade them that Louis XIV's ambitions posed a serious threat to their liberties. By contrast, a century and more of living close to powerful and threatening armies in the southern Low Countries had changed the Dutch, who had not possessed a martial tradition in the time of William I and Maurice of Nassau, into a nation which, while possessing a population less than half that of England and Wales, raised an army in the time of William II and III that included more native soldiers than the English military establishment.[30]

Other than to attempt to inculcate a fear of Louis XIV and the French, the English and Scottish governments did nothing in the way of persuading patriotic young men to volunteer for the army. William Sawle, an army chaplain with Robert Hodge's Regiment of Foot, tried to make military service in Flanders look attractive by assuring his readers that living in a tent in the summer was very pleasant, but he could think of little that was tangible except the remote possibility that a private soldier might get a share of 'the spoils and plunder of the field'. Military service was originally a mark of free status, but during the seventeenth century soldiers who were not gentlemen volunteers were recruited from marginal social groups, and were regarded as persons who had been deprived of free status by a kind of bonded servitude. This was because until the end of the reign of William II and III there was no time-limit on service in the English army, and

---

[29] Jones, *War and Economy*, 1–21; A. Corvisier, *Armies and Societies in Europe, 1494–1789*, trans. A. T. Siddall (1979), 76; HMC, *Thirteenth Report*, Appendix, Pt. V (House of Lords) (1892), 400; *Fourteenth Report*, Pt. VI (House of Lords) (1894), pp. iii–iv, 62.

[30] Childs, *BAW* 102, 127; R. E. Scouller, *The Armies of Queen Anne* (1966), 125, 293.

soldiers served at the king's pleasure. Except in a few cases, no man could quit the king's army without permission without committing the crime of desertion, which was a felony. There were a few instances of limited-service enlistments in the army of the East India Company or the Tangier garrison. An Act of the Scottish Estates of 1696 authorizing forced enlistment also specified limited terms of three years. Otherwise, the usual lawful way of leaving the army was the same way one got out of indentured servitude—by buying one's way out.[31]

Little is known concerning the motivation of those who volunteered to enlist in the army other than gentlemen volunteers, who apparently only committed themselves to one campaigning season at a time. We do, however, possess a detailed account of one 'brisk, genteel fellow' who was bold enough to speak up after his colonel had concluded a speech just before his regiment embarked for Flanders. He states that he enlisted for seven years, and, despite being described as 'genteel' (which may have been a sarcasm), it seems doubtful that he was accepted as being a gentleman. He states that he was born the son of an English yeoman who possessed an income of £80 per year, who now called himself a gentleman, and had sought to raise him as a gentleman by sending him to school and to Cambridge University. But the increase in taxes since King William's wars began had become extremely burdensome to his father, and he could no longer continue at Cambridge. So, he went home and found that the standard of comfort in his parish had declined to such an extent as a consequence of the disruption of trade that many honest tradesmen were reduced to living on a diet of garlic, onions and cabbage. He had considered becoming a 'knight of the pad', that is, a highwayman, or joining a 'company of clippers and coiners', or counterfeiters, but he noticed that many such young gentlemen 'made the trip up High Holborn [to Tyburn]'. He also thought of going to Wapping and trying his fortune at sea, but found that there was little trade because the crews of ships had been impressed into the navy, leaving many widows and orphans cursing 'press masters, the Navy Office and . . . Whitehall and Kensington [Palace, William III's favourite residence]'. The young volunteer insisted that he joined the army only for bread and pay: 'It was necessity which brought me hither; I neither regard the justice nor injustice of the cause; I neither fight for King William nor against King James.' He only promised loyalty to the colonel of the regiment, whom he said enjoyed a good reputation among his men.[32]

---

[31] Sawle, *Impartial Relation*, 13–14, 20–1; Corvisier, *Armies and Societies*, 36; C. Walton, *History of the British Standing Army, 1660–1700* (1894), 486–7.

[32] *Speech made by an English Colonel*, 9–12. It is difficult to see how the authorities could have avoided regarding this speech as seditious, so the possibility remains that this pamphlet was issued as a clever piece of Jacobite propaganda. However, since recruiting officers were begging for recruits from prisons, the decision could have been made to just send our 'brisk, genteel fellow' to Flanders, since, likely as not, he would have been dead within a few months. The problem with accepting this pamphlet as Jacobite propaganda is that the first eight pages of the pamphlet contain Williamite propaganda which would hardly have helped the Jacobite cause.

In England in the seventeenth century it was lawful to impress men for the navy, but not for the army. Nevertheless, the army was so desperate to fill up newly raised regiments that press-gangs were very active—especially in London—and were frequently involved in clashes with judicial, parliamentary and local authorities. In late February 1692/3 the officers of a regiment that was to be posted to the Netherlands were anxious to fill up their ranks. They appear to have attempted to press men themselves, but they also bribed a deputy provost-marshal and a naval press-gang to provide them with additional recruits. The impressed men were locked up in the deputy provost-marshal's house in Parkers Lane and another house in Drury Lane until they could be marched off to a port of embarkation. Members of Parliament were vigilant about detecting such illegal acts, and they ordered three military officers, the provost-marshal and the deputy provost-marshal to appear before the House of Commons with those whom they held in custody. The officers brought with them nine men in irons; their shackles were struck off and they were discharged. After examination, one Captain Winter was ordered to be prosecuted by the lord chief justice, and the other officers were released. This was not an isolated instance. In the same month, one Captain Cook impressed a bricklayer and confined him to the Tower of London. His friends applied to the lord chief justice for a writ of habeas corpus directed to the captain who had him in custody, but the captain refused to obey. The lord chief justice then ordered the sheriffs of London to seize the captain—'which will be a trial of skill between the civil and military power'.[33]

Press-gangs were heedless of the persons whom they assaulted. In January 1690/1 Peregrine Osborne, earl of Danby, heir to the marquis of Carmarthen and the commander of a naval ship, was returning home late one night when a press-gang, assisted by a constable, set upon the servants riding behind his carriage. When Danby tried to stop them, the press-masters assaulted him, knocked him down and beat him severely. A month later members of the press-gang were tried and convicted of assault at Hicks Hall: 'his lordship being in court was pleased to forgive some of them, but two were ordered to stand in the pillory, and the constable was fined.'[34]

Undeterred, the provost-marshals and their deputies continued to cooperate with press-gangs to impress men for land service. In February 1693/4 the House of Commons formed itself into a committee of the whole house to investigate the continuing abuses of impressment into the army. One press-gang consisted of two midshipmen and six members of the crew of the *Sandwich*, who had been bribed to furnish recruits for the army who were kept in a number of houses of detention scattered through London and the suburbs. Besides accepting bribes to release men whom they had impressed, they were also accused of allowing one man to die in detention for want of medical attention. Another man cut his throat rather

---

[33] *Journals of the House of Commons, 1693–1697* (1803), vol. x, p. 836a & b; Walton, *British Standing Army*, 482–3; Luttrell, *RSA* iii. 26, 37, 45.   [34] Luttrell, *RSA* ii. 167, 184, 186.

than face life in the army, and others suffered injuries and incurred disabilities as a result of ill treatment. In addition to using force, the press-masters got their victims drunk and falsely promised all sorts of inducements to persuade the men to accept the king's shilling. The light punishments inflicted upon the provost-marshals and press-masters had little effect, because their illicit trade appears to have been quite lucrative. Parliament tried a different approach and inserted in the Mutiny Act of 1694 a provision that specified that no man could be considered a soldier and subject to the Mutiny Act, not being an officer, unless he was brought before a justice of the peace, who was not a naval or military officer, and there formally declared that he wished to be enlisted. Penalties for violation of the statute were to be inflicted upon the officer responsible for the offence. This provision continued in legal force until the end of the Nine Years War.[35]

The contest between the civil and military authorities grew more sharp in 1695. In early April the under-sheriff and high constables of Middlesex went to the home of Michael Tooley, an army deputy provost-marshal in Holborn, with an order to release unlawfully impressed men who were kept in detention at his house. The deputy provost-marshal ordered the sentinels posted at the door to open fire, wounding the under-sheriff. When news of this spread, a crowd gathered at the wrestling ring in Lincoln's Inn Fields and broke open the deputy provost-marshal's house and freed 200 men who were being held for service in Flanders. The crowd then removed the furniture from the house and made a bonfire in the street. Soldiers were summoned who opened fire, killing one and wounding several rioters. The next night the crowd attacked two more provost-marshals' houses and attempted to break into the Marshalsea Prison in Southwark in order to release more unlawfully impressed soldiers. The horse and foot guards were called out to deal with the rioting, and orders were given to open fire. The tumults continued for two more days. The following week Michael Tooley was committed to Newgate Prison. In July Tooley was tried for murder at Hicks Hall and acquitted—perhaps on the instructions of a royal judge. Because of the threat of more anti-impressment riots and the Jacobite riots that occurred in early June, the London trained bands were kept standing to guard London and the suburbs for much of the summer.[36]

Besides impressment, another source of military manpower was the enlistment of prisoners. However, Ned Ward exaggerated when he defined a regiment as 'a corporation which consists of several individuals detached from Bridewell, the Queen's Bench, the Fleet, Newgate and the Compters'.[37] The English army appears not to have enlisted the most hardened and incorrigible felons. For

---

[35] *Journals of the House of Commons, 1693–1697*, xi. 93, 108, 110, 117–18; C. M. Clode, *The Military Forces of the Crown: Their Administration and Government*, 2 vols. (1869), ii. 7.

[36] Luttrell, *RSA* iii. 462–3, 483, 494.

[37] [Ward], *Mars stript of his Armour*, 2. The London Bridewell was a house of correction for vagrants, prostitutes and other minor offenders. Generically, a bridewell was a parish house of correction. The Compters of London and provincial towns were debtors' prisons.

example, at the Sessions of Oyer and Terminer for London and Middlesex held at the Old Bailey in February 1701/2, out of forty-one persons who were convicted at their trials, four were sentenced to hang, seventeen were to be burnt in the hand, eight were ordered to be whipped, three were enlisted in the navy and seven were impressed into the army, while two were fined. At the July 1701 Assizes at the Old Bailey, none were sentenced to death, 'seven or eight were burnt in the cheek, five or six, to prevent the same, desired to be listed in the king's service, which was granted'. In March 1706, at the request of the duke of Marlborough, three men in Northampton Gaol who were accused of 'several notorious crimes, but... convicted of deer stealing only' were enlisted in Marlborough's Regiment. Probably, a local landowner informed Marlborough of this recruiting opportunity as an alternative to having the poachers 'set at liberty again'.[38]

In 1698 Andrew Fletcher of Saltoun complained about this 'long and tedious war, which has cost this nation much blood'. Scotland had contributed a disproportionate amount of manpower to the armies and navies of England and the Netherlands. 'Seven or eight thousand of our seamen were on board the English fleet, and two or three thousand in that of Holland; we had twenty battalions of foot and six squadrons of dragoons here and in Flanders. Beside, I am credibly informed that every fifth man in the English forces were either of this nation, or Scots-Irish, who are a people of the same blood with us. All of these by a modest computation, may amount to thirty thousand men.'[39]

The Scottish Privy Council had long employed impressment for service in mainland European armies as a solution to the problems of vagrancy and cateran bands in a land that afforded few economic opportunities to its people. However, the Scottish Estates did not recognize the legality of conscription until 1694, when an Act authorizing the conscription of 3,000 men was passed. In 1696 another Act of the Scottish Parliament allowed an annual levy of 1,000 to be raised from the burghs and shires of Scotland. Those defined as most eligible for compulsory enlistment were young, unmarried men, who were not servants, but worked for 'daily wages or termly hire'. They were to assemble when summoned, and cast dice to see who was to be enlisted. Sheriffs and commissioners would throw the dice for those who failed to show.[40]

In the past methods of enlistment had been violent and even brutal. Andrew Marvell mentions the case of a certain Mr Harrington who was imprisoned in the Tower of London during the Third Anglo-Dutch War on a charge of sedition. Harrington had allegedly repeated a story told to him by two Scots soldiers, who had recently returned from Flanders. They complained that many of their countrymen had been seized by force, enlisted in the French army and detained in prison until put aboard transports. Those who offered resistance 'were heaved on

[38] Luttrell, *RSA* v. 72, 147–8, 165–6, 214: Clode, *Military Forces*, ii. 385–6.
[39] Andrew Fletcher of Saltoun, *Two Discourses concerning the Affairs of Scotland* (1698), in *Political Works*, ed. J. Robertson (1997), 42. Fletcher's estimates are accepted by Childs, *BAW* 15.
[40] Walton, *British Standing Army*, 482–3.

board fast tied and bound like malefactors; some struggling and contesting it were cast into the sea or maimed'.[41] Despite the Act of the Scottish Parliament of 1694 authorizing the enlistment of 3,000 soldiers, unlawful impressment continued until at least 1695, and probably thereafter. William II and III's soldiers were especially unpopular in Scotland where they incurred odium for the Glencoe Massacre and their illegal and violent methods of impressment, and they were frequently attacked and insulted. In April 1694 one Maclauchlan, a Glasgow schoolmaster, was sentenced to be whipped, pilloried and banished to the colonies for inciting soldiers to desert. Recruiting officers knew how difficult it was to persuade municipal corporations to cooperate in the matter of impressing men; they themselves would frequently refuse to surrender men, who, it was alleged, had been impressed unlawfully. A series of violent encounters occurred in Glasgow in December 1694, when three citizens of Glasgow were tried for the murder of Major James Menzies of John Lindsay, third earl of Lindsay and nine-teenth earl of Crawford's Regiment of Foot. The defence that the three citizens presented at their trial was that Menzies had imprisoned them upon the false accusation that they were deserters, and that he had refused to yield them to the magistrates of Glasgow when officially requested to do so. The provost of Glasgow, the two bailies and the town clerk demanded a conference with Menzies. The major was accompanied to the meeting by three captains, and when he was again asked to free the imprisoned citizens, he ran the town clerk through with his sword and killed him. Menzies then ordered the guard out to cover his escape. Francis Montgomery, a lord of the Privy Council, ordered a posse to pursue Menzies, and he was killed by the three defendants while resisting arrest. The jury that tried the three defendants returned the Scottish verdict of 'not proved', and they were discharged.[42]

After new recruits had been enlisted, they were detained under lock and key until they could be shipped overseas. Any training in drill and the manual of arms would necessarily have been quite limited. A manuscript copy of 'A Method of Discipline for the Behaviour of a Regiment of Foot upon Action', probably written by Richard Kane of the Royal Regiment of Ireland in the reign of Queen Anne, states that there was no standard method of drilling soldiers—even on the battlefield, where the space for marching and manoeuvering tens of thousands of men could be quite cramped—and each regiment clung to its own idiosyncrasies despite efforts to standardize the drill. The author states that a drill manual was finally issued for use by the horse, dragoons and foot, but it was intended for the parade ground only, and did not address the question of battlefield drill. The author thought that this was amazing considering the fact that the British army had already fought two extended wars on the continent, the Nine Years War and

---

[41] *An Account of the Growth of Popery and Arbitrary Government in England* (1678), in A. B. Grosart (ed.), *The Complete Works of Andrew Marvell, M.P.*, 4 vols. (1875; repr. 1966), iv. 333–4.

[42] J. Grant (ed.), *Seafield Correspondence from 1685 to 1708*, SHS NS 3 (1912), 134–5; Peter Burke, *Celebrated Naval and Military Trials* (1866), 50–7; Luttrell, *RSA* iii. 389.

the War of Spanish Succession, and the officer corps, which in both conflicts consisted mostly of young and inexperienced subalterns, had little guidance in how to prepare their men for battle. It was difficult to get two platoons together in battalion formation who understood the same commands.[43] An unofficial manual of drill published in 1690 also limits itself to parade-ground drill for the foot, and one is struck by its complexity. Before the replacement of screw and plug bayonets by the socket bayonet allowed musketeers to repel cavalry attacks as soon as they had fired their muskets, infantry companies and battalions had been obliged to retain pikemen, although in diminishing proportions. To march and drill pikemen and musketeers together was complicated, since the manual of arms for the former consisted of thirty-six separate commands and the latter forty-four commands. Orders could be effectively transmitted only by beat of the drum or sound of the trumpet. Officers assumed different positions on the parade ground, marching onto the battlefield and during the course of battle in order to observe, exhort and direct their men, or to deter them from desertion.[44]

Evidence for the lack of drill and training before a battalion was sent overseas is provided by *The Memoirs of Capt. Peter Drake*. Drake, an Irishman who passed for a gentleman, enlisted in Belcastel's Regiment in Dublin at the beginning of the War of Spanish Succession. The regiment was newly raised by Pierre, marquis de Belcastel, and was supposed to consist of Huguenot veterans who had settled in Ireland at the end of the last war. In fact, only the officers and non-commissioned officers were French Huguenots, and the private soldiers were Irish and English— all above five feet nine inches in stature. It also appears that all were volunteers who had received four guineas as an enlistment bounty. Those who could not provide security were confined to prevent desertion. Although carried on the English establishment, they were to be paid by the States General of the Netherlands, and posted to Gorcum. They were put aboard a transport ship at Rings End, where they remained at anchor for two weeks. Discipline began to break down when a French sergeant and his wife began selling ale and spirits aboard ship, and drunken brawling broke out—especially between two 'prize-fighters'. The officers came on board and managed to get the men below decks, and the hatches were battened down. The air below became stifling, and at this point Drake, a thorough rogue but not without attributes of charm and leadership, incited the first of his many mutinies. He led the men packed below in forcing their way on deck. Next day the officers returned on board, and held an inquiry into the mutiny. The two 'prize-fighters' were discharged, and the officers attempted also to get rid of Drake. He insisted that he wanted to remain in the regiment, and the remainder of the men declared that they would not serve if Drake was put ashore. Discipline still had not been restored when Belcastel's Regiment arrived at their quarters in

[43] BL, Add. MS. 41,141 ('A Method of Discipline for the Behaviour of a Regiment of Foot upon Action'), fo. 3r & v.

[44] *The Exercise of the Foot: With the Evolutions according to the Words of Command* (1690), 1–2, 52, 71; H. H. Turney-High, *Primitive War: Its Practice and Concepts* (1971), 11–12.

Gorcum. Here, Drake led his second mutiny when he discovered that the soldiers were required to purchase their bread within the town walls at double the price that bread sold for outside the walls. In the dispute that followed, Drake dangled the officer of the guard over the moat surrounding the town walls, and he and thirty companions bought loaves of bread and returned with them impaled on staves like banners. The officers were at a loss concerning what to do with Drake and his fellow mutineers, until the colonel arrived, discharged Drake and expelled him from Gorcum.[45]

William III did little to reform the English army, but he did impose more strict discipline—especially among those troops serving in Flanders. When soldiers were in England the various annual Mutiny Acts were carefully observed, but punishments were harsher overseas, where the authority of courts martial derived from the articles of war. Before the Mutiny Act of 1689 the English army had been 'an unconstitutional force', but not strictly speaking an illegal one, since Parliament had authorized 'guards and garrisons' as part of the Restoration settlement, and Parliament had also from time to time voted subsidies for new regiments in time of war. What was illegal was the failure of Charles II and James II to disband those regiments with the return of peace, and the devious way in which James II transferred Scottish and Irish regiments back and forth between those armies and the English establishment. Before the Mutiny Act of 1689, military law and courts martial had no legal foundation in England. The Articles of War of 1686 directed that all offences committed by military personnel in peacetime in England that were punishable by loss of life or limb were to be tried in common-law courts only. The Mutiny Act of 1689 authorized the officers of the army while in garrison in England to try before a court martial any offence as long as it did not involve civilians, but such military courts were confined to imposing the death penalty only for the offences of mutiny, desertion or sedition. The penalties allowed by the Mutiny Act were exacted against deserters in the home army as early as June 1689, when several soldiers were shot at the head of their regiments. As the war dragged on, desertions increased and the recruiting pool was diminished, and the practice of having condemned men draw lots or pardoning them at the last moment while standing before the firing squad came to prevail.[46]

William III applied a strict regimen to his highest-ranking officers as well as to the rank and file. When, during the Allied Siege of Namur in 1695, Major-General Johan Anton Ellenberger, a Hessian in Danish service who had begun his career as a private, proposed to surrender the fortified camp at Dixmuide without putting up a resistance—even before a breach was made in the walls—he was opposed by some of the younger officers of the four British regiments under his command, who insisted 'that it would not be consistent with their honour to deliver up the town so soon'. Ellenberg overruled his council of war, and surrendered

---

[45] *Memoirs of Capt. Peter Drake* (1755), 31–7.
[46] Childs, *BAW* 124–5; Walton, *British Standing Army*, 529, 531, 533–4, 538, 825; Luttrell, *RSA* i. 553.

because he thought resistance was hopeless, although it would have relieved pressure exerted by the French during the Confederate Siege of Namur. At the end of the campaigning season, an Allied council of war was convened in Ghent to look into the surrender of Namur. Ellenberg was sentenced to be beheaded, and a number of foreign colonels were broken and cashiered.[47]

Following the disastrous Battle of Landen, William III decided that an example had to be made of deserters. Thirty English and Scots deserters were swept up in the Dutch ports and returned to the British camp in Flanders by the grand provost-marshal. The king pardoned twenty-four of them, and the other six drew lots for death. Three more were pardoned, and the other three hanged at the head of their regiments the following day. Deserters included those who did not possess the stomach to face the slaughter on the battlefield, but others were drifters who had never stayed in any one place or occupation very long. Considering how the army recruited its soldiers, this hardly seems very surprising. During the War of Spanish Succession one in four of French soldiers deserted, and the problem persisted in all armies through the eighteenth century. The failure to pay soldiers in timely fashion, to feed them adequately and to provide permanent housing all exacerbated the problem. The question of unsettled allegiance also persisted in the army that William III took over after the invasion of 1688. When Jacobites or crypto-Jacobites deserted, officers and men usually defected together in larger groups to join the French army. In April 1691 sixteen Scots soldiers, including five officers, having landed in Ostend, deserted to the French; in December 1692 forty-six English and Irish were discovered in a batch of French prisoners. They were sent to Portsmouth, under guard, to be tried by a council of war.[48] Recruiting their regiments up to strength was a perpetual concern to colonels and recruiting officers, and the offer of enlistment bounties was a great temptation to desert one regiment and enlist in another. Allied generals squabbled with one another about deserters from one army to another. When the landgrave of Hesse sought to reclaim and try by court martial some British soldiers whom he claimed had deserted from the Hessian forces, Sir Charles O'Hara, colonel of the First Foot Guards, maintained the principle that to yield to the landgrave's claim would make men reluctant to enlist in the guards. O'Hara cited the practice that soldiers should remain in the regiment that brought them to Flanders, whatever their previous history. It would have been very difficult to sort out Peter Drake's enlistment history. In 1702 he was serving in the duke of Marlborough's Regiment in Flanders at the beginning of the War of Spanish Succession. To his horror, he was recognized by a sergeant of General William Stewart's Regiment, which he had deserted at the Tower of London, and tried by court martial. Brought before the presiding officer

---

[47] D'Auvergne, *Campaign in Flanders for . . . 1695*, 76–7, 181; Richard Kane, *Campaigns of King William and the Duke of Marlborough* (1747), 21–8, 26–8.

[48] D'Auvergne, *Campagne in the Spanish Netherlands, 1693*, 108; Luttrell, *RSA* ii. 218, 633; iii. 285, 288, 300; Corvisier, *Armies and Societies*, 70–1; *A Journal of the . . . Actions of the Confederate Forces against the French in the United Provinces and the Spanish Netherlands* (1690), 8.

in chains and guarded by eight grenadiers, Drake was asked why he had deserted. Drake answered that he had heard that the regiment was to be shipped to the West Indies, to which he had an aversion. The general told Drake that he deserved to die, but would 'be pardoned this time'. He was then asked what regiment he wished to serve in, and he chose to remain with Marlborough's. Drake thought that his life was spared because he was recovering from a duelling wound, and the officers of Marlborough's Regiment valued him as a courageous man for that reason.[49] When regiments or independent companies were ordered to the West Indies, there was a strong likelihood that men would desert. A whole company of Colonel John Tidcomb's Regiment garrisoned in Ireland deserted in 1701 and fled to the mountains rather than serve in the West Indies. The next year Colonel Faringdon and most of the officers of his regiment resigned their commissions rather than go to there. Brigadier Columbine's Regiment mutinied at Tilbury, and refused to board ship for the West Indies unless they were paid first.[50]

Desertion was only one variable that could reduce the strength of a battalion to the point where it could not fight in the line. The first campaign season that British units spent in Flanders in 1689 saw four of the fifteen infantry battalions removed from the line and sent into winter quarters in early September because of widespread dysentery, consequent upon the soldiers gorging themselves with the abundance of fruit—hardly surprising in an army that felt no obligation to supply soldiers with much more than bread and biscuit. The men had to be watched constantly to keep them from slipping away to plunder the country-folk. Individual soldiers were frequently killed by boors seeking revenge for the army's depredations. In 1692 a cartel signed by representatives of the emperor, the king of France and several German princes regulated the size of parties sent out to collect contributions in the war zones, and specified that an officer was to be in charge. This was intended to maintain discipline among foraging parties, and to avoid conflicts with peasants. Soldiers who failed to observe the regulations of this cartel were to be dealt with as robbers. It was also common practice in the Nine Years War for the generals of opposing armies to make a variety of cartels or agreements with one another concerning other questions, such as the treatment and exchange of prisoners of war. These agreements might be enforced by the courts martial of the respective armies.[51]

The English Parliament had become committed to a policy of defending the Glorious Revolution settlement, accepting William of Orange as their legitimate monarch and entering into a mainland European war to defend his title to the crowns of the Three Kingdoms. As the war dragged on, many members became convinced that England's interests were being subordinated to those of

---

[49] BL, Add. MS. 9,723 (Blathwayt Papers), fos. 55v–56r; *Memoirs of Capt. Peter Drake*, 49–50.
[50] Luttrell, *RSA* v. 83, 223, 245.
[51] *Motions and Actions of the Confederate Forces*, 8, 17, 25–32; S. H. F. Johnston, 'A Scots Chaplain in Flanders, 1691–97', *JSAHR* 27 (1949), 4–5; Sir George Clark, 'The Character of the Nine Years War, 1688–97', *CHJ* 11 (1954), 174–6.

the United Provinces. Participation in the War of the Grand Coalition required enlarging the army to nearly 70,000 horse and foot from the British Isles in 1694, together with some 23,000 Dutch, Danish and German troops who were carried on the English establishment and paid by Parliament. However, as Daniel Defoe argued, the power of the purse had grown stronger than the power of the sword in seventeenth-century England. Parliament and much of the political nation, having had bad experiences with the absolutist tendencies of Stuart monarchs, lord protectors and Presbyterian armies in the past, as well as having read Tacitus, Machiavelli, Harrington and Fletcher of Saltoun, could not be reconciled to the notion of a permanent standing army. Therefore, when the Nine Years War ended in 1697 Parliament set about dismantling that army, leading to what is called the 'Great Disbandment'. King William and others knew full well that the Treaty of Rijswijk had led to nothing more than a truce with Louis XIV, who intended to place a Bourbon on the Spanish throne and gain control of the Spanish Netherlands as soon as the ailing King Charles II of Spain died, which came to pass in 1700. William III did not manage Parliament well, and his advice about maintaining a standing army in order to be prepared for the next war was ignored. William had neglected to specify the size of the army that he wished to retain, and the very fact that he had offered an opinion in the matter was resented as being prescriptive and likely to bias the debates in the House of Commons. William had hoped to retain a standing army of 30,000 men in England, plus additional troops in Scotland and Ireland. Parliament determined to reduce the peacetime force to the level of Charles II's army in 1680, which was 10,000 men.[52]

In early 1698 Parliament voted to disband fifty-two English regiments together with the foreign regiments that were carried on the English establishment. Parliament did allow disbanded officers half pay, and William found ways of retaining most officers on full pay or half pay, which provided a cadre around which to rebuild the army during the War of Spanish Succession. He also resorted to the old Stuart trick of hiding regiments in Ireland. During the Nine Years War the home army had never exceeded 10,000 men, but now the remainder of the army was brought home, paid off and disbanded regiment by regiment. Generally speaking, the pay for most of the army was current, but the soldiers of some regiments had not been fully paid or the officers had made off with monies owing to their men, and mutinies broke out in a couple of them as a result.[53] Ned Ward offered the opinion that many private soldiers were once honest tradesmen who had been ruined by drink, whereby they became poor and were pressed for soldiers by the overseers of the poor. If they survived the wars and returned home, they then thought of themselves as gentlemen soldiers, and could not degrade themselves by becoming mechanics and artisans again. When Parliament

---

[52] [Daniel Defoe], *An Argument Shewing that a Standing Army with the Consent of Parliament is not Inconsistent with a Free Government* (1698), 17–21; Burnet, *History*, iv. 376–7; Childs, *NYW* 72; id., *BAW* 197.   [53] Luttrell, *RSA* iv. 285–6, 318–19, 518; Childs, *BAW* 199–200.

disbanded the army, all discharged soldiers were granted the privilege of becoming free of any municipal corporation and practising trades whether they had served an apprenticeship or not. As so often happened after wars in early modern Europe, discharged soldiers did not readily settle down into the routines of civilian life, and enough turned to dishonest occupations to constitute a crime wave. Cavalry troopers were allowed to keep their mounts and saddles, thus equipping them with everything they needed to pursue careers as highwaymen except a brace of pistols. A number of former Life Guards became notorious highwaymen after the Great Disbandment. In July 1699 Charles Sackville, sixth earl of Dorset, was set upon by a band of ten highwaymen between Chelsea and Fulham. All were former soldiers. Another band of thirty highwaymen made up of disbanded soldiers built huts and established a colony in Waltham Forest, and preyed upon travellers along the Newmarket Road and the Great North Road.[54]

The disbandment of the army following the end of the Nine Years War in 1697 also revived the standing-army controversy that had been smouldering since the time of the Restoration. Some of the Radical Whig opponents of a standing army began meeting at the Grecian Tavern in Devereux Court, which ran off of Essex Street in London. Those attending these discussions included John Trenchard, an Irish political pamphleteer, John Toland the deist, Walter Moyle, MP for Saltash, and Andrew Fletcher of Saltoun. They published a number of pamphlets against maintaining a permanent, professional military establishment in time of peace. What is striking about their line of argument is how little they had learned from the diplomatic background of the War of the Grand Coalition concerning Louis XIV's continuing ambitions and expansionism, and how little they knew of the methods of warfare at the end of the seventeenth century. The Radical Whigs had expressed their fear and distrust of Louis XIV since the time of the Third Anglo-Dutch War, when England was an ally of France, and English and Scots soldiers served in the French army. Apparently the fear that Louis XIV continued to harbour designs upon the Low Countries had evaporated among the Grecian Tavern Whigs, and it is difficult to avoid the conclusion that their former distrust of the French had been little more than a stick with which to beat Charles II and James II. Although all of them had a hand in helping William of Orange to the thrones of the Three Kingdoms, they had since learned to distrust his militarism, autocracy and deviousness.[55]

John Trenchard claimed that the disbandment of regiments and the discharge of foreign troops on the English establishment had not been carried out as

---

[54] [Ward], *Mars stript of his Armour*, 16; Luttrell, *RSA* iii. 537; iv. 540–1, 697, 715; J. Childs, 'War, Crime Waves and the English Army in the Late Seventeenth Century', *War and Society*, 15 (1997), 10–11, 13–14, 16.

[55] C. Robbins, *The Eighteenth-Century Commonwealthman* (1959; repr. 1968), 6, 103; Schwoerer, *NSA* 155–64, 167–9, 174–84; J. Black, 'The Revolution and the Development of English Foreign Policy', in E. Cruickshanks (ed.), *By Force or by Default: The Revolution of 1688–89* (1989), 136–40, 150–1.

officially stated. Whereas King William had promised to disband the army, his ministers and supporters were now warning of a new war with France:

Their arguments were turned topsy turvy, for as during the [Nine Years] war the people were prevailed upon to keep up the army in hopes of a peace, so now we must keep them up for fear of a war. The condition of France, which they have been decrying for many years was now magnified. We were told that it is doubtful whether the French king would deliver up any of his towns; that he was preparing a vast fleet for Lord knows what design; that it was impossible to make a militia useful; that the warlike King Jemmy [James VII and II] had an army of eighteen thousand Irish heroes in France, who would be ready when called for; and that the king of Spain was dying. The members of Parliament were discoursed with as they came to town; 'twas whispered about that the Whigs would be turned out of employments; a new plot was said to be discovered for murdering the king, and searches were made at midnight through the whole city to the discovery of plenty of fornication, but no traitors.[56]

Much of Trenchard's polemic was devoted to irrelevant and questionable technicalities. He thought that William III should have retained James II's army which was lawfully raised, rather than to raise forces illegally without the consent of Parliament. Despite the need to conquer Scotland and Ireland and to fight Louis XIV in order to preserve the Glorious Revolution Settlement and keep a hostile power out of the Low Countries, many MPs still believed that William's army had been raised without the consent of Parliament. The slogan of the Grecian Tavern Whigs was that 'freedom can be maintained only where the sword is in the hands of the people [i.e., the propertied classes], whereas tyrannies are supported by mercenaries'. The corollary of this was, as John Toland pointed out, that wars fought by freemen are soon finished, but it was in the interest of mercenaries to drag out conflicts. Toland distrusted armies composed of gentlemen (by which he meant a professional and salaried officer class) under an arbitrary monarch. The nobility must be restored to their former privileges so that they might command freemen in the militia, as their ancestors had done. It would appear that the Grecian Tavern Whigs, having lived through William of Orange's invasion of England, conquest of Scotland and Ireland, a long mainland European war with attendant high taxes and disruption of trade, now had trouble seeing the difference between the armies of James II and William III.[57]

Andrew Fletcher of Saltoun's perspective on the standing-army controversy was distinctly Scottish. He argued that there was no need to keep a standing army in Scotland after the Williamite conquest and the reduction of the Highlands. Scotland's small standing army had been used during the Nine Years War as a military manpower reserve for the English forces fighting in Flanders. The troops levied and the taxes raised in Scotland benefited only the two wealthy trading nations of England and the Netherlands without Scotland deriving any benefit by

---

[56] John Trenchard, *A . . . History of Standing Armies in England* (1698), 23–4.

[57] [John Trenchard], *The Militia Reformed* (1698), 22–3; Anon., *True Account of Land Forces in England* (1699), 8.

way of trade. Although he was willing to admit that the political communities of the Three Kingdoms had benefited from the Glorious Revolution, Fletcher insisted that they must be careful to preserve their liberties by not allowing the crown to maintain standing armies or any military forces in foreign armies that owed allegiance to the ruler of the Three Kingdoms.[58]

Daniel Defoe, who had been a soldier and a supporter of William III, replied that standing armies did not pose the threat to England's liberties that they had in the past, that England's domestic peace now seemed secure, but that it was necessary to maintain the Grand Coalition against Louis XIV. A widely accepted maxim of warfare stated that it was better strategy to carry the war into the enemy's country and keep it out of one's own country. The king's subjects should understand that the Low Countries served as a barrier against French armies. A militia would be of no use in a mainland European war, because the king lacked the constitutional authority to send the militia overseas. Even if he did possess that authority, the Allies would not accept the assistance of an English militia because of their lack of training and experience. In the international affairs of Europe, much depended upon the reputation in martial affairs of the monarch. Defoe appealed to a sense of national honour and Protestant sentiment in arguing that the outbreak of war over the question of the Spanish royal succession could turn into a religious war. For Parliament to contribute to that war only by subsidizing German mercenaries would bring the kind of dishonour upon the country that James VI and I's half-hearted and inept assistance to the elector palatine in the 1620s had done, and would display an indifference to the Protestant cause.[59]

In the 1640s the Wars of the Three Kingdoms had introduced the concept of standing armies and the theory and practice of the military revolution into the British Isles. The recollection of how these armies had been employed to impose absolutism in church and state haunted the memory of those who had lived through those troubled times, and contributed to the standing-army controversy of the years following the Great Disbandment. The wars of the 1690s laid the foundations of the fiscal-military state that enabled England (and after 1707) Great Britain to wage war on a European and a global scale. William of Orange's invasion of England, followed by the Glorious Revolution settlement, was supposedly directed at James VII and II's use of an enlarged standing army to introduce and support popery and absolutism. There were those in the English Parliament—especially the Radical Whigs and a few Tories—who wondered if they had not traded one tyrant for another, who further increased the size of the British army and drew England into the War of the Grand Coalition. Besides many other foreign contrivances, the Nine Years War introduced Dutch state-building into England. These institutions and

---

[58] Andrew Fletcher of Saltoun, *Two Discourses concerning the Affairs of Scotland* (1698) and *A Discourse of Government with Relation to Militias* (1698), in *Works*, ed. J. Robertson (1997), 17, 45.

[59] [Defoe], *Standing Army with the Consent of Parliament*, 5–8; id., *A . . . Reply to the History of Standing Armies in England* (1698), 19–20.

practices included the founding of the Bank of England (modelled on the Bank of Amsterdam) in 1694 and an array of new taxes collected directly by government revenue officers rather than by tax-farmers that Sir George Downing at the Treasury had devised as a result of his close study of Dutch fiscal and economic policy. This new fiscal system involved the establishment of a permanent national debt which was underwritten by a partnership of Parliament, the Bank of England and the London stock market. The Dutch fiscal system, which provided the model for this new British military-fiscal state, had arisen out of the need to finance the Dutch struggle for independence from Spain during the Eighty Years War, and later, the wars to contain Louis XIV's expansionism. Because the concept of a state bank was distinctly Dutch, it had originally been opposed as something 'only fit for republics' and incompatible with the institution of monarchy.

In the short run, the Nine Years War had a disastrous effect upon English trade and the economy, but in the early eighteenth century the combination of war and trade would prove more successful. The acceptance of the standing army in Britain as a permanent institution was dependent upon this financial revolution and better management of the army. The latter included subjecting not only the rank and file to stricter discipline, but also the officers, who earlier in the century would have regarded such a degree of control as incompatible with their military honour.[60]

The acceptance of a permanent standing army in Great Britain in the early eighteenth century also arose out of a greater awareness of the international politics of mainland Europe. Except perhaps for the Radical Whigs, most members of Parliament had come to realize that England's security and the defence of the Glorious Revolution settlement could not be divorced from involvement in continental affairs. The events of the Nine Years War and the War of Spanish Succession were well covered by books, pamphlets and newspapers, and free discussion was assured by the lapse of the Licensing Act in 1695. There were other considerations as well. Many had come to believe that participation in the Nine Years War restored England's martial honour, and these sentiments were shared to a degree in Scotland and Ireland too, and would become an important force in nation-building and in the integration of the British army prior to the Act of Union of 1707. Despite the fact that he had brought a Dutch army with him, there were also supporters of William III who took pride in the image of a soldier-king who had gained honour and glory in defying the French.

---

[60] J. Scott, *England's Troubles: Seventeenth-Century English Political Instability in European Context* (2000), 474–90; J. Robertson, *The Scottish Enlightenment and the Militia Issue* (1985), 12–13; J. Brewer, *The Sinews of Power: War, Money and the English State, 1688–1783* (1989), 133, 137–54; D. Hoak, 'The Anglo-Dutch Revolution of 1688–89', and J. G. A. Pocock, 'Standing Army and Public Credit: The Institutions of Leviathan', in D. Hoak and M. Feingold (eds.), *The World of William and Mary: Anglo-Dutch Perspectives on the Revolution of 1688–89* (1996), 13–14, 87–8, 97–8.

17

Conclusion: military professionalism

No profession in the world is more built on true reason and sound judgment than the military is, for both of those are essentially requisite to generals and the chief officers under them.

Roger Boyle, 1ˢᵗ earl of Orrery, *A Treatise of the Art of War* (1677), sig. B1r.

The same spirit that brings us into the army, should make us apply ourselves to the study of the military art, the common forms of which may be easily attained by a moderate application as well as capacity. Neither is it below any military man, let his birth be ever so noble, to be knowing in the minute parts of the service. It will not cramp his genius (as some have pleased to say, in order, as I suppose, to excuse their own ignorance) but rather aid and assist them in daring enterprises.

Humphrey Bland, *A Treatise of Military Discipline* (1727), 115.

The expertise of military officers is directed towards the management of violence in as rational and disciplined a manner as possible. In order to do this effectively, they must keep a cool head under fire, so it was not inappropriate that, during time of war, officers were still recruited from the ranks of gentlemen volunteers.[1] Commissions were also given to those who could recruit a company or a regiment, provided that they were gentlemen and could deliver their units to the battlefield clothed and equipped. Battlefield commissions and promotions were becoming more rare in the armies of the Three Kingdoms as the practice of purchasing commissions spread in times of relative peace. Monarchs such as William II and III and Queen Anne disapproved of the purchase system, but the English Parliament, which insisted upon joint control of armies raised in England and Ireland, thought that the system helped to weed out mercenaries and to ensure political loyalty and stability, which certainly were important considerations in the late seventeenth century. Some observers believed that the existence of the purchase system for commissions discouraged the acquisition of a high degree of military expertise based upon scientific study. There were a number of proposals for the

---

[1] Manning, *Swordsmen*, ch. 4.

establishment of military academies on the continental model, but such schemes did not begin to bear fruit in England until the middle of the eighteenth century when the Royal Military Academy, Woolwich, was founded for the technical training of artillery and military engineer officers. It was not thought necessary to give professional training to line officers until they ran up against the armies of Napoleon. By contrast, the English navy had made more progress towards professionalization during the latter part of the seventeenth century because a greater degree of technical proficiency was required to integrate navigational and military skills under one command.

Despite the centrifugal pull of conflicting allegiances during the period of dynastic change at the end of the seventeenth century, there is good reason to believe that serving officers became more committed to the court, the government and the state in England and Scotland after the Revolution of 1689. An increasing number of peers and gentlemen had experience of military service and shared a sense of belonging to one profession and one military organization, even before the Act of Union of 1707 formally created the British army.[2] Although conflicts between social and military hierarchies and between gentlemen and professional officers had persisted through most of the seventeenth century, these distinctions showed signs of lessening in the reigns of William II and III and Anne. However, the fear and distrust of standing armies commanded by career officers persisted much longer and retarded the full professionalization of the British officer class, which came only in the latter part of the nineteenth century.

Few historians of the British experience have addressed the question of how military professionalism developed or could be defined at the end of the seventeenth century. The phenomenon of the emergence of a professional officer class has been largely left to political and social scientists, who have attempted to conceptualize the problem of military professionalism based upon their reading of the works of historians of the early modern world who derive their knowledge of the subject from research in primary sources, but who have yet to develop a rigorous analytical model for investigating this question.[3] The result has been a paradigm better suited to investigating late eighteenth-century armies than earlier ones. The British and Irish experience of standing armies during the Wars of the Three Kingdoms had been an unhappy one, and consequently permanent military forces were associated with political absolutism. This prejudice was confirmed by reading the works of Tacitus, Machiavelli, Harrington and Algernon Sidney. Knowledge of contemporaneous armies, such as those of France and Spain offered little reassurance, and although the Dutch army provided the most attractive model of a well disciplined standing army led by a professional officer corps, the fact that the States' Army served a republic rather than a monarchy was

---

[2] Ibid. 17–20.

[3] A notable exception is David Trim ('Introduction', in Trim (ed.), *The Chivalric Ethos and the Development of Military Professionalism* (2003), 3–11), who discusses military professionalism in a broad European and western context.

thought to render the Dutch model inappropriate. However, the good behaviour of the Dutch soldiers who came to England with William III's invasion force helped to persuade some that a standing army could be well disciplined and made to respect the rights and property of civilians. Thus, sometime after *c*.1675 the term 'standing army' changed its meaning and came to convey the concept of an army comprising professional officers and long-service soldiers under an effective system of military discipline paid by and loyal to the state.[4]

Thus, one can say that a permanent standing army emerged in England under James VII and II, drawing its manpower from the military establishments of the Three Kingdoms. This proved to be a false start because of the unresolved question of political and religious allegiance, but it did help to lay the foundation for the British army which emerged in the reigns of William II and III and Anne. Full professionalism would come only much later, but some issues had been resolved by the reign of William III, and we can establish a set of criteria to judge the extent to which the officer class of the British army had become professionalized. The first and the most important criterion was the assertion of the primacy of military over social hierarchies. It had become indisputable that the king's commission gave primacy of command to his most senior officers whatever their social rank, although the conferring of patents of nobility often recognized their achievement of the highest levels of military and naval command. By way of a corollary, officers who commanded armies in the field were expected to pursue stated political and military objectives rather than being driven by heroic values and the quest for personal honour and glory. Also, by the end of the seventeenth century the custom of admitting noblemen to councils of war regardless of their military rank had fallen into disuse. At the same time, the process of professionalization was retarded by the purchase system which the landed aristocracy in Parliament imposed upon the armies of William and Anne in order to exclude mercenaries and ensure that places were reserved for themselves and their sons. The offices of ensign and cornet, lieutenant, captain and colonel were bought and sold, but the command of battalions in the field fell to lieutenant-colonels who were invariably men of experience who had undergone an apprenticeship in arms. William II and III would have preferred to prohibit the purchase of commissions, as was the practice in the Dutch army, but the manpower needs of the Nine Years War necessitated commissioning officers who could raise companies and regiments, and William took the easy way out rather than requiring higher standards of technical competence from the officers of the British army. William spent much of the year in Flanders, and he never had the time to impose his will upon his ministers or to manage Parliament effectively. Moreover, since many naval and military officers sat in the two houses of Parliament and were related to

---

[4] J. G. A. Pocock, *The Machiavellian Moment: Florentine Political Thought and the Atlantic Republican Tradition* (1975), 410–12. Among the more well-known studies of the emergence of professional officer corps are: S. P. Huntington, *The Soldier and the State: The Theory and Practice of Civil–Military Relations* (1967) and G. Teitler, *The Genesis of the Professional Officers' Corps* (1977).

other members of Parliament, this made it difficult to keep politics out of the fighting forces.

Since advancement in the British army depended upon the purchase of a commission rather than skill or merit, there was little incentive to acquire a military education.[5] Professionalism in the armies of the Three Kingdoms and, after 1707, the British army was also retarded by the question of allegiance and the competing loyalties associated with king and Parliament and the rival houses of Stuart, Orange-Nassau and Hanover. The dual control of the armed forces by king and Parliament in matters of finance, the validity of military law as well as the purchase of commissions also delayed the impact of professionalization in the British army.[6] Many of the armies of mainland Europe had been polyglot in both their officer classes and in the rank and file. Unless there existed a serious shortage of military manpower among the subjects and citizens of the ruler, a preference developed for native-born subjects to fill the officer ranks, which trend was manifested in the armies of the French and Dutch republics at the end of the eighteenth century. A sense of shared nationality among English and Scots increasingly characterized the officer class of the British army after 1689, but significant numbers of French Huguenot and, under the Hanoverians, German officers were also to be found holding commissions.[7]

Technical competence in military matters is another criterion for measuring the progress of professionalization that all scholars agree upon. Morris Janowitz argues that 'the development of the military profession has been the outcome of a continuous struggle to be rational and scientific in the context of military requirements'.[8] The late sixteenth and seventeenth centuries had seen a proliferation of military treatises and manuals of arms as well as textbooks on gunnery, fortification and engineering which were addressed to those undergoing an apprenticeship in arms and which sought to inculcate mathematical and scientific reasoning, calculation and measurement. These were supplemented by English translations of the works of Tacitus, Livy and Vegetius to teach the apprentice martialist about war in antiquity. The classical authors could be supplemented by reading military memoirs published during the late sixteenth and seventeenth centuries.[9]

An officer corps cannot be said to have existed in the British army until attendance at military colleges standardized the entrance requirements into the officer class and became obligatory for everyone regardless of social rank. The senior practitioners of

[5] J. Childs, *Armies and Warfare in Europe, 1648–1789* (1982), 90–1.

[6] Huntington, *Soldier and the State*, 35–6.

[7] J. R. Hale, 'The Military Education of the Officer Class in Early Modern Europe', *Renaissance War Studies* (1983), 227; K. M. Brown, 'From Scottish Lords to British Officers: State Building, Elite Integration and the British Army in the Seventeenth Century', in Macdougall, *S&W* 148; L. Colley, *Britons: Forging the Nation, 1707–1837* (1992), 11–18; Childs, *BAW* 132–8.

[8] M. Janowitz, 'Armed Forces and Society: A World Perspective', in J. van Doorn (ed.), *Armed Forces and Society* (1968), 23.

[9] This literature is discussed in: D. Eltis, *The Military Revolution in Sixteenth Century Europe* (1995); H. Webb, *Elizabethan Military Science: The Books and the Practice* (1965); M. J. D. Cockle, *A Bibliography of Military Books up to 1642* (1900; repr. 1978); Manning, *Swordsmen*, 73–9, 103–22.

other recognized professions in England had all succeeded in demanding an apprenticeship as a prerequisite for entry into practice, as was the case with surgeons, attorneys, apothecaries and the like. Physicians had long been trained in universities. Indeed, entry into the officer ranks in armies and corps raised in the British Isles was more likely to require the actual experience of battle, obtained as a gentleman volunteer in an apprenticeship in arms served in mainland European armies before the establishment of royal standing armies in the Three Kingdoms at the time of the Restoration, than was the case afterwards. Charles II had many loyal followers to reward and limited means to do so, and he awarded military commissions to supporters whether or not they had served an apprenticeship in arms. Since Charles's royal army consisted mostly of guards and garrisons, with a preponderance of the former, the better part of his military officers were amateurs corrupted by residence at court and in London, and who gained little useful military experience. An exception to this military indolence were those officers that served in the Tangier garrison, who had to contend with the hostility of the Moors on a daily basis, or those who were posted to the British brigades of the French, Dutch and Portuguese armies. These contrasting conditions of military service served only to perpetuate the dichotomy between the privileged officers in the guards regiments at court and those, such as the 'Tangerines', who gained battle experience and served apprenticeships in arms in distant, foreign posts. William II and III missed the opportunity to impose higher professional standards on the officer class of the British army, and gave out commissions to peers and country gentlemen in order to attach them and their houses to his regime. The ability to raise companies and regiments for service in the Nine Years War was a more important criterion for commissioning officers than military competence. William was also slow to recognize military talent among British officers and long gave out the highest commands in the British and Confederate armies to his German and Dutch cousins who had accompanied him in his invasions of England and Ireland.[10]

The professionalization of the officer class of the English navy proceeded more rapidly in the seventeenth century because the navy, unlike the army, became a standing naval force at an earlier date. The offices of sailing master and military commander had long been merged, and discharging the duties of a ship's captain required much greater technical skill than those of a line officer in the land forces. Most of these duties could be learned only in the school of experience, so the need for a naval apprenticeship had been recognized since Elizabethan times. Members of both the peerage and the gentry were attracted to naval careers, while persons of more humble birth, such as Sir Francis Drake, could achieve gentry status through sea service. Although tensions between gentlemen officers and tarpaulins persisted, the two had come to view themselves as belonging to the same profession by the

---

[10] Huntington, *Soldier and the State*, 2–5, 11, 20–1, 26; Teitler, *Genesis*, 6–8; G. Holmes, *Politics, Religion and Society in England, 1679–1742* (1986), 334–5; Sir John Dalrymple, *Memoirs of Great Britain and Ireland*, 2 vols., 2nd edn. (1771–3), I. ii. 87–8.

Restoration period. Parliament never viewed the navy as a threat to its own liberties or those of Englishmen, and being an island and commercial nation, it was always easier to persuade Parliament to provide funds for the navy than for a standing army.[11] A more formal naval apprenticeship was initiated by that great advocate of professional expertise Samuel Pepys, while he was secretary to the Navy Board. Pepys laid it down that a midshipman must serve a minimum of three years as a 'volunteer per order' or a captain's servant before he could take the examination to qualify for a commission as a lieutenant. The length of this apprenticeship was gradually increased to six years. J. D. Davies argues that it was evidence of the growing professionalism and esprit de corps among naval officers—both gentlemen and 'tarps'—that they conspired together to defeat regulations drawn up by civilian administrators such as Pepys and William Coventry, and to provide one another with alibis at courts martial. Both kinds of naval officers behaved as if they were answerable only to the lord admiral or the king. The hierarchy of civilian administrators and dockyard officials did not correspond to the hierarchy of naval rank, and there were frequent conflicts between the two. At the same time, an attempt was made to provide for continuity among naval officers during peacetime by giving demobilized captains preference for appointments as lieutenants and providing employment for discharged lieutenants as midshipmen. The gradual introduction of half-pay after the Second Anglo-Dutch War, first as a reward for senior naval officers, but gradually as a means of retaining a cadre of experienced officers, also promoted professional continuity.[12]

Rationalist modes of thought played an important role in promoting military professionalism. As more than one military intellectual pointed out, commanders and officers were not excused from thinking. Roger Boyle, first earl of Orrery, said that far too many commanders preferred to attribute their victories to 'good fortune', when they ought to have been pursuing military objectives on the basis of 'right reason' and good judgement. Orrery was a well read man, and a dramatist and man of letters as well. Like many military intellectuals, he remained dependent on Greek and Roman military commentaries, probably because they were more readily available than the works of contemporaneous military writers. He was familiar with the commentaries of only one English general—those of Sir Francis Vere. He must have heard of the memoirs of Robert Munro, Blaise de Monluc and François de La Noue,[13] but perhaps they were beneath his attention because they

[11] N. A. M. Rodger, *The Safeguard of the Sea: A Naval History of Britain, 660–1649* (1998), 298–305; Teitler, *Genesis*, 73; Charles Louis de Secondat, baron de la Brède et de Montesquieu, *The Spirit of the Laws* (1748), trans. and ed. D. M. Cohler, B. C. Milller and H. S. Stone (1989), 329.

[12] Holmes, *Politics, Religion and Society*, 335–6; J. D. Davies, *Gentlemen and Tarpaulins: Officers and Men of the Restoration Navy* (1991), 42–3, 52–3; R. Ollard, *Pepys: A Biography* (1984 repr. edn.), 74–6, 184 n.

[13] Robert Monro, *Monro, his Expedition with the Worthy Scots Regiment called Mac-keys*, ed. W. S. Brockington (1637; repr. 1999); Blaise de Lasseran-Massencome, seigneur de Monluc, marshal of France, *The Commentaries of Messire Blaize de Montluc, Mareshal of France*, trans. C. Cotton (1674); François de La Noue, *The Politicke and Military Discourses of the Lord De La Nowe*, trans. E. Aggas (1587).

were not English. He appears to have placed no value upon military commentaries and memoirs unless the authors were generals, and he scorned the writings of those who were not military men. Orrery recommended to King Charles II that military and naval commanders be required to submit written commentaries describing their 'actions, observations and motives' in their campaigns, expeditions and voyages. (Actually, naval commanders had been required to keep journals of their voyages since the days of the Commonwealth.)[14] Another important military intellectual was Edward Montagu, first earl of Sandwich. The cousin and patron of Samuel Pepys until his tragic death at the Battle of Solebay, he was far more than a 'gentleman admiral', and took his duties very seriously. His *Journal*, which for the most part he wrote himself, reveals that he took a keen interest in topography, astronomy and navigation. He was capable of original thought in naval tactics, and proposed ideas which were in advance of their time. He adhered to the custom sanctioned by long usage of consulting councils of war aboard his flagship, but he did not feel bound by the recommendations of the councils unless he found their conclusions to be rational and persuasive.[15]

The rise of professional standing armies in Great Britain and Ireland presented the aristocracies of the Three Kingdoms with new career opportunities, but modern warfare and military professionalization also had a corrosive effect upon aristocratic society and culture. When members of the older landed aristocracy took up the king's commission they were less likely to command soldiers drawn from among their own loyal tenants, retinues and neighbours, and more likely to be leading troops recruited or impressed from among vagrants and masterless men who could be brought to obey commands and accept discipline only by the threat of punishment. The methods of fighting which they had learned, employing traditional edged weapons, were altered by changing military technology, the enlarged scale of warfare and the need to deal with expanding bureaucracies. In the more competitive sphere of London, the court and the military camp, they were thrust into a theatre of honour where all distinctions between gentlemen and peers were levelled, and an earl might find himself challenged to appear on the field of honour by a mere knight. Increasingly, scientific and mathematical thinking and concepts of merit challenged the traditional values of nobility and honour, and forced the aristocrat continually to confront new intellectual, cultural and social realities. The rationalization of the politics of a standing army left little room for swaggering

---

[14] Roger Boyle, 1ˢᵗ earl of Orrery, *A Treatise of the Art of War* (1677), sigs. A1*v*–A2*v*. Two important works which appeared shortly after Orrery's *Treatise* were: Sir James Turner, *Palas Armata: Military Essayes of the Ancient Grecian, Roman and Modern Art of War, Written in the Years 1670 and 1671* (1683) and James Touchet, 2ⁿᵈ earl of Castlehaven, *The Earl of Castlehaven's Review: Or his Memoirs... of the Irish Wars* (1684).

[15] R. C. Anderson (ed.), *The Journal of Edward Montagu, First Earl of Sandwich, 1659–1665*, NRS 64 (1929), pp. x, 158–64; R. Ollard, *Cromwell's Earl: A Life of Edward Montagu, 1ˢᵗ Earl of Sandwich* (1994), 150.

by swordsmen who increasingly had to submit to military hierarchies with king and Parliament at the apex.[16]

An increasing emphasis upon military rather than social hierarchies can be detected aboard the fleet during the Second Anglo-Dutch War, and probably can be attributed to the influence of the lord admiral, James, duke of York. When the earl of Castlehaven came aboard Sir Thomas Allin's ship in May 1665 in the capacity of gentleman volunteer, Allin felt obliged to offer him the captain's cabin. Castlehaven politely declined, but did not hesitate to take the lieutenant's cabin instead. During the same war, when the second duke of Buckingham went aboard the *Royal Charles* in other than an official capacity, he assumed that he would be summoned to participate in a council of war. He and many other titled volunteers were not invited, and when Buckingham complained that the duke of Monmouth was always present at councils of war, he was informed that only flag officers and the commanders of the most important ships of the line were asked to attend. No explanation was offered concerning why the duke of Monmouth, although not holding the king's commission to command a ship, was present, but Buckingham ought to have been able to infer the answer.[17] When the duke of York became king, he gave command of the army to the earl of Feversham. Christopher Monck, second duke of Albemarle, who was colonel of all of the troops of the Horse Guards and who thought that he 'had a patent to command all the forces', complained that he had been slighted. Referring to the earl of Feversham, he added that he did 'not know how to serve those I have commanded'. As commander of the militia forces in Devonshire, Albemarle had failed to halt the advance of the duke of Monmouth's forces during the Rebellion of 1685, and was blamed for not being more active in his resistance. Albemarle had backed himself into a corner, and had to resign. By the beginning of the eighteenth century the laws of honour allowed precedence over knights to colonels and higher ranks in the army even though the holders of such military rank might not have been born gentlemen. However, Jonathan Swift continued to worry that the expansion of the army promoted social mobility and raised up *nouveaux riches* officers, and that the high rate of casualties during the War of Spanish Succession hastened this process.[18]

Professional soldiers without the means to purchase commissions in Charles II's armies had served in the armies of mainland Europe or in the Tangier garrison before it was abandoned. The professionalization of the English army began in the reign of James VII and II, when these officers began returning to the Three

[16] J. Dewald, *Aristocratic Experience and the Origins of Modern Culture: France 1570–1715* (1993), 46; H. Speier, 'Militarism in the Eighteenth Century', *Social Order and the Risks of War: Papers in Political Sociology* (1952), 232–3.

[17] R. C. Anderson (ed.), *Journals of Sir Thomas Allin, 1660–1678*, 2 vols., NRS 79–80 (1939–40), i. 233; Anderson (ed.), *Journal of Edward Montagu*, 179–80.

[18] *The Autobiography of Sir John Bramston*, CS OS 32 (1843), 205–7; *ODNB, sub* Christopher Monck, 2nd duke of Albemarle (1653–1688); *The Laws of Honour* (1714), 3; *The Examiner*, no. 13 (2 Nov. 1710), quoted in Holmes, *Politics, Religion and Society in England*, 345–6.

Kingdoms during James's expansion of the English and Irish armies. These men, such as John, Lord Churchill, Percy Kirke, Sir John Lanier and David Colyear, were itinerant soldiers in a variety of armies, whose allegiances shifted easily; their ambition to take advantage of the prospects for promotion and a more settled career under William II and III kept James's English army from dissolving after the Williamite invasion. It was also during William's reign that professional officers came to form the core of the British army. At the same time, in the short interludes of peace their presence in England as half-pay officers began to challenge the political and social exclusivity of the landed aristocrats, who had previously scorned professional soldiers as mercenaries. Because opportunities for professional officers did not expand at the same rate in the Scottish and Irish armies, many from those nations had to continue to seek opportunities in mainland European armies.[19]

Soldiers found full employment during the Nine Years War, which lasted most of William's reign, but the king conceived a poor opinion of British officers, whether gentlemen or professionals. Some of the experienced professionals turned out to be incompetent when given high command, and William thought that English peers were not amenable to military discipline. He disliked courtiers, and believed that only military men could claim noble status. He must have taken great pleasure in ordering the band of gentlemen pensioners to go to Flanders and fight. Part of William's difficulties in communicating with English peers can be explained by the difficulty in bridging the gap between martial culture and the world of the English court. Court and camp were almost indistinguishable in the Netherlands. This helps to explain why he did not attempt to reform the British army as he had done in the case of the Dutch in the 1680s, and why he did not reward and punish officers as he did in the Dutch army. Compared to his predecessors on the English throne, William dubbed fewer knights than any monarch in the previous century, including Elizabeth.[20]

William of Orange began to introduce reforms into the Dutch army soon after he was made captain-general in the early 1670s. He forbade colonels of regiments to chose their own regimental agents—a source of financial peculation—and prohibited false musters and dead-pays, which kept the commanders of field armies from accurately estimating their resources of military manpower. He executed one colonel who chose to ignore those orders, and the problem did not occur again. William also reversed the decisions of courts martial of officers where he thought the sentences were too lenient, and he punished officers who did not maintain secure watches or sleep in camp with their soldiers. Medical care was provided free to Dutch soldiers in field hospitals, whereas English soldiers had to pay for treatment. Consequently, the Dutch army reached its peak of efficiency during the Nine Years War. Dutch soldiers were well disciplined, did not plunder and returned to their colours after the heat of battle so that they could fight again.

[19] Childs, *BAW* 14, 39–42; id., *Profession of Arms*, p. xi.
[20] Childs, *BAW* 42–3, 53–4; Baxter, *William III*, 248–9; Luttrell, *RSA* ii. 395; Manning, *Swordsmen*, 94–6; William A. Shaw, *The Knights of England*, 2 vols. (1906), ii. 136–272.

William may not have been as great a general as some of the French military leaders whom he fought, but the Dutch army was better organized and disciplined and was paid more regularly than the French.[21]

The immediate necessity of sending British troops to assist the Confederate Allies in Flanders and the task of conquering Scotland and Ireland deflected William II and III from thoroughgoing reforms of the British army, and again, this delayed the process of professionalization. William's government desperately needed the help of English peers in a political and administrative as well as a military capacity. William picked officers for high command on the basis of experience and tended to favour officers such as Hugh Mackay, John Cutts and David Colyear who had served in the Scots and Anglo-Dutch Brigades of the Dutch army. For the very highest levels of command, he chose well born men such as the second duke of Ormonde or even Thomas Tollemache, whose mother was a Scottish duchess, because he could not imagine the princes who led the armies of the Grand Coalition speaking to someone below that exalted rank. John, Lord Churchill, was man that William regarded as an upstart and certainly no gentleman. Of course, William thought that his cousins were the fittest persons to command, and Ormonde was, after all, a cousin.[22]

In May 1689 a royal commission was established to reform 'abuses in the army'. This was a cynical and half-hearted attempt at reform on William's part. The commissioners, who conducted the very first general inspection of the English army, were sent out to various garrisons and to the newly established regimental depots with the authority to cashier officers and disband ineffective and disloyal regiments. The officers who were suspected of Jacobite sympathies had already been purged or had retired overseas of their own volition. Little was accomplished to stop the practice of false musters, and enlisted men who testified against their officers suffered retaliation. Officers in John Coy's Regiment of Dragoons, Princess Anne's Regiment of Foot (commanded by John Beaumont) and several other regiments were tried by court martial for returning false musters. Six or seven officers are known to have been punished by being fined or cashiered. But the rankers who testified against their officers suffered severe retaliation from those who remained. Several soldiers were flogged or made to run the gauntlet; one who was accused of desertion from another regiment was made to run it twice, while two soldiers who had the temerity to testify against the lieutenant-colonel of Colt's Regiment for making false returns of musters were condemned to be shot for having deserted other regiments. In the First Troop of Life Guards, four gentlemen troopers who had sent a letter of complaint against their superior officers to the king were cashiered.[23] The royal commissioners sought to compel officers not to withhold pay from their men, not to absent themselves from drill on the parade ground without permission, and ordered all officers in the foot

---

[21] Baxter, *William III*, 93–4, 102, 281–2; ten Raa and F. Bas, *Staatsche Leger*, vi. 8–9.
[22] Childs, *BAW* 53–4; Baxter, *William III*, 288–9.
[23] Childs, *BAW* 27–30, 42–3; Luttrell, *RSA* ii. 513; iii. 133, 193, 277, 373, 393, 396, 492; iv. 85.

except the regimental major not to appear on the parade ground on horseback. Other abuses by officers that the commissioners sought to reform included the failure to provide adequate clothing and equipment to their soldiers and the refusal to discharge debts to innkeepers for billeting. Many of these and other abuses were found in mainland European armies, and William probably had no illusions about his ability to effect army reforms if he wanted to ensure enough loyalty in British and Irish regiments to get them embarked for Flanders to fight the war against France. Although no regiments are known to have refused this service, most of the officers of Lillingstone's Regiment had to be cashiered for refusing to go to Jamaica in 1695. Professor Childs concludes that the royal commission to reform army abuses was simply a nod to the Whigs in Parliament.[24]

Since many officers had a proprietary interest in their offices, it is hardly surprising that some believed that those offices should produce a financial return. Charles Mordaunt, first earl of Monmouth (and later third earl of Peterborough), one of the king's commissioners to reform the army, although himself a gentleman officer rather than a professional, strongly disapproved of the purchase system because 'it disobliges all good officers that expect to rise by their service and diligence'. Monmouth was surprised and shocked to learn that there were two particular coffee-houses in London where colonels met to broker commissions as if they were taking bids on a public stock exchange. 'They sell most scandalously to any man without the least pretence (against all the just ones) that gives them the most money.' Such officers did not submit easily to military discipline, and Monmouth complained that they could not be counted upon to embark with their regiments for Flanders. But, it must be added, most people thought Monmouth was mad, and his was a minority voice.[25]

The English Parliament's main concern was to weaken royal authority over the army. This was a consequence of the recollections of members of how Charles II and James II had used their armies to strengthen royal power. The annual Mutiny Acts and parliamentary control over taxation provided the means to maintain this parliamentary oversight, as did the purchase system. Proprietary military offices were sold at a price-level high enough to maintain aristocratic influence and to make the army officer class primarily a preserve of gentlemen amateurs rather than an officer corps of professional soldiers. Because the purchase of commissions gave greater weight to proprietary rights than patronage, it may also have helped to protect the army against political interference during a time of political instability before the officer class was fully professionalized. Recognizing that Parliament was the ultimate source of military authority,

---

[24] Childs, *BAW* 27–30; *Exercise of the Foot: With the Evolutions according to the Words of Command* (1690), 222–6; Luttrell, *RSA* iii. 429.

[25] HMC, *Reports of the Manuscripts of Allan George Finch*, 4 vols. (1913–), iv. 98; *ODNB*, *sub* Charles Mordaunt, 3rd earl of Peterborough and 1st earl of Monmouth (1658?–1735).

British officers in the eighteenth century came to accept the legal subordination of the British army to civilian control.[26]

As long as the Nine Years War continued, the high casualty rates among company- and field-grade officers ensured that there would be opportunities for commissioning and promotion based at least in part upon competence demonstrated on the battlefield. Sir Daniel Fleming obtained an ensign's commission for his son Michael in James Stanley's Regiment of Foot after raising twenty men. Michael demonstrated courage and competence on the battlefield, and in a little more than a year he had been promoted to the rank of captain. Colonels had the right of nomination, but the king reserved the right to approve all promotions. Under William II and III, promotion within the company- and field-officer ranks was by seniority.[27] Charles Gerard, second earl of Macclesfield, claimed that he did not grant commissions in his cavalry regiment to any officer who did not possess military experience. However, there were other colonels who accepted bribes for commissions and who concealed vacancies in the officer ranks by returning false musters in order to collect the dead-pays for vacant military offices. William attempted to stop the practice in 1695 by cashiering the most egregious offender, Colonel Fernando Hastings.[28] In Scotland, Brigadier R. Maitland, commander of the garrison at Fort William, told the Scottish secretary of state, when recommending a cadet and two young officers for a commission and promotions, that he had always subscribed to King William II and III's criteria of merit and seniority. On the other hand, an earlier Scottish secretary of state, James Johnston, writing in 1693, had favoured drawing colonels of regiments from high-ranking and politically loyal members of the nobility, while employing experienced professional officers to serve as majors and lieutenant-colonels.[29] Despite the attempts of King William and Queen Anne to prevent the sale and purchase of military commissions, the practice had become entrenched by the early eighteenth century. By 1727 Humphrey Bland noted that the practice of serving an apprenticeship in arms in the ranks as a gentleman volunteer was in decline. He thought that the system of promotion on the basis of merit and experience that prevailed in the Dutch army, where the sale of commissions was forbidden, was the best one.[30]

Before the Williamite invasion of the British Isles, young gentlemen acquired military expertise and experience by serving an apprenticeship in arms in various armies and garrisons at home or in mainland European armies. This hands-on

---

[26] M. L. Bush, *The English Aristocracy: A Comparative Synthesis* (1984), 205–6; Childs, *BAW* 57–8; Humphry Bland, *A Treatise of Military Discipline* (1727), preface.

[27] HMC, *Twelfth Report*, Appendix, Pt. VII (Le Fleming MSS.) (1890), 331–6; HMC, *Finch MSS.*, iv. 20, 30, 41, 345; Childs, *BAW* 60–1.

[28] Luttrell, *RSA* iii. 280; Childs, *BAW* 49–50: C. Walton, *History of the British Standing Army, 1660–1700* (1894), 452–3.

[29] J. Grant (ed.), *Seafield Correspondence from 1685 to 1708*, SHS NS 3 (1912), 231; Joseph McCormick (comp.), *State Papers and Letters Addressed to William Carstares* (1774), 160.

[30] Luttrell, *RSA* v. 209; Bland, *Military Discipline*, 115, 145.

experience was sometimes supplemented, for those whose parents could afford it, by taking the grand tour or by attending military academies—especially those of France. Attending foreign military academies in Catholic countries, where there might be Jacobite agents lurking, became unacceptable after the Calvinistic William II and III became the ruler of the Three Kingdoms, and mounted a propaganda campaign declaring himself the defender of Protestant liberties in Europe. This led to proposals to erect a military academy in the vicinity of London and Westminster, which was contained in a bill introduced into Parliament in 1689 to license and regulate hackney coaches, and to use licensing fees as a source of revenue for the project. The bill never passed, and like other projects to establish an academy to provide professional training for military officers, the proposal withered and died. Most members of the English aristocracy had no desire to promote an institution to train a class of career professionals who would gain commissions and promotions on the basis of technical qualifications and merit alone. Daniel Defoe attempted to revive the project for a military academy in 1697, and pointed out that during the Nine Years War most of the military engineers and general officers in the British army were foreigners. He concluded that, given the lack of professional military training in England, this could hardly have been otherwise.[31] An apprenticeship in arms served in the ranks had been a useful way of training officers for the infantry and cavalry, but the practice was falling into disuse in the early eighteenth century, and there was nothing to take the place of that practice for many decades. The experience of service in foreign armies had been quite common among soldiers of the British Isles in the seventeenth century, but a Swiss visitor to England in the 1720s thought that the practice, except among the Irish, was dying out for the same reason that English aristocrats were less likely to resort to court than formerly. Independent wealth was easier to come by through managing one's estates, and the English did not particularly esteem military titles. The Scots were less likely to serve in mainland European armies in the eighteenth century because of expanding opportunities in the British army.[32]

The increasing difficulties that a gentleman volunteer serving in the ranks faced in obtaining a commission can be illustrated from the career of Robert Parker, an Irish Protestant from Kilkenny. Parker had been a schoolboy friend of James Butler, later second duke of Ormonde, and he had acquired an interest in military matters as a member of Butler's school cadet company. In 1683, at age 17, Parker joined Captain Frederick Hamilton's independent company—later part of William Steward, first Viscount Mountjoy's Regiment of Foot—but he was

---

[31] Childs, *BAW* 54; *Cal. S.P., Dom., 1700–1702*, 540–1; [Daniel Defoe], *An Essay upon Projects* (1697), 252.

[32] C. M. Clode, *The Military Forces of the Crown: Their Administration and Government*, 2 vols (1869), ii. 457–61; [Béat Louis de Muralt], *Letters Describing the Character and Customs of the English and French Nations* (1726), 3–4.

dismissed from the Irish army in 1687 because of his religion. In April 1689 Parker rejoined Hamilton's company, now part of the earl of Meath's Regiment, at the age of 23. He was not commissioned ensign until he was 29 years of age, after he had been through most of the major battles and sieges in Ireland and Flanders, and had demonstrated bravery on the battlefield at the Siege of Namur. Promotion came very slowly: he was made lieutenant at age 36, and finally was promoted captain of grenadiers in the Royal Regiment of Ireland when he was 42. In 1718 he sold his captain's commission and retired to Ireland.[33]

The shared experience of serving together in foreign and colonial wars (not forgetting those Englishmen and Scots who fought together for the Royalist cause during the Wars of the Three Kingdoms) was an important means of integrating the aristocracies of those two British kingdoms, and certainly helped to pave the way for an increasingly integrated British army, both before and after the Act of Union of 1707.[34] The poetry of George Lauder, a Scot who had accompanied the first duke of Buckingham's expedition to the Isle of Rhé, served as a colonel in the English Royalist army, gone into exile after the Royalist defeat and served as an officer in the Dutch army, conveys these sentiments and loyalties. Although offered a commission by the duke of Lauderdale, the need to feed a large family kept him abroad after the Restoration. One of his poems, published not long after the disastrous Isle of Rhé expedition, celebrates this sense of a common nationality that arose from shared military experiences:

> And this island all hath but one name,
> One king, one faith, one language, and one law,
> So let one love your hearts together draw
> That all Scots, English, all English Scots may be
> Possessed with the same mind which ruleth me.[35]

There were few opportunities for establishing careers in Charles II's army except in foreign forces and colonial garrisons, but many of the experienced English, Scots and Irish veterans of the French, Portuguese and Dutch armies began returning home when James VII and II began expanding the English army in 1685, and younger men also had the opportunity to begin military careers. Under both James and William, the distinction between professional and gentlemen officers began to abate, although it never did entirely disappear. The Irish and Scots armies did not expand like the English army, and most Scots and Irish officers who successfully pursued careers were able to do so because their

---

[33] Robert Parker, *Memoirs of the Most Remarkable Military Transactions From the Year 1683 to 1718 . . . in Ireland and Flanders* (1747), 2–3, 11–14; *ODNB, sub* Robert Parker (*fl.* 1718).

[34] K. M. Brown, 'The Origins of a British Aristocracy: Integration and its Limitations Before the Treaty of Union', in S. G. Ellis and S. Barber (eds.), *Conquest and Union: Fashioning a British State, 1485–1725* (1995), 224–5.

[35] [George Lauder], *The Scottish Souldier, by Lauder* (1629), sig. B2r & v; *ODNB, sub* George Lauder (*fl.* 1622–1677).

regiments were carried on the English establishment. Thus, the English army became more British in the years before the Act of Union, and, for the officers involved, this promoted interest in and loyalty to a British state. The accession to the thrones of the Three Kingdoms of William II and III brought foreign officers into the British army whose presence was resented, but that prejudice did not extend to Scottish and Irish Protestant officers. The Protestant Irish were considered to be more inclined to martial pursuits than the Catholic Irish, and more loyal. It would be another century before the British army began to perceive the Catholic Irish as a source of reliable military manpower.[36]

[36] Childs, *AJGR* 27–8; Brown, 'From Scottish Lords to British Officers', 148–9, 152; Sir William Petty, *The Political Anatomy of Ireland* (1691), 27.

Select Bibliography

Limitations of space necessitate a selective bibliography. Those frequently cited works contained in the List of Abbreviations are omitted.

I. MANUSCRIPT SOURCES

British Library, London

Additional MS. 9,723 (Blathwayt Papers).

 MS. 11,133 (Correspondence of Henry Cary, Viscount Falkland, lord deputy of Ireland).

 MS. 18,979 (Fairfax Correspondence).

 MS. 41,141 (Richard Kane, 'An Account of the Most Remarkable Military Transactions which happened in the Campaigns made from the 1689 to the Conclusion of the Peace of Ryswick in1697'; 'A Method of Discipline for the Behaviour of the Foot upon Action').

 MS. 46,188.

Harley MS. 945 ('Maxims and Observations of War', by Col. Thomas Culpeper, engineer general to James II).

 MS. 3638 (Sir Francis Vere, 'The Journey of Cadiz'; Sir Edward Cecil, Lord Wimbledon, 'The Duty of a Private Soldier'; id., 'Journal of the Spanish Expedition').

Royal MS. 18. C. xxiii ('Of Divers Parts of War, Especially the Cavalry').

Stowe MS. 133.

 MS. 459 ('Diary of John Richards' Travel from Dublin to Venice').

 MS. 466 ('Letterbook of John Richards, 1703–4').

Huntington Library, San Marino, Calif.

Ellesmere MSS., EL 8527.

Hastings MSS., HA (Military Box), 2 (3).

Stowe-Nugent MSS. (Spec. Subjects, War of 1689–91), 1.

Public Record Office (National Archives), London

SP 16 (State Papers, Domestic, Charles I).

SP 84 (State Papers, Holland).

II. PRINTED PRIMARY SOURCES

AINSWORTH, J. (ed.), *The Inchiquin Manuscripts*, IMC (1961).

ANDERSON, R. C. (ed.), *The Journal of Edward Montagu, First Earl of Sandwich, 1659–1665*, NRS 64 (1929).

BELL, R. (ed.), *Memoirs of the Civil War: The Correspondence of the Fairfax Family*, 2 vols. (1849).

CARTE, THOMAS (ed.) *A Collection of Original Letters and Papers... found among the Duke of Ormonde's Papers* (1739).

'The Correspondence of Francis Taaffe, Earl of Carlingford', *Memoirs of the Family of Taaffe* (1856).

Count Taaffe's Letters from the Imperial Camp to his Brother the Earl of Carlingford (1684).

FIRTH, C. H. (ed.), *The Clarke Papers*, 4 vols., CS NS 49, 54, 61, 62 (1891–1901).

—— *Scotland and the Commonwealth: Letters and Papers Relating to the Military Government of Scotland, 1651–1653*, SHS 18 (1895).

FLETCHER of Saltoun, ANDREW, *Political Works*, ed. J. Robertson (1997).

HMC, *Calendar of the Manuscripts of the... Marquis of Salisbury*, 24 vols. (1883–1976).

—— *Fourteenth Report*, Pt. VI (House of Lords) (1894).

—— *Lord De L'Isle and Dudley* (1925), vol. i.

—— '... Life and Memoirs of John Lord Belsyse, Written... by his Secretary, Joshua Moone', *Ormonde MSS.*, NS 2 (1903).

—— *Report on the Manuscripts of the Marquis of Ormonde*, ed. J. S. Gilbert, 2 vols., OS (1895, 1899).

—— *Thirteenth Report*, Appendix, Pts. II (Portland MSS.) and V (House of Lords) (1892).

JENNINGS, B. (ed.), *Wild Geese in Spanish Flanders, 1587–1700: Documents Relating Chiefly to Irish Regiments, from the Archives Générales, Brussels*, IMC (1964).

KAUFMAN, H. A. (ed.), *Tangier at High Tide: The Journal of John Luke, 1670–1673* (1958).

KNOWLER, WILLIAM (comp.), *The Earl of Strafforde's Letters and Dispatches*, 2 vols. (1739).

LATHAM, R., and W. MATTHEWS (eds.), *The Diary of Samuel Pepys*, 11 vols. (1971).

MORRICE, THOMAS (comp.), *The State Letters of Roger Boyle, 1ˢᵗ Earl of Orrery* (1742).

Passages from the Diary of General Patrick Gordon of Auchleuchries, 1635–1699, SC 20 (1849).

POCOCK, J. G. A. (ed.), *Political Works of James Harrington* (1977).

RAZZELL, E. and P. (eds.), *The English Civil War: A Contemporary Account*, 5 vols. (1996).

THURLOE, JOHN, *A Collection of State Papers*, ed. Thomas Birch, 7 vols. (1742).

VENABLES, ROBERT, *The Narrative of General Venables... Relating to the Expedition to the West Indies and the Conquest of Jamaica, 1654–1655*, ed. C. H. Firth, CS NS 60 (1900).

VERNEY, F. P. and M. M., *Memoirs of the Verney Family during the Seventeenth Century*, 2 vols. (1907).

The Works of Francis Bacon, ed. J. Spedding, 14 vols. (1857–74; repr. 1963).

III. BOOKS WRITTEN OR PRINTED BEFORE 1800

ABERCROMBY, PATRICK, *The Martial Achievements of the Scots Nation*, 2 vols. (1711, 1715).

An Abridgement of English Military Discipline (1682).

An... Account of the Siege of Namur (1695).

ADDISON, LANCELOT, *A Discourse of Tangier under the Government of the Earl of Teviot*, 2ⁿᵈ edn. (1685).

Advice to a Soldier... Written by an Officer in the English Army (1680), repr. in J. Malham (ed.), *HM*, 12 vols. (1808–11).

A.U., *Historie of the... Siege of Ostend... translated out of French by Edward Grimeston* (1604).

The Autobiography of Sir John Bramston, CS os 32 (1845).

BACON, Sir FRANCIS, *The Essayes and Counsells, Civill and Morall*, ed. M. Kieran (1985).

BARRY, GERRAT, *A Discourse of Military Discipline* (1634).

BERNARDI, JOHN, *A Short History of the Life of Major John Bernardi* (1729).

BINGHAM, JOHN, *The Art of Embattailing an Army, or the Second Part of Aelian's Tacticks* (1629; repr. 1968).

[BINGHAM, JOHN], *Tactics of Aelian* (1616; repr. 1968).

[BORLASE, EDMUND], *The History of the Irish Rebellion* (1743).

—— *The Reduction of Ireland to the Crown of England* (1675).

BOTELER, NATHANIEL, *War Practically Performed* (1663).

BOYLE, ROGER, 1ˢᵗ earl of Orrery, *A Treatise of the Art of War* (1677).

BROWNING, A. (ed.), *Memoirs of Sir John Reresby* (1936; repr. 1991).

BRUCE, THOMAS, 2ⁿᵈ earl of Ailesbury and 3ʳᵈ earl of Elgin, *Memoirs*, 2 vols., RC (1890).

[BURGH, ULICK DE, marquis of Clanricarde], *Memoires of the... Marquis of Clanricarde, Lord Deputy of Ireland* (1744).

BURNET, GILBERT, bishop of Salisbury, *The Memorials of James and William, Dukes of Hamilton and Castle-Herald* (1852).

—— *History of His Own Time*, ed. M. J. Routh, 6 vols. (1833; repr. 1969).

CAVENDISH, MARGARET, duchess of Newcastle, *The Life of William Cavendish, Duke of Newcastle*, ed. C. H. Firth (1906).

CECIL, Sir EDWARD, VISCOUNT WIMBLEDON, *A Journal and Relation of the Action... upon the Coast of Spaine* (1626).

CHILDS, J. (ed.), 'Captain Henry Herbert's Narrative of his Journey through France with his Regiment, 1671–3, and ane Account of Our Regiment's March from their winter Quarters to their Entrance into France', *CM XXX*, CS 4ᵗʰ ser. 39 (1990).

CHOLMLEY, Sir HUGH, *An Account of Tangier* (1787).

—— *Memoirs* (1787).

Colonel Joseph Bampfield's Apologie (1685).

The Commentaries of Sir Francis Vere (1657), in C. H. Firth (ed.), *Stuart Tracts, 1603–1693* (1903; repr. 1973).

COX, Sir RICHARD, *Hibernia Anglicana: or the History of Ireland*, 2 vols., 2ⁿᵈ edn. (1692).

[CRUSO, JOHN], *Militarie Instructions for the Cavallrie* (1692).

DALRYMPLE, Sir JOHN, *Memoirs of Great Britain and Ireland*, 2 vols. (1771–3).

D'AUVERGNE, EDWARD, *The History of the Campagne in Flanders for the Year 1691* (1735).

—— *The History of the Campaign in Flanders for the Year 1695* (1696).

—— *The History of the Campagne in Flanders... 1696* (1696).

—— *The History of the Campagne in Flanders... 1697* (1698).

—— *The History of the Campagne in the Spanish Netherlands, 1694* (1694).

—— *The History of the Last Campagne in the Spanish Netherlands, 1693* (1693).

—— *A Relation of... the Last Campaigne... in the Spanish Netherlands, 1692* (1693).

DAVIES, EDWARD, *The Art of War and England's Traynings* (1619; repr. 1968).

DAVIES, G. (ed.), *Autobiography of Thomas Raymond*, CS 3ʳᵈ ser. 28 (1917).

DAVIES, Sir JOHN, *A Discovery of the True Causes Why Ireland was never Entirely Subdued*, ed. J. P. Meyers (1612; repr. 1988).

[DEFOE, DANIEL], *An Argument Shewing that a Standing Army, with the Consent of Parliament, is not Inconsistent with a Free Government* (1698).

[DEFOE, DANIEL], *A Brief Reply to the History of Standing Armies in England* (1698).

—— *An Essay upon Projects* (1697).

DIGGES, LEONARD and THOMAS, *An Arithmeticall Militaire Treatise named Stratioticos* (1579; repr. 1968).

DIGGES, THOMAS and DUDLEY, *Foure Paradoxes, or Politique Discourses* (1604).

[DRUMMOND OF BALHALDY, JOHN], *Memoirs of Sir Ewen Cameron of Locheill*, ed. J. Macknight, MC 59 (1842).

The Earl of Castlehaven's Review: or His Memoires of... the Irish Wars (1684).

ELTON, RICHARD, *The Compleat Body of the Art Military* (1650).

An Exact Journal of the... Progress of their Majesties' Forces under the Command of Gen. Ginkel (1691).

The Exercise of the Foot: With Evolutions according to the Words of Command (1690).

FAIRFAX, THOMAS, Lord, *Short Memorials* (1699).

FERGUSON, J., *Two Scottish Soldiers: A Soldier of 1688 and Blenheim and a Soldier of the American Revolution* (1888).

FLEETWOOD, WILLIAM, *An Unhappy View of the Whole Behaviour of my Lord Duke of Buckingham at... the Isle of Rhee* (1648), in Sir W. Scott (ed.), *Somers Tracts*, 13 vols. (1809–15), vol. v.

The Foure Bookes of Flavius Vegetius Renatus, trans. John Sadler (1572; repr. 1968).

FRASER, JAMES, *Chronicles of the Frasers*, ed. W. Mackay, SHS 1st ser. 47 (1905).

[FRASER,] SIMON [11th] Lord Lovat, *Memoirs*, trans. W. Godwin (1797).

GORDON, JAMES, parson of Rothiemay, *History of Scots Affairs*, 3 vols., SC 1, 2, 4 (1841).

GRAHAM OF DEUCHRIE, JOHN, *The Expedition of William Ninth Earl of Glencairn*, Miscellanea Scotica, 4 (1819).

GRENVILLE, Sir RICHARD, *Two Original Journals of Sir Richard Grenville... II. Of the Expedition to the Isle of Rhee in France, Anno 1627* (1724).

GRIMSTONE, EDWARD, *A Generall Historie of the Netherlands* (1627).

GROTIUS, HUGO, *The Law of War and Peace* (1925; repr. 1962).

GUMBLE, THOMAS, *The Life of General Monck, Duke of Albemarle* (1671).

HALE, J. R. (ed.), *On a Tudor Parade Ground: The Captain's Handbook of Henry Barrett, 1562* (1978).

HEWITSON, A. (ed.) *Diary of Thomas Bellingham, an Officer under William III* (1698).

HEXHAM, HENRY, *The Principles of the Art Militarie Practiced in the Warres of the United Provinces* (1637).

—— *The Second Part of the Principles of the Art Militaire Practized in the Warres of the United Provinces* (1638).

An Historical Account of the British Regiments Employed since the Reign of Queen Elizabeth and James I in the Formation and Defence of the Dutch Republic (1794).

HOBBES, THOMAS, *Behemoth: The History of the Causes of the Civil Wars of England*, ed. William Molesworth (1682; repr. 1963).

H[OGAN], E. (ed.), *The History of the Warr of Ireland from 1641 to 1653 by a British Officer of the Regiment of Sir John Clotworthy* (1873).

HOLLES, GERVASE, *Memorials of the Holles Family, 1493–1656*, ed. A. C. Wood, CS 3rd ser. 60 (1937).

HOPTON, Sir RALPH, Lord Hopton, *Bellum Civile: Hopton's Narrative of his Campaigne in the West, 1642–1644*, ed. C. E. H. Chadwyck Healey, SRS 18 (1902).

HOWELL, JAMES, *Epistolae Ho-Elianae, or the Familiar Letters of James Howell*, 2 vols. (1907).

HUTCHINSON, LUCY, *Memoirs of the Life of Colonel Hutchinson*, ed. C. H. Firth (1906).

HYDE, EDWARD, earl of Clarendon, *The History of the Rebellion and Civil Wars in Ireland* (1719–20).

JENNER, H. (ed.), *Memoirs of Viscount Dundee... by an Officer of the Army* (1714; repr. 1903).

KANE, RICHARD, *Campaigns of King William and the Duke of Marlborough*, 2ⁿᵈ edn. (1747).

LAUDER OF FOUNTAINHALL, Sir JOHN, *Historical Notices of Scottish Affairs*, ed. D. Laing, 2 vols., BC 87 (1848).

—— *Historical Observations... October 1680 to April 1686*, ed. D. Urquhart and D. Laing, BC 66 (1837).

LINDSAY, COLIN, 3ʳᵈ earl of Balcarres, *Memoirs touching the Revolution, 1688–1690*, BC 71 (1841).

MACKAY, HUGH, *Memoirs of the War Carried on in Scotland and Ireland, 1689–1691*, BC 48 (1833).

MACKAY, J., *The Life of Lieut.-General Hugh Mackay, Commander in Chief of the Forces in Scotland, 1689 and 1690*, BC 53 (1836).

MACKENZIE, JOHN, *A Narrative of the Siege of London-Derry* (1690).

[MALTHUS, THOMAS], *Historical Memoires of the Life and Death of... Rupert, Prince Palatine of the Rhine* (1683).

MARKHAM, FRANCIS, *Five Decades of Epistles of Warre* (1622).

MARKHAM, GERVASE, 'The Muster-master', ed. C. L. Hamilton, *CM XXVI*, CS 4ᵗʰ ser. 14 (1975).

—— *The Souldier's Accidence, or an Introduction into Military Discipline* (1635).

MARKHAM, ROBERT, *Memoirs of the Military Transactions of Sir John Burroughs, Knt* (1758).

—— *The Description of that ever to be famed Knight, Sir John Burgh, Colonel-General of his Majestie's Army* (1628).

The Memoirs of Capt. Peter Drake (1755).

Memoirs of Denzil Lord Holles (1699).

The Memoirs of James II: His Campaigns as Duke of York, 1652–1660, trans. A. L. Sells (1962).

Memoirs of Sir Andrew Melvill, trans. T. Ameer-Al (1918).

METERAN, EMMANUEL VAN, *A... Discourse Historicall of the Succeeding Governors in the Netherlands and the Civill Warres*, trans. Thomas Churchyard (1602).

MICHELBOURNE, JOHN, *An Account of the Transactions in the North of Ireland... with a... Relation of the... Besieging and Taking of the Town of Sligoe* (1692).

The Military Memoirs of Capt. George Carleton (1728).

MONCK, GEORGE, 1ˢᵗ duke of Albermarle, *Observations upon Military and Political Affairs* (1671).

MURRAY, R. H. (ed.), *The Journals of John Stevens Containing a Brief Account of the War in Ireland, 1689–1691* (1912).

NAUNTON, Sir ROBERT, *Fragmenta Regalia, or Observations upon Queen Elizabeth, Her Times and Favourites*, ed. J. S. Cervoski (1641; repr. 1985).

NEVILL, HENRY, *Plato Redivivus* [*c*.1681], repr. in C. Robbins (ed.), *Two English Republican Tracts* (1969).

[OLDMIXON, JOHN], *The History and Life of Robert Blake* (*c*.1740).

Original Memoirs Written during the Great Civil War, Being the Life of Sir Henry Slingsby (1806).

Original Memoirs Written during the Great Civil War . . . Memoirs of Captain John Hodgson (1806).

OSBORNE, PEREGRINE, marquis of Carmarthen and duke of Leeds, *A Journal of the Brest Expedition* (1694).

PALMER, THOMAS, *Bristol's Military Garden* (1635).

PARKER, ROBERT, *Memoirs of the Most Remarkable Military Transactions from the Year 1683 to 1718 . . . in Ireland and Flanders* (1747).

REID, H. M. B. (ed.), *One of King William's Men . . . The Diary of Col. William Maxwell of Cardoness, 1685–1697* (1898).

RICH, BARNABE, *Alarme to England foreshewing What Perilles are Procured where the People live without regarde of Martiall Lawe* (1578).

—— *Path-Way to Military Practice* (1587).

RICHARDS, JACOB, *A Journal of the Siege and Taking of Buda by the Imperial Army* (1687).

SAWLE, WILLIAM, *An Impartial Relation of . . . Last Summer's Campaign in Flanders* (1691).

SHUTTLEWORTH, J. M. (ed.), *The Life of Edward, First Lord Herbert of Cherbury, Written by Himself* (1976).

SIDNEY, ALGERNON, *Court Maxims*, ed. H. W. Blom, E. H. Mulier and R. Janse (1996).

—— *Discourses concerning Government* (1698; repr. 1979).

SMYTHE, Sir JOHN, *Certain Discourses Military*, ed. J. R. Hale (1964).

SOMERVILLE, JAMES [by right 11th Lord], *Memorie of the Somervilles* [ed. Sir W. Scott], 2 vols. (1815).

SOMERS, JOHN, 1st Lord, *A Letter Ballancing the Necessity of Keeping a Land-Force in Times of Peace* (1697).

SPALDING, JOHN, *The History of the Troubles and Memorable Transactions in Scotland and England, 1625–1645*, 2 vols., BC 25 (1828–9).

SPALDING, RUTH (ed.), *The Diary of Bulstrode Whitelocke, 1605–1675*, BARSEH NS 13 (1990).

SPRIGGE, JOSHUA, *Anglia Rediviva: England's Recovery*, ed. H. T. Moore (1647; repr. 1960).

STORY, GEORGE, *A Continuation of the Impartial History of Ireland* (1693).

—— *A True and Impartial History of . . . the Kingdom of Ireland during the Last Two Years with the Present State of Both Armies* (1691).

SUTCLIFFE, MATTHEW, *The Practice, Proceedings and the Lawes of Armes* (1593).

The Swedish Discipline, Religious, Civile and Military (1632).

[TOLAND, JOHN], *The Militia Reformed: Or an Easy Scheme of Furnishing England with a Constant Land Force* (1698).

[TRENCHARD, JOHN], *A Short History of Standing Armies in England* (1698).

—— *The Militia Reformed* (1698).

The Triumphs of Nassau, trans. W. Shute (1590).

TUCKER, N. (ed.), *The Military Memoirs of Captain John Gwyn* (1822), in P. Young (ed.), *Military Memoirs: The Civil War* (1967).

TURNER, Sir JAMES, *Memoirs of his own Life and Time, 1632–1670*, BC 31 (1829).

—— *Pallas Armata: Military Essayes of the Ancient Grecian, Roman and Modern Art of War* (1683; repr. 1968).

VENN, THOMAS, *Military and Maritime Discipline* (1672).

The Vindication of Richard Atkyns (1669), in P. Young (ed.), *Miltary Memoirs: The Civil War* (1967).

WALSINGHAM, EDWARD, *Alter Britannia Heros: Or the Life of . . . Sir Henry Gage* (1645).

—— *Britannicae Virtatis Imago: Or the Effigies of... Major-Generall Smith* (1644).

—— 'Life of Sir John Digby (1645)', ed. G. Bernard, *CM XII*, CS 3rd ser. 18 (1910).

WARD, EDWARD, *Mars Stript of his Armour: Or, the army Displayed in all its True Colours* (1709).

WARD, ROBERT, *Animadversions of Warre* (1639).

WEBB, W. (ed.), *Military Memoirs of Colonel John Birch... Written by Roe his Secretary*, CS NS 7 (1873).

WHITELOCKE, BULSTRODE, *Memorials of English Affairs*, 4 vols. (repr. 1853).

WHITTLE, JOHN, *Constantius Redivivus: or... the Wonderful Providences and Unparalleled Successes of... William the 3rd* (1693).

[——] *An Exact Diary of... the Late Expedition of the Prince of Orange* (1689).

[——] *A Short Review of the remarkable Providences attending Our Gracious Sovereign William III* (1699).

WILLIAMS, Sir ROGER, *The Actions of the Low Countries*, ed. D. W. Evans (1618).

WILSON, ARTHUR, *The Life and Reign of James I, The First King of Great Britain* (1653), in [White Kennett,] *Complete History of England*, 3 vols. (1706), vol. ii.

—— 'The Life of Arthur Wilson the Historian... Written by Himself', in Francis Peck (ed.), *Desiderata Curiosa*, 2 vols. (1732–5).

WISHART, GEORGE, *The Memoirs of James Marquis of Montrose, 1639–1650*, trans. A. D. Murdoch and H. F. M. Simpson (1893).

WYATT, GEORGE, 'Treatise of the Militia (*c.*1590)', in D. M. Loades (ed.), *The Papers of George Wyatt, Esquire*, CS 4th ser. 5 (1968).

IV. BOOKS AND ARTICLES PRINTED AFTER 1800

ADAMS, S., *Leicester and the Court: Essays on Elizabethan Politics* (2002).

ADAMSON, J. S. A., 'Chivalry and Political Culture in Caroline England', in K. Sharpe and P. Lake (eds.), *Culture and Politics in Early Stuart England* (1993).

AILES, M. E., *Military Migration and State Formation: The British Military Community in Seventeenth-Century Sweden* (2002).

ALLEN, D., 'The Role of the London Trained Bands in the Exclusion Crisis, 1678–1681', *EHR* 87 (1972).

BARNARD, T., and J. FENLON (eds.), *The Dukes of Ormonde, 1610–1745* (2000).

BECKETT, I. W. F., *The Amateur Military Tradition, 1558–1945* (1991).

BITTON, D., *The French Nobility in Crisis, 1560–1640* (1969).

BLACK, J., *A Military Revolution? Military Change and European Society, 1500–1800* (1991).

BOYNTON, L., *The Elizabethan Militia, 1558–1638* (1967).

BREWER, J., *The Sinews of Power: War, Money and the English State, 1688–1783* (1989).

CANNY, N. P., *The Elizabethan Conquest of Ireland: A Pattern Established* (1976).

—— *Kingdom and Colony: Ireland in the Atlantic World, 1560–1800* (1988).

CARSWELL, J., *The Descent on England: A Study of the English Revolution of 1688 and its European Background* (1969).

CHANDLER, D. (ed.), *The Oxford Illustrated History of the British Army* (1994).

CHILDS, J., 'The British Brigade in France, 1672–78', *History*, 69 (1984).

—— *Nobles, Gentlemen and the Profession of Arms in Restoration Britain, 1660–1688: A Biographical Dictionary of British Army Officers on Foreign Service*, SAHR, spec. publication, 13 (1987).

CHILDS, J., 'War, Crime Waves and the English Army in the Late Seventeenth Century', *War and Society*, 15 (1997).

CLODE, C., *The Military Forces of the Crown: Their Administration and Government*, 2 vols. (1869).

COGSWELL, T., *The Blessed Revolution: English Politics and the Coming of War, 1621–1624* (1989).

—— *Home Divisions: Aristocracy, the State and Provincial Conflict* (1989).

COWAN, E. J., *Montrose: For Covenant and King* (1977).

COWARD, B., 'The Lieutenancy of Lancashire and Cheshire in the Sixteenth and Early Seventeenth Centuries', *THSLC* 119 (1967).

CRICHTON, A., *The Life and Diary of Lieut. Col J. Blackader of the Cameronian Regiment* (1824).

CRUICKSHANK, C. G., *Elizabeth's Army*, 2nd edn. (1968).

CRUICKSHANKS, E. (ed.), *By Force or By Default: The Revolution of 1688–89* (1989).

DALTON, C., *The Life and Times of General Sir Edward Cecil, Viscount Wimbledon*, 2 vols. (1885).

—— *The Scots Army, 1661–1688* (1909; repr. 1989).

DEWALD, J., *Aristocratic Experience and the Origins of Modern Culture: France, 1590–1715* (1993).

DONAGAN, B., 'Atrocity, War Crime and Treason in the English Civil War', *AHR* 104 (1994).

—— 'Codes and Conduct in the English Civil War', *P&P* no. 118 (1994).

—— 'Halcyon Days and the Literature of War: England's Military Education Before 1642', *P&P* no. 147 (1995).

—— 'The Web of Honour: Soldiers, Christians and Gentlemen in the English Civil War', *HJ* 44 (2001).

EDWARDS, P., *Dealing in Death: The Arms Trade and the British Civil Wars, 1638–52* (2000).

ELTIS, D., *The Military Revolution in the Sixteenth-Century Europe* (1995).

EMBERTON, W., *Skippon's Brave Boys: The Origins, Development and Civil War Service of London's Trained Bands* (1984).

FURGOL, E. M., *A Regimental History of the Covenanting Armies, 1639–1651* (1990).

—— 'Scotland Turned Sweden: The Scottish Covenanters and the Military Revolution', in J. Morrill (ed.), *The Scottish National Covenant and its British Context* (1990).

FERGUSON, J. (ed.), *Papers Illustrating the History of the Scots Brigade in the Service of the United Netherlands, 1572–1782*, 2 vols. (1899).

FIRTH, C. H., 'Royalist and Cromwellian Armies in Flanders', *TRHS* NS 17 (1903).

FISCHER, T. A., *The Scots in Germany* (1902).

—— *The Scots in Sweden* (1907).

FISSEL, M. C., *The Bishops' Wars: Charles I's Campaigns against Scotland* (1994).

GLOZIER, M., *The Huguenot Soldiers of William of Orange and the 'Glorious Revolution' of 1688: The Lions of Judah* (2002).

—— *Scottish Soldiers in the Reign of the Sun King: Nursery of Honour* (2004).

GRANT, J., *Memoirs and Adventures of Sir John Hepburn* (1851).

GRIMBLE, I., *Chief of Mackay* (1965).

GROENVELD, S., ' "J'equippe une flotte tres considerable": The Dutch Side of the Glorious Revolution', in R. Beddard (ed.), *The Revolutions of 1688* (1991).

GROSJEAN, A., *An Unofficial Alliance: Scotland and Sweden, 1569–1654* (2003).

HAINSWORTH, R., *The Swordsmen in Power: War and Politics under the English Republic, 1649–1660* (1997).

HALE, J. R., 'The Military Education of the Officer Class in Early Modern Europe', *Renaissance War Studies* (1983).

HAMMER, P., *The Polarisation of Elizabethan Politics: The Political Career of Robert Devereux, 2nd Earl of Essex, 1585–1597* (1999).

HARDACRE, P. H., 'The English Contingent in Portugal, 1662–1668', *JSAHR* 38 (1960).

'T HART, M., *The Making of a Bourgeois State; War, Politics and Finance during the Dutch Revolt* (1993).

HENRY, G., *The Irish Military Community in Flanders, 1586–1621* (1992).

HILL, J. M., *Celtic Warfare, 1595–1763* (1986).

HOAK, D., and M. FEINGOLD (eds.), *The World of William and Mary: Anglo-Dutch Perspectives on the Revolution of 1688–89* (1996).

HOLMES, C., *The Eastern Association in the English Civil War* (1974).

HOPKINS, P., *Glencoe and the End of the Highland Wars* (1986).

HUNT, W., 'Civic Chivalry and the English Civil War', in A. Grafton and A. Blair (eds.), *The Transmission of Culture in Early Modern Europe* (1990).

HUTTON, R., *The Royalist War Effort, 1642–1646* (1982).

ISRAEL, J., *The Dutch Republic: Its Rise, Greatness, and Fall, 1477–1806* (1995).

—— (ed.) *The Anglo-Dutch Moment: Essays on the Glorious Revolution and its World Impact* (1991).

JOHNSON, J. T., *Just War Tradition and the Restraint of War: A Moral and Historical Inquiry* (1981).

JONES, D. W., *War and Economy in the Age of William III and Marlborough* (1988).

JONES, G. H., *Charles Middleton: The Life and Times of a Restoration Politician* (1967).

—— 'The Recall of the British from Dutch Service', *HJ* 25 (1982).

KENYON, J., and J. OHLMEYER (eds.), *The Civil Wars: A Military History of England, Scotland and Ireland, 1638–1660* (1998).

KISHLANSKY, M., *The Rise of the New Model Army* (1979).

KNEVEL, P., *Burgers in het geweer: De Schutterijnen in Holland, 1550–1700* (1994).

LENIHAN, P., *Confederate Catholics at War, 1641–49* (2001).

LENMAN, B., *England's Colonial Wars, 1550–1688: Conflicts, Empire and National Identity* (2001).

—— *Jacobite Risings in Britain, 1689–1746* (1980).

LLOYD, H. A., *The Rouen Campaign, 1590–92: Politics, Warfare and the Early Modern State* (1973).

LOCKYER, R., *Buckingham: The Life and Political Career of George Villiers, first Duke of Buckingham* (1981).

LYNCH, K., *Roger Boyle, First Earl of Orrery* (1965).

LYNN, J. A., *Giant of the* Grand Siècle: *The French Army, 1610–1715* (1997).

McGURK, J., *The Elizabethan Conquest of Ireland: The 1590s Crisis* (1997).

MACINNES, A. I., *Charles I and the Making of the Covenanting Movement, 1625–1641* (1991).

MACKAY, J., *An Old Scots Brigade, Being the History of Mackay's Regiment* (1885).

MAGUIRE, W. A. (ed.), *Kings in Conflict: The Revolutionary War in Ireland and its Aftermath, 1689–1750* (1990).

MALCOLM, J. L., *Caesar's Due: Loyalty and King Charles, 1642–1646* (1983).

MILLER, J., 'The Militia and the Army in the Reign of James II', *HJ* 16 (1973).

—— *Popery and Politics in England, 1660–1688* (1973).

MORGAN, H. (ed.), *Political Ideology in Ireland, 1541–1641* (1999).

—— *Tyrone's Rebellion: The Outbreak of the Nine Years War in Tudor Ireland* (1993).

MORRAH, P., *Prince Rupert of the Rhine* (1976).

MORRILL, J. (ed.), *The Scottish National Covenant in its British Context* (1990).

MURDOCH, S., *Britain, Denmark-Norway and the House of Stuart, 1603–1660* (2000).

—— and A. MACKILLOP (eds.), *Fighting for Identity: Scottish Military Experience, c.1550–1900* (2002).

NEWMAN, P. R., *The Old Service: Royalist Regimental Colonels and the Civil Wars, 1642–46* (1993).

—— 'The Royalist Officer Corps, 1643–1660: Army Command as a Reflexion of Social Structure', *HJ* 26 (1983).

NOLAN, J. S., 'The Militarization of the Elizabethan State', *JMH* 58 (1994).

—— *Sir John Norreys and the Elizabethan Military World* (1997).

OHLMEYER, J., *Civil War and Restoration in the the Three Kingdoms: The Career of Randall MacDonnell, Marquis of Antrim, 1609–1683* (1993).

—— (ed.), *Ireland from Independence to Occupation, 1641–1660* (1995).

OLLARD, R., *Cromwell's Earl: A Life of Edward Mountagu, 1ˢᵗ Earl of Sandwich* (1994).

PARKER, G., *The Army of Flanders and the Spanish Road, 1567–1695: The Logistics of Spanish Victory and Defeat in the Low Countries War* (1972).

—— 'War and Economic Change: The Economic Costs of the Dutch Revolt', in J. M. Winter (ed.), *War and Economic Development* (1975).

PARROTT, D., *Richelieu's Army: War, Government and Society in France, 1624–1642* (2001).

PERCEVAL-MAXWELL, M., *The Outbreak of the Irish Rebellion* (1994).

PINCUS, S. C. A., *Protestantism and Patriotism: Ideologies and the Making of English Foreign Policy, 1650–1688* (1996).

PORTER, S. (ed.), *London and the Civil War* (1996).

QUINN, D. B., *The Elizabethans and the Irish* (1966).

TEN RAA, F. J. S., and F. DE BAS, *Het Staatsche Leger*, 8 vols. (1911–80).

ROBERTS, M., *Gustavus Adolphus: A History of Sweden, 1611–1632*, 2 vols. (1953, 1958).

ROBERTSON, J., *The Scottish Enlightenment and the Militia Issue* (1985).

ROY, I., 'England Turned Germany? The Aftermath of the Civil War in its European Context', *TRHS* 5ᵗʰ ser. 28 (1978).

—— 'The English Civil War and English Society', in B. Bond and I. Roy (eds.), *War and Society: A Yearbook of Military History*, 2 vols. (1975), vol. i.

RUBINSTEIN, H. L., *Captain Luckless: James Hamilton, First Duke of Hamilton, 1606–1649* (1975).

SCOULLER, R. E., *The Armies of Queen Anne* (1966).

—— 'Purchase of Commissions and Promotions', *JSAHR* 62 (1984).

SCHWOERER, L. G., *The Revolution of 1688–89* (1992).

SIMMS, J. G., *Jacobite Ireland, 1685–1691* (1969; repr. 2000).

—— *War and Politics in Ireland, 1649–1730*, ed. D. W. Hayton and G. O'Brien (1986).

SIMPSON, G. G. (ed.), *The Scottish Soldier Abroad, 1247–1967* (1992).

SMUTS, R. M., *Court Culture and the Origins of a Royalist Tradition in Early Stuart England* (1987).

SNOW, V. F., *Essex the Rebel: The Life of Robert Devereux, Third Earl of Essex, 1591–1646* (1970).

SPECK, W. A., 'The Orangist Conspiracy against James II', *HJ* 30 (1987).

STATER, V. L., *Noble Government: The Stuart Lord Lieutenancy and the Transformation of English Politics* (1994).

STEARNS, S. J., 'Conscription and English Society in the 1620s', *JBS* 11 (1972).

STEVENSON, D., *Alasdair MacColla and the Highland Problem in the Seventeenth Century* (1980).

—— *Revolution and Counter-Revolution in Scotland, 1644–1651* (1977).

STEWART, D., 'Sickness and Mortality Rates of the English Army in the Sixteenth Century', *Journal of the Royal Army Medical Corps*, 91 (1948).

STOYE, J. W., *English Travellers Abroad, 1604–1667: Their Influence in English Society and Politics* (1952).

STRADLING, R. A., *The Spanish Monarchy and Irish Mercenaries: The Wild Geese in Spain, 1618–68* (1994).

SZECHI, D., *The Jacobites: Britain and Europe, 1688–1788* (1994).

TAYLER, A. and H., *The House of Forbes*, SC 3rd ser. 8 (1937).

TEITLER, G., *The Genesis of the Professional Officer Corps* (1977).

TERRY, C. S., *The Life and Campaigns of Alexander Leslie, First Earl of Leven* (1899).

TREADWELL, V., *Buckingham and Ireland, 1616–1628* (1998).

TRIM, D. J. B., *The Chivalric Ethos and the Development of Military Professionalism* (2003).

UNDERDOWN, D., *Somerset in the Civil War and Interregnum* (1973).

WALTON, C., *History of the British Standing Army* (1894).

WARBURTON, E., *Memorials of Prince Rupert and the Cavaliers*, 3 vols. (1849).

WAUCHOPE, P., *Patrick Sarsfield and the Williamite War* (1992).

WEBB, H. G., *Elizabethan Military Science: The Books and the Practice* (1965).

WERNHAM, R. B., *After the Armada: Elizabethan England and the Struggle for Western Europe, 1588–1595* (1984).

—— *Before the Armada: The Emergence of the English Nation, 1485–1588* (repr. 1972).

—— (ed.), *The Expedition of Sir John Norris and Sir Francis Drake to Spain and Portugal, 1589*, NRS 127 (1988).

WESTERN, J. R., *The English Militia in the Eighteenth Century: The Story of a Political Issue, 1660–1802* (1965).

—— *Monarchy and Revolution: The English State in the 1680s* (1972).

WHEELER, J. S., *Cromwell in Ireland* (1999).

—— *The Making of a World Power: War and the Military Revolution in Seventeenth-Century England* (1999).

WIJN, J. W., *Het Krijgswezen in den Tijd van Prins Maurits* (1934).

WILSON, Sir C., *Queen Elizabeth and the Revolt of the Netherlands* (1970).

WOOLRYCH, A., *Britain in Revolution, 1625–1660* (2003).

WORTHINGTON, D., *Scots in Habsburg service, 1618–1648* (2004).

YOUNG, J. R. (ed.), *The Celtic Dimensions of the British Civil Wars* (1997).

ZWITZER, H. L., *De Militie van den Staat: Het Leger van de Republiek der Verenigde Nederlanden* (1991).

Index